When We Ruled

When We Ruled

The Ancient and Mediæval History of Black Civilisations

Robin Walker

Afterword by
Fari Supiya

Black Classic Press

Baltimore

When We Ruled
The Ancient and Mediæval History of Black Civilisations

Copyright 2006 Robin Walker
Published 2011 Black Classic Press
All Rights Reserved.

Library of Congress Control Number: 2010937063
ISBN: 978-1-58073-045-7

Printed by BCP Digital Printing,
an affiliate company of Black Classic Press, Inc.

To review or purchase Black Classic Press books,
visit: **www.blackclassicbooks.com**

You may also obtain a list of titles by writing to:
Black Classic Press
c/o List
P.O. Box 13414
Baltimore, MD 21203

Egypt. Temple of Abu Simbel, Kush. Built by Pharaoh Rameses II (ruled 1394-1328 BC), Nineteenth Dynasty, by carving it out of a mountainside. Each statue is 66 feet tall. (Photo: Alan Mitchell).

That Other African and the Lion's Historian an Introduction to the Black Classic Press Edition of *When We Ruled*

When We Ruled: The Ancient and Mediæval History of Black Civilisations, by Robin Walker, is the broadest single survey of early African humanity and civilizations yet compiled by a scholar of African descent. It is a grand overview of what Dr. Ivan Van Sertima referred to as "that other African"—not the stereotypical Black savage so graphically depicted in the early Hollywood movies nor the aimless, clueless, babbling slave incapable of deliberate action without instruction from his White master. No, the "other African" described in this major, sweeping work is the African who first populated the earth and who gave birth to and significantly influenced the world's oldest and most magnificent civilizations throughout time. It is the African who entered history not as slave but as a master or mistress in control of his or her own destiny. And *When We Ruled* is the powerful chronicle of their longstanding and broad-reaching legacy.

In Walker's own words, *When We Ruled* "brings together over two hundred years of research on the early history and heritage of Black people." Indeed, the book references and incorporates the works of a wide range of African and non-African scholars, fully embracing Kwa David Whitaker's maxim that, "What you do for yourself depends on what you think of yourself, and what you think of yourself depends on what you know of yourself, and what you know of yourself depends on what you have been told."

In twenty-two chapters, *When We Ruled* examines the nature of what we call "Black history," critically surveying the often-shoddy documentation of that history. It exhumes the truth about African roots of humanity, the origins and evolution of human culture, and the early peopling of Africa. Importantly, it focuses upon African civilization in the Valley of the Nile and analyzes the key historical phases of Ancient Egypt—critical exercises for any professed scholar of African history and vital pieces of Africa's legacy. These are key elements that Walker notes so many scholars of European descent have chosen, quite deliberately it seems, to distort, delete, or ignore.

Though Walker maintains that the ancient Nile Valley was the site of classical African civilization at its highest point, he makes it clear that it was the Upper Nile Valley, the land of "the burnt-faced people" of Ethiopia, that gave birth to the world's oldest monarchy: the Ta-Seti of Ancient Egypt, then known as "Kmt." Kmt was the greatest nation of antiquity, Walker emphasizes, and Ethiopia's most celebrated successor.

Walker knowledgably asserts that Kmt has long enthralled scholars throughout the world and throughout history—and why should it not be? He further claims that the examination of Kemetic civilization is the examination of perhaps the proudest and loftiest accomplishments in the whole of human annals, and that it probably will continue to be the primary focus of human studies for some time to come. To its credit, *When We Ruled* presents a lengthy and strikingly notable list of Kemetic society's achievements. Walker offers conclusive evidence that not only were Kmt's origins African, but also that African people endowed with dark complexions, full lips, broad noses, and tightly curled hair were dominant in both the general population and in the reigning elite through the mass of its dynastic period.

Walker further makes it clear that as important as ancient Egypt was, civilization in Africa was not confined to the Nile Valley. After his sweeping examination of Kmt, he focuses on two other great North African civilizations: ancient Carthage and Numidia. Carthage, of course, is familiar to most of us for the much-heralded exploits of that great African warrior, King Hannibal Barca. Walker explains, however, that Numidia is also important, although not nearly as well known.

After an exhaustive focus on the ancient African civilizations of the Nile Valley, *When We Ruled* shifts its attention to West Africa, the Sahel, and Central Africa, home to the great African kingdoms of Nok, Igbo-Ukwu, Yorubaland, Great Benin, Kongo, Kanem-Bornu, and the Hausa Confederation. It also examines the empires of ancient Ghana, Mali, and Songhai, meticulously confirming Walker's assertion that civilization in Africa was continent-wide. Walker next adroitly turns his attention east and south to examine the ancient civilizations of the Swahili states,

Medieval Nubia, and Zimbabwe, again confirming that ancient Egypt, though it remains the centerpiece of the study of early African civilizations, does not constitute the totality of Africa's ancient greatness.

When We Ruled also details the influence and impact of African civilizations beyond the continent of Africa. Following the tradition of many early scholars and paralleling my own writings, *When We Ruled* traces the imprint of African on the development of ancient civilizations in Sumer in southern Iraq, the kingdom of Elam in early Iran, the Harappan or Indus Valley civilization in Pakistan and India, and Arabia Felix in Yemen in the southwest Arabian Peninsula. It also makes a brief foray into Moorish Spain to bask in the glory of African people's influence in and on southern Europe. Other important chapters in this masterwork include one examining the role of Islam in African culture. Another chapter, "The Fall of Africa and the Resistance," follows in the footsteps of Chancellor Williams to highlight the role of the Arabs as precursors to the European invasion of Africa. Following an extensive Afterword by Fari Supiya, *When We Ruled* closes with a superb historical chronology and a comprehensive bibliography.

When We Ruled is a timely and immensely important work of benefit to scholars and students alike. I am proud to add it to my library. Robin Walker should be saluted for this massive study, and Black Classic Press should be commended for publishing it. Their efforts give tooth to the African proverb that says, "Until the lion has his historian, the hunter will always be a hero." Clearly, with the publication of this work, it can be hailed firmly and with certainty that the lion, at last, has his historian. To both Robin Walker and Black Classic Press: well done!

Runoko Rashidi

CONTENTS

ACKNOWLEDGEMENTS

In writing *When We Ruled*, there are just too many people to thank. Nevertheless some people deserve special mention. Mr Benaebi Benatari is probably the biggest single influence on the book. His unpublished paper *The Document of African Civilisation* was a great inspiration and produced a model of African history that has forever revolutionised my thinking. He was the first to demonstrate to me that it is possible to write a history of Africa focussed on its sciences, industry and technology. My colleague, Mr Fari Supiya, brought an unparalleled rigour to African historiography that few researchers have ever equalled. He introduced me to the juice concept of research - the idea that nearly all material, even if overtly hostile to Black people, will often contain juice that can be squeezed out. I believe that his contribution will set the very highest standards in African historical research for the future that one day will fill the immense gap left by the late Professor Diop. Mr Siaf Millar is a colleague with whom I have worked since our college days. His theories are not too different from those of Mr Benatari. He has also been a great inspiration. Mr Alan Mitchell encouraged me to bring more colour into my writing. Even more importantly, Mr Mitchell encouraged me to develop my own theories about what Black history should really be about. These ideas form the *Foreword* of the book. Dr Femi Biko is a brilliant academic - one of the very best ever to have emerged from among our people. His ideas are all over the first half of the book. Dr Kimani Nehusi and Ms Ammittai Lumumba taught me a great deal about the Slave Trade. Their imprint has greatly shaped Chapter 18. I would also like to thank Dr Stephen Howe who has provided me and my colleagues with many hours of mirth.[1] Finally, I would like to thank Mr Rey "you-must-do-the-reading" Bowen. He saw potential in me many years ago. I have listened carefully to his often severe criticisms of my work and it is my hope that this work fulfils some of that potential that he believed was there.

This work would not have been possible without the assistance of many other individuals. Chief among these were Ms Patricia Mills, who designed the book, and Ms Andrea McLeod, who designed the front cover. Others contributed financial assistance to make the book possible. I was moved by the generosity of Ms Judine Alleyne, the A. S. K. Team, Ms Marjorie Burke, the British Museum, Mr Michael Cohen, Mr Rod Chung, Ms Aminatta Diaby, Mr

Alistair Fell, Mrs Merthia Fell, Ms Jan Francis, Mr Desmond Holloway, Kindle UK, Ku-Amka Productions, Mambo Press, Mr Musi Katangaza, Mr Sebastian Lattouche, Dr Asher John-Baptiste, Ms J. J. Parker, Mr Michael Richmond, Mrs Sharron Richmond, Mr Stephen Roach, Ms Joan Sengati, Mr Mark Simpson, Mr Paul Soso, Ms Margaret Tonge, Ms Chantelle Warner, Ms Charmaine Williams, Ms Rosemary Yacobi and Ms Margaret Young. Special thanks go to Ms Avril Nanton and Ms Patricia Reid.

Note

[1] Alarm Promotions, *The Great Debate* (video), UK, Nekhebet Productions, 1998

FOREWORD

When We Ruled is a unique work. It brings together over two hundred years of research on the early history and heritage of Black people. Previous writers have established a *context* for the writing of African history. Others have established its *theoretical basis* and also its *scope*. Some have developed an appropriate *methodology*. It has been 30 years since a proper study has been published that combines all four elements. Professor John Jackson, author of *Introduction to African Civilizations,* wrote the best work on Black history there has ever been. The recovery of the African Data, however, was never a finished product even in his meticulous hands. It is well known that history evolves as new discoveries shatter old beliefs. It is less well known that long forgotten sources that revisit the light of day also challenge presently held certainties. For these reasons, our knowledge of Black history has advanced greatly since the publication of the Jackson *opus.*

The context surrounding the study of the African heritage, however, has changed little since Jackson's time. The profile of Black history is still low and astounding levels of ignorance persist. It was gratifying to follow a recent debate in the *Metro,* a widely read London daily, concerning this issue. David Bolton fired the first shot on 21 February 2001 with his claim that Africa lacked societies and therefore benefited from European colonialism. Shouted down the following day, seven letters were published to rebut Mr Bolton's ignorance. One such letter (by Bola Asiru) retorted that:

> How can anyone claim Africa did not have societies before the arrival of colonialism? Political, economic and social structures existed in African society well before the 19th century. Frederic Caillaurd, during his quest to discover the source of the Nile, marvelled at the structure of Egyptian society.[1]

Describing the cultures of West Africa, Diane Stokes, another well informed respondent, mentioned that: "Africa had universities before Oxford and Cambridge were founded, high art before Britain was populated and strict laws. These were broken down, destroyed and efforts were made to eradicate the indigenous cultures. Is the rape and pillage of these lands and their peoples civilised?"[2] Graeme Broster wrote that in southern Africa: "Massive empires existed in Zimbabwe and Zululand (to name but two) and were crushed by the land grab of the colonial empires in the 19th century".[3]

The fact that seven people could reply constructively to Mr Bolton indicates that awareness of African history is greater now than it would have been 30 years ago. This at first sight seems to be a development. But is it really? More than fifty years ago, Thomas Hodgkin, a fellow of Balliol College, Oxford, wrote an article for a periodical called *The Highway*. Part of this article reads as follows:

> It is no doubt flattering to our vanity to imagine that the peoples of Africa were "primitive" and "barbarous" before the penetration of the Europeans, and that it is we [i.e. Europeans] who civilised them. But it is a theory that lacks historical foundation. The Empire of Ghana flourished in what is now French West Africa during the dark ages of Western Europe. By the fifteenth century there was a university at Timbuktu. The Ashantis of the Gold Coast [i.e. Ghana] and the Yorubas [of Nigeria] possessed highly organised and complex civilizations long before their territories were brought under British political and military control. The thesis that Africa is what Western European missionaries, traders, technicians and administrators have made it is comforting (to Western Europeans) but invalid.[4]

In the light of the Hodgkin article, published in 1952, the recent debate in the *Metro* becomes all the more intolerable. The relevant information should have long been in the public domain. Mr Hodgkin, however, explained the context to why this did not happen:

> [M]ost of the available material on African affairs is presented from a European standpoint - either by imperial historians (who are interested in the record of European penetration into Africa), or by colonial administrators (who are interested in the pattern of institutions imposed by European governments upon African societies), or by anthropologists (who are often, though not always, mainly interested in the forms of social organization surviving in the simplest African communities, considered in isolation from the political developments in the world around them).[5]

Even earlier than Hodgkin putting pen to paper, Dr Victor Robinson, noted that:

> It is one of the paradoxes of history that Africa, the Mother of Civilisation, remained for over two thousand years the Dark Continent. To the moderns Africa was the region where ivory was sought for Europe, and slaves for America. In the time of Jonathan Swift (1667-1745), as the satirist informs us, geographers in drawing maps fill in the gaps with savage pictures. Where towns should have been they placed elephants.[6]

Scholars had raised this issue even earlier than Dr Robinson. Professor Leo Frobenius, the learned German historian of the early twentieth century, wrote:

> Let there be light in Africa. In that portion of the globe to which the stalwart Anglo-Saxon Stanley gave the name "dark" and "darkest". Light upon the people of that continent whose children we [i.e. Europeans] are accustomed to regard as types of natural servility with no recorded history. (But) the spell has been broken. The buried treasures of antiquity again revisit the sun.[7]

Light fell on one such buried treasure of antiquity a few years ago. *The Sunday Times* on 23 May 1999 carried an astonishing article entitled *Jungle reveals traces of Sheba's fabled kingdom.* Over the next few days many other papers followed suit. Even the *Daily Mail* on 24 May asked: *Was the Queen of Sheba really a Black woman from Nigeria?*[8]

As the evidence emerged, however, the Queen of Sheba link proved to be hype. The real Sheba was an Ethiopian or possibly half-Yemeni queen who lived three thousand years ago on the opposite side of the Continent. What was undeniable, however, was that the southern Nigerian rainforests concealed an even more amazing secret. During the Middle Ages, Africans built by far the largest city the world had ever seen. In size, it dwarfed Baghdad, Cairo, Cordova and Rome. The achievement was on a scale even bigger that that of the Great Pyramid of Giza, Africa's most celebrated monument.

At one time, scholars used to divide the three thousand-year history of southern Nigeria into four great cultural periods. They used to speak of the Nok Culture, the Igbo-Ukwu Culture, the Yoruba Kingdoms, and the Benin Empire. This view was boldly challenged by the findings of a Bournemouth University archaeological team led by Dr Patrick Darling. Since 1994 the team discovered and mapped the remains of yet another Nigerian kingdom previously covered by centuries of forest overgrowth. Barnaby Phillips of the BBC described the discoveries as possibly "Africa's largest single monument."[9] As we shall see, this is typical British understatement.

At Eredo, in southwest Nigeria, Darling's team found a huge earthen wall with moated sections. This encircled an ancient kingdom or city. From the base of the ditch to the summit of the rampart measured a towering 70 feet. According to Mark Macaskill of *The Sunday Times,* the rampart was "100 mile[s]" long and formed a rough circle, enclosing "more than 400 square miles."[10] The building was on a truly epic scale. The builders shifted 3.5 million cubic metres of earth to build just the rampart alone. According to the BBC this is, incidentally, "one million cubic metres more than the amount of rock and earth used in the Great Pyramid at Giza." Therefore Eredo's construction is estimated to have "involved about one million more man-hours than were necessary to build the Great Pyramid."[11] The ramparts may indicate the boundary of the original Ijebu kingdom that was ruled by a spiritual leader called the "Awujale". Macaskill, however, disagrees. He describes Eredo as a "city". If correct, this would make Eredo one of the very largest cities in all of human history. Comparable in size to modern London, it was the largest city built in the ancient and mediæval world.

Among the discoveries, a three-storey ruin has been identified tentatively as the royal palace. It had living quarters, shrines and courtyards. It is possible that thousands of smaller buildings are still concealed by the forests and will be mapped in time. Radiocarbon dating has so far established that the buildings and walls were more than 1,000 years old. Dates such as 800 AD have been suggested.

People who live near the ruined kingdom or city today have traditions that a wealthy and childless queen, Bilikisu Sungbo, built the city. Some say that she built the city as a religious offering. It is also claimed that Sungbo's territory had a gold and ivory trade. Portuguese documents dating back 500 years allude to the power of an Ijebu kingdom that some scholars think is possibly this very one. Today, the ruins continue to be of some importance. There are yearly pilgrimages to Sungbo's grave.

Dr Darling, the leader of the archaeological team, suggested that Eredo might well gain World Heritage Status. This will put the Eredo kingdom, or city, on an equal footing with other African marvels such as the Pyramids of Giza and the city of Djenné. It also places this great achievement on a footing with other marvels from around the world such as Stonehenge.

Since the nineteenth century and after much groping in the dark, pioneering African-American scholars evolved a theoretical structure to analyse Black history. More recently one of them crystallised it. "History" writes Professor Maulana Karenga, "is the struggle and record of humans in the process of humanizing the world, i.e., shaping it in their image and interests." It is a collective account of humans giving the world a human form and character that serves human interests rather than jeopardise, distort or destroy those interests. Black history is therefore the collective record of people of African descent in Africanising the world around them. "This", asserts Karenga, "adds to the richness and beauty of human diversity and contributes to the overall effort of humans to transform the world from control by nature to control by humanity."[12]

History contains five main elements. It is human, social, conflictual, fluid & changeable, and also manageable.[13] Besides, Karenga identifies four constraints that impede and shape the onward march of history. These are nature, society, other humans, and one's own personal limitations.[14] The example of Eredo demonstrates how Africans in that region shaped the world around them to reflect and serve their cultural images and interests. Through human genius and social organisation, they achieved a major engineering feat. They overcame the physical constraints of nature, internal opposition to the building programme, and also their individual limitations in engineering skills. Through struggle against these constraints, they made history.

Karenga further shows that history has clear social functions. It is a source of group understanding that enables a people to reflect on their strengths and weaknesses. It is a source of understanding for an individual of his or her society and also the world at large. Furthermore, history imposes modesty, especially if the example under discussion surpasses one's own achievements. Finally, history is a source of useful models to emulate.[15]

Professor John Clarke, the venerable African-American historian, wrote that history is always relevant because:

> History is the clock that people use to tell them their time of day. It is also a compass that people use to find themselves on the map of human geography. The role of history is to tell a people what they have been, where they have been, what they are and where they are. The most important role that history plays is that it has the function of telling a people where they still must go and what they still must be.[16]

Supporting this view, Professor Ivan Van Sertima, a Guyanese anthropologist, says that whether something happened ten minutes ago or ten thousand years ago, if you remember it, it occupies the same space in the consciousness.

The scope of Black history is to trace the documents, traditions, and archaeology concerning the Ethiopians, Libyans, Kushites, Hamites, Moors, Zanj, and Sudanese. In the ancient and early mediæval periods, these designations were applied strictly to Negroes, often without the geographical limitations implied by modern countries of the same name. For instance, Richard Jobson, the seventeenth century author of *The Golden Trade or A Discovery of the River Gambra, and the Golden Trade of the Aethiopians,* uses this term "Aethiopians" to refer to West Africans.[17] The point is these terms were not originally applied to non-Negroes. In later historical periods through to the modern period, however, some of these terms have changed their application. The Arabs conquered North Africa beginning in 639 AD and are still to this day the dominant population in Egypt, Sudan, Libya, Algeria, Tunisia and Morocco. Furthermore, the Arabs conquered East Africa in the eighteenth century and are still dominant in Zanzibar. The terms Libyans, Moors, Zanj, and Sudanese are now applied to the Arabs, creating the illusion that the ancient and mediæval documents that use these designations actually refer to Arabs, when they actually refer to Negroes.

Since the nineteenth century African-American historians began mapping the history of the Negroes.[18] Great advances were made in the 1920's. Mrs Drusilla Houston, Professor William Hansberry, and the Jamaican historian, Mr J. A. Rogers, made cutting edge research. Professor W. E. B. DuBois penned the landmark *The World and Africa.* Published in 1946, he told the story of Negro civilisations in North, South and West Africa. He also told of ancient Negro civilisations that used to exist in Asia. Professor DeGraft-Johnson, a Ghanaian historian, wrote *African Glory.* Published in 1954, it advanced the state of knowledge by including a strong account of the civilisation of the Moors in Spain. Like DuBois before him, however, DeGraft-Johnson was weak on the civilisations of East Africa. Englishman Dr Basil Davidson plugged this gap with his classic *Old Africa Rediscovered,* issued in 1959. Davidson, and later English scholars, alerted historians to the growing wealth of archaeological material available on the African past. *Introduction to African Civilizations,* the Jackson classic, was a 1970 synthesis and update of DuBois, DeGraft-Johnson and Davidson, together with research Jackson conducted with Willis Huggins, a colleague from the 1930's and 1940's. In particular, Professor Jackson shows that the human race was of African origin. In addition, the early civilisation of Sudan, Egypt, Sumer, Elam and India were Negro. He further demonstrated that Africans voyaged to America well before the time of Christopher Columbus.

Professors Cheikh Anta Diop and Yosef ben-Jochannan greatly advanced the methodology of researching and writing about the African heritage. With the publication of *Precolonial Black Africa,* Dr Diop, a Senegalese scholar, demonstrated the importance of reconstructing the social, political, economic, intellectual, technical, and aesthetic elements of the old African civilisations. This brings colour and vividness to those remote times totally lacking when history is presented as dry dates and dusty kings lists. His *African Origin of Civilization: Myth or Reality?* was concerned with a single question: Who were the Ancient Egyptians? In addressing this controversy, Diop presented an invaluable masterclass of how to interpret primary and secondary source material. Moreover, he demonstrated the key importance of confronting problem areas in Black history rather than retreating from them. Professor ben-Jochannan, author of *Africa! Mother of Western Civilization,* also teaches how to interpret source material. Additionally, Dr Ben introduces his readers to long forgotten works on African history written since the late eighteenth century. He empowers his readers to examine these works for themselves and to follow the leads that they give.

Mr Hodgkin, cited earlier, concluded that: "We shall probably have to wait a little while for the real history of Africa to be written by African scholars for an African reading public".[19] Since these words were written, great books have emerged from the pen of Black scholars. Among these were Professor Chancellor Williams' *The Destruction of Black Civilization,* Dr Charles Finch's *The Star of Deep Beginnings,* Dr Nnamdi Elleh's *African Architecture: Evolution and Transformation,* and the books and journals associated with Professor Ivan Van Sertima, Dr Runoko Rashidi, and their team at the *Journal*

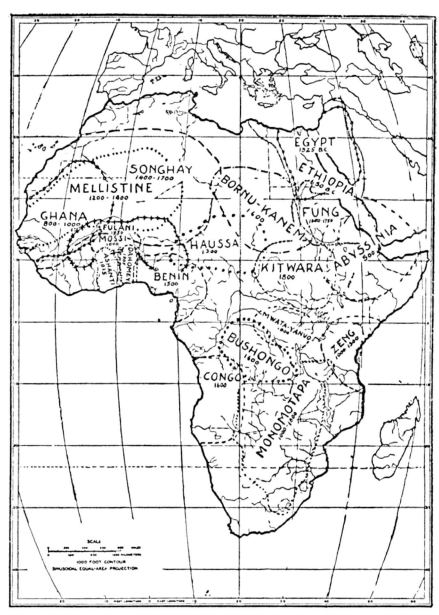

Map of African States (1325 BC-1850 AD). Originally published in W. E. B. DuBois, *The World and Africa* (US, International Publishers, 1965, p.109). It was a pioneering and laudable attempt to show the old African states at their point of greatest political expansion. Subsequent research has, however, improved upon this data. Moreover, Mellistine is now more usually called Mali, Bornu-Kanem is usually called Kanem-Borno, Ethiopia is Kush, Abyssinia is Axum, and Zeng (i.e. Zanj) is the Swahili Confederation.

of African Civilizations. These authors were fully aware of the importance of context, theoretical basis, scope and methodology. Other texts, more detailed and specialised, but lacking in the four key elements, have emerged from the pens of African and European scholars such as Stride, Ifeka, Oliver, Hornung, Usman, Eyo, Koslow, Watterson, etc. What was needed now was a work that could bring together and update the findings of these scholars and also the scholarship produced over the last two hundred or so years. *When We Ruled* attempts precisely this aim.

Notes

[1] Bola Asiru, *Africa had societies,* in *Metro,* UK, 22 February 2001, p.15.

[2] Ibid.

[3] Ibid.

[4] Quoted in J. C. DeGraft-Johnson, *African Glory,* UK, Watts & Co., 1954, p.ix.

[5] Quoted in ibid., pp.ix-x.

[6] Quoted in Yosef A. A. ben-Jochannan, *Africa! Mother of Western Civilization,* US, Black Classic Press, 1971, p.191.

[7] Quoted in ibid., p.196.

[8] See also Roger Highfield (Science Editor), *Britons explore 'Queen of Sheba's monument',* in *The Daily Telegraph,* 26 May 1999, p.13.

[9] Barnaby Phillips (BBC News), *Nigeria's hidden wonder,* BBC Online (Internet), 9 June 1999.

[10] Mark Macaskill, *Jungle reveals traces of Sheba's fabled kingdom,* in *The Sunday Times,* 23 May 1999, p.10.

[11] Barnaby Phillips (BBC News), *Nigeria's hidden wonder.*

[12] Maulana Karenga, *Introduction to Black Studies,* US, University of Sankore Press, 1982, pp.43-4.

[13] Ibid., p.44.

[14] Ibid., pp.44-7.

[15] Ibid., pp.47-52.

[16] Quoted in Anthony T. Browder, *Nile Valley Contributions to Civilization,* US, Institute of Karmic Guidance, 1992, p.29.

[17] Richard Jobson, *The Golden Trade or A Discovery of the River Gambra, and the Golden Trade of the Aethiopians,* UK, The Penguin Press, 1932.

[18] See Runoko Rashidi & James E. Brunson, *A Tribute to the Pioneer Contributors to the African Presence in Early Asia from 1883 to 1918,* in *African Presence in Early Asia,* ed Runoko Rashidi, US, Transaction Publishers, 1995, pp.254-268.

[19] Quoted in J. C. DeGraft-Johnson, *African Glory,* p.x.

INTRODUCTION

The Commission for Africa (2005)

"This year is of great significance for Africa", assert the authors of the 2005 British government report - *Our Common Interest: Report of the Commission for Africa.* The Commission aims to address the general issue of world poverty. In addition, to update and report on previous pledges made by rich countries to halve world poverty by the year 2015. In assisting Africa, the Commission brought together 17 people, the majority Africans, under the chairmanship of Mr Tony Blair, the British Prime Minister. Their role was to "define the challenges facing Africa, and to provide clear recommendations on how to support the changes needed to reduce poverty."[1]

Elsewhere in the report, we are informed that: "one of the commissioners warned us all that ideas and actions not premised on the cultures of Africa would not work."[2] Clearly the history of Black people had to be a key issue in understanding the present situation facing Africa and would be a key guide to understanding the cultures of Africa. This raises questions: What was the history of Africa? What were the cultures of Africa that need to be taken into account?

In the third chapter of the report, the reader is warned against "Misunderstandings about Africa". In contrast, the reader is advised to consider "The inheritance of history". Specifically:

> History is of more than academic interest here. In pre-colonial Africa, clans - groups of people who claim the same ancestor, either through birth or kinship - were the central units of administration, although immediate family units took precedence in the more sparsely populated areas. Clans had a variety of customary practices and social and political structures. Some of these customs were developed through consensus and/or commonly accepted principles of mutual accountability and susceptibility, such as between elders and non-elders and the wealthy and the poor … These structures were not static, so it is wrong to think in terms of some fixed 'traditional' or homogeneous culture. However, some features of this organisation persist today, including strong kinship ties, rules based on custom, and agreed principles including mutual accountability between elders and non-elders. The 'big man' culture in which powerful individuals are expected to offer patronage to other members of the clan is significant here … Influences from specific phases of African history must also be factored into the analysis. The Atlantic slave trade, missionaries and

colonialism disordered many of those traditional features, subtly altering them.
The demarcation of new colonial boundaries disrupted many existing clan,
ethnic and religious boundaries ... But what history shows, throughout all this,
is the tremendously interactive and evolving nature of African cultures. They
have been able to absorb a wide range of outside influences and impositions,
and have found ways to survive often difficult natural, environmental and
social conditions including conflict and disease. For many Africans, the
strength and resilience of African cultures give a real sense of pride and coming
opportunity, in stark contrast to pessimism about Africa that often dominates
outside the continent.[3]

Unfortunately, the above extract raises far more issues than it addresses. For
example: Is it accurate to portray pre-colonial Africa as merely clan-based
societies with customary practices? Did African societies not have official
legal and constitutional systems? Is it true that the only Black history worth
considering is the Atlantic slave trade, the missionary enterprises and
colonialism? For us the bigger question was undoubtedly: Why did the Black
commissioners who helped to compile the report sign their names to such
unscholarly and ahistorical nonsense? The extract gives the impression that
African culture today is a fair reflection of what was there in pre-colonial
times. Nothing could be further from the truth.

The truth is that no properly educated person can afford to overlook the real
history of one of the three great branches of the human family. History is a vast
umbrella subject. It encompasses all disciplines, not just political and cultural
history. It therefore includes literature, religion, the social and natural sciences,
the arts, technology, and mathematics. To be ignorant of the political and
cultural history of a people is also to be ignorant of the contributions of that
people to all areas of intellectual activity. Many people, unaware of the history
of African people, justify their position using arguments that echo the famous
Oxford University historian Professor Hugh Trevor-Roper. In a 1965 text he
wrote: "Perhaps in the future there will be some African history to teach. But
at present there is none, or very little: there is only the history of Europe in
Africa. The rest is largely darkness like the history of pre-Columbian America,
and darkness is not a subject for history."[4] Statements such as this actually
reduce Trevor-Roper to the status of the semi or quasi-educated. Do you want
to be among them? Clearly the commissioners held the same view as the
distinguished professor. More importantly, the Commission will fail in its
overall objectives for assisting Africa due to the fact that they have a false
understanding of African history and, as they themselves admit: "one of the
commissioners warned us all that ideas and actions not premised on the
cultures of Africa would not work."

Genuine humanity is demonstrated where individuals can share an authentic
delight in human achievement. That is, all human achievement. As the great

Terence of Rome put it: "I am a man and nothing human is alien to me."[5] In this vein, one does not have to be an African-American to delight in the profundity of Duke Ellington's *Diminuendo and Crescendo in Blue*. In a similar vein, one does not have to be Chinese to be impressed by the subtle and sophisticated teachings of Confucius. We, for example, are genuinely inspired by the struggle of the great Scotsman Sir William Wallace. The true citizen of the world recognises things of value no matter where found or among whom it originated. True distinction in human endeavour is a success for all of the world's people.

Serious scholarship works in the same way. In researching this book, we discovered the work of many authorities who, through background and conservative upbringing, seemed unlikely to give a fair appraisal to African history. Time and again these scholars demonstrated that a true respect for human achievement was more important than reinforcing the comfortable prejudices of their time and background. Some of the very best works were written by the most unlikely of historians. We were disappointed to find, by contrast, that it was the self-proclaimed Liberals who fell short in this respect. The history of Black people amounts to much more than just the Atlantic slave trade, the missionary enterprises, and colonialism.

About the Book

It is to be expected that for many people Black history is a new and unfamiliar subject. Furthermore, many may find a 713 page book somewhat daunting to read. We therefore recommend that all readers familiarise themselves with the first three chapters of the book. Chapter 1 asks: What is Black History? Chapter 2 is a short survey of the literature written about Africa before 1936. Chapter 3 concerns the history of Black women. We recommend that these chapters be read several times until the basic data has been grasped. In addition, the reader should study the maps carefully and also the images. After this, we recommend that the reader should examine each and every map and image in the book with a view to placing all the maps and images within the context of where and when. Only then do we recommend that readers who are new to this attempt the other chapters of the book.

It is important to note the following: *Readers will be comforted to find that portions of the material in these three early chapters reappear elsewhere in the book. This is an innovation to ensure that the later chapters are not all new to the reader. It is much easier to learn new material if one has already been introduced to portions of it. The hardcore and the academics, on the other hand, may already be familiar with this data and may therefore want to begin the book at Chapter 4 to avoid any repetition of material.*

Chapter 4 discusses the peopling of Africa. This is a key chapter for dealing with the civilisations of North and East Africa. In particular, North Africa in the present period belongs to the Arabians. This was not the case in the ancient world.

Chapter 5 concerns the very beginnings of humanity and human culture. The human race is of African origin. Skeletons of humans have been found in East Africa that date back 195,000 years. Skeletons of pre-humans have been found that date back 5 million years or more. Moreover, Africans were the first to organise fishing expeditions 90,000 years ago, they engaged in mining 43,000 years ago, they pioneered basic arithmetic 25,000 years ago, they invented animal husbandry 15,000 years ago, they cultivated crops 12,000 years ago, they mummified their dead 9,000 years ago and they carved the world's first colossal sculpture 7,000 years ago.

Chapters 6 and 7 cover the ancient civilisations of Sudan and Egypt. These civilisations, the lands of the pharaohs, were the oldest states on earth. Kings and Queens ruled in these regions from 5900 BC until 350 AD. Their achievements were great and their monuments continue to astonish the world. As late as 670 BC, one of the pharaohs could still justifiably describe himself as the "Emperor of the World."

Chapters 8 and 9 are of a somewhat technical nature and deal with two of the most controversial issues concerning the Ancient Egyptians: (1) Who were they? and; (2) How old is Ancient Egypt? Some readers may, however, find these chapters somewhat difficult. In our view they can be omitted without losing out on too much.

Chapter 10 concerns the North African civilisations of Carthage and Numidia. Carthage flourished from 814 BC to 146 BC. It was the richest city in antiquity with a population of 700,000. Numidia bloomed from the fifth century BC to 46 BC. At its height, it was a vast kingdom whose influence stretched from western Algeria in one direction to Libya in the other. Like Carthage, it was a place of libraries and scholarship.

Chapter 11 covers the civilisations of the West African coast. The Nok Culture was the first to emerge in 1000 BC. Statuary of great aesthetic power were produced there whose stylistic canons influenced art from all over Africa. Following this came the Yoruba kingdoms in 600 AD. Their achievements were so impressive that one pioneering scholar erroneously believed that he had encountered remnants of the lost civilization of Atlantis. Igbo-Ukwu began to flourish around 850 AD. Its artefacts continue to baffle and astonish historians. Great Benin emerged in 900 AD. Its capital city was built on an incredible scale. One writer compared its construction to that of the Great Wall of China. Finally, we encounter Kongo. Its earliest history is lost to us, but its mediæval history can be reconstructed in some detail.

Chapter 12 concerns the West African superstates. Ancient Ghana began as a kingdom in 300 AD. It became an empire in 700 AD and its ruler was described as the richest king on the face of the earth in 951 AD. Mali became the new superpower in the region after 1240. Its wealth was astonishing. The BBC claimed that it became the richest state in the fourteenth century world. Its institutions were gathering places for intellectuals, and its monuments continue to impress with their power and originality. Songhai became the new regional superpower after 1464. It controlled a territory as large as all of Europe combined. Its power was felt from Senegal to Niger.

Chapter 13 covers the civilisation of the Moors. African converts to Islam built a great civilisation in Northwest Africa. In addition, they helped to build one in Spain. The culture in Spain lasted from 711 AD until 1492. This culture proved pivotal to the birth of the European Renaissance. Great monuments built by Africans continue to stand in the cities of Marrakech, Fez, Rabat, Algiers, Tlemcen, and also Seville. Some of these are among the architectural treasures of the world.

Chapter 14 concerns the civilisations of the Central Sahara. The Sao Culture began in around the fourth century BC. Their political structures, technology and architectural ideas shaped the states that succeeded it after 800 AD. The Kanem-Borno Empire and the Hausa Confederation were places where it was possible to cash a cheque, converse with scholars familiar with Greek and Islamic philosophy, and buy writing-paper as well as goods made in England and Germany.

Chapter 15 covers the antiquities of East Africa. Ethiopia has monuments that date back before the fifth century BC. It was a kingdom of obelisks, castles, cathedrals and monasteries. In the early Christian era, it was ranked as the third most powerful empire in the world. The Swahili States were a number of major cities that flourished on the East African coast from the eighth century AD. The cities were splendid with houses of three or four storeys. They had indoor toilets and piped water controlled by taps.

Chapter 16 concerns the history of Mediæval Nubia. By the sixth century AD, three kingdoms flourished - Nobadia, Makuria and Alwa. This was one of the greatest periods in human history. Opulence was widespread in the villages, not just the towns and cities. Archaeological excavations found villages that possessed two storey houses, common sanitary and drainage systems, and also highly developed irrigation.

Chapter 17 covers the history of the southern African cultures, particularly the Empire of Munhumutapa. From the twelfth or thirteenth centuries AD, its rulers brought much of southern Africa under a single authority. The empire was rich in gold, iron, copper, bronze and ivory. They imported Chinese porcelain, Persian glazed wares, Indian textiles, and glass.

Chapter 18 concerns the fall of the African states, mass enslavement and the resistance that followed. North Africa suffered invasion, destruction and enslavement at the hands of the Persians in 525 BC, the Greeks in 332 BC, the Romans after 146 BC, the Vandals (i.e. Germans) in the fifth century AD, and the Arabs after 639 AD. These actions largely cleared Black people out of North Africa. Much of Africa, particularly the West, was devastated in another round of enslavement after 1441. Following this in the late nineteenth century Europe colonised almost the whole of Africa. Black people resisted. Most notably, some of the Blacks of Brazil set up their own independent all-Black kingdom after 1595.

Chapter 19 discusses the peopling of western and southern Asia. This is a key chapter for dealing with the Negro civilisations that used to exist in Arabia, Iran and Pakistan/Western India. To this day, Negro-Australoid populations descended from the Sabaeans of Arabia, the Elamites of Iran, and the Indus Valley Civilisation of Pakistan/Western India, can still be found.

Chapter 20 concerns the western Asian civilisations of Sumer and Elam. Sumer entered history around 3300 BC. Elam emerged a few years later. They built great monuments such as ziggurats that still stand today.

Chapter 21 covers the history of the Indus Valley Civilisation of Pakistan/Western India and the Sabaeans of Arabia. The Indus Valley Civilisation emerged around 3000 BC. It had planned cities laid out on a horizontal/vertical grid. Its houses were of two or more storeys and boasted chutes to dispose of rubbish or waste. The Sabaean Civilisation emerged around 1500 BC. By the time of the Greeks, it was the richest nation in the world where gold and silver drinking vessels were not uncommon.

Notes

[1] Tony Blair et al, *Our Common Interest: Report of the Commission for Africa,* UK, March 2005, p.1.
[2] Ibid., p.121.
[3] Ibid., p.125.
[4] Quoted in *news.telegraph.co.uk,* internet article, see
http://www.telegraph.co.uk/news/main.jhtml?xml=/news/2003/01/27/db2701.xml
[5] Quoted in J. A. Rogers, *Nature Knows No Color-Line,* US, Helga M. Rogers, 1952, p.4.

CHAPTER ONE: WHAT IS BLACK HISTORY?

Introduction

What is Black history? Malcolm X? Mary Seacole? Slavery? Clannic societies? The man who invented the traffic lights? Clearly the history of Black people dates back to a period well before they were enslaved and colonised. That there is such a history worth discussing was well stated many years ago by Professor William Hansberry, the venerable African-American historian. In a lecture entitled *Early African Civilizations,* he informed us that:

> Between the years 1834 and 1908, there occurred a revolution in academic thinking about Africa's place in the outlines of world geography and world history. And in the past 150 years, European explorers and archaeologists have found in the valleys of the Niger, Benwezi, Limpopo and Nile Rivers, in the basin of Lake Chad and the Sahara, extensive remains of hundreds of ruins which bear witness to the existence of former civilizations hundreds and thousands of years ago.[1]

Professor Cheikh Anta Diop, the noted Senegalese scholar, expressed a similar view more recently:

> In … Nubia [i.e. Sudan] … we still find a profusion of stone monuments, such as obelisks, temples, pyramids … In Zimbabwe [i.e. in Southern Africa] … we find ruins of monuments and cities built of stone … "over a radius of 100 to 200 miles around Victoria" … In other words, those ruins extend over a diameter almost as great as that of France. In the region of [ancient] Ghana … [was] the site of Kumbi, excavated by a French district officer, Bonnel de Mézières, who discovered tombs of great dimensions, "sarcophagi of schist, metallurgical workshops, ruins of towers and of various buildings" … In the Lake Debo region (in Mali, on the Niger), pyramids are found … [2]

We have already discussed the recent discovery of Eredo. Archaeology has unearthed two other civilisations in the Nigeria region, Nok and Igbo-Ukwu. Artefacts from the Nok culture were first stumbled upon in 1928 by tin miners who were digging in the region. Various dating techniques showed that the artefacts belonged to a civilisation dated at between 1000 BC and 300 BC.[3] Iron smelting was conducted in the Nok culture from at least 900 BC. There is evidence of iron slag and also a blast furnace wall.[4] Isaiah Anozie, a Nigerian

Hausa (Nigeria). Entrance to the Royal Palace of Daura. Mediæval date. Originally published in Garba Ashiwaju ed, *Cities of the Savannah* (Nigeria, The Nigeria Magazine, no date given for publication, p.36). The reader will note that this book, *When We Ruled,* is particularly well illustrated. This photograph (and all the others in this book) was reproduced to provide evidence that this mediæval heritage still exists and can be seen today. This challenges the idea that 'Africa,' outside of Egypt, 'has no history.' It also gives us a picture of life in mediæval Hausaland that enables an appreciation of the history presented in Chapter 14 of this book. Finally, this photograph (and all the others in this book) gives a picture of the art and aesthetics of the different African civilisations.

gentleman, discovered the Igbo-Ukwu culture in 1938. He unearthed a number of artefacts, quite by accident, when digging in his backyard. Archaeologists have since dated the Igbo-Ukwu culture at 800-1000 AD.[5] According to one writer: "The Igbo-Ukwu finds showed evidence of metal working, weaving, and pottery making of unusual skill. The metal work included 110 major and 575 minor copper and bronze objects of very high quality and a very distinctive design".[6] The Jos Museum in Nigeria and many other institutions continue to house the rediscovered artefacts, but our focus for this chapter is actually quite different ...

In Nigeria, great monuments of historical importance exist. The royal palace in the northern city of Daura is known to date to the mediæval period. Professor Dmochowski, an authority on Nigerian architecture, wrote: "[I]t is reasonable to presume that most of the original plan of the residence has not changed for several centuries".[7] He continues:

> The most impressive building [within the palace complex] was the *kofar zaure,* the entrance hall ... Its walls were extremely thick - up to 2.8 metres. The structure and three-dimensional design were most imaginative and proved the proficiency of the builders in spatial composition. The roughly square interior was covered by a flat roof, supported by an elaborate system of four main corbelled arches. They were supplemented by a number of semi-elliptical consoles or cantilevered beams, all reinforced with timber. The main arches, the *bazan gizo,* sprang from eight pillars: the four pillars standing on both sides of the main axis were square; the four along the transverse axis were round. All of them stood independently for only one-third of their height; the upper two thirds of each pillar joined with the walls of the *kofar,* thus forming an extremely powerful system of supports. It could be compared with the structural concept of flying buttresses but set inside, rather than outside the building, and leaving a free passage along the walls all around the *kofar zaure.* This passage could be compared with the ambulatory of a medieval cathedral, to borrow once again from the vocabulary of European gothic. This comparison, it must be emphasised, applies insofar as each problem was solved by similar thinking on the part of the designers. The structure, form and purpose had no similarity to any European device.[8]

The royal palace in the city of Kano dates back to the fifteenth century. Begun by Muhammad Rumfa (ruled 1463-99), it has gradually evolved over generations into a very imposing complex. A colonial report of the city from 1902 described it as "a network of buildings covering an area of 33 acres and surrounded by a wall 20 to 30 feet high outside and 15 feet inside ... in itself no mean citadel".[9] Furthermore, the southern gate of the first millennium palace of Dala, the original capital, still exists today and is a part of the Kano complex.[10] The royal palace in the city of Zaria dates to the sixteenth century. Begun by Bakwa Turunku (died 1566), though there is some doubt here, it too has evolved into a great complex (see page 93). Dr Dmochowski says of it: "the palace should be preserved as one of the most important monuments of Nigerian national culture".[11]

There are old mosques and minarets that are still in existence. Of these, the most celebrated are the Gobirau Minaret of Muhammad Korau (ruled *c.*1444-94) and the Friday Mosque of Zaria. Mallam Mika'ilu, the Babban Gwani ('Great Builder'), built this latter construction between 1834 and 1846. Made of egg-shaped clay bricks, the building was surrounded by an enclosure that contained a court and an adjoining sanctuary. The sanctuary possesses six domes but bears no resemblance to those of oriental buildings. Complexes of clay arches that were reinforced with corbels of palm beams spanned the spaces within. Reliefs decorated the supporting piers and parts of the *qibla* wall.[12] Professor Moughtin, author of *Hausa Architecture,* wrote:

> The Friday Mosque, Zaria, is probably the high point of Hausa architecture, built during a puritanical fervour … The relief patterns were … sober and formal, the dignified work of religious reformers, the very antithesis of the arabesque-like spirals, interlacing knots and chevrons typical of Hausaland for much of this [i.e. twentieth] century. The first impression on entering the mosque is of big sculptural forms. Decoration is restrained and in the background.[13]

North Africa

Egypt and other countries of North Africa are today considered integral parts of the Arab world. The Arabians have dominated North Africa since their victorious *jihad* of 639-708 AD.[14] Before that conquest, however, North Africa was basically Negro, just like the rest of the African continent. The most ancient monuments in this region were built when North Africa was under indigenous African rule.[15]

Pharaoh Djoser, the second king of the Third Egyptian Dynasty, ruled between 5018 and 4989 BC. He built the earliest monument in the world still celebrated today. Every year, thousands of tourists visit his Funerary Complex in the city of Saqqara. Imhotep, his celebrated Prime Minister, designed the Complex. An outer wall, now mostly in ruins, surrounded the whole structure. It was built on a rectangular plan one mile long and with one entrance (see page 161). Through the entrance are a series of columns, the first stone-built columns known to historians. Connected to walls, they are ornamental having been modelled on plant stems grouped together. The North House also has ornamental columns built into the walls that have papyrus-like capitals. Also inside the complex is the Ceremonial Court. Like everything else these buildings are solid and are thus symbolic. The Court is made of limestone blocks that have been quarried and then shaped. In the centre of the complex is the Step Pyramid, the first of 90 Egyptian pyramids. Made of limestone blocks, it is 197 feet high. Unlike the later pyramids, this structure is built on a rectangular plan measuring 345 by 414 feet - equivalent to a base of 14,000 square yards. It has 6 steps and may represent a stairway. The building slopes at an angle of 72° 30'.[16] Under the Pyramid were a series of rock-hewn chambers and corridors. They are ornamented with panels of colourful tiles. In these hidden quarters, Djoser and eleven others are said to have been buried.[17] On the importance of the Djoser complex, Dr Charles Finch, a leading African-American scholar, noted that: "[It] was humanity's first great architectural triumph. It established architectural forms, styles, and canons still in use today. The practical building technique and masonry evident in the entrance temple were never surpassed, though ... they were realized on a grander scale."[18]

The monuments "on a grander scale" include the structures built by the Fourth Dynasty Pharaohs - the Step Pyramid of Meidum, the Bent and Red Pyramids of Dashur, and the three Great Pyramids of Giza - monuments built between 4872 and 4615 BC. Of these, the most impressive is the first Great Pyramid of Giza. It was 481 feet tall, the equivalent of a 40 storey building. It was made of 2.3 million blocks of limestone and granite, some weighing 100 tons.[19] The accuracy of the construction work is astonishing. Dr Alfred Russell Wallace, a famous British scientist, commented on this more than a hundred years ago in an address before the British Association for the Advancement of Science:

> 1. That the pyramid is truly square, the sides being equal, and the angles right angles;
> 2. That the four sockets on which the first four stones of the corners rested are truly on the same level;
> 3. That the directions of the sides are accurate to the four cardinal points [of north, south, east and west];
> 4. That the vertical height of the pyramid bears the same proportion to its circumference at the base as the radius of a circle does to its circumference [i.e. the Egyptians understood π].[20]

Further south lay the complex of temples in the city of Waset. The Karnak and Luxor temples, now in partial ruin, were built over many years with contributions from different pharaohs of the Twelfth, Eighteenth, Nineteenth and Twenty-Fifth Dynasties (3405-664 BC). The Karnak Complex was a place of culture and business. It should be thought of as an abbey since people lived and worked there and the complex was self-contained. The treasures of the ancient world passed through its corridors; gold and precious woods from

Kush, tribute from Syria, and vases from Crete. A procession of sphinxes led to the outer pylon, itself 370 feet across, 143 feet high, and 49 feet thick at the base, but becoming narrower at the top. Behind the pylon was the Temple of Amen, which originally had huge doors to close it off (see page 193). A place of unbelievable luxury, the Hypostyle Hall, just one of its many temples, was 171 feet long and 338 feet wide, covering an area of 56,000 square feet. It was the largest enclosed space in Egyptian architecture, even larger than Durham Cathedral by 5,000 square feet. It contained 134 sandstone columns, covered with bas-reliefs and hieroglyphics.[21] An architect described the Hall as follows:

> No language [says Fergusson] can convey an idea of its beauty, and no artist has yet been able to reproduce its form so as to convey to those who have not seen it any ideas of its grandeur. The mass of its central piers, illuminated by a flood of light from the clerestory, and the smaller pillars of the wings gradually fading into obscurity, are so arranged and lighted as to convey an idea of infinite space; at the same time the beauty and massiveness of the forms, and the brilliancy of their coloured decorations, all combine to stamp this as *the greatest of man's architectural works* ... [22]

There were huge obelisks that stood before the façades of the Karnak and Luxor temples. They were made of a single piece of stone that was hewn from a quarry and then transported to the required position. Pharaoh Hatshepsut erected one such obelisk. It was 90.2 feet tall and weighed an astonishing 302 tons. There is a huge and unfinished obelisk that is 41.78 metres long that was left at Aswan, presumably because it did not meet exacting standards of accuracy.[23] The importance of these monuments are such that one authority has argued that there is a typological and symbolic link between the obelisks of ancient times and the skyscrapers of today. As Elleh put it: "Several texts exist of Pharaohs boasting that they erected obelisks which reached, pierced, or mingled with the sky."[24]

Pharaoh Hatshepsut (1650-1600 BC) of the Eighteenth Dynasty was builder of one of Egypt's most popular monuments. Senenmut, the Overseer of Works, constructed her temple in the region now known as Deir-el-Bahri (see page 81). Rather than build upwards from a base, the Mortuary Temple was built downwards, being cut out of a mountain. The whole building was hewn from the rocks by hammer and chisel. The result is a pillared terrace structure that rises in three stages with 2 central ramps, also carved and sculpted. The ramps are long and slope with a gentle gradient. Their position divides the temple into two symmetrical halves. Entrance halls of limestone columns lead to the interior chapels dedicated to the deities Anubis, Hathor, Osiris and Ra. Through the colonnade, the interior has wall reliefs that depict Hatshepsut's maritime voyages to Punt (i.e. possibly Somalia or Ethiopia) showing also the

Kush (Sudan). Pyramids at Gebel Barkal. c.100 BC. There are at least 223 pyramids in Sudan as a whole. Sudan has more pyramids than any other country on earth - even more than Egypt. (Photo: Louis Buckley, Black Nine Films).

round houses of that country. In its time, great sculptures embellished the building. There were over 100 limestone sphinxes, 22 granite sphinxes, 40 limestone statues of Hatshepsut, and 28 granite statues of Hatshepsut.[25]

Rameses II of the Nineteenth Dynasty also built a temple carved out of a hill. The Temple of Abu Simbel, in Nubia, is of an incredible scale (see page 197). The façade is 108 feet wide and contains four colossal statues of the pharaoh, each 66 feet high. What is remarkable here is the organisational feat involved. The carved images of Rameses are so large that each builder/sculptor would be so close to their work that none of them would be able to see the bigger picture as they worked. For this reason, accuracy was critical and not just for artistic reasons. The building was oriented to the east to catch the first rays of sunlight that illuminated its icons at the end of a 208 feet corridor. Inside the entrance to the temple are statues of the deity Osiris. This led to a smaller hall that led to an inner chamber.[26]

Further south, the Kushites (of southern Egypt, and northern and central Sudan) had a very long and ancient history. In their earliest periods, they had a pharaonic culture, much like ancient Egypt but beginning earlier than that of the Egyptians. Five thousand artefacts were recovered from a series of early pharaonic tombs in Qustul.[27] Other great periods were centred at cities like Kerma, Gebel Barkal, Meroë and Naqa.

Kerma contains monuments that were built before 1500 BC. Most impressive are the mighty *deffufas* (buildings of clay bricks), the largest of which was 150 feet long, 75 feet wide, and a towering 60 feet tall. Its walls were 12 feet thick and were straight and even. The functions of these buildings are somewhat unclear. Some writers see them as warehouses. In support of this view, archaeologists have found various trade and luxury goods, including pottery and jewels in their vicinity. Other writers claim they were temples, drawing attention to the quartz altar and also columns and faience tiles in one of the buildings.[28]

There are at least 223 pyramids in Kush in the cities of Al Kurru, Nuri, Gebel Barkal and Meroë. They are generally 20 to 30 metres high and steep sided, sloping at around 70°. They were made of smaller blocks than their Giza counterparts. The pyramids were used for royal burials and were entered by underground stairways on the eastern side.[29] Meroë became the capital of the Kushite Empire from around 590 BC until about 350 AD, a period well attested by monuments. There are, for example, 84 pyramids in this city alone,[30] many built with their own miniature temple. Moreover, there are ruins of a bath house sharing affinities with those of the Romans.[31] Two leading Africanists, Professors Roland Oliver and Brian Fagan assure us that:

> Even today the ruins of Mero[ë] make an impressive sight. Six low hills of iron slag mark the southern and western perimeters of the town, bearing witness to what must surely have been the main industry of its inhabitants [i.e. iron smelting]. To the east of the main housing areas are the ruins of a whole series of temples and cemeteries, while the burial pyramids of the royal family crown the summit of a low ridge overlooking the site. Only a small part of the town has so far been cleared and excavated - the royal cemeteries, some scattered temples, and the so-called Royal City, which extends along the banks of the Nile near the main landing stage. Here, the Temple of Amun [sic] was found to be 450 feet long, built of brick and sandstone blocks, and forming a series of courts and halls enclosing a central shrine.[32]

In Musawarat there is a very large and curious complex generally called the Great Enclosure. Dated at 220 BC, it has a series of walled enclosures and edifices that surround a central temple, itself built on a raised platform. Encircling the temple is a colonnade and outside of this is a series of ramps and corridors connecting the different parts of the building. Decorating the structure are elephant motifs.[33] Dr Davidson, an English Africanist, suggested that the building functioned as a place to train, and thus tame, African elephants.[34] Other scholars, just as convincingly, see it as a religious centre for accommodating pilgrims.

The Sudanese city of Naqa contains three important temples, the Temple of Amen, the Lion Temple, and the Kiosk. They date to between 1 AD and 20 AD.

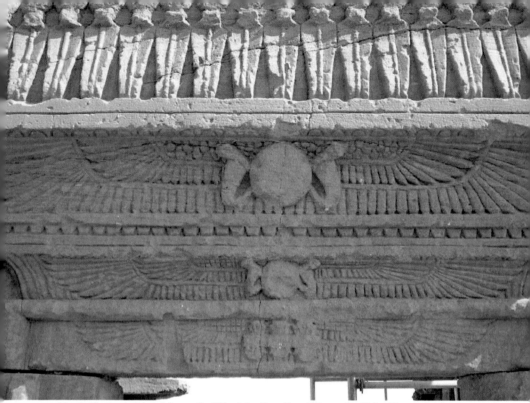

Kush (Sudan). Lintel from the Kiosk in the city of Naqa. Built by Pharaoh Natakamani and Queen Amanitore between 1 and 20 AD. (Photo: Louis Buckley, Black Nine Films).

Pharaoh Natakamani and Queen Amanitore built the Temple of Amen and the Lion Temple. The Temple of Amen has a columned hall leading to an inner sanctuary as in Egyptian temples. In addition, there were 12 sculpted rams that lined the avenue to the entrance. The Lion Temple was dedicated to Apedemak, a local deity. It has a typical Egyptian-like pylon with the King and Queen depicted as conquerors bashing the heads of their enemies. The depiction of the Queen doing the same thing may represent a powerful role for the Queen Mother in the society or may even represent matriarchy. Behind the pylon is a one-room structure, a design unique to Kush. Finally, the Kiosk is a strange building that seems to have incorporated many cultural influences. There are arches, possibly reflecting Roman influence, and the capitals of the columns show traces of Greek influence. Some writers describe them as "pseudo-Corinthian". It is important to note, however, that there is no evidence that the Romans (or Greeks) built this temple. Many writers have hinted at this possibility, but in the absence of solid evidence, we must conclude that this is a Kushite monument built by Kushites.[35]

West Africa

In West Africa, in the Tichitt-Walata region of Mauritania, archaeologists have

Songhai (Mali). House in the city of Djenné. Of two storeys. Originally published in Susan Denyer, *African Traditional Architecture* (UK, Heinemann, 1978, p.169). Possibly 15th or 16th century AD. Is there a connection between this type of architecture and that of the Nile Valley? Compare the façade of this house with the chapel connected to the Pyramid of Amanishakheto (see page 206).

found "large stone masonry villages" that date back to 1100 BC. The villages consisted of roughly circular compounds connected by "well-defined streets". Between 1000 and 800 BC, four times as many villages flourished where "each village [wa]s encircled by a masonry wall over 2m high and 1m thick".[36] By 250 BC, the foundations of West Africa's oldest cities were established such as Old Djenné.[37]

Kumbi Saleh, the capital of Ancient Ghana, flourished from 300 to 1240 AD. Located in modern day Mauritania, archaeological excavations have revealed much. There were houses, almost habitable today, for want of renovation and several storeys high. They had underground rooms, staircases and connecting halls. Some had nine rooms. One part of the city alone is estimated to have housed 30,000 people.[38] We can only speculate on the total city population, but it was several times the size of Mediæval London. There were many other great cities from the Middle Ages that are very much alive today, and have preserved some of their ancient buildings, such as Djenné, Timbuktu (see page 376), Gao, Agades, San, Boré, etc. William Winwood Reade, an English historian, saw some of them in the nineteenth century and commented that in Africa:

> There are ... thousands of large walled cities resembling those of Europe in the
> Middle Ages, or of ancient Greece, or of Italy before the supremacy of Rome,
> encircled by pastures and by arable estates, and by farming villages ... with

their villeggiatura, their municipal government, their agora or forum, their fortified houses, [and] their feuds and street frays of Capulet and Montague.[39]

One such example of a mediæval metropolis is the city of Djenné in modern-day Mali. Djenné's houses have been widely praised for their aesthetic hand sculpted outer walls and terracotta appearance. They are typically of two storeys, with battlements along the summits of the terraces. On the terraces were the latrines, which according to Major Felix Dubois, a pioneering authority, had "perfectly constructed drainage". The interiors had a system of baked pipes to carry away household water.[40] The exterior façade looks much like the façades of the temples attached to the Kushite pyramids or those of the Karnak and Luxor Temples, a fact noticed by both Major Dubois and Professor Diop.[41] Another "Nile Valley" feature is the obelisks. They are not free standing but are built into the house walls of the most substantial houses. Dubois also notes that: "The summits of their dwellings are ornamented by those triangular battlements which may be seen on the palaces of Rameses Meiamoun."[42]

Like Djenné, the houses in Timbuktu are typically of two storeys. They were made of regular sun dried bricks of various shapes - flat, long and rounded. They were set with mortar and then covered with a rough casing. According to Major Dubois, the houses defy "the heaviest tornadoes of rain and wind" and can "last for centuries".[43] The use of clay bricks was dictated by factors such as the availability of alternative building materials, as noted by Dr Finch: "The western Sudan [i.e. West Africa], unlike the Nile Valley or Zimbabwe, is not blessed with abundant building stone such as granite or limestone. Thus, the building material of choice is a particular clay native to the Sudan that allows the fashioning of … bricks."[44] The roofs of the houses were built by constructing a grid of wooden planks on top of the upper walls. The ends of the planks projected through the walls and could be seen from outside the building. A layer of clay was laid over the wooden grid that became the roof.[45]

There are mosques, still in use today, that date back to the glory days of the Mali and Songhai empires. Timbuktu had a famous university, the Sankoré Mosque, and two other important temples, the Djinguerebere and the Sidi Yahya. The minarets of all three fourteenth century monuments dominate the Timbuktu skyline (see page 379). The Djinguerebere Mosque is a nine-aisle building. It was made of round bricks and stone rubble with clay rendering. It has a flat roof sanctuary supported by arcades of mud piers. The minaret is 16 metres high and has an internal staircase. Mansa Musa built this monument in around 1326.[46] The Grand Mosque of Djenné, described as "the largest adobe [i.e. clay] building in the world",[47] was first raised in 1204 as a mosque. It is built on a square plan where each side is 56 metres in length. It has three large towers on one side, each with projecting wooden buttresses, as is typical of

Mali and Songhai (Mali). The Grand Mosque of Djenné. Dedicated by Koi Konboro as a mosque in 1204 AD, it probably predates this as a palace. Although it has been rebuilt several times, always on the same plan, it gives a reasonable picture of 13ᵗʰ (or indeed 11ᵗʰ) century architecture. This is the largest clay brick building on earth. (Photo: Copyright Musée de l'Homme, Paris, Armée de l'Air).

West African monuments from that period. The Grand Mosque of San is particularly noteworthy, as is the Mausoleum of Askia the Great, a weird sixteenth century edifice that resembles a step pyramid.[48] There are many other pyramidal structures in the Lake Debo region. A French archaeologist described them as follows:

> These are massive clusters of clay and stone, in the form of truncated pyramids, with a terra cotta summit of red brick. All of them date from the same period and were built for the same purpose … They rise 15 to 18 metres high on a base of 200 square metres.[49]

Thousands of these tumuli have been found across West Africa. Nearly 7,000 were discovered in north west Senegal alone spread over nearly 1,500 sites. They were probably built between 1000 and 1300 AD.[50]

Recent excavations at Gao, carried out by Tim Insoll of Cambridge University, revealed some intriguing information. One of the finds is well worth meditating on. It is entitled: "Fragments of alabaster window surrounds and a piece of pink window glass, Gao 10ᵗʰ - 14ᵗʰ century."

Ethiopia

In Ethiopia, there are monuments dating back at least 2,500 years. The Temple of Almaqah in Yeha was probably built before the fifth century BC. It is a two

Axum (Ethiopia). Stele in Axum. *c.*100 AD. Carved from a single block of granite, it weighs an awesome 300 tons. This is about the same weight as 450 family sized cars. It has details carved into it that represent a doorway and nine storeys worth of windows. (Photo: Werner Forman Archives).

storey structure made of dry stone masonry, built on a podium.[51] The blocks
were precisely cut and up to three metres long. The Temple has a frieze of ibex
facing the front. Also on the site is a line of huge square pillars. These
monoliths were the remains of a second building.[52]

The city of Axum has a series of seven giant stelae that date from perhaps
300 BC to 300 AD. They have details carved into them that represent windows
and doorways of several storeys. The largest obelisk, now fallen, is in fact "the
largest monolith ever made anywhere in the world".[53] It is 108 feet long,
weighs a staggering 500 tons, and represents a 13 storey building (see page
457). The largest standing obelisk is 75 feet tall and represents a nine storey
building. These monolithic towers may have been placed to mark the sites of
royal burials.[54] Their sizes and weight is worth pondering over when it is noted
that even modern technology would be taxed by the technological problem of
moving and erecting such sizeable structures. Two modern scholars have
discussed the problem of moving a 200-ton block which it must be noted, is
less than half the weight of the fallen monolith:

> Such loads simply cannot be hoisted by the typical tower and hydraulic cranes
> that we are familiar with from building sites in our cities. These cranes, which
> are pieces of advanced technology, can generally 'pick' a maximum load of 20
> tons … Loads exceeding 50 tons require special cranes. Furthermore, there are
> few cranes in the world today that would be capable of picking 200-ton blocks
> … In the United States there are presently only two land-based cranes of the
> 'counterweight and boom' type able to handle loads in the 200-ton range … To
> get this problem into perspective it is helpful to realize that a block of 200 tons
> represents a load roughly equivalent to 300 family-sized automobiles.[55]

Axum contains the Cathedral of Saint Mary of Zion, one of the world's
oldest Christian cathedrals. Dating to the fourth century, this monument was
later rebuilt in late mediæval times.[56]

In the twelfth and thirteenth centuries, Roha became the new capital of the
Ethiopians. Conceived as a New Jerusalem by its founder, Emperor Lalibela
(c.1150-1230), it contains 11 churches, all carved out of the rock of the
mountains by hammer and chisel. All of the temples were carved to a depth of
11 metres or so below ground level. The largest is the House (or Church) of the
Redeemer, a staggering 33.7 metres long, 23.7 metres wide and 11.5 metres
deep. It is entirely surrounded by a forest of columns, all carved and sculpted.
It is one of four churches that give the illusion of being freestanding in Roha
(also called Lalibela), connected only by their bases to the rock from which
they were hewn.[57] The other seven are almost hidden away. An Ethiopian
tourist manual informs us that:

> Physically prised from the rock on which they stand, these towering edifices
> seem superhuman in scale, workmanship, and concept. Some lie almost

Abyssinia (Ethiopia). House of Saint George in Lalibela/Roha. Built by Emperor Lalibela between 1180 and 1220 AD. It was one of eleven churches in the city carved out by chiselling and hollowing the living rock! Ethiopians call Lalibela/Roha the Eighth Wonder of the World. (Photo: Werner Forman Archives).

completely hidden in deep trenches, whilst others stand in open quarried caves.
A complex and bewildering labyrinth of tunnels and narrow passageways with
offset crypts, grotto[e]s, and galleries connects them all. Throughout this
mysterious and wonderful settlement, priests and deacons go about their
timeless business.[58]

The House of Mary is another of the 'freestanding' churches (see page 465).
The Emperor considered it one of his favourites and the royal family used it to
hold mass. It is 15 metres long, 11 metres wide and 10 metres deep. In its
courtyard is a deep square baptismal pool.[59]

Perhaps the most celebrated of the Lalibela churches is the House of Saint
George. From the top of the monument, looking downwards, the church is in
the shape of a concentric cross. It is more than 12 metres deep and its outer
wall seems to indicate four storeys. Like the Temple of Almaqah, the church
was built on a podium. The bottom rows of windows are similar in design to
those seen on the old Axum monoliths. Other windows have pointed arches.
Internally, there is a dome over the sanctuary.[60]

The architects of Lalibela seem to have absorbed or developed a wide range
of styles. The House of Golgotha has pointed arch windows, with a tendrille-
like tracery topped by a cross, similar to a Maltese cross. The House of Abba
Libanos has plain pointed arch windows but also cross-shaped openings. The
House of Mascal has Romanesque arches and windows of twinned crosses.
The House of Mary has swastika-shaped windows.[61]

Lalibela is not the only place to have such wonders (see also page 49). Peter
Garlake, author of *Early Art and Architecture of Africa,* reports research that
was conducted in the region in the early 1970's when:

> startling numbers of churches built in caves or partially or completely cut from
> the living rock were revealed not only in Tigre and Lalibela but as far south as
> Addis Ababa. Soon at least 1,500 were known. At least as many more probably
> await revelation to the outside world. A whole realm of architectural history
> awaits recording, study, and understanding.[62]

Southern Africa

In Southern Africa, there are at least 600 stone built ruins in the regions of
Zimbabwe, Mozambique and South Africa.[63] These ruins "show today an
extraordinary cultural past".[64] Most of them are said to date from the Middle
Ages, but some authorities give much earlier dates for their construction. These
structures are called Mazimbabwe in Shona, the Bantu language of the
builders, and means great houses of stone. João de Barros, a Portuguese writer
of the mid-sixteenth century, tells us "Symbaoe" (more correctly "Zimbabwe")

Shona (Zimbabwe). The Temple at Great Zimbabwe. The outer wall was made of 100,000 tons of granite bricks held together without any use of mortar. (Photo: Werner Forman Archives). We here adopt the date of c.1335 AD for the building of these walls. Dr Charles Finch gave this date in *The Star of Deep Beginnings* (US, Khenti, 1998, p.149). Older authorities have given dates of the ninth century AD and the sixth century AD. R. N. Hall and W. G. Neal gave a construction date of between 2000 and 1100 BC. See *Ancient Ruins of Rhodesia: Second Edition* (UK, Methuen & Co., 1904, pp.109-112).

in Shona "signifies court".[65] Of the buildings themselves, Professor Diop, cited
earlier, informs us that:

> [T]hey are almost cyclopean structures, with walls several metres thick; five at
> the base, three at the top, and nine meters in height. Edifices of all types are to
> be found there from the royal palace, the temple, and the military fortification
> to the private villa of a notable. The walls are of granite masonry.[66]

The Great Zimbabwe was the largest of these ruins. It consists of 12 clusters
of buildings, spread over three square miles. Its outer walls were made from
100,000 tons of granite bricks. In the fourteenth century, the city housed
18,000 people, comparable in size to that of London of the same period. The
buildings housed warehouses and shrines.[67] Its industries included 4,000 gold
mines, iron smelting, copper and bronze manufacture, and an ivory trade with
the Swahili on the East African coast. Among the products imported were
stoneware and green glazed dishes from China, coloured glass from the Near
East, and glazed and painted bowls from Persia.[68]

The walls of the central enclosure, popularly known as the "Temple", reach
35 feet in height and 17 feet thick in places. They form an irregular ellipse with
a maximum diameter of 292 feet and a circumference of 830 feet. The bricks
are fashioned and arranged to hold together in regular courses without the use
of mortar. The floors are of crushed granite and contain drains.[69] One of the
earliest visitors to the site, J. Theodore Bent, commented that: "As a
specim[e]n of the dry builder's art, it is without a parallel."[70] The tops of some
walls have ornamental patterns, of which chevron and dentelle are the most
common. For over 250 feet of its length, the chevron pattern ornaments the
outer wall and is perfectly level. On the summit of the wall above the chevron
work, stood a series of granite and soapstone monoliths and also a double row
of small granite towers.[71] Some of the other ruins show check, sloping block,
and herringbone patterns.[72] The North Entrance has steps that curve inwards in
a semicircular fashion. This leads immediately inside to the great Parallel
Passage, a distance of 220 feet.[73]

Though succumbed to the passage of time, cottages once stood within and
outside these walls for an area of three square miles. They were circular and
thatched. Moreover, they had walls 12 to 18 inches thick and made of *daga,* a
clay and gravel mixture. According to Peter Garlake, a former Senior Inspector
of Monuments, the cottages "exhibited considerable technical proficiency that
achieved almost sculptural effects." He continues:

> The *daga* structures in the Ruins were in fact structural accomplishments of the
> same order as the masonry walls ... [Y]et fundamentally they are only
> developments and refinements of traditions that were almost ubiquitous in the

Shona (Zimbabwe). The Temple at Great Zimbabwe. *c.*1335 AD. The cottages that once stood inside these walls have since perished but a reconstruction is on page 522. (Photo: Werner Forman Archives).

cultures of this area and time. Both reflect a concern for appearance, ostentation, even luxury, achieved regardless of the cost in labour or material.[74]

Daga was also used to make steps, fireplaces, chairs, bedsteads, and tables, all to a high level of smooth glazed finish. It was used to coat floors, again to a fine finish. Dr Finch notes that this must have had a "dazzling" aesthetic effect.[75]

The cottages were richly decorated with carved wooden beams and painted walls. Among the typical designs were paintings of animals, birds, people, and black and white squares. Some cottages had wooden doors, beautifully carved from selected timbers. One authority informs us that: "Very few of these elaborate door panels survive, but some can still be found in very remote regions of the country".[76]

Perhaps the most well known part of the ruined complex is the Conical Tower. The Parallel Passage leads on to this curious edifice. It is 18 feet in diameter at the base and 30 feet high, though once higher. Next to the tower is

Shona (Zimbabwe, Mozambique, etc.). Typical styles of decorative walling used at the Munhumatapan sites. (i) check pattern (ii) dentelle pattern and (iii) chevron pattern. From R. N. Hall and W. G. Neal, *Ancient Ruins of Rhodesia: Second Edition* (UK, Methuen & Co., 1904, opposite p.184).

a much smaller cone structure.[77] The Conical Tower may symbolise a mound of grain and therefore reinforce the role of the king as provider for the people.

On a hill 350 feet above and overlooking the Temple is a castle, generally known as the "Acropolis". It has very thick walls, massive conical turrets, narrow entrances, and twisting passageways. The widths of the entrances vary from half a metre to just over a metre. The widths of the walls vary from 12 to 14 feet at the top to 19 to 22 feet thick at the base. The site may well have been chosen for security reasons, giving a panoramic view of the city and the surroundings. What is interesting here is that the hill contains huge stone boulders. The builders incorporated the boulders into the walls rather than clearing them. The "Eastern Temple" was another part of the complex. It was here that the famous soapstone bird sculptures were found. These birds were typically 14 inches long and stood at the top of three feet long columns.[78]

By the thirteenth century, or perhaps earlier, an empire was established in the region of Zimbabwe, Mozambique, and South Africa. In later times it became known as Munhumutapa. Its rulers controlled the trade with the East African coastal cities. Furthermore, they controlled the all-important gold mines. Great Zimbabwe functioned as its cultural capital until about 1550 but then it was gradually abandoned. Hundreds of other stone built structures associated with this and a successor empire exist in the region. The most notable of these courts were at Khami (see page 528), Naletale and Dhlo Dhlo. Like Great Zimbabwe, they have walls of dressed blocks, but they also have platforms and terraces where the cottages were built.[79] In the Naletale walls, there are small towers capping the outer wall that, again, may represent a pile of grain. These walls are regularly coursed and contain decorations of chevron, check, herringbone, dark stone, and panelled herringbone patterns. Patterns of various motifs became a regular feature of walls in this area.[80] Of the domestic goods at the courts, archaeology at Khami has revealed interesting data:

> At the Khami Ruins, late sixteenth- or early seventeenth-century Wan Li blue-and-white porcelain, Portuguese, German and North African glazed stonewares and earthenwares, and fragments of Iberian silverware have been found ... [81]

The East African Coast

The East Coast, from Somalia to Mozambique, has ruins of well over 50 towns and cities. They flourished from the ninth to the sixteenth centuries due to their role in the Indian Ocean trade.[82] One of these cities was Kilwa, a former seaport on the coast of Tanzania. In the fourteenth century, Kilwa was a very fine place. One visitor described it as "one of the most beautiful and well constructed cities in the world":[83]

Swahili (Kenya). Handsome carved wooden door from and old house in Lamu. Doors of this type have been made for hundreds of years all along the East African coast. My guide said this door dated to the 16th century AD. (Photo: Robin Walker).

Today [says a modern authority,] only a shabby village stands there. Yet beyond
the village can still be found the walls and towers of ruined palaces and large
houses and mosques, which is what the Moslems call their churches. A great
palace [the Husuni Kubwa] has been dug out of the bushes that covered it for
hundreds of years. It is a strange and beautiful ruin on a cliff over the Indian
Ocean. Many other ruins stand nearby. But the strangest thing about Kilwa and
the other towns nearby is that there is little to be found about them in the newer
history books. Even when the cities are described, they are said to be not
African, but the work of people from Arabia and Persia. History books saying
this are out of date, and they are wrong.[84]

The other cities included the likes of Sinna, Zanzibar, Lamu, Mombasa, Gedi
and Mogadishu. Their mosques were "as grand as the mediaeval cathedrals of
Europe". The city of Lamu (see also page 470) was apparently "as
sophisticated as mediaeval Venice".[85] Tradition has it that Lamu, the best
preserved of the Swahili cities, was founded in 699 AD. Near its harbour are a
number of splendid mansions, now deserted. They have reception rooms
whose walls have tiered decorated niches. Also of interest is a fluted pillar
tomb that may date back to the fifteenth century period. The city has over 20
mosques, all whitewashed, and also a few palaces.[86]

In Kilwa the ruined mosque was once the largest of the Swahili temples. It
was founded in the tenth or eleventh centuries AD, but it was enlarged in the
thirteenth and fifteenth centuries. The north prayer hall was built first. It had a
massive stone and concrete roof built on wooden rafters. Supporting the roof
were a series of nine wooden pillars of polygonal shape. The domed extension,
to the south, was built later. Between 1421 and 1430, it was rebuilt during the
time of Sulaiman ibn Muhammad al-Malik al-Adil. Its roof is a complicated
construction and has barrel vaults and domes over alternate bays. The interior
has a forest of composite octagonal columns of rubble and cut stone, set in
mortar. To the south of the mosque is a high wall that encloses an area for
ablutions. It has water-tanks, a well and stone slabs - on which feet were
washed and dried. In total, it was an admirable structure. One early Portuguese
visitor compared its domed ceiling to that of the Great Mosque of Cordova in
Spain.[87]

There are other buildings of historical interest in Kilwa. Located east of the
Husuni Kubwa is the Husuni Ndogo, a contemporaneous building raised by al-
Malik al-Mansur.[88] The structure has a massive wall enclosing a rectangular
plan and covers an acre. At intervals along the walls and at the corners, are
solid towers. They are polygonal in shape but circular at the base. The function
of this great edifice is presently unknown but it may have been a mosque or
even a market.[89] South and west of the Great Mosque, lay the graveyard. This
leads to a small domed fifteenth century temple. It is the best preserved and
ornamented of the old structures. The customary vaults and domes ornament

Swahili (Tanzania). Interior of the Great Mosque of Kilwa. Founded in the 10th or 11th centuries AD, it was much enlarged in the 13th and 15th centuries. It was the largest of the Swahili temples. (Photo: Werner Forman Archives).

its roof, but an octagonal pillar, a most curious feature, surmounts the central dome. Islamic ware, consisting of small bowls, was set into the ceilings of the vaults. Above the *mihrab* were recesses for tiles and bowls. The eastern side of the building has a room that may have functioned as a Koran school.[90]

Marco Polo described Zanzibar in the latter thirteenth century. Mentioning their trade in ivory, he portrayed Zanzibar as a port that attracted "many merchant ships".[91] Of Zanzibari architecture, Dr Elleh, author of the excellent *African Architecture: Evolution and Transformation,* makes the following observations:

> The island[s] of Zanzibar and Pemba have some of the best preserved classic architecture of [the] Swahili middle ages and are distinguished by the art deco that garnishes the walls and the notches of the buildings. As in Lamu, Kenya, the houses in Zanzibar were built of brick. They are self-contained one- or two-storey buildings with gardens, courtyards, servant quarters, walls of coral, and a prioritized degree of privacy in the location of the master bedrooms, the wives' rooms, and the parlor or living space. In most cases, the verandas are well decorated with plaster work, and careful attention is given to the openings which are decorated along the top and down the sides as pilasters.[92]

Gedi, near the coast of Kenya, is another ghost town. Its ruins, dating from the fourteenth or fifteenth centuries, some say earlier, include the city walls, the palace (see page 472), private houses, the Great Mosque, seven smaller mosques, and three pillar tombs.[93] The walls are nine feet high and had at least three gates. Approaching the mosque was a washing pool for the believers to perform ablutions. It had a purifier made of limestone for recycling water. The houses had roofs of coral tiles covered in lime, walls of mortar and coral rag, and finely cut doorways of coral. The early houses were of one storey. They had a court, leading to the main room, and behind that was the private quarter. Also there, were smaller adjoining rooms, such as the bathroom, the toilet, bedroom, kitchen and storeroom. Later houses, from the fifteenth or sixteenth centuries, had upper floors. The royal palace had a layout similar to a large cluster of these houses, but with the addition of a reception hall. The palace contains evidence of piped water controlled by taps, bathrooms and indoor toilets. Finally, a part of this three-gated city had streets laid out on a north-south, east-west grid.[94]

In summary, "Africa has a long and varied history of human settlement", wrote Dr Thomas Blair, an expert on Architecture and Planning:

> Its cities reach back to the thresholds of man's urban experience when the dominance of activities at sacred temples, armed camps, palaces, market places and caravanserai drew neighbouring peoples into complex productive systems. From the ninth century expansion of inland and ocean trade to the fifteenth

century - long before the penetration of European slavers, factors and
conquistadores - the port cities, market centres and city states of powerful
kingdoms enclosed large, densely populated permanent settlements within their
boundaries. Large mining centres and stone-building civilisations prospered in
the southern tier of Mapungubwe (Transvaal), Zimbabwe and Monomotapa
(Southern Rhodesia and Moçambique), north to the Lunda-Luba settlements
and beyond; they flourished in the kingdoms of the Rift Valley in East Africa
and westward to the empires of Mali, Songhai, Kanem, Ghana, and Kongo-
Angola states. Administrative and trade centres of Sudanic kingdoms were
located in capital cities like Ségou and Gao, Timbuctu [sic], Wagadugu,
Kumasi, and Kano were known for their influence and power. Seaport towns
grew along the East African coast at Mogadishu, Brava, Malindi, Mombassa
[sic], Pemba, Zanzibar, Kilwa, Kilimane and Sofala. In West Africa the cities
of Yoruba kingdoms rose to prominence as [rulers] ... expanded their control
over trade routes. The [ruler's] palace and the market-place dominated the
central areas of well-planned cities like Ile-Ife, Ilesha and Ekiti. In the old
quarters nearby the houses of the guilds, traders and important families nestled
between the major roads radiating to neighbouring towns. Newly-settled areas
were laid out in a rectilinear pattern. The populace lived in compounds each of
which had a large house set in a square-shaped space bounded by a high wall.
Some were more than a half acre in size and provided living space for a large
family and kinsmen. Groups of compounds were administered by elders and
together they formed the basis of an urban council responsible to the princely
authority. African pre-colonial cities of the Great Iron Age grew out of the
traditional past in response to self-generated political and technological
changes. They were urban expressions of emergent adaptive self-assured
political states whose economies developed with the increased production of
commodities for trade.[95]

Notes

[1] Quoted in John Jackson, *Introduction to African Civilizations,* US, Citadel Press, 1970,
p.9.
[2] Cheikh Anta Diop, *African Origin of Civilization: Myth or Reality?* US, Lawrence Hill
Books, 1974, pp.156-7.
[3] Werner Gillon, *A Short History of African Art,* UK, Penguin, 1984, p.75 and Francine
Maurer and Olivier Langevin, *Dating of Ancient Civilizations from Nigeria,* in Bernard de
Grunne, *The Birth of Art in Black Africa,* France and Luxembourg, Adam Biro & Banque
Generale du Luxembourg, 1998, p.114.
[4] Charles S. Finch, *The Star of Deep Beginnings,* US, Khenti, 1998, p.36.
[5] Ekpo Eyo, *Two Thousand Years of Nigerian Art,* UK & Nigeria, Ethnographica and The
National Commission for Museums and Monuments, 1977, pp.72, 80-2.
[6] David Northrup, *The Growth of Trade among the Igbo Before 1800,* in *Journal of
African History, Volume 13: No.2,* UK, Cambridge University Press, 1972, pp.217-9.
[7] Z. R. Dmochowski, *Northern Nigeria: An Introduction to Nigerian Traditional
Architecture, Volume 1,* Nigeria, National Commission for Museums and Monuments,
1990, section 5.3.

[8] Ibid, section 5.4.

[9] Quoted in ibid., section 5.20.

[10] Ibid.

[11] Ibid., section 5.48.

[12] Allan Leary, *West Africa,* in *Architecture of the Islamic World,* ed George Michell, UK, Thames and Hudson, 1978, p.276.

[13] J. C. Moughtin, *Hausa Architecture,* UK, Ethnographica, 1985, pp.85-6.

[14] J. C. DeGraft-Johnson, *African Glory,* UK, Watts & Co., 1954, pp.58-76.

[15] See Chapters 4 and 9.

[16] Dietrich Wildung, *Egypt from Prehistory to the Romans,* Germany, Taschen, 1997, pp.28-37 and Charles S. Finch, *The Star of Deep Beginnings,* pp.105-108.

[17] Emma Brunner-Trout, *Ancient Egypt,* in *Architecture of the Ancient Civilizations in Colour,* ed Bodo Cichy, UK, Thames and Hudson, 1966, p.75.

[18] Charles S. Finch, *The Star of Deep Beginnings,* pp.107-8.

[19] Ibid., pp.108-111.

[20] Quoted in John Jackson, *Man, God and Civilization,* US, Citadel Press, 1972, p.223.

[21] Dietrich Wildung, *Egypt from Prehistory to the Romans,* pp.79-81, 95-119, Rev. James Baikie, *The Life of the Ancient East,* UK, A. & C. Black, 1923, p.105 and George Rawlinson, *Ancient Egypt: The Story of the Nations,* UK, T. Fisher Unwin, 1888, p.245.

[22] Quoted in George Rawlinson, *Ancient Egypt: The Story of the Nations,* pp.245-6.

[23] Nnamdi Elleh, *African Architecture: Evolution and Transformation,* US, McGraw-Hill, 1997, pp.28 and 41.

[24] Ibid., p.41.

[25] Emma Brunner-Trout, *Ancient Egypt,* in *Architecture of the Ancient Civilizations in Colour,* pp.101-2 and Dietrich Wildung, *Egypt from Prehistory to the Romans,* pp.130-134.

[26] Emma Brunner-Trout, *Ancient Egypt,* in *Architecture of the Ancient Civilizations in Colour,* pp.124-125.

[27] Bruce Williams, *The Lost Pharaohs of Nubia,* in *Egypt Revisited,* ed Ivan Van Sertima, US, Transaction Publishers, 1989, pp.90-104.

[28] Charles Finch, *The Star of Deep Beginnings,* pp.142-3.

[29] Dietrich Wildung, *Egypt from Prehistory to the Romans,* pp.42-3, 180-6 and Vivian Davies and Renée Friedman, *Egypt,* UK, British Museum Press, 1998, pp.103-7.

[30] Cheikh Anta Diop, *Precolonial Black Africa,* US, Lawrence Hill Books, 1987, p.196.

[31] Basil Davidson, *Old Africa Rediscovered,* UK, Victor Gollancz, 1959, p.51.

[32] Roland Oliver & Brian Fagan, *Africa in the Iron Age,* UK, Cambridge University Press, 1975, p.39.

[33] Charles Finch, *The Star of Deep Beginnings,* p.146.

[34] Basil Davidson, *Africa,* television series part 1: *Different but Equal,* UK, Michael Beazley, Rm Arts, Channel Four Television & Nigerian Television, 1984.

[35] Dietrich Wildung, *Egypt from Prehistory to the Romans,* pp.186-9.

[36] Patrick J. Munson, *Archaeology and the Prehistoric Origins of the Ghana Empire,* in *Journal of African History, Volume 21: No.4,* UK, Cambridge University Press, 1980, pp.459-60.

[37] Basil Davidson, *Africa in History,* UK, Macmillan, 1991, pp.87-8.

[38] Basil Davidson, *Old Africa Rediscovered,* p.86 and Cheikh Anta Diop, *The African Origin of Civilization: Myth or Reality?* p.157.

[39] Winwood Reade, *The Martyrdom of Man,* UK, Watts & Co., 1934 edition, p.219.

[40] Major Felix Dubois, *Timbuctoo the Mysterious,* UK, William Heinemann, 1897, p.152.

[41] Ibid., pp.148-53 and Cheikh Anta Diop, *Precolonial Black Africa,* pp.200-2.

[42] Major Felix Dubois, *Timbuctoo the Mysterious,* p.150.

[43] Ibid., p.149.

[44] Charles S. Finch, *The Star of Deep Beginnings,* p.162.

[45] Ibid., p.164.

[46] Sergio Domian, *Architecture Soudanaise: Vitalite d'une tradition urbaine et monumentale,* France, Éditions L'Harmattan, 1989, pp.68-75.

[47] Jean-Louis Bourgeois, *The Great Mosque of Djenné, Mali,* US, Internet Article, 1996, p.1.

[48] Sergio Domian, *Architecture Soudanaise: Vitalite d'une tradition urbaine et monumentale,* pp.41, 50-6, 77-80 and 85-9.

[49] Quoted in Cheikh Anta Diop, *African Origin of Civilization: Myth or Reality?* p.158.

[50] Peter Garlake, *Early Art and Architecture of Africa,* UK, Oxford University Press, 2002, p.98.

[51] Graham Hancock, *The Beauty of Historic Ethiopia,* Kenya, Camerapix, 1996, pp.26-7.

[52] Peter Garlake, *Early Art and Architecture of Africa,* p.75.

[53] Camerapix, *Ethiopia: A Tourist Paradise,* Ethiopia, Ethiopian Tourist Commission, 1996, p.24.

[54] Nnamdi Elleh, *African Architecture: Evolution and Transformation,* pp.44-5, 133 and Graham Hancock, *The Beauty of Historic Ethiopia,* pp.40-3.

[55] Robert Bauval and Graham Hancock, *Keeper of Genesis,* UK, Mandarin, 1996, pp.28-31.

[56] Nnamdi Elleh, *African Architecture: Evolution and Transformation,* pp.46 and 135.

[57] Ibid., pp.134-5.

[58] Camerapix, *Ethiopia: A Tourist Paradise,* p.36.

[59] Graham Hancock, *The Beauty of Historic Ethiopia,* p.63 and Nnamdi Elleh, *African Architecture: Evolution and Transformation,* p.135.

[60] Graham Hancock, *The Beauty of Historic Ethiopia,* p.66 and Nnamdi Elleh, *African Architecture: Evolution and Transformation,* p.137

[61] Basil Davidson, *African Kingdoms,* Netherlands, Time-Life Books, 1967, pp.134-5.

[62] Peter Garlake, *Early Art and Architecture of Africa,* p.89.

[63] Nnamdi Elleh, *African Architecture: Evolution and Transformation,* p.209.

[64] W. E. B. DuBois, *The World and Africa,* US, International Publishers, 1965, p.172.

[65] João de Barros, *Mines and Fortresses,* in *African Civilization Revisited,* ed Basil Davidson, US, Africa World Press, 1991, p.182.

[66] Cheikh Anta Diop, *Precolonial Black Africa,* p.197.

[67] Nnamdi Elleh, *African Architecture: Evolution and Transformation,* pp.209-14 and David Dugan, *Time Life's Lost Civilizations,* video series, *Africa, A History Denied,* Holland, Time Life Video, 1995.

[68] See Chapter 17.

[69] F. M. C. Stokes, *Zimbabwe,* in *The Geographical Magazine, Volume II: No.2,* ed Michael Huxley, UK, The Geographical Magazine, December 1935, p.143.

[70] J. Theodore Bent, *The Ruined Cities of Mashonaland, 3rd Edition,* UK, Longmans, Green, and Co., 1902, pp.110-1.

[71] F. M. C. Stokes, *Zimbabwe,* in *The Geographical Magazine, Volume II: No.2,* pp.143-4 and 146.

[72] Charles S. Finch, *The Star of Deep Beginnings,* p.155.

[73] F. M. C. Stokes, *Zimbabwe,* in *The Geographical Magazine, Volume II: No.2,* p.144.

[74] Peter Garlake, *Great Zimbabwe,* UK, Thames and Hudson, 1973, p.119.

[75] Charles S. Finch, *The Star of Deep Beginnings,* p.155.

[76] H. Ellert, *The Material Culture of Zimbabwe,* Zimbabwe, Longman Zimbabwe, 1984, p.13.

[77] F. M. C. Stokes, *Zimbabwe,* in *The Geographical Magazine, Volume II: No.2,* pp.142 (map) and 143.

[78] Ibid., pp.144-53.

[79] See Chapter 17.

[80] Peter Garlake, *Great Zimbabwe,* plate 103.

[81] Ibid., p.170.

[82] Basil Davidson, *Africa,* television series part 3: *Caravans of Gold,* UK, Channel Four Television, 1984.

[83] Cf. Ibn Battuta quoted in G. S. P. Freeman-Grenville ed, *East African Coast, Select Documents,* UK, The Clarendon Press, 1962, p.31.

[84] Basil Davidson, *A Guide to African History,* US, Zenith Books, 1965, pp.30-2.

[85] David Dugan, *Time Life's Lost Civilizations,* video series, *Africa: A History Denied.*

[86] Nnamdi Elleh, *African Architecture: Evolution and Transformation,* p.149 and Ronald Lewcock, *East Africa,* in *Architecture of the Islamic World,* ed George Michell, UK, Thames and Hudson, 1978, p.278.

[87] H. N. Chittick, *A Guide to the Ruins of Kilwa,* Tanzania, Ministry of Community Development and Culture, 1965, pp.8-10 and Peter Garlake, *Early Art and Architecture of Africa,* pp.178-9.

[88] Ronald Lewcock, *Zanj, the East African Coast,* in *Shelter in Africa,* ed Paul Oliver, UK, Barrie & Jenkins, 1971, p.90.

[89] H. N. Chittick, *A Guide to the Ruins of Kilwa,* p.10.

[90] Ibid., pp.20-1.

[91] Marco Polo, *The Travels,* UK, Penguin, 1958, p.302.

[92] Nnamdi Elleh, *African Architecture: Evolution and Transformation,* pp.165-6.

[93] Ronald Lewcock, *Zanj, the East African Coast,* in *Shelter in Africa,* pp.81-87 and Ronald Lewcock, *East Africa,* in *Architecture of the Islamic World,* p.278.

[94] Ibidem and Charles S. Finch, *The Star of Deep Beginnings,* p.160.

[95] Thomas L. Blair, *Shelter in Urbanising and Industrial Africa,* in *Shelter in Africa,* ed Paul Oliver, UK, Barrie & Jenkins, 1971, pp.226-7.

CHAPTER TWO: SURVEY OF THE DOCUMENTS

Travellers, Merchants and Envoys

Professor Leo Frobenius was a pioneering German Africanist. Writing in the earlier part of the twentieth century, he produced several highly original volumes on early African history. Most have remained in the original German, but a few were translated into French. One such work was *Histoire de la Civilisation Africaine* which appeared in 1936. It contains a splendid summary of what the earlier European merchants, travellers, and explorers saw when they visited Africa five hundred years ago:

> When they arrived in the Gulf of Guinea and landed at Vaida [in West Africa] the captains were astonished to find streets well laid out, bordered on either side for several leagues by two rows of trees; for days they travelled through a country of magnificent fields, inhabited by men clad in richly coloured garments of their own weaving! Further south in the Kingdom of the Congo [sic], a swarming crowd dressed in 'silk' and 'velvet'; great States well-ordered, and down to the most minute details; powerful rulers, flourishing industries - civilized to the marrow of their bones. And the condition of the countries on the eastern coast - Mozambique, for example - was quite the same.[1]

All very impressive, tree lined streets, large farms, textiles industries, silk and velvet, etc., but how did the professor know any of this? Where is his evidence? How can we moderns check that this is indeed a fair picture of what the early travellers saw?

> And what they told [says Frobenius] - those old captains, those chiefs of expeditions, the D'Elbées, the De Marchais, the Pigafettas, and all the others, what they told is true. It can be verified. In the old royal Kunstkammer of Dresden, in the Weydmann collection of Ulm, in many another European "curiosity cabinets" one still finds collections of objects from West Africa dating from that epoch: wonderful plush-velvets, of an extreme softness, made from the tenderest leaves of a certain banana tree; stuffs, soft and pliant, brilliant and delicate as silks, woven with well prepared raffia fibre, ceremonial javelins - their blades to the very points inlaid with the finest copper, bows so graceful, and ornamented so beautifully that they would do honour to any museum of arms whatsoever; calabashes decorated with the most perfect taste; sculpture in ivory and wood, the workmanship of which reveals skill and style.[2]

Kongo (Democratic Republic of Congo). View of the Kongolese regional capital of Loango. Is this an example of urban planning? Originally published in Olfert Dapper, *Description de l'Afrique*, 1668.

One of the sources Dr Frobenius alluded to was that of Filippo Pigafetta. His *History of the Kingdom of Kongo* was published in Rome in 1591. He based it on first hand information supplied to him by the slave trader Duarte Lopez. The trader had sailed to Kongo far down the West African coast in April 1578. Master Abraham Hartwell made an English language translation of Pigafetta's work in 1597. Thomas Fowell Buxton made a modern translation in 1881.

Pigafetta informs us that the kingdom of Kongo measured 1,685 miles in circumference and was divided into six administrative provinces. The capital city, Mbanza Kongo, lay in the province of Mpemba. It had a population of over 100,000 people and was already cosmopolitan. Some Portuguese lived there. Moreover, Christianity had spread to the region. The Kongolese king, Nzinga a Kuwu, had been baptised and appears in Pigafetta's account under the Portuguese baptismal name of Dom Affonso. Modern scholars, however, identify the king as Dom João I. According to Pigafetta, Mbanza Kongo was:

> open to the south. It was Dom Af[f]onso [i.e. Nzinga a Kuwu], the first Christian king, who first surrounded it with walls. He reserved for the

Portuguese a place also surrounded by walls. He also had his palace and the royal houses enclosed, leaving between these two enclosures a large open space where the main church was built; a square was left in front of it. The doors of aristocratic homes and of the houses of the Portuguese face walls of the church. At the entrance to the square a few great lords of the court have their homes. Behind the church, the square ends in a narrow street provided with a gate. When you walk through this gate, you find a great many houses to the east. Outside the walls which surround the royal residences and the Portuguese town there are numerous buildings belonging to various lords, each of whom occupies whatever location pleases him, so he can live near the court. It was impossible to determine the area of this town outside the two enclosures, since all of the countryside is filled with rural houses and palaces. Each lord with his group of habitations encloses a little village. The circumference of the Portuguese town measures about a mile, and that of the royal quarter as much. At night the gates are not closed or even guarded.[3]

The Portuguese sailed around the tip of South Africa in 1499 and landed in the vast empire of Munhumutapa. Called Benametapa in some of the Portuguese accounts, they described its vast gold reserves, ivory trade, and curious architecture. The empire itself ruled the modern territories of Zimbabwe, Mozambique, and parts of South Africa. Assisting the administration was a sizeable bureaucracy financed by taxation, tribute and presents. The royal family and their officers used most of the bounty but a portion of it went to social welfare. Antonio Bocarro, a Portuguese contemporary, informs us that:

[The Emperor] shows great charity to the blind and maimed, for these are called the king's poor, and have land and revenues for their subsistence, and when they wish to pass through the kingdoms, wherever they come food and drinks are given to them at the public cost as long as they remain there, and when they leave that place to go to another they are provided with what is necessary for their journey, and a guide, and some one to carry their wallet to the next village. In every place where they come there is the same obligation, under penalty that those who fail therein shall be punished by the king.[4]

In the 1520's Francisco Alvarez, a Portuguese friar, visited Ethiopia. In 1542 he published his report on the country as *Verdadera Informaçam das terras de Preste Joam.* From his account, we learn that the Portuguese sent him there on a mission to convert the Ethiopians to Roman Catholic Christianity. The Ethiopians were already Christians but they observed Coptic Christianity. On his visit, the Portuguese missionary saw the Ethiopian city of Lalibela. The city contained eleven underground churches. Clearly flabbergasted by their workmanship and ingenuity, Alvarez was worried that his fellow Portuguese citizens were not going to believe his account of this city. He wrote:

Abyssinia (Ethiopia). Old European engraving of the Church of Dongolo. 13th century. Clearly Lalibela was not the only place in Ethiopia to have such wonderful rock cut churches.

I swear by God, in whose power I am, that all that is written is the truth, and there is much more than I have already written, and I have left it [out] that they may not tax me with its being falsehood.[5]

In 1602 Pieter de Marees' *Description of Guinea,* was published. It contained first hand accounts of various travellers to Africa and what they found. Diereck Ruyters, a Dutch visitor, wrote one such account. He entered Benin City, in what is now southern Nigeria, and reported that:

At first the town seems to be very large; when one enters it one comes into a great broad street which appears to be seven or eight times broader than the Warme Street in Amsterdam; this extends straight out, and when one has walked a quarter of an hour along it he still does not see the end of the street ... The houses in this town stand in good order, one close to the other, like houses in Holland.[6]

In 1817 Thomas Bowditch, an Englishman, visited the Ashanti Empire in what is now Ghana and Ivory Coast. Sent on official business by the British government, his book, *Mission from Cape Coast Castle to Ashantee,* was published in 1819. It contains a vivid account of his impressions on entering Kumasi, the capital city:

We entered Kumasi at two o'clock ... Upwards of five thousand people, the greater part warriors, met us with awful bursts of martial music ... The smoke which encircled us from the incessant discharges of musquetry confined our glimpses to the foreground ... The dress of the[ir] captains was a war cap, with gilded rams' horns projecting in front, the sides extended beyond all proportion by immense plumes of eagles' feathers ... Their vest was of red cloth, covered with fetishes [i.e. symbols] and saphies in gold and silver ... They wore loose cotton trousers, with immense boots of a dull red leather, coming half way up the thigh ... The king, his tributaries, and captains, were resplendent in the distance, surrounded by attendants of every description ... At least a hundred large umbrellas, or canopies which could shelter thirty persons, were sprung up and down by the bearers with brilliant effect, being made of scarlet, yellow, and the most shewy [sic] cloths and silks, and crowned on the top with crescents, pelicans, barrels, and arms and swords of gold ... The caboceers, as did their superior captains and attendants, wore Ashanti cloths, of extravagant price from the costly foreign silks which had been unravelled to weave them in all varieties of colour, as well as pattern; [these cloths] were of an incredible size and weight, and thrown over the shoulder exactly like a Roman toga; a small silk fillet generally encircles their temples, and massy gold necklaces, intricately wrought.[7]

In 1822 Captain Clapperton and two of his colleagues set off across the Sahara from the Mediterranean coast. Travelling through what was the Kanem-Borno Empire, they headed for the Sokoto Caliphate of Northern Nigeria.

Benin (Nigeria). View of the Benin capital city during the once yearly procession of the Oba (i.e. King) and dignitaries. Originally published in Olfert Dapper, *Description de l'Afrique*, 1668.

Arriving there in 1824, they met the Sultan at the royal residence in the city of Gobir. The particulars, including meeting Sultan Bello, were published in 1826 under the name *Narrative of Travels and Discoveries in Northern and Central Africa:*

> March 17th [wrote Clapperton]. After breakfast, the sultan sent for me; his residence was at no great distance. In front of it there is a large quadrangle, into which several of the principal streets of the city lead … [and we] were immediately ushered into the presence of Bello, the second sultan of the Felatahs [i.e. Fulani]. He was seated on a small carpet, between two pillars supporting the roof of a thatched house, not unlike one of our cottages. The walls and pillars were painted blue and white in the Moorish taste; and on the back wall was sketched a fire-screen, ornamented with a course painting of a flower-pot. An armchair, with an iron lamp standing on it, was placed on each side of the screen. The sultan bade me many hearty welcomes, and asked me if I was not much tired … [8]

The English sent yet another fact-finding mission into West Africa. Led by the meticulous German Dr Henry Barth, the findings were published between

1857 and 1858. Five large scholarly volumes were issued entitled *Travels and Discoveries in North and Central Africa*. During his travels, word reached Dr Barth that an African historian in the 1600's had already mapped the early history of the region. The book, *Tarikh es Sudan*, was still in circulation, if only one could get one's hands on it:

> I passed the time during my residence in this place [Gando] not quite uselessly [wrote Dr Barth], especially as I was so fortunate as to obtain here from a learned man of the name of Bokhari, a son of the late Mohamed Wani, a copy of that most valuable historical work ... to which my friend 'Abd el Kader, in Sokoto [in Northern Nigeria], had first called my attention ... I spent three or four days most pleasantly in extracting the more important historical data of this work, which opened to me quite a new insight into the history of the regions of the middle course of the Niger ... exciting in me a far more lively interest than I had previously felt in a kingdom the greater power of which, in former times, I here found set forth in very clear and distinct outlines.[9]

William Winwood Reade wrote *The Martyrdom of Man* in 1872. It is a strange but beautifully written text that attempts to show that Africa was never far from the mainstream of history. Among other things, Reade wrote an admirable summary of what Captain Clapperton and his two colleagues witnessed when they visited Kanem-Borno and Northern Nigeria:

> Denham and Clapperton ... were astonished to find among the [N]egroes magnificent courts; regiments of cavalry, the horses caparisoned in silk for gala days and clad in coats of mail for war; long trains of camels laden with salt and natron and corn and cloth and cowrie shells - which form the currency - and kola nuts, which Arabs call "the coffee of the [N]egroes." They attended with wonder the gigantic fairs at which the cotton goods of Manchester, the red cloth of Saxony, double-barrelled guns, razors, tea and sugar, Nuremberg ware and writing-paper were exhibited for sale. They also found merchants who offered to cash their bills [i.e. cheques] upon houses at Tripoli; and scholars acquainted with Avicenna, Averroes, and the Greek philosophers.[10]

The Hon A. Wilmot, then a member of the Legislative Council of the Cape of Good Hope, wrote *Monomotapa: Its Monuments and its History*. Published in 1896, it was the first modern synthesis of the documents concerning the early history of the Munhumutapa Empire. Though far from perfect, Mr Wilmot presented enough source material to have allowed later historians to write a balanced history of this region. We have extracted the following from this work:

> In the historical description of the most wonderful countries of the world by Johnstone, published in 1603, we are supplied with a fair summary of what could be learned from Portuguese writers. He tells us that, "In the residue of

Kanem-Borno (Chad, Nigeria, Cameroon, Niger and Libya). Borno knight wearing chainmail. Chainmail and/or body armour was worn by soldiers and royals in Nupe, Hausaland, Benin and Songhai. Compare with page 432. Originally drawn by Major Dixon Denham and published in Major Dixon Denham et al, *Narrative of Travels and Discoveries in Northern and Central Africa* (UK, John Murray, 1826, opposite p.64).

Ethiope [i.e. Africa] raigne divers [i.e. many] powerful princes as the Kings of Adell, Monomugi, Monomotapa, Angola, and Congo. Monomotapa [i.e. Munhumutapa] is mightier and more famous than the rest. This kingdom containeth all that island [sic] which lieth between the river of Cuama [i.e. Zambezi] and Spirito Santo [i.e. Limpopo] (a territory of 150 leagues in compass), and from Spirito Santo it stretches to the Cape of Good Hope [i.e. southern tip of South Africa], for the viceroys of that huge tract do acknowledge him for their sovereign and superior governor. The soil aboundeth with corn and cattle. By the store of teeth [i.e. ivory] not less than 5,000 elephants must die yearly. Zimba [i.e. Great Zimbabwe] and Benemaraxa [i.e. Khami] are cities. There is no climate like it for plenty of gold, for by report there is 3,000 miles wherout gold is digged; gold is likewise found in the earth, in rocks, and in rivers. The mines of Manica, Boro, Quiticui, and Totoa (which some men call Butua) are the richest. The people are mean of stature, black, and well set. They converse with the king knealing. The offences most punished are witchcraft, theft, and adultery. The king beareth on his coat of arms a certain little spade with an ivory handle, and two small darts. He keepeth for his faithfullest guard two hundred dogs. He keepeth the heirs of the vassal princes to be secured of their father's loyalty."[11]

Major Dubois, a French scholar, synthesised the *Tarikh es Sudan* with a travelogue to produce the first modern account of the Songhai Empire of West Africa. His *Timbuctoo the Mysterious* appeared in New York in 1896 and London the following year:

As my boat approaches ... the banks and walls of the city [of Djenné in Mali] emerge in greater proportions from encircling water. At their feet I can distinguish a harbour filled with large boats that have nothing in common with the accustomed pirogue. They are large and strange in form, like the city that shelters them. When I climbed the banks and entered the walls, my surprise takes a definite form. I am completely bewildered and thrown out of reckoning by the novelty and strangeness of the town's interior. Surely the angel of Habakkuk has suddenly transported me a thousand leagues away from the Sudan [i.e. Africa]. For it is not in the heart of a country of eternally similar huts (childish in their simplicity and confusion) that I should look to find a real town. Yes, a real town in the European sense of the word; not one of those disorderly conglomerations of dwellings which we call towns in this country. Here were true houses; not primitive shelters crowned with roofs that are either flat or in the shape of an inverted funnel. Streets too; not seed-plots of buildings amongst which one wanders by paths that serpentine more than the most serpentine serpent. The idea suddenly occurs to me, perhaps this is Timbuctoo [sic] after all. This would explain everything. But it is impossible; the Bosos say we are still twelve days' journey distant from there. What is this town, then, with its wide, straight roads, its houses of two stories (some with a sketch of a third) built in a style that instantly arrests the eye? I am completely bewildered ... Where did this gathering of unknown life come from? What is this civilisation, sufficiently assured to possess a manner and style of its own?[12]

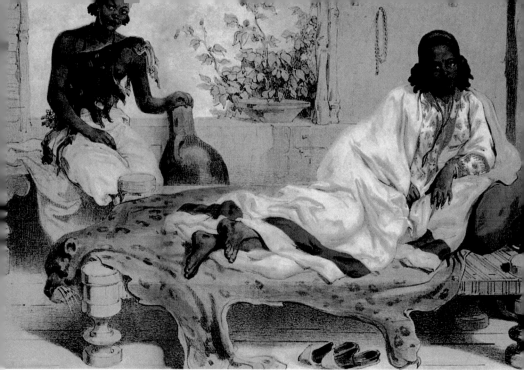

Abyssinia (Ethiopia). Noblewoman of Tigre with her equally graceful attendant as seen by Théophile Lefebvre. Originally published in his *Voyage en Abyssinie*, 1845.

The Songhai Empire flourished in the fifteenth and sixteenth centuries. A vast imperial system, it encompassed parts of the territories now called Mali, Mauritania, Niger, Northern Nigeria, Guinea, Senegal and Gambia.

In 1903 H. Ling Roth wrote *Great Benin: Its Art, History and Horrors*. This work was the first modern account of the Nigerian civilisation of Benin. The author, much like Wilmot, presented a great deal of raw material that could have allowed later historians to write a full history of this region. Mr Roth gave his reasons for writing the book as follows.

> At the time of the destruction of the city of Great Benin [by the British in 1897], we seemed to know very little about the city or the country, but its capture caused us to seek out what had once been known and long since forgotten.[13]

Thus by 1903 the student of Black history had three important works to draw upon, each containing a wealth of primary source material. Quite apart from this literature, however, another branch of historical research had produced important and relevant results.

Orientalist Scholarship

Count De Volney is, perhaps, best known for *The Ruins, or Meditations on the Revolutions of Empires and the Law of Nature*. Written in 1791 and enlarged in 1794, this book launched Orientalism, a whole new scholarly arena. Prior to this work, the *Bible* was considered the final word on ancient history in academic circles. The Count demonstrated that Christianity and all later religions could be traced back to early astronomical ideas based on the zodiac. Destroying the Biblical chronology, De Volney declared that Negroes in Ancient Egypt and the Sudan pioneered the study of the zodiac thousands of years ago. Moreover, Africans started civilisation. The Father of Orientalism wrote:

> [W]e have the strongest reasons to believe that the country neighbouring to the tropic [i.e. Sudan and Southern Egypt] was the cradle of the sciences, and of consequence that the first learned nation [on earth] was a nation of Blacks; for it is incontrovertible, that, by the term Ethiopians, the ancients meant to represent a people of black complexion, thick lips, and woolly hair. I am therefore inclined to believe, that the inhabitants of Lower Egypt [i.e. the northern Mediterranean coast] were originally a foreign colony imported from Syria and Arabia, a medley of different tribes of savages, originally shepherds and fishermen, who, by degrees formed themselves into a nation, and who, by nature or descent, were enemies of the Thebans [i.e. the southern Black capital now the ruined city of Karnak], by whom they were no doubt despised and treated as barbarians. I have suggested the same ideas in my *Travels into Syria,* founded upon the black complexion of the Sphinx. I have since ascertained that the antique images of Thebias [i.e. the old pharaonic sculptures in Thebes/Karnak] have the same characteristic; and Mr. Bruce has offered a multitude of analogous facts.[14]

The Father of Orientalism was, however, heavily influenced by the earlier research of his countryman M. Charles Dupuis. M. Dupuis, the French savant, published his *Memoirs on the Origin of the Constellations and on the Explanation of the Fable by Astronomy* in 1781. He expanded this work into the twelve-volume *The Origin of All Religious Worship* in 1794. In 1798 he abridged the twelve-volume book into a one-volume popular work. In 1872 an English language translation of the one-volume abridgement was published in the United States and was entitled *The Origin of All Religious Worship.* In this work, of the most profound scholarship, M. Dupuis shows that the veneration of the Sun, Moon, and other natural phenomena was and still is the foundation of all subsequent religions. These cultural ideas began in Africa and spread to other parts of the world:

> The Ethiopians [i.e. Sudanese], the fathers of the Egyptians, living in a burning climate, worshipped nevertheless the divinity of the Sun, but above all that of the Moon, which presided over the nights, the sweet coolness of which, made them forget the heat of the day. All the Africans offered sacrifices to these great Divinities. It was in Ethiopia [i.e. Sudan], where the famous table of the Sun

was found ... The same as the Incas of Peru, they called themselves the children of the Sun, which they regarded as their first progenitor ... The Troglodytes [i.e. of the Sahara] had a fountain, dedicated to the Star of Day. In the neighbourhood of the temple of Ammon, there was a rock, sacred to the south-wind, and a fountain of the Sun. The Blemmyes, situated on the confines of Egypt and Ethiopia, immolated human victims to the Sun. The rock of Bagia and the island of Nasala, situated beyond the territory of the Ichthyophagi [i.e. the Sahara], was dedicated to the same luminary ... The divinities, which were invoked as witnesses in the treaty of the Carthaginians [i.e. of Tunisia] with Philip, the son of Demetrius, were the Sun, Moon, the Earth, the Rivers, the Prairies, and the Water. Massinissa [a king of Numidia - see below], in thanking the Gods on the arrival of Scipio in his empire, addresses himself to the Sun. The natives of the island of Socotora [i.e. near Yemen] and the Hottentots [i.e. of South Africa] preserve to this day [i.e. in 1798 AD] the ancient veneration, which the Africans had always had for the Moon, which they regard as the principle of sublunary vegetation; they applied to her, when they wanted rain, sunshine or good crops. She is to them a kind and beneficent Divinity, such as was Isis with the Egyptians. All the Africans, who inhabit the coast of Angola and of Congo [sic], worship the Sun and the Moon. The natives of the island of Tenerif [sic] worshipped them also, as well as the planets and other stars, on the arrival of the Spaniards.[15]

Count De Volney and M. Dupuis began a reassessment of the early Greek and Roman sources, the oldest corpus of literature produced by Europeans. Herodotus, an ancient Greek historian, is also called the Father of History. While he did not pioneer the subject, he was the first European to write a history book that has come down to us today. Writing in around 450 BC, he synthesised historical material collected during visits to various countries, but much of what he wrote came from memory. Herodotus, as he himself admits, took few notes. In Egypt, his information came from the priests who told him particulars on some of the most important pharaohs:

The priests said that Mên [i.e. Mena] was the first king of Egypt ... Next, they read me from a papyrus the names of three hundred and thirty monarchs, who (they said) were his successors upon the throne. In this number of generations there were eighteen Ethiopian [i.e. Sudanese] kings, and one queen who was a native; all the rest were kings and Egyptians.[16]

Manetho, writing in around 240 BC, was an Egyptian priest from the city of Heliopolis. During his time, Egypt was under the imperial rule of the Greeks. The Greek monarch Ptolemy Philadelphus commissioned him to compile a full history of Egypt from the earliest times to the Greek conquest. This great work is now lost but later historians quoted from it. Josephus, the Roman Jewish historian, quotes an excerpt that reads as follows:

> A blast of God smote us; and unexpectedly, from the regions of the East, invaders of obscure race marched in confidence of victory against our land. By main force they easily seized it without striking a blow; and having overpowered the rulers of the land, they then burned our cities ruthlessly ... and treated all the natives with a cruel hostility, massacring some and leading into slavery the wives and children of others. Finally, they appointed as king one of their number whose name was Salitis.[17]

Contrary to Herodotus, not all of the pharaohs were Egyptians or Sudanese, some were Asians from the East. It is possible that the priests that Herodotus spoke to omitted these foreigners from the papyrus scroll. Josephus, who quoted the above passage, identifies these invaders as the Children of Israel. They conquered Egypt and ruled as the Fifteenth and Sixteenth Dynasties. If Josephus is correct in this assertion, the Old Testament is largely, if not completely, erroneous.

Plutarch was a Greek scholar of the late first century AD. He was interested in religious matters and wrote a brilliant and penetrating account of Egyptian philosophical and religious culture. This work, *Concerning Isis and Osiris,* drew heavily on Egyptian source material especially the writings of Manetho. Plutarch shows that the Ancient Greek scholars were very interested in Egyptian thought and studied it first hand from the priests of Egypt. The Greek scholars apparently visited the Egyptian cities of Memphis, Sais and Heliopolis in order to study:

> And the most wise of the Greeks also are witnesses - Solon, Thales, Plato, Eudoxus, Pythagoras, and, as some say, Lycurgus as well - through coming to Egypt and associating with her priests. And so they say that Eudoxus was hearer of Chonouphis of Memphis, and Solon of Sonchis of Sais, and Pythagoras of Œnuphis of Heliopolis. And the last especially, as it appears, being contemplated and contemplating, brought back to the memory of his men [i.e. the Greeks] their [i.e. the Egyptians] symbolic and mysterious (art), containing their dogmas and dark sayings. For most of the Pythagoric messages leave out nothing of what are called the hieroglyphic letters.[18]

Diodorus Siculus was another outstanding Greek historian of antiquity. In the first century BC, he wrote *General History,* an encyclopaedic work on world history. These volumes demonstrate the state of historical knowledge in Diodorus' time. We have extracted the following account of human origins:

> Now the Ethiopians [i.e. Africans], as historians relate, were the first of all men and the proofs of this statement, they say are manifest. For that they did not come into their land as immigrants from abroad but were natives of it and so justly bear the name of "autochthones" [i.e. sprung from the soil itself] is, they maintain, conceded by practically all men; furthermore, that those who dwell

> beneath the noon-day sun were, in all likelihood, the first to be generated by the earth, is clear to all; since inasmuch as it was the warmth of the sun which, at the generation of the universe, dried up the earth when it was still wet and impregnated it with life, it is reasonable to suppose that the region which was nearest the sun was the first to bring forth living creatures.[19]

It is astonishing to note just how 'modern' these ideas are. It is now generally accepted that Africa is the cradle of the human race. This is discussed in some detail in Chapter 5.

Carthage and Numidia were two important civilisations in North Africa in the regions now called Tunisia and Algeria. Most of what we know about these states comes from what the Greek and Roman writers have recorded on their behalf. Massinissa (238-149 BC) was king of Numidia during the Punic Wars. Polybius, a Roman author, recorded the following about this distinguished man:

> Massinissa was the greatest and the happiest sovereign of our epoch. He reigned more than sixty years in perfect health. Physically he was the strongest and most robust man of his time. Thanks to the harmony that reigned in his family, his kingdom was never troubled by intrigue or domestic strife. But this was his greatest merit, his most admirable work; before him, Numidia was wild, uncultivated and alien to all culture. He was the first to show that it could produce all kinds of fruit like any other country. He has, therefore, more title and rights than anyone that his memory should be honoured.[20]

Mr Bosworth Smith was the English author of *Carthage and the Carthaginians*. Writing in 1877, he penned a detailed account of the North African culture. He relies on the Greek and Roman source material because:

> No native poet, whose writings have come down to us, has sung of the origin of Carthage, or of her romantic voyages. No native orator has described, in glowing periods which we can still read, the splendour of her buildings and the opulence of her merchant princes. No native annalist has preserved the story of her long rivalry with the Greeks and Etruscans, and no African philosopher has moralised upon the stability of her institutions or the causes of her fall. All have perished.[21]

Strabo was an ancient geographer. He suggested that very early Greek sources indicate that Ethiopians, that is, Black people in general, used to inhabit a wide stretch of the ancient world, not just Africa. In his own words:

> I assert that the ancient Greeks, in the same way as they classed all the northern nations with which they were familiar as Scythians, etc., so, I affirm, they designated as Ethiopia the whole of the southern countries toward the ocean ... [I]f the moderns [i.e. in Strabo's time] have confined the appellation Ethiopians

to those who dwell near Egypt [i.e. Sudan], this must not be allowed to interfere
with the meaning of the ancients.[22]

Professor Arnold H. L. Heeren, a German historian, was the author of
*Historical Researches into the Politics, Intercourse, and Trade of the
Carthaginians, Ethiopians, and Egyptians.* Translated into English in 1832,
this two-volume work summarised the known data on Carthage, Nubia and
Egypt. Furthermore, Heeren developed a theory that Black people in Africa
and early western and southern Asia pioneered civilisation by establishing the
first trading networks. Concerning the distribution of these early Black
peoples, Professor Heeren wrote that:

> [A]ll those who were strikingly distinguished from Europeans by a very dark,
> or completely black skin, received the general appellation of Ethiopians. After
> these remarks it will not seem strange that we find Ethiopian nations scattered
> over a great part of the ancient world. Africa certainly contained the greatest
> number of them, yet they were not the only inhabitants of this part of the world,
> nor were they confined to it alone. A considerable tract of Asia was occupied
> by an Ethiopian race; and [the term] India was often made to comprise southern
> Africa, so, in like manner, [the term] Ethiopia is frequently made to include
> southern India.[23]

The notion that Negroes once occupied India and a considerable tract of Asia
may seem unusual, but it is not without corroboration. Many other scholars
have pointed out the same fact.

Godfrey Higgins, an English magistrate, wrote *Anacalypsis* in 1836. The
subtitle to this two-volume masterpiece is *An Attempt to Draw Aside the Veil
of the Saitic Isis.* Of astonishing erudition, Mr Higgins attempted to trace the
origin of nations, languages, and religions. Moreover, he synthesised the
research of the English Orientalists, led by Sir William Jones, with those of the
French Orientalists, led by Count De Volney. The following excerpt is
representative of his findings:

> No person who has considered well the character of the temples in India and
> Egypt, can help being convinced of the identity of their character, and of their
> being the production of the same race of people; and this race evidently
> Ethiopian. The Sphinxes [of Egypt] have all Ethiopian [i.e. Negro] faces. The
> bust of Memnon [i.e. Pharaoh Amenhotep III] in the British Museum is
> evidently Ethiopian. The worship of the Mother and Child is seen in all parts of
> the Egyptian religion. It prevails everywhere. It is the worship of Isis and the
> infant Orus [i.e. Horus] or Osiris. It is the religious rite prohibited at Rome, but
> which prevailed in spite of all opposition, as we find from the remaining ruins
> of its temples. It was perhaps through this country, Egypt, that the worship of
> the black virgin and child came into Italy, where it still prevails. It is the
> worship of the God Ιαω, the Saviour; Bacchus in Greece, Adonis in Syria,

> Cristna in India; coming into Italy through the medium of the two Ethiopias [i.e. Egypt and India], she was, as the Ethiopians were, *black,* and such she still remains.[24]

After 1821 Egyptology became a separate subject among the Orientalist disciplines. M. Jean-Francois Champollion founded the discipline by being the first to decipher the hieroglyphic script. The Father of Egyptology, however, failed to write a proper book on the subject of Egypt. He did, however, write a series of letters on his findings. His brother published these in 1839 under the title *Egypt Ancienne.*

In modern times, Egypt has three main populations - the ruling Arabs, the Copts, and the Nubians. The Copts, a relatively light-skinned population, are often presented as the descendents of the pharaohs because their language, used in church services, is closest to Ancient Egyptian. The Father of Egyptology refuted this view because:

> The ancient Egyptians belonged to a race quite similar to the Kennous or Barabras, present inhabitants of Nubia. In the [present] Copts of Egypt, we do not find any of the characteristic features of the ancient Egyptian population. The Copts are the result of crossbreeding with all the nations that have successively dominated Egypt [i.e. the Greeks and Romans]. It is wrong to seek in them the principal features of the old race.[25]

By the 1850's, a new discipline had emerged among the Orientalists called Assyriology. Focusing on the western Asian territories of Iraq, Iran and Syria, Sir Henry Rawlinson founded the discipline. He was the first modern scholar to decipher cuneiform, the long-dead script used by the ancient civilisations of the region. The Sumerians were the first civilised culture in the Middle East and the pioneers of cuneiform, followed by the Akkadians, the Babylonians, Assyrians and Chaldaeans. Deciphering cuneiform was an important achievement but like Champollion before him, however, the Father of Assyriology failed to write a proper book on the subject. His younger brother, Professor George Rawlinson of Oxford University, presented his findings in his own works. Sir Henry wrote *On the Early History of Babylonia* as a supplementary essay to one of George Rawlinson's books. From this essay, we cite the following:

> In regard to the language of the primitive Babylonians [i.e. Sumerians], although in its grammatical structure it resembles dialects of the Turanian family, the vocabulary is rather Cushite or Ethiopian, belonging to that stock of tongues which in the sequel were everywhere more or less mixed up with the Semitic languages, but of which we have probably the purest modern specimins [sic] in the Mahra of Southern Arabia and the Galla of Abyssinia [i.e. Ethiopia].[26]

Since the Cushite or Ethiopian languages originated in East Africa, Sir Henry theorised that the Sumerians evolved there and migrated to Iraq in prehistoric times through Southern Arabia.

Charles Darwin, the Father of Natural Selection theory, wrote *The Descent of Man*. This 1871 work contained the first ever attempt to apply natural selection theories to the origin of humanity. One of the topics Darwin discussed was *On the Birthplace and Antiquity of Man*. This section begins as follows:

> We are naturally led to enquire, where was the birthplace of man … In each great region of the world the living mammals are closely related to the extinct species of the same region. It is therefore probable that Africa was formerly inhabited by extinct apes closely related to the gorilla and chimpanzee; and as these two species are now man's nearest allies, it is somewhat more probable that our early progenitors lived on the African continent than elsewhere.[27]

That same year, Philip Smith wrote an instructive text called *The Ancient History of the East*. This work, also entitled *The Students Ancient History,* shows just how much of the cutting edge research had made its way into the mainstream of British scholarship. In an early chapter, Mr Smith assures us that:

> Four races are thus distinguished, the *White,* or *Caucasian;* the *Yellow,* or *Mongolian,* the *Black, Negro,* or *Nigritian;* and the *Red,* or *American.* The first was the sole possessor of ancient civilization; the second appears only occasionally on the scene of ancient history, when its nomad hordes came down from their homes in the plateaux of Central Asia, over which they have always wandered; the third is only represented by the slaves depicted on Egyptian monuments; the fourth does not yet appear at all.[28]

He does not leave the issue there. Concerning the ancient Egyptians:

> If we were left to form an opinion upon the subject by the description of the Egyptians left by the Greek writers, we should conclude that they were, if not Negroes, at least closely akin to the Negro race. That they were much darker than the neighbouring Asiatics; that they had hair frizzled either by nature or by art; that their lips were thick and projecting, and their limbs slender, rests upon the authority of eye-witnesses, who had travelled in the country, and who could have no motive to deceive.[29]

"But":

> the vast majority of the mummies are those of the native Egyptians, and their osteological character proves that they belonged to the Caucasian and not to the African race.[30]

Moreover:

> The monuments and paintings, however, show that the Egyptians possessed a
> peculiar physiognomy, differing from both races, approaching more nearly to
> the Negro type than to any of the other Caucasian races. The fullness of the lips,
> seen in the Sphinx of the Pyramids and in the portraits of the kings, is
> characteristic of the Negro, and the elongation of the eye is a Nubian
> peculiarity.[31]

In conclusion:

> New light has recently been thrown upon the whole subject by M. Mariette's
> discovery, in the north-easternmost part of Egypt, of a race of men of a type
> quite different from the Egyptians, both ancient and modern, who seem to
> represent a more ancient population. The distinct separation of classes, though
> it be incorrect to term them *castes,* is an indication that the dominant Egyptians
> had overcome a previous population; and it now appears that there was such a
> population, more nearly approaching the African type, but decidedly not
> Negroes.[32]

The only conclusion that one can draw is that Negroes occupied the top
caste, as represented by the Sphinx and the royal portraiture. The lower castes
were comprised of populations more nearly approaching the African type, "but
decidedly not Negroes", and also Caucasians, as represented by the mummies.

Concerning the Sumerians of Iraq, founders of the first civilisation in Asia,
Mr Smith describes them thus:

> The seat of this Cushite monarchy - the first which its monuments enable us to
> regard as properly historical - is placed by those monuments (as we have seen)
> in the southern tetrapolis of Babylonia. In that quarter, also, the oldest traditions
> make civilization enter from the sea. Accordingly the city, which the oldest
> extant inscriptions seem to mark as the capital, was *Hur* (now *Mugheir*), the
> furthest to the south of all the cities of Chaldæa. Its site (a little below 31° N.
> latitude) was no doubt originally on the shore of the Persian Gulf; and its *ships*
> are mentioned in connection with those of *Ethiopia*.[33]

These days, scholars no longer consider Hur (i.e. Ur) to have been the oldest
Sumerian city, but the other data is still relevant.

Mr Philip Smith describes the early peoples of India and Iran and their
subjugation by Caucasian invaders in early times:

> After a struggle, which lasted for centuries, [the Aryan invaders] conquered the
> Cushite aborigines of the Indian peninsula, and reduced them to the position of
> inferior castes ... The Iranian branch [of the Aryan invaders] ... overran Media,
> eastern Susiana, Persia [i.e. Iran], and the fertile parts of Carmania; expelling

from those countries or reducing the old Cushite inhabitants, whom the Iranian legends describe as men of a black complexion, with short and woolly hair.[34]

Finally, Mr Smith discusses ideas taken from the *Bible* concerning ethnic classifications. He uses them to group the Canaanites of Palestine together with the Lower Mesopotamians of Iraq:

> It appears to be very much, if not chiefly, by the test of *colour,* that the ethnic table of *Genesis X.* groups the children of Ham (i.e. *Cham,* "the swarthy".) By this test, the Canaanites of Palestine and Phœnicia, with the Syro-phœnicians and other dark Syrians further north, would be distinguished, on the one hand, from the lighter immigrants of the Hebrew race from Upper Mesopotamia, and, on the other, from the "White Syrians" of Cappadocia. And this distinction confirms their migration from the native land of a dark race, such as Lower Mesopotamia ... [T]he dark races of the Syrian coast [are alluded to] in Homer and other classic authors, who find *Ethiopians* on the Syrian coast ...[35]

By 1871 the mainstream position on ancient history credited Negroes, whether called Cushites or Ethiopians, with the origin of material civilisation. Whether in Sudan, Egypt, Canaan, Sumer, earliest Iran or India, it was impossible to escape from Negro origins.

Islamic Scholarship

In the Middle Ages, the Arabic term "Sudanese" entered the literature. In the seventh century AD, the Arabs conquered Egypt and the rest of North Africa. Equivalent in meaning to Ethiopia, Sudan was their main designation for Black people. Ibn Khaldun was a Tunisian historian of the fourteenth century. Of White Berber origins, he was also a Muslim. Considered one of the best historians of all time, he discussed the Arab invasion of North Africa and gave details of what the conquerors found in West Africa:

> At the time of the conquest of Northern Africa [by the Arabs between 639 and 708 AD], some merchants penetrated into the western part of the land of the Blacks [i.e. West Africa] and found among them no king more powerful than the king of Ghana. His states extended westwards to the shores of the Atlantic Ocean. [Kumbi-Saleh], the capital of this strong, populous nation, was made up of two towns ... and formed one of the greatest and best populated cities in the world. The author of the *Book of Roger* makes special mention of it, as does the author of *Roads and Kingdoms.*[36]

Al-Bakri was a Spanish geographer from the city of Granada. He wrote the *Book of the Roads and Kingdoms* in 1067. In this work is a description of the Emperor of Ghana's courtly ritual:

> When he gives audience to his people [says Al-Bakri] ... he sits in a pavilion around which stand his horses caparisoned in cloth of gold: behind him stand ten pages holding shields and gold-mounted swords: and on his right hand are the sons of the princes of his empire, splendidly clad and with gold plaited into their hair. The governor of the city is seated on the ground in front of the king, and all around him are his vizirs [i.e. ministers] in the same position. The gate of the chamber is guarded by dogs of an excellent breed, who never leave the king's seat: they wear collars of gold and silver.[37]

Al-Idrissi, a Moorish geographer, wrote the *Book of Roger.* This work, as Ibn Khaldun suggests, contains an excellent account of Ancient Ghana but also the East African coast. Writing in 1153, he also gave a clear picture of the state of Islamic geographical knowledge at that time:

> What results from the opinion of philosophers, learned men, and those skilled in observation of the heavenly bodies, is that the world is as round as a sphere, of which the waters are adherent and maintained upon its surface by natural equilibrium. It is surrounded by air, and all created bodies are stable on its surface, the earth drawing to itself all that is heavy in the same way that a magnet attracts iron. The territorial globe is divided into two equal parts by the equinoctial line. The circumference of the earth is divided into 360 degrees each of 25 parasangs.[38]

Al-Masudi, a distinguished Arab historian from Baghdad, visited the East African coast in 916 AD. He documented his extensive travels in a book called *Meadows of Gold and Mines of Gems.* He described the Zanj, that is, East Africans, as having an empire spread over a large territory divided by valleys, mountains, and deserts:

> The inhabitants of the people of Zendj [i.e. Zanj] extend to Sofala [i.e. Mozambique], which is the termination of the voyages of the mariners of Oman and Syraf ... It is a land abounding in gold, rich in wonderful things, and very fertile. The Zendjs have chosen it for the seat of their empire and have placed at their head a king, whom they name *Ouklimen* - that is the name [i.e. title] which the King of Zendj has borne throughout time. Eklimn, who is the chief of all the Zendj kings, marches at the head of three thousand cavaliers; they are mounted upon cows; they have neither horses or mules ... [39]

In 1331 Ibn Battuta, a Moroccan of White Berber origins, visited the same region. Battuta's book, *Travels in Asia and Africa,* contains much that is useful including the following account of his visit to the Tanzanian city of Kilwa:

> We spent a night on the island of [Mombasa], and then set sail for Kilwa, the principal city on the coast the greater part of whose inhabitants are Zanj of very black complexion. They have tattoo marks on their faces, like the Limiyyin of Janada [i.e. in West Africa]. A merchant told me that a fortnight's sail beyond

Kilwa lies Sofala, where powdered gold is brought from a place a month's journey inland called Yufi. Kilwa is one of the most beautiful and well-constructed cities in the world. The whole of it is elegantly built.[40]

He also left a detailed travelogue of his voyage to Mali in West Africa covering some of the same places that Dr Barth trekked 500 years later.

Early Twentieth Century Scholarship

In 1905 Lady Lugard wrote *A Tropical Dependency*. It was subtitled *An Outline of the Ancient History of the Western Soudan with an Account of the Modern Settlement of Northern Nigeria*. This masterpiece synthesised the findings of Heeren, Barth, Clapperton, Dubois and the Islamic scholars previously cited. In this undertaking, she recovered the early history of Ghana, Mali, Songhai, Kanem-Borno, and Hausaland. Among her many findings, she noted that:

It is interesting and remarkable that while Timbuctoo [sic] undoubtedly dominated the life of the Songhay [sic] Empire, and was the first town of the Soudan [i.e. that part of Africa] many other towns are almost equally noticed by travellers for their trade and for their learning of which they were the centre. Marmol, writing in the reign of Askia Daouad [sic], speaks of Melle [i.e. Mali] as not only rich in trade but also in learning, having its own schools of science and religion. The writers of Timbuctoo themselves made frequent allusions to learned doctors of Melle, Aiwalatin [i.e. Walata], Jenné, and Katsena. In Masina also there were an "immense number of distinguished men of letters and divines." Even the far distant Tekadda [sic] is named as the seat in which El [Maghili] chose to establish his school.[41]

In 1906 G. R. S. Mead wrote *Thrice Greatest Hermes* subtitled *Studies in Hellenistic Theosophy and Gnosis*. This three-volume masterpiece synthesised the findings of Manetho and Plutarch, as well as the work of various nineteenth century scholars such as Champollion. Mead's aim in writing the book was to elucidate the teachings of a body of Egypto-Greek literature called the *Hermetica*. He traced the prototype of this literature to the Egyptian doctrines taught at the schools of Hermopolis, Memphis and Heliopolis as synthesised in an eighth century BC inscription in the British Museum [also called the Shabaka Stone]. In the conclusion to this great work, Mead wrote the following:

And if we say that this Wisdom has come down to us in Greek tradition, we should ever remember that this Græcising or philosophising has to do with the form and not the substance. For whence did Thales and Pythagoras and Plato draw the inspiration for their philosophy or love of wisdom; was it not from

Egypt? At anyrate [sic] so say the Greeks themselves without a single dissenting voice. And can we think that the Greeks, who were always so proud of their own achievements and boasted their own genius so loudly, would have given the palm of wisdom to Egypt had they not been compelled by overwhelming evidence to do so?[42]

In 1913 Captain Stigand wrote *The Land of Zinj*. It was subtitled *Being an Account of British East Africa, its Ancient History and Present Inhabitants*. This work was the first to synthesise the documentation concerning the history of the Swahili or Zanj. The Captain explains the origin of this unusual word:

This word "Zinj [sic]," meaning "a black," was generally used to refer to the [B]lacks of the East African coast. Our word "Zanzibar" is derived from the Arabic "Zangibar," meaning "the country of the [B]lacks." It was originally used to refer to the greater part of the coast which was called the country of Zinj or Zenj, but it is now restricted to the island of Zanzibar. Zinj or Zenj, the Zingium of Cosmas and Zingis of Ptolemy, was originally south of the "Berbera" country as far as Sofala, roughly Juba River to Zambezi River, though different writers assigned it different limits. The country of "Berbera" was situated between Abyssinia [i.e. Ethiopia] and Zenj, and so consisted of the whole of Somaliland.[43]

Leo Wiener, a Harvard University philologist, wrote a provocative but well received work entitled *Africa and the Discovery of America*. It was a three-volume study that appeared between 1920 and 1922. In the final volume, the professor drew the following conclusion:

The presence of Negroes with their trading masters in America before Columbus is proved by the representation of Negroes in [early] American sculpture and design, by the occurrence of a Black nation at Darien early in the XVI. century, but more specifically, by Columbus' emphatic reference to Negro traders from Guinea [in West Africa], who trafficked in a gold alloy, guanin, of precisely the same composition and bearing the same name, as frequently referred to by early writers in Africa.[44]

Dr Wiener was a brilliant pioneer but his work contains a major flaw. There are mediæval documents that allude to these early African voyages to America but none mention "trading masters" of a different race to the Negroes.

Sir E. A. Wallis Budge, the great English Egyptologist, was the English translator of the *Kebra Negaste* and other important documents from Ethiopia, i.e. the modern country of this name. In addition, he studied the written accounts of the country by Francisco Alvarez and the other Portuguese authors of centuries ago. In 1928 Budge wrote *A History of Ethiopia, Nubia & Abyssinia*. This two-volume work mapped the history of Kush, Mediæval Nubia, and Ethiopia.

Ethiopia had a long and eventful history ruling from the cities of Yeha and then Axum. Between 1180 and 1220 AD, they built a new capital called Roha or Lalibela. Containing eleven churches, still in existence, Dr Budge commented on their architectural significance:

> Abyssinia [i.e. Ethiopia] contains the most remarkable churches in the world ...
> which certainly deserve to be reckoned with the Seven Wonders of the world.
> All who have seen them marvel, not at their beauty, but at the mind of the man
> who conceived their design, and the colossal labour which was expended in
> their making ... The rock-hewn temples of Rameses II at Kalabshah and Abu
> Simbel cannot be compared with the churches at Lalibala [sic], because no
> attempt was made to alter the shape of the hills of sandstone out of which the
> temples were hewn, and to make the temples resemble independent buildings.[45]

Cecilia Hill, an English writer, penned a fascinating travelogue entitled *Moorish Towns in Spain.* Published in 1931, it contained an excellent history of the Moorish civilisation. In the introduction, she asks of the Moors:

> Why were they so hated? Why did the Spaniards, when with the passage of
> centuries they had learnt all that the Moors could teach them, strive with an
> ever-increasing animosity to drive them out: first from Toledo; then, after a
> long interval, from Cordova and Seville; finally, after two more centuries of
> struggle, from their last fort, Granada? It was inevitable. It was instinctive. The
> Moors were a coloured race, and their occupation of a European country was
> an insult. They were heathens [i.e. non-Christians], and to suffer them was an
> offence before God. They were invaders, and they had no right to be in Spain.
> They occupied a valuable strip of seaboard, and might assist a further invasion
> from Africa. They were an obstacle to national unity and hampered
> participation in the affairs of Europe. They were an irritating anachronism.
> They were a thorn in the flesh.[46]

In England in 1931 "a coloured race" could only refer to Negroes. The Moorish civilisation was hardly discussed by scholars back then and thus Mrs Hill's book was a welcome addition to the frame of reference.

Coming full circle, Dr Leo Frobenius, cited earlier, summarised his findings thus:

> The revelations of the navigators of the fifteenth to the seventeenth centuries
> give incontrovertible proofs that Negro Africa stretching south from the edge
> of the Saharan deserts was still in full flower - the full flower of harmonious
> and well-ordered civilizations. And this fine flowering the European
> conquistadors annihilated as far as they penetrated into the country. For the new
> country of America had need of slaves, and they were to be had in Africa:
> hundreds, thousands, whole cargoes of slaves. However the traffic in Negroes
> was never an affair of an entirely easy conscience. It demanded a justification,
> and so the Negro was made into a half-animal, an article of merchandize. And

for this reason the notion of the fetich [sic] was invented, as the symbol of an African religion, (Portuguese - feticeiro) ... As for me I have not seen in any part whatsoever of Africa the natives worshipping fetiches.[47]

The professor, while an extraordinary pioneer, revealed his limitations when he claimed that Negro Africa extended only as far north as the Sahara. There was already enough literature to prove otherwise. Whichever be the case, it should be clear that most of what is now known about Black history was already known in European circles before 1936. By then, Darwin, the Father of Natural Selection Theory, had already argued that the human race was of African origin. Count De Volney, the Father of Orientalism, had already shown that Negroes in Egypt and Sudan founded civilisation. M. Jean-Francois Champollion, the Father of Egyptology, had already argued that the Ancient Egyptians were "quite similar to the Kennous or Barabras, present inhabitants of Nubia". Sir Henry Rawlinson, the Father of Assyriology, had already suggested that the Sumerians were "Cushite or Ethiopian". Philip Smith proves that these ideas were in the British intellectual mainstream as it stood in 1871. In fact, he shows that Cushites "whom the Iranian legends describe as men of a black complexion, with short and woolly hair" founded earliest Iran and India. Rulers "characteristic of the Negro" ruled in Egypt, and "a dark race" identified as "Ethiopians" inhabited Palestine. Nor was Smith alone in this view. On page 592 we cite a French schoolbook from 1907 that makes essentially the same points.

Other European scholars had begun the mapping of later chapters of the African heritage. Mr Bosworth Smith, as we have seen, documented the history of Carthage in 1877. After him, Mr Wilmot wrote a history of Munhumutapa. Major Dubois penned a history and travelogue of the Songhai Empire. Mr Roth documented the primary source material on Great Benin. Lady Lugard penned the history of Ghana, Mali, Kanem-Borno and Hausaland, among others. Mr Mead had shown the Egyptian origin of the ideas that became Greek philosophy and also Christian religion. Captain Stigand wrote of the history and culture of the East African coast. Professor Wiener documented the African voyages to America before Columbus. Sir Wallis Budge published a history of Ethiopia and Nubia. Finally, Mrs Hill penned a history of the Moors in Spain.

Issues Raised

The reader may well wonder why none of this information is common knowledge today but in 1871 (and 1907) most of it was in the mainstream. While the above is a small sample of the literature that is out there, it is sufficient to demonstrate that what now masquerades as World History is largely fictitious. The key issue is that in 1871 only Europeans would have been reading this material. It was for their eyes only. The current make-believe histories that locate Europeans (or "Mediterraneans") as the founders of civilisation itself were fabricated over the last one hundred years. This time, however, the material was aimed at a world readership. To pull this off, European scholars had to forget or pretend to forget all that they previously knew about Africans and their history.

By the year 1900 European control over the world by colonial conquest was almost complete. In addition, they seized control over the media and educational systems of the world. Therefore, what the world learned about itself came from or through a European source. Consequently, only stereotypes of non-Whites were ever going to escape the censorship. In the case of the Far East Asians, no scholarship ever located them as the original founders of civilisation itself. The mainstream could therefore tolerate Chinese history since it did not clash with the twentieth century fabrication that Europeans were the original founders of civilisation. The mainstream could not, however, tolerate Black history. Thus, it became important for the propagandists (a.k.a. "historians") to deny that the above literature even existed, or if not, deny that the terms Ethiopians, Libyans, Kushites, Hamites, Moors, Zanj, and Sudanese refer to Negroes, unless, of course, such people were captured slaves. If that failed, the mainstream bitterly attacked the credibility of the ancient and the modern scholars. This was not an entirely satisfactory approach since European historical scholarship is itself built upon the foundations laid by Herodotus, De Volney, Dupuis, Sir William Jones, Champollion, Rawlinson and Darwin. To attack these scholars was therefore equivalent to scoring an own goal. The final and most modern approach is to claim that modern authority is worth more than ancient documentation. It was all in vain because as Leo Frobenius put it, "the spell has been broken." Moreover, "the buried treasures of antiquity again revisit the sun."

We give the final word on this topic to Professor Yosef ben-Jochannan, an Ethiopian Egyptologist. This gentleman, one of the master teachers of our time, comments that:

> This ... should have made you (the student) aware of the fact that there is a preponderance of historical evidence showing the Nubians, Ethiopians, Puanits, Lebus (Libyans), Zimbab[weans], and other Africans along the Nile Valleys and African Great Lakes. It should have made you realize that there are thousands of volumes on the history of each of these African nations which have been purposefully kept from students of history (all colors) for the past two centuries or more. Unfortunately most of said volumes are alien to most of our "modern" professors of history and anthropology, including those bearing the title AUTHORITY OF AFRICA. This in no way exclude[s] most BLACK STUDIES PROFESSORS. Thus, you are aware of the problems all of us face;

that is, people who profess to speak "authoritatively" on Africa, and things African, without any knowledge of them except for certain aspects of the infamous SLAVE TRADE … [48]

Notes

[1] Leo Frobenius, *Histoire de la Civilisation Africaine,* quoted in Anna Melissa Graves, *Africa, the Wonder and the Glory,* US, Black Classic Press, (originally 1942), p.4.

[2] Ibid., pp.4-5.

[3] Filippo Pigafetta, *History of the Kingdom of Kongo,* quoted in Georges Balandier, *Daily Life in the Kingdom of the Kongo,* UK, George Allen & Unwin, 1968, p.150.

[4] Quoted in S. I. G. Mudenge, *Political History of Munhumutapa c 1400-1902,* Zimbabwe, Zimbabwe Publishing House, 1988, p.192.

[5] Francisco Alvarez, *Verdadera Informaçam das terras de Preste Joam,* quoted in Graham Hancock, *The Beauty of Historic Ethiopia,* Kenya, Camerapix, 1996, p.67.

[6] Pieter de Marees, *Description of Guinea,* quoted in H. Ling Roth, *Great Benin: Its Customs, Art and Horrors,* UK, F. King and Sons, 1903, pp.157-8.

[7] Thomas Bowditch, *At Kumasi,* in *African Civilization Revisited,* ed Basil Davidson, US, Africa World Press, 1991, pp.383-5.

[8] Hugh Clapperton, *Sultan Muhammad Bello,* in *African Civilization Revisited,* ed Basil Davidson, US, Africa World Press, 1991, p.381.

[9] Heinrich Barth, *The Western Sudan,* in *African Civilization Revisited,* ed Basil Davidson, US, Africa World Press, 1991, p.392.

[10] Winwood Reade, *The Martyrdom of Man,* UK, Watts & Co., 1934 edition, p.230.

[11] Hon A. Wilmot, *Monomotapa: Its Monuments and its History,* UK, T. Fisher Unwin, 1896, pp.138-9.

[12] Major Felix Dubois, *Timbuctoo the Mysterious,* UK, William Heinemann, 1897, pp.82-4.

[13] H. Ling Roth, *Great Benin: Its Customs, Art and Horrors,* UK, F. King and Sons, 1903, p.v.

[14] C. F. Volney, *The Ruins of Empires,* US, Peter Eckler, 1890 (original English edition 1802), p.17.

[15] Charles Dupuis, *The Origin of All Religious Worship,* US, New Orleans, 1872, pp.25-7.

[16] George Rawlinson (translator), *History of Herodotus: Volume II, Third Edition,* UK, John Murray, 1875, pp.163-5.

[17] W. G. Waddell (translator), *Manetho,* UK, William Heinemann, 1940, pp.79-81.

[18] Plutarch, *Concerning the Mysteries of Isis and Osiris,* in *Thrice Greatest Hermes, Volume I,* by G. R. S. Mead, UK, John M. Watkins, 1949, pp.274-5.

[19] C. H. Oldfather (translator), *Diodorus Siculus. Library of History, Volume II,* US, Loeb Classical Library, 1967, pp.89-91.

[20] Polybius quoted in J. A. Rogers, *World's Great Men of Color, Volume I,* US, Macmillan, 1972, p.116.

[21] R. Bosworth Smith, *Carthage and the Carthaginians, New Edition,* UK, Longmans, Green and Co., 1894, p.10.

[22] Strabo quoted in John G. Jackson, *Ethiopia and the Origin of Civilization,* US, Black Classic Press, (original 1939), p.8.

[23] A. H. L. Heeren, *Historical Researches into the Politics, Intercourse, and Trade of the Carthaginians, Ethiopians, and Egyptians, Volume I,* UK, D. A. Talboys, 1832, pp.291-2.

[24] Godfrey Higgins, *Anacalypsis, Volume I,* US, A & B Books, 1992 (original 1836), p.311.

[25] Quoted in Cheikh Anta Diop, *African Origin of Civilization: Myth or Reality?* US, Lawrence Hill, 1974, p.49.

[26] Henry C. Rawlinson, *On the Early History of Babylonia,* in George Rawlinson (translator), *History of Herodotus: Volume I, Third Edition,* UK, John Murray, 1875, p.433.

[27] Charles Darwin, *The Descent of Man, Volume I,* UK, John Murray, 1871, p.199.

[28] Philip Smith, *The Ancient History of the East,* UK, John Murray, 1871, p.6.

[29] Ibid., p.25.

[30] Ibid., p.26.

[31] Ibid.

[32] Ibid.

[33] Ibid., p.208.

[34] Ibid., p.395.

[35] Ibid., pp.551-2.

[36] Quoted in Cheikh Anta Diop, *Precolonial Black Africa,* US, Lawrence Hill, 1987, p.7.

[37] Quoted in J. Spencer Trimingham, *A History of Islam in West Africa,* UK, Cambridge University Press, 1962, pp.42-3.

[38] Al Idrissi, *The Book of Roger,* quoted in Lady Lugard, *A Tropical Dependency,* UK, James Nisbet & Co., 1906, pp.37-8.

[39] Al Masudi, *Meadows of Gold and Mines of Gems,* quoted in Hon A. Wilmot, *Monomotapa: Its Monuments and its History,* UK, T. Fisher Unwin, 1896, p.106.

[40] Cf. Quoted in John E. G. Sutton, *A Thousand Years of East Africa,* Kenya, British Institute of Eastern Africa, 1990, p.81 and Ibn Battuta, *Kilwa in 1331,* in *African Civilization Revisited,* ed Basil Davidson, US, Africa World Press, 1991, p.143.

[41] Lady Lugard, *A Tropical Dependency,* UK, James Nisbet & Co., 1906, p.209.

[42] G. R. S. Mead, *Thrice Greatest Hermes, Volume III,* UK, John M. Watkins, 1949 (original 1906), p.325.

[43] Captain C. H. Stigand, *The Land of Zinj,* UK, Constable & Company, 1913, pp.6-7.

[44] Leo Wiener, *Africa and the Discovery of America, Volume III,* US, Innes & Sons, 1922, p.365.

[45] E. A. Wallis Budge, *A History of Ethiopia, Nubia & Abyssinia, Volume I-B,* US, ECA Associates 1991 (original 1928), pp.164-5.

[46] Cecilia Hill, *Moorish Towns in Spain,* UK, Methuen & Co., 1931, pp.xii-xiii.

[47] Leo Frobenius, *Histoire de la Civilisation Africaine,* quoted in Anna Melissa Graves, *Africa, the Wonder and the Glory,* p.4.

[48] Yosef A. A. ben-Jochannan, *Africa! Mother of Western Civilization,* US, Black Classic Press, 1971, pp.299-300.

CHAPTER THREE: THE BLACK WOMAN

The Daughters of Lucy

In 1974 an important fossil was discovered in Ethiopia near the banks of the Awash River. The fossil was of an early ancestress of humanity belonging to a species called *australopithecus afarensis*. She was found to be upright walking, less than four feet tall, and weighed 60 pounds. She possessed a relatively small brain and had skull features resembling that of an ape. Her pelvis, legs and teeth, however, were much more like a modern human. Dated at 3.5 million years, the discovery suggested that the lineage that produced humans went back much further in time than previously thought. What name should we give to this ancestress? Professor Donald Johanson of the US Institute of Human Origins suggested the name 'Lucy'. Having been discovered in Ethiopia, however, others suggest giving her an African name. Ethiopians call her 'Dinquinesh' which means 'thou art wonderful'.[1]

In the 1980's scholars, led by Rebecca Cann of the University of Berkeley, conducted pioneering work with modern human DNA. Their findings, published in a 1987 edition of *Nature* magazine, suggested that all modern humans have a lineage traceable to a single female ancestor. Her theory is an example of monogenesis - the idea that all human groups are descended from the same parent population. Professor Cann's article was entitled *Mitochondrial DNA and human evolution*. In the abstract to this valuable paper, we read the following:

> Mitochondrial DNAs from 147 people, drawn from five geographic populations have been analysed by restriction mapping. All these mitochondrial DNAs stem from one woman who is postulated to have lived about 200,000 years ago, probably in Africa.[2]

Dr Cann drew conclusions on how her team's findings should be interpreted in the light of the fossil data:

> We infer ... that Africa is a likely source of the human mitochondrial gene pool ... Our tentative interpretation ... fits with one view of the fossil record: that the transformation of archaic to anatomically modern forms of Homo sapiens [i.e. *homo sapiens sapiens*] occurred first in Africa ... and that all present day humans are descendants of that African population.[3]

Newsweek, the widely read weekly journal, did much to popularise the new DNA research from the University of Berkeley. Concerning the African ancestress, they inform us that:

> Scientists are calling her Eve, but reluctantly. The name evokes too many wrong images - the weak-willed figure in Genesis, the milk-skinned beauty in Renaissance art, the voluptuary gardener in "Paradise Lost" who was all "softness" and "meek surrender" and waist-length "gold tresses." The scientists' Eve - subject of one of the most provocative anthropological theories in a decade - was more likely a dark-haired, black-skinned woman, roaming a hot savanna [of Africa] in search of food.[4]

In Britain, the well-established Conservative newspaper, *Daily Mail,* brought these research findings to the attention of their readership. They also reviewed *River Out of Eden,* a new book on the topic by Oxford University professor Richard Dawkins:

> Just imagine this: you me and every man, woman and child who walks the Earth is descended from the same African woman. Genesis gave us a version of the story with the Garden of Eden, as do most religions and tribal legends. But what if the existence of a shared ancestral mother could be *scientifically* proven, a matter of fact rather than faith? ... In his new book, River Out of Eden, the zoologist Richard Dawkins, author of The Selfish Gene, sets out to achieve this mind boggling goal. His compelling conclusions are rooted in Darwin's theory of natural selection. Dawkins does not just content himself with taking us step by step, back to our common ancestor; he goes much further, giving her an identity. She was a [B]lack woman who lived a quarter of a million years ago and we can trace our way back to her only through the female line.[5]

Archaeologists now believe that modern humans (i.e. *homo sapiens sapiens*) evolved from earlier hominid types in East Africa such as *australopithecus afarensis* but over an estimated period of five million years. Whichever be the case, the main point is still inescapable. Humanity is of African origin and the ancestors of humanity are also of African origin.

From Africa early humans migrated to other parts of the globe. Some of those early peoples, for example, entered Europe 39,000 years ago. They created a widespread culture that stretched from the Pyrenees to Siberia called the Aurignacian Culture. Mr Legrand Clegg, a well-known contributor to the *Journal of African Civilizations,* informs us of the importance of the African migration:

> One can state without exaggeration that the Grimaldis [referring to the early Africans] brought "civilization," such as it was, from prehistoric Africa to prehistoric Europe. Their invention of sculpting and their general contribution

to the field of art were universally recognized by scientists until the modern Grimaldi "blackout", which occurred because of the need of some Western authorities to deny "the area over which [N]egroids were scattered on the face of the globe." In addition to their invention of pendants, stone implements, certain styles of dress, an advanced symbol system, and perhaps even musical instruments, the Grimaldis were undoubtedly the first homo sapiens to bury their dead and they may have introduced to the world the use of the bow.[6]

Statuary from this early culture is scarce. Only twenty pieces have come down to us - fifteen of females and five of males. The females are shown to be fat, steatopygous (i.e. possess large buttocks), and have peppercorn hair. Professor Ernest Albert Hooton, a Harvard University anthropologist of the 1930's, wrote that: "It is interesting to note that the clearest cases of steatopygia occur in the representatives of females from the Aurignacian period of the European cave-cultures and among the modern Bushman-Hottentots [i.e. Black South-West Africans]".[7] Dr Charles Finch, one of our best scholars at the present time, says that:

These figurines are almost certainly mother figures model[l]ed on the African Grimaldi women, the standard-bearers of Aurignacian [C]ulture in Europe. In non-Western traditional cultures, particularly in Africa, obesity is often the mark of beauty and whenever an obese female is figuratively represented, she is invariably a mother figure.[8]

While the Aurignacian Culture flourished in Europe great advances were being made in Africa. From the Ishango region of Zaïre (now called Congo), near Lake Edward, a famous bone was found that had great significance. The Ishango bone was a tool handle with notches carved into it. Jean de Heinzelin, a Belgian archaeologist of the Royal Institute of the Natural Sciences, unearthed it in the late 1950's. The bone tool was originally thought to have been over 8,000 years old, but a more sensitive recent dating has given dates of 25,000 years old.[9] On the tool are 3 rows of notches, two of which add up to sixty. The number patterns represented by the notches are of great interest. Professor Claudia Zaslavsky, an American mathematician,[10] and more recently Dr Charles Finch[11] made independent studies of them.

Row 1 shows three notches carved next to six, four carved next to eight, ten carved next to two fives and finally a seven. The 3 and 6, 4 and 8, and 10 and 5, are believed to represent the process of doubling or $2n$. Row 2 shows eleven notches carved next to twenty-one notches, and nineteen notches carved next to nine notches. This is thought to represent 10 + 1, 20 + 1, 20 - 1 and 10 - 1. Finally, Row 3 shows eleven notches, thirteen notches, seventeen notches and nineteen notches. 11, 13, 17 and 19 are the prime numbers between 10 and 20. A prime number can only be divided by itself and by 1 to produce a whole

number. The early mathematician(s?) behind the Ishango Bone therefore understood doubling or *2n,* addition, subtraction and prime numbers. Furthermore, two of the rows add up to sixty (Row 2 consists of 11 + 21 + 19 + 9 = 60, and Row 3 consists of 11 + 13 + 17 + 19 = 60).

Dr Zaslavsky cites the work of Alexander Marshack, another authority on the bone. He noted a "close tally between the groups of marks and the astronomical lunar periods. A number of other readings in the long series of tests that were conducted gave even closer lunar approximations." On this basis, Marshack felt that the bone contained a lunar calendar. Elsewhere Dr Finch informs us that the female menstrual cycle was the first time-keeper in history. He wrote that: "Eventually, the moon, with its changing phases over a 29½-day period, became a celestial calendar linked to the menstrual cycle because of their seeming co-incidence."[12] Females would have been the first to have made the link between the menstrual cycle and the lunar month. We conclude, therefore, that since the Ishango bone may also have functioned as a lunar calendar, it is highly probable that the early mathematician(s) behind the bone were females.

Professor Fred Wendorf of the Southern Methodist University, and his colleagues, discovered that Africans were the first to grow crops. In the floodplains of the Nile, now part of Egypt's Western Desert, the people of Wadi Kubbaniya cultivated crops of barley, capers, chick-peas, dates, legumes, lentils and wheat. Their ancient tools were also recovered. There were grindstones, milling stones, cutting blades, hide scrapers, engraving burins, and mortars and pestles. The level of the Nile 12,000 years ago was higher than it is now. Each year during the summer, the Nile flooded, depositing rich silt into the Wadi Kubbaniya region. As the waters receded in late August and September, catfish were left stranded in ponds that were formed by the depressions. Since ash and charcoal were also uncovered, it seems that the ancients smoked the fish. As the fish stocks were depleted the people took the opportunity to plant crops on the silt. After the planting, it seems that hunter gathering was the main activity, judging from the recovered bones. They hunted wild cattle, hartebeest and sometimes, hippos. When December or January arrived, this was the time for the harvest. The cereals were ground to make flour. After the harvest, gazelles became the main source of subsistence. Also hunted were geese, ducks and wild game. By the time of summer, the Nile would flood again. The annual cycle was thus repeated.[13] Dr Finch, as usual, placed this data within the correct context:

> The greatest single invention in the history of civilization and the very thing that made it possible was agriculture. The ability to cultivate grains at seasonal intervals was probably the most decisive step in freeing mankind from the absolute, immediate grip of nature. It made possible settled communities, food

surpluses, population expansion, occupational diversification, and acquisition of specialized knowledge to boost productivity. Agriculture had to have been a female invention. It was the woman who collected most of the grains, seeds, roots, berries, and plants for the group's nutritional consumption and millenia of observing how seeds sprout when they spill onto the ground would have gradually led to purposeful cultivation … In Africa, the fields still belong to and are cultivated by the women.[14]

Prehistoric rock paintings have been found at various sites in North, East, West, Central and Southern Africa. The paintings in Namibia date back to a staggering 27,000 BC! In North Africa a remarkable tradition of art developed called the Saharan Rock Paintings. Artists would decorate and graffiti on cave walls, indeed on any suitable rock face, using the striking colours of red, yellow, black and white. The tradition in Algeria, in the Tassili n'Ajjer region, dates back to around 8000 or 7000 BC and continued for thousands of years.[15] In a television programme entitled *Africa: Different but Equal,* Dr Basil Davidson, its distinguished presenter, noted that the figures depicted in the prehistoric Algerian paintings looked to be "obviously African in origins".[16]

One distinguished painting is known as 'The Horned Goddess'. On the goddess' head is depicted a pot-shaped hat from which extend two horns. Some writers call this same painting 'The White Lady'. The image received this latter name because it depicts an extensive shower of light coloured grains of wheat that contrast against the figure's dark skin. The grains also complement the light coloured scarification dots in long rows of three or four on the goddess' skin. She is depicted as running, with an arched rainbow between her legs. Dr Rosalind Jeffries, our authority on these paintings, tells us that the horns represent an ancient belief that a goddess could transform herself into a cow or bull for the benefit of humans. Moreover, the up-turned pot represents a harvest offering as a sacrifice to the ancestors. The grain, of course, represents part of the evidence that women invented agriculture. Other images show women in combat roles with bows and arrows. In these images only one breast is depicted. This may indicate the origin of the stories concerning Amazonian warriors who removed one breast so as not to be hampered by it when using a bow and arrow. Other images are surprisingly modern. They depict sophisticated and elegant ladies wearing chic garments and supporting elaborate hairstyles. The garments, hairstyles, and quality of the paintings would not look too out of place in the twentieth century. Dr Jeffries concluded from her analysis of rock art from all over Africa that women are shown as:

primal mother, as giver of life, as virgin, symbol of purity, yet as destroyer, serpent and vulture, blessed rainmaker, herbalist and healer, warrior of Amazonic fierceness and power, protector of man, huntress and dancer, ringed and horned, wigged and hatted, veiled and masked.[17]

The Nile Valley

Ancient Egypt is the first major civilisation in Africa for which records are abundant. It was not, however, Africa's first kingdom. On 1 March 1979, the *New York Times* carried an article on its front page and page sixteen, written by Boyce Rensberger, that was entitled *Nubian Monarchy called Oldest.* In the article we were assured that:

> Evidence of the oldest recognizable monarchy in human history, preceding the rise of the earliest Egyptian kings by several generations, has been discovered in artifacts from ancient Nubia ... The discovery is expected to stimulate a new appraisal of the origins of civilization in Africa, raising the question of to what extent later Egyptian culture derived its advanced political structure from the Nubians.[18]

This ancient kingdom, generally called Ta-Seti, encompassed the territory of the northern Sudan and the southern portion of Egypt. It has sometimes been referred to as Ancient Ethiopia in some of the literature and as Cush (or Kush) in other literature.[19]

The first kings of Ta-Seti may well have ruled about 5900 BC. For three generations, these kings were the only attested kings on earth. During the time of the fifth generation of Nubian rulers, Upper (i.e. southern) Egypt may have united and became a greater threat to Ta-Seti. By the period of the seventh generation Nubian pharaoh, an important line of kings ruled in Upper Egypt. These kings were buried at Abydos - the sacred city of the Egyptians. With the rise of the Egyptian First Dynasty, Pharaoh Hor-Aha, its second pharaoh (5598-*c.*5581 BC), campaigned against Ta-Seti's ninth generation pharaoh. Hor-Aha's campaign destroyed the Nubian kingdom.[20]

Ancient Egypt was now the supreme power in the Nile Valley. Its next ruler was Queen Neith-Hotep (*c.*5581 BC). The single most powerful person in the world at the time, she ruled as Queen-Regent for Pharaoh Djer until he became of age to accept full political authority.[21] Pharaoh Mer-Neith (5524-*c.*5507 BC) succeeded Djer on the throne. She ruled as Egypt's first female pharaoh. Her name means 'beloved of Neith', named after the same goddess that the Greeks would, at a much later date, call Athena. She had two great tombs built, one in the southern Egyptian city of Abydos, the other in the northern city of Saqqara. Tradition dictated that these monuments be built to symbolise the authority of the pharaoh as ruler of the north and the south, Lower and Upper Egypt. Her monuments, especially the Saqqara tomb, are as large and impressive as those of the male pharaohs.[22]

Both Queen-Regent Neith-Hotep and Pharaoh Mer-Neith belonged to the First Egyptian Dynasty. From Dynasty One to the end of Dynasty Six (5660-

4188 BC) was the Old Kingdom period - Egypt's first golden age. This was the era when the solar calendar was invented, the Sphinx of Giza was built, the Great Pyramids were erected, and the first substantial literature in the world appeared. What is also extraordinary is that no other organised governments appeared anywhere else on the planet at this time of which historians are aware.

Two great females appeared during the Sixth Dynasty. Iput (c.4355 BC) ruled Egypt as Queen-Regent for Pharaoh Pepi I until he became of age.[23] Pharaoh Nitocris was the last ruler of the dynasty (4200-4188 BC). Rumours later circulated to the effect that she built the Third Great Pyramid of Giza, though this is probably false. In any case, the Old Kingdom collapsed after her rule.[24] Egypt went into a lengthy period of decline called the First Intermediate Period (4188-3448 BC). Kush, the land to the south of Egypt, became a great and powerful kingdom during this period.

Egypt entered its second golden age with the birth of the Middle Kingdom in 3448 BC. During this period, the Egyptians built the first planned city in the world at the site of Kahun. Furthermore, they built the largest monument in the ancient world - the Labyrinth, with its 3000 apartments. Finally, Egypt colonised Kush. Outside of the Nile Valley, states appeared for the first time in Asia. Of these, Sumer (located in modern Iraq) emerged first around 3300 BC. It was quickly followed by Elam (located in modern Iran), Akkad (in Iraq and Syria), and then the Indus Valley Civilisation (in western India and Pakistan). With the controversial exception of Crete, there were no other known civilisations on the planet at this date. There are, however, historians from the British Isles who claim that Stonehenge and also various structures built in Ireland and northern Scotland, deserve consideration as evidence of very early civilisation in Europe.

The Sumerian civilisation of Iraq contained an important and formative Negroid component. Ur, one of its great city-states, emerged in the fourth millennium BC. It had been greatly enriched by maritime and land trade with Egypt and Kush, amongst other places. The treasures buried with the rulers were superb. They include a dagger and sheath of pure gold, decorated with lapis lazuli. There was a ram in a thicket made of gold, silver, lapis lazuli, shell and red limestone. There was a bull's head made of gold leaf, wood and lapis lazuli. Finally, the jewellery of Chieftess Puabi (c.3200 BC), the earliest known great woman, was impressive.[25] It was comparable in style and quality with those of Twelfth Dynasty Egypt.

Another distinguished lady of Sumer was Ku-Baba. She was a ruler of the Third Dynasty of the city-state of Kish. The Sumerian King List, a crucial historical document, records her as the "barmaid" or woman of wine. This may indicate that she was originally an owner of a tavern or a vineyard before

becoming the ensi (i.e. king). A later account claims that she seized Kish from
the city of Akshak. Whichever be the case, she is said to have "consolidated the
foundation of Kish" and to have ruled 100 years, but this figure coming from
the King List may well be an exaggeration. The historical authorities are not
agreed on what dates to assign to her, but it is safe to say that she must have
ruled well before 2508 BC. After her passing, Kish became a lot less important
in the general history of the Sumerians.[26]

Returning to Egypt, the last pharaoh of the Twelfth Dynasty was
Sebekneferura. She ruled Egypt for an ephemeral 3 years and 10 months
(3186-3182 BC).[27] After her reign the Middle Kingdom collapsed. Egypt
entered her second dark age - known as the Second Intermediate Period. This
period of decline lasted from 3182 BC until 1709 BC. During this lengthy
period non-African invaders from Asia ruled Egypt. They were the first
Caucasians known to have ruled any part of African territory. The invaders
were joined by a second Asian horde - the Hyksos. They ruled the kingdom
from 2545 until 1709 BC. Kush, to the south, flourished during this period.

During the reign of the last Hyksos ruler, King Ipepi (1770-1709 BC), the
Egyptians rebelled, led by the indigenous monarchs of the Seventeenth
Dynasty. Queen Ahhotep was renowned for saving Egypt during these wars of
liberation against the Hyksos occupation. She rallied the Egyptian troops and
crushed a rebellion in Upper (i.e. southern) Egypt. For her part in the liberation
struggle, she received Egypt's highest military decoration at least three times -
the Order of the Fly.[28] After ruling as Queen-Regent, Kamose, her son,
succeeded her. He maintained the military pressure on the Hyksos until they
were finally evicted from Egypt.

The Eighteenth Dynasty (1709-1450 BC) is the most celebrated period of
Ancient Egyptian history today. From Dynasty Eighteen to Dynasty Twenty
(1709-1095 BC) was the New Kingdom period. Pharaoh Ahmose founded the
Eighteenth Dynasty. Ahmose-Nefertari, his wife, was highly distinguished and
did much to help reconstruct the country. She held the position of Second
Prophet of Amen and also that of Divine Wife. In these roles she performed
various civil and religious duties. She maintained a college of priestesses,
controlled the divine offerings to the deity Amen, was in charge of the workers
of the temple fields and also controlled a number of dignitaries. She later ruled
the country as Queen-Regent for Amenhotep I, her son. Some building projects
date back to her time such as the reconstruction of the Deir-el-Medina
necropolis. Amenhotep I succeeded her when he became of age.[29] Of this great
woman, Sir Flinders Petrie, master of the British archaeologists, wrote that she
was "the most venerated figure of Egyptian history."[30]

Hatshepsut was the next great woman of the dynasty. In September 1650 BC
Thutmose I, her father, elevated her to the position of co-regent. Following this

Egypt. Temple at Deir-el-Bahri. Built by Pharaoh Hatshepsut (1650-1600 BC), Eighteenth Dynasty, by carving it out of a mountainside. (Photo: B. Hungerford and R. Garner).

in 1628 BC she became the Great Royal Wife of Thutmose II. In 1615 BC she ruled as Queen-Regent for Thutmose III but later deposed him.[31] She proclaimed herself pharaoh in his place and took the religious titles the "female Horus" and the "daughter of Ra". She was deeply religious and did much to undermine the veneration of Set, the deity promoted by the Hyksos and identified as their deity Ba'al. Her leading statesmen, both of humble origins, Senenmut and Hapuseneb, oversaw her building activities. She also appointed Asians to powerful positions within the administration, the first pharaoh to do so.[32] At Karnak she erected two giant obelisks that rose to almost 100 feet:

> To make the obelisks still more conspicuous [says J. A. Rogers], she had their tops encased in electrum, a metal costlier than gold. (Electrum was a composition of silver and gold. Silver being rather rarer in Egypt, it was more precious.) In the bright sunlight of that rainless land the obelisks shone like glittering peaks. Their brilliancy, in the queen's own words, lit up the two lands of Egypt.[33]

In Deir-el-Bahri, she built her celebrated rock-hewn temple dedicated to Amen, Anubis and Hathor. In this temple are records of her famous maritime voyage to Punt (i.e. possibly Somalia or Ethiopia). In that land, the Egyptians bought incense, animals, animal skins, gum, gold, ivory and ebony. To pay for it, they brought weapons, jewellery and wares. On the cultural front, great lyric poetry was composed during her period.[34]

The period of Amenhotep III, a successor, was long and distinguished. Ascending the throne in 1538 BC, he ruled until 1501 BC. During his early years on the throne, the dominant influences came from his mother, Mutemwia, who ruled as Queen-Regent.[35] Later, he elevated Tiye to the position of Great Royal Wife. In later years, she became the real centre of power, as illness made Amenhotep III more and more dependent on her. Tiye built alliances by arranging diplomatic marriages. She also bought off Asian peoples through the gift giving of gold.[36] In return the Asians sold lapis lazuli and cedar wood. A period of much prosperity and stability, this allowed for the construction of great monuments.[37]

Amenhotep IV (1501-1474 BC) is best known as a religious reformer. His wife, Nefertiti, has become a somewhat enigmatic figure in Nile Valley history. Some writers have suggested that she was not a genuine Egyptian but had originated in the Middle East. Dr Asa Hilliard, for example, describes her as a "daughter of the Persian King Dushratta."[38] Dr Joann Fletcher, the distinguished English Egyptologist, found her mummy recently and used its skeletal structure to reconstruct her face. Georgina Littlejohn writing in the *Metro*, a London daily newspaper, commented on the reconstruction: "With her delicate features and striking dark eyes, she could easily pass as a top model.

But the next Naomi Campbell she is not - this is the face of legendary Egyptian queen Nefertiti."[39] We agree. The end result of the facial reconstruction, in our opinion, bears a much stronger likeness to Iman, the striking Somalian supermodel, than it does to Naomi Campbell. If Dr Hilliard is correct, the Fletcher reconstruction may provide evidence of the ethnic affinities of Nefertiti, Dushratta and their people in the Middle East of that period.

The Nineteenth Dynasty was also a great period of achievement. Tawosret (1243-1236 BC) was the last pharaoh of the dynasty. Again, she ascended the throne as the most powerful individual in the world. She, however, had a favourite named Bey, a man of Syrian origins. She elevated him to power where he became the Great Chancellor. During her time the turquoise mines of the Sinai region were dug. Additionally, she built a funerary complex near the Ramesseum, another great Nineteenth Dynasty monument. After her death, she was buried in the Valley of the Kings.[40]

After the Twentieth Dynasty (1236-1095 BC) Egypt again fell apart. More and more regional power ended up in the hands of the Libyans to the west and the Kushites to the south. Central authority in Egypt disappeared. Eventually the Kushites seized control over all Egypt during the period of Twenty Fifth Dynasty (785-664 BC). Kashta, the ruler of Kush, took control of the Egyptian city of Waset in 760 BC and received the divine mandate of Amen to rule. Following this, he installed his daughter as the successor to the post of High Priestess of Amen.[41] Charles Finch and Larry Williams argue that it became the standard practise for the Kushite pharaohs to place their female relatives in this position:

> These women, working through their own prime ministers, were in effect rulers of Upper Egypt. They undertook massive restoration and public works in Thebes [i.e. Waset] and throughout Upper Egypt. Their names are on scores of monuments, buildings, and statues ... The Cushite [sic] pharaohs ruled mainly from Napata and seemed to have had the utmost confidence in their female relatives to govern Upper Egypt.[42]

Amenirdas I, Kashta's daughter, gained various titles. She became "Chief Prophetess of Amen", "Queen of Thebes" and "Mistress of Egypt". Records from her reign have survived throughout Egypt. There are also statues, statuettes, etc. that have come down to us. She had quasi-royal privileges and her own prime minister. She restored buildings and commissioned public works programmes. Shepenoupet, her niece, succeeded her. There is confusion of names and details of this "dynasty", however. For example, it is known that a Shepenoupet was the last independent Negro ruler of Egypt, but we do not know which one. (It might have been Shepenoupet II).[43] After a great period of achievement, Egypt fell in 663 BC to the Assyrians. Shepenoupet (II) was deposed in 654 BC. After this, various other Caucasian peoples conquered Egypt. Egypt fell to the Persians in 525 BC, the Greeks 332 BC, the Romans in 30 BC and finally the Arabs in 639 AD. Pharaonic culture survived only in Kush. Meanwhile Egypt was gradually de-Africanised by the various conquests and occupations.

In Kush a number of women had the title Kentake. This title means Queen-Mother and was recorded in Roman sources as 'Candace.' Some of these women were heads of state. Kentake Qalhata (c.639 BC) had her own pyramid built at Al Kurru. It was notable that the colours used to depict males and females in the art closely followed the artistic canon of the Egyptians.[44] Pseudo-Callisthenes mentions that Alexander the Great visited "Candace, the black Queen of Meroe" in the fourth century BC. She was apparently a "wondrous beauty". No one seems to know the name of this Kentake, but she was evidently the ruler of Kush.[45] Kentake Shenakdakhete was the second known Kentake to rule Kush by herself (170-150 BC). Sculptures show her in front of her son or by herself. Monuments from her time show the first clearly dated examples of texts written in Meroïtic.[46] This was a new script that the Kushites invented to replace hieroglyphics. Kentake Nawidemak ruled around 50 BC. Little is currently known about her.[47]

The Roman conquest of Egypt in 30 BC brought a new challenge to Kush. Augustus Caesar threatened an invasion, following his Egyptian campaign.[48] According to Strabo, a famous geographer, sometime between 29 and 24 BC the conflict with Kush began. Queen-Mother Amanirenas, the Kushite ruler, gave the order to march into Egypt and attack the invaders. Akindad led the campaigns against the Roman armies of Augustus. The Kushites sacked Aswan with an army of 30,000 men and they destroyed the statues of Caesar in Elephantine. The Romans, under Petronius, counterattacked. Though described as a strong and fortified city, they captured Qasr Ibrim in 23 BC after their first assault. The Romans invaded as far as Napata and sacked it, though Amanirenas evaded their clutches. Petronius returned to Alexandria with prisoners and booty leaving behind a garrison in Lower Nubia. Amenirenas ordered her armies to march a second time with the aim of seizing the Roman garrison. This time, however, a standoff with Petronius was reached without fighting. The Roman army retired to Egypt and withdrew their fort declaring *Pax Romana* (peace). In fact, the full extent of the Roman humiliation has yet to be disclosed since the relevant Kushite account of the affair has yet to be published. The Meroïtic account of this encounter cannot as yet be fully understood.[49]

Kentake Amanishakheto (10-1 BC), a successor, had a palace at Wad ben Naqa. It was 61 metres square and had columned halls, corridors and long narrow rooms. It had at least two storeys with the palatial apartments on the

Kush (Sudan). Queen-Mother Nawidemak (*c.*50 BC) depicted on a now destroyed chapel at Gebel Barkal. Painted by Linant in the early nineteenth century.

upper floor. From her pyramid (see page 206), treasures were found made of gold, silver, gemstones, wood and copper alloy. Amongst the most spectacular of these treasures were a golden armlet and also a ring - both were made of gold and also inlaid glass.[50]

Pharaoh Natakamani and Queen Amanitore were the last great builders in Kush. They lived somewhere around 1 AD to 20 AD. Their buildings were raised in Keraba, an area between the Nile and the Atbara Rivers. Besides, they built in Naqa. In this city, the Temple of Apedemak (see page 217), one of their best known monuments, is in a good state of preservation. Naqa also contains a famous Kiosk (see page 25). This temple mixes architectural motifs from Nile Valley, Roman and Greek influences. The royal palace of Natakamani and Queen Amanitore was in Gebel Barkal.[51] Finally, they dug reservoirs around Meroë, restored its huge Temple of Amen, and rebuilt the Amen Temple of Napata previously destroyed by the Romans.[52]

The period of decline dates from 200 AD. Hungry nomads from the desert obstructed vital trade routes and also infiltrated the country.[53] Kentake

Maleqereabar was a ruler of Kush during this period (266-283 AD), but little is currently known about her. The following century, Kush was faced by a more important challenge than just nomads. This came from the kingdom of Axum located in the present day regions of Eritrea and Ethiopia. Under King Ezana, their armies marched on Kush in 350 AD. They destroyed the towns of masonry and seized a vast amount of livestock.[54] Kush collapsed. This ended the 6,000 year cycle of pharaonic culture.

Ethiopia

In and around Axum, the old Ethiopian capital, there are over 50 obelisks, many of them undecorated. Some are believed to be very old, but firm dates have not been established. Near to some of these obelisks, one kilometre from Axum on the road to the city of Gondar, is a massive building containing a drainage system with "finely-mortared stone walls, deep foundations and an impressive throne room".[55] Ethiopian tradition establishes this building as the palace of Empress Makeda, the fabled Queen of Sheba (1005-955 BC). Tradition also establishes one of the obelisks, carved with four horizontal bands, each topped with a row of circles in relief, as the marker of the Queen's grave.[56] It was probably due to this evidence that J. A. Rogers, the famous Jamaican historian, declared that: "A few years ago her tomb, as well as the ruins of a great temple and twenty-two obelisks of her period, were excavated at Axum".[57]

The Queen of Sheba was one of the most powerful women in history. She is named as Makeda in the Ethiopian chronicle, the *Kebra Negaste,* or Bilqis, in the Koran. She presided over Ethiopia and Yemen (Saba or Sheba) and thus controlled the Red Sea, a great trade route. The evidence of the tomb and the obelisks indicate that the Queen of Sheba was an Ethiopian. There are also obelisks that seem to be intermediate in date and style between those of the Makeda period and those of the early Christian era.

There is another theory, which is worthy of discussion, to the effect that the Queen was half-Ethiopian and half-Yemeni. Professor William Hansberry, master of the African-American historians, draws attention to a mediæval manuscript of Al-Hamdani. This Muslim scholar died in the Arabian city of Sana in the middle of the tenth century AD. His account portrays Bilqis as the daughter of Shar Habil, the king of Yemen, and Ekeye Azeb, an Ethiopian princess. Moreover, she was born in the Yemenite city of Marib, but spent her youth in Ethiopia. She returned to Marib just before her father's death.[58]

The Queen was famous as a trader. She established trading networks carried by 520 camels and 370 ships. Tamrin, her chief merchant, headed the operation. The book of *Ezekiel* 27: 22-24 says:

> The merchants of Sheba and Raamah were thy merchants; they traded in thy fairs with the best of all spices, and with all precious stones, and gold. Haran, and Calneh, and Eden, the merchants of Sheba, Asshur, and Chilmad were thy merchants. These were thy merchants in all sorts of things, in blue clothes, and embroidered work, and in chests of rich apparel, bound with cords, and made of cedar, among thy merchandise.

Unlike some other personalities in African history, there is an abundance of documents surrounding Makeda. This has made it difficult to separate fact from legend. For example Josephus, the great Roman Jewish historian, portrays her as Queen of Ethiopia but also Egypt. Other sources give her sovereignty over parts of Syria, Armenia, India and Indonesia. We take the more prudent view that she ruled just Ethiopia and Yemen.[59]

In the early Christian era, Ethiopia was still a great power. It was perhaps the third most powerful empire in the world, after Syria and Rome. In the early fourth century AD, it became a Christian state. The city of Axum continued to be a great city. It had a cathedral, an imposing castle complex, obelisks and multi-storey buildings. Rulers issued gold and silver coins. Trade continued to flourish with Persia, Arabia, India, Byzantium and Roman-ruled Egypt.

In 940 AD, though some authorities give slightly earlier dates, Judith, a Falasha conqueror, seized the throne of Axum and proclaimed herself Queen. Inspiring dread in many Christian minds, she destroyed the churches, killing thousands in the process. Her campaigns ended both the thousand-year supremacy of Axum and also an era in Ethiopian history. An old history book, *History of the Patriarchs of Alexandria,* mentions that the King of Axum begged the Patriarch of Alexandria for help - but none came. Judith ruled unchallenged for around 40 years. Succeeding her was the Zagwe Dynasty,[60] who ushered in a golden age. They ruled from Roha, their new capital, in the south, later renamed Lalibela. Their empire controlled a vast territory, much of it mountainous, but still larger than that controlled by Axum.

North Africa

In the ninth century BC the city-state of Carthage was established. It was situated on the North African coast of modern Tunisia. Incoming Phœnicians, the early people of Palestine, founded it and called it Qart Hadasht (cf. Carthage). Other influences in the culture came from different sources. The Libyans, the indigenous people of North Africa, played an important, and ultimately, the dominant role. In addition, other people and cultural practices came from the Nile Valley. What was the resulting mix?

Archaeologists have recovered skeletons from a Carthaginian cemetery. Professor Eugène Pittard, then at the University of Geneva, reports: "Other bones discovered in Punic [cf. Phœnician] Carthage, and housed in the Lavigerie Museum, come from personages found in special sarcophagi and probably belonging to the Carthaginian elite. Almost all the skulls are dolichocephalic." Moreover, the sarcophagus of the highly venerated Priestess of Tanit, "the most ornate" and "the most artistic yet found," is also housed in the Lavigerie Museum. Pittard says: "[T]he woman buried there had Negro features. She belonged to the African race!"[61]

Kingdoms have existed in Numidia since at least the fifth century BC. Originally there were several Numidian kingdoms of which two became important. Both were located to the west of Carthage in the regions of Algeria and western Tunisia. These too were Negro civilisations. The Carthaginian and Numidian kingdoms flourished for hundreds of years before they were finally conquered by the Romans in 146 BC and 46 BC respectively. Though under Roman occupation, notable Africans emerged during the early Christian era.

When Christianity began to spread as a new religion, many Africans from these regions converted to it. The Roman authorities were not pleased and developed a policy to combat the religion. On 17 July 180 AD, they executed the first martyrs of the African Church. Five women and seven men were put to death in a single day. The leader of the martyrs was a 22 year old woman called Perpetua. She was married and had a child. At a later date, a chapel was built for her memory in Carthage dedicated to St Perpetua. All twelve martyrs were Numidians, however, who were taken in chains to Roman-controlled Carthage to be tried and punished. Perpetua's brother was also executed as was a slave-girl called Felicitas. She gave birth just before being put to death.[62]

In 639 AD a new conquering force swept into Africa. The Arabians seized Egypt, Cyrenaica, Tripoli, and pushed on to Carthage and Numidia. The invasion swept away 600 years of Roman occupation. The new conquerors spread Islam from Egypt to Morocco and also into Spain. The Spanish conquest was achieved with African help. The invaders also destroyed many Africans, enslaved many, and caused others to flee further south to evade their clutches. Kuseila of Mauritania resisted but he was defeated and killed in 688 AD. Dahia al-Kahina (cf. Cohen) became leader of the African resistance. She is generally held to have been a Jewess but we believe that she could just as well have followed the old Carthaginian religion. This differs from Judaism but also shares some affinities with it. There are, of course, Negro Jews in many parts of Africa such as the Falasha of Ethiopia and the Lemba of South Africa. Arab records describe her as having "dark skin, a mass of hair and huge eyes" - the comment referring to her hair may refer to an afro or perhaps dreadlocks. Dr John Clarke describes her as a nationalist who favoured no particular religion. This may explain her effectiveness in bringing together a united front against the invaders. She counterattacked the invaders and drove them into

Tripolitania. This was so effective that some Arabs doubted whether Africa could be taken. As one African army was beaten another replaced them. The Arabs seized Carthage in 698 AD. Dahia defeated them and instituted a scorched earth policy to prevent the Arabs from being able to find crops to feed on in the region. That desolation can be seen even today in southern Tunisia. Eventually, however, the Arabs returned. Dahia was finally defeated in battle in 705 AD.[63] North Africa was overrun. Today Black people are a minority in North Africa. Furthermore, Africans in Mauretania and Sudan continue to face the threat of enslavement.

The Western and Central Sahara

A golden age existed in West Africa dating from an early period. Ancient Ghana was situated in today's Mali and southern Mauritania region between the Senegal and Niger rivers. By the eleventh century AD, at the height of its power, the empire also included parts of Senegal and Guinea.[64] The capital was Kumbi-Saleh, but Nema, Walata, and Audoghast were important cities.[65] The first kings of Ghana ruled from around 300 AD. By the year 700 AD, the kingdom had expanded into an empire - the first one known to have existed in West Africa. Concerning sexual politics, Dr Finch notes that: "Arab writers were profoundly shocked to find that the fabulously wealthy West African empire of Ghana was ruled by the matrilineal principle [i.e. where descent is traced through the female line] as were numerous other African kingdoms."[66]

After 1240 Ghana declined but it was succeeded by another kingdom in approximately the same geographical region. This state was Mali. By the fourteenth century Mali became a large and important empire - the second largest on earth.[67] The BBC, in a splendid documentary, claims that it was the richest kingdom in the fourteenth century world, due to its large gold reserves.[68]

Ibn Battuta, the most acclaimed traveller of the age, visited the empire. Not only is his *Travels in Asia and Africa* a classic, it contains some of the best eyewitness details of life in Mali during this period. For this reason, we feel justified in reproducing the following extracts from this work:

> I travelled [says Ibn Battuta] ... with travel companions whose leader was Abu Muhammad Yandakan al-Massufi, may God have mercy on him. In the company was a group of merchants of Sidjilmessa and others. We arrived after twenty five days at Taghaza. It is a village with no good in it. Amongst its curiosities is the fact that the construction of its houses and its mosques is of rock salt with camel skin roofing ... In it is a salt mine. It is dug out of the ground and is found there in huge slabs ... A camel can carry two slabs of salt. The [B]lacks [i.e. Malians] arrive from their country and carry away the salt. A

camel load of it is sold in Iwalatan (Walata) for from eight to ten *mithqals,* and in the town of Malli [i.e. Niani] for twenty to thirty *mithqals* perhaps the price reaches up to forty. The [B]lacks exchange the salt as money as one would exchange gold and silver. They cut it up and trade with it in pieces.[69]

Ibn Battuta witnessed various festivals while in the empire. On Fridays, the ruler held festivals after the late afternoon prayers. Ibn Battuta tells us in lush and exquisite detail what happened:

> The sultan holds sessions during the days associated with the two festivals after the 'asr (late afternoon) prayers on the *banbi* [i.e. platform]. The men-at-arms come with wonderful weaponry: quivers of silver and gold, swords covered with gold, their sheaths of the same, spears of silver and gold and wands of crystal. Four of the *amirs* stand behind him to drive off flies, with ornaments of silver in their hands which look like riding stirrups. The *farariyya* (commanders), the *qadi* [i.e. judge], and the preacher sit according to custom, the interpreter Dugha brings in his [i.e. the Mansa's] four wives and his concubines, who are about a hundred in number. On them are fine clothes and on their heads they have bands of silver and gold with silver and gold apples as pendants. A chair is set there for Dugha to sit on and he beats an instrument which is made of reeds with tiny calabashes below it, praising the sultan, recalling in his song his expeditions and deeds. The wives and the concubines sing with him and they play with bows. There are with them about thirty of his pages wearing red woollen robes and white caps on their heads. Each one of them has a drum tied to him and he beats it. Then come his retinue of young men who play and turn in the air as they do in Sind [i.e. India]. They have a wonderful gracefulness and lightness in this. They juggle with swords beautifully and Dugha performs a marvellous game with a sword. At that point, the sultan orders that a gift be given him, they bring him a purse of two hundred *mithqals* of gold dust. An announcement of its contents is made to him over the heads of the people. The *farariyya* (commanders) get up and twang their bows, thanking the sultan. On the following day every one of them makes a gift to Dugha according to his means.[70]

After his visit to Walata, Ibn Battuta described the women as "extremely beautiful and are more important than the men". He continues in a like vein:

> The condition of these people is strange and their manners outlandish. As for their men, there is no sexual jealousy in them. And none of them derives his genealogy from his father but, on the contrary, from his maternal uncle. A man does not pass on inheritance except to the sons of his sister to the exclusion of his own sons. Now that is a thing I never saw in any part of the world except in the country of the unbelievers of the land of Mulaibar (Malabar) among the Indians.[71]

Some scholars believe that Ibn Battuta appears to be describing a matriarchal social order operating in Mali. Other evidence that supports this interpretation comes from an anecdote, again from Ibn Battuta's pen:

> It came about that in the days of my stay in Malli [sic] that the sultan [i.e. Mansa Suleiman] was angry with his senior wife, the daughter of his paternal uncle, who was called Qasa which signifies the queen among them. The queen is his partner in the kingship, following the custom of the [B]lacks. Her name is mentioned with his in the pulpit.[72]

Saïd Hamdun and Noël King, the translators of Ibn Battuta's narrative, comment on this passage as follows:

> The 'woman-king' is often important in African kingship. She was a sovereign in her own right. Often she was not in fact the king's spouse but a female monarch chosen from the princesses of the blood royal. We may be in this narrative witnessing the sultan's attempt to replace the African type of queen by the consort-type of queen, a person who owed her position to her husband.[73]

To the east of Mali and located in the central Sahara was the Kanem-Borno Empire. At its height it controlled northeastern Nigeria, eastern Niger, western Chad, northern Cameroon, and southern Libya. Once horse-borne nomads, the Zaghawa built this culture. They created a state renowned for its longevity and political stability. From the late eleventh century onwards its rulers came from the same family - the Sefuwa. The empire's known history takes us from the early ninth century of our era, well into the nineteenth century.

The So Culture (also called Sao) was an earlier and vastly superior civilisation that thrived in the same region. "Remains of Sao settlements to the southeast of Lake Chad" says a modern scholar, "have been traced back to the 4th century B.C."[74] Zaghawa nomads immigrated to the lands of the So and lived among them. Using trickery, the Zaghawa gradually took them over and later absorbed them into their state. G. T. Stride and Caroline Ifeka presented the relevant facts about the So civilisation with characteristic accuracy:

> [T]he So people possessed considerable political and artistic genius. Although they never combined effectively to form an empire, they developed city-states which were the centres of intense local patriotism. Each city was surrounded by strong defensive walls and dominated the life of the surrounding countryside which it both protected and governed. Government was by an elaborate hierarchy, headed by a divine ruler … Except on ceremonial occasions, the rulers made few public appearances and even then remained concealed from the common gaze by a screen. Women occupied a respected position in society and the Queen Mother and senior sister of the ruler exercised considerable political influence on the government of the state. The So people were mainly settled farmers but among them were craftsmen of considerable industrial and artistic merit. They were able to work in both clay and metals to manufacture household utensils, tools, and works of art for religious purposes. Impressive

objects found by archaeologists include burial urns and naturalistic figures of animals and human beings both in clay and bronze. All this had been achieved ... before about A.D. 700 ... [75]

During the time of King Arku (1023-67), the Zaghawa extended their domain northwards into the Sahara. They established control over the trading activities of Muslims in the region. Islam came to have an influence in the royal court itself though it had little influence anywhere else in the kingdom. Queen Hawwa, Arku's successor, became the first Islamic sovereign of Kanem, ruling for four years. An equally short reign followed.[76]

In the thirteenth century Njimi became the new capital. From here, official and cultural contacts were established with the world at large.[77] Lady Lugard commented that: "The thirteenth century would seem to have been a brilliant period".[78] Sir Richmond Palmer, the pioneering and erudite authority on Kanem-Borno, seemed equally impressed. In his own words: "[T]he degree of civilisation achieved by its early [rulers] would appear to compare favourably with that of European monarchs of that day" especially when it is understood that "the Christian West had remained ignorant, rude, and barbarous".[79]

It is interesting to consider the administration of this vast territory. Dr Oliver and Dr Fagan's account of how it worked produced useful information that also throws light on old African matriarchy. Moreover, Oliver and Fagan's research demonstrates the extent to which Kanem-Borno copied its institutional structures from the conquered So:

> Despite the evident Muslim piety of many of the *mais* [i.e. kings], the political structure which emerged in medieval Kanem retained strong traces of the pre-Islamic sacral kingship attributed by al-Muhallabi [sic] to the Zaghawa, and having many features in common with other states of the Sudanic belt [of West Africa]. The ruler led a ritually secluded existence, surrounded by titled office-holders and palace slaves. As in so many African kingdoms, the highest positions of all were held by two women, known as the Queen Mother and the Queen Sister, each of whom had her own court and officers. The highest male dignitaries were the provincial governors theoretically responsible for the north, the east, the south and the west.[80]

The Hausa Confederation consisted of seven independent cities and their surrounding territories. Known as the Hausa Bakwai, or "pure" Hausa States, the cities were Gobir, Biram, Katsina, Kano, Daura, Rano and Zazzau. Gobir was the most northerly and Zazzau the most southerly. They flourished in the region of northern Nigeria from the eleventh or twelfth centuries[81] to the early twentieth century. Though linked by language, for most of their history the Hausa never formed a unified territory. Scholars thus describe them as a confederacy of independent states. Hausa historians also claim kinship with

Hausa (Nigeria). Entrance Gate of the Royal Palace of Zaria. Probably founded by Queen Bakwa (ruled 1536-1566 AD). (Photo: National Commission for Museums and Monuments, Lagos).

other states in the Nigeria region known as the Banzai Bakwai, or "impure" Hausa States. These were Zamfara, Kebbi, Gwari, Nupe, Yoruba and Kwararafa.[82]

Zazzau in the fifteenth century had various fortified places, such as Turunku and Kufena. Zaria city, however, dates back to 1536. Bakwa Turunku founded it after conquering Kufena. Apparently Turunku, her previous capital, lacked sufficient sources of water to support the growing needs of her commercial centre.[83] She probably founded the royal palace of Zaria, which remains an impressive structure. Dr Dmochowski, an architectural authority, says of it: "the palace should be preserved as one of the most important monuments of Nigerian national culture".[84]

On her death in c.1566, Karama, a soldier, succeeded her. Princess Amina, Turunku's daughter, accompanied him on campaigns. She was born around 1533 in Zazzau. In 1549 she became the heir apparent (Magajiya) to her mother. With the title came responsibility for a ward in the city where she convened daily councils with other officials. She also began training in the cavalry. In 1576 she became the undisputed ruler of Zazzau. Distinguished as a soldier and an empire builder, she led campaigns within months of becoming ruler. She built walled forts as area garrisons to consolidate the territory conquered after each campaign. Some of these forts still stand today. She is credited with popularising the earthen city wall fortifications, which became characteristic of all Hausa city-states since then. Towns grew within these protective walls, many of which are still in existence called "ganuwar Amina", or Amina's walls. Amina subdued the whole area between Zazzau and the Niger and Benue rivers, absorbing the Nupe and Kwararafa states. The *Kano Chronicle* says: "Every town paid her tribute. The Sarkin Nupe [i.e. king of Nupe] sent her forty eunuchs and ten thousand kolas ... In her time all the products of the west came to Hausaland". The southern expansion provided large supplies of slave labour. Moreover, Zazzau came to control the trade route from Gwanja and began to benefit from the trade previously enjoyed only by Kano and Katsina, two other Hausa city-states.[85] Amina's achievement was the closest that any ruler had come in bringing the region now known as Nigeria under a single authority (see page 445).

The West African Coast

In central Nigeria a hitherto unsuspected culture flourished between 1000 BC and 1000 AD.[86] Tin mining operations conducted in 1928 brought this civilisation out into the open. Lt-Colonel J. Dent Young, an Englishman, led mining operations in the Nigerian village of Nok located in the Jos region. During these operations, one of the miners found a small terracotta of a monkey head. Other finds included a terracotta human head and a foot.[87] The Colonel, at a later date, had these artefacts placed in a museum in Jos.[88] In 1942 another artefact, clearly belonging to this same culture, was found, but this time in Jemaa some distance away. This find was brought to the attention of Bernard Fagg, an English cadet administrative officer. Mr Fagg had a background as an archaeologist and by the mid-forties he wrote on this and other finds in the region. The ancient culture was now called the Nok Civilisation, named after the village in which the small terracotta monkey head was discovered.[89] Since then, around four hundred pieces of Nok art have been recovered.[90]

The artefacts are mostly human statues made of terracotta. From a few inches in height to almost life size, they depict people wearing rows of bracelets, necklaces, skullcaps, and in at least one instance, a cape. Most show the hair exposed - the coiffeurs are inventive and bold with highly individual plaits, ridges, locks and buns.[91] Mr Fagg wrote that: "The Nok people must have taken just as many hours as the chic Lagos ladies of the twentieth century do arranging their coiffures, or, to put them into their own historical period, the Mediterranean ladies who were living in their villas north of the Sahara".[92]

Another major development in the southern Nigeria region concerns the building of the city of Eredo in 800 AD. *The Sunday Times* on 23 May 1999 carried a valuable article entitled *Jungle reveals traces of Sheba's fabled kingdom*. Over the next few days many other papers followed suit. Even the

Daily Mail on 24 May asked: *Was the Queen of Sheba really a Black woman from Nigeria?*[93]

As the evidence emerged, however, the Queen of Sheba link proved to be hype. The real Sheba was an Ethiopian or half-Yemeni queen, as we have seen, who lived three thousand years ago on the opposite side of the Continent. What was undeniable, however, was that the southern Nigerian rainforests concealed an even more amazing secret. During the Middle Ages, Africans built by far the largest city the world had ever seen. In size, it dwarfed Baghdad, Cairo, Cordova and Rome. The achievement was on a scale even bigger than that of the Great Pyramid of Giza, Africa's most celebrated monument.

At Eredo, in southwest Nigeria, archaeologists found a huge earthen wall with moated sections. This encircled an ancient kingdom or city. From the base of the ditch to the summit of the rampart measured a towering 70 feet. According to Mark Macaskill of *The Sunday Times,* the rampart was "100 mile[s]" long and formed a rough circle, enclosing "more than 400 square miles."[94] The building was on a truly epic scale. The builders shifted 3.5 million cubic metres of earth to build just the rampart alone. According to the BBC this is, incidentally, "one million cubic metres more than the amount of rock and earth used in the Great Pyramid at Giza." Therefore Eredo's construction is estimated to have "involved about one million more man-hours than were necessary to build the Great Pyramid."[95] The ramparts may indicate the boundary of the original Ijebu kingdom that was ruled by a spiritual leader called the "Awujale". Macaskill, however, disagrees. He describes Eredo as a "city". If correct, this would make Eredo one of the very largest cities in all of human history. Comparable in size to modern London, it was the largest city built in the ancient and mediæval world.

Among the discoveries, a three storey ruin has been tentatively identified as the royal palace. It had living quarters, shrines and courtyards. It is possible that thousands of smaller buildings are still concealed by the forests and will be mapped in time. Radiocarbon dating has so far established that the buildings and walls were more than 1,000 years old. Dates such as 800 AD have been suggested.

People who live near the ruined kingdom or city today have traditions that a wealthy and childless queen, Bilikisu Sungbo, built the city. Some say that she built the city as a religious offering. It is also claimed that Sungbo's territory had a gold and ivory trade. Portuguese documents dating back 500 years, allude to the power of an Ijebu kingdom that some scholars think is possibly this very one. Today, the ruins continue to be of some importance. There are yearly pilgrimages to Sungbo's grave.

By the eleventh century AD, the Yoruba, ruling from the city of Ife (also called Ile-Ife), were the leading cultural force in southern Nigeria. Their civilisation has been widely admired by many scholars. Professor Cheikh Anta Diop, for example, wrote that: "It is impossible to describe here all the riches of the civilization of Ife".[96] Ile-Ife became a powerful city some time after 1000 AD. Home to the divine ruler, the Oni, it was also the centre of trade routes.[97] Professor Ekpo Eyo, the former head of the Nigerian museums network, narrates a curious oral tradition concerning Oni Oluwo, a distinguished Yoruba ruler. Apparently she was walking around the capital when her regalia got splashed with mud. Oluwo was so upset by this that she ordered the construction of pavements for all the public and religious places in the city.[98] Archaeology confirms that:

> Pavements … are widespread in Africa. Potsherd pavements are the most common types of pavements known in West Africa … The most consistent reports about excavated pavements in West Africa have so far come from Ife, specifically the sites at: Oduduwa College, Lafogido, Ita Yemoo, Obalara's Land and Woye Asiri Land.[99]

As early as 1913, Dr Frobenius, the German savant, speculated that there was a link between the Yoruba culture and the cultures of ancient America. He believed that this connection was forged at a date well before Christopher Columbus' so-called discovery of America:

> I cannot finish [wrote Frobenius] without devoting a word or two to a certain symptomatic conformity of the Western Atlantic civilisation with its higher manifestations in America. Its cognate features are so striking that they cannot be overlooked, and as the region of Atlantic African culture is Yoruba … it seems to be a present question, whether it might not be possible to bring the marvellous Maya monuments … into some prehistoric connection with those of Yoruba.[100]

Strangely enough, recent archaeological evidence lends support to some of Frobenius' ideas. Scholars have discussed and debated the validity of many pieces of evidence for ancient connections between Africa and America. Dr David Kelley is one such example. In his own words:

> The kind of evidence field archaeologists like is the pavement of Île Ife [sic], a former Yoruba capital (Van Sertima 1976: 264-267). This is made from broken potsherds that were decorated by rolling corncobs over their surface before firing. Paul Mangelsdorf, who had seen some of the sherds assured me (about 1954) that they were indeed Zea mays [i.e. an American plant]. Another interpretation of Yoruba tradition is that the capital was moved from Île Ife to Old Oyo about A.D. 1100 or earlier (M. D. W. Jeffreys, 1953). If so, this site provides the hard evidence that archaeologists want for American plants in Africa in pre-Columbian times [i.e. before Columbus].[101]

No one knows whether Native Americans sailed across the Atlantic and visited Ile-Ife bringing the maize with them. It is equally possible that Yorubas visited ancient America and returned with the maize. One thing is certain - contact between the two cultures occurred before 1100 AD or before whatever date is accepted for the paving of the city. Scholars today routinely speak of the Pre-Pavement period as between 800 and 1000 AD and the Post-Pavement period as after 1000 AD.[102] On this basis, contact between the two cultures, Yoruba and Native American, must therefore had taken place before 1000 AD. That leaves one key question: Was Oni Oluwo responsible for the Yoruba/Native American connection? On present evidence this appears to be probable but more research in this area is always welcome.

From the fifteenth century onwards, West Africa began to face the rigours of the Slave Trade. The challenge first came from the Portuguese. Later challenges came from other European peoples. In the region now known as Angola, there was a kingdom called Ndongo. Kabasa was its capital city. Portuguese traders exerted a great pressure on this kingdom. After 1608 their army commander-in-chief instituted a new policy of repression. Bento Cardoso devised a system whereby every Ndongo notable would be owned by a Portuguese official and was responsible for delivering a certain quantity of slaves to that official. Should the Ndongo notable fail therein, he too would be enslaved. Over a hundred notables were enslaved in a single year. In addition, the Portuguese killed a further one hundred. Even the ruler of Ndongo, himself a slave trader, resisted the aggression. War dragged on for years but the Portuguese were forced to sue for peace.[103]

In 1622 Ann Nzinga (see page 352), the Ndongo royal sister, attended a peace conference with the Portuguese convened in the coastal city of Luanda. She demanded (1) that the Portuguese evacuate Kabasa, the Ndongo capital; (2) that the Portuguese wage war on the Jaga, an African people much involved in the Slave Trade; (3) all Ndongo notables who had become vassals of the Portuguese must return to their former loyalty to the Ndongo crown. In return, Nzinga promised to hand over Portuguese prisoners of war. The provisions of the treaty were designed to end all fighting in the region, but alas the Portuguese breached it almost immediately by invading Kongo, the kingdom to the north.

In 1623 Ann Nzinga officially became the Ngola (which means King) [sic], and in this capacity made the regional alliances necessary to fight the Portuguese. She even made common cause with the Jaga. Ndongo was declared a free country the following year. All slaves entering the country were legally declared to be free. By 1629 her forces and allies captured Matamba, the neighbouring state to the east. Incidentally, this state had a tradition of being ruled by females. This too was declared a free country. The fragile alliance with the Jaga ended when their ruler betrayed her and attacked Matamba. Fortunately, dissention among the Europeans - the Dutch were encroaching on Portugal's share of the slave trade - created an opportunity for Nzinga. She established a strategic alliance with the Dutch, pitting them against the Portuguese. After the Portuguese defeated the Dutch, Nzinga retreated to the hills of Matamba, where she established a formidable resistance movement against the Portuguese. One key strategy was to get Black slave soldiers to desert to her side. She promised them land and freedom. She was the only African leader in history known to have attempted this. In 1641 Garcia II, a vigorous king, emerged in Kongo, to the north. He made alliances with the Dutch to fight Portuguese aggression. His death in 1661 ended the great era of Kongolese culture. In Ndongo, the death of Nzinga in 1663 marked a turning point. Her extraordinary and brilliant reign only delayed the inevitable.[104]

Towards the end of the seventeenth century, both the combined states of Ndongo and Matamba, and also Kongo, fell victim to European predator activities where "executions, treachery, robbery, and violence became the order of the day."[105] Even under these trying circumstances, another great woman emerged. Kimpa Vita also called Dona Beatriz continued the resistance against the Portuguese slave traders. She was a Kongolese aristocrat born in 1682. By 1704 she began to get national recognition as a prophetess. Though a Christian, she led an interpretation of Christian doctrine that her opponents called the Antonian Heresy. This theology created a national religion in Kongo that owed little to the Church of Rome. Vita preached that (1) Kongo was the Holy Land described in the Bible; (2) The Kongolese capital, Mbanza Kongo, is the real site of Bethlehem; (3) Christ and all the other saints were Black; and (4) Heaven was for Africans only. Thus, she called on Africans not to listen to White missionaries. Her political programme was to find the new king of Kongo who would lead the next golden age of Kongo civilisation. Unfortunately, it was not to be. She was eventually captured and executed by the Portuguese in 1706.[106]

The Slave Trade continued well into the nineteenth century with millions of Africans deported and many more killed. Black history, in the sense defined by Dr Karenga, re-emerged in the Maroon societies of Brazil, Jamaica, the United States and the Haitian Revolution. Great women emerged during this period such as Acheampong Nanny of Jamaica and Harriet Tubman of the United States. In Britain, Mary Prince wrote a devastating book on her life as a former slave that made a large social impact. Following the Slave Trade and without much opportunity to recover, almost the whole of Africa was conquered and colonised by Europe at the end of the nineteenth century. Again great women emerged in the twentieth century to challenge this state of affairs such as the glorious Amy Jacques Garvey.

Notes

[1] Graham Hancock, *The Beauty of Historic Ethiopia,* Kenya, Camerapix, 1996, p.14 and Ivan Van Sertima, *The African Eve: Introduction and Summary,* in *Black Women in Antiquity,* ed Ivan Van Sertima, US, Transaction Publishers, 1988, p.5.

[2] Rebecca Cann et al, *Mitochondrial DNA and human evolution,* in Nature, UK, 1 January 1987, p.31.

[3] Ibid., pp.33-5.

[4] *The Search for Adam and Eve,* in *Newsweek,* US, 11 January 1988, p.38.

[5] Jessica Davies, *Is this the Mother of us all?* in *Daily Mail,* UK, 11 May 1995.

[6] Legrand Clegg II, *The First Invaders,* in *African Presence in Early Europe,* ed Ivan Van Sertima, US, Transaction Publishers, 1985, p.32.

[7] Quoted in J. A. Rogers, *Sex and Race: Volume I,* US, Helga M. Rogers, 1968, pp.31-2.

[8] Charles Finch, *Echoes of the Old Darkland,* US, Khenti, 1991, p.61.

[9] Charles Finch, *The Star of Deep Beginnings,* US, Khenti, 1998, pp.2-4 and 56.

[10] Claudia Zaslavsky, *Africa Counts,* US, Lawrence Hill & Co., 1973, pp.17-8.

[11] Charles Finch, *The Star of Deep Beginnings,* pp.55-7.

[12] Charles Finch, *Echoes of the Old Darkland,* p.67.

[13] Fred Wendorf, Romauld Schild, and Angela E. Close, *An Ancient Harvest on the Nile,* in *Blacks in Science: Ancient and Modern,* ed Ivan Van Sertima, US, Transaction Publishers, 1983, p.58.

[14] Charles Finch, *The Star of Deep Beginnings,* pp.77-8.

[15] Werner Gillon, *A Short History of African Art,* UK, Penguin, 1984, pp.36-51.

[16] Basil Davidson, *Africa,* television series part 1: *Different but Equal,* UK, Michael Beazley, Rm Arts, Channel Four Television & Nigerian Television, 1984.

[17] Rosalind Jeffries, *The Image of Woman in African Cave Art,* in *Black Women in Antiquity,* ed Ivan Van Sertima, US, Transaction Publishers, 1988, pp.121-2. See also pp.105-119 and Basil Davidson, *African Kingdoms,* Netherlands, Time-Life Books, 1967, pp.43-54.

[18] Boyce Rensberger, *Nubian Monarchy Called Oldest,* in *New York Times,* 1 March 1979, pp.1 and 16.

[19] 'Ethiopia' in this sense is in a different location to the modern country of the same name. The two should not be confused with each other.

[20] Bruce Williams, *The Lost Pharaohs of Nubia,* in *Egypt Revisited,* ed Ivan Van Sertima, US, Transaction Publishers, 1989, p.103.

[21] Deidre Wimby, *The Female Horuses and the Great Wives of Kemet,* in *Black Women in Antiquity,* ed Ivan Van Sertima, US, Transaction Publishers, 1988, p.38.

[22] Ibid., pp.38-9.

[23] Ife Jogunosimi, *The Role of Royal Women in Ancient Egypt,* in *Kemet and the African Worldview,* ed Maulana Karenga & Jacob Carruthers, US, University of Sankore Press, 1986, p.36.

[24] Deidre Wimby, *The Female Horuses and the Great Wives of Kemet,* in *Black Women in Antiquity,* pp.39 and 41.

[25] Alastair Service, *Lost Worlds,* UK, Marshall Cavendish, 1981, pp.96-7 and 100.

[26] Runoko Rashidi, *More Light on Sumer, Elam and India,* in *African Presence in Early Asia,* ed Runoko Rashidi, US, Transaction Publishers, 1995, p.166.

[27] Ife Jogunosimi, *The Role of Royal Women in Ancient Egypt,* in *Kemet and the African Worldview,* pp.38-9.

[28] *Women in Ancient Egypt,* Internet article, see
http://www.crystalinks.com/egyptianwomen.html
[29] Deidre Wimby, *The Female Horuses and the Great Wives of Kemet,* in *Black Women in Antiquity,* pp.42-4.
[30] Quoted in W. E. B. DuBois, *The World and Africa,* US, International Publishers, 1965, p.126.
[31] Duncan MacNaughton, *A Scheme of Egyptian Chronology,* UK, Luzac & Co., 1932. pp.208-9.
[32] Erik Hornung, *History of Ancient Egypt,* UK, Edinburgh University Press, 1999, pp.82-5.
[33] J. A. Rogers, *World's Great Men of Color, Volume I,* US, Macmillan, 1972, p.46.
[34] Erik Hornung, *History of Ancient Egypt,* pp.85-8.
[35] Ife Jogunosimi, *The Role of Royal Women in Ancient Egypt,* in *Kemet and the African Worldview,* p.37.
[36] Erik Hornung, *History of Ancient Egypt,* pp.94-5.
[37] Vivian Davies and Renée Friedman, *Egypt,* UK, British Museum Press, 1998, p.136.
[38] Asa G. Hilliard III, *Bringing Maat, Destroying Isfet,* in *Egypt: Child of Africa,* ed Ivan Van Sertima, US, Transaction Publishers, 1988, p.128.
[39] Geogina Littlejohn, *Revealed: Face of an ancient beauty,* in *Metro,* UK, 14 August 2003, p.3.
[40] Deidre Wimby, *The Female Horuses and the Great Wives of Kemet,* in *Black Women in Antiquity,* p.46.
[41] Derek A. Welsby, *The Kingdom of Kush,* US, Markus Wiener, 1996, p.63.
[42] Larry Williams & Charles S. Finch, *The Great Queens of Ethiopia,* in *Black Women in Antiquity,* ed Ivan Van Sertima, US, Transaction Publishers, 1988, p.23. See also p.21.
[43] Ibid., pp.21-6.
[44] Timothy Kendall, *Kingdom of Kush,* in *National Geographic, Volume 178, Number 5,* ed William Graves, US, National Geographic Society, November 1990, pp.112-4.
[45] Larry Williams & Charles S. Finch, *The Great Queens of Ethiopia,* in *Black Women in Antiquity,* pp.31-2.
[46] Ibid., p.30.
[47] Ibid.
[48] Ibid.
[49] Ibid., pp.30-1 and Derek A. Welsby, *The Kingdom of Kush,* pp.39, 47 and 68-9.
[50] Derek A. Welsby, *The Kingdom of Kush,* pp.124-5 and 185-6.
[51] Ibid., pp.34, 77, 119, 122 and 124.
[52] Roland Oliver & Brian M. Fagan, *Africa in the Iron Age,* UK, Cambridge University Press, 1975, p.40.
[53] Basil Davidson, *African Kingdoms,* p.38.
[54] Ibid.
[55] Graham Hancock, *The Beauty of Historic Ethiopia,* p.43.
[56] Camerapix, *Ethiopia: A Tourist Paradise,* Ethiopia, Ethiopian Tourist Commission, 1996, p.28.
[57] J. A. Rogers, *World's Great Men of Color, Volume 1,* p.86.
[58] Joseph E. Harris ed, *Pillars in Ethiopian History: The William Leo Hansberry African History Notebook, Volume 1,* US, Howard University Press, 1974, pp.51-2.
[59] Larry Williams & Charles S. Finch, *The Great Queens of Ethiopia,* in *Black Women in Antiquity,* pp.16-20.

[60] Ibid., p.33.

[61] Quoted in Cheikh Anta Diop, *The African Origin of Civilization: Myth or Reality?* US, Lawrence Hill, 1974, p.122.

[62] J.C. DeGraft-Johnson, *African Glory,* UK, Watts & Co., 1954, p.32.

[63] Ibid., pp.66-8 and John Henrik Clarke, *African Warrior Queens,* in *Black Women in Antiquity,* ed Ivan Van Sertima, US, Transaction Publishers, 1988, pp.128-9. Also H. Monès, *The conquest of North Africa and Berber resistance,* in *UNESCO, General History of Africa: Volume III,* ed M. El Fasi, UK, Heinemann, 1988, p.238.

[64] John G. Jackson, *Introduction to African Civilizations,* US, Citadel Press, 1970, p.199.

[65] Cheikh Anta Diop, *Precolonial Black Africa,* US, Lawrence Hill Books, 1987, pp.199-200.

[66] Charles Finch, *Echoes of the Old Darkland,* p.58.

[67] Basil Davidson, *African Kingdoms,* p.84.

[68] Jeremy Isaacs (producer), *Millennium: The 14th Century,* Television Series, UK, BBC Television, 1999.

[69] Saïd Hamdun and Noël King, *Ibn Battuta in Black Africa,* US, Markus Wiener, 1994, p.30.

[70] Ibid., pp.52-3.

[71] Ibid., p.37.

[72] Ibid., p.55.

[73] Ibid., p.91.

[74] Philip Koslow, *Kanem-Borno: 1,000 Years of Splendor,* US, Chelsea House, 1995, p.13.

[75] G. T. Stride & Caroline Ifeka, *Peoples and Empires of West Africa,* UK, Thomas Nelson and Sons, 1971, pp.113-5.

[76] Philip Koslow, *Kanem-Borno: 1,000 Years of Splendor,* pp.21-2.

[77] J. Spencer Trimingham, *A History of Islam in West Africa,* UK, Oxford University Press, 1962, p.117.

[78] Lady Lugard, *A Tropical Dependency,* UK, James Nisbet & Co., 1906, p.270.

[79] Quoted in Basil Davidson, *Old Africa Rediscovered,* UK, Victor Gollancz, 1959, pp.81-2.

[80] Roland Oliver & Brian M. Fagan, *Africa in the Iron Age,* p.153.

[81] J. Spencer Trimingham, *A History of Islam in West Africa,* p.126.

[82] G. T. Stride & Caroline Ifeka, *Peoples and Empires of West Africa,* pp.86-7.

[83] Sule Bello, *Birnin Zaria,* in *Cities of the Savannah,* ed Garba Ashiwaju, Nigeria, The Nigeria Magazine, no date given, p.77 and G. T. Stride & Caroline Ifeka, *Peoples and Empires of West Africa,* p.97.

[84] Z. R. Dmochowski, *Northern Nigeria: An Introduction to Nigerian Traditional Architecture, Volume 1,* Nigeria, National Commission for Museums and Monuments, 1990, section 5.48.

[85] G. T. Stride & Caroline Ifeka, *Peoples and Empires of West Africa,* p.97, J. Spencer Trimingham, *A History of Islam in West Africa,* p.129 and Philip Koslow, *Hausaland: The Fortress Kingdoms,* US, Chelsea House, 1995, pp.23-4.

[86] Bernard de Grunne, *The Birth of Art in Black Africa,* France and Luxembourg, Adam Biro & Banque Generale du Luxembourg, 1998, p.15.

[87] Werner Gillon, *A Short History of African Art,* p.75.

[88] Ekpo Eyo and Frank Willett, *Treasures of Ancient Nigeria,* UK, William Collins & Sons, 1980, pp.3-4.

[89] Bernard de Grunne, *The Birth of Art in Black Africa,* p.15.

[90] Ibid., p.21.

[91] Ibid., pp.26-8 and 90-7.

[92] Bernard Fagg, *Nok Terracottas,* UK & Nigeria, Ethnographica and The National Commission for Museums and Monuments, 1990, p.27

[93] See also Roger Highfield (Science Editor), *Britons explore 'Queen of Sheba's monument',* in *The Daily Telegraph,* 26 May 1999, p.13.

[94] Mark Macaskill, *Jungle reveals traces of Sheba's fabled kingdom,* in *The Sunday Times,* 23 May 1999, p.10.

[95] Barnaby Phillips (BBC News), *Nigeria's hidden wonder.* BBC Online (Internet article), 9 June 1999.

[96] Cheikh Anta Diop, *The African Origin of Civilization: Myth or Reality?* p.158.

[97] Alastair Service, *Lost Worlds,* p.137.

[98] Ekpo Eyo and Frank Willett, *Treasures of Ancient Nigeria,* p.10.

[99] Nwanna Nzewunwa, *Prehistoric Pavements in West Africa,* in *West African Journal of Archaeology: Volume 19,* ed Bassey W. Andah and Ikechukwu Okpoko, Nigeria, Association Quest Africaine d'Archaeologie, 1989, pp.93-100.

[100] Leo Frobenius, *The Voice of Africa: Volume I,* UK, Hutchinson & Co., 1913, p.348.

[101] David Kelley quoted in Ivan Van Sertima, *Early America Revisited,* US, Transaction Publishers, 1998, p.7.

[102] Robin Polynor, *The Yoruba and the Fon,* in *A History of Art in Africa,* by Monica Blackmun Visonà et al, UK, Thames and Hudson, 2000, p.229.

[103] Chancellor Williams, *The Destruction of Black Civilization,* US, Third World Press, 1987, pp.260-1.

[104] Ibid., pp.262-72 and Christopher Ehret, *The Civilizations of Africa,* UK, James Currey, 2002, p.368.

[105] J. C. DeGraft-Johnson, *African Glory,* p.143.

[106] Georges Balandier, *Daily Life in the Kingdom of the Kongo,* UK, George Allen & Unwin, 1968, pp.257-63 and Jan Vansina, *Kingdoms of the Savanna,* US, University of Wisconsin Press, 1966, p.154.

CHAPTER FOUR: THE LAND OF THE BLACKS

The Peopling of Ancient Egypt

Africa is the ancestral homeland of Black people. Indeed, Africa was once called The Land of the Blacks.[1] The Ancient Greek historians and scholars called the entire continent of Africa 'Ethiopia' in their literature. This literally meant The Land of the Burnt Faces.[2] In the Mediæval period the Arabian scholars called the continent 'Bilad es-Sudan', meaning The Land of the Blacks.[3] It is evident that Ethiopia for the Greeks, and Bilad es-Sudan for the Arabs refers to the same territory. A cursory look at the peopling of the continent will reveal that the Blacks are not predominant throughout Africa. South Africa is under the domination of the Dutch and the British,[4] while North Africa is under the domination of the Arabians and the White Berbers.[5] The Arabs, White Berbers, British and the Dutch are not indigenous to the continent. They are all descendents of invaders that seized territories originally occupied by Black people. How and when did this happen?

There has been considerable population replacement in North Africa due to invasions and occupations. The Arabians attacked and occupied North Africa between 639 and 708 AD.[6] They are still there today and are still the politically and economically dominant people. This is so much the case that the typical picture that most people have of a North African is the Arab. Even earlier than the Arab invasion and occupation, North Africa was invaded and occupied by the Vandals, a Germanic speaking people. They seized North Africa in the fifth century AD. Before the Vandal occupation, however, the Romans ruled North Africa. Their occupation began in 146 BC. By 30 BC, they were the masters of North Africa. The descendents of the Romans and Vandals today live as part of the 'Berber' peoples of North Africa. Before the Roman period, however, the Greeks occupied Egypt in 332 BC and the Persians occupied Egypt in 525 BC. These invasions led to Indo-European people ruling Egypt. The Ancient Egyptian civilisation, however, is thousands of years older than 525 BC.

In North Africa today, the Arabians have become the main population, as already stated. There are also large light-skinned populations that are descendants of the Vandals, Romans and Greeks. In Egypt, the Coptic or Christian population, generally claimed to be descendants of the Pharaohs, are mostly of Egyptian-Greek ancestry. As with many mixed populations some are dark and others are pale. Even the Coptic script illustrates the reality of cultural admixture. The Coptic script is largely based around the ancient Egyptian language, but it is written using the Greek alphabet. Clearly, the Ancient Egyptians could not have been Arabs, Vandals, Romans, Greeks or Persians, so … who were they?

The Classical writers were the ancient Greek and Roman scholars. They described the Ancient Egyptians during the periods of Persian, Greek and Roman ascendancy. The term "Egyptian" in their writings only referred to the indigenous people and not the foreign ruling classes in Egypt such as the Persians, the Greeks and the Romans. Another term that the Classical writers use is "Ethiopian". It literally means the "burnt-faced" people and is an ancient term for Negro.

Pliny the Elder was a Roman naturalist. In 77 AD he wrote his voluminous *Natural History*. In Book 2 of this work, there is an attempt to show the link between physical appearance of the peoples of Africa, northern Europe, and southern Europe, and also the climate in which these peoples lived:

> For it is beyond question that the Ethiopians [i.e. Africans] are burnt by the heat of the heavenly body near them, and are born with a scorched appearance, with curly beard and hair, and that in the opposite region of the world [i.e. Northern Europe] the races have white frosty skins with yellow hair that hangs straight; while the latter [i.e. Northern Europeans] are fierce owing to the rigidity of their climate but the former [i.e. Africans] are wise owing to the mobility of theirs … [I]n the middle of the earth [presumably Italy] owing to a healthy blending of both elements … men are of medium bodily stature, with a marked blending, even in the matter of complexion.[7]

It is worth noting that Africans and Northern Europeans are seen as polar opposites. Besides, the Italians considered themselves intermediate in complexion between the two extremes. These days, of course, the Romans are considered Caucasians without reservation. Moreover, Africans were considered wise. Why was this? Who were these wise Ethiopians of which Pliny speaks?

Vitruvius, the Roman architect, wrote *De Architectura,* in the first century BC. In Book 6, Chapter 1, we read the following:

> This is why people of the north are so large in stature, so light in complexion, and have straight red hair, blue eyes, and are full of blood for they are formed by the abundance of the moisture, and the coldness of their country. Those who live near the equator, and are exactly under the sun's course, are, owing to its power, low in stature, of dark complexion, with curling hair, black eyes, weak legs [and] deficient in quantity of blood … [F]rom the clearness of the atmosphere, aided also by the intense heat … the southern nations are quick in understanding and sagacious in counsel … [8]

Vitruvius has advanced a similar theory to that of Pliny. Vitruvius' "southern nations" are the same as the people from "near the equator". Incidentally, the countries on the equator are Kenya, Congo, Uganda, Gabon and Somalia. The countries near the equator are Nigeria, Ghana, Sudan and Ethiopia. His "southern nations" were identical to Pliny's "Ethiopians". They were considered "quick in understanding and sagacious in counsel". Why was this? Which "southern nations" was Vitruvius writing about?

Diodorus Siculus was a very important Greek language historian writing in the first century BC. His voluminous writings appear under the title *General History*. From Book 3, we have extracted the following:

> Now the Ethiopians, as historians relate, were the first of all men and the proofs of this statement, they say, are manifest … They say also that the Egyptians are colonists sent out by the Ethiopians, Osiris having been the leader of the colony. For, generally speaking, what is now Egypt, they maintain, was not land but sea … however, as the Nile during the times of its inundation carried down the mud from Ethiopia, land was gradually built up from the deposit.[9]

Diodorus' theory that Egypt was originally swamplands is widely accepted today. As the land became habitable, the land was colonised from Ethiopia (i.e. from the south of Egypt). It therefore followed that the Egyptians were Ethiopians. The Egyptians were therefore one of the "southern nations" who were similar to people from "near the equator". It was probably in part due to Egypt that Africans were considered "wise", "quick in understanding" and "sagacious in counsel". This raises an important question: Can we prove that the Egyptians looked like Pliny's "Ethiopians" or Vitruvius' "equator[ial]" Africans?

Herodotus was one of the most important historians of all time. In the European tradition, he is called the Father of History. He wrote the first history book by a European that is still in circulation today. In around 450 BC, Herodotus wrote his famous *The Histories*. In Book 2 of this valuable work, we are assured that:

> There can be no doubt that the Colchians are an Egyptian race. Before I heard any mention of the fact from others, I had remarked it myself … My own conjectures were founded, first, on the fact that they are black-skinned and have woolly hair, which certainly amounts to but little, since several other nations are so too; but further and more especially, on the circumstance that the Colchians, [and] the Egyptians … are the only nations who have practised circumcision from the earliest times.[10]

Clearly the Egyptians had black skins and woolly hair. These features are similar to the "dark complexion[s]" and "curling hair" that Vitruvius ascribes to equatorial Africans.

Galen was an important writer from the Classical period. He wrote *Mixtures* in the first century AD. In Book 2 of this work, we are assured that: "[I]t is a matter of observation that hairs themselves, in proximity to a fire, immediately curl. Thus Ethiopians, for example, are all curly-haired." On the following page we are informed that:

> The hair of Egyptians ... and in general all peoples who inhabit hot, dry, places, has poor growth and is black, dry, curly, and brittle. That of the inhabitants of cold, wet places ... has reasonably good growth and is thin, straight, and red. Those who live in some well-balanced land [presumably Italy] which is between these in quality have hair with extremely good growth, which is strong, fairly black, moderately thick, and neither completely curly nor completely straight.[11]

Galen has a related theory that corroborates that of Pliny and also Vitruvius. According to him, Egyptian hair was black, dry, curly and brittle. We note that this is slightly different to Somalian hair, which is relatively soft rather than brittle. Furthermore, Egyptian hair was different to Italian and presumably Mediterranean hair. Notice also that even Mediterranean hair was fairly black in colour.

Lucian was a Greek writer. In 160 AD he wrote a famous dialogue called *Navigations*. An extract from this dialogue between Lycinus and Timolaus reads as follows:

> Lycinus: "This [Egyptian] boy is not merely black; he has thick lips and his legs are too thin ... his hair worn in a plait behind shows that he is not a freeman."
> Timolaus: "But that is a sign of really distinguished birth in Egypt."[12]

Lucian shows that thick lips and thin legs existed among the Egyptians. Lucian's "thin legs" corroborates the "weak legs" that Vitruvius ascribes to equatorial Africans - a slight and lanky appearance.

Aristotle was an important Greek scientist from the period. Martin Bernal of Cornel University paraphrases some of Aristotle's ideas in his controversial work, *Black Athena: Volume 1:* "[I]n a very early example of modern racial discrimination against Ancient Egyptians [writes Bernal], Winckelmann followed Aristotle's claim that they were mostly bandy-legged and snub-nosed."[13] This is evidence of snub noses and bandy legs among the Egyptians. This data corroborates the findings of other writers. For example, Aristotle's bandy legs are similar to the "weak legs" that Vitruvius ascribes to equatorial Africans.

Other Classical writers say the following about the Ancient Egyptians. Aeschylus in *The Suppliants* described the Egyptians as "sable limb[ed]".[14] Heliodorus in *An Æthiopian History* refers to them as "blacke [sic] coloured".[15]

Appolodorus in *The family of Inachus* calls them "the black footed ones".[16] Finally, Aristotle in *Physiognomy* wrote that they were "too black".[17]

We can therefore conclude that the Ancient Egyptians were black skinned, black-footed or too black and they had sable limbs. They had black, woolly, dry, brittle and curling hair. Their hair is also an authentic example of Ethiopian hair. They possessed snub noses and thick lips. They had bandy or thin legs i.e. a slight and lanky appearance. They also were of the same race as Ethiopians and equatorial Africans and were descended from them. The one equatorial people they may not have resembled were Somalians, due to a slight difference in hair type. Finally, the Ancient Egyptians bore no resemblance to southern Europeans or other 'Mediterraneans' in the following respects. They had a different skin colour, a different hair type and texture, a different build, and a different lineage.

Analysing the physical remains supports the evidence supplied by the Classical writers. In this vein, Professor Diop, a Senegalese historian, carried out research on Egyptian mummy skin. He presented his findings at a debate called The Cairo Symposium in January and February 1974 to discuss "The Peopling of Ancient Egypt". The debate was published in *UNESCO's General History of Africa: Volume 2,* edited by G. Mokhtar in 1990. In the essay entitled *Annex to Chapter 1: Report of the symposium on The Peopling of Ancient Egypt and the Deciphering of the Meroitic Script,* we read the following:

> Skeletons with fragments of skin attached ... had been discovered by Elliot-Smith. These fragments, stated Professor Diop, contain melanin in sufficient quantity to establish them as [N]egro skin. In the quest for positive proof, Professor Diop had studied a number of preparations being subjected to laboratory examination in Dakar. These consisted of samples of skin taken from mummies found in the Mariette excavations. They all revealed - and Professor Diop invited the specialists present to examine the samples - the presence of a considerable quantity of melanin between the epidermis and the dermis.[18]

The skin analysis shows that all of the Mariette excavation mummies had Negro skin. This data was presented in the context of a debate. All of the scholars present including the opponents were invited to check the samples - none of them challenged the findings. This evidence therefore stands unchallenged.

There is evidence that supports the view that the Egyptians had a lanky and slight appearance. There is a difference between tropical and temperate adaptation. It affects stature (slightness and lankiness) and also skin colour. In 1996 Marc R. Feldesman and Robert L. Fountain wrote a paper on this topic for the *American Journal of Physical Anthropology* called *"Race" Specificity and the Femur/Stature Ratio.* In this essay, they conclude that:

The aforementioned results leaves no doubt that the "Black" sample presents a significantly different and distinct femur/stature ratio. At the same time, the results fail to justify any claim that "Whites" and "Asians" evidence any proportional differences in their femur lengths relative to their statures.[19]

In the conclusion to their article, they assure the reader that:

There is no doubt that different geographic "races" present different body proportions, and these body proportions translate into different femur/stature ratios. Every result presented here corroborates that point, and strongly suggests that "three-race" (or "two race") ratios should be used wherever possible.[20]

Gay Robins and C. C. D. Shute, both of Cambridge University, wrote an article on Egyptian body proportions for the *Journal of Human Biology*. In their essay, we read the following:

Robins (1983) has recently analyzed Warren's data on predynastic bones and has measured photographs and X-rays of some dynastic skeletons from the Middle Kingdom. She has shown that, for males at least, plausible estimates of stature that are reasonably consistent when different long bones are used only result from [N]egro equations, and that the most satisfactory equations are those of Trotter and Gleser.[21]

Robins and Shute gathered measurements on the statures of pharaonic mummies from the great Eighteenth and Nineteenth Dynasties. The mummies studied were Ahmose, Amenhotep I, II, and III, Smenkhare, Thutmose I, II, III, and IV, Tutankhamen, Seti I and II, Rameses II, Merneptah and Siptah. The evidence led to the following conclusion:

It can be seen that all the pharaonic values, including those of 'Smakhare' [sic], lie much closer to the [N]egro curve than to the [W]hite curve. Since stature equations only work satisfactorily if the individuals to whom they were applied have similar proportions to the population group from which they were derived, this provides justification for using [N]egro equations for estimating stature from single bones of the New Kingdom pharaohs, reinforcing the previous findings of Robins (1983).[22]

The anthropological analysis of Robins and Shute demonstrates that the Ancient Egyptians of all periods (Predynastic, Middle Kingdom and New Kingdom) were tropically adapted in appearance. This provides additional support and corroboration for the black skin colour. The abstract to their paper reads in part: "It is shown that the limbs of the pharaohs, like those of other Ancient Egyptians had [N]egroid characteristics".[23]

There is evidence that the Egyptians of antiquity had woolly hair. Dr F. D. P. Wicker is a contemporary English Egyptologist. He is author of an interesting work called *Egypt and the Mountains of the Moon.* This work was published in 1990 and contains the following data:

> That the ancient Egyptians had black curly hair is evident from their own illustrations and from their hieroglyph for hair ... which shows three tight braids as still worn by many African tribes. One such braid was recovered from a tomb at Abydos by Flinders Petrie, it is now in the Ashmolean Museum in Oxford, No.E1669.[24]

Later on, Dr Wicker tells us that: "The Egyptians had a number of possessions that are still found across equatorial Africa ... [such as] head-rests (which are uncomfortable for people with straight hair)."[25]

Michael Rice is a contemporary English historian. He is best known for his work, *Egypt's Making,* which was published in 1990. Rice tells us that the Egyptians "also manufactured a very striking range of combs in ivory: the shape of these is distinctly African and is like the combs used even today by Africans and those of African descent."[26]

The research of the two modern English historians, Wicker and Rice, show that Egyptian art and the hieroglyph for hair suggests Afro hair. Also, Egyptian head rests were only compatible with Afro hair and finally, the Egyptians had afro combs.

Further support for this view comes from a physical anthropological analysis of Ancient Egyptian hair. We are indebted to our colleague Fari Supiya whose research provided a basis for this topic. It is generally accepted that there is a difference between round (Mongolian), oval (Caucasian) and flattened (Negro) hair cross-sections. Mr Supiya has analysed five studies of Ancient Egyptian hair based on a total of 53 individuals (Predynastic and Dynastic periods). The five studies were those of Pruner-Bey (1877) which yielded 6 hair samples (and an average cross section index of 64.35), Eugene Strouhal (1971) had 7 samples (average 55), E. Rabino-Massa *et al* (1972 and 1980) both giving a total of 26 samples (average of 66.54) and finally Titlbachová and Titlbach (1977) gave 14 samples (53.85). The total sample of 53 gives an average cross section index of 61.4. The Negro average index is 60, the Western European average is 71, the Indian average is 73, the Chinese average is 83, the Zulu average is 55 and the Australian Aborigine average is 68. Supiya concludes that Egyptian hair is close to the Negro average and may represent internal variation within a single population. It is intermediate between Zulu and Australian Aborigine hair. One of the individuals had an index of 22 - flatter and presumably more tightly curled than the tightest Negro hair today. Moreover, three of the hair samples presented by Titlbachová and Titlbach were from the Christian era and may therefore be from Greek or Roman individuals, rather than genuine Egyptians. If they were subtracted from the pooled average the result would be 60.02. This is almost exactly the Negro average.

There is evidence that the Egyptians of antiquity had Negro facial features. Johannes Winckelmann, an art historian of the eighteenth century, wrote *History of Ancient Art* in 1764. Professor Martin Bernal quoted his findings in *Black Athena: Volume 1,* where we read the following:

> How can one find even a hint of beauty in their figures, when all or almost all of the originals on which they were based had the form of the African? That is they had, like them, pouting lips, receding and small chins, sunken and flattened profiles. And not only like the African but also like the Ethiopian, they often had flattened noses and a dark cast of skin.[27]

W. G. Palgrave, author of *Dutch Guiana,* published in 1867 had a more positive view of Egyptian art. In his own words:

> [T]he peculiarities of the Negro countenance are well known in caricature; but a truer pattern may be seen by those who wish to study it any day among the statues of the Egyptian rooms in the British Museum; the large gentle eye, the full but not overprotruding lips, the rounded contour, and the good-natured, easy, sensuous expression. This is the genuine African model ... Rameses [see also page 197] and his queen were cast in no other mould.[28]

We made a number of visits to the British Museum. This building continues to house statues from the Egyptian times, though some of the "Egyptian" exhibits were also from the periods of Greek and Roman domination, and therefore depict Greeks and Romans. We found that 16 out of the 18 pharaonic statues of indigenous rulers on display in the British Museum at the time of our visit in 1999 have clear Negro profiles.[29] For comparison, we visited the Royal Museum of Edinburgh. In this institution, 11 out of 13 of the pharaonic statues and figurines on display also have clear Negro profiles.[30] Furthermore, the British Museum has 3 statues of the Kings of the Twenty-Fifth Dynasty, a dynasty of foreign origin universally held to have been Negro.[31] If anything, the Egyptian portraits looked at least as Negroid as two of these "Negro" portraits and considerably more Negro than the third, portrait statue EA 633. The non-Negro profiles of the carvings of the two Egyptian kings, Pharaoh Amenhotep I (EA683) and Horemheb (EA21) is consistent with internal variation within a single population and need not imply another race nor admixture. It is well known that in all racial groups, there will be a small minority of members that share some phenotypical resemblances to members of another racial group, without there being any admixture between the two.

In January and February 1974 UNESCO called The Cairo Symposium to discuss "The Peopling of Ancient Egypt". At that time UNESCO was in the process of compiling a multi-volume history of Africa. One sticking point was the Egyptian question. UNESCO staged the debate to resolve the controversy once and for all. Two African scholars, Professors Diop and Obenga, presented the case for a Negro Ancient Egypt. Eighteen European and Arab scholars presented (or tried to present) a case for a Caucasian Ancient Egypt. In fact, they actually claimed that the "people who lived in Ancient Egypt were 'white', even though their pigmentation was dark, or even black ... Negroes made their appearance only from the Eighteenth Dynasty onwards".[32] It is difficult to believe that 18 sober scholars signed their name to this nonsense, but truth can sometimes be stranger than fiction. The conclusion of the debate was published in *UNESCO's General History of Africa: Volume 2,* edited by G. Mokhtar in 1990. The debate was reproduced in an essay entitled *Annex to Chapter 1: Report of the symposium on The Peopling of Ancient Egypt and the Deciphering of the Meroitic Script,* where we read the following:

> It is to be expected that the overall results of the symposium will be very differently assessed by the various participants. Although the preparatory working paper sent out by Unesco gave particulars of what was desired, not all participants had prepared communications comparable with the painstakingly researched contributions of Professors Cheikh Anta Diop and Obenga. There was consequently a real lack of balance in the discussions.[33]

In other words, Professors Diop and Obenga soundly defeated the 18 opponents by proving that the Ancient Egyptians were Negroes.

The Peopling of North Africa

In North Africa, outside of Egypt, a remarkable tradition of prehistoric art developed called the Saharan Rock Paintings. Artists would decorate and graffiti on cave walls, indeed on any suitable rock face, using the striking colours of red, yellow, black, white, and others. The tradition in Algeria, in the Tassili n'Ajjer region, dates back to around 8000 or 7000 BC and continued for thousands of years.[34]

Henri Lhote, author of *The Search for the Tassili Frescoes,* was the major authority on these paintings. In this work he asked of the peoples depicted in the frescoes: "Were these people Negroes or 'whites'?" He presented his summary thus:

> The profiles were astonishing in their diversity. Some were prognathous, others of 'European' type, so that perhaps we may conclude that the physique of this people were not uniform and that several different human types lived side by

side - just as do today the Tuareg and their Negro slaves. The variety of costume (which included long tunics, short loin cloths, garments of fibre, etc.) tends to confirm this assumption. All the same, the most common profile suggested that of Ethiopians ... [35]

Since the most common profile suggested that of Ethiopians, Mr Lhote considers these paintings to "afford us the most ancient data that we have concerning Negro art."[36] Likewise "the paintings ... prove ... that in prehistoric times Black Africa stretched much farther north than it does now."[37] Just how far north was this?

Specialists in ancient African geography who took their stand on the texts of Pliny and Ptolemy thought indeed (and some of these specialists still think) that the 'Land of the Blacks' referred to by these authors was situated, not on the latitude of the Niger, but that it began on the edge of the North African cultivatable areas.[38]

In a television programme entitled *Africa: Different but Equal,* Dr Basil Davidson, its distinguished presenter, drew conclusions that echoed those of Lhote. As far as Davidson was concerned, the figures depicted in the prehistoric Algerian paintings looked to be "obviously African in origins".[39]

The only points that we need to add here concerns the minority of Saharans depicted with non-Negro profiles. Concerning skin colour, Mr Lhote is clear that the figures were "all executed in similar colours".[40] Only the structure of the faces differed from the Negro. Lhote, himself, identifies the non-Negro profiles as belonging to the Peul (also called Fulani). The Peul/Fulani are a population of West Africa that show a marked resemblance to the Masai of Kenya. They are Negroes but they typically have narrower faces and lips. As with the Egyptian example of Pharaoh Horemheb, discussed above, this again indicates internal variation within a single population. Finally, we cannot agree with Lhote's hint that the Tuaregs are a separate population from Negroes. Contrary to Lhote, the majority of Tuaregs are either Negroes or Mulattoes. Almost none are White.

In the old European literature the indigenous North Africans to the west of Egypt were called Moors meaning 'Dark' or 'Black'.[41] Moor may originally have been derived from the name of the Ancient Kushite (Sudanese) city of Meroë.[42] A number of early Latin speaking scholars commented on the origin of the Moors. Juvenal, for example, wrote: "Your cups will be handed to you by ... the bony hand of some Moor so black you'd rather not meet him at midnight."[43]

Continuing this theme, the African-American anthropologist, Ms Dana Reynolds-Marniche, wrote a highly informative paper on the peopling of North Africa:

In one of the Martial's writings ... we read the phrase "woolly hair like a Moor." Silius Italicus, an early writer around the beginning of the Christian era, describes the Maures [sic] as "Nigra" or black. Corripus, a 6th century historian in his Johannid comedy speaks of their "facies nigroque colourus" and their blackness as "horrida" or "horrifying". Procopius, another 6th century Byzantine historian, says the Moors (Maurusioi) were a people composed of a number of "black-skinned" tribes who had gained domination over all of North Africa after the period of the Vandals' [i.e. Germans] ascendancy in Africa.[44]

Clearly the Moors of the Roman times were a woolly-haired and black-skinned population who were midnight coloured. This shows continuity between the Moors and the much earlier peoples of the Saharan Rock paintings who were obviously African in origins.

Richard Hakluyt, an English traveller of the fifteenth century, wrote that: "In old times, the people of Africa were called aethiops [i.e. Ethiopians] and nigritae [i.e. Blacks] which we now call Moores, Moorens and Negroes".[45] Andrew Boorde, an English writer of the early sixteenth century, noted that:

There be many Moors brought into Christendom into great cities and towns to be sold ... They have great lips and notty [sic] hair, black and curled; their skin is soft and there is nothing white but their teeth and the white of the eye.[46]

William Shakespeare uses the term Moor to refer to Negroes in his dramas, most notably *Othello, Merchant of Venice,* and *Titus Andronicus.* Adam Lively, the Welsh author of *Masks: Blackness, Race and the Imagination,* comments that:

The presence of 'Moors' and the practice of 'blacking up' [by White actors] in the Elizabethan theatre are but part of a broader and older folk tradition that testifies to an African presence at the very roots of European culture. A central feature of the English mummers' play, which had its origins in village festivals marking the stages of the agricultural year, was the enactment of a ritual battle in which St George slays an infidel opponent. These elements of blacking up and ritual battle were originally shared with the morris (or 'Moorish') dance.[47]

A traveller who visited Benin (southern Nigeria), known to historians by the initials D. R., recorded that: "The noblemen go with great respect and reverence to the court [of Benin], and are accompanied by many [N]egroes or common [M]oors ..."[48]

As late as 1646, Sir Thomas Browne continued to use the term Moor to mean African or Negro.

Beauty is determined by opinion ... Thus flat noses seem comely unto the Moor, an Aquiline or hawked one unto the *Persian,* a large and prominent nose unto the Romaine; but none of these is acceptable in our opinion.[49]

Atgier, writing in 1904, argued that:

> The word, Mauretania, inhabited by black populations and was later called
> Nigritia, or Negro-land. Moor, therefore, was the equivalent of Negro ... The
> word, Moor or More, signifies a primitive black population.[50]

Dr Welsby of the British Museum suggested a similar idea more recently. He
points out that some old documents confuse Mauritania with Nobadia, one of
the Nubian kingdoms of mediæval Sudan. This shows that Nubians were easily
confused with Moors:

> In *The Life of the Patriarch Isaac* (690-93) written by Bishop Mena ... it is
> recorded that the king of Makuria was unable to get bishops for his country on
> account of the enmity of the king of Mauritania ... It has been suggested that
> for Mauritania we should read Nobadia, and that this literary evidence and the
> epigraphic evidence just noted provides the chronological parameters within
> which the unification of the two kingdoms lie.[51]

J. A. Rogers, the Jamaican historian, made a special study of the coat-of-
arms of European families of distinguished lineages. Some of these depict
Moors' heads. He found that: "Families with Negro in their coat-of-arms range
from Sicily to Finland."[52] Mr Rogers discussed various theories as to why so
many European family crests contain Negroes. While not producing a
definitive answer on this question, Rogers' research clearly shows that when
the Europeans depicted a Moor's head, they clearly had the Negro in mind.[53]

The term Libyan appears from time to time in the ancient European
literature. It can describe the North Africans west of Egypt but can also have a
bigger meaning. It can, in certain contexts, refer to the entire African continent.
It is certain, however, that the Libyans were ethnically related to the Ethiopians
as the Roman Emperor Julian explained in the fourth century:

> For different natures must have existed in all those things that among the
> nations were to be differentiated [says Justinian]. Thus, at any rate is seen, if
> one observes how very different in their bodies are the Germans and Scythians
> from the Libyans and Ethiopians.[54]

Emperor Julian's perspective is clearly in line with the ideas of Pliny,
Vitruvius and Galen, cited earlier. Likewise, the physical appearance of the
Libyans was in the starkest contrast with that of the northern Europeans. No
doubt Italians were intermediate between the two extremes.

In Arabic records, the terms Moor and Libyan do not usually appear. The
favoured term for the indigenous North Africans seems to have been 'Berber'.[55]
Dr Basil Davidson, that able English Africanist, paraphrased the eighth century
AD Arab writer Wahb Ibn Munabbeh, as saying that:

Carthage. (Tunisia). These coins, housed in the Museo Kircheriano, are four of six known coins struck during the Carthaginian invasion of Italy *c.*217 BC (See Chapter 10). All of them show Hannibal's personal Indian elephant on one side. On the other side are likenesses of Hannibal, the great Carthaginan leader. All have different Punic characters written on them. Originally published in P. Raffaele Garrucci, *Le Monete Dell'Italia Antica* (Rome, 1885, plate T. LXXV).

> The descendants of the posterity of Kush, who was the son of Ham and the grandson of Noah … include the peoples of the Sudan; and these are the Qaran (perhaps the Goran, east of Lake Chad), the Zaghawa (who still inhabit Wadai and Western Darfur), the Habesha (Abyssinians), the Qibt (the Copts) [i.e. Egyptians], and the Barbar (the Berbers).[56]

Ibn Munabbeh's use of Biblical allegory should not cause confusion. It is generally understood that Ham is the mythical ancestor of the Blacks (Hamites), since the Hebrew word 'Ham' (hot or burnt) was probably derived from the Egyptian 'Kam' (black).[57] Moreover, he describes all of these people as being "of the Sudan". This can only mean Black. Just in case the point was missed, Ibn Munnabeh calls these same peoples "the posterity of Kush".

Writing in the ninth century AD, the brilliant Black Arab scholar, Al-Jahiz, stated that: [A]mong the Blacks are counted the Negroes, the Ethiopians, the Fezzan, the Berbers, the Copts, the Nubians … [58]

Summarising the information, the original Moors/Berbers/Libyans were black skinned, such that only the whites of their teeth and eyes stood out. In addition, any white actor that played them had to black up. They had black, woolly, curly or knotted hair. They considered flat noses to be comely and they also possessed great lips. They were racially akin to the Ethiopians, Kushites, Nubians, Nigritae and Negroes. Furthermore, their ethnic appearance made them polar opposite to that of the Northern Europeans. Finally, their history in

North Africa can be traced back at least 10,000 years to the earliest rock art of the region, which, as Lhote put it "[wa]s apparently the work of Negro artists."[59]

Despite the evidence, some modern authors, who really ought to know better, have attempted to construct a false picture of ancient North Africa. They attempt to portray the White Berbers, who are really descendants of the Romans and the Vandals (i.e. Germans), as if they were the original Moors or Berbers. These European groups invaded and occupied North Africa in the second century BC and the fifth century AD, respectively.[60] The Berbers today are consequently a very mixed ethnic group of Blacks, Whites, and the resulting Mulattoes. Mrs Erskine, author of *Vanished Cities in Northern Africa,* wrote that "there are tall, fair Berbers to be found in certain regions, and there is the more general well-set-up dark type that we meet in the Kabyle mountains and the desert".[61] Among the more general "dark type" are the Harratin of Morocco and the Chouchen of Algeria. A further source of confusion concerns the presence of Negroes of West African descent living in North Africa. Some of these peoples are descended from groups captured and enslaved after the sixteenth century AD in Arab-led raids against West Africa. Some historians deliberately muddle these groups with the Harratin and Chouchen to create the false impression that all Negroes in North Africa are descended from post sixteenth century slaves from West Africa. In this way, it is possible for dishonest historians to deny the original inhabitants of the region their credit in building the Carthagian and Moorish civilisations.

The True Negro Hypothesis

Other writers have opined that the only authentic Black Africans (True Negroes) are the people of West Africa. There is no racial distinction between West Africans and Blacks in any other part of Africa, but the reason why this absurd claim is made, is to restrict the scope of African history to West Africa in general and the Slave Trade in particular. Meanwhile, these dishonest historians can claim that the rest of Africa was inhabited by Caucasians, or at least non-Negroes, and can set about stealing its history and passing it off as a Caucasian achievement. Some of these writers label the non-West African peoples as Pygmies, Bushmen, Hottentots, Bantus, Hamites, Semites, Danakils, Cushites, Moors, Berbers, etc. Following this reclassification, the same scholars allege that the other groups have part or full Caucasian ancestry. If some members of these groups, for example, display long and narrow faces, narrow noses, less thick lips, etc. the racists can have a field day.[62] Dr Chancellor Williams gave an excellent explanation of how such writers have attempted to accomplish this:

> Much of the history of Africa has been written by anthropologists. They have written it within the theoretical framework of their own ethnology, and historians and others have relied almost entirely on their classification of peoples ... The main thrust of their findings is to make Africa Caucasian from the very beginning of its history, and to give the Blacks not just a subordinate role but no significant role at all in that history. Hence their emphasis on (1) the "Caucasoid" identity of this or that African tribe and, (2) failing that, in a highly advanced all-black setting where no such classification could be made, to allege Caucasian influence in one way or another ... In line with their presumption in taking over the continent and reordering its racial composition, the anthropologists and their historian followers have declared that the "true Negroes" (Black Africans) are concentrated in West Africa only![63]

To illustrate what Dr Williams was writing about, we cite the "research" of Professor M. D. W. Jeffreys of South Africa's Witwatersrand University. He wrote a famous and widely discussed essay in 1951 for a West African magazine. Entitled *The Negro Enigma,* this paper informs us that theories of "the origins and distribution of the Negro race" are as "plentiful as flowers in spring." This is apparently because Black people were not the original inhabitants of Africa! Instead, he proposed that Caucasians were the original Africans and the Blacks came later, perhaps in around 6000 BC. For this reason, the origin of the Negro is an enigma that the good professor attempts to explain. Moreover, the Whites in the old *apartheid* South Africa could claim, on the basis of Jeffreys' theories, that the land had always belonged to them for tens of thousands of years:

> The Caucasian comes from an old human stock - a stock that is to-day called Modern Man [says Professor Jeffreys]. Modern Man goes back a long way in time. The Swanscombe skull found in Great Britain is dated as 250,000 years and is our stock, not Negro. The skeletal remains dug up by the Leakeys in East Africa [sic] are us, not Negro. Boskop man, found in the Cape [sic], is dated at 50,000 years and falls into our group, not that of the Negro. There are no Negro skulls of any antiquity - the oldest known is about 6,000 B.C. [sic] The two Grimaldi skulls, one of a woman and the other a boy, are not Negro skulls. They merely show some Negro features. So the enigma deepens: all the evidence points to the Negro being a comparatively recent race ... [64]

These days it has become fashionable, even for the racists, to laugh at Professor Jeffreys' nonsense. Later scholars, however, learned the value of presenting equally ridiculous ideas in a more subtle and sophisticated way. One thinks of Dr Donald L. Wiedner, the author of *A History of Africa South of the Sahara* in 1962. In this work Wiedner presented a map preposterously entitled *Ethnography of Africa* that claims to shows the origin and distribution of Africa's different races. The map shows the dispersal of races from a common

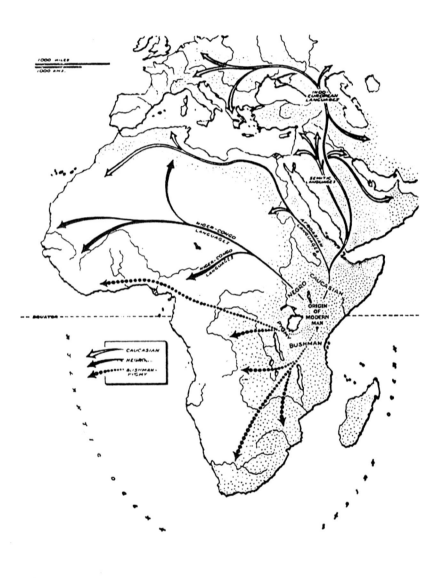

ETHNOGRAPHY OF AFRICA BEFORE 300 B.C. *(HYPOTHESIS)*

From Donald L. Wiedner, *A History of Africa South of the Sahara* (US, Random House, 1962, there are no page numbers in this part of the book). Notice the dishonest attempt to Caucasianise ancient North and Eastern Africa. Moreover, Wiedner attempts to restrict Negro history to West Africa only!

centre in the equatorial regions of East Africa around Uganda and Kenya. Wiedner calls this region the "Origin of Modern Man". From here the "Bushman" migrated to Southern Africa, the "Pygmy" to Central and West Africa, the "Negro" to Central, West Africa and Algeria, and finally, the "Caucasian" [sic] to Ethiopia, Sudan, Egypt, Arabia and North Africa.[65]

Other writers would follow suit. In 1975 Professors Oliver and Fagan, authors of the otherwise admirable *Africa in the Iron Age,* used linguistics to make essentially the same argument as Wiedner:

> In general, the settled peoples to the north and east of the [Sahara] desert were of Afro-Mediterranean or Caucasian stock, speaking languages of the Afro-Asiatic family - ancient Egyptian, Berber, Chadic, Cushitic. Those to the south were Negroes, speaking languages of the Niger-Congo, Saharan, Central Sudanic and Nilotic (including Paranilotic) families.[66]

We can only marvel at how the Chadic speaking people, such as the Hausas, made it into their Caucasian stock. They are one of the very darkest peoples in Africa.

Mr Colin McEvedy writing in 1980 produced the *Penguin Atlas of African History*. In this work, he described the peopling of Africa in about 8000 BC by noting that:

> [E]very continent has one or more easily distinguishable races. Africa has a particularly large number, five in all ... The Negroes' original homeland was the forest and bush country of West Africa ... The Nilo-Saharans ... were probably confined to the middle third of the Nile valley ... The rest of sub-Saharan Africa (bar the Horn) was divided between the Pygmies and the Bushmen ... Africa north of the Sahara was then as now quite a different world. It was inhabited by white races ... loosely grouped together by linguists under the name Hamites.[67]

As recently as 1983 there were still scholars trying to argue that Africa is not the original and exclusive homeland of Black people. Barbara G. Walker, feminist author of the *Women's Encyclopedia of Myths and Secrets,* repeated this racist claim. Part of her entry for *Pygmies* reads as follows:

> Like their relatives the Bushmen, [P]ygmies are [C]aucasoid people [sic]: thin-lipped, light-skinned, often blue eyed [sic]. Anthropological investigation show the [P]ygmies were not true primitives but remnants of a formerly sophisticated race, the proto-Berber people inhabiting what Hallet called "old [W]hite Africa."[68]

More recently still, Professor Martin Bernal's 1987 work *Black Athena* was widely and prematurely acclaimed as a Liberal and anti-racist approach to the

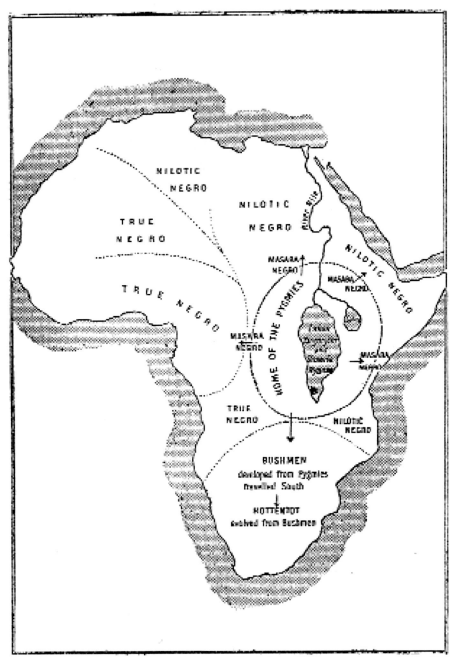

From Albert Churchward, *The Origin and Evolution of Freemasonry connected with the Origin and Evolution of the Human Race* (UK, G. Allen and Unwin, 1921, p.84). Although written years before Dr Wiedner, Churchward's scholarship and honesty compare favourably.

writing of ancient history. He presents a subtle and politically correct spin on the same ideas presented more bluntly by Donald Wiedner and Colin McEvedy. Like them, he singles out West Africans as being more authentic representatives of the Black race and uses it to claim that the Ancient Egyptians were not Negroes:

> I am happy to be in the excellent company of Dubois, Mazrui and the others [says Professor Bernal] who, while they do not picture all Ancient Egyptians as resembling today's West Africans, do see Egypt as essentially African.[69]

He is not alone in this view. Dr Barbara Watterson, author of an otherwise useful history entitled *The Egyptians,* wrote that:

> The racial typing of the earliest Egyptians is a vexed question. They were certainly people of north-east Africa but, whether this means, as some claim, that they were black is open to question. One has to define what is meant by 'black', the popular conception of which is the physical type that is today typically found in West Africa.[70]

The problem here is that older and more overtly racist scholarship has proved itself to be more reliable on this point than its Liberal and Feminist successors. Dr Albert Churchward's 1921 *The Origin and Evolution of Freemasonry Connected with the Origin and Evolution of the Human Race* presented a map of Africa "[s]howing the home of Primary Man". He presented Central East Africa as the "Home of the Pygmies". Some of these Pygmies migrated south and evolved into the "Bushmen" and later the "Hottentot". Some migrated to West Africa and evolved into the "True Negro". Some migrated to North and East Africa and evolved into the "Nilotic Negro". Finally, others in Central East Africa evolved into the "Masaba Negro". Churchward thus presented the peopling of Africa as having been accomplished by one race, the Pygmies, who have since differentiated into different sorts of Negroes.[71] Unlike Jefferys, Wiedner, McEvedy, Bernal, Watterson and Walker, he has not attempted to repopulate early Africa with Caucasian and other non-Negro races that did not exist. However, even he singles out the West Africans as true members of the race. Since the human race originated in East Africa, surely it should have been the East Africans who were the true Negroes.

Since so many writers have suggested a special status for the West Africans, it is worth investigating whether there is any substance to it. Lady Lugard was the author of the otherwise splendid *A Tropical Dependency,* a work that covers the ancient history of the West African empires of Ghana, Mali, Songhai and also the history of Hausaland. She informs us that: "The Haussa [sic] and the Songhay [sic] are other races which, though [B]lack, are absolutely distinct from the pure [N]egro type".[72]

Her Ladyship was not alone in holding this opinion. Peter Garlake writes of the authority that the "Hamitic speaking Hausa sultans and emirs" exercised over their "Negroid subjects".[73] He thus makes it clear that the Hausa are not Negroid. Major Dubois, author of the otherwise flawless *Timbuctoo the Mysterious,* informs us that the Songhai were not Negroes either since:

> [T]heir physical type owns nothing in common with that of the West African [N]egro ... In short, the Songhois [sic] recalls the Nubian rather than the West African [N]egro, and I have studied both at leisure.[74]

Lady Lugard went on to explain that to the south of the great empires of Ghana, Mali and Songhai, were "inferior" races. These people, Lugard's "pure Negroes," inhabited the coastal regions of West Africa and built civilisations such as the Benin Empire. In this, Wiedner contradicts her. His map identifies the Saharan Blacks, builders of Ghana, Mali, Songhai, and Hausaland, as the authentic Negroes! F. George Kay partly supports this view. He wrote that: "The people of Kano [the main Hausa city] ... were true Negroes, very black and very tall".[75] Moreover, racists can be found to specifically deny that the Bini were genuine Negroes. Mr Cyril Punch, for example, wrote that: "I must say the Benin type of features was distinctly more refined than any other Negroes in West Africa. They were lighter in colour and the features were much cleaner cut."[76] Even Mr Frank Willett was not above such nonsense. In an article on the Yorubas of southwest Nigeria for the *Journal of African History,* he wrote that: "The Yoruba are racially very mixed, ranging from typical Sudanese Negroes to what an earlier generation would have called 'pure Hamites'."[77] Although Hamites mean Blacks, Willett, here, like Garlake, follows the standard anthropological party line that they are dark skinned extensions of the Caucasian race, with "refined" features. This, of course, implies that Negro features lack refinement!

In other words, Lugard, Garlake, Dubois, Punch, and Willett have reproduced the same argument used to deny the Negroes their history in West Africa that M. Champollion-Figeac used to deny the Negroes their history in ancient Egypt. Writing in 1839, Champollion-Figeac, brother of the founder of Egyptology, suggested that:

> The opinion that the ancient population of Egypt belonged to the Negro African race, is an error long accepted as the truth ... A serious authority declared himself in favor of this view and popularised the error. Such was the effect of what the celebrated Volney published on the various races of men he had observed in Egypt ... To support his opinion, Volney invokes that of Herodotus who, apropos the Colchians, recalls that the Egyptians had black skin and had woolly hair. Yet these two physical qualities do not suffice to characterize the Negro race and Volney's conclusions as to the Negro origin of the ancient Egyptians is evidently forced and inadmissible.[78]

This neatly illustrates why Professor Chancellor Williams wrote:

> Laughter and Tragedy. For, of course, a racism so extreme that it becomes
> ridiculous also becomes amusing, even though it is at the same time the tragedy
> of an unabashed twentieth century assault on the Blacks.[79]

The dishonest anthropologists and historians, however, were rational in trying to claim East Africa as Caucasian. The glories of Ethiopian, Sudanese, Egyptian, Swahili, and Zimbabwean civilisations were located there. The human race, as we shall see, originated there. Moreover, the Semitic language family originated there. Nor can we overlook the genuine confusion over racial identity that does in fact exist among some East Africans. This confusion can and has been exploited to falsify the history of East Africa. To illustrate the problem, Professor Williams informs us that:

> Ethiopia (the new name for Abyssinia), like the Republic of Sudan, is ... ruled
> by a people of mixed blood who not only do not consider themselves African
> by race, but who maintain a privileged class society based upon colour. To
> them, all black-skinned Africans are "Bantu." To these they feel superior by
> reason of "white blood," and their discriminatory practices are just as subtle
> and just as real as those of the whites. And although the enslavement of black-
> skinned Africans continues in both countries even in our times, both the Sudan
> and the new Ethiopia have adopted the "Brotherhood Front" since the sudden
> rise of so many independent African states.[80]

Similar confusion exists among the Swahili of the East African coast. Captain C. H. Stigand drew attention to this issue in his pioneering work on the East African culture, *The Land of Zinj*:

> Who are the Swahili? Are they a race, a tribe, a mixture, or what? A black "boy"
> with [N]egroid features, slightly flattened nose and black, African curly hair in
> patches on his head, comes up to ask for employment. "What is your tribe?"
> you ask. He answers, "Swahili." "What was your mother?" "A Makoa" (a tribe
> in Portuguese East Africa). "And your father?" "Oh, he was killed long ago in
> a war at home, and then my mother was brought to Mombasa while I was still
> a child." He does not mention that she was a slave. "Well then, if both your
> father and mother were Makoa, you are a Makoa." "Yes, that was my origin.
> We Swahilis are all like that; each one is a Swahili, but he has his own tribe as
> well. I have been a Swahili as long as I can remember." "What is your name?"
> "Jamezi (James). I was educated in the mission." Now let us tackle a reverent-
> looking old gentleman, dressed in a long flowing joho and turban, as to his
> antecedents. He has a grey beard of straight hair and the light complexion of an
> Arab. Under his arm is a Koran, as he is making his way to the mosque to read
> and pray. "Good evening, Sheikh." "Good evening, master." "What is your
> name?" ["]Ali bin Fullani bin Fullani" (Ali, son of So-and-so, son of So-and-
> so). "Oh, you are an Arab?" ["]No, I am a Swahili," he says with some pride.

"What is your descent?" "I am sprung from the Nabahans; my grandfather was Bwana Mkuu of Pate. See, here is my descent from the time the Nabahans left Arabia," and he produces a slip of paper from his Koran, showing a line of ancestors reaching back about level with Magna Carta. Now ask him if Jamezi is a Swahili, and he says, "No, he is a slave from the savages of the interior." Ask Jamezi if this man is a Swahili, and he says, "No, he is an Arab."

On who is the true Swahili, Captain Stigand concluded that:

If Jamezi's father had been an Arab or a true Swahili, Ali would have said, "Yes, he is a Swahili," in spite of the fact that his mother was an African slave, but then his name would not have been Jamezi, but he would be called by an Arab name, and still bear his father's name. A Swahili, then, in the more confined sense of the word, is a descendant of one of the original Arab or Persian-Arab settlers on the coast. In the broader sense of the word it includes all who speak a common language, Swahili.[81]

The Captain, as we shall see in a later chapter, drew the wrong inference. The Swahilis were originally Negroes. Ibn Battuta, a Moroccan traveller, visited the region at its peak in the early fourteenth century. He described the more northerly people of the coast as Berbers - "a people of the Blacks". The more southerly people he calls Zanj - "of very black complexion".[82] Marco Polo, writing some years earlier, describes the Zanzibari as Negroes.[83] Today, the term Swahili encompasses Negroes, Arabs, Persians, and the resulting Mulattoes that live on the East African Coast. The Arabs and Persians only became dominant since the eighteenth century.[84] Stigand is, however, correct to infer that the Makoa and other indigenous East Africans have suffered recent enslavement at the hands of the Arabs.

Conclusion

In *When We Ruled* we are only interested in Negro achievement. We therefore disregard the later periods of East African history (and for that matter North African history) where people of doubtful ethnicities and allegiances become dominant in that history. This does not imply that their history is of no value. We, for example, greatly admire the standing monuments built in North Africa by the Romans and the Arabians. However, Roman and Arabian achievement is not relevant in a book designed to discuss the history and achievements of the African, using the definition of history established in an earlier chapter.

Many African scholars, most notably ben-Jochannan, have taken the strongest exception to the use of terms like Bushmen, Hottentot, Hamite, Bantu, Pygmy, and even Negro, to describe African peoples. He correctly argued that all these terms are either inappropriate or derogatory.[85] Professor

Jackson agrees and argued for the use of the term Ethiopoid to cover all the indigenous Black people of Africa.[86] More recently Professor Keita, a physical anthropologist, argues for the use of Africoid,[87] a term gaining wide acceptance among African-American historians. In this work, however, we shall stick to the term Negro. While not acceptable to all, this term offers a certain degree of what Dr Bernal calls "anatomical precision".

On the other hand, European scholars who try to Caucasianise early Africa are on precarious grounds. There are large and easily recognisable physical differences between different European tribes. Mr J. A. Rogers recorded that:

> On a recent visit to Denmark I was struck with the difference in the complexion of the Danes and the English. Brunets were very rare among the Danes. Of scores of school children I saw only one whose hair was a trifle darkish; the rest was almost cottonly white. In London and to the south, on the other hand, the people were considerably darker. Among American whites the difference to the Scandinavians is still more noticeable.[88]

Continuing this theme, Dr Cheikh Anta Diop remarked that:

> If the African anthropologist made a point of examining European races "under the magnifying glass," he would be able to multiply them *ad infinitum* by grouping physiognomies into races and sub races as artificially as his European counterpart does with regard to Africa. He would, in turn, succeed in dissolving collective European reality into a fog of insignificant facts.[89]

Following the precedent set by Colin McEvedy, it is possible to divide European peoples into races and thus allege recent Negroid ancestry for the darkest European peoples, the Mediterraneans. Following Bernal and Watterson, it is further possible to classify the Danes as the True Caucasian and thus deny any racial affinity between them and the Greeks or the Romans. One could claim that any European that does not have "cottonly white" hair is really a Mulatto. Furthermore, any achievement made by such a European people is in reality due to the mixed or Negro ancestry in the population. In addition, one could introduce concepts such as "Europe North of the Alps" to refer to White Europe and claim any achievement south of the Alps belongs to Africa. In this way, all of European history becomes Mediæval or Post-Mediæval. In addition, the dolmens and stone circles of Northern Europe, the earliest major achievements in this part of the world, lack convincing archaeological evidence of Caucasian involvement. One could exploit this fact to deny any prehistoric Caucasian progress. Finally, African anthropologists could invent terms for some White groups such as Iceman, every bit as insulting and dubious as their term Bushman (correct name 'Khoisan'). Thus the McEvedys, Bernals, Wattersons and other European scholars who try to racialise the history of Africans, stand to lose much more than they could possibly gain if their own ideological weapons were turned against them.

We give the final word on this issue to the Reverend Dr Isaac Osabutey-Aguedze, a Ghanaian scholar. In a remarkable book written as a thesis as a young man called *Rationale of African Religious Rites,* he notes that:[90]

> It does appear evident that partly for the convenience of exotic imperialism and partly for fostering a discordant and contemptible atmosphere in African communities ... modern ethnologists have adopted methods which tend to unsolder ... the unity of the aborigines [i.e. original inhabitants] of Africa. The conventional nomenclature: Hamitic, Ethiopic, Negro all of which mean "Black", and two of which could be eliminated on the score of needlessness ... Thus ... one finds in the Encyclopedia Britannica: the *Hamitic,* the *Ethiopic,* the *Negro,* the *Somalian,* the *Bushman,* the *Kaffir,* the *Lybian* [sic], and what not; then we hear the anthropologist say the Hamitic is not Negro, the Ethiopian is not Hamitic, the Negro is not Hamitic, the Somalian is not Ethiopian, the Bushman or Kaffir is not Negro, et cetera; which is tantamount to saying the Blackman is not black, the Blackman is not black, the Blackman is not black, an endless series of *circulus in definindo* of a negative and ludicrous type.[91]

Notes

[1] Chancellor Williams, *The Destruction of Black Civilization,* US, Third World Press, 1987, pp.23 and 33-4.

[2] Yosef A. A. ben-Jochannan, *Africa! Mother of Western Civilization,* US, Black Classic Press, 1971, p.454 and W. E. B. Du Bois, *The World and Africa,* US, International Publishers, 1965, p.115.

[3] Chancellor Williams, *The Destruction of Black Civilization,* p.44.

[4] Ibid., pp.33-4 and 288-9.

[5] Cheikh Anta Diop, *The African Origin of Civilization: Myth or Reality?* US, Lawrence Hill Books, 1974, pp.69-70. See also Yosef A. A. ben-Jochannan, *Africa! Mother of Western Civilization,* p.713.

[6] J. C. DeGraft-Johnson, *African Glory,* UK, Watts & Co., 1954, pp.58-76.

[7] Pliny the Elder, *Natural History, Book II,* UK, William Heinemann, 1938, p.321.

[8] Joseph Gwilt (translator), *The Architecture of Marcus Vitruvius Pollio,* UK, Priestly and Weale, 1826, pp.166-8.

[9] Diodorus Siculus, *Library of History, Book III,* US, Loeb Classical Library, 1967, quoted in John Jackson, *Man, God, and Civilization,* US, Citadel Press, 1972, p.91.

[10] George Rawlinson (translator), *History of Herodotus, 3rd Edition, Volume II,* UK, John Murray, 1875, pp.169-171.

[11] Galen, *Mixtures,* in *Selected Works,* translated by P. N. Singer, UK, Oxford University Press, 1997, p.253. See also p.252.

[12] Lucian, *Navigations,* quoted in Cheikh Anta Diop, *Origins of the Ancient Egyptians,* in *Egypt Revisited,* ed Ivan Van Sertima, US, Transaction Publishers, 1989, p.17.

[13] Martin Bernal, *Black Athena: Volume I,* UK, Free Association, 1987, p.212.

[14] Quoted in Godfrey Higgins, *Anacalypsis, Volume I,* US, A & B Books, 1992 (original 1836), p.434.

[15] Heliodorus, *An Æthiopian History, 2nd Edition,* UK, Chapman & Dodd, no date given for publication, p.10.

[16] Quoted in Cheikh Anta Diop, *Origins of the Ancient Egyptians,* in *Egypt Revisited,* p.17.

[17] Ibid.

[18] G. Mokhtar, *Annex to Chapter 1: Report of the symposium on The Peopling of Ancient Egypt and the Deciphering of the Meroitic Script,* in *UNESCO General History of Africa, Volume II,* UK, James Currey, 1990, p.37.

[19] Marc R. Feldesman and Robert L. Fountain, *"Race" Specificity and the Femur/Stature Ratio,* in *American Journal of Physical Anthropology, Volume 100,* June 1996, p.219.

[20] Ibid., p.220.

[21] Gay Robins and C. C. D. Shute, *The Physical Proportions and Living Stature of New Kingdom Pharaohs,* in *Journal of Human Biology, Volume 12,* 1983, p.455.

[22] Ibid., p.461.

[23] Ibid., p.455.

[24] F. D. P. Wicker, *Egypt and the Mountains of the Moon,* UK, Merlin Books, 1990, p.13.

[25] Ibid., p.35.

[26] Michael Rice, *Egypt's Making,* UK, Routledge, 1990, p.28.

[27] Quoted in Martin Bernal, *Black Athena: Volume I,* p.244.

[28] W. G. Palgrave, *Dutch Guiana,* UK, Macmillan & Co., 1876, pp.192-3.

[29] Senwosret III (Number EA608, EA684, EA685, EA686), Amenemhet III (EA1063), Amenemhet IV (EA58892), Sobekemsaf I (EA871), Amenhotep I (EA683), Thutmose I (EA1238), Amenhotep III (EA4, EA5), Amenhotep III or Thutmose III (EA15), Amenhotep II or Thutmose III (EA61), Horemheb (EA21, EA75), Rameses II (EA19) and Rameses VI (EA140). There was another pharaonic statue that we could not identify.

[30] Mentuhotep II (1965.2), Amenemhet III (1905.2842), Ahmose I (1900.212.10), Amenhotep II (1951.346), Thutmose IV (1965.3), Amenhotep III (1956.139), Akhenaten (1972.94), Tutankhamen (1910.81), Horemheb (1953.288), Seti I (1956.261), Rameses II (1965.5 and 1971.130) and Rameses IX (1965.1).

[31] Taharka (EA1770, EA1779), and one unidentified ruler (EA633).

[32] G. Mokhtar, *Annex to Chapter 1: Report of the symposium on The Peopling of Ancient Egypt and the Deciphering of the Meroitic Script,* in *UNESCO General History of Africa, Volume II,* p.35.

[33] Ibid., p.55.

[34] Werner Gillon, *A Short History of African Art,* UK, Penguin, 1984, pp.36-49.

[35] Henri Lhote, *The Search for the Tassili Frescoes,* UK, Hutchinson of London, 1959, p.63.

[36] Ibid., p.13

[37] Ibid., p.194.

[38] Ibid., p.127.

[39] Basil Davidson, *Africa,* television series part 1: *Different but Equal,* UK, Michael Beazley, Rm Arts, Channel Four Television & Nigerian Television, 1984.

[40] Henri Lhote, *The Search for the Tassili Frescoes,* p.220.

[41] Ivan Van Sertima, *The Moor in Africa and Europe,* in *Golden Age of the Moor,* ed Ivan Van Sertima, US, Transaction Publishers, 1992, p.4 and David Mac Ritchie, *Ancient and Modern Britons: A Retrospect, Volume I,* US, William Preston, 1985, pp.46-58.

[42] Ivan Van Sertima, *The African Presence in Early Europe: The Definitional Problem,* in *African Presence in Early Europe,* ed Ivan Van Sertima, US, Transaction Publishers, 1985, p.140.

[43] Quoted in J. A. Rogers, *Nature Knows no Color Line,* US, Helga M. Rogers, 1952, p.45.

[44] Dana Reynolds, *The African Heritage and Ethnohistory of the Moors,* in *Golden Age of the Moor,* ed Ivan Van Sertima, US, Transaction Publishers, 1992, p.95.

[45] James Brunson & Runoko Rashidi, *The Moors in Antiquity,* in *Golden Age of the Moor,* ed Ivan Van Sertima, US, Transaction Publishers, 1992, p.36.

[46] Quoted in J. A. Rogers, *Nature Knows no Color Line,* p.99.

[47] Adam Lively, *Masks: Blackness, Race and the Imagination,* UK, Vintage, 1998, p.15.

[48] Quoted in H. Ling Roth, *Great Benin: Its Customs, Art and Horrors,* UK, Routledge & Kegan Paul, 1968 (original 1903), p.108.

[49] Thomas Browne, *Pseudoxia Epidemica or Vulgar Errors,* quoted in Adam Lively, *Masks: Blackness, Race and the Imagination,* pp.22-3.

[50] Atgier, *Bulletin and Memorandum: Society of Anthropology,* quoted in J. A. Rogers, *Nature Knows no Color Line,* p.72.

[51] Derek A. Welsby, *The Medieval Kingdoms of Nubia,* UK, The British Museum Press, 2002, p.84.

[52] J. A. Rogers, *Nature Knows no Color Line,* p.99.

[53] Ibid., pp.69-108.

[54] Quoted in J. A. Rogers, *Nature Knows no Color Line,* p.10

[55] James Brunson & Runoko Rashidi, *The Moors in Antiquity,* in *Golden Age of the Moor,* pp.36-7.

[56] Basil Davidson, *The Lost Cities of Africa,* UK, Little, Brown, & Co., 1987, p.54.

[57] Charles S. Finch, *Echoes of the Old Darkland,* US, Khenti, 1991, p.133. See also Cheikh Anta Diop, *The African Origin of Civilization: Myth or Reality?* pp.7-9.

[58] Abu 'Ulthman 'Amr Ibn Bahr Al-Jahiz, *The Book of the Glory of the Blacks Over the Whites,* (Translated by Vincent J. Cornell), US, ECA Associates, 1990, pp.36-7.

[59] Henri Lhote, *The Search for the Tassili Frescoes,* pp.12-3.

[60] Yosef A. A. ben-Jochannan, *Africa! Mother of Western Civilization,* p.713 and Cheikh Anta Diop, *The African Origin of Civilization: Myth or Reality?* pp.69-70.

[61] Mrs Stuart Erskine, *Vanished Cities in Northern Africa,* UK, Hutchinson & Co., no date given for publication, pp.15-6.

[62] Yosef A. A. ben-Jochannan, *Africa! Mother of Western Civilization,* pp.70-83.

[63] Chancellor Williams, *The Destruction of Black Civilization,* pp.179-180.

[64] Professor M. D. W. Jeffreys, *The Negro Enigma,* in *The West Africa Review,* September 1951, p.1049.

[65] Donald L. Wiedner, *A History of Africa South of the Sahara,* US, Random House, 1962, there is no page number attached to this page.

[66] Roland Oliver & Brian Fagan, *Africa in the Iron Age,* UK, Cambridge University Press, 1975, p.3.

[67] Colin McEvedy, *Penguin Atlas of African History,* UK, Penguin, 1980, p.20.

[68] Barbara G. Walker, *Women's Encyclopedia of Myths and Secrets,* US, Harper & Row, 1983, p.831.

[69] Martin Bernal, *Black Athena: Volume I,* p.437.

[70] Barbara Watterson, *The Egyptians,* UK, Blackwell, 1997, p.13.

[71] Albert Churchward, *The Origin and Evolution of Freemasonry connected with the Origin and Evolution of the Human Race,* US, ECA Associates, 1990 (original 1921), p.84.

[72] Lady Lugard, *A Tropical Dependency,* UK, James Nisbet & Co., 1906, p.22.

[73] Peter Garlake, *The Kingdoms of Africa,* UK, Elsevier-Phaidon, 1978, p.40.

[74] Felix Dubois, *Timbuctoo the Mysterious,* UK, William Heinemann, 1897, p.97.

[75] F. George Kay, *The Shameful Trade,* UK, Frederick Muller, 1967, p.17.

[76] Quoted in H. Ling Roth, *Great Benin: Its Customs, Art and Horrors,* p.18.

[77] Frank Willett, *Ife and its Archaeology,* in *Papers in African Prehistory,* ed J. D. Fage and R. A. Oliver, UK, Cambridge, 1970, p.304.

[78] Champollion-Figeac, *Egypte Ancienne,* quoted in Cheikh Anta Diop, *The African Origin of Civilization: Myth or Reality?* pp.50-1.

[79] Chancellor Williams, *The Destruction of Black Civilization,* pp.85-6.

[80] Ibid., p.29.

[81] Captain C. H. Stigand, *The Land of Zinj,* UK, Constable & Company, 1913, pp.116-7.

[82] Cf. Said Hamdun & Noël King, *Ibn Battuta in Black Africa,* US, Markus Wiener Publishers, 1993, pp.15 and 22. See also Ibn Battuta, *Kilwa in 1331,* in *African Civilization Revisited,* ed Basil Davidson, US, Africa World Press, 1991, p.143.

[83] He, however, uses language that we cannot repeat here. See Marco Polo, *The Travels,* UK, Penguin, 1958, pp.300-1.

[84] David Dugan, *Time-Life's Lost Civilizations,* video series, *Africa: A History Denied,* Holland, Time-Life Video, 1995.

[85] Yosef A. A. ben-Jochannan, *Africa! Mother of Western Civilization,* pp.199-227.

[86] John Jackson, *Man, God, and Civilization,* US, Citadel Press, 1972, pp.205-8.

[87] S. O. Y. Keita, *Further Analysis of Crania from Ancient Northern Africa,* in *American Journal of Physical Anthropology, Volume 87,* 1992, p.246.

[88] J. A. Rogers, *Nature Knows no Color Line,* p.3

[89] Cheikh Anta Diop, *The African Origin of Civilization: Myth or Reality?* p.275.

[90] Originally written in 1933, now issued as Isaac D. Osabutey-Aguedze, *Principles Underlying African Religion and Philosophy,* Kenya, Maillu Publishing House, 1990.

[91] Ibid., p.17.

CHAPTER FIVE: THE CRADLE OF THE HUMAN RACE

Human Origins

Africa has a key role in the early history of humanity. It was, in fact, the cradle of the human race. Diodorus Siculus, an outstanding Greek historian of antiquity, wrote an encyclopaedic work on world history in the first century BC. These volumes demonstrate the state of historical knowledge in Diodorus' time. We have extracted the following account of human origins:

> Now the Ethiopians [i.e. Africans], as historians relate, were the first of all men and the proofs of this statement, they say are manifest. For that they did not come into their land as immigrants from abroad but were natives of it and so justly bear the name of "autochthones" [i.e. sprung from the soil itself] is, they maintain, conceded by practically all men; furthermore, that those who dwell beneath the noon-day sun were, in all likelihood, the first to be generated by the earth, is clear to all; since inasmuch as it was the warmth of the sun which, at the generation of the universe, dried up the earth when it was still wet and impregnated it with life, it is reasonable to suppose that the region which was nearest the sun was the first to bring forth living creatures.[1]

Charles Darwin, the Father of Natural Selection theory, wrote *The Descent of Man*. This 1871 work contained the first ever attempt to apply natural selection theories to the origin of humanity. One of the topics Darwin discussed was *On the Birthplace and Antiquity of Man*. This section begins as follows:

> We are naturally led to enquire, where was the birthplace of man ... In each great region of the world the living mammals are closely related to the extinct species of the same region. It is therefore probable that Africa was formerly inhabited by extinct apes closely related to the gorilla and chimpanzee; and as these two species are now man's nearest allies, it is somewhat more probable that our early progenitors lived on the African continent than elsewhere.[2]

The erudite Albert Churchward, author of the masterly *Signs and Symbols of Primordial Man*, developed a theory of the origin and evolution of humanity and culture in 1910. The research of this great English scholar advanced the theories of Darwin and also those of his mentor, Gerald Massey:

> [R]esearch has led us to bring forward such evidence, as furnished by the records and monuments of the country or nations of the world, where we find

the same myths and legends, the same sacred ceremonies and identical religious beliefs, which, when correctly interpreted, proves that only one conclusion can be definitely arrived at, which we have set forth in this work - *viz.* the first or Paleolithic man was the Pygmy, who was evolved in Central Africa at the sources of the Nile, or Nile Valley, and that from here all originated and were carried throughout the world.[3]

In 1961 Robert Ardrey, an American writer, wrote an important popular work on evolution called *African Genesis*. This book opens with a wonderful poetic introduction where we are assured that:

Not in innocence, and not in Asia, was mankind born. The home of our fathers was that African highland reaching north from the Cape to the Lakes of the Nile. Here we came about - slowly, ever so slowly - on a sky-swept savannah glowing with menace.[4]

The archaeological evidence broadly supports the position taken by Diodorus, Darwin, Churchward, and Ardrey. The oldest known skeletal remains of anatomically modern humanity (*homo sapiens sapiens*) were excavated at four sites in Africa. Human remains were discovered at Omo in Ethiopia that were dated at 195,000 years old.[5] Skeletons have also been found at Laetoli in Tanzania, Klasies River Mouth in South Africa, and Border Cave in South Africa. These finds have been dated at between 130,000 and 110,000 years old.[6] The oldest *homo sapiens sapiens* remains excavated in Asia were dated at 95,000 years old.[7] The oldest found in Europe were dated at 39,000 years old.[8] Finally, the oldest found in Australasia were dated at 32,000 years old though it is believable that humans have inhabited that continent for 70,000 years.[9] Human skeletons outside Africa are, therefore, much younger than the oldest African finds. This evidence supports the notion that humanity originated in Africa and gradually spread out over the globe.

All of the remains so far discussed, including the Asian, the European, and the Australasian finds, were of the Negroid type.[10] The oldest known skeletons of non-Negroes that have so far been excavated are among the Cro-Magnon remains found in both southern France and the Caucasus region of Russia.[11] These finds, some of which are Caucasians or at least ancestors of Caucasians, have been dated at 20,000 years old.[12] The oldest known remains of the Mongolian type (Chinese, Japanese, Malaysian, etc.) are younger still.[13]

Professor Rebecca Cann and her colleagues at the University of Berkeley, California, conducted pioneering work with mitochondrial DNA. Their findings, published in a 1987 edition of *Nature* magazine, suggested that all modern humans have a lineage traceable to a single female ancestor. Her theory is an example of monogenesis - the idea that all human groups are descended from the same parent population. Dr Cann's article was entitled

Mitochondrial DNA and human evolution. In the abstract to this valuable paper, we read the following:

> Mitochondrial DNAs from 147 people, drawn from five geographic populations have been analysed by restriction mapping. All these mitochondrial DNAs stem from one woman who is postulated to have lived about 200,000 years ago, probably in Africa.[14]

Professor Cann drew conclusions on how her team's findings should be interpreted:

> We infer ... that Africa is a likely source of the human mitochondrial gene pool ... Our tentative interpretation ... fits with one view of the fossil record: that the transformation of archaic to anatomically modern forms of Homo sapiens [i.e. *homo sapiens sapiens*] occurred first in Africa ... and that all present day humans are descendants of that African population.[15]

Newsweek, the widely read weekly journal, did much to popularise the new mitochondrial DNA research from the University of Berkeley. Concerning the African ancestress, they inform us that:

> Scientists are calling her Eve, but reluctantly. The name evokes too many wrong images - the weak-willed figure in Genesis, the milk-skinned beauty in Renaissance art, the voluptuary gardener in "Paradise Lost" who was all "softness" and "meek surrender" and waist-length "gold tresses." The scientists' Eve - subject of one of the most provocative anthropological theories in a decade - was more likely a dark-haired, black-skinned woman, roaming a hot savanna in search of food.[16]

In Britain, the well-established Conservative newspaper, *Daily Mail,* brought these research findings to the attention of their readership. They also reviewed *River Out of Eden,* a book on the topic by Oxford University professor Richard Dawkins:

> Just imagine this: you me and every man, woman and child who walks the Earth is descended from the same African woman. Genesis gave us a version of the story with the Garden of Eden, as do most religions and tribal legends. But what if the existence of a shared ancestral mother could be *scientifically* proven, a matter of fact rather than faith? ... In his new book, River Out of Eden, the zoologist Richard Dawkins, author of The Selfish Gene, sets out to achieve this mind boggling goal. His compelling conclusions are rooted in Darwin's theory of natural selection. Dawkins does not just content himself with taking us step by step, back to our common ancestor; he goes much further, giving her an identity. She was a [B]lack woman who lived a quarter of a million years ago and we can trace our way back to her only through the female line.[17]

It has been suggested that *homo sapiens sapiens* evolved from earlier hominid types in East Africa over an estimated period of five million years. New research is already starting to challenge this position. Some claim that hominid fossils dating back seven million years have been found in the Sahara. The reader must therefore be aware that new finds will quickly make the archaeological details presented in this chapter out of date. In addition, each new find will trigger debates about whether the hominid represented is really a human ancestor or an evolutionary dead end. Whichever be the case, the main point is still inescapable. Humanity is of African origin and the ancestors of humanity are also of African origin. Only the details will change as new discoveries are made and discussed.

The oldest ancestral type of humanity is generally thought to have been the *australopithecus ramidus,* who lived at least 4.4 million years ago. They were typically around 4 feet 6 inches in height. They walked upright and were robust in appearance. Unable to make stone tools, they probably used sticks and branches instead. Their diet was mainly vegetarian, though they may have scavenged for meat and also ate small animals.[18]

Australopithecus afarensis, who flourished about four million years ago, is said to have evolved from the *ramidus* type. They were fully bi-pedal, of small stature, and had small skulls with a size of around 480 cc.[19] This type of hominid was in turn superseded by another australopithecine type, but the details are hazy. The possible candidates for succession were the lightly built *australopithecus africanus,* the massive and heavy-featured *australopithecus robustus* or the hyper-robust *australopithecus bosei.* In general, all of the australopithecine types were short in stature, dark or black coloured and were relatively hairless. Their culture flourished from 5 million until 2 million years ago in east and southern Africa. None of their remains have been found outside of the continent. They were forager-scavengers and used sticks and stones as tools. By one million years ago, the australopithecines had died out entirely.[20]

The *homo* family succeeded the australopithecines, possibly 2.5 million years ago. *Homo habilis* was the first of the pre-humans to make tools. Dr Ehret continues:

> The tools … belong to what we call the Olduwan industry. ("Industry" as used by archaeologists of early humans refers to the kit of tools and the toolmaking techniques used by a particular human population.) This tool kit was rudimentary; it consisted simply of sharp flakes broken off of stones by striking them with other stones. The sharp flakes, however, could efficiently cut and skin even thick-skinned animals, and the making of Olduwan tools would have greatly facilitated the meat-collecting capabilities of their makers.[21]

Homo habilis was typically dark coloured, short of stature and had a skull capacity of 600-800 cc. They existed for over a million years in east Africa alongside the later australopithecines. Moreover, like the australopithecines, there is no evidence that this species had ever left Africa. *Homo habilis* finally died out around 1.6 million years ago.[22]

Homo erectus became the next species to emerge about 1.7 million years ago. This was the first of the pre-humans to travel away from Africa. Skeletons of them were found in Asia, such as Java Man and Peking Man. Members of this species were much closer in appearance to modern humans. The tallest of them stood six feet tall. In appearance they were dark coloured and their skulls were 800 to 1200 cc in size. Though not as large as modern human skulls, there is some overlap in size with the smaller modern skulls. The main difference was that *homo erectus* skulls were lower, flatter, and with more pronounced brow-ridges. Of their culture, they invented fire and were highly proficient as toolmakers. They are also thought to have been ancestors of the modern human type that succeeded them about 195,000 years ago (or 200,000 years ago according to the DNA evidence).[23]

The Caucasian people of Europe originated about 20,000 years ago. They were descendants of African migrants to Europe who entered the continent 39,000 years ago. These migrants, called Grimaldis or Cro-Magnons in the literature, left an important cultural impact known as the Aurignacian Culture. Mr Legrand Clegg, a well-known contributor to the *Journal of African Civilizations,* informs us of the importance of the African migration:

> One can state without exaggeration that the Grimaldis [referring to the early Africans] brought "civilization," such as it was, from prehistoric Africa to prehistoric Europe. Their invention of sculpting and their general contribution to the field of art were universally recognized by scientists until the modern Grimaldi "blackout", which occurred because of the need of some Western authorities to deny "the area over which [N]egroids were scattered on the face of the globe." In addition to their invention of pendants, stone implements, certain styles of dress, an advanced symbol system, and perhaps even musical instruments, the Grimaldis were undoubtedly the first homo sapiens to bury their dead and they may have introduced to the world the use of the bow.[24]

Art historian, H. G. Spearing of Oxford University, commented upon the early art from Europe. He confirms that nearly all of the persons depicted were similar to the Bushman and Hottentots. These are the Negro inhabitants of south-western Africa who are more correctly called Khoisan:

> It is unfortunate [laments Mr Spearing] that the head of Fig. 12 is missing, for it might have shown what race was represented. The shape of the body indicates a better race [sic] than most of the other statuettes, some of which are so fat that they almost seem to represent a steatopygous [i.e. large buttocked] race like the Bushmen or Hottentots.[25]

Europe, during this period, however, was in an Ice Age. A one-mile thick block of ice that extended across southern Russia, Poland, northern Germany, and southern England, covered much of the continent.[26] During this period, it was a great evolutionary disadvantage to be dark-skinned. Not only is dark-skin more prone to frostbite and other forms of cold-injury, dark skin also protects the skin from ultraviolet light. Sunlight, a great source of ultraviolet light, can prove injurious to skin and cause cancers in extreme cases. Sunlight is, however, a great source of Vitamin D, which is useful for the proper development of bones. A dark-coloured skin under normal conditions protects the individual from the deleterious effects of ultraviolet light but still allows some Vitamin D to penetrate the skin. This allows for proper bone formation. An Ice Age, by contrast, is characterised by reduced sunlight and also many sunless days. The ability of dark-skin to shield sunlight becomes a disadvantage under these conditions as the reduced supply of Vitamin D is also shielded out. In addition, people in extremely cold environments are likely to cover their bodies from head to foot in thick clothing of one sort or another. This too reduces the skin's exposure to Vitamin D. In such situations, dark-coloured people are more likely to suffer the debilitating effects of Vitamin D deficiency. This causes osteomalachia in adults and rickets in children. The affected individual's bones become prone to fracture and deformities. This is exactly what was observed among the early skeletons found in Europe.[27]

For the albinos among these early Black migrants, their situation would have been markedly different. It is well known that albinism is present in small numbers among all of the world's populations. The whitened skin colour is usually a disadvantage in a hot climate, but it is not a disadvantage in a cold climate. Therefore, while Vitamin D deficiency would have reduced the life expectancy of the early dark-skinned Europeans, it would not have caused problems for the few albinos among them. They would therefore have had normal life expectancies. The longer one lives the more descendants one is more likely to produce on average. Over thousands of years of extreme climatic pressure, the albinos would gradually have become the majority in Europe. The range of skin shades among albinos, the hair colours, and also the eye colours correspond well with those of modern Europeans. As Dr Charles Finch, author of an impressive book on human origins and prehistory, explains: "Thus, a mutation, deleterious in one environment, confers a distinct advantage in another and swiftly propagates for that reason".[28] Summing up his analysis, Dr Finch proposes:

> that the *H. sapiens sapiens* population that survived the last glaciation … was largely a group of albinoids who were better adapted to the ecology than their darker relatives who had originally colonized the area. These latter were gradually replaced by albinoids, though small groups of African aboriginal

types long persisted on the North Atlantic seaboard because of the availability of Vitamin D-rich salt-water fish.[29]

Other than white skin colour, the other traits associated with Caucasians such as lank hair and narrow facial features, also evolved to suit the environment. Dr Finch explained how this worked:

> Eighty-five percent of the heat loss from the human body comes from the head and face. In equatorial Africa, the kinky, and particularly the peppercorn, hair of the early human types would expose more of the scalp to the atmosphere and so promote heat loss. The typical Negroid broad nose and flaring nostrils would enhance the loss of moisture, and therefore heat, during respiration. The thick Negroid lips would increase the surface area of the face and further facilitate heat loss. Bodily leanness, so characteristic of the East African Nilotic types, would also promote heat loss. Among Caucasians of the frigid north, by contrast, body heat would have to be conserved. The characteristic Caucasian narrow nose and thin lips, by reducing surface area, would help preserve heat. The narrowed nostrils would also aid in warming inspired air. Caucasian straight hair, falling down on the back of the neck, would help preserve heat in the head and neck region. The tendency in the male Caucasian to more profuse body hair may have also been an aid to heat preservation on the hunt away from his campfires. We have already noted that hominids, like other warm-blooded animals, are regulated by the effects of Gloger's Law, which states that the closer an animal is to the equator, the darker his coat; the closer to the Arctic Circle, the whiter his coat. The polar bear, the arctic fox, and the snowshoe rabbit are all examples of winterized white-coated Arctic animals who illustrate Gloger's Law. The Caucasian phenotype among *H. sapiens sapiens* also follows it.[30]

The Mongolian peoples of Asia (the Chinese, Japanese, Malaysian, etc.) probably emerged as some mixture of Black and White. The similarity in features of the Mongolian peoples to some of the Negroes of southern Africa (the so-called Bushman or Hottentot type) is somewhat striking. Both groups are scant of body hair, short in stature and have epicanthic folds over their eyes, perhaps the most well known stereotype of the Mongolian face. The Japanese scholar Dr Nobuo Takano developed a theory that the South African type of Negro crossbred with Europeans to produce the Mongolian type. Since "Bushmen or Hottentots" were all over prehistoric Europe, as attested to by the Aurignacian art, it is likely that they were also in Asia. The admixture with the newly emerged Caucasian lightened the colour of the population and straightened their hair. This must have taken place within the last 20,000 years.[31] Some of these peoples, a few thousand years later, migrated from Asia to America across the Bering Straights. They became the first human inhabitants of North, South and Central America - the Native Americans. Thus the Native peoples of the Americas, and the Mongolians, are ethnically related.

Everywhere else on the planet where there were no Caucasians or Mongolians, the populations remained purely Negro. This was the case with prehistoric southern Asia, western Asia, Australasia, as well as Africa. Furthermore, remnants of these early Negro populations are still around today in Asia and Australasia. Alluding to the wide distribution of the Blacks in prehistoric times, Professor Chancellor Williams of Howard University, notes that:

> This fact alone indicates the great tasks of future scholarship on the real history of the race … How do we explain such a large population of Blacks in Southern China, powerful enough to form a kingdom of their own? Or the black people of Formosa, Australia, the Malay peninsula, Indo-China, the Andaman and numerous other islands? The heavy concentration of Africans in India [sic] … opens still another field for investigation … The African populations in Palestine, Arabia and Mesopotamia [i.e. Iraq] are better known, although the many centuries of [B]lack rule over Palestine, South Arabia, and in Mesopotamia should be studied and elaborated in more detail. All of this will call for a new type of scholarship, a scholarship without any other mission than the discovery of truth.[32]

There have been many objections to the data presented above. In the western world many people are brought up on the Genesis account of human origins from the Good Book. Even today, the *Bible* story continues to feed the 'common sense idea' that humanity evolved in the Middle East, which was, of course, where the fabled Garden of Eden was supposedly located. Moreover, ideas taken from the book of Genesis, such as the Semitic race and the Hamitic race, continues to inform modern linguistics. In 1650 the Irish cleric, Archbishop James Ussher, declared that the world was created in 4004 BC basing his conclusion on a study of the *Holy Bible.* A few years later Dr John Lightfoot, one time Vice-Chancellor of Cambridge University, offered greater precision. He suggested that the creation took place on 23 October 4004 BC at 9 AM![33]

Of greater importance, are the objections of a school of anthropological thought called Polycentrism. This school, while disagreeing with each other over the particulars, agree that the human race has many different origins, not just one. In the nineteenth century there were scholars who claimed that the Africans evolved from the gorilla, the Europeans from the chimpanzee, and the Mongolians from the orang-utan. This nonsense convinced no-one, not even racists, and it was back to the drawing board. In the 1930's, Franz Weidenreich, himself a victim of racism, proposed a more sophisticated dressing up of the nineteenth century ideology. A generation later, his student, Professor Carleton Coon, was able to win respectability for Weidenreich's ideas.[34] Professor Milford H. Wolpoff, of the University of Michigan, repackaged Coon's ideas into a concept called multiregional evolution. This theory states that the different peoples of the world, such as Africans, East Asians, Europeans, Australomelanesians (i.e. Black people of Asia and Australia), Mongolians, etc. each evolved separately from different man-like apes. From this it follows that the racial differences between peoples are larger than they may at first appear because each race involved a separate evolution.

To illustrate Professor Wolpoff's ideas, it is instructive to take the example of the evolution of Europeans. It has been pointed out that some *homo erectus* left Africa at least 500,000 years ago and wandered all over the globe. In Europe, some of these evolved into Swanscombe Man in England, and Steinheim Man in Germany, both around 300,000 years ago. These types evolved into Neanderthal Man around 80,000 years ago and this type, it was argued, evolved into the modern European. In this way, Wolpoff and his followers can teach that Europeans are not descended from anatomically modern Africans but from Neanderthal Man.[35]

There are, however, serious problems with this hypothesis. Firstly, the distribution of early *homo sapiens sapiens* remains found across the world show that there are no remains of Caucasians comparable to 195,000 years old. In fact, the oldest known Caucasian skeletons, giving the most generous dates, are only 20,000 years old. Even in Europe, there are older remains going back 39,000 years, but these are of Negroes not Caucasians. Secondly, African *homo sapiens sapiens,* emerging at least 195,000 years ago, is older than Europe's Neanderthal Man, emerging only 80,000 years ago.[36] There have been recent attempts to reclassify Swanscombe Man and Steinheim Man as Neanderthals. We believe that this is misinformation designed to fool the uninitiated into believing than the Neanderthals are much older than modern humanity, when in fact they are younger. Finally, the University of Munich have produced research that has ended the pretensions of the Wolpoff School. *A Washington Post* staff writer usefully presented this data, as follows:

> Neanderthals - the brawny enigmas who mysteriously disappeared 30,000 years ago after coexisting with modern humans in Europe for tens of thousands of years - were not close relatives or even ancestral forms of existing people, a new study has found. Instead, unprecedented DNA tests on a famous Neanderthal skeleton indicate that the creatures were almost certainly a separate species that contributed little, and probably nothing, to the present human gene pool. The finding, by veteran ancient DNA researcher Svante Paabo of Munich and colleagues, could help bring down the curtain on one of the longest-running and feud-prone disputes in anthropology; whether Neanderthals disappeared after nearly 300,000 years [sic] because they evolved gradually into modern humans; or whether they were abruptly superseded by an evolutionary upstart that left Africa only a few dozen millennia ago and from which all people now alive are descended.[37]

The article ends with the following data:

> Although the recent out-of-Africa hypothesis is now the predominant theory
> among experts, the debate will continue, and Paabo's lab is looking for other
> [DNA] sequences. Meanwhile, DNA specialist Tomas Lindahl of Britain's
> Imperial Cancer Research Fund observes in an companion article in Cell. "the
> present recovery ... represents a landmark discovery, which is arguably the
> greatest achievement so far in the field of ancient DNA research".[38]

Early Human Culture

The oldest known human culture developed in Katanda, a region in
northeastern Zaïre (now Congo). Alison Brooks of George Washington
University and John Yellen of the National Science Foundation made the
discovery in 1988. From the site they recovered a finely wrought series of
harpoon points, all elaborately polished and barbed. Also uncovered was a tool,
equally well crafted, believed to be a dagger. The discoveries suggested the
existence of an early aquatic or fishing-based culture.[39] The Katanda people
organised annual fishing expeditions during the rainy seasons. They caught
catfish. "What's exciting is that we're seeing strategic planning for subsistence
by people who lived so long ago," says Brooks. "Humans in Africa invented
sophisticated [tool] technologies long before their European counterparts, who
have often been credited with initiating modern culture".[40] Initially, Brooks and
Yellen dated the artefacts to 70,000 years old. Subsequently, they revised the
dating of the Katanda culture to 90,000 years old.[41]

Early humanity made other significant advances that have come to light. In
1964 a hematite mine was found in Swaziland at Bomvu Ridge in the Ngwenya
mountain range. An iron-mining company, quite by accident, first made the
discovery. Professor Raymond Dart, a scholar at the University of
Witwatersrand in Johannesburg, made a scholarly study of the site. His team
discovered a large cache of ancient mining tools as well as tunnels and adits.
This suggested that the ancients of this region were engaged in systematic
mining. In time 300,000 artefacts were recovered including thousands of stone-
made mining tools. Adrian Boshier, one of the archaeologists on the site, dated
the mine to a staggering 43,200 years old, within an error range of plus or
minus 1,600 years. The ancient miners dug for a metal called specularite. This
is a type of hematite, an iron containing ore. Specularite comes in two distinct
colours - red and black. Used as a cosmetic and a body dye, it may also have
been used in funeral rituals.[42]

Dr Raymond Dart is associated with another important discovery. In 1930 his
archaeological team discovered a manganese mine at Chowa in Zambia. They

found thousands of ancient manganese tools, such as axes, chisels, choppers, grindstones, hammers and wedges. The Chowa mine was dated at 28,000 years old. The manganese was probably used as a cosmetic because of the blackish colour of its ore. It was also used for tool making.[43]

The Ishango bone is a tool handle with notches carved into it. Jean de Heinzelin, a Belgian archaeologist of the Royal Institute of the Natural Sciences, unearthed it in the late 1950's. He excavated in the Ishango region of Zaïre (now called Congo) near Lake Edward. The bone tool was originally thought to have been over 8,000 years old, but a more sensitive recent dating has given dates of 25,000 years old.[44] On the tool are 3 rows of notches, two of which add up to sixty. The number patterns represented by the notches are of great interest. Professor Claudia Zaslavsky, an American mathematician,[45] and more recently Dr Charles Finch[46] have made independent studies of them.

Row 1 shows three notches carved next to six, four carved next to eight, ten carved next to two fives and finally a seven. The 3 and 6, 4 and 8, and 10 and 5, is believed to represent the process of doubling or $2n$. Row 2 shows eleven notches carved next to twenty-one notches, and nineteen notches carved next to nine notches. This is thought to represent 10 + 1, 20 + 1, 20 - 1 and 10 - 1. Finally, Row 3 shows eleven notches, thirteen notches, seventeen notches and nineteen notches. 11, 13, 17 and 19 are the prime numbers between 10 and 20. A prime number can only be divided by itself and by 1 to produce a whole number. The early mathematician(s?) behind the Ishango Bone therefore understood doubling or $2n$, addition, subtraction and prime numbers. Also, two of the rows add up to sixty (Row 2 consists of 11 + 21 + 19 + 9 = 60, and Row 3 consists of 11 + 13 + 17 + 19 = 60). Dr Finch believes that this represents an understanding of base 60, which is, incidentally, the mathematical concept on which modern clocks and watches are based. For example, on a modern clock 60 seconds = 1 minute, and 60 minutes = 1 hour. Finally, the centrality of numbers ten and twenty for the calculations in Row 2 and Row 3, suggest an early understanding of base 10, the basis of the decimal system of counting. For example, on a modern decimal ruler 10 millimetres = 1 centimetre, and 10 decimetres = 1 metre.

Ishango is just four miles from Katanda, the site of the old harpoon-making culture. Moreover, Jean de Heinzelin discovered a cache of harpoon heads in Ishango, as well as the Ishango bone. De Heinzelin believed that the harpoon-making culture diffused northward to the Nile Valley region from Ishango. In his own words:

> From central Africa the [harpoon] style seems to have spread northward. At Khartoum near the upper Nile [in the Sudan] is a site that was occupied considerably later than Ishango. The harpoon points found show a diversity of styles … [other harpoons] have the notches that seem to have been invented

first at Ishango. Near Khartoum, at Es Shaheinab, is a Neolithic site that
contains harpoon points bearing the imprint of Ishango ancestry; from here the
Ishango technique moved westwards along the southern border of the Sahara
… The technology also seems to have followed a secondary branch northward
from Khartoum along the Nile Valley to Nagada [sic] in Egypt … Other
[Egyptian harpoons] show the influence of the Near Eastern Natufian culture
[i.e. the prehistoric Negro culture of Palestine] and the Fayum [in Egypt]
technique which is closely related to it.[47]

In 1980 Professor Charles Nelson, an anthropologist at the University of
Massachusetts, announced an important find in the *New York Times.*[48] Evidence
had come to light of the domestication of cattle in Kenya 15,000 years ago. Dr
Nelson's team found teeth and cattle bones spread over a limited area
suggesting that the animals were not wild. Had the cattle been wild, the
remains would have been more widely distributed over a larger area.
Furthermore, evidence suggests that tsetse flies would have killed off any wild
cattle. The highland regions where the cattle bones were discovered were
generally free of flies, thus protecting them from this menace. Professor
Nelson discovered the cattle bones at three sites in the Lukenya Hill District of
the Kenyan highlands. The region was approximately 25 miles from Nairobi.[49]

The first known advances in agriculture took place before 12,000 years ago.[50]
Professor Fred Wendorf and his colleagues discovered that Africans were the
first to grow crops. In the floodplains of the Nile, now part of Egypt's Western
Desert, the people of Wadi Kubbaniya cultivated crops of barley, capers, chick-
peas, dates, legumes, lentils and wheat. Their ancient tools were also
recovered. There were grindstones, milling stones, cutting blades, hide
scrapers, engraving burins, and mortars and pestles. The level of the Nile
12,000 years ago was higher than it is now. Each year during the summer, the
Nile flooded, depositing rich silt into the Wadi Kubbaniya region. As the
waters receded in late August and September, catfish were left stranded in
ponds that were formed by the depressions. Since ash and charcoal were also
uncovered, it seems that the ancients smoked the fish. As the fish stocks were
depleted the people took the opportunity to plant crops on the silt. After the
planting, it seems that hunter gathering was the main activity, judging from the
recovered bones. They hunted wild cattle, hartebeest and sometimes, hippos.
When December or January arrived, this was the time for the harvest. The
cereals were ground to make flour. After the harvest, gazelles became the main
source of subsistence. Also hunted, were geese, ducks and wild game. By the
time of summer, the Nile would flood again. The annual cycle was thus
repeated.[51] Bayard Webster, in an article originally for the *New York Times,*
explained Professor Nelson's view on the significance of these two important
archaeological discoveries - agriculture and animal husbandry:

Such findings suggest that many of the elements necessary for the development of civilization - agriculture and animal husbandry and their accompanying technologies - may have originated in surrounding areas and were exported to the Middle East through trade and cultural diffusion of information and ideas.[52]

The next major development in culture concerns a mummy found in the Acacus Mountains of south western Libya. Forty years ago a mummified infant was found under the Uan Muhuggiag rock shelter. The infant was buried in the fetal position and was mummified using a very sophisticated technique that must have taken hundreds of years to evolve. The technique predates the earliest mummies known in Ancient Egypt by at least 1,000 years. Carbon dating is controversial but the mummy may date from 7438 ($\pm$220) BC at the earliest, to 3500 BC at the latest.[53] Dr Savino di Lernia of the University of Rome has taken an interest in the mummy and also the culture that produced it. He believes that a widespread culture existed across a large part of Africa that encompassed the regions now designated as Mali, Niger, Chad, Sudan, Algeria, Libya and Egypt before this vast area became a desert. The rock art, for example, depicts elephants, giraffes, lions, crocodiles and hippopotami - many of these animals can only survive in savannah regions. Some of the earliest pottery associated with this culture dates back to around 7000 BC. In this widespread culture, cattle had a religious and ritualistic significance. There were circular temples built where cattle were sacrificed. Moreover, cattle appear in up to 50% of the rock art. There were also religious rituals involving humans wearing jackal headed masks depicted in the rock art. Also humans were typically buried in the fetal position. Initially Italian archaeologists believed this culture was unique to Libya but French archaeologists showed a similar culture existed in Niger 500 miles to the south. Dr Joann Fletcher, the noteworthy English Egyptologist, believes that the mummification techniques of this culture informed later Egyptian mummification. She further believes that its cattle cult informed Egyptian religious ideas of a later period. Finally, she believes that its jackal mask rituals informed the Egyptian concept of Anubis, the god of embalming - depicted in Egyptian art as a jackal. Moreover, there is archaeological evidence that Uan Muhuggiag decorated pottery later appeared in the southern Nile Valley region. Dr di Lernia suggests that the Uan Muhuggiag people migrated to the Nile Valley when the region became a desert. Also, they became an integral part of the Ancient Egyptian culture. Dr Fletcher summarised the importance of these findings thus:

I find it quite extraordinary that this central Saharan civilisation shows all the features we generally associate with later Egyptian pharaonic culture and mummification is a prime example. There are definite links between the two cultures.[54]

The construction of the Great Sphinx of Giza in northern Egypt represents another major cultural advance. One of the grandest showpieces of early African technology, this colossus was fashioned with the head of a man combined with the body of a lion. At first the builders carved only the head and the fore part. At a later date the builders sculpted the body, in particular the hind part. The builders also carved out a rectangular ditch around the body. In the process, tons of limestone were quarried and removed. A key and important question raised by this monument was: How old is it?

In October 1991 Professor Robert Schoch, a geologist from Boston University, demonstrated that the Sphinx was sculpted between 7000 BC and 5000 BC, dates that he considered conservative. He arrived at this conclusion by checking the patterns of rain wear on the body of the statue. Egypt is a dry country where there has been no significant rainfall for thousands of years. The Sphinx, however, is partly disfigured by rain wear. Dr Schoch concluded that the rain damage must have occurred many thousands of years ago when Egypt was a wet country. With the help of the geophysicist, Thomas Dobecki, Professor Schoch was able to arrive at solid but conservative dates for the construction of the building.[55] The reaction to this data in Egyptological circles, however, was not encouraging. In the *International Herald Tribune,* of 25 October 1991, we read the following:

> The research findings were announced Wednesday at the annual meeting of the Geological Society of America in San Diego. They immediately drew fire from Mark Lehner, an Egyptologist at the University of Chicago who is a leading expert on the Sphinx.[56]

Even today Professor Lehner's emotional outburst has become the typical response to this data by Egyptologists although no reliable counter evidence has ever been offered by them to challenge Professor Schoch's findings. Dr Schoch's dating therefore stands unchallenged. Baron D. V. Denon, a French traveller, made a famous first hand sketch of this statue in 1798 AD. He also commented on it: "The character is African … the lips are thick … Art must have been at a high pitch when this monument was executed".[57] African civilisation, the oldest in the world, was firmly established with the construction of this monument at least 7,000 years ago. Civilisation had to wait another 1,000 years to emerge in Asia and 4,000 years to emerge in mainland Europe.

Mr Peter Eckler, an American publisher, beautifully summarised the importance of this sculptural masterpiece. In 1890 he issued an English language translation of *The Ruins, or Meditations on the Revolutions of Empires and the Law of Nature,* by Count De Volney, one of the glories of enlightenment literature. In the *Publisher's Preface,* Mr Eckler declared that:

Egypt. The Sphinx of Giza. *c.*5000 BC. By itself, this monument is sufficient to prove the African origin of civilisation. This is the earliest known collosal sculpture anywhere on earth. (Photo: Fari Supiya).

> We are in reality indebted to the ancient Ethiopians, to the fervid imagination of the persecuted and despised [N]egro, for the various religious systems now so highly revered by the different branches of both the Semitic and Aryan races. This fact, which is so frequently referred to in Mr. Volney's writings ... may even suggest a solution to the secret so long concealed beneath the flat nose, thick lips, and [N]egro features of the Egyptian Sphinx.[58]

Count De Volney himself wrote a fine summary of the stages that humankind passed through on the long road from savagery to civilisation. We give him the last word on this topic:

> Formed naked in body and in mind, man at first found himself thrown, as it were by chance, on a rough and savage land: an orphan, abandoned by the unknown power which had produced him ... Like to other animals, without experience of the past, without foresight of the future, he wandered in the bosom of the forest, guided only and governed by the affections of his nature. By the pain of hunger, he was led to seek food and provide for his subsistence; by the inclemency of the air, he was urged to cover his body, and he made him clothes; by the attraction of a powerful pleasure, he approached a being like himself, and he perpetuated his kind. Thus the impressions which he received from every object, awakening his faculties, developed by degrees his understanding, and began to instruct his profound ignorance: his wants excited industry, dangers formed his courage; he learned to distinguish useful from noxious plants, to combat the elements, to seize his prey, to defend his life; and thus he alleviated its miseries. Thus self-love, aversion to pain, the desire of happiness, were the simple and powerful excitements which drew man from the savage and barbarous condition in which nature had placed him ... Wandering in the woods and on the banks of rivers in pursuit of game and fish, the first men, beset with dangers, assailed by enemies, tormented by hunger, by reptiles, by ravenous beasts, felt their own individual weakness; and, urged by a common need of safety, and a reciprocal sentiment of like evils, they united their resources and their strength; and when one incurred a danger, many aided and succored him; when one wanted subsistence, another shared his food with him. Thus men associated to secure their existence, to augment their powers, to protect their enjoyments; and self-love thus became the principle of society ... And men, aiding one another, seized the nimble goat, the timid sheep; they tamed the patient camel, the fierce bull, [and] the impetuous horse ... When, therefore, men could pass long days in leisure, and in communication of their thoughts, they began to contemplate the earth, the heavens, and their own existence, as objects of curiosity and reflection; they remarked the course of the seasons, the action of the elements, the properties of fruit and plants; and applied their thoughts to the multiplication of their enjoyments. And in some countries, having observed that certain seeds contained a wholesome nourishment in a small volume, convenient for transportation and preservation, they imitated the process of nature; they confided to the earth rice, barley, and corn which multiplied to the full measure of their hope; and having found the means of obtaining within a small compass and without removal, plentiful

subsistence and durable stores, they established themselves in fixed habitations; they built houses, villages, and towns; [and] formed societies and nations.[59]

Notes

[1] C. H. Oldfather (Translator), *Diodorus Siculus. Library of History, Volume II,* US, Loeb Classical Library, 1967, pp.89-91.
[2] Charles Darwin, *The Descent of Man, Volume I,* UK, John Murray, 1871, p.199.
[3] Albert Churchward, *Signs and Symbols of Primordial Man, 2nd Edition,* UK, George Allen & Co., 1913, p.3.
[4] Robert Ardrey, *African Genesis,* UK, William Collins, 1961, p.9.
[5] *We've all just got 40,000 years older,* in *Metro,* UK, 17 February 2005, p.9.
[6] Charles S. Finch, *Echoes of the Old Darkland,* US, Khenti, 1991, p.15.
[7] Ibid., p.56. See also Richard Leakey & Roger Lewin, *Origins Reconsidered,* UK, Little, Brown & Co., 1992, pp.223-4.
[8] Charles S. Finch, *Echoes of the Old Darkland,* p.37.
[9] Ibid., p.41.
[10] Ibid., pp.40-3. See also Cheikh Anta Diop, *Civilization and Barbarism,* US, Lawrence Hill Books, 1991, p.60.
[11] Charles S. Finch, *Echoes of the Old Darkland,* p.37.
[12] Cheikh Anta Diop, *Civilization and Barbarism,* pp.26, 28-9.
[13] Ibid., pp.53-5.
[14] Rebecca Cann et al, *Mitochondrial DNA and human evolution,* in *Nature,* UK, 1 January 1987, p.31.
[15] Ibid., pp.33-5.
[16] *The Search for Adam and Eve,* in *Newsweek,* US, 11 January 1988, p.38.
[17] Jessica Davies, *Is this the Mother of us all?* in *Daily Mail,* UK, 11 May 1995.
[18] David Keys, *Fossils could reveal origins of humanity,* in *The Independent,* UK, 22 September 1994.
[19] Charles S. Finch, *Echoes of the Old Darkland,* p.9.
[20] Ibid., pp.9-10.
[21] Christopher Ehret, *The Civilizations of Africa,* UK, James Currey, 2002, p.18.
[22] Charles S. Finch, *Echoes of the Old Darkland,* pp.10-2.
[23] Ibid., pp.11-2.
[24] Legrand Clegg II, *The First Invaders,* in *African Presence in Early Europe,* ed Ivan Van Sertima, US, Transaction Publishers, 1985, p.32.
[25] H. G. Spearing, *The Childhood of Art,* UK, Kegan Paul, Trench, Trübner & Co., 1912, p.37.
[26] Charles S. Finch, *Echoes of the Old Darkland,* pp.28-31, 37 and Cheikh Anta Diop, *Civilization and Barbarism,* pp.13-6.
[27] Charles S. Finch, *Echoes of the Old Darkland,* pp.32-6.
[28] Ibid., p.35.
[29] Ibid.
[30] Ibid., p.36.
[31] Ibid., pp.38-9 and Cheikh Anta Diop, *Civilization and Barbarism,* pp.16 and 55.

[32] Chancellor Williams, *The Destruction of Black Civilization,* US, Third World Press, 1987, pp.41-2.

[33] John G. Jackson, *Christianity before Christ,* US, American Atheist Press, 1985, p.5.

[34] Charles S. Finch, *Echoes of the Old Darkland,* pp.12-3.

[35] Ibid., pp.14-8 and 47-9.

[36] Ibid., pp.14-7 and 29.

[37] Curt Suplee, *DNA Refutes Neanderthal Link,* in *washingtonpost.com,* 11 July 1997, http://www.washingtonpost.com

[38] Ibid.

[39] Charles Finch, *The Star of Deep Beginnings,* US, Khenti, 1998, pp.2-3.

[40] Bruce Boyer, *African finds revise cultural roots,* in *Science News Online: Editors' Picks,* 29 April 1995, http://www.sciencenews.org/sn_edpik/aa_2.htm

[41] Charles Finch, *The Star of Deep Beginnings,* pp.2-3.

[42] Ibid., pp.25-6 and Yosef A. A. ben-Jochannan, *Africa! Mother of Western Civilization,* US, Black Classic Press, 1971, p.56 and Charles S. Finch, *Africa and The Birth of Science and Technology: A Brief Overview,* US, Khenti, 1992, p.2.

[43] Charles Finch, *The Star of Deep Beginnings,* pp.25-7.

[44] Ibid., pp.2-4 and 56.

[45] Claudia Zaslavsky, *Africa Counts,* US, Lawrence Hill & Co., 1973, pp.17-8.

[46] Charles Finch, *The Star of Deep Beginnings,* pp.55-7.

[47] Quoted in ibid., p.4.

[48] Ivan Van Sertima, *The Lost Sciences of Africa: An Overview,* in *Blacks in Science: Ancient and Modern,* ed Ivan Van Sertima, US, Transaction Publishers, 1983, p.20.

[49] Bayard Webster, *African Cattle Bones Stir Scientific Debate,* in *Blacks in Science: Ancient and Modern,* ed Ivan Van Sertima, US, Transaction Publishers, 1983, pp.65-6.

[50] Charles S. Finch, *Echoes of the Old Darkland,* p.86.

[51] Fred Wendorf, Romauld Schild, and Angela E. Close, *An Ancient Harvest on the Nile,* in *Blacks in Science: Ancient and Modern,* ed Ivan Van Sertima, US, Transaction Publishers, 1983, p.58.

[52] Ibid.

[53] Michael J. Carter, *The Infant Mummy of Uan Muhuggiag,* in *Egypt: Child of Africa,* ed Ivan Van Sertima, US, Transaction Publishers, 1994, pp.278-9.

[54] See Gillian Mosely (producer), *The Black Mummy Mystery,* (television programme), UK, Fulcrum TV, 2003.

[55] Charles S. Finch, *The Star of Deep Beginnings,* pp.18-22.

[56] John Noble Wilford, *The Latest Riddle of the Sphinx,* in *International Herald Tribune,* US, 25 October 1991.

[57] *Travels in Upper and Lower Egypt,* quoted in Yosef A. A. ben-Jochannan, *Africa! Mother of Western Civilization,* p.194.

[58] C. F. Volney, *The Ruins of Empires,* US, Peter Eckler, 1890, pp.iii-iv.

[59] Ibid., pp.22-4.

CHAPTER SIX: THE EARLY HISTORY OF THE NILE VALLEY

Ta-Seti Civilisation

Ancient Egypt is the first major civilisation in Africa for which records are abundant. It was not, however, Africa's first kingdom. On 1 March 1979, the *New York Times* carried an article on its front page and also page sixteen, written by Boyce Rensberger, that was entitled *Nubian Monarchy called Oldest*. In the article we were assured that:

> Evidence of the oldest recognizable monarchy in human history, preceding the rise of the earliest Egyptian kings by several generations, has been discovered in artifacts from ancient Nubia ... The discovery is expected to stimulate a new appraisal of the origins of civilization in Africa, raising the question of to what extent later Egyptian culture derived its advanced political structure from the Nubians.[1]

This ancient kingdom, generally called Ta-Seti, encompassed the territory of the northern Sudan and the southern portion of Egypt. It has sometimes been referred to as Ancient Ethiopia in some of the literature and as Cush (or Kush) in other literature.[2] It was the first known society on earth to have evolved through the stages described by Count De Volney to civilisation.

Mr Rensberger explained that the discovery of this lost kingdom was based on interpreting artefacts from long lost tombs excavated in 1962. An international archaeological campaign headed by Keith C. Seele, a professor at the University of Chicago, uncovered the remains from a graveyard. The archaeologists worked quickly to rescue the deposits before the rising waters of the Aswan Dam covered them forever. The cemetery was located in the ancient city of Qustul on the Nile near the modern boundary between Sudan and Egypt. It was found to contain 33 tombs. The importance of these artefacts, however, went unappreciated until relatively recently. They were kept in storage at the university's Oriental Institute.

In 1978 Bruce Williams, a research associate at this institution, made a systematic study of the finds and demonstrated their great importance. From noticing the quantity and quality of the painted pottery and the jewellery, Bruce Williams concluded that the buried individuals were distinguished. Just how distinguished was answered by an incense burner. This artefact depicts a

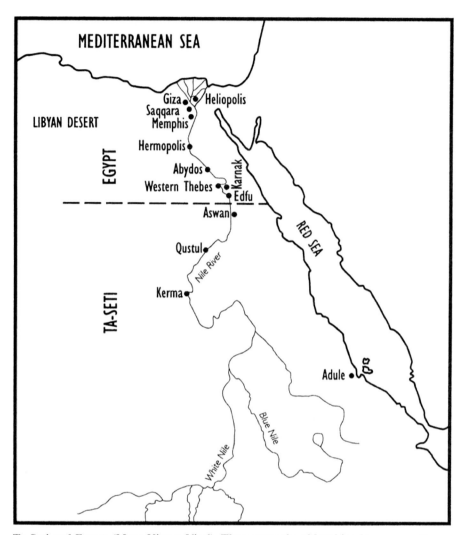

Ta-Seti and Egypt. (Map: Kieron Vital). These were the oldest kingdoms on earth.

crowned individual together with a palace façade, a royal ship, and a falcon totem - all symbols of royalty. Dr Williams was unable to name the crowned king. He could confirm, however, that this royal personage ruled three generations before the first known Egyptian ruler, King Scorpion.[3] Apparently Nubia had writing at this early time, to cite Rensberger:

> [Bruce Williams] said some of the Nubian artifacts bore disconnected symbols resembling those of Egyptian hieroglyphics that were not readable. "They were

on their way to literacy," Dr. Williams said. "Probably quite close to Egypt in this respect."[4]

Mr Rensberger's splendid article closes with the following intelligence: "A detailed monograph on the discovery is in preparation, but there is no deadline and publication is expected to be a few years away".[5] A year later, Bruce Williams delivered. He published a valuable paper on his discoveries in *Archaeology Magazine* (Volume 33, Number 5: 1980). The article was entitled *The Lost Pharaohs of Nubia,* from which we have extracted the following:

> A newly discovered kingdom is always a matter of intense interest, but when it precedes the earliest known monarchy, the unification of Egypt … then history itself is reborn. The place is an[c]ient Nubia at Qustul, where the investigation of archaeological materials recovered during the great 1960's rescue effort has recently unveiled a birthplace of pharaonic civilization several generations before the rise of the first historic Egyptian dynasty.[6]

In 1962 an archaeological team set out to unearth ancient remains before the newly built Aswan Dam flooded the sites. Professor Keith C. Seele led the University of Chicago's Oriental Institute Nubian Expedition. His team excavated an area of Qustul near the river. Towards the end of their campaign they found a cemetery consisting of A-Group (Northern Nubian) tombs. These tombs were as large as those of Egyptian pharaohs Narmer and Qaa from the Egyptian city of Abydos. Recognising the importance of this site, Professor Seele named it Cemetery L.[7]

From this graveyard over 1,000 painted pots, many of fine quality, were retrieved. Some were complete but others had long since fragmented. The pottery represented five styles of decoration or manufacture. Three of these styles were of Sudanese or Lower (i.e. northern) Nubian origins. Also represented, were vessels of Syro-Palestinian origins. Most of the foreign pottery, however, came from Egypt. Of Egyptian manufacture were miniature flasks, narrow-necked bottles, jars - cylindrical and spouted, and also large storage jars. Four of the storage jars "were incised with inscriptions that clearly represent an early form of hieroglyphic writing".[8] Dr Williams demonstrates that the writing was partly an Egyptian and partly a Nubian development:

> The fragments of art and writing in Cemetery L parallel most of the developments of late Naqada civilization in Egypt. Enough of them are of local materials, are local type objects, or are of such a nature that an Egyptian origin is precluded … The marks, inscriptions, and representations incised on pottery include simple marks made for the control of production or transportation. Except for the inscription of Pe-Hor major writing groups incised before firing were of Egyptian origin, but a number of stereotyped symbols incised after firing do not occur in Egyptian potmarks [i.e. they are of Nubian origin].[9]

The only comment that needs to be added is that Dr Williams may be incorrect to assume a part Egyptian origin for the development of writing. This point will be discussed later.

Aside from the pottery, a startling variety of objects were excavated. Gold was found in five of the tombs. As well as a golden bracelet, there was a necklace consisting of a golden pendant shaped like a fly connected to gold sheet beads.[10] We note that its appearance reminds us of the later Egyptian military decoration the Order of the Fly. There were copper artefacts. These included maceheads, spearheads, rings, a copper tray and a copper cap for a furniture leg.[11] There were artefacts of ivory. These included ivory spoons and gaming pieces. Incidentally, gaming boards were also recovered.[12] There were art pieces of great naturalism. There were hippopotami fashioned in terracotta and limestone.[13] There were mortars and pestles, and also palettes, highly polished, made of coloured quartz. They were used to grind malachite for application as eye paint. Moreover, high quality jewellery was recovered including finely crafted pieces of amethyst, carnelian, faience and rock crystal.[15] Finally, there were 100 stone vessels and more than 4,000 other objects made from seashells.[16] With this level of wealth surviving after millennia of plundering, it was not difficult to see why Dr Williams inferred that: "The range of these and other fragments from the plundered cemetery began to indicate a wealth and complexity that could only be called royal".[17]

In one of the earliest tombs a Horus incense burner was unearthed incised with symbols similar to those of Egyptian royalty but predating Egypt! The incisions, though stylised, depict an important personage sitting in a boat. Dr Williams explains that:

> Although the figure in the middle ship is almost completely destroyed, the white crown [supposedly] of Upper Egypt clearly stands out above the ship. In front of it is the tail of a falcon - another sign of kingship. The crown indicates that the figure is a king ... In front of the falcon is a rosette, a symbol of royalty before the First Dynasty [of Egypt] ... The early date of the Qustul incense burner is further reflected by other figures that have connections to middle and later Predynastic [Egyptian] art - an un-named feline deity ... a man saluting in a pose and style typical of Naqada II vase painting; and two animals, an antelope and carnivore, cavorting around the central royal ship. They pose in the characteristic manner of early [Egyptian] palettes which show groups of struggling animals; this type precedes those with scenes of historical events [i.e. it is pre-historic or pre-Egyptian First Dynasty]. Its date provided by context, style and composition, the Qustul burner furnishes the earliest definite representation of a king in the Nile Valley or anywhere.[18]

On this evidence Bruce Williams concluded that the ruler depicted above is the first attested king in world history. There existed, however, earlier

archaeological evidence that had been known about for nearly a century. This
data could have been used long ago to produce the same conclusion.
Predynastic tombs excavated in Sayala show that the Nubian elite were buried
with a rich collection of goods. These included copper ingots, axes of copper,
huge bird shaped palettes, and two huge maces with golden handles. According
to a modern scholar, one of these mace-heads was a "superlative object and
would have been a prized possession in the Treasury of an Egyptian King; in
fact hardly anything quite so fine has been recovered from Egypt of the same
period".[19] Dr Williams interprets other evidence from Sayala (i.e. Siali) that Ta-
Seti was a territorial state. The first such state to be established in history:

> [A] seal impression found in a[n] A-Group storage cache at Siali far to the north
> of Qustul … [has] a concentric serekh surmounted by the familiar falcon
> symbol … [There are also] representations of incense burners in use; D-shaped
> altars or pylons associated with the Heb-Sed festival, the jubilee celebrated by
> a pharaoh first in his thirtieth year and periodically thereafter; and a man seated
> in a chair saluting the bow symbol … [T]he bow hovers over a shortened
> rectangle which in this period represents land. The obvious interpretation is that
> the man is saluting the name for Nubia - Ta-Seti, or "Land of the Bow" - as a
> kingship and territorial state.[20]

The range of pottery in the tombs offers evidence of trading links. Ta-Seti
traded goods with lands to the south, with Egypt and also 1,000 miles away in
the Middle East. The copper artefacts, including the cap for a furniture leg, the
jewellery of gold or precious stones, the ivory spoons and the quartz palettes
all give clues to some of the industries in Ta-Seti. The ships, "with their tall
sterns and bent prows",[21] gives an indication of how trade over such distances
could well have been conducted. The gaming pieces give some clues to some
of their recreation activities.

Incense burning is usually associated with religious activities. Bruce
Williams writes that: "The presence of Horus emphasizes the development of
official religion at Qustul of a type later characteristic of dynastic Egypt".[22]
Horus is generally associated with the ancient Egyptian religion. He is
portrayed as a God or Saint and is sometimes depicted as a falcon in the
iconography. The Qustul evidence shows that the Horus story came from
Nubia and was only inherited by the Egyptians. Interestingly, an Egyptian text,
which may well date from the Third Dynasty, makes the same point:

> The Edfu Text [says Professor Jackson] is an important source document on the
> early history of the Nile Valley. This famous inscription, found in the Temple
> of Horus at Edfu, gives an account of the origin of Egyptian civilization.
> According to this record, civilization was brought from the south [i.e. Nubia]
> by a band of invaders under the leadership of King Horus. This ruler, Horus,
> was later deified and ultimately became the Egyptian Christ.[23]

The Greeks, towards the end of Ancient Egyptian history, restored the Temple of Horus. The Greeks, however, maintained the authenticity of the original monument as Professor Breasted explains: "The priests who conducted the rebuilding of Edfu under the Ptolmies [i.e. the Greek rulers of Egypt], claimed to be reproducing the structure formerly erected there after the plans of Imhotep [i.e. a Third Dynasty prime minister]".[24]

The other key God or Saint in the "Egyptian" religion was Osiris. His worship would also seem to have originated in Nubia. Dr Williams offers evidence that suggests the Heb-Sed festival was performed in Ta-Seti. Sir Flinders Petrie, the great British Egyptologist, wrote that this festival was performed to identify "the king with Osiris".[25] Diodorus Siculus, the noted Greek historian, recorded that Ethiopians (i.e. Nubians) who had come from the south initially peopled Egypt, "Osiris having been the leader of the colony". Diodorus further affirms that the historians of his time:

> say that ... [the Ethiopians] were the first to be taught to honour the gods and to hold sacrifices and processions and festivals and the other rites by which men honour the deity; and that in consequence their piety has been published abroad among all men, and it is generally held that the sacrifices practised among the Ethiopians are those most pleasing to heaven. As witness to this they call upon the poet who is perhaps the oldest and certainly most venerated among the Greeks [i.e. Homer]; for in the *Iliad* he represents both Zeus and the rest of the gods with him as absent on a visit to Ethiopia [i.e. Nubia] to share in the sacrifices and the banquet which were given annually by the Ethiopians for all the gods.[26]

The notion that Osiris came from Nubia is also supported by an Egyptian religious text called the *Leyden Papyrus*. In this text we read the following: "I looked out before ... to observe Osiris the Ethiopian". The original Egyptian word given as Ethiopian in the translation is *Ks* or Kush.[27] Therefore the sentence is more accurately rendered as "I looked out before ... to observe Osiris the Kushite". Kush, Ethiopia and Nubia are, of course, nearly synonymous and generally refer to the same territory that was to the south of Ancient Egypt.

Professor Amélineau was one of the early pioneers in archaeology. He also taught History and Religion in Paris. He concurs with the above ideas contained in the *Leyden Papyrus* and adds that Set and Isis were also of Nubian origins:

> If Osiris was of Nubian origin ... it would be easy to understand why the struggle between Set and Horus took place in Nubia. In any case, it is striking that the goddess Isis, according to the legend, has precisely the same skin color that Nubians always have, and that the god Osiris has what seems to me an ethnic epithet indicating his Nubian origin.[28]

Sir E. A. Wallis Budge, Britain's greatest Egyptologist of all times, noted that Amen-Ra, Shu, Tefnut, Hathor and Nut - other Egyptian Gods, Goddesses, or Saints, were also of Nubian origins. From the *Hymn of Amen-Ra,* translated by Budge, we read the following:

> The gods love the smell of him when he, the eldest born of the dew, cometh from Punt [i.e. Somalia or Ethiopia], when he traverseth the land of the Metchaiu [i.e. Nubia], the Beautiful Face coming from the land of the god (*i.e.,* the South-Eastern Sudan).[29]

Concerning Shu, Tefnut and Hathor, Budge informs us that:

> These "forms" of Ra were Shu, Tefnut, Keb, Nut, Osiris, Isis, Set, and Nephthys. Now Shu and Tefnut were Sudani [i.e. Nubian] deities, the original seat of whose worship was Bukem ... a country in the Eastern Sudan, and they were introduced into Egypt in very early times with the worship of the Sudani Cow-goddess Hathor.[30]

Emphasizing this point, he adds that:

> From an inscription published by Brusch ... we see plainly that Shu and Tefnut were gods of Sudani or Nubian origin, and that their worship was introduced into the Island of Senmut, in the First Cataract, from the South.[31]

Concerning Nut, he notes that in one representation: "She has a Sudani crown of plumes on her head, and wears armlets and bracelets".[32]

Finally, Mr J. A. Rogers, the pioneering Jamaican researcher, points out that: "According to Sir E. A. W. Budge and others most of the earliest Egyptian gods [such] as Ptah, "Father of the Gods" and Bes, god of war, mischief, and comedy, originated in the Sudan."[33]

The Qustul incense burner offers a clue to the royal architecture of Ta-Seti. Professor Diop in *Civilization or Barbarism* noticed that the palace serekh incised on the incense burner resembles part of the outer wall of a famous Egyptian monument of the Third Dynasty that is still extant. This monument, known as the Funerary Complex of Saqqara, has an entrance that seems to have taken its design directly or indirectly from the serekh idea (see page 161). This indicates that the palaces of Ta-Seti may have partly resembled the Saqqara Complex.[34]

Returning to the research of Bruce Williams, he wrote that "the continued reevaluation of the Qustul objects began to indicate a sequence that led generation by generation from Cemetery L to the time of the last pre-First Dynasty tombs at Abydos".[35] The dating of this period, however, is controversial. Cemetery L contains the tombs of twelve pharaohs ruling over nine generations. Bruce Williams believes that the dating of the first pharaoh can only be accomplished in relation to the First Dynasty of Egypt. He believes that the twelve kings ruled for a total period of 300 years, most of which elapsed before the First Dynasty. This is not a fixed date but is relative to and dependent on the chronology accepted for the dating of Ancient Egypt.[36] We date the first Nubian kings to around 5900 BC. Our justification for this dating will be given in Chapter Eight.

Dr Williams found that three generations of pharaohs ruled Ta-Seti as the only attested kings on earth. During the fourth generation, a Ta-Seti pharaoh successfully marched against Hierakonpolis in Egypt. This was the "earliest known recorded event" in world history.[37] A storage jar at Qustul attests to this victorious campaign. Furthermore, there is an A-Group (i.e. Nubian) tomb in Hierakonpolis "of royal size and design", adding further substance to a Nubian conquest.[38] The Gebel Sheikh Suleiman monument boasts of other military victories over the Egyptians.[39] Another bowl from Qustul records Nubian campaigns against Ta-Shemau (Upper Egypt) and against Ta-Tjemeh (Libya).[40] During the time of the fifth generation of Nubian rulers, Upper Egypt may have united and became a greater threat to Ta-Seti. By the period of the seventh generation Nubian pharaoh, an important line of kings ruled in Upper (i.e. southern) Egypt. These kings were buried at Abydos, the sacred city of the Egyptians. With the rise of the Egyptian First Dynasty, Pharaoh Hor-Aha, its second pharaoh (5598-c.5581 BC), campaigned against Ta-Seti's ninth generation pharaoh. Hor-Aha's campaign destroyed the Nubian kingdom. At a much later date, Dr Williams believes that the fleeing Nubians created the Kerma culture much further south.[41] (See pages 174-176).

Richard Poe, author of *Black Spark: White Fire,* introduces new archaeological evidence that he feels undermines or modifies the data that Bruce Williams has presented:

> An impressive royal tomb [says Poe] was excavated, for example, near the [Upper] Egyptian city of Abydos. The early date of the tomb - which appears to have been roughly contemporary with the Qustul incense burner - increases the probability that Egyptian and Nubian monarchies may have evolved at roughly the same time.[42]

Physical anthropological data, however, places this evidence into a very different light. Tracy L. Prowse and Nancy C. Lovell of the University of Alberta in Canada wrote a useful paper entitled *Concordance of Cranial and Dental Morphological Traits and Evidence for Endogamy in Ancient Egypt.* The abstract to this document reads as follows:

> A biological affinities study based on frequencies of cranial nonmetric traits in skeletal samples from three cemeteries at predynastic Naqada, Egypt, confirms

the results of a recent nonmetric dental morphological analysis. Both cranial and dental traits analyses indicate that the individuals buried in a cemetery characterized archaeologically as high status are significantly different from individuals buried in two other, apparently non-elite cemeteries and that the non-elite samples are not significantly different from each other. A comparison with neighbouring Nile Valley skeletal samples suggests that the high status cemetery represents an endogamous ruling or elite segment of the local population at Naqada, which is more closely related to populations in northern Nubia than to neighbouring populations in southern Egypt.[43]

This evidence indicates that the elites of Upper (i.e. southern) Egypt at this early date, in contrast to the commoners, were in fact Nubians. Moreover, the Nubian elite buried at Naqada intermarried with others from Nubia and not with the Upper Egyptians. This may well show that the royal tomb referred to by Poe belonged to a Nubian elite personage, or if Egyptian, its existence was sanctioned by the Nubian elite. The Abydos tomb therefore, is unlikely to undermine nor significantly modify the Williams data. On the other hand, Prowse and Lovell's evidence may indicate that developments in the Egyptian city of Naqada were due to the influence exerted by the Nubian elite. One of these developments, as Dr Williams explained, was the birth of writing. It may well turn out that the birth of writing was entirely a Nubian accomplishment, contrary to Williams, who believed that it was partly a Nubian and partly an Egyptian accomplishment.

In closing, the archaeological evidence lends great support to what the classical writers had said all along. Stephanus of Byzantium, writing in the fifth century AD for example, accurately recorded that: "Ethiopia [i.e. Nubia] was the first established country on earth and the Ethiopians were the first to set up the worship of the gods, and who established laws".[44] Dr Williams penned a good summary on the importance of the Ta-Seti achievement that we have reproduced as follows:

> For nine generations or more, according to the sequence of tombs of Cemetery L, some twelve kings at Qustul participated with other kings in Upper Egypt in the creation of a unified culture. For Egypt, they helped fashion pharaonic civilization and thus a legacy for the First Dynasty which the world has marvelled at for millennia. For Nubia, they established an early political unity and led that country to its first cultural distinction.[45]

Old Kingdom Egypt

Ancient Egypt was entirely dependent on the River Nile for its very existence. This was so much the case that the Egyptians had a deeply held belief that the Nubians could, in theory, bring them to their knees by diverting its course.[46]

The Nile flows from Lake Victoria in present-day Uganda, north through the Sudan, and ultimately through Egypt. Along the way, the river passes through six naturally occurring geographical markers called cataracts. By tradition, scholars call the first cataract, which is also the most southerly, number six. In addition, they call the last one, also the most northerly, number one. Professor Yosef ben-Jochannan, an Ethiopian Egyptologist, long proposed abandoning this strange tradition, but his ideas have not caught on as yet. In this chapter, we use the traditional numbering, though we are well aware that it is perverse. After a trek of 3400 miles, the Nile reaches the Egyptian Nile Valley, which stretches 650 miles through the desert. For the last 100 miles of the Nile's journey, the river divides. It fans out before emptying into the Mediterranean. These swamplands of northern Egypt are also called the Delta, a Greek name, referring to the Greek letter delta or 'd'. This letter is written as a triangle. The swamplands received this name because the rivers subdividing on a map looks triangular (See map on page 149).

Once every year the Nile River overflows. In Ethiopia, monsoon rains flood the banks of the Nile. As the Nile flows from south to north, rich soils are carried along the river, which are eventually deposited in Egypt. Bringing great fertility to the land, these soils made Egypt one of the most fertile places on earth. The Nile dominated every aspect of Egyptian life. Their calendar was divided into three agricultural seasons based on the annual flooding. The first season was called Inundation, the time of the summer floods. During this period, the Egyptians could be employed on construction projects since there was no agricultural work for them to do. There was another season called Emergence where crops could be planted as the water receded. Finally there was a season of the Dry Time where it was possible to harvest. The Nile year was 12 months long, each month consisting of 30 days. They added five festival days at the end of the year to complete the 365-day cycle. The government levied taxes according to the height of the Nile during the inundation. The inundation affected the amount of land that could be watered and fertilised by the Nile. Herodotus, the Greek historian, claimed that the annual flooding of the Nile made Egypt so fertile that very little farming effort was required to reap such bountiful crops.[47]

Manetho, an Egyptian priest, wrote a history of Egypt towards the very end of the Ancient Egyptian period. He divided the history of the pharaohs into 30 dynasties. Unfortunately this great work is now lost. What is known about it today comes from excerpts that later writers have quoted, such as Africanus and Eusebius. There are, however, other records of Egyptian history. The Temple of Pharaoh Seti I (ruled 1450-1395 BC) dedicated to Osiris, the Egyptian god of death and resurrection, contains a special Hall of the Ancestors. Seventy-five royal ancestors were listed there in chronological

Egypt. Handsome limestone portrait of Pharaoh Narmer/Mena (ruled 5660-5998 BC), First Dynasty. He was the founder of the Egyptian Old Kingdom. (Photo: Courtesy of the Petrie Museum of Egyptian Archaeology, University College London, UC 15989).

order. There are other sources from similar temples that are of great importance in the reconstruction of Egyptian history.[48]

Geographically, Egypt was divided into two, Upper Egypt and Lower Egypt. Each had its own capital city. The southern part of Egypt, from the First Cataract of the Nile to the region now known as Cairo, was called Upper Egypt. Nekhen (also called Hierakonpolis) was its greatest early city. The Nile flows further north from Cairo to the Mediterranean. This northern region is called Lower Egypt. Buto was its greatest early city. Each of the two lands had their own heraldic flower, crowns, kingly titles, demigods, and goddesses.

Each land was unified in the person of the ruler. Upper Egypt was the land of the lotus flower whose rulers wore the White Crown. The Upper Egyptians believed that Nekhbet, the vulture goddess, protected their land. Lower Egypt was the land of the papyrus plant whose rulers wore the Red Crown. The Lower Egyptians believed that Wadjet, the snake goddess, protected their land.[49]

Both crowns, however, had a very different origin. The White Crown of Upper Egypt made its earliest known appearance on the heads of the Ta-Seti pharaohs, as we have already seen. The Red Crown of Lower Egypt made its earliest known appearance on an Upper Egyptian artefact from the city of Naqada.[50] We believe this shows the powerful influence of Ta-Seti on early Egypt.

Hierakonpolis, the capital of Upper Egypt, was the city of Horus - the falcon deity. Archaeologists discovered it over 100 years ago and have systematically studied it. In 1978 scholars found that it existed 400 years before the First Egyptian Dynasty. The city stretched for over two miles along the edge of a plain. Containing many neighbourhoods, its population included skilled people such as craftsmen, farmers, officials and potters. Of particular interest was a house and workshop that once belonged to a potter who made cooking pots for his neighbours. Fragments of 300,000 pots were found in the vicinity. On the north side of town was located the industrial zone. One of the things produced there was beer. The brewery could well have served the needs of 200 people per day.[51] Also discovered was Egypt's first known temple. The Temple of Horus had a large oval courtyard. In its midst stood a pole with a large image of Horus, the falcon. Adjacent to the courtyard was a three-room shrine, whose facade was made up of four huge timber pillars, 20 feet high. Covering the walls were lavish coloured mats. The shrine dominated both the temple complex and the central part of the city.[52]

Buto was the capital of Lower Egypt. Archaeological excavations in 1983 showed that the city was very ancient and was occupied for over 500 years. The early pottery found there seems to have been influenced from models coming in from the Middle East. The later pottery was of an indigenous Upper Egyptian style. As in Upper Egypt, the early houses in this region were made of mud bricks.[53]

The earliest king of a unified Egypt was Mena from the Upper Egyptian city of Thinis. Different historians of antiquity quote Manetho as saying slightly different things about this great monarch. Africanus, however, quotes Manetho as saying that Mena reigned 62 years.[54] Herodotus, the excellent Greek historian of antiquity, collected other information on this king during his visit to the country:

> The [Egyptian] priests said that Mên [i.e. Mena] was the first king of Egypt,
> and that it was he who raised the dyke which protects Memphis from the
> inundations of the Nile. Before his time the river flowed entirely through the
> sandy range of hills which skirts Egypt on the side of Libya. He, however, by
> banking up the river at the bend which it forms about a hundred furlongs south
> of Memphis, laid the ancient channel dry, while he dug a new course for the
> stream half-way between the two lines of hills ... Besides these works, he also,
> the priests said, built the temple of Vulcan [i.e. Ptah] which stands within the
> city [i.e. in Herodotus' time], a vast edifice, very worthy of mention.[55]

There is a famous palette associated with an Egyptian king called Narmer.
Most historians believe that he is the same person as Mena. This document,
exquisitely carved, shows the king wearing the White Crown of Upper Egypt
and he stands with his arm raised holding a mace just about to strike an enemy.
On the other side of the palette the king is seen wearing the Red Crown of
Lower Egypt. He is in procession with the company of high officials. This
document shows that the king has defeated the rulers of Lower Egypt. On the
palette are lions with serpent-like heads intertwined symbolising unification.
From this date onwards, the kings of Egypt wore the Double Crown - the White
and the Red Crown combined.[56] He was thus the first king to take the title of
the "Two Ladies" referring to the goddesses Nekhbet and Wadjet.[57] Finally,
Mena led expeditions southeast to the mountain regions where the stone
quarries stood. From here, building materials were obtained.[58]

The city of Abydos was important. The kings of the first two dynasties of the
Old Kingdom were buried there.[59] The research in 1988 showed that an even
earlier dynasty reigned in Abydos. Of the many discoveries was an elaborate
tomb lined with bricks. The tomb had 12 rooms with doors and windows,
resembling a palace in almost every way. In the palace was an ivory sceptre
that demonstrates the incumbent was a king. Some scholars call this period
Dynasty 0. During this period the ancient Egyptians (and for that matter the
Nubians) developed writing. This script is the famous hieroglyphic system.
Some of the documents from the tomb contained place names that existed in
Lower Egypt. Scholars interpret this as evidence that the Lower Egyptians paid
taxes and tribute to these early rulers of Abydos. Also found were wine jars
brought in from Canaan. King Scorpion was the great ruler from this period.[60]

Out of the unification of the two lands emerged the new capital city of
Memphis. This city was also called 'The White Walls', probably in reference
to the walls that surrounded the royal palace. Memphis was also called 'The
Balance of the Two Lands'.[61] The period from Mena to the end of the Sixth
Dynasty is called the Old Kingdom. During this period, the Egyptians built the
Great Pyramids, wrote the Pyramid Texts, and pioneered the Solar Calendar.

There is much controversy surrounding the actual dating of this period,
however. Egyptian records, documented by Manetho and cited by Julius

Egypt. Entrance to the Funerary Complex of Saqqara. Built by Pharaoh Djoser (ruled 5018-4989 BC). Prime Minister Imhotep designed the building. The entrance was originally part of a one mile wall that surrounded the Complex. (Photo: Alan Mitchell).

Africanus, gave the beginning of the Old Kingdom period as 5717 BC. Some contemporary scholars, for no good reason, prefer the Berlin Chronology of Professor Eduard Meyer. He dates the beginning of the Old Kingdom period as 3180 BC. Meyer had, in effect, erased two and a half thousand years off African history with the stroke of a pen! His chronology has become the standard one used by Egyptologists, through the dominance of the Oriental Institute in the world of Egyptology founded by Meyer's disciple, James Henry Breasted. Their chronology is supported by no records whatsoever and actually contradicts those records. Since history must be based on the available documentation, we follow Professor Jackson in using the Manetho-Africanus chronology, as modified and corrected by the Scottish Orientalist, Duncan MacNaughton. We do, however, have minor disagreements with this scholar, but we accept his basic edifice. We date the ascension of Narmer/Mena at 5660 BC.[62] We present a fuller discussion of Egyptian chronology in Chapter Eight.

In 5598 BC Hor-Aha succeeded Mena. During his time, there were trade links with Lebanon and Syria. Coniferous timber was obtained from these countries that were used in building projects. Hor-Aha built a castle in Memphis and also its first tomb. Gargantuan in size, it was constructed of sun-dried bricks and had five underground rooms carved out of the rock. In Abydos, the religious capital, he built a false tomb. Later kings would do likewise.[63] According to Michael Rice, an able English historian: "The monumental tombs of the First Dynasty are, by any standards, very remarkable buildings".[64] Another important development from the period was the evolution of hieratic (i.e. cursive) writing, written on papyrus. Of the few tid-bits of information that has come down to us specifically on this king, it is recorded that he visited the sanctuary of the Goddess Neith in Lower Egypt and had a divine statue of her carved. Despite this piety, however, he ordered military campaigns. Hor-Aha led a devastating raid on Ta-Seti, ending its dynasty and closing a chapter in African history.[65]

Djer, the next ruler, held sway in Nubia as far south as the Second Cataract. He also campaigned against the Libyans at the edge of the Delta.[66] In addition, later traditions claimed that the Djer period was one where the sciences flourished. Apparently Djer wrote books on anatomy and medicine, himself, that were still popular thousands of years later. A treatment for baldness was among his achievements.[67] Important physical remains survive from Djer's time that demonstrates "the sumptuousness of the King's accoutrements and the opulence of his court."[68] In Saqqara stands an extensive building 56 metres long and 24 wide, surrounded by 300 bulls heads with horns, finely sculpted of clay. Originally inlaid with strips of gold plating, the central chamber consisted of a room with wooden panels. Inside were found a wealth of copper vessels, tools, weapons, and a fine gold-handled knife. Finally, from his Abydos tomb, a stunning collection of jewels were recovered - still attached to a human arm.[69]

Egypt. Part of an inner temple in the Funerary Complex of Saqqara. Built by Pharaoh Djoser (ruled 5018-4989 BC). Despite the hoary age of the monument, some of the construction work challenge our notions of what we consider to be modern construction standards. (Photo: Fari Supiya).

Pharaoh Mer-Neith, his successor, was the first woman in history to run a country in her own right.[70] Djet, the next ruler, is known primarily for the artistic merits of his tomb stela, now housed in the Louvre Museum in Paris.[71] "Above all else," says Mr Rice:

> what Djet's stela demonstrates is restraint, exceptional refinement, and an understanding of form which is not to be repeated by artists of other nationalities until the coming of the Greeks … Even then, the Greeks hardly ever achieved the monumental simplicity that the unknown master of the stela of King Djet produced with such divine assurance.[72]

Den succeeded Djet on the throne in around 5476 BC. Like Djer, he had a medical background. Medical studies on bone fractures carried out during his reign were quoted in much later Egyptian medical documents.[73] The Edwin Smith Papyrus, now housed in the New York Academy of Medicine, is one of ten surviving ancient Egyptian medical texts. The text gives an account of 48 cases of bone surgery and of external pathology. The text demonstrates a detailed knowledge of anatomy, gives remarkably accurate descriptions of traumatic surgical lesions and describes their treatments where applicable. Professor Cheikh Anta Diop, the great Senegalese Egyptologist, informs us that "[i]ts scientific conciseness has won the admiration of modern scientists."[74] The Papyrus, though written during the Eighteenth Egyptian Dynasty, is a copy of a much older Egyptian text from this period. The Eighteenth Dynasty copyist was forced to include glossaries for the readers because the original language nearly 3,000 years earlier was just too archaic; the meanings had become impenetrable. What has survived, however, is only one third of the original manuscript that stops at the 48th case. Consequently it deals only with the skeleton and soft tissue parts of the head and neck - the upper portion of the body. The original was probably a complete manual of traumatic surgery covering all of the body. Each of the 48 surviving cases is written out as (i) an examination, (ii) a diagnosis, (iii) a treatment (iv) and finally, glossaries to explain the First Dynasty language to an Eighteenth Dynasty surgeon.[75] Dr Charles Finch, a medical doctor who has made a special study on this papyrus, was somewhat baffled by the standards of medical knowledge achieved. He notes that:

> Cases 29-33 all represent additional case descriptions of vertebral dislocations and sub-luxations and their clinical consequences. At present, some of these conditions are almost impossible to detect or describe fully without X-ray studies. The question then arises is how did our ancient surgeon, living a[n]d practicing [thousands of] years ago, manage to diagnose and describe these problems *without* benefit of X-rays?[76]

On the military front, Den successfully campaigned against the people of the Sinai Peninsula. Finally, he innovated in building technique. His tomb had a stela of diorite with a floor of red granite. Previously these stones were only used to make vessels.[77]

Political turmoil interrupted the technical and cultural achievements made during the reigns of the last three kings of this dynasty. Royal names were erased from inscriptions as a political and magical weapon. This reflected disputes in the royal lineage that prepared the way for a change in dynasty.[78]

As with the First Dynasty, the Second Dynasty rulers originated from the Thinis region. As far as modern historians are concerned, this is an obscure period where little is currently known. What can be deduced, however, is that perhaps twelve rulers held the crown of Egypt from 5386 to 5046 BC. During this period, pottery was turned on a wheel for the first time. Pharaoh Baneter, perhaps the fourth king of the dynasty, ruled for 47 years. He is depicted as celebrating the Heb-Sed festival at least once during his reign. This festival rejuvenated the king as the deity Osiris, the god of death and resurrection.[79] Peribsen may well have been the sixth king of this line. Unlike the earlier kings, he was a worshipper of Set, an ancient god of the south. He also restored the old practise of having royal burials in the city of Abydos.[80] Pharaoh Khasekhemui, the last king of the dynasty, presided over a brilliant 48 years of political and religious stability. Icons from his period depict both the Horus and Set animals above his name implying his allegiance to both deities. Stone sculpture developed greatly during his time. Private individuals as well as

Egypt. Composite columns in the Funerary Complex of Saqqara. Built by Pharaoh Djoser (ruled 5018-4989 BC). These are the first known columns in history but they are attached to walls since Imhotep had not yet worked out how to make columns free standing. (Photo: Fari Supiya).

royalty had portrait sculptures carved. Finally, there is evidence of trade with Byblos in Palestine.[81]

Agriculture was, of course, the key economic activity during this period. Taxes were paid to the government in kind, mostly grain and foodstuffs. Collected grain was stored in warehouses and the surplus paid for royal building and also relief activities. It could be distributed as and when necessary. Surplus food production was also sold into the Middle East. From there, the Egyptians imported wood from Lebanon and Syria, olive oil from Palestine, and lapis lazuli from Afghanistan. The very ancient city of Nekheb (sic), near Hierakonpolis, controlled trade routes to the Red Sea. From here the Egyptians obtained flint, gold, lead and tin. They spent the wealth generated on lavish monuments based on their ancestralist religious belief that buildings for the dead should be more important than those of the living.[82] Sir E. A. Wallis Budge, the venerable English Egyptologist, also alludes to trade between Egypt and the lands to the south. In his view:

> Of the relations which existed between the Nubian sheks [sic] and Narmer and Aha, conquerors of Egypt, and its earliest dynastic kings, we know nothing, but that intercourse went on between Egypt and Nubia at this period for trading purposes is quite certain. There is a possibility that the people of Upper Egypt were descendants of settlers from the south-eastern parts of the Sudan, and Naville and Maspero believed that the Egyptians and the people of Punt belonged to the same race. Punt ... was a country near Somaliland, and many dynastic Egyptians regarded it as their original home. The long plaited beards of the Egyptian gods resemble those worn by the men of Punt, and certain funerary ceremonies were of Puntite origin.[83]

The Egyptian court was well organised at this time with the institution of a number of key office holders. The Reverend Baikie, a fine historian and a most charming wordsmith, explained how this worked:

> The Court Chamberlain appears as early as the reign of Narmer. The Commander of the Inundation, who is mentioned in the reign of Zer [i.e. Djer], is evidence of the early date at which the Egyptian organised the resources of the state for the purpose of dealing with the life-giving bounty of the Nile ... A little later in the dynasty comes the Commander of the Elders, while in the reign of King [sic] Merneit [sic] we have the appearance of a functionary with whom the Bible-stories of our childhood made us familiar, - Pharaoh's Chief-Butler, who figures as the Keeper of the Wine. Still in the 1st Dynasty we have the Royal Seal-Bearer, the Royal Architect, and the Keeper of the King's Vineyards; and the grouping round the king of a regular aristocracy is attested by the names of the Leader of the Peers and the Master of Ceremonies. Evidently Egyptian society ... had already stiffened into something of the minute ritual of court etiquette which marked it in later days ... For purposes of administration the country was at first provided with two treasuries, one for the North, "the Red House," and one for the South, "the White House."[84]

Egypt. The Step Pyramid of Saqqara. This monument, of six steps, was the centrepiece of the Funerary Complex. Built by Pharaoh Djoser (ruled 5018-4989 BC), the Step Pyramid is the first of ninety Egyptian pyramids. Note also that there are two people in the photograph giving a sense of scale. (Photo: Alan Mitchell).

The kings of the first two dynasties were buried in deep underground tombs lined with bricks. Over these burials stood mud brick structures called mastabas. In time, these buildings became elaborate. Khasekhemui built the largest royal tomb in the city of Abydos. Shaped like a trapezium, it was 230 feet long and over 33 feet wide. Some distance away is the remains of the king's palace. Its mud bricks undulated and wound into a number of niches and recesses. In its day it boasted white panelled walls. In size, it was an awesome 400 feet long and 213 feet wide. Standing 36 feet high, its walls were a staggering 18 feet thick. Khasekhemui built another palatial enclosure, this time at Hierakonpolis.[85] Finally, there exists an interesting and important monument built near the city of Memphis. An astounding 1150 by 2130 feet with walls 49 feet thick, this structure was probably the world's very first building in stone. Scholars do not as yet know who built this monument but they have reason to credit King Khasekhemui.[86]

With the Third Dynasty (5046-4872 BC) there was a change in public administration. The Prime Minister now led the bureaucratic structure.[87] The great ruler of this dynasty was Pharaoh Djoser. During his 29 years, Egyptian power was felt in Lower Nubia and in the Sinai region. In the latter region, Egyptian miners worked the copper and turquoise mines.[88] There were developments in art. Statues for the first time were made life-sized. Some stone statues were carved for private persons. There were other developments in relief sculpture. As an example of this, the wooden plaques recovered from the tomb of Hezyre were distinguished and show this artistic development.

The city of Saqqara was originally south of the Memphis necropolis. Here Djoser built a complex that replaced an older temple of wood, brick and woven mats. Imhotep, his Prime Minister, designed the building. This structure contained Egypt's first pyramid. The Step Pyramid and its surrounding complex represent major developments in technological achievement and artistic sensibility.[89] The Step Pyramid was built of six steps. Its shape represents the primeval mound of creation. It contained chapels of blue tiles that depict the Heb-Sed festivals. There was also a life-sized statue of the king, which Mr Rice feels "deserves to be recognized as one of the wonders of the world."[90] The symbolic meaning behind the construction is that the pharaoh was continually having his vitality renewed and has thus become immortal.[91] Mr Rice further notes that:

> The Djoser complex is unique. Once again, it is totally without precedent, not merely in Egypt but in the entire world. For centuries its high white limestone curtain walls and the elegant, superbly proportioned kiosks, magazines, and shrines which were built within the walls made it the most remarkable building in the world: perhaps indeed it remains the most remarkable ever built.[92]

This period was not always tranquil and positive, however. There is a famous document called the Famine Stela associated with Pharaoh Djoser. It describes a famine that lasted seven years caused by low Nile floods. At the end of the famine the king offered land to the priests of Khnum of Nubia. They helped to end the famine.[93]

Imhotep was an able and praiseworthy figure. Mr Rice believes it "entirely possible that no more remarkable creative talent ever lived".[94] He was born in Memphis to a highborn family. His father, Kanofer, was a distinguished royal architect and master builder. Under Djoser, Imhotep served as Prime Minister, but he was also an astronomer, physician, poet, philosopher and Chief Lector Priest of Heliopolis. As an architect and medical doctor, his reputation was unassailable. By 525 BC, Imhotep was deified. A temple was later dedicated to him in Karnak.[95]

King Huni (4898-4872 BC) was the last monarch of the Third Dynasty. He had 8 smaller step pyramids built across the country. It is possible that these buildings were important for more administration reasons. They may have been used for census collection or tax collection.[96]

The three great pyramids of Giza are perhaps the most visited attraction in the world. The three monuments have been attributed to three kings of the Fourth Dynasty, Khufu, Khafra and Menkaura. There are over 90 royal pyramids in Egypt, however. The pyramids themselves symbolise a daily religious meaning. The Egyptians had accounts of creation where creation begins through a primeval watery void called Nun. Out of this void emerged the sun god considered the embodiment of life, energy and light. This sun god emerges in the shape of a hill that emerges out of the water, also called Ptah. The pyramids represent this shape and are thus symbolic of the God Ptah.[97]

Also built during the Fourth Dynastic period, was the Helwan Dam. A most impressive engineering feat, the dam consisted of stone, rubble and other walling. It was over 321 feet wide at the bottom and 184 feet across at the top. It was originally designed to be 46 feet high and 361 feet long. It is possible that 500 workmen were employed to build it. The dam demonstrated great hydrological knowledge.[98]

The Fourth Dynasty had its origin in Memphis or Elephantine (see Chapter Eight). Pharaoh Sneferu, its founder, was perhaps the most important builder of the entire Pyramid Age. Ascending the throne in 4872 BC, he ruled for a possible 48 years. During this time there are records of 40 ships laden with cedar wood arriving from Byblos in a single year. The ships from this period were impressive, being 150 feet long. Their harbours were located in the Delta. There are also records of military campaigns. Sneferu marched against Nubia and Libya, seizing prisoners and cattle. From Nubia, he took 7,000 prisoners and 200,000 heads of cattle. From Libya, he brought back 11,000 prisoners and 13,100 heads of cattle.[99] The raids boosted the treasury through tribute and taxation. There was also stone quarrying conducted on a large scale.[100] Sneferu built three grand pyramids and possibly also two smaller ones. He built the Pyramid at Meidum, the Bent Pyramid of Dashur and the Red Pyramid. Prince Kanefer, his architect, designed these buildings.[101] Their mortuary temples consisted of an altar and two stelae inscribed with the royal titulary. The Bent Pyramid, by contrast had statues and wall reliefs. The scenes depicted include foundation rituals, the Heb-Sed festival and also the first known examples of the king being embraced by a deity.[102] In later times, the Egyptians would remember Sneferu as a beneficent ruler that presided over great general prosperity. The ruling class also benefited greatly:

> The[ir] quality of life ... can be gauged by the extraordinarily sumptuous elegance of the furnishings found in the tomb of [Sneferu's] consort Queen Hetepheres ... Once more it is not only their richness of materials and precision of craftsmanship which amazes: it is, overwhelmingly, the certainty and restraint with which they are designed. The hoard of objects from Hetepheres' burial, a fraction of what originally it contained, are amongst the most splendid to survive from the Old Kingdom ... What did survive however, was a magnificent alabaster sarcophagus, a carrying chair, exquisitely inlaid with gold, a gold-encased bed and gossamer-fine canopy, gold implements, and silver bracelets inlaid with butterflies.[103]

The houses of this time were typically one or two storeys with front courtyards. The one storey houses had three rooms with a veranda. By contrast, the two storey houses had six rooms, an outside staircase, and a roof loggia. Walls were typically of sun-dried brick with floors of beaten earth. The roofs were usually flat, but there were also domed roofs and barrel-vaulted roofs. Wood was used for columns, ceiling beams, and stair supports. The British historian, Dr Watterson, informs us that: "Wood was also used as a sort of damp course: wooden poles, set at intervals along the upper part of a wall, kept the mud-brick dry by allowing moisture to permeate through them until it reached the outside air."[104] The window and door-frames were of stone. Sometimes the inhabitants slept on the roof, as it was cooler. They would sometimes erect a parapet of wood or reeds, or else a wooden pavilion for privacy.

The rooms typically contained couches, stools and chests. There were single beds of wooden frames that contained leather or string webbing. The furniture legs were carved to resemble the legs and feet of animals. The houses of the wealthy had stone-window gratings. At nights, stone or pottery lamps, burning castor oil or animal fat, illuminated the insides. Surrounding these houses were pools and gardens with flower beds.[105] For the royal family, their houses were likely to be even larger but no evidence of palaces from the Old Kingdom period exists today.[106] On this basis, some authorities conclude that the Egyptians of this period did not have palaces.

In 4824 BC Pharaoh Khufu succeeded Sneferu to the royal throne. He built the first Great Pyramid of Giza. This building, though noteworthy due to its great size, accuracy, and orientation, was no more impressive than the other two Giza pyramids. The great pyramid complexes all consisted of a causeway, a valley temple, a mortuary temple, and the pyramids themselves. Surrounding the first Great Pyramid were 5 rock-hewn pits that contained boats. One such boat was 143 feet long. The distinguished Egyptologist, Professor Hornung, observed that:

> The immense expenditure entailed was intended not for the glorification of a king but rather the welfare of the state, which in any case depended on the monarch: his creative powers, which held together the very order of the world, had to be preserved even behind death's doorstep. The construction of the pyramid was thus a communal religious effort on the part of the Egyptians of the old Kingdom, who were certainly not "free" in our sense of the world but rather were in various ways bound to and dependant on the king and the other divine powers.[107]

Of the Great Pyramid, Mr Marsham Adams, an Oxford University historian of the nineteenth century, wrote that:

> The Monument in stone is unique, solid almost to indestructability, incapable of variation, and standing unchanged and unchanging, regardless of the assaults, whether of time or of man. That extraordinary pile, the most majestic and most mysterious ever erected by the hand of man, stands close to the verge of the immense desert which stretches its arid wastes across the whole breadth of the African continent to the shore of the western ocean, just at the spot where the busy life of the earliest civilisation on record was bordered by the vast and barren solitude. Of all the other structures which made the marvels of the ancient world, scarcely a vestige is left. Where are the hanging gardens, the boast of the monarch of Babylon? Where is the far-famed Pharos of Alexandria? Centuries have passed since earthquake laid low the Colossus which bestrode the harbour of Rhodes; and a madman's hand reduced to ashes the temple of Artermis, the pride of Ephesus. But the Grand Pyramid of Ghizeh [sic] still remains, undestroyed and indestructible, ages after the lesser marvels have passed away, as it stood ages before ever they came into being.[108]

Finally, Khufu built the first Temple of Hathor at Denderah. This monument has since been restored several times.[109]

Djedefra succeeded Khufu to the throne in 4761 BC. He was the first pharaoh to take the religious title Son of Ra. He began a pyramid at Abu Rawash, but left it incomplete.[110]

It is interesting to estimate the population of Egypt during the Pyramid Age. Egypt was primarily an urban civilisation. Cities, towns and ports were dotted along the Nile River. Indeed, the Nile could have been described as one long urban strip. Cities were constructed around temples, craft specialities, graveyards, commercial, and also governmental buildings.[111] And "with a population of perhaps five million crowded into a habitable area the size of Belgium," writes Professors Oliver and Fagan, two contemporary Africanists: "it is clear that the Egypt of 2500 years ago was as urbanised as most modern industrial societies."[112] While it is noted that Oliver and Fagan refer to a much later period in Egyptian history, the importance of their contribution can be judged by comparing it to the following statement by Peter Tompkins, author of the excellent *Secrets of the Great Pyramid.* Mr Tompkins specifically addresses the Pyramid Age:

> Statisticians estimate that eight million people were crowded into a space of only 11,500 square miles, giving a population density of 695 per square mile - which is more than modern Belgium, the most densely populated part of Europe.[113]

Pharaoh Khafra built the Second of the Great Pyramids of Giza and also a temple. The Temple, built of limestone, consisted of huge granite blocks. Through the doors of this structure were 23 diorite statues of Khafra, all life sized. Also on the same site, was the Great Sphinx. The diorite came from

Tushka in Nubia. At this time, the Egyptians controlled these quarries and also the gold mines of Nubia.[114]

Menkaura inherited the throne from Khafra in around 4678 BC. He built the Third Great Pyramid of Giza. During his time, the different nomes (regions) were allowed greater autonomy from the crown. Each nomarch (regional ruler) claimed that their right to govern came from the protection of a local divinity. The nomarchs passed on their positions to their children. This had the effect of challenging royal power, since the king's ability to appoint the office holders of his choice had now been undermined.[115]

Pharaoh Shepseskaf, his successor, broke with recent tradition and raised a mastaba as opposed to a pyramid.[116]

The Fifth Dynasty (4599-4402 BC) had its origins in Elephantine. The kings built important pyramids in the city of Abusir located south of Giza. Though stripped of their casing, these buildings were once important. In 1893, 300 fragments of papyrus were discovered in one of the tombs. An analysis of these fragments revealed that the temples had scribes, priests and purifiers, as well as members of the local town, drawn from all social classes. The priests had an important role in helping to maintain, transport and guard the possessions of the pyramid complex. In the mornings and evenings a sacred ceremony would take place. The people would clean and bathe the statues. At the same time, the priests would chant and fill the place with burning incense. The aim was to prepare the spirit of the dead king for a ritual meal, which would be gradually shared out among the people.[117] Vivian Davies and Renée Friedman, two modern Egyptologists, conclude that this was "part of a massive redistribution scheme and one that was highly successful".[118]

Pharaoh Userkaf, the founder of the dynasty, ruled for 28 years. During his time contacts with the international world were widespread.[119] Maintaining international contacts, Pharaoh Sahura, his successor, sent the first fully documented expeditions to Punt (i.e. possibly Somalia or Ethiopia). Trading with Syria, the Egyptians imported Syrian bears for the Royal Zoo. Furthermore, there were political relations with Crete and also records of a campaign against Libya. Finally, in his Mortuary Temple, Sahura's artists depicted the transportation of his gilded pyramidion.[120]

Prime Minister Ptah-Hotep wrote a famous philosophical text offering practical advice on good conduct in the presence of superiors, inferiors and equals. It also discusses ethical and social responsibility.[121] His ideas are still timely:

> If you are a leader [says Ptah-Hotep], be courteous and listen carefully to the presentations of petitioners. Stop not their speech until they have poured out their heart and spoken that which they came to say ... Not all that is asked for can be granted, but a fair hearing satisfies the heart.[122]

Inside some of the Fifth Dynasty pyramids are bright and highly coloured inscriptions. The walls of the pyramid of Pharaoh Unas (4435-4402 BC) contain the famous *Pyramid Texts.* Representing the oldest surviving corpus of religious literature in the world, the texts contain spells, religious utterances, and hymns. They were believed to chart the journey of the king into his afterlife.[123] On a practical note, Unas also ordered campaigns. He battled the Asiatic Bedouins of Sinai or southern Palestine.[124]

In 4402 BC Pharaoh Teti founded the Sixth Dynasty. During his time, the nomarchs became more and more powerful. Some were able to significantly undermine royal authority. Izi, nomarch of Edfu, and Heqaib, of Elephantine, became very powerful and were later deified.[125]

Pharaoh Pepi II, the fifth king of the dynasty, became an important ruler. Inheriting the throne as a young child, he ruled the nation for a lengthy 94 years, the longest of any king in history.[126] In his time, a man called Harkhuf made four important voyages into Central Africa from Elephantine. From the inscriptions in Harkhuf's tomb, we learn that he brought back a number of foreign goods including ebony, incense, ivory, oils and panther skins. He also returned with a person: a Pygmy. Very impressed with his voyage, Pepi II, the child king, wrote to Harkhuf saying how keen he was to meet with him.[127] His letter reads as follows:

> Come forth to the palace at once! Hurry and bring with you this [P]ygmy whom you brought from the land of the horizon dwellers who does the dances of the gods. When he goes with you into the ship, place worthy men around him on deck, lest he fall into the water! When he sleeps, surround him with worthy men in his tent. Inspect him ten times at night. My Majesty wishes to see this [P]ygmy more than the gifts of the mine-lands. Orders have been given to the town mayors and overseers of priests that supplies are to be furnished for you from every storage depot and every temple.[128]

Years later, Pepi II became a great conqueror, seizing control of countries to the south such as Wawat, Irthet and Punt.[129] In later years, however, things fell apart. Pepi's nine decades on the throne was accompanied by the growth in power of the nomarchs and the weakening of the central administration. On the domestic front, the early decades of his reign were quiet and uneventful. In later years, the nomarchs and priests took advantage of the king's senility to press for greater power and concessions. The king practically gave land away tax-free to the priests.[130] This spelled trouble. Professor Hornung offers a fine and incisive analysis of the situation:

> The decisive factor was that the archaic, patriarchal structure of the administration was no longer adequate to meet the more specialized demands of the era and thus not suited in all respects to the tenor of the times ... The

increases in the number of cultic endowments freed by royal decree from taxes
and other obligations put a strain on the economy of the state ... A weak central
administration could no longer provide the state-conducted trade with the
rational planning or the armed protection it needed. The consequences were
economic difficulties and ultimate catastrophe, famine, and struggle for life
itself.[131]

After Pepi II, came Merenre II who ruled for one year. Succeeding him was
Nitocris, a female pharaoh. She was the last ruler of the dynasty and presided
for 12 years. The Old Kingdom fell in 4188 BC.

Kush

The city of Kerma was at the heart of the Kushite state. Its authority was felt
from the Second Cataract of the Nile, down to the Fourth. This city goes back
a long way in history. Some authorities claim that it was probably settled as
early as the fourth millennium BC. However, as in Egypt, there are clearly
problems with the chronology of Kush.

Charles Bonnet, an important Swiss archaeologist, believes that there were
clear divisions that can be made in Kushite history basing his ideas on the
research of Brigitte Gratien. The divisions she proposes are the Ancient Period
of 2500/2400 to 2050 BC, the Middle Period of 2050 to 1750 BC and the
Classic Period of 1750 to 1500 BC.[132] Throughout these periods Kush was
often in political conflict with Egypt. It is unfortunate, however, that Gratien
has dated the Kerma artefacts in conformity to the short chronology of Meyer
and Breasted. The Meyer-Breasted chronology does not stand up to critical
scrutiny and it is therefore likely that the Kerma artefacts are much older than
the dates given there. Bonnet believes that the beginning of the Ancient Kerma
period was contemporaneous with Harkhuf. Manetho dates this period to
c.4200 BC. Bonnet believes that the Middle Period is contemporaneous with
the Theban Period in Egypt. Manetho gives this as about 3500 BC. Finally,
Bonnet gives 1750 BC for the Classic Period but it is not at all clear how this
date was arrived at. We cannot therefore offer a firm Manetho date for the
beginnings of this period.

By around 4200 BC, or perhaps earlier, Kerma had emerged as the capital of
a unified state. Bonnet believes that it lasted intact for nearly a thousand years
but we think this is conservative. Tellingly, Bonnet believes that this state may
well have been the Land of Yam that was Harkhuf's destination in the voyage
previously described.[133] Between Kush and Egypt lay another kingdom ruled
from the city of Sai.[134]

By the Middle Period, beginning in say 3450 BC, Kush was a powerful state.
Its rulers wore the long White Crown of Ta-Seti. Its burial practices may well

Kush (Sudan). After the great age of Kerma, Kush was conquered by Egypt. The Kushites began to build temples influenced by Egyptian styles. A good example is reproduced here - the Temple of Bes at Gebel Barkal, built by Pharaoh Taharqo (ruled 690-664 BC). Painted by Linant in the early nineteenth century.

indicate that their main deity was Amen, as in Egypt at the same period. Its soldiers gained an important reputation for their skills in warfare. They were armed with bows and arrows. Kushite power was indirectly reflected in the massive fortresses built by the Egyptian pharaohs of later dynasties to keep the Kushites at bay. In later years, the Kushites pillaged these forts and carried away Egyptian artefacts.[135]

The great epoch in Kushite history was the Classic Period, which began in 1750 BC according to Bonnet. Kush became a powerful and very large state. They seized control of the Sai kingdom and therefore dominated the whole of the Nubian Nile from the First Cataract.[136] Professor Hansberry, the great African-American historian, informs us of an Egyptian inscription in the city of Waset that names 242 towns, cities, and districts in Kush and also Punt.[137]

Kerma became a great city. At this time, it was the largest city in Africa that lay outside Egyptian territory. At the peak of its power it covered 65 acres. Surrounding the central parts of the city was a wall of massive size with a ditch in front of it. The walls were 30 feet high and made of mud bricks. They had rectangular towers that projected and also had four fortified gates. Inside the city lay the gardens, the palace of the king, the houses of the nobility and the *deffufa*, a large white temple. There was also a second religious complex separated by a 16 foot wall. This complex consisted of bronze workshops, storerooms, housing for the priests, and also chapels. Archaeologists working in the city have detected a large audience hall that probably dates from the Middle Period. This building was circular and may have been thatched. Also found were thousands of mud blanks that would have been used for making seals. This gives evidence that business transactions took place. There was also a great palace. It had an audience hall that included a throne on a raised platform. The king sat here and received delegations. Several large columns supported the roof and the building is believed to have been 25 feet high.[138]

In its time, the kingdom of Kush controlled gold mines and also major trade routes between Egypt and the rest of Africa. The goods sold into Egypt were incense, ebony, ivory, ostrich eggs, animal skins and slaves. Kush itself produced high-quality pottery that was eggshell thin. It was the finest ceramics industry produced in the ancient world. They also produced bronze implements of exceptional quality.[139]

The kings were buried in huge tombs over 262 feet in diameter. These tombs were filled with luxury products such as jewellery, weaponry, pottery and inlaid furniture. Some of the products were of Egyptian manufacture such as vessels and stone sculptures.[140]

It seems that the decline of the kingdom of Kush was related to the drying up of its water supply. The two Nile channels that used to feed the city dried up and consequently the city went into decline.[141] As will be explained, the final blow came with the rise of Egypt's Eighteenth Dynasty whose destructive campaigns destroyed the city.

Notes

[1] Boyce Rensberger, *Nubian Monarchy Called Oldest,* in *New York Times,* 1 March 1979, pp.1 and 16.
[2] 'Ethiopia' in this sense is in a different location to the modern country of the same name. The two should not be confused with each other.
[3] Boyce Rensberger, *Nubian Monarchy Called Oldest,* pp.1 and 16.
[4] Ibid., p.16.
[5] Ibid.
[6] Also reprinted as Bruce Williams, *The Lost Pharaohs of Nubia,* in *Egypt Revisited,* ed Ivan Van Sertima, US, Transaction Publishers, 1989, p.90.
[7] Ibid., p.92.
[8] Ibid., pp.93-4.
[9] Bruce Beyer Williams, *The A-Group Royal Cemetery at Qustul: Cemetery L,* US, The Oriental Institute of the University of Chicago, 1986, p.158.

[10] Ibid., p.131 and plates 64 and 110.

[11] Ibid., plates 64-65.

[12] Ibid., plates 63 and 66-7.

[13] Ibid., plates 98-104.

[14] Ibid., plates 39-48 and Bruce Williams, *The Lost Pharaohs of Nubia*, pp.94 and 102.

[15] Bruce Williams, *The Lost Pharaohs of Nubia*, p.100.

[16] Ibid., pp.94-5.

[17] Ibid., p.93.

[18] Ibid., p.97.

[19] Michael Rice, *Egypt's Making*, UK, Routledge, 1990, p.136.

[20] Bruce Williams, *The Lost Pharaohs of Nubia*, p.99.

[21] Ibid., p.96.

[22] Ibid.

[23] John Jackson, *Introduction to African Civilizations*, US, Citadel Press, 1970, p.93.

[24] James Henry Breasted, *A History of Egypt*, US, Bantam Books, 1967, p.95.

[25] Quoted in John Jackson, *Man, God, and Civilization*, US, Citadel Press, 1972, p.145.

[26] Diodorus Siculus, *Library of History, Volume II*, US, Loeb Classical Library, 1967, pp.89-91.

[27] Francis Griffith & Herbert Thompson ed, *The Leyden Papyrus: An Egyptian Magical Book*, US, Dover Press, 1974, pp.74-5.

[28] Quoted in Cheikh Anta Diop, *African Origin of Civilization: Myth or Reality?* US, Lawrence Hill Books, 1974, pp.76.

[29] E. A. Wallis Budge, *The Book of the Dead*, US, University Books, 1960, p.108.

[30] Ibid., p.116.

[31] Ibid., p.175.

[32] Ibid., p.131.

[33] J. A. Rogers, *100 Amazing Facts about the Negro*, US, Helga M. Rogers, 1957, p.30.

[34] Cheikh Anta Diop, *Civilization or Barbarism*, US, Lawrence Hill Books, 1991, pp.105-7.

[35] Bruce Williams, *The Lost Pharaohs of Nubia*, p.97.

[36] Charles Finch, *The Star of Deep Beginnings*, US, Khenti, 1998, p.17.

[37] Bruce Williams, *The Lost Pharaohs of Nubia*, p.103.

[38] Ibid., pp.100 and 103.

[39] Ibid., p.103.

[40] Ibid., pp.95, 101-2.

[41] Ibid., p.103.

[42] Richard Poe, *Black Spark: White Fire*, US, Prima Publishing, 1997, p.428.

[43] Tracy L. Prowse and Nancy C. Lovell, *Concordance of Cranial and Dental Morphological Traits and Evidence for Endogamy in Ancient Egypt*, in *American Journal of Physical Anthropology, Volume 101*, October 1996, p.237.

[44] Quoted in Drusilla Dunjee Houston, *Wonderful Ethiopians of the Ancient Cushite Empire*, US, Black Classic Press, 1985, pp.17-8.

[45] Bruce Williams, *The Lost Pharaohs of Nubia*, p.102.

[46] Chancellor Williams, *The Destruction of Black Civilization*, US, Third World Press, 1987, p.123.

[47] Vivian Davies and Renée Friedman, *Egypt*, UK, British Museum Press, 1998, pp.11-3.

[48] Ibid., p.16.

[49] Ibid., pp.17-8.

[50] Michael Rice, *Egypt's Making,* UK, Routledge, 1991, p.149.

[51] Vivian Davies and Renée Friedman, *Egypt,* pp.23-7.

[52] Ibid., pp.27-8.

[53] Ibid., pp.29-30.

[54] See E. A. Wallis Budge, *Egypt in the Neolithic and Archaic Periods,* UK, Kegan Paul, Trench, Trübner & Co., 1902, p.130.

[55] George Rawlinson (translator), *History of Herodotus: Volume II, Third Edition,* UK, John Murray, 1875, pp.163-4.

[56] Vivian Davies and Renée Friedman, *Egypt,* pp.32-3.

[57] Barbara Watterson, *The Egyptians,* UK, Blackwell Publishers, 1997, pp.42-3.

[58] Erik Hornung, *History of Ancient Egypt,* UK, Edinburgh University Press, 1999, p.6.

[59] Vivian Davies and Renée Friedman, *Egypt,* p.35.

[60] Ibid., pp.35-8.

[61] Ibid., p.38.

[62] John Jackson, *Man, God, and Civilization,* pp.218-9.

[63] Erik Hornung, *History of Ancient Egypt,* pp.6-8.

[64] Michael Rice, *Egypt's Making,* p.116.

[65] Erik Hornung, *History of Ancient Egypt,* pp.6-8.

[66] Ibid., p.8.

[67] Michael Rice, *Egypt's Making,* pp.120-1.

[68] Ibid., p.126.

[69] Ibid., pp.122-4 and 162.

[70] Diedre Wimby, *The Female Horuses and Great Wives of Kemet,* in *Black Women in Antiquity,* ed Ivan Van Sertima, US, Transaction Publishers, 1988, pp.38-9.

[71] Erik Hornung, *History of Ancient Egypt,* pp.8-9.

[72] Michael Rice, *Egypt's Making,* pp.125-6.

[73] Ibid., p.126.

[74] Cheikh Anta Diop, *Civilization and Barbarism,* p.284.

[75] Charles S. Finch, *Science and Symbol in Egyptian Medicine: Commentaries on the Edwin Smith Papyrus,* in *Egypt Revisited,* ed Ivan Van Sertima, US, Transaction Publishers, 1989, pp. 325-351.

[76] Ibid., p.349.

[77] Erik Hornung, *History of Ancient Egypt,* pp.4 and 10.

[78] Ibid., p.10.

[79] Ibid., pp.10-1.

[80] Ibid., p.11.

[81] Ibid., pp.11-2.

[82] Barbara Watterson, *The Egyptians,* pp.45 and 67.

[83] Sir E. A. Wallis Budge, *A History of Ethiopia, Nubia & Abyssinia, Volume I,* UK, Methuen & Co, 1928, p.7.

[84] Rev. James Baikie, *The Life of the Ancient East,* UK, A. & C. Black, 1923, pp.44-6.

[85] Vivian Davies and Renée Friedman, *Egypt,* pp.57-63.

[86] Ibid., pp.64-69.

[87] Erik Hornung, *History of Ancient Egypt,* p.21.

[88] John Ruffle, *Heritage of the Pharaohs,* UK, Phaidon Press, 1977, p.31.

[89] Erik Hornung, *History of Ancient Egypt,* pp.13-6.

[90] Michael Rice, *Egypt's Making,* p.178.

[91] Erik Hornung, *History of Ancient Egypt,* pp.13-6.

[92] Michael Rice, *Egypt's Making,* p.172.
[93] John Ruffle, *Heritage of the Pharaohs,* p.31.
[94] Michael Rice, *Egypt's Making,* p.173.
[95] Alan Mitchell, *Imhotep: He Who Comes in Peace,* in *The Alarm Journal,* ed Robin Walker, UK, Alarm Promotions, Spring/Summer 1997, pp.9-11.
[96] Vivian Davies and Renée Friedman, *Egypt,* p.70.
[97] Ibid., pp.53-6.
[98] Ibid., pp.44-6.
[99] Barbara Watterson, *The Egyptians,* p.51.
[100] Erik Hornung, *History of Ancient Egypt,* pp.20-1.
[101] Vivian Davies and Renée Friedman, *Egypt,* pp.70-7 and Erik Hornung, *History of Ancient Egypt,* pp.17-9.
[102] Erik Hornung, *History of Ancient Egypt,* p.19.
[103] Michael Rice, *Egypt's Making,* pp.198-99.
[104] Barbara Watterson, *The Egyptians,* p.72.
[105] Ibid., pp.70-1 and 75.
[106] Ibid., p.74.
[107] Erik Hornung, *History of Ancient Egypt,* p.24.
[108] W. Marsham Adams, *The Book of the Master,* US, ECA Associates, 1990 (original 1898), pp.105-6.
[109] Erik Hornung, *History of Ancient Egypt,* pp.22-5.
[110] Ibid., pp.26-7.
[111] Jacob Carruthers, *Essays in Ancient Egyptian Studies,* US, Timbuktu Press, 1984, p.95.
[112] Roland Oliver & Brian Fagan, *Africa in the Iron Age,* UK, Cambridge University Press, 1975, p.4.
[113] Peter Tompkins, *Secrets of the Great Pyramid,* US, Harper Colophon, 1978, p.117.
[114] Vivian Davies and Renée Friedman, *Egypt,* pp.77-82 and Erik Hornung, History of Ancient Egypt, pp.27-8.
[115] Erik Hornung, *History of Ancient Egypt,* pp.30-1.
[116] Ibid., p.31.
[117] Vivian Davies and Renée Friedman, *Egypt,* pp.88-92.
[118] Ibid., p.92.
[119] Michael Rice, *Egypt's Making,* p.209.
[120] Erik Hornung, *History of Ancient Egypt,* p.33.
[121] Ibid., p.37.
[122] Maulana Karenga, *Selections from The Husia,* US, The University of Sankore Press, 1984, p.43.
[123] Vivian Davies and Renée Friedman, *Egypt,* pp.92 and 95.
[124] Erik Hornung, *History of Ancient Egypt,* p.37.
[125] Ibid., pp.38-9.
[126] Norris & Ross McWhirter, *Guinness Book of Records, 21st Edition,* UK, Guinness Superlatives Limited, October 1974, p.183.
[127] Vivian Davies and Renée Friedman, *Egypt,* pp.49-50.
[128] Quoted in Vivian Davies and Renée Friedman, *Egypt,* p.50.
[129] Wayne Chandler, *Of Gods and Men: Egypt's Old Kingdom,* in *Egypt Revisited,* ed Ivan Van Sertima, US, Transaction Publishers, 1989, p.175.
[130] A. Joseph Ben-Levi, *The First and Second Intermediate Periods in Kemetic History,* in *Kemet and the African Worldview,* ed Jacob Carruthers and Maulana Karenga, US, University of Sankore Press, 1986, p.56.

[131] Erik Hornung, *History of Ancient Egypt*, p.41.

[132] Charles Bonnet, *The Kingdom of Kerma*, in *Sudan: Ancient Kingdoms of the Nile*, ed Dietrich Wildung, France, The Institut du monde arabe, 1997, pp.89-90.

[133] Ibid.

[134] Christopher Ehret, *The Civilizations of Africa*, UK, James Currey, 2002, p.149.

[135] Charles Bonnet, *The Kingdom of Kerma*, in *Sudan: Ancient Kingdoms of the Nile*, p.90.

[136] Christopher Ehret, *The Civilizations of Africa*, pp.149-50.

[137] Joseph E. Harris ed, *Africa and Africans as Seen by Classical Writers: The William Leo Hansberry African History Notebook, Volume II*, US, Howard University Press, 1981, p.12.

[138] Vivian Davies and Renée Friedman, *Egypt*, pp.122-9.

[139] Ibid., p.127 and Charles S. Finch, *The Star of Deep Beginnings*, US, Khenti, 1998, p.31.

[140] Vivian Davies and Renée Friedman, *Egypt*, p.127.

[141] Ibid., pp.128-9.

CHAPTER SEVEN: THE LATER HISTORY OF THE NILE VALLEY

The First Intermediate Period

After the fall of the Old Kingdom the public monuments were plundered. Temples were violated, tombs were pillaged, statues were shattered,[1] and the central economy collapsed. This period of chaos is generally called the First Intermediate Period. During this time, nomarchs organised raids on other regions to plunder food. Peasants were forced to arm themselves. The middle classes, by contrast, lived in the relative safety of their walled residences.[2] In the midst of this upheaval a new literature developed. It was quite unlike the old mortuary literature and biographies. These works, on the social and political turmoil, became classics to be studied at school in much later pharaonic periods when stability returned. *The Admonitions of Ipuwer,* for example, describes the revolt of the poor, and the invasions from Asia:

> A man regards his son as his enemy ... the tribes of the desert have become Kemites [i.e. Egyptians] everywhere ... what the ancestors foretold has arrived at fruition ... the land is full of confederates, and a man goes to plow with his shield ... Indeed, hearts are violent, pestilence is everywhere, blood is throughout the land, death is not lacking, and the mummy-cloth speaks even before one comes near it. Indeed, the land turns round like a potter's wheel; the robber is a possessor of riches and a rich man has become a plunderer ... barbarians from abroad have come to Kemet. Those who were Kemites have become foreigners and are thrust aside ... and the man of rank can no longer be distinguished from him who is nobody ... All is ruined.[3]

There were also developments in sacred literature. *The Coffin Texts* were partly a restatement of the *Pyramid Texts* but with new developments added. Preserved on wooden coffins, their function was to accompany the dead person with all the spells they would need in the journey through their afterlife.[4]

In 4188 BC a group of oligarchs tried to establish hegemony over the city of Memphis. Manetho identifies these rulers as the Egyptian Seventh Dynasty. According to Africanus, 70 kings ruled in 70 days. Doubtless an exaggeration, but it highlights the extent of the political instability. Eusebius, another scholar, records Manetho as saying that this dynasty consisted of 4 kings that ruled in 75 days. This seems far more believable to us.[5]

The Eighth Dynasty also ruled from Memphis. Consisting of 27 kings, they ruled for 146 years (4188-4042 BC).

The Ninth Dynasty (4042-3633 BC) ruled from Herakleopolis as did the Tenth Dynasty (3633-3448 BC) that followed them. The latter dynasty built modest sized pyramids at Saqqara.[6] Of the 38 rulers of the two dynasties, the best acknowledged today are Kheti I, Kheti II, Neferkare, Kheti VII and Merikare, all of the Ninth Dynasty.[7] Pharaoh Kheti VII wrote the famous *Instruction of Merikare* for Merikare, his young son. It advised the young man on how to be a good ruler when he inherited the throne. A reading of this text shows that stability had certainly been achieved during this period. Pharaonic hegemony was firmly established from Thinis in the south to the Mediterranean in the north. The text describes conflicts with the Libyans in the western Delta and the Bedouins of the eastern Delta, but this is no different to the problems faced by earlier kings. The lands to the south of Thinis, it seems, belonged to Kush.[8] This document, in any case, refutes the notion fashionable among current historians and Egyptologists that Egypt at this time was in total chaos ruled by simultaneous dynasties. The Herakleopolitans stayed in power until 3448 BC but a rival dynasty did in fact arise to challenge them. These rivals ruled from the southern city of Waset.

Little seems to be known about Mentuhotep I, the founder of the rival Eleventh Dynasty. In 3548 BC, Antef I succeeded him. Antef II was the first ruler of Waset to assume the full insignia of royalty. His forces challenged the power of the Herakleopolitans to the north probably making Tefibi the northern boundary. He seized the city of Abydos and the entire Thinite nome to the south, extending his power to the First Cataract. After a distinguished rule of nearly fifty years, his son succeeded him.[9]

Middle Kingdom Egypt

A successor ruler, Mentuhotep II, completed the reunification of Egypt after finally defeating his Herakleopolitan rivals and expelling the troublesome Asiatic element. This marks the beginning of the Middle Kingdom. Waset was now established as the capital.[10] Mentuhotep II ruled for 51 years. During his career, he created the office of Overseer of Lower Egypt, his ships sailed to Byblos to collect wood, and monuments were built in Upper Egypt. The Mortuary Temple in Deir-el-Bahri combined a rock cut tomb with a pyramid tomb. Also built were rock-cut tombs for his important officials.[11] At a much later period, his Mortuary Temple inspired Pharaoh Hatshepsut to build her temple, currently one of Egypt's most celebrated monuments.[12]

Mentuhotep III ascended the throne in 3424 BC. He built monuments in the Delta. One of his officials made an expedition to Punt.[13] During the period of

Egypt. Admirable portrait statue of Pharaoh Mentuhotep II (ruled 3475-3424 BC), Eleventh Dynasty. He was the founder of the Egyptian Middle Kingdom. (Photo: Fari Supiya).

his successor, Mentuhotep IV, quarrying was resumed in Hammamat. Some ten thousand men were recruited to work in this region from all over the country. We are informed, from an inscription, that during this campaign: "My soldiers returned without loss; not a man perished, not a troop was missing, not an ass died, not a workman was enfeebled."[14] This king, however, seems to have been an ineffectual ruler who failed to check the growing power of the nomarchs. Some of the problems of decentralisation associated with Pepi II re-emerged.[15]

Amenemhet I was of the nomarchy of Elephantine. At first, he was the Prime Minister of Mentuhotep IV, but overthrew him in 3405 BC.[16] He moved the royal residence to a site near the modern town of el-Lisht, near to Memphis. Returning to old ideas, he built a mortuary temple of fluted columns. He also erected a pyramid. Rising to a lofty 352 feet, it was the largest built since the Fifth Dynasty.[17] His officials were buried nearby in mastabas. Waset remained the centre of Amen worship. In this city, he built the statues and altar in the Temple of Amen in Luxor. In the Nubian cities of Buhen and Wawat, he built great castles with walls 16 feet thick and nearly 30 feet high. These monuments guarded Egyptian control over the Nubian gold mines and quarries. In the eastern Delta, he built fortifications to secure routes to the Sinai peninsular. This led to Egyptian control of the copper and turquoise mines. Amenemhet I, however, was unable to secure the western border with Libya. He thus resorted to occasional campaigns to deal with this element.[18] The king's palace was astonishing - a veritable fever of the gods. Its doors were overlaid with sheet copper fitted with bolts of bronze. The floors were inlaid with silver. Its walls were embellished with gold leaf. The roof was made of sycamore. Finally, lapis lazuli decorated its ceilings.[19]

Canon Rawlinson was the Camden Professor of Ancient History at the University of Oxford. He was very impressed by the Twelfth Dynasty, and wrote the following précis of its achievements:

> The wise rulers of the time devoted their energies and their resources, not, as the earlier kings, to piling up undying memorials of themselves in the shape of monuments that "reached to heaven," but to useful works, to the excavation of wells and reservoirs, the making of roads, the encouragement of commerce, and the development of the vast agricultural wealth of the country. They also diligently guarded the frontiers, chastised aggressive tribes, and checked invasion by the establishment of strong fortresses in positions of importance. They patronized art, employing themselves in building temples rather than tombs, and adorned their temples not only with reliefs and statues, but also with the novel architectural embellishment of the obelisk, a delicate form, and one especially suited to the country.[20]

Before the Twelfth Dynasty period historians know of only two organised states on the planet earth - Nubia and Egypt. During the Twelfth Dynasty period, states would appear for the first time in Asia. Of these, Sumer (located in modern Iraq) emerged first around 3300 BC. It was quickly followed by Elam (located in modern Iran), Akkad (in Iraq and Syria), and then the Indus Valley Civilisation (in western India and Pakistan). With the controversial exception of Crete, there were no other known civilisations on the planet earth at this date. There are, however, historians from the British Isles who claim that Stonehenge and also various structures built in Ireland and northern Scotland, deserve consideration as evidence of very early civilisation in Europe.

According to Dr Hornung, Senwosret I (3376-3331 BC) "would be first surpassed as an architect only by the great kings of Dynasty 18".[21] He built the Kiosk for Amen in Karnak. It was a fine building with finely executed reliefs of reused blocks. He commissioned the Temple of Ra in Heliopolis where he added two red granite obelisks. In Abydos, he constructed important buildings. In the country of Wawat, far to the south, he completed the colonisation. He built the castles of Quban and Aniba. His armies penetrated Kushite territory.[22] In year 38 of his reign, Ameny, his herald, led a force of 17,000 men to carry 150 statues and 60 sphinxes as part of the royal construction programme. Donkeys were used as beasts of burden.[23]

Amenemhet II, the following king, came to power in 3331 BC. He built a shrine to Hathor in Sinai and the White Pyramid of Dashur.[24] From this period, trade goods were discovered among the Treasures of Tod. Archaeologists found four copper chests in the foundations of the Temple of Mountu at Tod, near Waset. In the chests were precious metals and stones, and also works of art from Sumer and Crete. Also found were cylinder seals from the Third Sumerian Dynasty of Ur.[25] This evidence may indicate that the Amenemhet II period was contemporaneous with Ur Dynasty III but this is controversial and we will discuss this issue in a later chapter. Unfortunately, however, slave trading was going on at this time, to cite Professor Hornung once more: "[U]nlike the Old Kingdom, we can distinguish a brisk trade in slaves in this period; there were not enough military undertakings to explain the ever-growing number of Asiatic slaves in Egypt."[26]

Senwosret II ruled over an eventful nineteen years. He built dams and canals around Lake Moeris to allow irrigation of the Fayum region. He erected a pyramid tomb near el-Lahun. Nearby, he constructed Kahun, a town of officials, priests and workers. It had over a hundred houses where even the smallest homes for people of the lowest rank had 4 to 6 rooms and an area of 1,022 square feet or larger.[27] Excavations revealed that this city was the world's first known example of town planning. Kahun was rectangular and walled. Inside, the city was divided into two parts. One part housed the wealthier inhabitants - the scribes, officials and foremen. The other part housed the ordinary people. The streets of the western section in particular, were straight,

Egypt (Sudan). Reconstruction of Semnah Castle in Kush. Built by Pharaoh Senwosret III (ruled 3280-3242 BC), Twelfth Dynasty. Despite the age of this monument, it looks very ahead of its time. From Adolf Erman, *Life in Ancient Egypt* (UK, Macmillan and Co., 1894, p.525).

laid out on a grid, and crossed each other at right angles. A stone gutter, over half a metre wide, ran down the centre of every street. Positioned to benefit from the cool north winds, five single storey mansions were found along the northern edge of the city. Their doorways were arched. Each boasted 70 rooms, divided into four sections or quarters. There was a master's quarter, quarters for women and servants, quarters for offices and finally, quarters for granaries, each facing a central courtyard. The master's quarters had an open court with a stone water tank for bathing. Surrounding this was a colonnade. Of the maze of rooms, some were barrel vaulted in brick but others were wooden and thatched. The ceilings were supported by wooden and stone columns some with palmiform capitals. Limewash coated the walls, but some rooms contained frescoes.[28]

Senwosret III had a long and illustrious career on the throne, ruling for 38 years.[29] In Egypt he undermined the power of the nomarchs. In Wawat he built a string of castles spread over a distance of 30 miles. Throughout Nubia he was worshipped as a god. In Palestine his armies marched, spreading Egyptian writing and the Egyptian calendar. Finally, on the cultural front, there were great developments of expressive portrait sculpture during his time.[30]

Amenemhet III, the last great ruler of the dynasty (3242-3195 BC), built two important pyramids, at Hawara and Dashur. The former monument had a sepulchral chamber weighing a staggering 110 tons of yellow quartzite.[31] He built a hall of granite pillars for Sobek. At Medinet Madi he built a temple to Renenutet, the Goddess of the harvest. At Hawara he built the Labyrinth with its massive layout, multiple courtyards, chambers and halls. The very largest building in antiquity, it boasted 3,000 rooms. One thousand five hundred were above ground and the other one thousand five hundred were underground. Our old friend, Herodotus, saw it in ruins three thousand years later. He was still somewhat impressed:

> I visited this place, and found it to surpass description; for if all the walls and other great works of the Greeks could be put together in one, they would not equal, either for labour or expense, this Labyrinth; and yet the [Greek] temple of Ephesus is a building worthy of note, and so is the temple of Samos. The pyramids likewise surpass description, and are equal to a number of the greatest works of the Greeks; but the Labyrinth surpasses the pyramids.[32]

Amenemhet III's daughter, Nefruptah had a rich burial.[33] After this impressive period, Amenemhet IV ruled for nine years and was succeeded by Queen Regent Sebekneferura, the last ruler of the dynasty. This obscure reign spelled the end of the Middle Kingdom. "The glory of the Middle Kingdom, however," says a modern authority, "had been firmly implanted in the Kemetic [i.e. Egyptian] consciousness and did not fade. Over the centuries it was regarded as Kmt's [i.e. Egypt's] classical period."[34]

The Second Intermediate Period

The Thirteenth Dynasty began to rule in 3182 BC. Manetho tells us that it consisted of 60 kings of Waset that ruled for a lengthy 453 years. A period of great political upheaval, modern historians call this the Second Intermediate Period. The weakening of pharaonic authority meant more power was concentrated into the hands of the viziers. In the far south the castles of Buhen were burned. The Nubians became independent. Egypt's southern boundary returned to Elephantine.

In the north nomadic Semites infiltrated the eastern Delta. These foreigners probably worshipped Ba'al, later to be identified with Set, the Nile Valley god of the south. The nomads built the city of Avaris. Asiatic slaves and freemen, already in the country, increased the numbers and influence of the Semites. Asians building pyramids at Dashur and Saqqara reflected this power. In time the Delta became independent under the Asian Dynasty Fourteen.[35] They were the first White kings to rule any part of African territory. Manetho implies that it consisted of 76 kings, some of whom ruled independently for 184 years after the fall of Dynasty Thirteen. We do not know the dates for the earliest kings, but they were contemporary with Dynasty Thirteen except ruling from the north. We can certainly deduce that the Asians ruled from 2729 BC, the date for the fall of the Thirteenth Dynasty, until 2545 BC, as the sole masters of Egypt.

Modern Egyptologists under the spell of Meyer and Breasted tend to mystify then dismiss this period as if it did not exist. However, Manetho claims 136 kings for Dynasties Thirteen and Fourteen. The *Royal Papyrus of Turin,* another Egyptian source, names 116 of them. Moreover, the time periods given by the Papyrus, although fragmentary and in need of interpretation, corroborate Manetho. We shall discuss this in a later chapter.

In 2545 BC Egypt was conquered by a new set of rulers - the Hyksos. Manetho informs us that:

> A blast of God smote us; and unexpectedly, from the regions of the East, invaders of obscure race marched in confidence of victory against our land. By main force they easily seized it without striking a blow; and having overpowered the rulers of the land, they then burned our cities ruthlessly ... and treated all the natives with a cruel hostility, massacring some and leading into slavery the wives and children of others. Finally, they appointed as king one of their number whose name was Salitis.[36]

These conquerors, of west Semitic origin, dominated the lands for over 669 years ruling as the Fifteenth and Sixteenth Dynasties. We believe, however, that Manetho muddled the order of the dynasties, incorrectly placing Dynasty Sixteen before Fifteen. In our view, Salitis, named above, was actually the first king of the *Sixteenth* Dynasty. Dynasty Fifteen consisted of 32 Hyksos kings. Twenty-four of these are named in a Greek language document called the *Book of Sothis.* We believe that the lengths of reigns given by this source are overly generous, but the order is reliable. Dynasty Sixteen (1993-1709 BC) consisted of six rulers from Salitis to Ipepi. Of all the Hyksos kings, however, Khyan and Ipepi were probably the most important. It should be noted, however, that the origin of the Hyksos remains controversial. Many writers echoing Josephus, the great Roman Jewish historian, identify them as the Ancient Israelites. If this is true then the Old Testament of the Bible is largely, if not completely, false.

The Hyksos established their capital city at the Asian-dominated site of Avaris.[37] Excavations reveal that it was nearly one square mile and had houses, tombs, palaces, and temples. A wall of mud bricks, 26 feet thick, surrounded the city. The buildings within the walls show some affinity with those of Canaan or perhaps those of Western Asia. The position of Avaris allowed the Hyksos to control trade routes that led to the Mediterranean and the Middle East by sea and by land.[38]

The conquering rulers made overtures to the Kingdom of Kush. They hoped to secure their southern border and also build trade links with the rest of Africa. However, some Egyptians, led by Seqenenre Tao II, rebelled against them. Seqenenre, of the Seventeenth Dynasty, began a war of liberation. The foreign rulers had military advantages, however. With stronger chariots, giving greater speed, they also had powerful weapons. The Hyksos possessed a new type of bow design that could fire over a much greater distance than an ordinarily wooden bow. Seqenenre Tao II died in the battle. Kamose succeeded him on the throne.[39]

A famous inscription, written by Pharaoh Kamose, gives an account of his campaign against the elderly Hyksos king Ipepi.[40] Part of which reads as follows:

> Behold, I have come, I am successful … As the mighty Am[e]n endures, I will not leave you alone, I will not let you tread the fields without being upon you. O wicked of heart, vile Asiatic, I shall drink the wine of your vineyard … I lay waste your dwelling place, I cut down your trees.[41]

The Egyptians were worried about an alliance between the foreigners and the Kingdom of Kush. The *Kamose Stela* tells us that the Hyksos ruler of Egypt wrote a letter to the King of Kush asking him to intervene in Egyptian affairs. Part of the letter reads as follows:

> He [i.e. Kamose] chose the two lands to persecute them, my lands and yours, and he has ravaged them. Come, navigate downstream, do not be afraid. Behold he is here with me. There is no one who will be waiting for you in this Egypt, for I will not let him go until you have arrived. Then we shall divide the towns of this Egypt, and the lands of Khent-hen-nefer [i.e. Nubia] will be in joy.[42]

The messenger entrusted to carry this letter never got to his destination. The Egyptian army intercepted him. This letter is, however, evidence that the Kushites were literate. Kamose did not see the final defeat of the foreign rulers of Egypt. He died before his campaign could be completed. He did, however, conquer as far as the Faiyum.[43]

New Kingdom Egypt

Ahmose I, his brother (1709-1683 BC), defeated the Hyksos and drove them out of the north, having stormed Memphis and then Avaris. By this conquest, Ahmose founded a new dynasty. Although a continuation of the Seventeenth Dynasty, historians call it the Eighteenth Dynasty, marking the beginning of the New Kingdom period. This was the last great era when Negro Egyptians ruled an independent Egypt. Egypt (and for that matter Libya) had, however, changed. Both countries now contained large Asian and Afro-Asian populations who had become part of the society over the previous one thousand years. Many of these Asian populations were White or near White. In addition, the political landscape to the east had changed. Civilisations and states emerged all over western and southern Asia. Some of these would challenge Egypt. Moreover, the Twelfth Dynasty was seen as a lost bygone era where the only remains were now crumbling monuments then over 1,400 years old. The New Kingdom Egyptians would look to this era as a source of inspiration and also a source of building materials - to be plundered!

Ahmose led other campaigns. He marched into Canaan and successfully captured the city of Sharuhen. There, he gained control over the copper mines. This conquest signified the beginnings of the Egyptian Empire.[44] After this campaign, he seized Wawat to the south encountering little resistance. Egypt now controlled the gold mines and the quarries of the region.[45] Further south, however, the Kushites put up a stronger resistance. Only after several campaigns of a successor king did the Egyptians finally triumph there.[46] Ahmose created the new post of Viceroy to administrate the south - King's Son of Kush and Overseer of the Southern Foreign Countries - titles that would be in use for hundreds of years. The viceroy ruled from the city of Aniba. Guarding Egyptian power, he built a huge fortified complex in Buhen. Besides, he restored the older Twelfth Dynasty castles. In Egypt, he introduced a new administration system. Offices were inherited, and he took steps to limit the power of the nomarchs. Waset, the city of Amen, once more became the religious capital of the empire. Finally, in Abydos, he built a mortuary complex.[47]

Amenhotep I ascended the throne in 1682 BC. He gathered about him a creative elite of scientists, artists, architects, poets and theologians. This elite created the greatest intellectual and cultural flowering since the glorious Twelfth Dynasty. The *Ebers Papyrus,* the famous medical text, was written during this time as was the *Book of the Hidden Chamber,* a religious text. The latter book is noteworthy because it depicts the concept of Hell. Another achievement concerns the astronomer, Amenemhet. He constructed a water clock. Finally, Amenhotep I commissioned constructions at Karnak. The rulers from this time would attempt to outdo each other in religious piety demonstrated by how much they could contribute to the building programme in the city of Waset.[48]

Pharaoh Thutmose I, his successor, became the decisive conqueror of Kush in 1661 BC. He burnt the capital city of Kerma after having it sacked.[49] In Asia, he marched as far as the river Euphrates taking Palestine and Syria with little resistance. The Egyptian Empire had Memphis as its military headquarters meanwhile Karnak remained the seat of the intellectuals and theologians.

Inene, the Mayor of Waset, oversaw the construction of the Temple of Amen. He also supervised the building of tombs in the Valley of the Kings. Thutmose's young son, Amenmesse, was given a military upbringing in Memphis and was later appointed Generalissimo of the army.[50]

Hatshepsut was the next great ruler of the dynasty. In September 1650 BC Thutmose I, her father, elevated her to the position of co-regent. Following this in 1628 BC she became the Great Royal Wife of Thutmose II. In 1615 BC she ruled as Queen-Regent for Thutmose III but later deposed him.[51] She proclaimed herself pharaoh in his place and took the religious titles the "female Horus" and the "daughter of Ra". She was deeply religious and did much to undermine the veneration of Set, the deity promoted by the Hyksos and identified as their deity Ba'al. Her leading statesmen, both of humble origins, Senenmut and Hapuseneb, oversaw her building activities. She also appointed Asians to powerful positions within the administration, the first pharaoh to do so.[52] At Karnak she erected two giant obelisks that rose to almost 100 feet:

> To make the obelisks still more conspicuous [says J. A. Rogers], she had their tops encased in electrum, a metal costlier than gold. (Electrum was a composition of silver and gold. Silver being rather rarer in Egypt, it was more precious.) In the bright sunlight of that rainless land the obelisks shone like glittering peaks. Their brilliancy, in the queen's own words, lit up the two lands of Egypt.[53]

In Deir-el-Bahri, she built her celebrated rock-hewn temple dedicated to Amen, Anubis and Hathor (see page 81). In this temple are records of her famous maritime voyage to Punt (i.e. possibly Somalia or Ethiopia). In that land, the Egyptians bought incense, animals, animal skins, gum, gold, ivory and ebony. To pay for it, they brought weapons, jewellery and wares. On the cultural front, great lyric poetry was composed during her period.[54]

Early in the reign of Thutmose III, the next ruler, there were threats from Asia. Asian rulers were unifying against Egyptian interests and siding with the Mitanni. In 1599 BC Thutmose III attacked the Asian coalition in the first of seventeen campaigns to retake the lands to the Euphrates (i.e. Syria). He set up a strict system of administration for the Asian territories headed by General Djehuty. Asian princes who submitted to Egyptian rule kept some control over their territories. Their sons were raised at the Egyptian court.[55]

His campaigns increased Egyptian power further south as far as the Fourth Cataract in Kush. On the site of an old Kushite settlement, Thutmose III built a new regional capital. This city, known as Napata, had a famous hill nearby today called Gebel Barkal. Believed to be the dwelling place of the great god Amen-Ra, this hill maintained a sacred importance.[56] Thutmose III and his successor, Amenhotep III, established Egyptian control over the Nubian sources of gold. Over 100 mines and gold working sites have been discovered

situated in the eastern deserts of Sudan, 150 miles from the Nile.[57] The god Ra
was often portrayed in gold showing his divine qualities. Kings who wanted to
partake of those divine qualities were buried in golden coffins as was the case
with Pharaoh Tutankhamen.[58] Thutmose III received huge quantities of gold
from the Kushite mines. He imported the annual equivalent of 794 kg of gold,
which would be worth many millions today. From Kush, the pharaohs also
received huge quantities of ebony, ivory, slaves and cattle. As with the Asian
princes, the Egyptians had a policy of assimilation for the defeated princes of
Kush. Their children were taken to the Egyptian court to be indoctrinated with
Egyptian culture. At a later date these Kushites became part of the
administrative class of the Egyptian-dominated government.[59] Finally,
Thutmose III built temples throughout the empire from Gebel Barkal in the
south to Byblos in the north. He also restored the very ancient Upper Egyptian
temples of Esna, Dendera and Kom Ombo.[60]

Professor Hornung tells us that Amenhotep II, a successor, placed great
emphasis on his martial abilities. In his inscriptions, his war-like mentality is
much in evident:

> The brutality that accompanied this attitude, though, seems to have been a
> personal trait of this king; he conducted his wars with a cruelty that was foreign
> to his father, and he had the bodies of slain princes hung from the bow of the
> royal ship. The adoption of warlike Asiatic deities was well suited to this new
> atmosphere.[61]

The period of Amenhotep III, his successor, was long and distinguished.
Ascending the throne in 1538 BC, he ruled until 1501 BC. During his early
years on the throne, the dominant influences came from his mother,
Mutemwia. Later, he elevated Tiye to the position of Great Royal Wife. She
became the real centre of power in later years as illness made Amenhotep III
more and more dependent on her. Tiye built alliances by arranging diplomatic
marriages. She also bought off Asian peoples through the gift giving of gold.[62]
In return the Asians sold lapis lazuli and cedar wood. A period of much
prosperity and stability, this allowed for the construction of monuments.
Amenhotep III commissioned a brilliant new temple in the city of Luxor
containing hundreds of statues of Amen-Ra and himself. The Colossi of
Memnon stood in front of his great temple at Waset.[63] They were 65 feet high
and an awesome 720 tons each.[64] During this prosperity, members of the
administrative and ruling class shared in the wealth of the land. They had great
statues built of themselves and many could afford luxurious tombs.
Overlooking the Nile from the West Bank, these private tombs were carved
into the hills. A high official under Amenhotep II owned one of these tombs. It
had three chapels decorated with coloured paintings showing daily life
activities.[65] In Nubia, Amenhotep III built the temples of Soleb and Sedeinga.[66]

Egypt. Temple of Amen, Karnak. Built by Pharaoh Seti I (ruled 1450-1395 BC), Nineteenth Dynasty. One architectural scholar considered this monument to have been the finest one ever built by man. (Photo: Alan Mitchell).

This period was indeed a Golden Age. Goods entered Egypt from Asia Minor, Crete, Cyprus, and elsewhere in Africa paid for by Egyptian grain, papyrus, linen and leather. From Asia Minor came coniferous woods. From Syria came oils, resins, weapons of metal, and wine. From Crete came vases. From Cyprus came copper. From the Aegean came silver. From Nubia, and the lands to the south, came ebony, elephant ivory, gums, leopard and panther skins, ostrich plumes and eggs, resins, and a variety of animals. Caravan trails of donkeys, mules and asses carried goods to and from Egypt, the Western Desert, and the Isthmus of Suez. Goods changed hands with the payment of silver, gold, grain or copper. One unit or *deben* (9.1 grams) of gold, equalled two units of silver, equalled two hundred units of copper or two hundred bushels of grain.[67]

The city of Waset had a population of one million people.[68] It spread out six square miles on both sides of the Nile. On the edge of the metropolis lay the houses of the nobles. Typically of 50 or 60 rooms, they had lakes and flower-gardens, all accessed by cool, tree-shaded avenues. Inside were beautifully painted walls, exquisitely inlaid furniture, gorgeous vases and fine sculptures. These craft pieces were in gold, bronze, ebony, ivory and glass. Towards the centre of the city stood the royal palace, the House of Rejoicing, which occupied an astounding 32 hectares. Along the Nile, in the epicentre of the city, stood the great temples of Karnak and Luxor, which towered over everything. Their massive pylons, obelisks, and gates of gold and bronze, made a huge statement. In their time, the temples were animated by the activities of students and priests. Horse-drawn chariots, sometimes twenty abreast, traversed the sphinx-lined avenues. On the river, lay quays where the merchant ships of the Nile mingled with those from the Mediterranean. Across the river to the western plain stood other temples, equally magnificent, and from there led to the Valley of the Kings, the royal graveyard.[69] Professor Breasted, master of the American Egyptologists, described the buildings associated with Amenhotep III:

> He raised a massive pylon before the temple of Karnak, adorned with unsurpassed richness; stelas of lapis-lazuli were set up on either side and besides great quantities of gold and silver, nearly twelve hundred pounds of malachite were employed in the inlay work … The king also built a temple to Mut, the goddess of Thebes [i.e.Waset], where his ancestors had begun it, on the south of Karnak, and excavated a lake beside it. He then laid out a beautiful garden in the interval of over a mile and a half, which separates Karnak from the Luxor temple and connected the great avenues of rams … carved in stone, each bearing a statue of the Pharaoh between the forepaws. The general effect must have been imposing in the extreme; the brilliant hues of the polychrome architecture, with columns and gates overwrought in gold and floors overlaid with silver, the whole dominated by towering obelisks clothed in glittering

metal, rising high above the rich green of the nodding palms and tropical foliage which framed the mass, - all this must have produced an impression both of gorgeous detail and overwhelming grandeur, of which the sombre ruins of the same buildings, impressive as they are, offer little hint at the present day.[70]

Nor can the scale of the temple complexes be overlooked, to cite Reverend Baikie once more:

Comparisons may help us a little. St. Peter's, Rome, Milan, and Notre Dame, Paris, are three of the most familiar and imposing of European cathedrals - the whole three put together just equal in area the actual temple building of Karnak. Into the sacred enclosure, you could pack St. Peter's, Milan, Seville, Florence, St. Paul's, Cologne, York, Amiens, and Antwerp; while Notre Dame would go comfortably into one of the halls of Karnak, and that not the largest, though the most complex and imposing. We are dealing with by far the largest complex of religious building in the world, though the famous Labyrinth of the XIIth Dynasty Pharaoh, Amenemhat III, now almost totally destroyed, was still larger in its day.[71]

Amenhotep IV (1501-1474 BC) is best known as a religious reformer. Of this great man J. A. Rogers says the following:

Lord Supreme of the then civilized world, with the mightiest army at his command, he preached a gospel of peace and preached it so consistently that when subject nations rebelled he refused to attack them. Living centuries before King David, he [Amenhotep IV] wrote psalms as beautiful as the Judean monarch. Thirteen hundred years before Christ [i.e. using the short chronology] he preached and lived a gospel of perfect love, brotherhood, and truth. Two thousand years before Mohammed he taught the doctrine of the One God. Three thousand years before Darwin, he sensed the unity that runs through all living things. Akhenaton [sic], too was the richest man on earth.[72]

Having dispatched the High Priest of Amen to oversee a quarrying expedition, he promoted the minor deity, Aten, to the position of sole deity throughout the country. In Karnak, he built a temple to this deity enforcing a more strict monotheism. The king surrounded himself with a new set of officials. Many of these were foreigners or Egyptians of the lower orders. In this way the Amen priesthood/civil service were sidestepped. Unhappy with Waset, the king built a new capital further north called Akhetaten. The American urban planner, Earl Faruq, in an interesting essay, noted that:

Great importance was attached to cleanliness in Amarna [i.e. Akhetaten], as in other Egyptian cities. Toilets and sewers were in use to dispose waste. Soap was made for washing the body. Perfumes and essences were popular against body odor. A solution of natron was used to keep insects from houses ... Amarna was

landscaped with flowers and beautiful gardens as part of Akhenaton's [sic] land
use scheme. Amarna may have been the first planned "garden city" ... The
temples and personal chapels built throughout the city were open to the air. This
allowed for the worship of the sun which was contrasted with the closed
temples of Thebes [i.e. Waset]. Officials laid out great estates, attractively
incorporating nature into their plans. Workman['s] houses were erected on well
ordered streets in grid iron fashion.[73]

By 1493 or 1492 BC the king's religious revolution was complete. He
changed his name from Amenhotep IV to Akhenaten and instituted a revolution
in Egyptian art. Gone were the old stylised representations. In some of the new
statues, Akhenaten is portrayed as father and mother to the nation with an
appropriate synthesis of male and female body shapes. However, all was not
going well with the empire. Egypt was losing its grip on its Asian colonies.[74]

During this difficult period, Tutankhaten inherited the throne as a boy. Aya,
his chief priest, exercised authority almost as Regent. Aya led a non-violent
restoration of Amenism. In 1478 BC Waset, the city of Amen veneration,
regained its former status as capital. The young pharaoh changed his name to
show this change in religious devotion. Tutankhaten became Tutankhamen.[75]
The life and treasures of this young man has attracted the imagination of many
writers. Madame Christiane Desroches-Noublecourt wrote a splendid text on
him where she describes, among other things, his childhood education. We
could not fail to cite the following intelligence:

> Children's education began very early in Egypt at that time ... they began
> learning to read at the age of four. In the mornings, they were taught to
> recognize and pronounce the several hundred hieroglyphs representing
> everything alive and real ... When they could read the basic signs, had learned
> to conjugate verbs and to set pronouns in their proper places; when they could
> make agreements in number and gender, use figures and do mental arithmetic,
> they were then taught the hieratic script used on papyruses and *ostraca*. After
> this they were introduced to the literary language, its specialized vocabulary
> and the system used for transcribing foreign, mainly Asian, nouns. For his
> exercises the little prince was privileged to use papyrus, manufactured in Egypt
> from the time of the 1st Dynasty of fibres from the great marsh-reeds, which
> ordinary schoolchildren could not afford - this royal material was most
> expensive and generally used for making scroll-books. Schoolchildren wrote
> on calcareous slivers or potsherds, known today as *ostraca*. The teacher
> corrected the young prince as strictly as his school mates and, when their copies
> of phrases from popular fables or books of social instruction were faulty,
> marked them in red ink.[76]

On the political front, however, neither Tut nor his immediate successors,
effectively challenged the break up of the Asian Empire. Rameses I ascended
the throne in 1456 BC. During his year on the throne, he built additions in the
Karnak Complex.[77]

Egypt. Temple of Abu Simbel, Kush. Built by Pharaoh Rameses II (ruled 1394-1328 BC), Nineteenth Dynasty, by carving it out of a mountainside. Each statue is 66 feet tall. (Photo: Alan Mitchell).

Pharaoh Seti I, founder of the Nineteenth Dynasty, ruled from 1450 to 1395 BC. Unlike previous rulers, his court was principally based at Memphis. From here, he led campaigns into Asia, Nubia, and against the Libyans. His greatest architectural achievement has impressed architects for many years. He built the 134 columned Hypostyle Hall at Karnak.[78] James Fergusson, a widely respected architectural scholar, described the hall as "the most magnificent on which the eye of man has ever rested".[79] Seti, as his name suggests, was also a devotee of Set, the ancient god of the South.[80] The burial chamber of Seti I was decorated with heavenly constellations.[81] Together with the planisphere in the Temple of Denderah, we believe that this shows the Egyptian understanding of the zodiac. The period of Seti I was a great period of continued internal wealth and political stability.[82]

Rameses II became king in 1394 BC and ruled for 66 years. In the swamplands of the Delta, he built the city of Pi-Rameses, the new capital. It boasted sphinxes, obelisks and statues. In Waset, he commissioned major buildings in Karnak and Luxor. In Kush, he built the two rock cut temples of Abu Simbel.[83] According to Professor Hornung, Rameses II's building activities were such that: "In Egypt and Nubia alike, there is scarcely an excavation site where monuments of this king has not come to light".[84] There was, however, a negative side:

We have to acknowledge the tireless architects of Rameses II for the fact that nothing is left of the absolutely enormous buildings of Egypt's Middle Kingdom. They plundered the temples of the Fayum, particularly the Pyramid temples at El-Lahun and Hawara, just as they plundered those in Memphis of the White Walls and Heliopolis. The remarkable Labyrinth of Amenemhet III at Hawara, perhaps the largest single building in antiquity according to eyewitness accounts, suffered severely during Ramses' reign.[85]

However, problems emerged with the Hittites, the great military empire in the Turkish region. This state threatened Egypt's Asian interests. A great battle between the two powers took place in 1389 BC in Syria near a town called Qadesh. Though the outcome is disputed, it seems clear that the Egyptians lost control of their northern territories in the Near East. A century later, the Egyptian Empire in the east had all but collapsed. Meanwhile the supply of gold from the south was in decline.[86]

Merneptah, the next ruler, was the thirteenth son of Rameses II. Dissatisfied with Pi-Rameses, he re-established Memphis as the new royal residence. Under his direction, Memphis, that most ancient city, gained a new prestige. Building a palace complex near to the Temple of Ptah, Merneptah was venerated for this piety in later times. On the practical front, new challenges emerged. A sinister alliance between various European peoples and the Libyans had been forged. They attempted an invasion of Egypt. Mereneptah's forces crushed this invasion party in 1323 BC.[87]

Seti II succeeded Merneptah in 1308 BC and had a long reign. During his career, Messui, the Nubian viceroy, rebelled against him and became the ruler of Upper Egypt. Seti II defeated him in battle.[88] Queen Regent Tawosret became the next ruler and brought some stability since Siptah, the direct descendent of Seti II, was merely a child. The boy's early death, however, elevated Tawosret to the status of Pharaoh. She, in turn, elevated Bay, her favourite, to be the real power holder in the country. Bay was a man of Syrian origins.[89] Like Pharaoh Hatshepsut before her, Tawosret was buried in the Valley of the Kings after her death.[90]

Setnekht founded the Twentieth Dynasty in 1236 BC. After six years on the throne, Rameses III succeeded him. Rameses III modelled himself on Rameses II in many ways. He went as far as to copy reliefs depicting the Battle of Qadesh from Rameses II's temple into his own structure. In any case, his Mortuary Temple at Medinet Habu was an architectural triumph.[91]

Evidence exists to show that roughly contemporaneous with the time of Rameses III, if not much earlier, the Egyptians, or else some other group of Negroes, engaged in maritime activities across the Atlantic. Documents from the time of Rameses III mention voyages to "the ends of the earth"[92] and also voyages to the mountain in the far west of the world. Mr Rafique Jairazbhoy, an Indian scholar of considerable erudition, identified this region as Ancient Mexico and the African voyagers as Egyptians. He pointed out a huge number of cultural continuities between the Nile Valley and those in Olmec Mexico.[93]

There are colossal stone carvings of human heads produced by the Olmecs, the formative Native American civilisation. Sixteen such heads have been found. Two were recovered from Tres Zapotes, four from La Venta, six from San Lorenzo and four from other sites. All weighed between 10 and 40 tons. All of them have African facial features, and one has a braided hairstyle. The earliest has been dated at about 1160 BC and some to 580 BC.[94] Jose M. Melgar, a Mexican, found one of the carvings in 1862. In 1869 he wrote a bulletin on it for the *Mexican Society of Geography and Statistics:* "[W]hat astonished me [says Melgar] was the Ethiopic type represented. I reflected that there had undoubtedly been Negroes in this country, and that this had been in the first epoch of the world."[95] In 1963 the Museum of Fine Arts in Houston, Texas, held an exhibition of Olmec artefacts between 18 June and 25 August. Alfonso Medellin Zenlil wrote the introductory essay for the exhibition catalogue, *The Olmec Tradition.* In this essay, we are assured that:

> The colossal heads and "Monument F" of Tres Zapotes, principally, have vigorous and precise Negroid physical characteristics, such as prominent cheek bones, thick lips and platyrrhine noses. For a long time there was concern as to what their hair is, or was, since, in the case of the colossal heads, they are invariably covered by a cap or helmet. This doubt has gone on indefinitely, but finally some light has been thrown on the problem with the discovery of two heads, .75 meters tall, which are identified as "Numbers 1 and 2" of Laguna de los Cerros, on which, together with the characteristic cheek bones and platyrrhine nose, there is a hair arrangement or head of curly hair.[96]

Supplementing this iconographic evidence are a vast number of artefacts that depict Africans in Native American art. In 1966 Count Alexander Von Wuthenau, a German art historian, held an exhibition for President Senghor of Senegal in Dakar, the Senegalese capital. A number of ancient African faces clearly emerged. Von Wuthenau published twice on this issue. In 1969 his *Art of the World: Pre-Columbian Terracottas* emerged in English. In 1976 he followed this with *Unexpected faces in Ancient Mexico.* A number of his images appear in books by Professor Ivan Van Sertima.[97] Count Von Wuthenau's books are profound and wide reaching in their implications for Ancient American history and are thus difficult to summarise. Below we have reproduced a good statement from his 1969 text of what he sought to convey:

> The Negroid element ... is well proven by the large Olmec stone monuments as well as the terracotta items and therefore cannot be excluded from the pre-Columbian history of the Americas. Furthermore, it is precisely the Negroid

representations which often indicate personalities of high position, who can unhesitatingly be compared to the outstanding Negroes who served as models for great works of art in Egypt and in Nigeria.[98]

According to Van Sertima, the cultural impact of the Africans on the Olmecs was considerable. The Native Americans built pyramids with a north, south orientation. The Nile Valley pyramids have a north, south orientation.[99] At Cerro de la Piedre there is an image of a Native American dignitary wearing a double crown. This can be compared to the pharaonic double crown. At Oxtotitlan there is a painting of a man holding a flail in an African manner. This can be compared to the royal flail of the pharaohs. In San Lorenzo there is a head of a man painted purple. In the Nile Valley this was a colour for the priests and the royalty. Finally, there are several images from ancient American art of distinguished people sporting false beards. In Ancient Egypt the false beard of the pharaoh was regarded as a sign of wisdom. Even Hatshepsut, the female ruler, was depicted in the art wearing a false beard.[100]

Professor Andrej Wiercinski, a Polish authority on craniometry, drew attention to the skeletal remains of the African presence. He presented a paper at the 41st International Congress of the Americanists in 1974 based on research he completed in 1972. 13.5% of the skulls at the earlier Olmec site of Tlatilco were of Africans. At Cerro de las Mesas, a later Olmec site, 4.5% of the skulls were found to be of Africans. The burials were arranged with African males buried next to Native American females. The evidence suggests that the Africans and the Native Americans progressively intermarried.[101] However, it is important to note that Wiercinski's methodology is far from perfect and thus his findings are very far from conclusive. We feel that more research in this area is required to clean up the physical anthropology of the Olmec period cemeteries.

Returning to Egypt, however, political problems emerged with the Sea Peoples. Of European origins, they invaded Egypt from the Sea. Other problems emerged with the Libyans. Rameses III repelled both groups of invaders.[102] On the domestic front, in addition, there was great discontent. Workers went on strike in 1200 BC when their payments-in-kind were in arrears by over two months. They marched on the Ramesseum.[103] More problems emerged. There were attempts at grave robbing. Many of the strikers were implicated in this activity.

From a later period, the time of Rameses IX (after 1173 BC), there is a transcript of a court case involving a grave robber and his gang.[104] Amenpnufer, the gang leader, confessed after being tortured by the Egyptian authorities:

We went to rob the tombs in accordance with our regular habit [says Amenpnufer], and we found the pyramid tomb of King Sekhemreshedtawy,

Son of Ra, Sob[e]kemsaf, this being not at all like the pyramids and tombs of the nobles we habitually went to rob. We took our metal tools and forced a way into the pyramid of this king through its innermost part. We found its underground chambers, and we took lighted candles in our hands and went down. Then we broke through the rubble … and found this god lying at the back of his burial-place. And we found the burial-place of Queen Nubkhaas, his queen, situated beside him … We opened the sarcophagi and their coffins … and found the noble mummy of this king … We collected the gold we found on the noble mummy of this god together with that on his amulets and jewels … We collected all that we found upon her likewise and set fire to their coffins … Thus I, together with the other thieves who are with me, have continued down to this day in the practice of robbing the tombs of the nobles and people of the land in the west of Thebes.[105]

There were severe penalties for these types of activities, but tomb robbery proved unrelenting. As is well known, only Pharaoh Tutankhamen escaped this plunder from the ancient times. The persistence of tomb robbery was almost a by-product of corruption among the governing classes, especially during the Twentieth Dynasty. All of the reigns of the kings, Rameses IV to Rameses X, were weak and unstable, characterised by crime waves and famine.[106] After the fall of this dynasty, central authority collapsed. Egypt became split into two powers, the north and the south. The High Priest of Amen Ra at the Temple of Karnak became the ruler of the south. After this period, Panehesy, the viceroy of Kush, declared independence for his territory. The Egyptians lost their supply of gold.[107] Another Panehesy became the ruler of Upper Egypt. General Piankh succeeded him, followed by Herihor. Rameses XI, the last king of this dynasty, exercised no power in the south.[108]

Smendes of the Twenty-First Dynasty ascended the throne in 1089 BC ruling from the city of Tanis. Egypt had some semblance of stability under his rule but in reality the High Priest of Amen continued to dominate Upper Egypt. Amenism flourished in Tanis as it did in the south, but politics continued to split the land into two countries for generations. Friendly relations between the two territories, however, were the norm. Historians call this epoch the Third Intermediate Period.[109]

The Libyans finally achieved power over the north in around 940 BC with the ascension of Shoshenq I. He established the Twenty-Second Dynasty after the death of Pharaoh Psusennes II, the last Tanite king. Shoshenq I made some effort to bring greater unity to the country. Sometime around 936 BC, he appointed his son to the post of High Priest of Amen. Later kings would do the same. Another branch of his household ruled Herakleopolis under Prince Nimrut. Consequently, Libyan power emanating from the same family was felt all over the country. In 924 BC Shoshenq I launched a raid on Jerusalem.[110] Despite the appellation 'Libyan' to the dynasty, it is not yet known whether or not they were genuine Africans since Libya also had populations descended from the Hyksos and also the Sea Peoples.[111] In the south, however, there was no such confusion.

Kush

Immediately to the south of Egypt lay the land of Wawat. It was a territory of great wealth due to the presence of gold mines. To the south of Wawat lay the land of Kush. The Egyptians called the people of Kush 'Nehesi' meaning the people who inhabited the river valley as against the 'Medjay,' the people who occupied the wadis of the Eastern desert. The term Kush comes from the Egyptian Kas or Kash/Kesh. The term was clearly acceptable to the Kushites who also used it.[112] Dr Welsby, of the British Museum, informs us that: "During the XXVth Dynasty (c.747-656 BC), at a time when the Kushites ruled Egypt, at least one inscription refers to Kush by the old Egyptian term for the area south of the frontier, Ta Sety [sic], meaning 'the Land of the Bow'."[113] In our view, this indicates some connection between this Kushite kingdom and the much earlier pharaonic kingdom that predated Egypt. Dr Welsby explained the global importance of the Kushites as follows:

> Consideration of the Kushites alongside such giants of the ancient world as the Greeks, Romans and Egyptians is justified on account of the longevity of the kingdom and of its size, if for no other reasons. At the time when Rome was a small village on the banks of the Tiber and the Greek city states held sway over minuscule territories, the Kushites ruled an empire stretching from the central Sudan to the borders of Palestine.[114]

Of this new Kushite kingdom, archaeologists know the earliest royal burial as Lord A of the tomb Ku.Tum.1. He was buried with a large number of objects that included pottery and golden jewellery.[115] The capital of this kingdom was at Al Kurru. This city had monumental buildings and was walled for defensive purposes. Surrounding it were wide tracts of irrigable land.[116] The dating of this period, however, is controversial. Some say that Lord A ruled around the eleventh century BC others say the ninth century BC:

> Reisner and his supporters [continues Dr Welsby] favour a 'short' chronology where the burials at el Kurru [sic], prior to the historically dated king Piye [i.e. Piankhy], are assumed to be six rulers, the other graves being those of the members of the royal family. He [Reisner] writes, ... 'if we take the beginning of Piankhy's [Piye's] reign at about 740 BC, we get 860-920 BC for the date of the oldest ancestor, he of Ku.Tum.1.' The proponents of the 'long' chronology believe that many more of the graves are those of rulers and, therefore, that the time span involved must be considerably greater.[117]

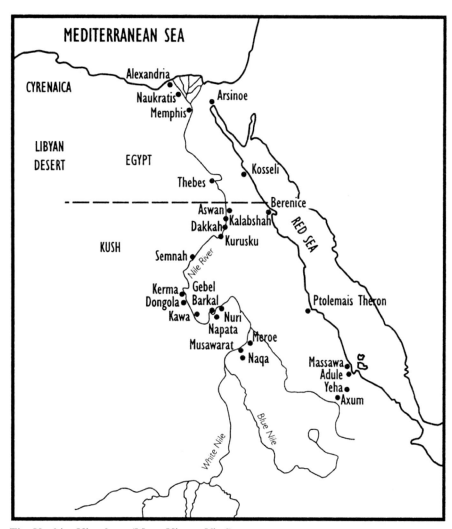

The Kushite Kingdom. (Map: Kieron Vital).

The second Kushite capital was Napata (also named after its famous hill Gebel Barkal). Originally an Egyptian religious centre, it was sacred to Amen and the home of his *ka* (i.e. vital force or spirit). The Egyptians built an important temple there during the Eighteenth Dynasty. Pharaoh Thutmose III raised a stela that informs us that his divine mandate to rule came from both Amen in Waset and Amen in Gebel Barkal. The Kushites shared this religious belief and thus Napata regained its importance. The Kushite rulers were buried at Nuri, a short distance upstream.[118]

King Alara, or perhaps a predecessor, built a temple to Amen in Kawa. He, or his successor, may have built Temple B800 in Gebel Barkal.[119] Kashta was the next ruler. His name means the Kushite.[120] Extending Kushite power into Egypt, he took control of Waset in 760 BC and received the divine mandate of Amen to rule. He installed his daughter as the successor to the post of High Priestess of Amen.[121] After his death, he was buried in a gilded wooden anthropoid coffin, from which fragments of gold foil, lapis lazuli and coloured glass are still in existence.[122] Charles Finch and Larry Williams argue that it became the standard practise for the Kushite pharaohs to place their female relatives in this position:

> These women, working through their own prime ministers, were in effect rulers of Upper Egypt. They undertook massive restoration and public works in Thebes [i.e. Waset] and throughout Upper Egypt. Their names are on scores of monuments, buildings, and statues … The Cushite [sic] pharaohs ruled mainly from Napata and seemed to have had the utmost confidence in their female relatives to govern Upper Egypt.[123]

At a later date, however, Queen-Mothers Shanakdakhete and Amanishakheto ruled Kush as pharaohs with the full insignia. Reliefs on temple walls depict these rulers with special iconographies that integrate these females into the role of kings.[124]

Pharaoh Piye (also known as Piankhy), Kashta's successor, continued to exercise power over Egyptian affairs. His troops occupied much of Upper Egypt. A stela in Gebel Barkal suggests that the Egyptians petitioned Piye to intervene in Egypt probably to counter the power of Tefnakhte, a local dynast in Lower Egypt. Piye is not portrayed as a conqueror of Egypt but as a protector of its ancient religion. After his victory he spared Tefnakht and gradually withdrew Kushite power from Egypt.[125]

Piye was also an important builder. He refurbished and enlarged the old Egyptian temple of Amen at Gebel Barkal. Considered the single most important religious building in Kush, he extended it towards the Nile. He raised a substantial hypostyle hall entered through an enormous pylon. The building was 500 feet long and about 135 feet wide. Piye may also have been responsible for extending Temple B800. He built a palace next to this temple.[126] Since neither Kasta nor Piye's invasions of Egypt resulted in destruction nor looting, Dr Welsby feels that this "suggests that they were motivated more by piety than by territorial ambitions".[127] Professor Hansberry, the pioneering African-American historian, was also of this opinion:

> [I]n almost every instance where we are able to get a glimpse of the Ethiopian [i.e. Kushite] sovereigns, great warriors though they were, we find them free of those rapacious and piratic habits that have so often sullied the otherwise

> brilliant careers of so many monarchs of other nations … [I]n [Piye's]
> triumphant march through Egypt, we are told that before he would attack a city
> he would first offer it the most favourable terms of peace to avoid fighting, for
> it was his desire that harm should come to no one, that "not even a babe might
> have cause to cry" … [W]hen he left Egypt to return to Ethiopia "he did not
> leave behind a land filled with the slain and ruins of towns which he had
> burned," nor were there "fields blackened with the ashes of the crops which he
> had set on fire." The spirit of tolerance and forbearance was also evident on the
> part of … Shabaka; the same statesmanlike qualities are expressed in the
> activities of the Ethiopian king Taharka … Here were true representatives of
> Homer's "blameless" and Hesiod's "high-souled Ethiopians."[128]

Piye was buried at Al Kurru on his death in 716 BC. His tomb was the first
among the Kushites to be marked by a pyramid. For the next thousand years,
pyramids were built in cemeteries in Nuri, Gebel Barkal and Meroë. In total
there are at least 223 pyramids in Kush, far more than in Egypt. These haughty
monuments had steep sides that sloped at between 60° and 73° giving the
buildings a more slender appearance. An exception to this is pyramid Nu.7 at
Nuri which is a bent pyramid recalling the Bent Pyramid of Dashur. The
Kushite pyramids usually had an offering chapel on the eastern side. Originally
constructed of clay bricks, the later chapels progressed to the use of sandstone
blocks. They were rectangular buildings entered by a central door. Some had
the same 'standard' pylonic design typical of many Kushite temples. In their
time, these monuments were covered in white plaster, usually painted red or
white. They possessed circular plaques inserted as surface decoration and also
had a band of stars painted around their bases.[129] Lady Lugard wrote: "On the
base of one of the monuments a zodiac has been found".[130] Professor Diop
adds:

> Lepsius later discovered [in Meroë] the foundation of an astronomical
> observatory there; on the walls of this edifice was found a scene representing
> persons operating an instrument which it might not be inappropriate to call an
> astrolabe … There was also found a series of numerical equations relating to
> astronomic events which occurred two centuries B.C.[131]

Shabaqo (also called Shabaka), Piye's brother and successor, re-conquered
Egypt and is generally credited with founding the Twenty-Fifth Dynasty. We,
however, believe that the credit for starting the dynasty should go to Alara, a
predeccessor. Before becoming king Shabaqo served in the army and was
stationed in the Delta for some years. After ascending to the throne, he built a
huge empire. Memphis became a royal residence of the Kushite pharaohs and
Waset became the capital of the empire.[132] Inscriptions inform us that Kush was
divided into nomes, as was Egypt, each with its own capital.[133] As ruler,
Shabaqo abolished the death penalty and replaced it with hard labour, to cite

Kush (Sudan). View of the Pyramid and Chapel of Kentake Amanishakheto (ruled 10-1 BC) in Meroë. This is one of at least 223 Sudanese pyramids. Originally published in Frédéric Cailliaud, *Voyage à Meroé*, 1826.

Herodotus: "When an Egyptian was guilty of an offence, his plan was not to punish him with death: instead of so doing, he sentenced him, according to the nature of his crime".[134]

In the Near East, the Assyrians, a near White Semitic power, rose to imperial prominence at this time ruling from their city of Nineveh. As their armies conquered territories to the west of Mesopotamia, conflict with the Kushite pharaohs of Egypt seemed inevitable. Initially, there were diplomatic relations between the Kushites and the Assyrians, but things came to a head. The Assyrians attempted to invade the kingdom of Judah, an ally of Kush. The Assyrian invasion, however, came to naught. Plague destroyed the Assyrian armies.[135]

Taharqo (also called Taharka) ruled from 690 until 664 BC. He inherited a huge empire from Qebh-Hor in Asia to the lands south of Napata. In addition, Erathosthenes claimed that he conquered a vast territory in North Africa and "penetrated into Europe as far as the 'Pillars of Hercules' (Gibraltar)."[136] Corroborating this, Professor Ivan Van Sertima wrote that:

> We [also] have a clear and indisputable reference to this in a [Spanish] manuscript by Florian de Ocampo *Cronica General* published in 1553. The name of the invading general is given as Tarraco [cf. Taharqo]. He is not only identified as head of the Ethiopian [i.e. Kushite] army. The reference is more specific. It says he was later to become King of Egypt. The name, the period, the historical fact of his generalship and his later kingship in Egypt ... all attest to the validity of this reference.[137]

Moreover, there is some evidence, to be discussed in a later chapter, that the newly founded North African city of Carthage was part of his sphere of influence. Thus, his imperial activities give substance to his boast of being the "Emperor of the World".[138] Of this great man, Professor Rawlinson wrote the following:

> The reign of Tirhakah (Tehrak) [sic] during this period appears to have been glorious. He was regarded by Judea as its protector, and exercised a certain influence over all Syria as far as Taurus, Amanus, and the Euphrates. In Africa, he brought into subjection the native tribes of the north coast, carrying his arms, according to some, as far as the Pillars of Hercules. He is exhibited at Medinet-Abou in the dress of a warrior, smiting with a mace ten captive foreign princes. He erected monuments in the Egyptian style at Thebes, Memphis, and Napata. Of all the Ethiopian [i.e. Kushite] sovereigns of Egypt he was undoubtedly the greatest.[139]

One authority described him as "a great builder approaching the scale of Rameses II".[140] According to Vivian Davies and Renée Friedman:

Taharqo was a great builder, erecting temples, shrines and statues throughout the Nile Valley, and turning Gebel Barkal into an architectural showpiece, its central temple a southern version of Karnak in Thebes, though on a smaller scale. High up on the great pinnacle he had an inscription recording his dominance carved in hieroglyphs and sheathed in gold - to be visible far and wide, no doubt a spectacular sight as it glistened in the sun.[141]

In Kawa Taharqo restored a temple by clearing the sand from around it. He also built a large temple for Amen. This building was of sandstone blocks. It had an outer colonnaded court entered between two pylons. Beyond the court lay a hypostyle hall. This led into a sanctuary that was flanked by a number of ancillary rooms. In Gebel Barkal he expanded the Temple of Amen B500 into a formidable monument, 150 metres long.[142] There are similar temples at Sanam and Tabo that were probably commissioned by him.[143] These buildings share affinities with those of Egypt from the Old Kingdom period. At Qasr Ibrim he built the earliest Kushite temple there. Additionally, in Nuri he built the largest pyramid in Kush (N.1). It was 51.75 metres square at the base, and rose to a soaring height of 49 metres. In Egypt he built the six-columned kiosk situated in the forecourt of the Temple of Amen of Karnak.[144] Dr Brooks-Bertram, an African-American scholar, notes that Taharqo did much to reclaim the artistic and religious ideas that had lain dormant since the time of Egypt's Old Kingdom:

> Taharka [sic] sought sculptors who probably belonged to the workshops which produced the reliefs in the Theban tombs of officials of the reign of Taharka and the beginning of the Saite dynasty. It is in this temple [of Kawa] that we find raised reliefs decorating the Hypostyle Hall, and sunken reliefs copied after, or reviving, Old Kingdom reliefs ... The use of Old Kingdom royal models at Kawa is the most striking and one of the earliest examples of this type of relief ... In the temple of Kawa, Taharka was also responsible for the revival of the Pyramid Texts in literature and the old text of the Memphite Theology ... Not only were the Kawa Temples a treasure trove of Nubian royal inscriptions second only to Jebel [sic] Barkal, Kawa was a local centre of considerable importance ... At Qasr Ibrim, a temple with some few extant frescoes from this epoch was also constructed.[145]

Taharqo resided at Tanis in northern Egypt probably to keep watch on its northeastern frontier. In 671 BC the Assyrians invaded Kushite controlled territory and captured as far as Memphis. Taharqo re-occupied the city in 669 BC and re-established Kushite rule in Lower Egypt. The Assyrians marched once more and established Egyptian vassals as far south as Waset without taking control of the city. Tanwetamani was the next ruler of Kush. He re-established Kushite control over the city of Memphis. The Assyrian response was to invade south once more. They reached Waset and devastated it in 663

BC. They placed Psammetik I, a vassal, on the throne. Psammetik in turn installed his daughter as the successor High Priestess of Amen in 654 BC replacing the Kushite Priestess who held that position.[146] The destruction of the glorious city of Waset was a turning point. It ended the dominance of Blacks in world history.[147] Even in ruins, however, the city tells a timely story. "For if the Blacks had never left a single written record of their past greatness," observes Chancellor Williams, the late African-American historian:

> the record would still stand, defying time, in the deathless stones of Thebes [Waset], of her fallen columns from temples, monuments, and her pyramids; a city more eternal than Rome because its foundation was laid before the dawn of history, and its plan was that copied by other cities of the world. If the Blacks of today wish to measure the distance to the heights from which they have fallen, they need go no farther than Nowe [Waset].[148]

Egypt had fallen under the foreign rule of the Assyrians. From then until now, the land was repeatedly occupied and looted by different Middle-Eastern and European peoples. The occupations changed the character of Egyptian culture. From being purely African before the Second Intermediate period, it became African and Asian afterwards. Eventually it became the Arab dominated Afro Eurasian mix that characterises North Africa in the present era. For this reason, the Copts of modern Egypt no longer resemble the Ancient Egyptian skulls, mummies or sculptures. There are, of course, Coptic populations in Sudan and Ethiopia, and also Nubian populations in Egypt and Sudan, who do resemble the Ancient Egyptians in these respects. Lieutenant Francis Wilford, a pioneering English Orientalist, made the following observation many years ago:

> [T]he modern Copts [of Egypt] are far from answering to the description given by Herodotus, and their features differ from those of the mummies, and of ancient statues brought from Egypt, whence it appears, that their ancestors had large eyes with a long slit, projecting lips, and folded ears of a remarkable size.[149]

Dr R. R. Madden, after studying thousands of mummy heads and many other ancient skulls from different civilisations, made a similar observation a few years later:

> Herodotus, whose *own* observations are deemed veracious, describes the old Egyptians, among whom he was residing, as a people of black skins, and short woolly hair; the Copts [of Egypt] have neither one nor the other; and above all, what, in my opinion, is the strongest of all evidence on the subject, is the utter dissimilarity in the form of the heads of both people ... It is among the [modern] Nubians we are to search for the descendants of the Egyptians; a

swarthy race, with wiry hair; surpassing in the beauty of their slender forms, all
the people of the East; [now] living on the [southern] confines of Egypt, where,
probably, their ancestors had been driven by the Persians ... [150]

Kushite power was restricted to the First Cataract - the old Egyptian/Nubian
border. It was in Kush that pharaonic culture was preserved. Kush's southerly
location saved it from the invasions that undermined and whitened Egypt.
Professor Williams continues:

> The Africans, eventually barred from further rule in Egypt, continued Piankhi's
> [i.e. Piye's] line first from the capital at Napata and then at Meroe where they
> promoted a broad reconstruction program ... Having lost both Upper and
> Lower Egypt, Ethiopia's [i.e. Kush's] border had been pushed to the First
> Cataract at Assuan [sic] ... Other invasions came. The Persians ... took over,
> and their domination of Egypt lasted from 525 to 404 B.C. ... They returned in
> 343 B.C. ... Alexander [of the Greeks] reached Egypt in 332 B.C. ... Upon his
> death, one of his most outstanding generals became Pharaoh as Ptolemy I, thus
> beginning 300 years of Macedonian-Greek rule. Towards the end of Greek
> domination, the expansion of the Roman empire had transferred the real center
> of power to Rome. Assyria, Persia, Greece, Rome - the continuing process of
> transforming a black civilization into a near-white civilization ... Ethiopia [i.e.
> Kush] now began at the First Cataract in the north and extended south into
> present-day Ethiopia. It was now bounded by Upper Egypt, the Red Sea and the
> Libyan desert. [151]

Egypt under Psammetik II invaded Kush in 593 BC marching as far as the
Third Cataract. Some authorities believe that this invasion destroyed the city
of Napata. He also had the names and special insignia of the Twenty Fifth
Dynasty rulers removed from Egyptian monuments. [152] Napata was the original
religious capital of Kush but this religious role was gradually transferred to the
more southerly city of Meroë, following this invasion. [153] Pharaoh Aspelta (593-
568 BC) commissioned the famous Temple of the Sun and the Temple of
Amen, both raised in the city of Meroë. [154] The Sun Temple was built on a
podium approached by an inclined ramp. It had a colonnade running around
the edge. [155]

The earliest occupation of Meroë dates back to the tenth century BC. [156] A
solid wall made of dressed stone blocks encircled its Royal City. Over three
meters thick, the walls had towers that projected at the angles and the enceinte.
Similar towers probably flanked some of the gates. [157] In addition, the city
contained a famous building that shared affinities with a Roman bath. Its
central feature was a large pool approached by a flight of steps. The
waterspouts were decorated with lion heads and the edge of the basin had
inlaid faience roundels and panels. [158] In its heyday Meroë supported 200,000
soldiers and 4,000 artisans. [159]

In 525 BC the Persians, under King Cambyses, conquered Egypt. A year later the Persians attempted to invade Kush. Herodotus described the expedition as an embarrassment. It failed miserably in the desert.[160] Before this attempted invasion, however, Derek Welsby tells us that: "Cambyses had … sent a mission to the Kushite court, the members of which were blatantly spying".[161] The source of this intelligence is Herodotus' *The Histories.* In this work, Herodotus informs us that the Kushite king showed the Persian-paid agents a number of things during their stay in the country:

> [H]e led them to a fountain, wherein when they had washed, they found their flesh all glossy and sleek, as if they had bathed in oil - and a scent came from the spring like that of violets … When they quitted the fountain the king led them to a prison, where the prisoners were all of them bound with fetters of gold. Among these Ethiopians [i.e. Kushites] copper is of all metals the most scarce and valuable. After they had seen the prison, they were likewise shown what is called "the table of the Sun." Also, last of all, they were allowed to behold the coffins of the Ethiopians, which are made (according to report) of crystal.[162]

Professor William Leo Hansberry, formerly of Howard University, demonstrated that many of the more startling details of Herodotus' account stand up to critical scrutiny and can be corroborated with other evidence. Concerning the violet scented fountain, for example, Dr Hansberry wrote that:

> [T]he excavations at Mero[ë] by the Liverpool expedition revealed … not only the remains of elaborately constructed baths and beautifully decorated swimming pools, but in one of the pools there has been found a column of plaster within whose centre has been embedded an earthenware pipe apparently designed to convey water through the column. The pipe is threaded through the column, says W. S. George, the engineer of the expedition, and is similar in character to other pipes which were used in connection with the heating and conveying of water through the pipes; however, it is smaller than the pipes used for such purposes, and such pipes are not embedded in columns of plaster. This pipe-threaded column, therefore, must have had some other use. George hinted that it might once have stood upright in the pool and, by some system of hydraulics, water may have been forced up through the column to its top, thus producing a fountain-like cascade in the center of the pool. With such a pool in mind, and by assuming that the waters used in the baths were treated with some aromatic spices or salts for which Ethiopia [i.e. Kush] has long been noted, it becomes easy enough to believe … Herodotus' account.[163]

On the question of golden fetters used to enchain prisoners, Hansberry wrote:

> [G]old was beyond any question a most plentiful commodity … In the Asian kingdoms contemporary with the Eighteenth dynasty there was a belief that

gold was in Egypt "as common as dust" ... yet the truth of the matter is that practically no such precious metal was native to Egypt ... [it] was for the most part of Ethiopian [i.e. Kushitic] origin, and there are many Egyptian documents which shed considerable light on the ways and means by which this metal reached the northern kingdom out of the south. In the tomb of Huy, a viceroy in Ethiopia in the reign of King Tutankhamen (c.1350 B.C.),[164] there is a painting showing the products sent to Egypt by this official. Along with hundreds of other precious things, there is an enormous quantity of gold represented in a variety of forms; in rings in bags, and sacks of gold dust. A letter dating from the reign of Rameses II (c.1292-1225 B.C.) addressed to an Egyptian official on duty in Ethiopia instructs this officer to procure for the royal treasury, among other things, "much good gold," including "fans of gold, gold wrought in dishes, and refined gold in bushels."[165]

Finally, concerning the coffins of crystal, Hansberry tells us that:

[A]rchaeological research in Ethiopia has as yet revealed no evidence of the existence of such a practice. However, some seeming confirmation does exist. Ctesias of Cindus, a Greek physician living at the court of the Persian King Artaxerses Memnon in 415-398 B.C., and the author of an anciently famous but long-lost history of Persia and India, has preserved through the pages of Diodorus an interesting notice supplementary to Herodotus' account of burial practices in Ethiopia. The wealthier Ethiopians, so the story goes, after embalming the body of the dead, placed it in a hollow statue of gold made to resemble the deceased. The statue was covered with melted glass and set up in some conspicuous place where it could be viewed for a time by the living relatives. The Ethiopians of lesser fortune followed the same general practice except that the hollowed statue, instead of being made of gold, was composed of silver or of potter's clay.[166]

The basis of this wealth was a dynamic economy. Animal husbandry and agriculture formed the backbone. The Kushites grew crops of vines, cotton, sorghum, date palms, wheat, barley, beans, lentils, and vegetables. Moreover, they reared sheep, goats and cattle. There were civil engineering activities to harness water for irrigation and animal husbandry.[167] Kushite genius is attested to by their construction of a national system of reservoirs. Strategically located at Musawarat, Naqa, Hordan, Umm, Usuda, in the Gezira region, at Duanib, Basa, etc., they were built to survive the ever-encroaching desert. Oxen-powered wheels operated the irrigation.[168]

Gold and iron working were important economic mainstays. In 1834 AD the famous Italian grave robber and vandal, Guiseppe Ferlini, unearthed some important examples of Kushite gold work from the Pyramid of Kentake Amanishakheto (see page 206). Among other things, a golden armlet and ring were recovered made of gold and inlaid glass. They were superlative pieces of work that incorporated a complex mix of Nile Valley religious symbols with

Kush (Sudan). View of the Royal Cemetery at Meroë, 250 BC-350 AD, from an 1832 document. There are a total of at least 84 pyramids in this city.

Kush (Sudan). Detail from the Chapel of Meroïtic Pyramid number 11, showing the Queen and her Consort from an 1844 document.

perhaps some Greek design influences.[169] Apart from these treasures, many other golden pieces were recovered from Kush, including ornate amulets, wadjet eyes, knives, decorated cylinder sheaths, tweezers, gold flower necklaces and earrings.[170] Gold was also used to decorate temples. One writer reported that: "Recent excavations at Meroe [sic] and Mussawwarat es-Sufra [sic] revealed temples with walls and statues covered with gold leaf".[171] Intriguing examples of steel tools have been discovered from the time of the Twenty-Fifth Dynasty. According to Dr Finch:

> Five specimens were analyzed by Williams and Maxwell-Hyslop. The tools were notable for their "remarkably good condition" and for their "surprisingly modern appearance." Two of the five tools analyzed were composed of low carbon steels (0.1-0.2% carbon content) but even this low carbon level was sufficient to convey a hardness three times greater than iron.[172]

Meroë became the centre of an iron working industry that produced metal of a superior quality. Based on the huge scale of the iron working activities, one early archaeologist described this city as the "Birmingham of Africa". A more recent archaeologist, A. J. Arkell, visited the site and witnessed for himself the remains of iron slag left by the old manufacturing processes. On the comparison with Birmingham, he concluded that: "I think this is a fair description".[173] In addition to iron, they produced bronze works.[174] There were trade routes connecting Meroë to ports on the Red Sea, such as Aidhab. There was trade to the north with Egypt and also southwards to the hill regions of Ethiopia. It is also likely that Kush traded westward towards the Niger River region.[175] The Kushites imported Egyptian pottery, wine, honey and olive oil. In later years they imported Greek and Roman luxury products, and also goods from the East.[176] To pay for these products, they exported gold, ivory and iron. Barges, donkeys and more rarely, camels were employed to move these goods to the markets.[177]

There were royal palaces at Wad ben Naqa, Musawarat, Meroë, Gebel Barkal/Napata, Sanam, Kawa and Pnubs. Furthermore, there were fortified settlements at Sheikh Daud, Faras, Sabaqura, Kalabshah and Ikhmindi. These forts have an identical gateway design.[178] Amanishakheto's palace at Wad ben Naqa has been excavated. It was 61 metres square and had columned halls, corridors and long narrow rooms. It had at least two storeys with the palatial apartments on the upper floor.[179]

In Northern Nubia very small houses have been excavated. In Gaminarti housing complexes have been found that consisted of two-room apartments. At Abu Geili the entire village was discovered to be an interconnected complex consisting of dwellings of two or more storeys where each of the dwellings must have been apartments. Houses near Abu Simbel were vaulted structures

Kush (Sudan). Temple of Apedemak at Musawarat. Built by Pharaoh Arnekhamani between c.235 and 221 BC. There is also a very similar temple to this one still standing in the city of Naqa. (Photo: Louis Buckley, Black Nine Films).

with alcoves and niches. They had staircases, some internal and others external. At Karanog a castle has been excavated. Of three storeys high, its rooms were arranged around a central internal courtyard. Scholars do not think royalty resided there but more ordinary people.[180] Archaeology has also turned up an interesting surprise. A tavern was discovered at Qasr Ibrim. It was a rectangular building consisting of six interconnecting rooms. Also found were fragments of goblets and amphorae numbering thousands.[181]

Pharaoh Harsiyotef of the fourth century BC rebuilt a temple in the southern city of Tara. He decorated the Amen temple of Napata with gold. He covered the statues of Amen with golden rings and commissioned golden figures of saints, rams heads and beads. He added a new sanctuary to this monument of acacia wood overlaid with gold. This extension boasted vessels of bronze and silver including the censers, lamp stands and shovels. The temple was well provided with honey, incense and myrrh.[182] Harsiyotef also led campaigns. His bowmen made nine raids against regional enemies, probably with the aim of seizing all the caravan routes from Axum into Egypt. He ruled for at least thirty-five years.[183]

The period that began with Pharaoh Natasen (328-308 BC) was highly remarkable. It was distinguished by originality in architecture and also pottery.[184] Besides this, the Kushites had developed another script. The Meroïtic script had twenty-three letters of which four were vowels and there was also a word divider.[185] They developed a numerical system for mathematics. Writing was generally done on purposefully designed wood and skins, but examples are also found on walls, vases, etc.[186] Hundreds of old texts survive in this script. Diodorus Siculus, a Greek contemporary, says that unlike in Egypt, universal literacy was achieved in Kush.[187] During this period the capital was moved from Napata to Meroë although the pharaohs continued to be crowned on the golden throne of Napata.[188]

According to Dr Basil Davidson, one of the notable achievements of the Kushites was the taming of the African elephant. African elephants are not nearly as pliable as their Indian cousins. His evidence for this was from the enormous Temple Complex of Musawarat dated at 220 BC.[189] Dr Derek Welsby offers evidence that supports this position:

> The area to the south of the Egyptian frontier was an important source of elephants for the armies of the Ptolemies, allowing them to match the Indian elephants of the Seleucids. It is likely that many of these animals came from the realm of the Kushites. Arrian records that before elephants were employed in warfare by the Macedonians and Carthaginians, they were used by the Ethiopians [i.e. Kushites] and the Indians. There were also other references to the use made by the Ethiopians of war elephants and their prowess as mahouts, but whether we are justified in equating these Ethiopians with the Kushites is unclear. The elephant is depicted in Kushite art. At Musawwarat es Sufra reliefs of elephants are common. One of these shows a king riding an elephant. On the northwest wall of the Lion Temple a file of elephants leads prisoners on ropes.[190]

Incidentally, there are reliefs that depict processions where people are shown riding two-wheeled horse-drawn chariots.[191]

The Kushites maintained a keen interest in the political developments in Egypt, their northern neighbour. Upper Egypt revolted against the rule of the Greeks in 204 BC. Though re-conquered in 185 BC, Lower Nubia fell into the hands of Kush. Pharaohs Arkamani II and Adikhalamani built monuments in Dakka, Debod and Philae.[192] In around the first century BC the Upper Egyptians again revolted amongst the Greek rulers. The Kushites offered their support.[193]

There were also armed campaigns against the Romans in 24 BC. The Roman conquest of Egypt in 30 BC brought a new challenge to Kush. Augustus Caesar threatened an invasion, following his Egyptian campaign.[194] According to Strabo, the famous geographer, sometime between 29 and 24 BC the conflict with Kush began. Queen-Mother Amanirenas, the Kushite ruler, gave the order to march into Egypt and attack the invaders. Akindad led the campaigns against the Roman armies of Augustus. The Kushites sacked Aswan with an army of 30,000 men and they destroyed the statues of Caesar in Elephantine.

Kush (Sudan). Detail from the Temple of Apedemak in the city of Naqa showing Queen Amanitore. From Sir E. A. Wallis Budge, *The Egyptian Sudan, Volume II* (UK, Kegan Paul, Trench, Trübner & Co., 1907, p.133).

The Romans, under Petronius, counter attacked. Though described as a strong and fortified city, they captured Qasr Ibrim in 23 BC after their first assault. The Romans invaded as far as Napata and sacked it, though Amanirenas evaded their clutches. Petronius returned to Alexandria with prisoners and booty leaving behind a garrison in Lower Nubia. Amenirenas ordered her armies to march a second time with the aim of seizing the Roman garrison. This time, however, a standoff with Petronius was reached without fighting. The Roman army retired to Egypt and withdrew their fort declaring *Pax Romana* (i.e. peace). In fact, the full extent of the Roman humiliation has yet to be disclosed since the relevant Kushite account of the affair has yet to be published. The Meroïtic account of this encounter cannot yet be fully understood.[195]

Pharaoh Natakamani and Queen Amanitore were the last great builders of Kush. They lived somewhere around 1 AD to 20 AD. Their buildings were raised in Keraba, an area between the Nile and the Atbara Rivers. Moreover, they built monuments in Naqa. In this city, The Temple of Apedemak, one of their best known monuments, is in a good state of preservation. Naqa also contains a famous Kiosk. This temple mixes architectural motifs from Nile Valley, Roman and Greek influences (see page 25). The royal palace of Natakamani and Queen Amanitore was in Gebel Barkal.[196] Finally, they dug reservoirs around Meroë, restored its huge Temple of Amen, and rebuilt the Amen Temple of Napata previously destroyed by the Romans.[197]

The period of decline dates from 200 AD.[198] Hungry nomads from the desert obstructed vital trade routes and also infiltrated the country. A more important challenge came from the kingdom of Axum located in the present day regions of Eritrea and Ethiopia. Under King Ezana, their armies marched on Kush in 350 AD. They destroyed the towns of masonry and the cotton fields, and also seized a vast amount of livestock.[199] After a brilliant one thousand years, the Kushite state collapsed. This ended the 6,000 year cycle of pharaonic culture. We give the final word on this topic to Mr George Wells Parker, who wrote a moving dedication to the Nile Valley legacy:

> For thousands of years Egypt dwelt happily in the Valley of the Nile, till her warriors crossed the emerald mountains with sword in hand, inviting luxury, decay and death, and though these inevitable human consequences came, as they must always come, Horus has never ceased his vigil ... Egypt has lived and played her part in the human wonder drama. But I believe that the memory that we have of her may hold one lesson among the many, and that is there have been and are great potentialities in that race which gave Egypt to the sum of human things. Perhaps that Hebrew sage was truly inspired when he told how in the days to come the children of Ethiopia [i.e. Nubia/Kush] and Egypt should again stretch forth their hands and bring back to their immortal race the glory which lies sleeping and forgotten.[200]

Notes

[1] James Henry Breasted, *A History of Egypt,* US, Bantam Books, 1967, p.147.

[2] Erik Hornung, *History of Ancient Egypt,* UK, Edinburgh University Press, 1999, p.42.

[3] A. Joseph Ben-Levi, *The First and Second Intermediate Periods in Kemetic History,* in *Kemet and the African Worldview,* ed Jacob Carruthers and Maulana Karenga, US, University of Sankore Press, 1986, pp.56-7.

[4] Erik Hornung, *History of Ancient Egypt,* p.42.

[5] Cf. ibid., p.44.

[6] Ibid.

[7] Runoko Rashidi, *Black Land of Antiquity,* in *Egypt: Child of Africa,* ed Ivan Van Sertima, US, Transaction Publishers, 1994, p.85.

[8] Adolf Erman, *The Literature of the Ancient Egyptians,* UK, Methuen & Co, 1927, pp.75-84.

[9] James Henry Breasted, *A History of Egypt,* p.151.

[10] Ibid., pp.151-2.

[11] Erik Hornung, *History of Ancient Egypt,* pp.46-9.

[12] Runoko Rashidi, *The Middle Kingdom of Kemet,* in *Egypt Revisited,* ed Ivan Van Sertima, US, Transaction Publishers, 1989, p.185.

[13] Erik Hornung, *History of Ancient Egypt,* p.49.

[14] James Henry Breasted, *A History of Egypt,* p.152.

[15] Runoko Rashidi, *The Middle Kingdom of Kemet,* in *Egypt Revisited,* p.187.

[16] Ibid., pp.187-9.

[17] Ibid., p.189.

[18] Erik Hornung, *History of Ancient Egypt,* pp.50-2.

[19] Barbara Watterson, *The Egyptians,* UK, Blackwell Publishers, 1997, p.74.

[20] George Rawlinson, *Ancient Egypt: The Story of the Nations,* UK, T. Fisher Unwin, 1888, pp.100-1.

[21] Erik Hornung, *History of Ancient Egypt,* p.56.

[22] Ibid., pp.56-8.

[23] Erik Hornung, *History of Ancient Egypt,* pp.58-9.

[24] Runoko Rashidi, *The Middle Kingdom of Kemet,* in *Egypt Revisited,* pp.189-191.

[25] Erik Hornung, *History of Ancient Egypt,* p.61.

[26] Ibid.

[27] Ibid., pp.61-3.

[28] Barbara Watterson, *The Egyptians,* pp.72-3.

[29] Runoko Rashidi, *The Middle Kingdom of Kemet,* in *Egypt Revisited,* p.192.

[30] Erik Hornung, *History of Ancient Egypt,* pp.65-6 and 70.

[31] Runoko Rashidi, *The Middle Kingdom of Kemet,* in *Egypt Revisited,* p.194.

[32] George Rawlinson (translator), *History of Herodotus: Volume II, Third Edition,* UK, John Murray, 1875, pp.226-7.

[33] Erik Hornung, *History of Ancient Egypt,* pp.66-7.

[34] Runoko Rashidi, *The Middle Kingdom of Kemet,* in *Egypt Revisited,* p.198.

[35] Erik Hornung, *History of Ancient Egypt,* pp.70-1.

[36] W. G. Waddell (translator), *Manetho,* UK, William Heinemann, 1940, pp.79-81.

[37] Erik Hornung, *History of Ancient Egypt,* pp.71-2.

[38] Vivian Davies and Renée Friedman, *Egypt,* UK, British Museum Press, 1998, pp.114-5.

[39] Ibid.

[40] Ibid.

[41] Quoted in Vivian Davies and Renée Friedman, *Egypt*, p.112.

[42] Quoted in ibid., p.115.

[43] Erik Hornung, *History of Ancient Egypt*, pp.74-5.

[44] Vivian Davies and Renée Friedman, *Egypt*, pp.119-120.

[45] Ibid., p.129.

[46] Ibid., pp.97 and 129.

[47] Erik Hornung, *History of Ancient Egypt*, pp.75-7.

[48] Ibid., pp.78-80.

[49] Vivian Davies and Renée Friedman, *Egypt*, pp.97 and 129.

[50] Erik Hornung, *History of Ancient Egypt*, pp.80-2.

[51] Duncan MacNaughton, *A Scheme of Egyptian Chronology*, UK, Luzac & Co., 1932. pp.208-9.

[52] Erik Hornung, *History of Ancient Egypt*, pp.82-5.

[53] J. A. Rogers, *World's Great Men of Color, Volume I*, US, Macmillan, 1972, p.46.

[54] Erik Hornung, *History of Ancient Egypt*, pp.82-8.

[55] Ibid., pp.88-91.

[56] Vivian Davies and Renée Friedman, *Egypt*, pp.97-9.

[57] Ibid., p.130.

[58] Ibid., p.109.

[59] Ibid., p.135.

[60] Erik Hornung, *History of Ancient Egypt*, p.90.

[61] Ibid., pp.91-2.

[62] Ibid., pp.94-5.

[63] Vivian Davies and Renée Friedman, *Egypt*, p.136.

[64] Erik Hornung, *History of Ancient Egypt*, pp.94-5.

[65] Vivian Davies and Renée Friedman, *Egypt*, p.138.

[66] Erik Hornung, *History of Ancient Egypt*, pp.94-5.

[67] Barbara Watterson, *The Egyptians*, pp.131-3.

[68] Asa Hilliard, *Waset, the Eye of Ra and the Abode of Maat: The Pinnacle of Black World Leadership in the Ancient World*, in *Egypt Revisited*, ed Ivan Van Sertima, US, Transaction Publishers, 1989, p.212.

[69] Chancellor Williams, *The Destruction of Black Civilization*, US, Third World Press, 1987, p.94, Joseph McCabe, *The Golden Ages of History*, UK, Watts & Co., 1940, p.4, Rev. James Baikie, *The Life of the Ancient East*, UK, A. & C. Black, 1923, p.96 and Barbara Watterson, *The Egyptians*, p.151.

[70] James Henry Breasted, *A History of Egypt*, pp.344-5.

[71] Rev. James Baikie, *The Life of the Ancient East*, pp.98-9.

[72] J. A. Rogers, *World's Great Men of Color, Volume I*, p.57.

[73] Earl Walter Faruq, *The Power of Spiritual Determinism in Ancient Egyptian City Life*, in *Kemet and the African Worldview*, ed Jacob Carruthers and Maulana Karenga, US, University of Sankore Press, 1986, p.76.

[74] Erik Hornung, *History of Ancient Egypt*, pp.98-103.

[75] Ibid., pp.103-4.

[76] Christiane Desroches-Noblecourt, *Tutankhamen*, UK, Penguin, 1971, pp.110-1.

[77] Erik Hornung, *History of Ancient Egypt*, pp.107-8.

[78] Ibid., pp.108-9.

[79] Quoted in George Rawlinson, *Ancient Egypt: The Story of the Nations*, p.245.

[80] Erik Hornung, *History of Ancient Egypt,* pp.108-9.
[81] Vivian Davies and Renée Friedman, *Egypt,* p.143.
[82] Ibid., p.147.
[83] Erik Hornung, *History of Ancient Egypt,* pp.109-113.
[84] Ibid., p.113.
[85] Runoko Rashidi, *Ramses the Great,* in *Great Black Leaders,* ed Ivan Van Sertima, US, Transaction Publishers, 1988, pp.244-5.
[86] Vivian Davies and Renée Friedman, *Egypt,* p.147.
[87] Erik Hornung, *History of Ancient Egypt,* pp.113-6.
[88] Ibid., p.116.
[89] Ibid., pp.116-7.
[90] Ife Jogunosimi, *The Role of Royal Women in Ancient Egypt,* in *Kemet and the African Worldview,* ed Jacob Carruthers and Maulana Karenga, US, University of Sankore Press, 1986, pp.39-40.
[91] Erik Hornung, *History of Ancient Egypt,* pp.117-8.
[92] Rafique Jairazbhoy, *Rameses III: Father of Ancient America,* UK, Karnak House, 1992, p.25.
[93] Ibid., pp.9-75.
[94] Anthony T. Browder, *Nile Valley Contributions to Civilization,* US, Institute of Karmic Guidance, 1992, p.210.
[95] Quoted in Anthony T. Browder, *Nile Valley Contributions to Civilization,* p.209.
[96] Alfonso Medellin Zenlil, *The Olmec Culture,* in *The Olmec Tradition* (catalogue), US, The Museum of Fine Arts, Houston Texas, 1963, there are no page numbers in this catalogue.
[97] Ivan Van Sertima ed, *African Presence in Early America,* US, Transaction Publishers, 1992 and Ivan Van Sertima, *Early America Revisited,* US, Transaction Publishers, 1998.
[98] Alexander Von Wuthenau, *Art of the World: Pre-Columbian Terracottas,* UK, Methuen & Co., 1969, p.187.
[99] Beatrice Lumpkin, *Pyramids - American and African: A Comparison,* in *African Presence in Early America,* ed Ivan Van Sertima, 1992, pp.136-154.
[100] Ivan Van Sertima, *Egypto-Nubian Presences in Ancient Mexico,* in *African Presence in Early America,* ed Ivan Van Sertima, US, Transaction Publishers, 1992, pp.71-5.
[101] Keith M. Jordan, *The African Presence in Ancient America: Evidence from Physical Anthropology,* in *African Presence in Early America,* ed Ivan Van Sertima, US, Transaction Publishers, 1992, pp.106-9.
[102] Erik Hornung, *History of Ancient Egypt,* pp.118.
[103] Ibid., p.120.
[104] Vivian Davies and Renée Friedman, *Egypt,* pp.147-8.
[105] Ibid., p.148.
[106] Erik Hornung, *History of Ancient Egypt,* pp.120-3.
[107] Vivian Davies and Renée Friedman, *Egypt,* p.148.
[108] Erik Hornung, *History of Ancient Egypt,* pp.123.
[109] Ibid., pp.125-6.
[110] Ibid., pp.128-9.
[111] Cf. Chancellor Williams, *The Destruction of Black Civilization,* p.112.
[112] Derek A. Welsby, *The Kingdom of Kush,* US, Marcus Wiener, 1996, p.7.
[113] Ibid.
[114] Ibid., p.9.

[115] Ibid., pp.13, 83 and 207.
[116] Ibid., pp.13-14 and 17.
[117] Ibid., p.14.
[118] Ibid., pp.14 and 62-3.
[119] Ibid., pp.15-6.
[120] Ibid., p.7.
[121] Ibid., p.63.
[122] Ibid., p.82.
[123] Larry Williams & Charles S. Finch, *The Great Queens of Ethiopia,* in *Black Women in Antiquity,* ed Ivan Van Sertima, US, Transaction Publishers, 1988, p.23. See also p.21.
[124] Derek A. Welsby, *The Kingdom of Kush,* p.26.
[125] E. A. Wallis Budge, *A History of Ethiopia, Nubia & Abyssinia, Volume I,* UK, Methuen & Co., 1928, pp.27-32.
[126] Ibidem and Derek A. Welsby, *The Kingdom of Kush,* p.16.
[127] Derek A. Welsby, *The Kingdom of Kush,* p.63.
[128] Joseph E. Harris, *Africa & Africans as seen by the Classical Writers: William Leo Hansberry Notebook, Volume Two,* US, Howard University Press, 1977, pp.112-3.
[129] Derek A. Welsby, *The Kingdom of Kush,* pp.105, 106 and 110, and Vivian Davies and Renée Friedman, *Egypt,* pp.102-5.
[130] Lady Lugard, *A Tropical Dependency,* UK, James Nisbet & Co., 1906, p.220.
[131] Cheikh Anta Diop, *Precolonial Black Africa,* US, Lawrence Hill Books, 1987, p.196.
[132] Derek A. Welsby, *The Kingdom of Kush,* p.64.
[133] Ibid., pp.33 and 37.
[134] George Rawlinson (translator), *History of Herodotus Volume II,* p.216.
[135] Derek A. Welsby, *The Kingdom of Kush,* p.64.
[136] Quoted in Phaon Goldman, *The Nubian Renaissance,* in *Egypt Revisited,* ed Ivan Van Sertima, US, Transaction Publishers, 1989, p.267.
[137] Ivan Van Sertima, *The Moor in Africa and Europe,* in *Golden Age of the Moor,* ed Ivan Van Sertima, US, Transaction Publishers, 1992, p.2.
[138] Phaon Goldman, *The Nubian Renaissance,* in *Egypt Revisited,* pp.267-8.
[139] George Rawlinson, *Ancient Egypt: The Story of the Nations,* p.330.
[140] Quoted in Peggy A. Brooks-Bertram, *The Sixth Napatan Dynasty of Kush,* in *Egypt: Child of Africa,* ed Ivan Van Sertima, US, Transaction Publishers, 1994, p.156.
[141] Vivian Davies and Renée Friedman, *Egypt,* p.99.
[142] Derek A. Welsby, *The Kingdom of Kush,* pp.17, 19, 20, 64, 117 and 118.
[143] Ibid., p.33.
[144] Ibid., pp.17, 107, 108, 115 and 118.
[145] Peggy A. Brooks-Bertram, *The Sixth Napatan Dynasty of Kush,* p.157.
[146] Derek A. Welsby, *The Kingdom of Kush,* pp.64-5.
[147] Cheikh Anta Diop, *The African Origin of Civilization: Myth or Reality?* US, Lawrence Hill Books, 1974, p.221.
[148] Chancellor Williams, *The Destruction of Black Civilization,* pp.89-90.
[149] Lieutenant Francis Wilford, *On Egypt and the Nile From the Ancient Books of the Hindus,* in *Asiatick Researches, Volume III,* ed Sir William Jones, India, 1792, p.536.
[150] R. R. Madden, *Travels in Turkey, Egypt, Nubia and Palestine in 1824, 1825, 1826, and 1827, Volume II,* UK, Henry Colburn, 1829, p.95.
[151] Chancellor Williams, *The Destruction of Black Civilization,* pp.117-120.
[152] Derek A. Welsby, *The Kingdom of Kush,* p.65.

[153] Chancellor Williams, *The Destruction of Black Civilization*, p.125.

[154] Ibid., p.127.

[155] Derek A. Welsby, *The Kingdom of Kush*, p.119.

[156] Ibid., p.17.

[157] Ibid., p.45.

[158] Ibid., pp.122-3.

[159] W. E. B. DuBois, *The World and Africa*, US, International Publishers, 1965, p.139.

[160] Derek A. Welsby, *The Kingdom of Kush*, pp.65-6.

[161] Ibid., p.70.

[162] George Rawlinson (translator), *History of Herodotus, Volume II*, pp.423-4.

[163] Joseph E. Harris, *Africa & Africans as Seen by the Classical Writers: William Leo Hansberry Notebook, Volume Two*, p.111.

[164] He is using the 'short' Egyptian chronology.

[165] Ibid., pp.109-110.

[166] Ibid., p.110.

[167] Derek A. Welsby, *The Kingdom of Kush*, pp.99, 153-160.

[168] Chancellor Williams, *The Destruction of Black Civilization*, p.131.

[169] Vivian Davies and Renée Friedman, *Egypt*, pp.106-7.

[170] Timothy Kendall, *Kings of the Sacred Mountain*, in *Sudan: Ancient Kingdoms of the Nile*, ed Dietrich Wilding, France, Flammarion, 1997, pp.186-7, 198 and Dietrich Wilding, *The Kingdom of Napata and Meroe*, in *Sudan: Ancient Kingdoms of the Nile*, ed Dietrich Wilding, France, Flammarion, 1997, pp.226-35.

[171] A. A. Hakem, *The civilization of Napata and Meroe*, in UNESCO, *General History of Africa, Volume II*, ed G. Mokhtar, UK, James Currey, 1990, p.311.

[172] Charles S. Finch, *The Star of Deep Beginnings*, US, Khenti, 1998, p.38.

[173] A. J. Arkell, *The Valley of the Nile*, in *The Dawn of African History*, ed Roland Oliver, UK, Oxford University Press, 1961, p.10.

[174] Charles S. Finch, *The Star of Deep Beginnings*, p.31.

[175] Basil Davidson, *Africa in History*, US, Macmillan, 1991, pp.40-1.

[176] Roland Oliver & Brian M. Fagan, *Africa in the Iron Age*, UK, Cambridge University Press, 1975, pp.38-9.

[177] Derek A. Welsby, *The Kingdom of Kush*, pp.171, 174-6.

[178] Ibid., pp.34 and 47.

[179] Ibid., p.124.

[180] Ibid., pp.124-7.

[181] Ibid., p.54.

[182] E. A. Wallis Budge, *A History of Ethiopia, Nubia & Abyssinia, Volume I*, p.47.

[183] Ibid., pp.47-8 and Derek A. Welsby, *The Kingdom of Kush*, pp.34, 40 and 51.

[184] Basil Davidson, *African Kingdoms*, Netherlands, Time-Life Books, 1967, p.37.

[185] Chancellor Williams, *The Destruction of Black Civilization*, p.127. See also Basil Davidson, *Africa*, television series part 1: *Separate But Equal*, UK and Nigeria, Michael Beazley, Rm Arts, Channel Four Television and Nigerian Television, 1984.

[186] Chancellor Williams, *The Destruction of Black Civilization*, p.127.

[187] Derek A. Welsby, *The Kingdom of Kush*, p.193.

[188] W. E. B. DuBois, *The World and Africa*, p.138.

[189] Basil Davidson, *Africa*, television series part 1: *Separate But Equal*.

[190] Derek A. Welsby, *The Kingdom of Kush*, p.43.

[191] Ibid.

[192] Karl-Heinz Priese, *The Kingdom of Napata and Meroe,* in *Sudan: Ancient Kingdoms of the Nile,* ed Dietrich Wilding, France, Flammarion, 1997, p.216.

[193] Derek A. Welsby, *The Kingdom of Kush,* p.67.

[194] Larry Williams & Charles S. Finch, *The Great Queens of Ethiopia,* in *Black Women in Antiquity,* p.30.

[195] Ibid., pp.30-1 and Derek A. Welsby, *The Kingdom of Kush,* pp.39, 47 and 68-9.

[196] Derek A. Welsby, *The Kingdom of Kush,* pp.34, 77, 119, 122 and 124.

[197] Roland Oliver & Brian M. Fagan, *Africa in the Iron Age,* p.40.

[198] Basil Davidson, *African Kingdoms,* p.38.

[199] Ibid.

[200] George Wells Parker, *The Children of the Sun,* US, Black Classic Press, 1981 (original 1918), p.11.

CHAPTER EIGHT: EGYPTIAN CHRONOLOGY

Introduction

Just how old is Ancient Egypt? A survey of contemporary textbooks on this ancient culture gives a First Dynasty date of 3180 to 2900 BC. Dr F. D. P. Wicker, for example, gives a first Dynasty date of 2920 BC and advises his readers that: "Pharaonic dates are generally accepted as ± 75 years at the start of the dynastic period to precision from the 26th dynasty onwards".[1] The confidence that his dates are maximally only 75 years out is totally unjustified. Nor should readers be fooled by the apparent unanimity of scholars or their apparent refusal to discuss the problem. This shows little more than the pernicious effects of academic peer group pressure and the ability to put a brave face on contrary data. Professors Jackson and ben-Jochannan are to be commended for continually raising this problem in their works.[2] Despite the best efforts of historians and archaeologists over the last two hundred years, the Egyptian chronology has yet to be settled in a way that synthesises the known data. We propose to place the relevant conflicting information on the table with no attempt to paper over the cracks.

The following table presents the chronological ideas of various authorities and show a great divergence of opinion. Only the chronologies of Champollion-Figeac, Petrie in 1906, MacNaughton, Pochan,[3] and the present author, bear any resemblance to the Egyptian record as preserved by Manetho.

| | DYNASTIES | | | |
	I	VI	XII	XVIII
Manetho (3rd century BC)	5717	4426	3440	1674
Wilkinson (1836)	2320			1575
Champollion-Figeac (1839)	5867	4426	3703	1822
Lepsius (1858)	3892	2744	2380	1591
Brugsch (1877)	4400	3300	2466	1700
Meyer (1887)	3180	2530	2130	1530
Breasted (1906)	3400	2625	2000	1580
Petrie (1906)	5510	4206	3459	1580
Petrie (1929)	4553	3282	2586	1587
MacNaughton (1932)	5776	4360	3389	1709

Pochan (1971)	5619	4326	3336	1595
Brunson & Rashidi (1989)	3200	2345	1991	1560
Rohl (1998)	2789	2224	1800	1193
Chinweizu (1999)	4443	3162	1994	1788
Author (2006)	5660	4402	3405	1709

The Documentary Evidence

Perhaps the best overall source of Egyptian chronology would have been the *Royal Papyrus of Turin*. This document contained the names of three hundred and thirty kings from the First Dynasty to the New Kingdom, also the order in which they reigned, and the lengths of each reign. Unfortunately, the papyrus crumbled into pieces while being transported to the Museum in Turin. There have been various attempts to re-assemble the fragments, but this remains a controversial exercise. In its present form the document can only be very imperfectly read.[4] In the 1950's Sir Alan Gardiner, an English Egyptologist, made an important attempt to reconstruct the document. Modern historians now have at their disposal a fairly useful king's list but problems and omissions exist.

The lengths of reigns given by this document for some of the earliest kings seem very unlikely, however. Merbiapen (Anejib) and Semesen (Semerkhet) of the First Dynasty, for example, are given 74 years and 72 years on the throne respectively. Bawnetcher and Baneter of the Second Dynasty are given 95 years on the throne each. The pyramid builders, on the other hand, are given reigns that seem unusually short. Djoser is given 19 years, Sneferu is given 24 years, Khufu is given 23 years, and Menkaura is given 18 years.[5] This is problematic because when Herodotus visited Egypt, he was informed that the Great Pyramid took thirty years to build,[6] a figure widely used today. In the light of this tradition, the low figures cannot be accepted. The strength of the *Royal Papyrus of Turin,* however, is that from the Fifth Dynasty onwards through the Intermediate Periods, a great deal of useful data is preserved. In our chronology, we rely on this document for reconstructing the Eleventh through to the Fourteenth Dynasties.

Another Egyptian source is the Tablet of Abydos. This Tablet shows Pharaoh Seti I, of the Nineteenth Dynasty, accompanied by his young son, Rameses II, paying homage to seventy-five royal ancestors. The seventy-five kings are in chronological order, but the lengths of their reigns are not given on the Tablet. Moreover, the scribe who compiled the text presented only a selection of the available kings. For example, none of the kings of the Thirteenth through to the Seventeenth Dynasties are included on the Tablet. No one knows what criteria the scribe used to choose who got mentioned from those who were to be omitted.[7] The Tablet of Saqqara comes from the period of Rameses II. It contains a list of forty-seven kings but the order and detail still corroborates the information given on the Tablet of Abydos.[8] The Tablet of Karnak shows Thutmose III paying homage to sixty-one royal ancestors. The kings are listed in approximately chronological order but it peters out during the Thirteenth Dynasty.[9] When combined, the three tablets name over a hundred kings from Mena to Rameses II.[10] These tablets have proved invaluable in reconstructing the Tenth Dynasty.

The Egyptian scribe, Manetho of Sebennytus, was a high priest of Heliopolis. He wrote his work, *Aegyptiaca,* during the period of Ptolemy Philadelphus. In this great work, Manetho was the first to divide the history of Egypt into the rise and fall of thirty dynasties. Unfortunately, this valuable text is now lost. Today, what has survived from it are quotations that appear in the writings of Julius Africanus, Eusebius, Josephus and Syncellus. These writers, however, fail to agree on what they claim Manetho wrote. According to Africanus, for example, 561 kings ruled in Egypt over 5524 (or 5373) years. According to Eusebius, about 361 kings ruled over a period of 4480 or 4470 years. Worse than this, there is no absolute agreement between them over the arrangements of the dynasties, the number of kings within each dynasty, or the lengths of their reigns. It is generally agreed, however, that the Africanus quotations best corroborate the other known facts about Egyptian history than the quotations of Eusebius.[11] It seems certain, however, that Africanus double counted the Seventeenth Dynasty. Adjusting for this and assuming a date of 343 BC for the fall of Nektanebos II, this yields a date of 5717 BC for the earliest kings of the First Dynasty, quoting Africanus. The first kings of the Sixth Dynasty would be 4426 BC, the Twelfth Dynasty would be 3440 BC (from the time of Amenemhet I) and the Eighteenth Dynasty would be 1674 BC. An assessment of Manetho's work contains no lengths of royal reigns that are improbable or unlikely. His account of the early rulers of the first four dynasties, for example, is clearly superior to that given by the Turin Papyrus. For this reason, we rely on this document to reconstruct the early dynastic periods. In addition, we regard it as a reliable guide to the general reconstruction of Egyptian chronology.

There are, however, slight differences between what we have presented here and that recorded by Africanus. Evidence exists, here and there, to show that there are some missing kings from Manetho's First and Second Dynasties. Manetho fails to mention Hor-Aha, Mer-Neith, Hotepsekemui, Peribsen, etc. We have added these kings into the basic structure recorded by Africanus. On the other hand, evidence for three of the kings recorded for Manetho's Third Dynasty is weak. We have therefore deleted them from our kings' list. Nor have we accepted Africanus' view that Dynasty Seven consisted of 70 kings ruling in 70 days though it seems evident that he was not alone in holding this belief.

Herodotus is another useful source on Egyptian chronology. He recorded that during his visit to Egypt, one of the priests read to him a list of kings from Menes to Sesostris (in this context Rameses II). There were 312 Egyptian kings and 18 Ethiopian kings. Evidently the priest did not inform Herodotus of the Hyksos Dynasties. What is surprising, however, is just how closely this data corroborates Manetho. According to him, or more exactly Africanus and Eusebius, the number of kings from Mena to Rameses II are given as follows.[12]

Dynasty 1	8 Thinites
Dynasty 2	9 Thinites
Dynasty 3	9 Memphites
Dynasty 4	8 Memphites (Eusebius gives 17 Memphites)
Dynasty 5	9 Elephantines
Dynasty 6	6 Memphites
Dynasty 7	4 Memphites (Africanus gives 70 Memphites)
Dynasty 8	27 Memphites
Dynasty 9	19 Herakleopolitans
Dynasty 10	19 Herakleopolitans
Dynasty 11	16 Thebans
Dynasty 12	7 Thebans + Amenemhet I
Dynasty 13	60 Thebans
Dynasty 14	76 Kings of Xois
Dynasty 17	43 Thebans
Dynasty 18	16 Thebans
Dynasty 19	2 Thebans (i.e. Seti I and Rameses II)
Total	*339 kings*

Our reckoning is slightly different to that of Manetho but our conclusions are even closer to those of Herodotus.

Dynasty 1	9 Thinites
Dynasty 2	12 Thinites
Dynasty 3	6 Memphites
Dynasty 4	7 Memphites or Elephantines
	(Eusebius gives 17 Memphites)
Dynasty 5	9 Elephantines
Dynasty 6	6 Memphites
Dynasty 7	4 Memphites (Africanus gives 70 Memphites)
Dynasty 8	27 Memphites

Dynasty 9	19 Herakleopolitans
Dynasty 10	19 Herakleopolitans
Dynasty 11	7 Thebans
Dynasty 12	8 Thebans
Dynasty 13	60 Thebans
Dynasty 14	76 Kings of Xois
Dynasty 17	43 Thebans
Dynasty 18	15 Thebans
Dynasty 19	2 Thebans (i.e. up to Rameses II)
Total	*329 kings*

The 18 Ethiopian kings spoken of by Herodotus are explicable. Eusebius records 17 kings for Dynasty Four. He further states that Khufu was the *third* king of this dynasty. Presumably Sneferu and some other, as yet, unidentified king preceded him. Africanus records 8 kings for Dynasty Four and 8 kings for Dynasty Five. Moreover, he lists Khufu as the *second* king of the Dynasty. Africanus' view is the one generally accepted today except that most writers allow 7 kings for Dynasty Four and 9 kings for Dynasty Five. Dynasty Five originated in Elephantine. In the time of Herodotus, Elephantine was considered part of Ethiopia (i.e. Nubia). This would explain 8 of the Ethiopian kings. It seems evident that the Fourth Dynasty of Eusebius is equivalent to the Fourth and Fifth Dynasties of Africanus but with the mysterious king added to the beginning of the dynasty. It also seems evident that the Egyptian priest who Herodotus consulted shared the same view as Eusebius in classifying them all as part of the same dynasty. It therefore followed that the Fourth as well as the Fifth Dynasty shared the same Elephantine origins. The notion that the Fourth Dynasty is from Ethiopia (i.e. Nubia) finds support from the fact that Khufu is also called Khnum Khuf in some of the inscriptions. Khnum is, of course, an "Ethiopian" deity. This would explain 17 of the Ethiopian kings (i.e. 7 + 1 + 9). We believe that the 18th Ethiopian king is Nehesi of the Fourteenth Dynasty. Dynasty Fourteen is generally considered to be Asian, a view that we share. It is evident that Herodotus considered it indigenous.

Herodotus, however, drew very different conclusions from those that we draw. He believed that the dynastic history of Egypt spanned 11,340 years on the basis that 341 generations multiplied by just over 33 years for a generation gives a total of 11,340 years.[13] There is evidence that we shall discuss that approximately supports his view but we hold a very different position.

Diodorus Siculus is another useful early source. He reckoned that Egyptian history spanned more than 4,700 years, counting back from the Persian conquest of 525 BC. This results in a First Dynasty date of earlier than 5225 BC. Moreover, he stated that 470 kings ruled, of which four were Ethiopians and five were queens.[14] There were indeed five Queen Pharaohs in Egyptian history. They were Mer-Neith of the First Dynasty, Nitocris of the Sixth Dynasty, Sebekneferura of the Twelfth Dynasty, Hatshepsut of the Eighteenth Dynasty and Tawosret of the Nineteenth Dynasty. Concerning the four Ethiopian kings, evidently Diodorus only considered the Twenty Fifth Dynasty to have been Ethiopian. These kings were Piye, Shabaqo, Shebitqo and Taharqo. However, we do not fully agree with his figure of 470 kings from Menes to the conquest of the Persians. We think the correct figure, including the Hyksos Dynasties, was 415. Perhaps Diodorus accepted the view shared by Africanus that Dynasty Seven consisted of 70 kings. This would produce a total of 481 kings showing a discrepancy between his reasoning and ours of just 11 kings.

Birth of the Short Chronology

Contemporary Egyptology uses the thirty-dynasty model that Manetho pioneered. Many writers, however, hold great reservations of using the Manetho-Africanus chronology unmodified. The notion that Egyptian history began 5,000 years before that of the Greeks, for example, proved difficult to swallow. The fact that Greek scholarship corroborates it was neither here nor there. Scholars influenced by the *Holy Bible* also had problems accepting it. In the early nineteenth century, Sir John Gardiner Wilkinson, a British Egyptologist, proposed a First Dynasty date of 2320 BC!

In 1887 Professor Eduard Meyer of the University of Berlin proposed a First Dynasty date of 3180 BC. Meyer correctly argued that very few Egyptian monuments are known to modern scholarship that date from the Seventh Dynasty through to the Tenth Dynasty. Few monuments are also known from the period of the Thirteenth Dynasty through to the Seventeenth Dynasty. Meyer concluded that these periods must have represented prolonged social and political chaos. For these reasons, few monuments were built. Controversially, he concluded that the many hundreds of years Manetho gave to these periods could not have been so. Meyer reasoned that many kings of the different dynasties must have ruled simultaneously over different parts of the country. The effect of Meyer's theories was to compress the Manetho chronology by over 2000 years.[15]

In England, however, scholars free from the spell of Wilkinson remained unimpressed. Sir Flinders Petrie, the dean of the British archaeologists, wrote an eloquent defence of the Manetho chronology in 1906 and proposed a First Dynasty date of 5510 BC.[16] Sir Wallis Budge, then Keeper of Egyptian Antiquities at the British Museum, preferred a chronology in between the ideas of Meyer and Petrie. He proposed a First Dynasty date of 4483 BC.[17]

One obvious problem with using the simultaneous dynasty argument to compress the chronology is that it flatly contradicts the research of Herodotus and Manetho, two of our most important ancient authorities. According to Herodotus:

> Thus far I have spoken on the authority of the Egyptians and their priests. They declare that from their first king to this last-mentioned monarch, the priest of Vulcan [i.e. Ptah], was a period of three hundred and forty-one generations; such, at least, they say, was the number both of their kings, and of their high priests, during this interval.[18]

The priests offered Herodotus visual evidence of this. To cite Herodotus once more:

> They led me into the inner sanctuary, which is a spacious chamber, and showed me a multitude of colossal statues, in wood, which they counted up, and found to amount to the exact number they had said: the custom being for every high-priest during his lifetime to set up his statue in the temple. As they showed me the figures and reckoned them up, they assured me that each was the son of the one preceding him; and this they repeated throughout the whole line.[19]

Mena founded the Temple of Ptah in the First Dynasty, as we have seen. Five thousand years later, the priests of that institution were able to show Herodotus proof of 341 uninterrupted generations of priests who had presided there. This eloquently refutes the notion held by Meyer that one can compress Egyptian history by claiming simultaneous dynasties. Or are we supposed to accept that there were simultaneous dynasties of priests of Ptah also?

Sir Flinders Petrie offers evidence that Manetho was quite capable of dealing with simultaneous dynasties when they occurred without the suppositions of modern scholars:

> Manetho has been often accused of double reckoning, by stating two contemporary dynasties or kings separately. Every instance in which this has been supposed has broken down when examined in detail. Not a single case of overlapping periods can be proved against him. On the contrary, there are two excellent proofs of his care to avoid such errors. The XIth dynasty we know by the monuments to have covered at least one century, and probably two. Yet Manetho only gives 43 years, evidently because he reckoned the Xth dynasty as legitimate, and until that ended he did not count the XIth dynasty, which was partly contemporary. Again, in the case of a single reign, we find the same treatment. It is well known that Taharqa was reigning about 29 years before the accession of Psametek I. Manetho places three ancestors of Psametek before him, reigning 21 years in all. Here, it has been said, is a clear case of double reckoning of overlapping reigns. But just here is Manetho's care shown, for he cuts down the well-known reign of Taharqa to 8 or 18 years, according to

different readings; and this 8 years, with the 21 of the three other kings, makes
the 29 years of Taharqa. In fact, he has only counted Taharqa until he takes up
what he regards as the legitimate line, and thus he ignores the 21 years of the
reign which overlapped those of the other kings.[20]

On this reasoning, we think that Dynasty Ten and Eleven were
contemporaneous but with the latter dynasty outlasting the former by 43 years.
Similarly, we think that Dynasty Thirteen and Fourteen were contemporaneous
but with the latter dynasty outlasting the former by 184 years. Finally, we think
that Dynasty Sixteen and Seventeen were contemporaneous. They both ended
at the same date.

Professor James Henry Breasted, an American Egyptologist, was a disciple
of Meyer. He founded the University of Chicago's Oriental Institute, soon to
become the leading Egyptological body in the world. In 1906 Breasted
proposed a First Dynasty date of 3400 BC. Due to the dominance of the
Oriental Institute in the world of Egyptology, this chronology became the
standard one used by Egyptologists. These days it has been inched down to
3100 BC or 3000 BC. Some textbooks now carry a First Dynasty date of 2920
BC. Even though the modern chronologies are starting to approach that of Sir
Gardiner Wilkinson, the celebrated nineteenth century bigot, modern historians
still derive their basic ideas on this issue from Breasted. We therefore let the
masterly American scholar defend his ideas in his own words:

> [T]he calendar is of inestimable value to us in establishing the chronology of
> Egyptian history. Where the heliacal rising of Sothis [i.e. Sirius] is recorded in
> terms of the calendar, it is a matter of the simplest arithmetic to determine,
> within a margin of four years, in what B. C. the rising occurred. As we have
> seen, three such dates are preserved to us, two of which each give the year of
> the king's reign, and from these the entire Twelfth Dynasty, and the reign of
> Amenhotep I in the Eighteenth Dynasty, are established within four years in
> terms B.C. They show that the Twelfth Dynasty began in 2000 B.C., and the
> reign of Amenhotep I in 1557 B.C., thus determining the accession of the
> Eighteenth Dynasty as 1580 B.C.[21]

The Kahun Papyrus and the Ebers Calendar, it was argued, gave objective
astronomical dates for the ninth year of Amenhotep I and also the seventh year
of Senwosret III. These dates can be judged from the rising of the star Sothis
which can be objectively calculated by astronomy. Fixing these two dates, and
adding up the lengths of the reigns for the other kings of Amenhotep I's and
Senwosret III's dynasties, fixes the Twelfth Dynasty at 2000 to 1788 BC, and
the Eighteenth at 1580 to 1320 BC. However, it remains to be seen if Breasted
is correct in assuming that Sothis is the star Sirius. In defence of the Breasted
position, we can cite Leo Depuydt, a modern authority on the Egyptian
calendar, who wrote the following:

Unlike agriculturally significant events such as the inundation and the harvest, *astronomical* events often occur at fixed times in the year. An example of an astronomical event that naturally presents itself as a yearly beginning is the heliacal rising in July of the star Sirius, Sothis in Greek, *spdt* in Egyptian. The fact that Sirius rises approximately when the Nile does only reinforces its role as marker of a new beginning. The Sothic rising came to be viewed as the herald of the inundation ... There is much evidence that the rising of Sirius was conceived of as a yearly beginning ... No evidence is more explicit than a passage from the decree of Canopus.[22]

There is, however, another major problem but Breasted was aware of it. The fall of the Twelfth Dynasty in 1788 BC and the rise of the Eighteenth Dynasty in 1580 BC leaves a time span of just 208 years. The *Royal Papyrus of Turin* and other documentary evidence shows that at least 116 kings reigned during Breasted's proposed 208 years. Breasted himself put the total at 118 kings. This seems to be far too short a period to accommodate such a large number of kings. Breasted, like Meyer, claims that several kings ruled at the same time in different parts of the country. To show that this was possible, he adds that:

Under the Moslems 77 viceroys held the throne of Egypt in 118 years, from 750 to 868 A. D. In Europe some 80 Roman emperors after Commodus ruled in a period of 90 years (193-283 A. D.; see Meyer, *op. cit.*). The 118 kings enumerated in this confused age by the Turin Papyrus may have ruled no more than 150 years; 100 years is ample for the Hyksos, of which 50 years may be contemporary with the native dynasts.[23]

Believing this issue settled, Dr Breasted proposed 315 years for the period between the Seventh and the Tenth Dynasties but adds that "this estimate is extremely uncertain".[24] Breasted further allows 925 years for the first six dynasties and 160 years for the Eleventh Dynasty. This results in a First Dynasty date of 3400 BC calculated as 2000 BC + 160 + 315 + 925 = 3400 BC.

The truth is, however, the issue of the Thirteenth through to the Seventeenth Dynasties is not settled. Assuming simultaneous dynasties, as Meyer and Breasted claim, the time periods between the Twelfth and the Eighteenth Dynasties ought to be dictated by the longest dynasty of the period. Africanus informs us that the Thirteenth Dynasty lasted 453 years, the Fourteenth Dynasty lasted at least 184 years, the Fifteenth 284 years, the Sixteenth 518 and the Seventeenth 151 years. Therefore, the logic of the Meyer-Breasted position should give a period of at least 518 years for the fall of the Twelfth and the rise of Eighteenth Dynasties not a measly 208 years. Quoting Eusebius instead of Africanus won't help their case either. Eusebius gives 453 years for the Thirteenth Dynasty, fully 245 years more than Meyer and Breasted have allowed.[25]

In addition, the 925 years Breasted allowed for the first six dynasties is inadmissible. Both Manetho and the Turin Canon, Egyptology's only possible sources, allow more years for this period. The Turin Canon has missing values for over a dozen early kings but even if these are discounted, the total number of years given still totals 949 years.[26] Adding the missing values would certainly result in well over a thousand years. In addition, Diodorus informs us that Mena and 54 successors (i.e. Dynasties One through to Six) reigned for more that 1,400 years.[27] This corroborates Africanus' figure of 1,494 years and our figure 1,472 years. It should be clear then that the Meyer-Breasted position is not based, as they claim, on simultaneous dynasties but on whims and prejudices.

Manetho Resurrected

In 1932 Duncan MacNaughton, a Scottish Orientalist, vigorously challenged the Meyer-Breasted chronology. He argued that Meyer and Breasted were wrong to claim that Sirius was the only Sothic star the Egyptians used as the basis for their calendar. Before 2036 BC and even after, Spica, one of the stars of Virgo, was the chief star that was used. He further claims that the original new year of the Egyptians began with the month of Hathor and not with the month of Thoth. In support of this view, MacNaughton cites the following pieces of evidence:

At all times the Egyptians attached importance to the Isis-Sothis, Sirius, and in the late period regarded its rising as the commencement of the sidereal year. Their original Sothis, however, was Spica, the star from which both they and the Babylonians measured their zodiacs, and in the Calendar of Esneh the day of its [i.e. the Sothic star] Rising is referred to as the Beginning of the Year of the Ancients. In the Arthribis Zodiac A, the old Sothic symbol of the star in the horns of the Hathor Cow is opposite the beginning of Libra, thus confirming the importance of this sign as the first sign of the zodiac and of Spica as the measuring star. That Hathor (Libra rising) was the original first month of the fixed civil calendar is also indicated by references in the old inscriptions to the New Year ceremonies. From these Brusch deduced, according to Budge ... that "Sothis rose heliacally on the first day of the Egyptian New Year, and when the Sun-God Ra had entered his boat, Hathor, the goddess of the star Sothis, went with him and took up her place like a crown upon his forehead." Also, in the hymn to Ra in the *Book of the Dead,* the deceased officer Nekht says, "O thou beautiful being, thou dost renew thyself in thy season in the form of the Disk within thy mother Hathor," thus clearly showing that the original New Year began with Hathor, not Thoth.[28]

MacNaughton demonstrated that the astronomical date for the ninth year of Amenhotep I was not the 1557 BC postulated by Breasted. Rather it was 1674-

1673 BC using Spica as the Sothic star, not Sirius. In addition, Breasted *et al,* claim that Epet was the 11th month of the calendar, when clearly it was the 10th. In other words the "short" chronologists had to claim the Ebers calendar meant something other than it actually said. If Breasted *et al* used Sirius without re-interpreting the Ebers calendar, they would have produced an Amenhotep I date of 1424 BC, an unacceptable date - even to them:

> The Egyptologist Ebers [explains MacNaughton] discovered a papyrus dated on the reverse the 9th of the 11th month in the 9th year of [Amenhotep I] ... The script continues in the form of a calendar ...

New Year's Day	month 11, day 9	Rising of Sothis
Tekhi	month 12, day 9	
Menkhet	month 1, day 9	
Hathor	month 2, day 9	
Kaherka	month 3, day 9	
Shefbedet	month 4, day 9	
Rekeh	month 5, day 9	
Rekeh	month 6, day 9	
Renenouti	month 7, day 9	
Khonsou	month 8, day 9	
Khen Khat	month 9, day 9	
Epet	month 10, day 9	

> The calendar thus explicitly states that Menkhet was then the first month ... In the late calendar of Esneh two New Years were celebrated, one at the Rising of Sirius and the other, the New Year of the Ancients, at the Rising of Spica ... Calculation shows that Spica rose on the 9th of Re Hor Khouti the 11th month (then equivalent to 20th September) about 1676-4 B.C. ... We have seen how in other cases importance was attached to the great conjunctions of Jupiter and Saturn. Calculation shows that one of these fell in 1674 B.C. ... 9th Re Hor Khouti did not tally with the Rising of Sirius (14th July in South, 19th July in North) till about 1424-1404 B.C., which is incompatible with any system of chronology so far proposed [including the Meyer-Breasted one]. Consequently those who consider that "Rising of Sothis" is incapable of meaning anything else than the Rising of Sirius have felt compelled to postulate that though Menkhet is called the first month the calendar meant Thoth and thus the eleventh month was Epet though the calendar distinctly calls the tenth month Epet. This [falsely] yielded a date in the 16th century [BC] which seemed to them satisfactory.[29]

MacNaughton's new date for year 9 of Amenhotep I of 1674 or 1673 would lead to an Eighteenth Dynasty date of 1709 BC. Incidentally, Africanus gave the year 9 of Amenhotep I as 1661 BC. Compared to MacNaughton's view, this is a discrepancy of 13 years. On Breasted's chronology, the discrepancy is 104 years (i.e. 1661 - 1557).

In Mesopotamia (i.e. Iraq and Syria) a clay cylinder of King Nabonidus was found. On this document is the statement that King Sharaktishuriyash reigned in Mesopotamia 800 years before Nabonidus' time.[30] Since Nabonidus lived in 552 BC, this implies that Sharaktishuriyash flourished before 1352 BC. It is generally agreed among historians that a certain Burnaburiash lived over 120 years before Sharaktishuriyash. This places King Burnaburiash around 1475-1448 BC. However, Burnaburiash corresponded with Akhenaten of Egypt and his letters have come down to us. Akhenaten obviously must have lived at the same time as Burnaburiash. MacNaughton places Akhenaten between 1501 and 1474 BC and this harmonises well with the Nabonidus data. Breasted and all the other "short" chronologists place Akhenaten over a hundred years later. To appease the short chronologists, specialists in Mesopotamian history customarily claim that there is an error in the Nabonidus document. In other words, the scribe should have said that Sharaktishuriyash lived 680 years before Nabonidus's time instead of the 800 years specified.[31] It is on such make believe foundations that the short chronology was built.

At the Karnak Temple additional evidence was found. In 1904 an alabaster water clock was discovered there belonging to the time of Amenhotep III. The clock was essentially a water pot with an aperture for the outflow of water. On the inside rim of the pot are the numbers of the calendar months in order from 1 to 12. Under each sign of the month are calibrated intervals to show how far the water level has fallen to. The calibrated intervals indicate twelve hours of the night measured by the level of the water. The lower the water level, the greater the time period that had elapsed. However, the calibrated interval representing the 12th hour of time is lowest in the 3rd and 4th months and highest in the 9th and 10th months. This shows that a night in the 3rd or 4th month was longer than a night in the 9th or 10th months. Why was this?

An Egyptian hour of the night was defined as one-twelfth the period from sunset to sunrise and not as one-twenty fourth of the day. During the Summer Solstice, the night was at its shortest and therefore each hour of the night was at its shortest during that part of the year. On the other hand, during the Winter Solstice, the night was at its longest and therefore each hour of the night was also at its longest. Filling the clock with the same amount of water, the clock will empty itself more during a winter night than a summer night, simply because the winter night was longer. The 3rd and 4th months of the year must therefore be around the period of the Winter Solstice and the 9th and 10th months must be around the time of the Summer Solstice. For this reason, the calibrated intervals on the clock were further apart for the winter period and closer together for the summer periods.

Duncan MacNaughton demonstrates that during the period of Amenhotep III, 1538 to 1501 BC, the Summer Solstice did indeed occur between the period of the 9th and 10th months of the Egyptian year. Using the Julian calendar, the Solstice would fall on the 7th July. During the Amenhotep period, this date would tally as the 29th day of the 9th month and the intervening days to the 8th day of the 10th month. On the short chronology, however, the date of Amenhotep III is 120 years later. During this period, the 9th and 10th months correspond with late March to the beginning of May. Clearly this is the wrong date for the Summer Solstice. This elegantly refutes the short chronology date.[32]

David Rohl, a most unlikely contemporary source, presented archaeological evidence that supports this date. He also shows that the standard Egyptological chronology has an Eighteenth Dynasty date that is 120 years too late:

> [A]t the beginning of the [Eighteenth] dynasty we have the eruption of Thera, whose ash straddles the Late Minoan IA period (in Aegean archaeology terms). For many years archaeologists had tied LM IA into the early 18th Dynasty on the basis of their ceramic chronology. This dated the eruption to the reign of Ahmose [Amenhotep I's predecessor] or later. The date of the eruption, established by archaeologists, has recently received dramatic confirmation in M. Bietak's discovery of pumice within a stratified context at Tell ed-Daba (Ezbet Helmi) which spans the period from Ahmose to Thutmose III (OC [Old Chronology]- 1539-1425 BC). However, C-14 dates for short-lived materials from the Theran eruption span the period 1760-1540 BC with the great majority falling in the earlier period. As a result, in 1989 the Third International Thera Congress favoured an eruption date between circa 1680 and 1670 BC. Of course, this was before the discovery of pumice in a datable Egyptian context. In the conventional chronology, the earliest Ahmose could have reigned according to Egyptian dating is *circa* 1550 BC which is at least 120 years later than the date of the eruption established by the radiocarbon method. If the eruption took place sometime later than the reign of Ahmose, the chronological chasm between Egyptian archaeology and radiocarbon dating would be even greater.[33]

MacNaughton further proposes much earlier dates for the Twelfth Dynasty bearing in mind that any proposed date must harmonise with an astronomically based date for the seventh year of Senwosret III. He proposes a Spica date of 3274 BC. This is the latest possible date before Breasted's failed 1880 BC that meets the criteria, making the beginning of the Twelfth Dynasty 3373 BC (or 3389 including Amenemhet I). This date corroborates Manetho's Twelfth Dynasty date of 3440 BC. Updating MacNaughton's ideas, we offer a Twelfth Dynasty date of 3405 BC. Incidentally, Africanus gave the year 7 of Senwosret III as 3285 BC. This is a discrepancy of just 11 years compared to Breasted's discrepancy of 1405 years (i.e. 3285 - 1880).

Professor Breasted, however, dismisses such early dates for the Twelfth Dynasty as "hardly worthy of a serious answer". He feels that the gap of a thousand years between the fall of the Twelfth and the rise of the Eighteenth Dynasty is not credible because:

> It involves the assumption that nearly fifteen hundred years of history have been enacted in the Nile valley without leaving a trace behind! It is like imagining that in European history we could insert at will a period equal to that from the fall of Rome to the present![34]

This is a bogus analogy. It involves unfairly comparing Egypt, a single country, with Europe, a whole continent. Dr Breasted implies that it is impossible for Europe not to have left remains behind them from the Roman period to the present. Quite true for a continent but there are plenty of examples of individual countries that have large gaps in their archaeological records. The Professors' derision can therefore be ignored on this point. On the other hand the Egyptian written record is perfectly solid. It is quite easy and very likely that 116 or more kings really did rule in a thousand years, excluding the Hyksos and Seventeenth Dynasty kings. The erudite Scot wrote that Breasted's argument at best:

> shows that short reigns are possible. It does not show that they are probable. When we are compelled to choose between probability and possibility, it is the probability we must prefer. Manetho gave 60 kings for the Thirteenth Dynasty and 76 for the Fourteenth, 136 in all. About 118 [i.e. 116] of these have been found on the broken Turin Papyrus ... In my chronology they ruled 937 years or an average of slightly less than 7 years each. I have not discovered any period in history in which 136 consecutive rulers averaged less than 2 years. Yet Breasted's figures require an average of 1 1/3 years [if the date of 1580 BC is accepted for the Eighteenth Dynasty]. There are many periods in history where 136 consecutive rulers averages more than 7 years. It is safe to say that 48 different periods of 100 years in different countries could easily be found in which the average reign exceeded (often greatly exceeded) 7 years, while it is doubtful if any instances of average reigns under 2 years extending over a period of 100 years could be found except the two instanced by Breasted. The probability is therefore at least 48 to 2 against his chronology on this ground. (96 per cent. in favour of my theory, 4 per cent. in favour of his.)[35]

In addition, the Turin Papyrus, although fragmented, gives the reigns of 15 identifiable kings of the Thirteenth Dynasty (see page 258). They ruled an average of 6 years each. Manetho gives them an average of 7 1/2 years each, which seems to tally closely with the Turin average of 6 years. We fully agree with MacNaughton in rejecting Breasted's position, which requires each king to reign for an average of 1 1/3 years each. However, we draw a different conclusion to that of MacNaughton. In our view Dynasty Thirteen lasted 453 years, just as Manetho recorded, and Dynasty Fourteen lasted 184 years. This gives a total of 637 years. Since Dynasty Fourteen consisted of 76 kings, we believed they must have overlapped with Dynasty Thirteen at some uncertain date (possibly 3015 BC) and ruled as the sole kings of Egypt for 184 years after the fall of Dynasty Thirteen. We have selected the date of 3015 BC on two grounds. Dr Hornung informs us that Neferhotep I of the Thirteenth Dynasty continued to have political influence in Palestine.[36] This implies that he had no rival in the North. Dr Watterson informs us that Neferhotep I and two successors (Sihathorre and Sebekhotep IV) formed a mini dynasty.[37] This implies continued political stability until the death of Sebekhotep IV. We conjecture that the Fourteenth Dynasty began after his time hence 3015 BC at the earliest.

Clinching the argument over his Twelfth Dynasty date, MacNaughton informed us that:

> The Festival of the Beginning of the Seasons was on the 21st of the 8th month of Sen[wosret] III.'s 18th year. As we have seen the crude probability exceeded .99998+ in favour of 3263 B.C. It may be assumed that none would place the date at the previous Great Festival in 4176 B.C. (which was not on the 21st of the 8th month). The succeeding Great Festival was in 2409 but the date fell in the 3rd month and if any would like to see in this date the 18th year of Sen[wosret] III. they would require to postulate an artificial change of 5 months in the calendar, which seems exceedingly improbable. The Festival does not tally at all with the date postulated on the "short" chronology so that the probability here is 100 per cent. in favour of the earlier date.[38]

We conclude that Dynasties Thirteen, Fourteen, Fifteen, Sixteen and Seventeen lasted 1473 years calculated as 3182 BC for the end of Dynasty Twelve minus 1709 BC for the rise of Dynasty Eighteen. Incidentally, Africanus gave this figure as 1439 years, calculated as 453 + 184 + 284 + 518. This is a discrepancy between our view and that of Africanus of just 34 years (i.e. 1473 - 1439). This compares favourably with Breasted's discrepancy of 1231 years (i.e. 1439 - 208). Moreover, the *Royal Canon of Turin* names 116 of the 136 kings of Dynasties Thirteen and Fourteen. *The Book of Sothis* names 30 of the 38 kings of Dynasties Fifteen and Sixteen.

For the Old Kingdom period MacNaughton claims a date of 5714 BC for the ascension of Pharaoh Athothis I (i.e. Hor-Aha), the second ruler of the First Dynasty. He based this argument on an interpretation of an Egyptian royal chronicle called the *Palermo Stone*. On the second line of the stone, Professor Breasted interprets a ten-year period from the First Dynasty as follows:

1st year.	Birth of Anubis.
2nd year.	End of one king's year, and the accession of another.
3rd year.	Feast of Desher.

6th year.	Feast of Sokar.
7th year.	Birth of the goddess Yamet.
8th year.	Birth of Min.
9th year.	Birth of Anubis.
10th year.	First occurrence of the Feast of Zet.

Commenting on Breasted's findings, Duncan MacNaughton interprets the data thus:

> It is evident that these are recurring festivals, and probable that they recur at regular intervals. They all reappear on other parts of the stone, and in addition to the third line [of the Palermo Stone] the Births of Seshat and Mefdet are recorded. The fact that there are five "births" suggests that these celebrations have reference to the cycles of the five planets known to the ancients ... If the first year is 5715-4 (or perhaps 5714-3) the phenomena tally thus (the date of the Rising of Spica being then roughly 24th August):

5715-4 1st year.	Morning rising of Venus	c.17th July	5714 B.C.
5710-9 6th year.	Mercury invisible at inferior conjunction	c.15th September to 8th October	5709
5709-8 7th year.	Saturn rising	c.29th August	5708
5708-7 8th year.	Jupiter rising	c.9th August	5707
5707-6 9th year.	Morning rising of Venus	c.15th July	5706
5706-5 10th year.	Rising of Jupiter	c.6th October	5705
	Rising of Saturn	c.28th September	5705[39]

MacNaughton believes that the astronomical data presented above demonstrates that the First Dynasty period described on the *Palermo Stone* must refer to the period 5715 to 5705 BC. In no other period do we get the astronomical risings or conjunctions of Mercury, Venus, Saturn and Jupiter. He further supposes that the births of Anubis, Min, etcetera, that are recorded on the Stone, are references to these astronomical phenomena. In the second year, 5714 BC, the change of king is believed, by MacNaughton, to be the death of Pharaoh Mena and the accession of Pharaoh Athothis I (i.e. Hor-Aha). On this evidence, he proposed an accession date for Mena of 5776 BC. We disagree.

We believe that MacNaughton would have to prove that the Egyptians had this level of astronomical knowledge at this early date first. We accept the findings of Charles Dupuis, Count De Volney and Sir William Peck on the early Nile Valley origin of the Zodiac.[40] However, we believe that more evidence is required to show that the Egyptians knew of the planetary movements and held festivals in their honour at this very early date. We do, however, accept that they probably had this information from the Pyramid Age onwards. For this reason, we take an alternative position on the First Dynasty chronology.

Furthermore, Mr MacNaughton believes that the kings' list of Erathosthenes astronomically dates the periods of several Old Kingdom rulers, such as Bawnetcher, Kara, Nebka, Usekaf, Pepi I, Pepi II, etc. He feels that Eratosthenes recorded a list of kings whose dates correspond to the 119-year cycles of Jupiter-Saturn conjunctions. If MacNaughton is right, then this is a brilliant piece of deduction on his part. We are, however, much less confident about the Erathosthenes data and thus we are less happy relying on it.

Despite our minor disagreements, the MacNaughton chronology provides the best possible synthesis of the known facts about Egyptian history, in our view. It provides the best marriage of the research of Manetho, the *Royal Papyrus of Turin,* the research of Herodotus, the astronomical dating, the archaeological dating of Thera, and the new dates for the Sphinx. Nor is his chronology fazed by synchronisations with the Middle East or Crete.

For example, the Early Minoan I period of Crete is traditionally dated to the same period as Pharoah Mena. How dates were arrived at for the Cretan artefacts, before carbon dating had been invented, was to measure the depths where the artefacts were found. The deeper the artefacts were buried the earlier the period. Sir Arthur Evans, the early excavator of the site, gave the depths for the end of the Middle Minoan III period (or the beginning of Late Minoan) as 2.5 metres. This coincided with the Eighteenth Egyptian Dynasty. Moreover, he gave the Early Minoan I period as 5.33 metres. To cite MacNaughton once more:

> It will be seen that the depth to a period synchronising with the commencement of the Eighteenth Dynasty, 1709 B.C. by my chronology, (*c.* 1580 by Meyer's) was 2.5 metres. To the present time [i.e. 1932] this represents about 3600 (or 3500) years or approximately 1440 (or 1400) years per metre. As the depth to EM. [i.e. Early Minoan] I. was 5.32 metres this yields a date for the beginning of EM. I. about 7660 (or 7448) years before the present time, namely *c.* 5730 B.C., thus differing very little from my date for Menes [i.e. Mena] arrived at independently (*c.* 5776-5714).[41]

Discussion

There are, however, potential problems with this chronology. Dr Charles Finch discusses radiocarbon dates for pre-dynastic Egyptian sites that are younger than the dynastic dates given here. Professor Fekri Hassan, for example, published six radiocarbon studies on pre-dynastic Egyptian sites between 1980 and 1988. Using high-resolution radiocarbon instruments, he dates the pre-dynastic Badarian culture to 4400 BC at the earliest. His date does, however, contradict the thermoluminescent date of 5500 BC given by Hoffman, author of *Egypt before the Pharaohs.* Following Petrie, the Badarian culture should have been much earlier.[42] Both the Hassan and Hoffman dates potentially contradict the Manetho-MacNaughton chronology, but then again, they also contradict each other. What should one make of this?

Chinweizu and Finch both feel that Hoffman's thermoluminiscent dates refute the long chronology. According to Chinweizu:

> Mena's date cannot be earlier, or even as early as, the earliest stratum of farming settlement at Nekhen, the town from which he extended his rule to all of Kemet. In the absence of TL [i.e. thermoluminescent] and RC [i.e. radiocarbon] dates for that stratum at Nekhen, a probably adequate approximation is that he cannot be earlier than the earliest settlement stratum of any of the earliest farming villages of Upper Kemet. At present, the earliest known is at Hemamieh, with a TL date of ca. 5580 ± 420 BC. (Hoffman, 1984: 141) This would rule out all dates for Mena that are earlier than the mid-6th millennium BC. If we allow at least 1,000 years for the evolution of the oldest Nile Valley farming villages before their final unification by Mena, that would place Mena sometime after ca. 4580 BC. Now, would 1,000 years be too short for the predynastic period? Would it imply an impossibly rapid evolution? Probably not, especially when we consider similar evolutions elsewhere. In the case of Rome, it took just some four centuries (ca. 650-ca. 250 BC) for three not-long-settled farming villages to unify and dominate all of central and southern Italy. By that Roman yardstick, the march from Nile Valley farming villages to the Pharaonic state could have happened within 400 years! Hence, allowing at least 1,000 years for the predynastic period is comparatively quite conservative. This would put Mena, provisionally, after ca. 4580 BC.[43]

Dr Chinweizu's logic is impeccable. Clearly the Hoffman evidence harmonises well with his chronology. Nevertheless, a careful reading of the above data reveals that our chronology is *not* ruled out by the Hoffman data. We have been informed that the oldest known farming village in Upper Egypt is dated at 5580 BC plus or minus 420 years using thermoluminescent dating. This may mean 6100 BC, at the upper end, or 5160 BC at the lower end of the spread. We have also been informed that "the march from Nile Valley farming villages to the Pharaonic state could have happened within 400 years!" This means that this evolution could have taken place from 6100 BC to 5700 BC. This does *not* refute our First Dynasty Date of 5660 BC. Furthermore, Chinweizu presents evidence that the Predynastic period was probably not as long and drawn out as Petrie and Finch seem to think. It could therefore have evolved within a relatively short time span:

> It should not be presumed that the BAG [Badarian, Armatian and Gerzean] was entirely Predynastic, especially as there is considerable evidence of stylistic continuities between Predynastic BAG artefacts and Early Dynastic artefacts. In fact, as the following examples show, some Early Dynastic artefacts have indeed been indistinguishable from definitive BAG artefacts.

a) The Gebel el Arak knife, according to Hoffman, "apparently dates to the Late Gerzean or Protodynastic". (Hoffman, 1984: 340) This inability to place it in one and not the other period is evidence of the lack of a hard stylistic distinction between these periods.

b) Commenting on a photograph of a miniature groundstone vase, Hoffman says: "Stone vase grinding developed as a full-time craft during the Gerzean and reached a peak under the first two dynasties". (Hoffman, 1984: 342)

c) In emphasizing the continuities between Badarian, Amratian and Gerzean styles, Alan Gardiner points to their burial arrangements as basically unchanged. (Gardiner, 1961: 393). And Hoffman carries the picture of continuity forward into the protodynastic era when he notes that the tombs of "Protodynastic kings at Abydos, although much larger than the (Predynastic/Late Gerzean) Painted Tomb, are built according to the same plan". (Hoffman, 1984: 335)

d) Gardiner also notes that the commemorative palettes, of which the famous Narmer Palette is one, "belonged to the very latest predynastic times, if not in some cases to the protodynastic." (Gardiner, 1961: 393)

e) Similarly, there was a continuity in copper tools and ornaments, from Badarian into protodynastic times. Hammered and annealed copper objects were found in Badarian graves (Hoffman, 1984: 143); in both Badarian and Amratian sites (Hoffman, 1984: 207); and from Dyn. I at Saqqara (Hoffman, 1984: 153).

f) In architecture, Hoffman cites evidence of predynastic-to-protodynastic continuities, including the following: "At El Amrah ... Petrie found a miniature clay model of a house in a grave of Gerzean date that looks like a typical Dynastic mud-brick dwelling ... Baumgartel mentions a Gerzean rectangular house with typical dynastic room and forecourt plan under the temple at Badari" (Hoffman, 1984: 148)

Such continuities and, more importantly, the lack of clear discontinuities, support Hoffman's contention that "the change from Predynastic to Dynastic society was largely organizational and political, not technological and cultural" (Hoffman, 1984: 17.) In fact, no evidence of a technological break occurs until the transition from Dyn. II to Dyn. III ... We may therefore conclude that the BAG era spanned both the Predynastic and Early Dynastic periods, lasting from the beginning of Nile Valley farming villages, as at Hemamieh, till the end of Dyn. II. The BAG era was, thus, the cultural context for the evolution and consolidation of the Pharaonic state. The date for Mena's unification of Kemet, Mena's Year One, would thus lie within its full time span.[44]

Dr Hassan recently presented a television programme on the BBC entitled *Ancient Apocalypse*. In this programme, he repeatedly suggests a Sixth Dynasty date of 2200 BC without qualification or discussion.[45] His Old Kingdom dates are, therefore, younger than the only reasonable Twelfth Dynasty dates given as 3440 BC by Manetho. The Hassan chronology, therefore, cannot be accepted and there is worse to come. Of the thermoluminescent date given by Hoffman, on the other hand, we accept that, if fully verified, it would undermine the long chronology presented here.

Unfortunately he too is a supporter of the "short" chronology and thus presents Old Kingdom dates that are younger than the only acceptable Middle Kingdom dates.

The radiocarbon dates are not as impressive as they first seem. The *Radiocarbon Web Info Site* gave the following information on the origin of this dating technique:

> The radiocarbon method was developed by a team of scientists led by the late Professor Willard F. Libby of the University of Chicago after the end of World War 2. Libby later received the Nobel Prize in Chemistry in 1960 for the radiocarbon discovery. Today, there are over 130 radiocarbon dating laboratories around the world producing radiocarbon dates for the scientific community. The C14 method has been and continues to be applied and used in many, many different fields including hydrology, atmospheric science, oceanography, geology, palaeoclimatology, archaeology and biomedicine.[46]

There is a section on this web page entitled *How did Libby test his method and find out if it worked correctly?* In this section, we are informed that:

> Libby tested the new radiocarbon method on carbon samples from prehistoric Egypt whose age was known. A sample of acacia wood from the tomb of the pharaoh Zoser was dated for example. Zoser lived during the 3rd Dynasty in Egypt (2700-2600 BC). Libby figured that since the half-life of C14 was 5568 years, they should obtain a radiocarbon amount of about 50% of that which was found in living wood because Zoser's death was about 5000 years ago. The results they obtained indicated this was the case. Many other radiocarbon dates were conducted on samples of wood of known age. Again, the results were good. In 1949, Libby and his team published their results. By the early 1950s there were 8 new radiocarbon laboratories, and by the end of the decade more than 20.[47]

Among Libby's other data, included artefacts from the time of Hemaka (First Dynasty), given as 5,000 years old, Sneferu, given as 4,500 years old, and a boat dated to the time of Sesostris, given as 3,900 years old. Like his date for Djoser, his dates for Hemaka, Sneferu and Sesostris (probably one of the Twelfth Dynasty kings) were based on Egyptian samples "whose age was known". But how did Libby know that these dates were known? Known by whom exactly? In reality, Libby seems to have accepted the chronology of Breasted, who, incidentally worked at the same academic factory - the University of Chicago. Breasted's dates are, however, unreliable.

To assess the reliability of C14, consider the following dates reported by Schwaller De Lubicz in *Sacred Science*. He reports that Hemaka has been dated to 2923 BC ± 250 years, Zoser to 1830 BC ± 650 years, Sneferu 2852 BC ± 210 years, and Senwosret III 1671 BC ± 180 years. In other words 71 years separates the First and the Fourth Dynasties, Sneferu reigned 1032 years before Zoser, and finally 159 years separates the Third and Twelfth Dynasties! All of this is frankly embarrassing. Moreover, one of the dates for Sneferu of the Fourth Dynasty was given as 3598 BC.[48] This is over 600 years earlier than Hemaka of the First Dynasty! What is worse, none of these dates agrees with those of Professor Libby, who supposedly used the same method to date the same artefacts. In fact, few of the published carbon dates given by different authorities agree with each other. However, each time the carbon dates were published, they were presented to the public as though they were the final word on the subject.

Professor Lehner, Herbert Haas and colleagues, recently analysed organic remains from ten Old Kingdom monuments, using a new and improved radiocarbon dating technique. They found that the buildings were minimally 400 years older than the standard short chronology dates would lead us to expect. For example, they published 16 out of 50 samples taken from the Great Pyramid of Giza. The oldest sample published was found to date to 3809 BC but the youngest sample was 2853 BC. Lehner, Haas *et al* concluded that the pyramid was minimally 389 years older than the short chronology date of 2464 BC. On this basis, Dr Finch proposes moving the short chronology First Dynasty back from 3100 BC to 3500 BC.[49] We disagree.

We believe that if these dates are to be accepted, surely it should be the oldest or the median dates that should be used, and not the latest one. The oldest radiocarbon dates should reflect the oldest known piece of organic material on the monument. However, the younger pieces of organic material could have got there at any time since the monument was constructed. This is of some importance in the light of the research of Mark McCarron. In a provocative internet paper, Mr McCarron shows that recent research at Oregon University has demonstrated that C14 dates tend to be 15% too low when compared to tree ring dates. This effectively pushes the 3809 BC date for the Great Pyramid back to 4226 BC.[50] This is younger than our date of *c.*4794 BC, but it is much closer to it than the *c.*2877 BC of Breasted or the 2600 BC used today.

To explore all possibilities: should the median dates of Lehner *et al* be considered? The median date for the Great Pyramid may well turn out to be 3400 BC, accepting, for the sake of argument, Lehner's dates, or 3705 BC, according to McCarron. These dates may support a chronology in between the ideas of Petrie and Breasted, such as the one advocated by Budge or the chronology at one time advocated by Finch. In *Echoes of the Old Darkland,* Charles Finch advocated a First Dynasty date of 4300 BC. His theory is a fascinating and well-argued synthesis of Manetho, astronomy and religion.[51] More recently Dr Chinweizu has developed these ideas with even greater sophistication into a chronology with a First Dynasty date of 4443 BC.[52]

It is widely believed that the Egyptian calendar was established by at least 4241 BC. The evidence for this assertion is derived from the writings of Herodotus. In *The Histories,* the Greek historian alludes, in a very cryptic way, to a unique feature of the Egyptian calendar. The Egyptians invented the novel idea of having two calendars running simultaneously. One calendar lasted 365¼ days, which is close to the calendar we use today, and the other lasted 365 days. After four years the two calendars would diverge by one day. After eight years they would diverge by 2 days. Continuing the computations further, after 1460 years, the two calendars would diverge by a whole year. The two calendars would be so far apart that they would actually meet up with each other! A Roman historian, Censorinus, informs us that the two calendars agreed in 139 AD. The two calendars must therefore have met up in 1321 BC, since this is 1460 years earlier. In a statement analysed by many historians such as George Rawlinson and Walter Marsham Adams, Herodotus implied that the two calendars met up on two previous cycles. This gives 4241 BC as the first definite Egyptian date (calculated as 1321 + [1460 x 2] = 4241). The beginning of the Egyptian year was July 19, the first day of Thoth, associated with the rising of the star Sothis supposedly Sirius. Bringing the information together, a Sothic Cycle began on 19 July 4241 BC, a second one began on 19 July 2781 BC, and a third one began on 19 July 1321 BC, etc.[53] Dr Finch reproduces an ivory tablet associated with Pharaoh Djer of the First Dynasty. The tablet reads: "[Sothis] Opener of the Year, Inundation, 1". On this evidence, the learned scholar believes this fixes a date for when Pharaoh Djer flourished, i.e. 4241 BC.[54]

Unfortunately, Finch's seductive theory collapses over precisely the same hurdle as Breasted's. Dr Finch proposed an Eleventh or Twelfth Dynasty date that starts between 2238 and 2218 BC. This implies the same Middle Kingdom dates as given by Breasted with exactly the same consequence. The late date compresses the Thirteenth through Seventeenth Dynasties into an unlikely 208 years when the minimum he could logically argue for is 453 years. Chinweizu's chronology suffers from exactly the same problem except that his time gap is 211 years. Finally, are Rawlinson, Adams and Finch correct in their interpretation of Herodotus?

Following Duncan MacNaughton it seems that scholars have, again, confused Sirius with Spica. We note that even Leo Depuydt, the modern authority on the Egyptian calendar cited earlier, uncritically links Sirius with Sothis. Consequently, the enigmatic statement of Herodotus may well have a completely different interpretation. According to MacNaughton:

> The first cycle began about 5578 [BC], the second about 41[5]2, the third about 2736, and the fourth about 1314, so that the ... [period by which Herodotus was writing about] was half-way through the fourth cycle.[55]

We believe that 5578 BC is the true period that Pharaoh Djer flourished, a date consistent with the Manetho-Africanus chronology though disagreeing with MacNaughton's date. On this basis, we offer a First Dynasty date of 5660 BC. Incidentally, Africanus gave the final year of Djer as 5598 BC, a discrepancy between our view and his of 20 or more years. Breasted, on the other hand, does not use the Djer Tablet. It is possible that he was unaware of it. However, even if he was made aware of it, we shall show that it completely destroys his chronology. We conclude that considering the remote dates involved with the Djer Tablet, we believe that the Manetho chronology is vindicated. Moreover, we have demonstrated that using the Spica theory with the month of Hathor as the start of the new year consistently produces smaller discrepancies with Africanus than using the Sirius theory with Thoth as the start of the new year.

The Sphinx of Giza provides another problem concerning the Manetho-MacNaughton chronology. Professor Hornung tells us that: "The Great Sphinx of Giza … dates to the reign of Khephren [i.e. Khafra]".[56] According to Vivian Davies and Renée Friedman in a recent book published by the British Museum: "Khafra added something unique. This was the Sphinx, which presides over Giza (and art history) as the first royal statue in Egypt".[57] Professor Lehner, regarded as one of the world's foremost authorities on Giza, contextualises the Sphinx. In his view:

> The Sphinx does not sit out alone in the desert totally up for grabs … The Sphinx is surrounded by a vast architectural context which includes the Pyramid of Khufu, the Pyramid of Khafre [sic] and the Pyramid of Menkaure [sic], pharaohs of the Fourth Dynasty.

He continues by showing that the builders conceived of the Sphinx and Khafra's Temple as one unit:

> The south side of the Sphinx ditch forms the northern edge of the Khafre [sic] causeway as it runs past the Sphinx and enters Khafre's Valley Temple. A drainage channel runs along the northern side of the causeway and opens into the upper south-west corner of the Sphinx ditch, suggesting that the ancient quarrymen formed the ditch after the Khafre causeway was built.[58]

On the question of who built the Sphinx, Robert Bauval and Graham Hancock, two radical historians, take a distinctly minority view. They believe that Pharaoh Khafra merely restored the Sphinx "like many Pharaohs after him (Ramesses II, Thutmosis IV, Ahmoses I, etc., etc.)".[59] Finally Lieutenant Frank Domingo, senior forensic artist with the New York police department, made a special study on the facial portrait of the Sphinx and compared it with a famous sculpture of Pharaoh Khafra. He concluded that:

After reviewing my various drawings, schematics and measurements, my final conclusion concurs with my initial reaction, i.e. that the two works represent two separate individuals. The proportions in the frontal view, and especially the angles and facial protrusion in the lateral views convinced me that the Sphinx is not Khafre [sic].[60]

Synthesising the ideas of Davies and Friedmann, Hornung, Lehner, Bauval and Hancock, and Domingo, we believe that Khafra originally built the Sphinx. He constructed it during the Fourth Dynasty where it was part of the Giza complex of pyramids, causeways and temples. Later kings restored the monument and it is for this reason that the portrait no longer resembles Khafra. The date of the Sphinx, and therefore the Fourth Dynasty, has already been given as 5000 BC at the latest. As discussed in an earlier chapter, Professor Schoch's geological dating remains unrefuted by anyone. Schoch, however, regarded his dates as conservative. If the Sphinx could be shown to date back to say 6000 BC, or earlier, this would prove too early to harmonise with the Manetho-MacNaughton chronology.

The dating of Pharaoh Mena is the final problem of which we are aware concerning the Manetho-MacNaughton chronology. It is well known that northern Egypt was largely swamplands in the pre-dynastic periods that tended to discourage human habitation. Herodotus credits Mena with building a dam that diverted the course of the Nile and rendered Lower Egypt more suitable for human habitation. At what date did all this take place? Walter Fairservis wrote that:

During the Pliocene period, that is, the latest period before the coming of the Ice Age (Pleistocene), it has been noted that an arm of the ancient Mediterranean protruded along the Nile Valley. This arm or gulf reached almost to the present dam at Aswan, or at least four hundred miles along the present Nile Valley, and it was well over five hundred feet above the present sea level. During this period heavy rainfall caused the surrounding streams that fed into the proto-Nile Valley to empty their vast quantity of gravel and silts ... The gulf filled with erosional deposits and this caused a retreat of the sea arm. (This may have been helped by a fall of the sea as the Mediterranean found its modern bed) ... The Pleistocene and the so-called Ice Age are practically synonymous. The period began perhaps one million years ago and ended around 10,000 BC.[61]

The above data could be synthesised with the ideas of Herodotus to date the reign of Mena to a period before 10,000 BC. If Herodotus recorded correctly, Mena must have lived at a time when much of Egypt was swampland. Fairservis gives the latest possible date when this was the case as 10,000 BC. This is clearly a much earlier date than our 5660 or MacNaugton's 5776 BC. As with the Sphinx, this data may indicate that a much longer chronology is required than that given by Manetho.

Conclusion

Tying the arguments and evidence together, the Manetho-MacNaughton chronology is clearly the best synthesis known to Egyptology. In fact, it is the *only* logical chronology that has been presented to the academic world. Clearly it has to be updated in the light of new archaeological discoveries on the names, order, and length of reigns of the kings, especially from the Old Kingdom period. We believe that Professor Jackson, author of the masterly *Man, God, and Civilization,* was justified in popularising MacNaughton's work. On the other hand, there is no hiding from the problems of the long chronology. Thermoluminescent dates for the pre-dynastic period do not harmonise as well with it as with other chronologies, but the radiocarbon dates from the Old Kingdom monuments are hard to interpret. New dates for the Sphinx, however, may indicate that the Manetho-MacNaughton chronology is too conservative and an even longer chronology needs to be adopted. The issues surrounding the dating of Mena tends also to suggest a longer chronology. These issues remain unsettled but a clear position emerges.

The Meyer-Breasted chronology is a complete failure. There are four major problems with the "short" chronology that undermine its credibility. Firstly, the chronology involves a total rejection of the best Egyptian, and for that matter, the best Greek sources. Worthwhile history cannot be written in this way. The 925 years Breasted gives for the first six dynasties, for example, comes from nothing more than his imagination. Secondly, a minimum of 116 kings ruling in 208 years is highly improbable at best, and contradicts Meyer and Breasted's own arguments concerning simultaneous dynasties. Had these scholars been consistent, they should have proposed a minimum period for the Thirteenth to the Seventeenth Dynasties of 518 or 453 years, not 208 years. Additionally, there are three separate pieces of evidence that pulls the Eighteenth Dynasty back over a hundred years before Breasted's date - the Nabonidus document, the Karnak water clock and the eruption of Thera. Since the Eighteenth Dynasty began in 1709 BC, this allows a time gap of 71 years from the fall of the Twelfth Dynasty to the rise of the Eighteenth Dynasty. Since there are 15 recognisable kings on the Turin fragments with their length of reigns intact, we can account for 91 years of the Thirteenth Dynasty. This ALONE refutes the Breasted position since 91 years is greater than the 71 years that the evidence allows Breasted to claim. Thirdly, the Sothic Tablet for Pharaoh Djer completely demolishes the 3180 BC or 3400 BC First Dynasty dates. If the calendar was invented in 4241 BC, following the Sirius argument, the Egyptians must have had advanced record keeping at least 800 years before the writing system to document it emerged in the Dynastic period, following the Meyer-Breasted chronology.

H. E. Winlock, a former director of the Metropolitan Museum of Art, noticed the absurdity of this and proposed instead that the calendar must have been invented at the next Sothic cycle, i.e. 2781 BC. (He actually gave the date as 2773 BC). Winlock hinted, but was careful not to say, that Imhotep of the Third Dynasty invented the calendar. Since the Third Dynasty began in 2980 BC, following Breasted, Winlock proposed that the entire Third Dynasty should be moved forward to coincide with the birth of the calendar.[62] This involved cutting a further 200 years off the Old Kingdom chronology. If the Sothic calendar was invented in the Third Dynasty period of 2781 or 2773 BC, as Winlock claims, then how can he explain a First Dynasty tablet with a Sothic date on it? The First Dynasty period of Pharaoh Djer is still at least 200 years earlier than the proposed invention of the calendar. Moreover, using the Spica dates instead of the Sirius ones won't help Breasted, Meyer or Winlock. The nearest relevant dates are either 4182 BC or 2736 BC.

Finally, Professor Breasted himself revealed that he did not fully believe his own propaganda. In his influential *Ancient Records of Egypt, Volume One,* Breasted let his guard slip and wrote the following bizarre passage:

> [T]he calendar was introduced in the middle of the forty-third century B.C. (4241 B.C.). This is the oldest fixed date in history. This fact demonstrates not only a remarkable degree of scientific knowledge in that remote age, but also stable political conditions, and a wide recognition of central authority, which could gradually introduce such an innovation. The date employed was that for the rising of Sothis in the latitude of Memphis or the southern Delta.[63]

In other words, the unification of Egypt, the birth of kingship, and the foundation of Memphis were necessary conditions for the birth of the calendar! The earliest time Egypt is known to have met these conditions is during the First Dynasty. Consequently, this strange passage may indicate that Breasted's true position is not so far away from that of Finch or Chinweizu. But the damage had already been done. Generations of scholars regarded the "short" chronology as canonical when it should have merited little consideration.

Meyer and Breasted, according to Professor Jackson, had a more sinister reason for down dating the Egyptian chronology. "The reason why they clipped two thousand years off the other chronology" explains Jackson, "is in order to make Egyptian culture fit into the Bible".[64] Christian bigots had argued that the world was created in around 4004 BC using the Good Book as their main source. Any Egyptian dates older that this were unacceptable to Christian historians. Even today, newer texts are creeping closer and closer to the Wilkinson date of 2320 BC. Some radical historians, such as David Rohl, are defending very low dates and evoke the *Bible* as evidence to support this position. In *Legend - The Genesis of Civilisation,* Mr Rohl proposes a First

Dynasty date of 2789 BC.[65] In support of Mr Rohl, at least the Djer Tablet does not inconvenience his chronology.

The "medium" chronologies of Budge, Chinweizu, Finch in 1990, and Petrie in 1929, are also far less satisfactory than the chronology presented here. The Finch and Chinweizu chronologies are tied to Breasted's Middle Kingdom dates as we have seen. The chronologies of Budge and Petrie (in 1929), on the other hand, involve a total rejection of the Senwosret III Sothic date. This is clearly less acceptable than the MacNaughton chronology that incorporates it. The only advantages of the "medium" chronologies are that they are better able to incorporate the new carbon dates for the Old Kingdom monuments and harmonise better with the thermoluminescent dates given by Hoffman. This, of course, presumes that the carbon dates are reliable and there is no evidence in existence to show that they are. Furthermore, the thermoluminescent dates do not rule out the "long" chronology as Finch and Chinweizu seem to think. On the other hand, the medium dates are further away from the geological dates for the Sphinx than those of the "long" chronology. They are also further away from the date of the Pleistocene, which may give an independent date for Mena. In conclusion, as a synthesis of the available data, the "long" chronology clearly emerges as superior to its rivals.

Notes

[1] F. D. P. Wicker, *Egypt and the Mountains of the Moon,* UK, Merlin Books, 1990, pp.8-9.
[2] John Jackson, *Man, God, and Civilization,* US, Citadel Press, 1972, pp.218-9 and Yosef ben-Jochannan, *Abu Simbel to Gizeh,* US, Black Classic Press, 1989, p.13.
[3] André Pochan, *L'Enigme de la Grande Pyramide,* France, Éditions Robert Laffont, 1971, pp.309-315.
[4] E. A. Wallis Budge, *Egypt in the Neolithic and Archaic Periods,* UK, Kegan Paul, Trench, Trübner & Co., 1902, pp.114-9.
[5] Alan H. Gardiner, *The Royal Canon of Turin,* UK, Griffith Institute, 1959, plates I and II.
[6] George Rawlinson (translator), *History of Herodotus, Volume II,* UK, John Murray, 1875, pp199-201.
[7] E. A. Wallis Budge, *Egypt in the Neolithic and Archaic Periods,* pp.119-124.
[8] Ibid., pp.124-6.
[9] Duncan MacNaughton, *A Scheme of Egyptian Chronology,* UK, Luzac & Co., 1932, p.157.
[10] E. A. Wallis Budge, *Egypt in the Neolithic and Archaic Periods,* pp.126.
[11] Ibid., pp.126-146.
[12] See ibid., pp.130-6.
[13] See also John G. Jackson, *Ages of Gold and Silver,* US, American Atheist Press, 1990, pp.76-9.
[14] See Duncan MacNaughton, *A Scheme of Egyptian Chronology,* pp.2 and 44-5.
[15] Charles Finch, *Echoes of the Old Darkland,* US, Khenti, 1991, pp.117-8 and John Jackson, *Man, God, and Civilization,* pp.218-9.

[16] W. M. Flinders Petrie, *Researches in Sinai*, UK, John Murray, 1906, pp.163-185.

[17] E. A. Wallis Budge, *Egypt in the Neolithic and Archaic Periods*, p.149

[18] George Rawlinson (translator), *History of Herodotus, Volume II*, p.220.

[19] Ibid., p.222.

[20] W. M. Flinders Petrie, *Researches in Sinai*, pp.171-2.

[21] James Henry Breasted, *Ancient Records of Egypt Volume I*, US, University of Chicago Press, 1906, pp.31.

[22] Leo Depuydt, *Civil Calendar and Lunar Calendar in Ancient Egypt*, Belgium, Peeters Publishers & Department of Oriental Studies, 1997, p.14.

[23] James Henry Breasted, *Ancient Records of Egypt Volume I*, p.35.

[24] Ibid., p.37.

[25] W. G. Waddell (translator), *Manetho*, UK, William Heinemann, 1940, pp.73-99.

[26] Alan H. Gardiner, *The Royal Canon of Turin, plates I and II*.

[27] Duncan MacNaughton, *A Scheme of Egyptian Chronology*, p.109.

[28] Ibid., pp.28-9.

[29] Ibid., pp.192-4.

[30] *Inscription on a Clay Cylinder of Nabonidus*, in *Light from the East*, by Rev. C. J. Ball, UK, Eyre and Spottiswoode, 1899, pp.208-11.

[31] Duncan MacNaughton, *A Scheme of Egyptian Chronology*, pp.8-9 and 371-2.

[32] Ibid., pp.221-2.

[33] David M. Rohl, *A Test of Time (Volume One): The Bible - From Myth to History*, UK, Century, 1995, p.386.

[34] James Henry Breasted, *Ancient Records of Egypt Volume I*, p.36.

[35] Duncan MacNaughton, *A Scheme of Egyptian Chronology*, p.153.

[36] Erik Hornung, *History of Ancient Egypt*, UK, Edinburgh University Press, 1999, pp.70-1

[37] Barbara Watterson, *The Egyptians*, UK, Basil Blackwell, 1997, p.56.

[38] Duncan MacNaughton, *A Scheme of Egyptian Chronology*, pp.376-7.

[39] Ibid., pp.47-9.

[40] Charles Dupuis, *The Origin of All Religious Worship*, US, New Orleans, 1872, C. F. Volney, *The Ruins of Empires*, US, Peter Eckler, 1890 and William Peck, *A Popular Handbook and Atlas of Astronomy*, UK, Gall & Inglis, 1890.

[41] Duncan MacNaughton, *A Scheme of Egyptian Chronology*, p.186.

[42] Charles Finch, *The Star of Deep Beginnings*, US, Khenti, 1998, p.15.

[43] Chinweizu, personal communication.

[44] Ibid.

[45] Fekri Hassan, *Ancient Apocalypse* (television programme), UK, BBC Television, 2001.

[46] *Radiocarbon Web-Info*, http://www.c14dating.com/k12.html

[47] Ibid.

[48] R. A. Schwaller De Lubicz, Sacred Science, US, Inner Traditions, 1982, p.251.

[49] Charles Finch, *The Star of Deep Beginnings*, pp.15 and 17.

[50] Mark McCarron, *Khufu or NOT Khufu ... that is the Question?* Internet article, http://www.gizapyramid.com/McCarron-C14.htm.

[51] Charles Finch, *Echoes of the Old Darkland*, pp.115-128.

[52] Chinweizu, personal communication.

[53] W. Marsham Adams, *The Book of the Master*, US, ECA Associates 1990 (original 1898), pp.47-50 and 195-6.

[54] Charles Finch, *Echoes of the Old Darkland*, pp.119 and 126.

[55] Duncan MacNaughton, *A Scheme of Egyptian Chronology*, p.163.

[56] Erik Hornung, *History of Ancient Egypt*, p.27.

[57] Vivian Davies and Renée Friedman, *Egypt*, UK, British Museum Press, 1998, p.82.

[58] Quoted in Robert Bauval and Graham Hancock, *Keeper of Genesis*, UK, Mandarin, 1996, pp.14-5.

[59] Robert Bauval and Graham Hancock, *Keeper of Genesis*, p.12.

[60] Quoted in Robert Bauval and Graham Hancock, *Keeper of Genesis*, p.10.

[61] W. A. Fairservis, *The Ancient Kingdoms of the Nile*, US, New American Library, 1962, pp.42-5.

[62] H. E. Winlock, *The Origin of the Ancient Egyptian Calendar*, US, *Proceedings of the American Philosophical Society: Volume 83, No.3*, September 1940, pp.447-464.

[63] James Henry Breasted, *Ancient Records of Egypt Volume I*, p.30.

[64] James E. Brunson and Runoko Rashidi, *Sitting at the feet of a forerunner: An April 1987 Meeting and interview with John G. Jackson*, in *African Presence in Early Asia*, ed Runoko Rashidi, US, Transaction Publishers, 1995, p.198.

[65] David M. Rohl, *A Test of Time (Volume Two): Legend - The Genesis of Civilisation*, UK, Century, 1998, pp.422-4.

EGYPTIAN KINGS LIST

Introductory Note

The sources used to compile this list are: Africanus (see Budge 1902), Eusebius (see Budge 1902), the Book of Sothis (see Budge 1902), the Royal Canon of Turin (see Gardiner 1959), Breasted (1906), the British Museum (see Davies & Friedman 1998), Brunson & Rashidi (see Van Sertima 1989), Hornung (1999), MacNaughton (1932), Rice (1991) and Welsby (1996). If a source exists but we have specifically rejected it, that source has been placed in brackets. Finally, we have estimated the unknown reigns of the Old Kingdom pharaohs as 17 years.

Old Kingdom Period (5660 - 4188 BC)

FIRST DYNASTY (5660 BC - 5386 BC) Thinites   SOURCE

5660 - 5598	Mena	62	Africanus
5598 - c.5581	Hor-Aha	x	(Hornung 30)
5581 - 5524	Djer	57	Africanus
5524 - c.5507	Mer-Neith	x	
5507 - 5476	Djet	31	Africanus
5476 - 5456	Den	20	Africanus
5456 - 5430	Anejib	26	Africanus (Turin 74)
5430 - 5412	Semerkhet	18	Africanus (Turin 72)
5412 - 5386	Qaa	26	Africanus (Turin 63)

SECOND DYNASTY (5386 - 5046 BC) Thinites

5386 - 5348	Bawnetcher	38	Africanus (Turin 95)
5348 - c.5331	Hotepsekhemui	x	
5331 - 5292	Raneb	39	Africanus
5292 - 5245	Baneter	47	Africanus (Turin 95)
5245 - 5228	Wadjnes	17	Africanus (Turin 54)
5228 - c.5211	Peribsen	x	
5211 - 5170	Seneb	41	Africanus (Turin 70)
5170 - 5153	Kara	17	Africanus
5153 - 5128	Neferkara	25	Africanus
5128 - c.5111	Neferkasoker	x	(Turin 8)
c.5111 - c.5094	Hetchefa	x	(Turin 1)
5094 - 5046	Khasekhemui	48	Rice (Turin 27)

THIRD DYNASTY (5046 - 4872 BC) Memphites

5046 - 5018	Nebka	28	Africanus (Turin 19)
5018 - 4989	Djoser	29	Africanus (Turin 19)
4989 - 4970	Teta	19	Africanus
4970 - 4928	Ahtes	42	Africanus
4928 - 4898	Setches	30	Africanus
4898 - 4872	Huni	26	Africanus (Turin 24)

FOURTH DYNASTY (4872 - 4599 BC) Memphites (or possibly Elephantines)

4872 - 4824	Sneferu	48	British Museum (Turin 24)
4824 - 4761	Khufu	63	Africanus (Turin 23 or 24)
4761 - c.4744	Djedefra	x	(Turin 8)
4744 - 4678	Khafra	66	Africanus
4678 - 4615	Menkaura	63	Africanus (Turin 18 or 28)
4615 - 4608	Shepseskaf	7	Africanus (Turin 4)
4608 - 4599	Thampthis	9	Africanus (Turin 2)

FIFTH DYNASTY (4599 - 4402 BC) Elephantines

4599 - 4571	Userkaf	28	Africanus (Turin 7)
4571 - 4559	Sahura	12	Africanus
4559 - 4539	Neferikare	20	Africanus
4539 - 4532	Shepseskare	7	Africanus
4532 - 4512	Neferefre	20	Africanus
4512 - 4482	Niuserre	30	Breasted
4482 - 4474	Menkauhor	8	Turin
4474 - 4435	Isesi	39	British Museum
4435 - 4402	Unas	33	Africanus (Turin 30)

SIXTH DYNASTY (4402 - 4188 BC) Memphites

4402 - 4372	Teti	30	Africanus (Turin 6 months 21 days)
4372 - c.4355	Userkare	x	
4355 - 4302	Pepi I	53	Africanus (Turin 20)
4302 - 4295	Merenre I	7	Africanus (Turin may give 44)
4295 - 4201	Pepi II	94	Africanus
4201 - 4200	Merenre II	1	Africanus
4200 - 4188	Nitocris	12	Africanus

First Intermediate Period (4188 - 3448 BC)

SEVENTH DYNASTY (4188 - 4188 BC) Memphites

4188 - 4188   4 kings in 75 days   Eusebius (Africanus 70 days)

EIGHTH DYNASTY (4188 - 4042 BC) Memphites

4188 - 4042   27 kings in 146 years   Africanus

NINTH DYNASTY (4042 - 3633 BC) 19 Herakleopolitans in 409 years

4042 - c.4012	Kheti I	x (x = 29.2 years)
c.4012 - c.3983	Neferkare	x
c.3983 - c.3954	Kheti II	x
c.3954 - c.3925	Senen …	x
c.3925 - c.3895	Kheti III	x
c.3895 - c.3866	Kheti IV	x
c.3866 - c.3837	Shed …	x
c.3837 - c.3808	H …	x
c.3808 - c.3779	Kheti V	x
c.3779 - c.3749	Meri …	x
c.3749 - c.3720	Se … re Kheti	x
c.3720 - c.3691	Kheti VI	x
c.3691 - c.3662	Kheti VII	x
c.3662 - 3633	Merikare	x

NB These dates are approximate since there are 5 additional missing kings.

TENTH DYNASTY (3633 - 3448 BC) 19 Herakleopolitans in 185 years

3633 - c.3619	Netjerikare	x (x = 13.5 years)	
c.3619 - c.3605	Menkare	x	
c.3605 - c.3592	Neferkare	x	
c.3592 - c.3578	Neferkare Nebi	x	
c.3578 - c.3565	Djedkare Shema	x	
c.3565 - c.3551	Neferkare Khendu	x	
c.3551 - c.3538	Merienhor	x	
c.3538 - c.3524	Sneferka (Neferkamin)	x	
c.3524 - c.3511	Nikare	x	
c.3511 - c.3497	Neferkare Tereru	x	
c.3497 - c.3484	Neferkahor	x	
c.3484 - c.3470	Neferkare Papisenebu	x	
3470 - 3468	Neferkamin Anu	2	Turin
3468 - 3464	Kakaure (Kakare Ibi)	4	Turin

3464 - 3462	Neferkaure	2	Turin
3462 - 3461	Neferkauhor	1	Turin
c.3461 - 3448	Neferirkare	x	

NB These dates are approximate since there are 2 additional missing kings.

Middle Kingdom Period (3448 - 3182 BC)

ELEVENTH DYNASTY (c.3560 - 3405 BC) Thebans dominant for 43 years

The first two thirds of this dynasty overlapped with Dynasty Ten but ruled in the south. Strictly speaking, the Middle Kingdom actually began during the reign of Mentuhotep II after the Tenth Dynasty fell.

c.3560 - 3548	Mentuhotep I	12	Internet
3548 - 3532	Antef I	16	Hornung
3532 - 3483	Antef II	49	Turin
3483 - 3475	Antef III	8	Turin
3475 - 3424	Mentuhotep II	51	Turin
3424 - 3412	Mentuhotep III	12	Turin
3412 - 3405	Mentuhotep IV	7	Turin

TWEFLTH DYNASTY (3405 - 3182 BC) Thebans

3405 - 3376	Amenemhet I	29	Consensus
3376 - 3331	Senwosret I	45	Turin
3331 - 3299	Amenemhet II	32	Consensus
3299 - 3280	Senwosret II	19	Turin
3280 - 3242	Senwosret III	38	Derived from Turin
3242 - 3195	Amenemhet III	47	Derived from Turin
3195 - 3186	Amenemhet IV	9	Turin
3186 - 3182	Sebekneferura	4	Turin

Second Intermediate Period (3182 - 1709 BC)

THIRTEENTH DYNASTY (3182 - 2729 BC) 60 Thebans in 453 years

3182 - 3180	Wegaf	2	Turin
3180 - 3174	Sekhemkare	6	Turin
3174 - 3171	Amenemhet V	3	Turin
3171 - c.3163	Sehetepibre I	x (x= 8.04 years)	
c.3163 - c.3155	Iufeni	x	
c.3155 - c.3147	Senkhibre	x	
c.3147 - c.3139	Amenemhet VI	x	
c.3139 - c.3131	Sehetepibre II	x	
c.3131 - c.3123	Sewadjkare	x	
c.3123 - c.3115	Nedjemibre	x	
3115 - 3110	Sebekhotep I	5	Brunson & Rashidi
3110 - c.3102	Renseneb	x	
c.3102 - c.3093	Awibre Hor	x	(Brunson & Rashidi 7 months)
c.3093 - c.3085	Amenemhet VII	x	
c.3085 - c.3077	Sebekhotep II	x	
c.3077 - c.3069	Userkare	x	
c.3069 - c.3061	Imiramesha	x	
c.3061 - c.3053	Antef IV	x	
c.3053 - c.3045	Kesetre	x	
3045 - 3044	Sebekhotep III	1	Turin
3044 - 3033	Neferhotep I	11	Brunson & Rashidi
3033 - c.3025	Sihathorre	x	
3025 - 3016	Sebekhotep IV	9	Hornung
3016 - 3011	Khahetepre	5	Turin
3011 - 3000	Wahibre Yayebi	11	Turin (Brunson & Rashidi 10)
3000 - 2977	Menferre Iy	23	Brunson & Rashidi
2977 - 2975	Merhetepre Ini	2	Turin
2975 - 2972	Sewadjtu	3	Turin
2972 - 2969	Mersekhemre Ined	3	Turin
2969 - 2964	Sewadjkare Heri	5	Turin
2964 - 2962	Sebekhotep V	2	Turin
2962 - c.2930	4 missing kings	4x	
c.2930 - c.2922	Dedumes	x	
c.2922 - c.2914	Ibi II	x	
c.2914 - c.2905	Hor II	x	
c.2905 - c.2897	Se … kare	x	
c.2897 - c.2889	Senebmiu	x	
c.2889 - c.2873	2 missing kings	2x	
c.2873 - c.2865	Sekhaenre	x	
c.2865 - c.2857	Missing king	x	
c.2857 - c.2849	Merkheperre	x	
c.2849 - c.2841	Merkare	x	
c.2841 - 2729	14 other kings	14x	

FOURTEENTH DYNASTY (*c.*3015 - 2545 BC) 76 kings of Xois dominant for 184 years

The first two thirds of this dynasty was contemporaneous with Dynasty Thirteen but ruled in the north.

*c.*3015 - *c.*3008	Nehesi	*x* (*x* = 7.18 years)	
*c.*3008 - *c.*3001	Khatire	*x*	
3001 - 3000	Nebfautre	1	Turin
3000 - 2997	Sehebre	3	Turin
2997 - *c.*2990	Meridjefare	*x*	
2990 - 2989	Sewadjkare	1	Turin
2989 - *c.*2982	Nebdjefare	*x*	
*c.*2982 - *c.*2975	Webenre	*x*	
*c.*2975 - *c.*2967	Missing king	*x*	
2967 - 2963	. . . re	4	Turin
2963 - *c.*2956	. . . webenre	*x*	
*c.*2956 - *c.*2949	Awtibre	*x*	
*c.*2949 - *c.*2942	Heribre	*x*	
2942 - 2941	Nebsenre	0.5	Turin
*c.*2941 - *c.*2934	Missing king	*x*	
*c.*2934 - *c.*2927	Sekheperenre	*x*	
2927 - 2925	Djedkherure	2	Turin
*c.*2925 - *c.*2918	Seankhibre	*x*	
*c.*2918 - *c.*2911	Kanefertemre	*x*	
*c.*2911 - *c.*2904	Sekhem … re	*x*	
*c.*2904 - *c.*2896	Kakemure	*x*	
*c.*2896 - *c.*2889	Neferibre	*x*	
*c.*2889 - *c.*2882	I … re	*x*	
*c.*2882 - *c.*2875	Kha … re	*x*	
*c.*2875 - *c.*2868	Aakare	*x*	
*c.*2868 - *c.*2860	Semen … re	*x*	
*c.*2860 - *c.*2853	Djed … re	*x*	
*c.*2853 - *c.*2801	6 missing kings	6*x*	
*c.*2810 - *c.*2803	Senefer … re	*x*	
*c.*2803 - *c.*2796	Menibre	*x*	
*c.*2796 - *c.*2789	Djed …	*x*	
*c.*2789 - *c.*2760	4 missing kings	4*x*	
*c.*2760 - *c.*2753	Inenek	*x*	
*c.*2753 - *c.*2746	Ineb …	*x*	
*c.*2746 - *c.*2738	Ip …	*x*	
*c.*2738 - *c.*2731	Hab	*x*	
*c.*2731 - *c.*2724	Sa	*x*	
*c.*2724 - *c.*2717	Hepu …	*x*	
*c.*2717 - *c.*2710	Shemsu	*x*	
*c.*2710 - *c.*2702	Meni	*x*	
*c.*2702 - *c.*2695	Werqa	*x*	
*c.*2695 - *c.*2681	2 missing kings	2*x*	
*c.*2681 - *c.*2674	. . . ka	*x*	

c.2674 - c.2667	. . . ka	x
c.2667 - c.2659	Missing king	x
c.2659 - c.2652	Hepu	x
c.2652 - c.2645	Anati	x
c.2645 - c.2638	Bebenem	x
c.2638 - c.2631	Missing king	x
c.2631 - c.2623	Iuf ...	x
c.2623 - c.2616	Seth	x
c.2616 - c.2609	Sunu	x
c.2609 - c.2602	Hor ...	x
c.2602 - c.2588	2 missing kings	2x
c.2588 - c.2580	Nibef	x
c.2580 - c.2573	Mer ... en ...	x
c.2573 - c.2566	Penensetensepet	x
c.2566 - c.2559	Kheretheb Shepesu	x
c.2559 - c.2552	Khut ... hemet	x
c.2552 - 2545	Missing king	x

NB These dates are approximate since there are 6 additional missing kings.

FIFTEENTH DYNASTY (2545 - c.1993 BC) 32 Hyksos

2545 - c.2407	8 kings including Khyan	8x (x=17.25)
c.2407 - c.2389	Kurodes	x	(Book of Sothis 63)
c.2389 - c.2372	Aristarchos	x	(Book of Sothis 34)
c.2372 - c.2355	Spanios	x	(Book of Sothis 36)
c.2355 - c.2320	2 missing kings	2x	(Book of Sothis 72 total)
c.2320 - c.2303	Osirapis	x	(Book of Sothis 23)
c.2303 - c.2286	Sesonchosis	x	(Book of Sothis 49)
c.2286 - c.2269	Amenemes	x	(Book of Sothis 29)
c.2269 - c.2251	Amasis	x	(Book of Sothis 2)
c.2251 - c.2234	Akesephthres	x	(Book of Sothis 13)
c.2234 - c.2217	Anchoneus	x	(Book of Sothis 9)
c.2217 - c.2200	Armiyses	x	(Book of Sothis 4)
c.2200 - c.2182	Chamois	x	(Book of Sothis 12)
c.2282 - c.2165	Miamus	x	(Book of Sothis 14)
c.2165 - c.2148	Amesesis	x	(Book of Sothis 65)
c.2148 - c.2131	Uses	x	(Book of Sothis 50)
c.2131 - c.2113	Rameses	x	(Book of Sothis 29)
c.2113 - c.2096	Ramesomenes	x	(Book of Sothis 15)
c.2096 - c.2079	Usimare	x	(Book of Sothis 31)
c.2079 - c.2062	Ramesseseos	x	(Book of Sothis 23)
c.2062 - c.2044	Rammessameno	x	(Book of Sothis 19)
c.2044 - c.2027	Ramesse Iubassz	x	(Book of Sothis 39)
c.2027 - c.2010	Ramesse Uaphru	x	(Book of Sothis 29)
c.2010 - c.1993	Koncharis	x	(Book of Sothis 5)

SIXTEENTH DYNASTY (1993 - 1709 BC) Hyksos

1993 - 1974	Salitis	19	Consensus
1974 - 1930	Bnon	44	Consensus
1930 - 1869	Pachnon	61	Africanus
1869 - 1819	Staan	50	Africanus
1819 - 1770	Archles	49	Africanus
1770 - 1709	Ipepi	61	Africanus (Hornung 40)

SEVENTEENTH DYNASTY (1860 - 1709 BC) 43 Thebans in 151 years

This dynasty was contemporaneous with Dynasty Sixteen but ruled in the south.

1860 - c.1785	28 missing kings	$28x$ (x = 2.65 years)	
	(including Opehtiset Nubti)		
c.1785 - c.1783	Antef V	x	
c.1783 - c.1780	Rahotep	x	
c.1780 - c.1777	Sobekemsaf I	x	
c.1777 - c.1775	Djehuti	x	
c.1775 - c.1772	Mentuhotep V	x	
1772 - 1743	Nebiriawre	29	Turin
1743 - c.1740	Nebiretawre	x	
c.1740 - c.1738	Semenre	x	
1738 - 1726	Seuserre ...	12	Turin
1726 - c.1723	Sobekemsaf II	x	
c.1723 - c.1720	Antef VI	x	
c.1720 - c.1718	Antef VII	x	
c.1718 - c.1715	Seqenenre Tao I	x	
c.1715 - 1713	Seqenenre Tao II	x	
1713 - 1709	Kamose	4	Hornung

New Kingdom Period (1709 - 1095 BC)

EIGHTEENTH DYNASTY (1709 - 1450 BC) Thebans

1709 - 1683	Ahmose I	MacNaughton
1682 - 1662	Amenhotep I	MacNaughton
1662 - 1628	Thutmose I	MacNaughton
1650 - 1600	Hatshepsut	MacNaughton
1628 - 1615	Thutmose II	MacNaughton
1615 - 1561	Thutmose III	MacNaughton
1579 - 1569	Thutmose IV	MacNaughton
1569 - 1538	Amenhotep II	MacNaughton
1538 - 1501	Amenhotep III	MacNaughton
1501 - 1474	Akhenaten	MacNaughton
1489 - 1480	Smenkhare	MacNaughton
1480 - 1468	Tutankhamen	MacNaughton
1468 - 1456	Aya	MacNaughton
1456 - 1454	Rameses I	MacNaughton
1454 - 1450	Horemheb	MacNaughton

NINETEENTH DYNASTY (1450 - 1236 BC) Thebans

1450 - 1395	Seti I	MacNaughton
1394 - 1328	Rameses II	MacNaughton
1328 - 1308	Merneptah	MacNaughton
1308 - 1248	Seti II	Africanus
1248 - 1243	Amenmesse	MacNaughton
1243 - 1236	Tawosret	MacNaughton

TWENTIETH DYNASTY (1236 - 1095 BC) Thebans

1236 - 1230	Setnekht	MacNaughton
1230 - 1199	Rameses III	MacNaughton
1199 - 1193	Rameses IV	MacNaughton
1193 - ?	Rameses V	MacNaughton
? - ?	Rameses VI	MacNaughton
? - ?	Rameses VII	MacNaughton
? - 1173	Rameses VIII	MacNaughton
1173 - ?	Rameses IX	MacNaughton
? - 1113	Rameses X	MacNaughton
1113 - 1095	Rameses XI	MacNaughton

Third Intermediate Period (1095 - 716 BC)

TWENTY FIRST DYNASTY (1095 - 926 BC) Tanites

1095 - 1089	Herihor	MacNaughton
1089 - 1062	Smendes	MacNaughton
1062 - 1017	Psusennes I	MacNaughton
1017 - 968	Amenemope	MacNaughton
968 - 952	Menkheperre	MacNaughton
952 - 940	Pinudjem I	MacNaughton
940 - 926	Psusennes II	MacNaughton

TWENTY SECOND DYNASTY (940 - 803 BC) Libyans

The beginning of this dynasty was contemporaneous with Dynasty Twenty One.

940 - 906	Shoshenq I	MacNaughton
906 - 870	Osorkon I	MacNaughton
891 - 866	Takelot I	MacNaughton
888 - 860	Osorkon II	MacNaughton
c.884	Shoshenq II	MacNaughton
865 - 840	Takelot II	MacNaughton
884 - 831	Shoshenq III	MacNaughton
832 - 826	Pami	MacNaughton
840 - 803	Shoshenq IV	MacNaughton

TWENTY THIRD DYNASTY (809 - 729 BC) Tanites

809 - 769	Pedibast I	MacNaughton
769 - 761	Osorkon III	MacNaughton
761 - 729	Various petty rulers	

TWENTY FOURTH DYNASTY (729 - 716 BC) Saïtic

729 - 722	Tefnakhte	Hornung
722 - 716	Bakenrenef	Africanus

Renaissance Period (716 - 664 BC)

TWENTY FIFTH DYNASTY (785 - 664 BC) Kushites

The first half of this dynasty was contemporaneous with Dynasties Twenty Three and Twenty Four but ruled in Kush. Strictly speaking, the Renaissance actually began when the Twenty Fourth Dynasty fell.

785 - 760	Alara	Welsby
760 - 747	Kashta	Welsby
747 - 716	Piye	Welsby
716 - 702	Shabaqo	Welsby
702 - 690	Shebitqo	Welsby
690 - 664	Taharqo	Welsby

Egypt under non-African rule

INFLUENCE OF THE ASSYRIANS 663 BC

INFLUENCE OF THE PERSIANS 525 BC

INFLUENCE OF THE GREEKS 332 BC

INFLUENCE OF THE ROMANS 30 BC

INFLUENCE OF THE ARABS 639 AD

CHAPTER NINE: THE EGYPTIAN QUESTION

The racial classification of the Ancient Egyptians, even now, remains a thorny issue. Many writers and television documentary makers still depict them as Caucasians or Mulattoes, usually offering no evidence at all to support these unscientific portrayals. Professor Erik Hornung of the University of Basle, for example, makes the bizarre suggestion that the Egyptians did not encounter Negroes until well into the Eighteenth Dynasty period, echoing the argument refuted at the Cairo Symposium. We reproduce the Professor's own words on this point:

> At the south of his empire, Tuthmosis III [i.e. Thutmose III] also reached beyond the previous borders. The region of Napata at Gebel Barkal, where he had a stele set up in 1433 B.C.E., was included in the province of Kush, and the Fourth Cataract would remain the southern boundary of Egypt for a long time to come. Here, the Egyptians came into contact with [B]lack Africans, who were henceforth to appear in representations in tombs along with other foreigners.[1]

The English Egyptologist, Mr Michael Rice, takes a different position. His Ancient Egyptians were Negroes but after admitting this, Rice felt compelled to racially abuse them:

> The culture which grew and flourished in the Nile Valley was wholly autochthonous. It grew out of the lives and preoccupations of the cattle-rearing African peoples ([B]lack Africans, it must certainly be acknowledged) who were the true ancestors of the Pharaohs, in all their majesty and power. The Egyptians long held on to the recognition of their essentially African character, incidentally: even in the Middle Kingdom the King could be portrayed in all the barbaric splendour of an African chief … [2]

On the atypical occasions that writers attempt to present evidence of a non-Negro Ancient Egypt, they usually try to base their position on ten lines of argument. (1) Caucasians were the first people in North Africa. (2) Even if the prehistoric population of North Africa were Negroes, they were conquered and displaced by a "Dynastic Race" from Europe and Asia. (3) The Ancient Egyptians (and for that matter the Moors/Libyans/Berbers) spoke Semitic or Afro-Asiatic, i.e. languages that originated in the Middle East. This implies that the people were also of Middle-Eastern origins. (4) Herodotus' account of

Egypt cannot be trusted. (5) Egyptian skulls share affinities with Europeans. (6) Egyptian mummies, such as Yuya, Thuya and Rameses II, possess blond or red hair. Others mummies show straight hair. (7) Only some of the dynasties possessed kings that one can "usefully" call Black. (8) The Egyptians distinguished themselves from Negroes in their literature. (9) The Egyptians distinguished themselves from Negroes in their art. (10) Physical anthropology has shown the Egyptians cannot be classified as Black or White.

It is easy to show that all of these arguments are naïve, outdated, false or fraudulent. Furthermore, they can all be easily dismissed by counter-evidence. The evidence for human origins suggests that the first human inhabitants of all lands, except the Americas, were Negroes.[3] The Caucasians evolved in southern France or southern Russia from Negroes that migrated from Africa to those regions. The early Black migrants to Europe and Asia probably entered Spain via Morocco, and Israel via Egypt.[4] Since Morocco and Egypt are both in North Africa, it is difficult to see how the original inhabitants of North Africa could have been anything other than Negroes. Of course Oliver, McEvedy, and Wiedner do not need to bother offering evidence to prove that North Africa was originally Caucasian, presumably their say so is good enough! In any case, their views are refuted by the Saharan Rock Paintings, dating back ten thousand years. As Dr Davidson has noted, the paintings show people that are "obviously African in origins".[5] Finally, Henri Lhote remarked that the earliest art "[wa]s apparently the work of Negro artists."[6]

Concerning the identity of the prehistoric Egyptians we cite the outstanding research of Dr Keith Crawford, an African-American scholar. His essay, *The Racial Identity of Ancient Egyptian Populations based on the Analysis of Physical Remains,* contains the following anthropological evidence:

> The earliest modern human fossils found in Egypt was the skeleton of the Nazlet Khater man found near Tahter, Egypt which was dated at 35,000-30,000 B.C. (upper Paleolithic period). Regarding the racial affinity of this skeleton, Thoma (1984) concludes, "Strong alveolar prognathism combined with fossa praenasalis is suggestive of Negroid morphology ..." In 1982, Wendorf discovered a skeleton at Wadi Kubbaniya, located 10-15 km north of Aswan in Egypt. The skeleton dated to approximately 20,000 B.C. The wide nasal aperture, lower nasal margin morphology (presence of the sulcus praenasalis), wide interorbital distance and alveolar prognathism demonstrate affinities with Broad African variants (i.e. "Negroid" traits) (Stewart, 1985). Greene and Armelagos (1964) analysed a collection of crania from Wadi Halfa dating from 13,000 to 8,000 B.C. The skulls were dolichocephalic with bun-shaped occiputs, and they displayed extreme facial flattening in the orbital and nasal regions, massive browridges, sloping foreheads, great alveolar prognathism, large teeth and large, deep mandibles. Rightmire (1975) notes a similarity between this population and skeletons from West Africa (Tamaya Mellet, Niger and El Guettara, Mali).[7]

Dr Crawford uses the term Broad African to refer only to those African populations with broad faces, broad flat noses, and prominent jaws (alveolar prognathism). His research shows that from 35,000 BC to 8,000 BC only Negro skeletons have been found in Egypt. He goes on to discuss the Predynastic Egyptian cultures of Badaria and Nagada:

> [U]sing improved statistical analysis, Keita (1990) observed, "The Badarian crania have a modal metric phenotype that is clearly 'southern'; most classify into the Kerma (Nubian), Gaboon, and Kenyan groups." He further reports, "No Badarian cranium in any analysis classified into the European series ..." The Nagada cultural period that followed the Badarian period has also been shown to have consisted of populations with affinities to Broad African populations. One of the earliest studies to characterize Nagada crania was conducted by Fawcett (1902). She identifies the characteristics of the Nagada race commenting, "We are dealing therefore with a long-headed narrow-faced race with a flat nose and rather round orbits." Nutter (1958) compared Nagada, Badarian and Kerma (Upper Nubia) skulls and concluded the three groups were almost identical, all of them possessing Broad African phenotypic traits (see Keita, 1990).[8]

The view that invaders from Europe and Asia overwhelmed a predynastic Negro Egypt in early times is very deceptive. There are two Egyptian documents, which could be interpreted to imply that Caucasians invaded the northern coast at an early date - *Narmer's Tablet* and *The Instruction of Merikare*. *Narmer's Tablet* gives a pictorial record of the great First Dynasty monarch conquering enemies and uniting Egypt into a single state for the first time. Many scholars have suggested that Caucasians were among the defeated enemies of Narmer (i.e. Mena), therefore implying that they must have entered the land at an early date to become an enemy.[9] Pharaoh Kheti VII of the Tenth Dynasty wrote *The Instruction of Merikare* for his son, Merikare. It was a political guide for the young man, instructing him how to rule wisely when he inherited the throne. The text warns him of trouble that Asiatics (i.e. Caucasians) could cause and implied that they had always been a menace to the Egyptians from time immemorial. The phrase given is: "He [the Asiatic] has been fighting since the time of Horus (yet) he does not conquer nor is he conquered."[10] Our view is that even if these documents are interpreted to show that there were Caucasians in Egypt from before the First Dynasty, those same documents indicate that the Egyptians kept them at bay and considered them enemies.

The real evidence deflates even these pretensions, however. The surviving statues of the Old Kingdom Pharaohs, including Narmer, the founder of a unified Egypt, show unambiguous Negro faces.[11] We can only agree with Pierre Montet, a French Egyptologist, who described the Old Kingdom rulers as possessing: "unusually large, almost flat noses, thickish lips and somewhat low foreheads. Such were without exception the kings of Egypt at the time of the Old Kingdom.[12]

The Egyptian language was at one time classified as a non-African tongue. Scholars claimed that it belonged to a Middle-Eastern language family called Semitic. This position, however, was publicly refuted once and for all. In 1974 UNESCO called the now historic conference, the Cairo Symposium.[13] UNESCO's aim was to sponsor the writing of an authentic history of Africa but the ancient Egyptians and their place in African history was a major sticking point. Twenty of the world's leading Egyptologists participated, including Professor Cheikh Anta Diop and Professor Théophile Obenga.[14] The two Africans presented a mass of linguistic comparisons between Egyptian and Wolof (Senegalese), and Egyptian and Bantu languages. It was generally agreed among the participants that the Egyptian language was indeed an indigenous African tongue related to other African languages.[15]

Moreover, the Semitic or Afro-Asiatic language group did not, however, originate in the Middle East, as is popularly believed. Joseph Greenberg, a linguist of great distinction, demonstrated that their true origins were in Ethiopia. Ethiopia and Eritrea has the largest number of Semitic languages spoken today such as Tigrinia and Amharic. Cushitic languages are also spoken in this region:

> He [Greenberg] discarded as imprecise and illogical such familiar linguistic categories as "Semitic" and "Hamitic" [says a modern scholar] in favour of a more inclusive category, which he termed "Afro-Asiatic." In Greenberg's opinion, this category was justified by the demonstrable affinities between Semitic Hebrew, Arabic, Phoenician, Aramaic, and Amharic on the one hand and the northeast African group (formerly "Hamitic"), comprising Egyptian, Cushite, Chadic, and Hausa on the other. According to Greenberg, the long-dead mother tongue of all these languages would have originated in the highlands of Ethiopia. What this means, in effect, is that so-called Semitic languages are but branches of an original northeast African parent, of which Egyptian and Cushitic are "charter" members.[16]

Dr Christopher Ehret, another recent authority, comments that:

> The old Western and Middle Eastern presumption that the Afrasan (Afroasiatic) language family originated in Asia can simply no longer be sustained, now that we have large amounts of first-rate data from the African branches of the family. But this newer evidence is still almost unknown to most scholars of the Semitic and ancient Egyptian languages, with the consequence that an unbalanced understanding of the family continues to prevail in many quarters. Unfortunately the outdated view of Afrasan as having an Asian origin continues to affect not only popular thinking but also the interpretation of scholars in other fields, such as biological anthropology, who study Africa. Some readers

are disturbed by the idea that the Semitic and Egyptian languages are related, because they think such a relationship would make Egyptian an Asian language. Of course, that is not so. Semitic alone, among all the divisions of the [Afroasiatic] family, consisted in earlier times of languages of the far southwest corners of Asia, spoken even right next to Africa. All the rest of the divisions are entirely African, and the only reasonable interpretation of this evidence is that Semitic was a solitary Asian offshoot of the family, brought into Asia long ago by immigrants from Africa.[17]

It has always been a puzzle to us as to how Dr Greenberg located the parent of Semitic in the highlands of Ethiopia. We have an idea that he derived this view from Herodotus. Herodotus, as we shall see in the next chapter, reported that the Phoenicians (a Semitic speaking people), "according to their own account" originated in Eritrea before migrating to the Middle East. Eritrea is, of course, next door to Ethiopia.

Many modern writers have vented their anger against Herodotus for recording data such as this. Furthermore, they have taken particular exception to the Father of History describing the Egyptians as having black skins and woolly hair, as contained in Book II, section 104 of his *The Histories.* Sir John Gardiner Wilkinson, the noted English Egyptologist, fired the first shot in 1862:

> The hair he [i.e. Herodotus] had no opportunity of seeing, as the Egyptians shaved their heads and beards; and the blackness of colour is, and always was, a very conventional term; for the Hebrews even called the Arabs "black" *kedar,* the "cedrei" of Pliny; though … may only mean of a dark or a sunburnt hue … The Negroes of Africa in the paintings of Thebes, cannot be mistaken; and the Egyptians did not fail to heighten the caricature of that marked race by giving to their scanty dress of hide the ridiculous addition of a tail.[18]

Sir John went on to present an image of a Black woman with a tail that he claims was found in a Theban tomb or temple. This image, of course, does not exist. The distinguished Egyptologist fabricated it. Concerning Egyptian hair, even if all the men Herodotus saw shaved their heads, he would still have observed the hair and wigs of Egyptian women. A wig is, of course, hair taken off one Egyptian head and placed on another Egyptian head. Finally, we note that Wilkinson has unconsciously provided useful data on the race of the earliest Arabs, citing Pliny and the Hebrews as source material. We shall return to this question in a much later chapter.

W. W. How and J. Wells wrote *A Commentary on Herodotus,* in 1912. Commenting on Book II, Section 104, they wrote the following:

> H[erodotus]'s ideas of Egyptian appearance have been somewhat confused by the numerous [N]egro slaves he saw in the streets of Memphis. As the

Egyptians themselves shaved wholly or in part … the 'woolly hair' is the more inexplicable.[19]

If Herodotus, as How and Wells suggests, confused the Egyptians with Negro slaves, this merely implies that the two peoples were absolutely identical in every visible way. There could not have been any racial difference between them at all. It is possible to confuse Senegalese and Gambians for precisely the same reasons. Incidentally, Fari Supiya, our esteemed colleague, pointed out that part of the royal insignia of the pharaohs was an animal skin worn with the tail hanging down. Perhaps Sir John Wilkinson in faking the image described above, confused a Black woman with a pharaoh!

Professor Archibald H. Sayce proved equally upset by Herodotus' disclosure. Confusing the past with the present tense, Sayce declared that:

> The Egyptians are not black skinned nor have they woolly hair. This warns us against accepting Herodotos [sic] as an anthropological authority. As the Egyptians shaved, he had not much opportunity of observing their hair, but seems to have made his observations on their Negro slaves. It is equally difficult to believe that the Kolkhians [sic] were black and woolly haired. Certainly none of the numerous races now inhabiting the Kaukasos are so.[20]

Sayce correctly describes the modern Egyptians and the modern populations of the Colchis region (i.e. the Caucasus region or near southwestern Russia) as not being Negroes. This observation is, however, an irrelevance concerning the ancient peoples of both regions. Incidentally, Martin Bernal, author of *Black Athena* reproduces an almost identical argument to that given by Sayce. Just as Sayce requires "anthropological authority" before being able to say whether or not the ancient Egyptians were Black, Bernal requires "anatomical precision."[21] Just as Sayce confuses the ancient and modern peoples of Egypt and Colchis, Bernal tells us that: "I am convinced that, at least for the last 7,000 years, the population of Egypt has contained African, South-West Asian and Mediterranean types."[22] The last 7,000 years are, of course, interesting - but wholly irrelevant. It does not address the question of who the Ancient Egyptians were. Rather, it dodges the issue.

Since the time of Wilkinson, How, Wells and Sayce, the attacks on Herodotus have become increasingly tiresome and irritating, consisting of the same empty statements unsupported by counterevidence. Some writers, such as Bernal and Poe attempt to play it both ways by claiming the Colchians were Negroes but the Egyptians were not. This is an untenable scholarly position, since the Colchians descended from the Egyptians. The critics of Herodotus are yet to attack Aeschylus, Apollodorus, Aristotle, Diodorus, Galen, Heliodorus and Lucian - all of whom corroborate him on the Egyptian question. In fact, the critics do not have a single eyewitness description that contradicts Herodotus or any of the above named Classical writers. We give the final word on the Herodotus question to Wilhelm Spiegelberg, author of the fascinating lecture-essay *The Credibility of Herodotus's Account of Egypt in the Light of the Egyptian Monuments.* He concludes that:

> Our verdict, then, on the credibility of Herodotus (especially with regard to his statement on the history) is distinctly a favourable one. The view that he derived his accounts from books, or actually invented them, can only be described as ridiculous. That he was in Egypt cannot be doubted by any sane person. Why his observations do not always tally with the facts as we know them has already been explained; apart from the universal grounds for mistake expressed in *errare est humanum,* there must be taken into account, *inter alia,* the rapidity of his journey and the comparatively short sojourn in the country. In addition to all this there is another factor of great importance. Herodotus, as he himself more than once points out (chs. 73, 125), took no written notes, but relied upon his memory, which, remarkable though it was, could not suffice for a great quantity of details.[23]

One enterprising modern writer, Richard Poe, suggests a novel way of undermining the Classical writers' descriptions of the Ancient Egyptians. He believes that "contrary to the claim of some experts - Greek and Roman authors *offer no definitive answer* to whether we should call the Egyptians black, in the modern sense of the word."[24] As evidence, he cites the writings of the Roman poet Manilius, who felt that:

> The Ethiopians stain the world and depict a race of men steeped in darkness, less sunburnt are the natives of India, the land of Egypt ... darkens the bodies mildly ... its moderate climate imparts a medium tone. The Sun-god dries up with dust the tribes of Africans amid their desert lands [of the Sahara], the Moors derive their names from the faces, and their identity is proclaimed by the colour of their skins.[25]

Based on this, Mr Poe believes that Manilius describes five dark skinned populations ranging from the Ethiopians - the darkest in shade, through the Indians, Egyptians, Saharans, and finally the Moors - the lightest. Poe further reasons that the Egyptians were two shades lighter than the Ethiopians, but two shades darker than the Moors.[26] Poe concludes that the Egyptians, unlike the Ethiopians, were too light in complexion to be classified as real Negroes in the modern sense of the word.

We note that while Poe may be correct in suggesting a sliding scale of shades from Ethiopians to Moors, it still does not prove what he thinks it proves. Juvenal, as we have already seen, describes the Moors as midnight black. If the Egyptians were two shades darker that this, they and all the other groups, the

Saharans, Indians and Ethiopians included, must have been very dark indeed. Moreover, the Classical writers classify the Libyans as Ethiopians. The Libyans, as we have already seen in Chapter Four, were the same people as the Moors. D. E. L. Haynes, an authority on Libyan antiquities, was forced to admit: "Some ancient sources describe the Garamantes [a Libyan people] as 'Aethiopians'."[27] Herodotus collected information from the ancient Tunisian civilisation of Carthage about some of their trading voyages:

> The Carthaginians still relate the following story. Beyond the Pillars of Hercules there exists a Libyan country inhabited by men who they visit. They unload their goods and lay them neatly on the shore edge, then they reboard their vessels and send up signals of smoke to attract the notice of the natives. The latter, seeing the smoke, draw near to the sea, place next to the goods the gold they are offering in exchange, and withdraw. The Carthaginians disembark once more and examine what has been left. If they estimate that the amount of gold matches the value of the goods, they take it away and raise anchor. If not, they return to their ships and wait. The natives, coming back in their turn, add more gold until the Carthaginians are satisfied. Neither side does the other any wrong.[28]

All historians who have considered this question know that the "Libyan country" of which the Carthaginians spoke was Guinea in West Africa. The method of trade described is called dumb barter and two thousand years later this was still used in that part of the world. This makes the people of Guinea, the so-called True Negroes, authentic Libyans! Furthermore, Professor Serge Lancel of the University of Grenoble, paraphrased an ancient source that describes the trade between the Phoenicians and the people of Cerne, far to the north (sic) of Guinea along the coast of the Western Sahara: "Around the end of the sixth century [BC], a passage in the *Periplus* of the Pseudo-Scylax would be more precise about what the Phoenician traders were then offering the 'Ethiopians'."[29] Combining the two sources, notice that the Guineans to the south are called Libyans but the Saharans to the north are called Ethiopians. Synthesising the Classical sources, E. W. Bovill, the English author of *The Golden Trade of the Moors,* wrote that "ethnologically the Garamantes are not easy to place, but we may presume them to have been [N]egroid".[30] The Arab writers of the eighth and ninth centuries AD, as we have already seen, classify the Copts (i.e. Egyptians), the Fezzani (i.e. Saharans), and the Berbers (i.e. Moors) as peoples "of the Sudan [i.e. Black]". One such writer adds that they were of the "posterity of Kush."

In addition, Professor Diop wrote that: "Strabo goes even further in his *Geography* and attempts to explain why Egyptians are blacker than Hindus."[31] This contradicts the sliding scale of Manilius and places the Egyptians and Ethiopians one shade apart. However, Godfrey Higgins paraphrases Arrian as saying: "the inhabitants upon the Indus [i.e. Indians] are in their looks and appearance not unlike the Ethiopians" (see also pages 578-588). Arrian then goes on to state that among the Indians were darker people in the south and lighter people in the north. He correctly compares this difference to Egyptians being, on average, lighter than Ethiopians (i.e. Sudanese) in Africa.[32] But if the Indians were "not unlike the Ethiopians", including those of a lighter complexion, then the Egyptians were also "not unlike the Ethiopians". This corroborates Diodorus who stated that the Egyptians were originally an Ethiopian colony. Finally, Erathosthenes wrote: "On the left of the course of the Nile live Nubae [i.e. the Nubians] in Libya, a populous nation. They begin from Meroe, and extend as far as the bends [of the river]".[33]

We conclude, therefore, that the colour scale deduced by Poe has such a limited range of shades where the darkest (i.e. Sudanese), the lightest (i.e. Garamantes) and those in between (i.e. Egyptians and Indians) were called Ethiopians or were not unlike the Ethiopians. Bovill calls the Garamantes, who were part of Poe's lightest group, "Negroid". Moreover, this same relatively light coloured group - the Moors, were midnight coloured according to Juvenal. Furthermore, this same light coloured group - the Libyans, included the people of Guinea (the so-called True Negroes) and also the Nubians (i.e. Ethiopians). This destroys Poe's entire theoretical edifice with nothing left to support it.

Some writers allege that Egyptian skulls share affinities with those of Europeans. While this view contains particles of truth, it is really an argument presented by those who know nothing about human origins. The African origin of the human race implies that the facial or physical variations noted among the many peoples around the world first made their appearance on the African continent.[34] Many South African Negroes (the 'Khoisan'), for example, have a Chinese-like appearance with respect to their faces, in particular, their eyes. A good example is Nelson Mandela, the former South African Head of State. We have, of course, put the cart before the horse. The reality is that it is the Chinese who resemble South African Negroes in this respect, not the other way round.[35] Even facial features associated with Caucasians, such as thin lips and narrow noses existed among African Negroes independently of any intermarriage with Caucasians, and existed before Caucasians came into existence.[36] The Tutsi of central east Africa are a good example. Their narrow features have developed independently of any "exotic" admixture.[37] Therefore, skulls can sometimes be used to prove the existence of Negroes, when they have facial features unique to Negroes, and distinct from Caucasians or Mongolians. However, skulls cannot be used as the sole evidence to prove the existence of Caucasians. Caucasian skulls are not sufficiently distinct from those of many East African Negroes. It follows that Egypt, also in East Africa, contained thinner-lipped and narrower-nosed Negro types, resembling the Somalis or Ethiopians of today. Their skulls, when examined by the anthropologists were systematically misclassified, giving the false view that 30 or 40% of the Egyptian skulls were Caucasian when they should have been classified as East African.

In the early nineteenth century it used to be claimed that Negro skulls were the longest (dolichocephalic), Mongolian skulls were the shortest (brachycephalic), and Caucasian skulls were in-between (mesocephalic). Based on this classification, Dr Madden in the 1820's drew the following conclusion about the ethnicity of the Ancient Egyptians:

> The traveller, Dr R. R. Madden [says a modern writer] made a special study of skulls of different Eastern races at the beginning of the nineteenth century; in Upper Egypt he saw several thousand mummy heads and he 'opened the heads of fifty mummies'; they were all extremely narrow across the forehead and oblong in shape, like the heads of Nubians in measurement rather than like those of Copts. Herodotus was correct.[38]

Dr Madden was not alone in this view. In 1883 Captain Richard Burton wrote to the English Egyptologist Gerald Massey and remarked that: "You are quite right about the African origin of the Egyptians, and I have sent home a hundred skulls to prove it."[39]

In addition, Dr Madden demonstrated that there were no affinities between the skulls of the modern Copts and the skulls of the Ancient Egyptians. He concluded that:

> From this table it is evident that there is no affinity between the head of the [Ancient] Egyptian mummy and that of the [modern] Copt; but allowing, in all measurements, three quarters of an inch for difference of the scalp on the [modern] Nubian head, it follows that the measurement of the latter corresponds with that of the mummy head in every particular.[40]

The conclusions outraged the racists and therefore new criteria were added to what determines the ethnicity of a skull. It was now declared that Negro skulls had to be dolichocephalic but also contain a short broad face, Mongolian skulls were deemed to be brachycephalic with flat faces, and Caucasian skulls were mesocephalic with long faces. Based on this classification, Falkenburger arrived at the following conclusions:

> 'Falkenburger reopened the anthropological study of the Egyptian population in a recent work [says Professor Diop] in which he discusses 1,787 male skulls varying in date from the old Pre-Dynastic to our own day. He distinguishes four main groups' (p.421). The sorting of the predynastic skulls into these four groups gives the following results for the whole predynastic period: '36% Negroid, 33% Mediterranean, 11% Cro-Magnoid and 20% of individuals approximating either to the Cro-Magnoid or to the Negroid'.[41]

The conclusion drawn was still unacceptable. In the United States anyone with any African ancestry, no matter how remote, were legally classified as Negroes. Using this "one-drop rule", African-American historians claimed that Ancient Egypt was 56% Black. They arrived at this by adding the 36% of Negroes to the 20% of individuals "approximating either to the Cro-Magnoid or to the Negroid [i.e. Mixed Race]".

We disagree with their conclusions for two reasons. Firstly, modern American systems of classification have no place in the ancient world. Secondly, the African-Americans have failed to tackle either Falkenburger's Mediterranean or Cro-Magnoid categories.

The Mediterranean category in the popular mind implies Greeks, Spaniards, Italians, White North Africans, and Israelis. For a physical anthropologist, on the other hand, it implies dolichocephalic skulls with long narrow faces. There are two populations that generally possess these traits, some European populations and some East African populations. Since Egypt is also in East Africa, it is simpler to theorise that the 33% Mediterranean skulls resemble East Africans rather than Europeans. The Cro-Magnons are the earliest people to inhabit Europe, the ancestors of White skinned people. These early people, creators of the Aurignacian Culture, were Negroes as has already been seen in an earlier chapter. Falkenburger's 20% approximating either to the Cro-Magnoid or to the Negroid can only be a mixture of Negroes with Negroes. We therefore conclude that all of Falkenburger's predynastic skulls were of Negroes. Moreover, this is the simplest and therefore the most scientifically acceptable reading of the evidence.

Mr J. Michael Crichton, author of Jurassic Park, wrote an important study on Egyptian and East African crania in 1966 called *A Multiple Discriminant Analysis of Egyptian and African Negro Crania.* He concluded that

> As expected, the Negroes are distinguished from the Egyptians principally in the nasal region. The Negro nose is large, broad and flat ... The breadth of the Negro face is also distinctive ... This study does not agree, however, with Crewdson-Bennington's conclusion that Egyptians are more longheaded than Negroes. No significant differences in head length were discovered.[42]

Professor Shomarka Keita of Howard University has created something of a revolution in Egyptian physical anthropology. He has shown that the skull, like any other physical attribute of a people, will reflect the continual shaping influence of the environment upon it. Thus a population that starts out broad nosed can evolve narrow noses over thousands of years due to environmental selection pressure in a very cold climate. This has happened in Europe as Cro-Magnon evolved into its White skinned descendant. The same thing can happen in a very hot climate. Narrow noses can evolve to restrict the effect of breathing dry heat. As an example, Keita discusses the Tutsi of Central East Africa:

> Hiernaux (1975) has accounted for variation in Africa using a non-racial approach; he does not specifically address the northern Nile Valley in great detail, but his concepts, based on microevolutionary principles (adaptation, drift, selection), are applicable in this region in the light of recent archaeological data. For example, in living and fossil tropical Africans, narrow faces and noses (versus broad "Negro" ones) do not usually indicate European or Near Eastern migration or "Europoid" (Caucasian) genes, called Hamitic as once taught, but represent indigenous variation, either connoting a hot-dry climatic adaptation or resulting from drift.[43]

Dana Reynolds-Marniche, another African-American, wrote a useful paper entitled *The Myth of the Mediterranean Race,* where she noted that:

> Much of the problem [with the older craniometric studies] lay in the fact that scholars believed that the form of the human skull, as indicated by cephalic index, was a permanent racial character.[44]

Carlson and Van Gerven have shown that within a single population, it is possible for variation to occur in size and shape of noses. This reflects different environmental pressures in each locality rather than a different or mixed population:

> With regard to Crichton's (1966) analysis, it is important to consider that his earliest Egyptian groups were spatially separated 432 km to the south of his most recent series. There is the distinct alternative possibility that the differences detected between the earliest and latest groups reflect geographical variation. The nasal aperture, for example appears to be adaptively responsive to climatic variation (Woolpoff, 1968; Glanville, 1969) and appears to be clinally distributed. Interestingly, metric variation in the nasal aperture figured most prominently in distinguishing Egyptian from East African crania. Crichton's results demonstrate that the East African crania are smaller than the Egyptian series and have a broader nasal aperture. The Egyptian series presents a similar continuum, with the crania from the upper Nile being the smallest and having the broadest nasal aperture. That distribution is consistent with a geographical, ecological hypothesis.[45]

Drawing together the craniometric studies from Madden to Keita, and the summary of Crawford, we conclude that the ancient Egyptian population consisted of one people. They were originally broad featured and, over time, evolved through dry heat adaptation into a population showing a mixture of broad and narrow features. The narrow featured groups resembled the Tutsi, Somalis or Ethiopians. In addition, no research has ever suggested that any of the Ancient Egyptian crania resembled those of the modern Copts. Unlike some of the modern East African populations, however, other evidence indicates the Egyptians had brittle rather than soft hair. Or does it?

The hair of the Ancient Egyptian mummies has been used to claim that they were not Negroes. Sir John Gardiner Wilkinson, for example, wrote that:

> [T]he mummies prove that the Egyptians were *neither black nor woolly-haired,* and the formation of the head at once decides that they are of Asiatic, and not of African origin.[46]

Don Brothwell and Richard Spearman wrote a foundation article called *The Hair of the Earlier Peoples.* Written for archaeologists, this valuable paper shows how to interpret and handle ancient hair evidence. They mention, for example, that some surviving Egyptian hair samples are dark brown in colour, others are brown and some are now blond. Samples of hair from the Canary Islands dating from 700 to 1200 AD range in colour from dark brown to blonde. An eighteenth century sample of hair from Malawi was found to be dark brown. What should we make of this?

> The blond hair is particularly interesting [wrote Brothwell and Spearman], especially as the cases noted in early material are from Egypt, Peru and the Canary Islands, areas now generally associated with dark hair. As far as we can tell this fair hair colour was not the result of intentional bleaching ... Although burial can result in some degree of fading as evidenced by the changes in modern hair after burial for many months, it seems very unlikely that such a light colour could result from an originally dark specimen. A possible solution to this question might be in the examination of the actual melanin granules themselves under the electron microscope ... Even if some of the blond samples are the result of staining by the embalming fluid (as already suggested by Batrawi) or ground solutions this might indicate their true colour ... Ancient hair keratin was often stained with yellowish brown patches from the deposits in all burial sites but causes no confusion with melanin as this appears as dark granules under the microscope ... Transverse sections of hair from an Egyptian mummy ... were interesting in that there was a strong uniform reddish florescence of the keratin with acridine orange, but the melanin granules in the medulla and cortex were black.

Brothwell and Spearman draw a conclusion on the light hair colour of this particular mummy:

> In view of the covering of the body of the mummy with cloth it suggests that atmospheric oxidation was not responsible for this change, which may have been produced by the embalming preparation.[47]

The texture of the hair can also be affected. This produces the same effect as permanent waving (i.e. a perm). As an example, they show what can happen to sheep's wool:

> Hair is largely made up of the fibrous protein keratin. This substance is extremely resistant to decomposition and enzymatic digestion, mainly owing to the presence of disulphide cross linkages of the amino acid cystine. These join together the long polypeptide chains of the molecule. If these cross linkages are broken by reduction or oxidation, altered keratin is readily attacked by proteolytic enzymes … [T]he chief factors which alter keratin are probably atmospheric oxidation, soaking in water, and alkaline pH of the soil. These changes can occur in a living animal; thus atmospheric weathering of the fleece in sheep results in loss of cystine from the exposed tips of the fibres. Permanent waving [i.e. a perm] alters the keratin cross linkages, and these changes have been detected by florescence microscopy (Jarret, unpublished). It is probable that if the preparations employed during mummification contained reducing or oxidizing agents or alkaline substances the hair keratin would be damaged.[48]

This shows that hair that has suffered from preparations during mummification, atmospheric oxidation, soaking in water, or deleterious alkaline pH of the soil, can suffer damage similar to permanent waving. This would have the effect of straightening Negro hair just as it can straighten out sheep's wool.

Consequently, mummies such as Yuya, Thuya and Rameses II that possess seemingly blond or red hair are likely to have oxidised or stained hair. These mummies and the others that possess seemingly straight hair probably display similar and related hair damage that has resulted in permed or straightened hair. None of this is genuine Caucasian straight hair. The fact that a Malawi hair sample has turned dark brown in only 200 years or so supports this interpretation.

Professor Martin Bernal is author of a widely discussed work entitled *Black Athena*. It is difficult to draw any conclusions about the ethnicity of the Ancient Egyptians from this book, however, but he does appear to claim that four of the Egyptian dynasties consisted of "pharaohs whom one can usefully call black" whatever this means. He feels "convinced that many of the most powerful Egyptian dynasties which were based in Upper Egypt - the 1st, 11th, 12th and 18th - were made up of pharaohs whom one can usefully call black".[49] We do not know if "usefully call black" means Negro as used in this book, but we shall ask a slightly different question: Is it possible for a scholar to usefully blacken these dynasties without usefully blackening the other dynasties? Bernal appears to think so.

The venerable Carter G. Woodson wrote a handbook for the study of the Negro many years ago entitled *The African Background Outlined*. In this work we read the following: "The statues of Rahotep and Nefert [sic], of Khafra, Amenenhat [sic] I and III, Usertesen [sic] I, Tahatmes [sic] III, Queen Mutema [sic], and Ramses [sic] II show distinctly Negroid features."[50] Mr J. A. Rogers wrote: "I have seen Negroes here [i.e. in the US] and in Africa, who bore a striking resemblance to Seti the Great."[51] In addition to the portrait statues, Thutmose III (cf. Tahatmes III), Rameses II, and Seti I, were shown to have Negro body proportions by Robins and Shute. You may recall from the previous chapter that all three men raised monuments to venerate their ancestors - the Tablets of Karnak, Saqqara and Abydos. According to MacNaughton, the Karnak List has names of Kings from Dynasties IV, V, X, XI, XII and XIII. It may also have once possessed the names of Kings of Dynasties VI and VIII, but these names were erased from the first line of the document. MacNaughton believes that this list is approximately in chronological order and adds that: "The Karnak List probably does not extend further than to the end of the Thirteenth Dynasty."[52] According to Budge, the Abydos List mentions kings of Dynasties I, II, III, IV, V, VI, X, XI, XII, XVIII and XIX. The Saqqara List contains the same kings as those of Abydos, but a smaller number of kings are listed.[53] The three lists when combined, list about 100 kings from Dynasties I, II, III, IV, V, VI, X, XI, XII, XIII, XVIII and XIX. They may also have contained a name of a king or two from Dynasty VIII. The conclusion is inescapable. If Thutmose III, Seti I and Rameses II were Negroes, then all of the 100 or so ancestor kings were also Negroes.

It is possible that Bernal thinks that the four dynasties concerned were "usefully" black due to them being foreign i.e. Nubian or semi-Nubian in origin. He seems to suggest as much by highlighting the Upper Egyptian origins of these kings. If so, didn't Dynasty Two share the same Thinite origins of Dynasty One? Was it not Sir Flinders Petrie who wrote that a "conqueror of Sudani features founded the Third Dynasty, and many new ideas entered the country"?[54] Wasn't Dynasty Four among the 18 Ethiopian pharaohs mentioned by Herodotus? Wasn't Dynasty Five of Elephantine origins? Wasn't Dynasty Seventeen the ancestors of Dynasty Eighteen? How did these dynasties escape from being usefully called black? In conclusion, we note that it is not possible to give some of the ancient history of Egypt back to Africa without giving all of it back. Bernal's position here, as elsewhere, is untenable.

Some historians have pointed out that the Egyptians distinguished themselves from Negroes in their literature. In Nile Valley history, there were indeed conflicts between Egypt and Nubia, causing the Egyptians to take stern measures against the Nubians. These conflicts are reflected in Egyptian documents. One such document, associated with Senwosret III, reads as follows:

> I am the king; [my] word is performed. My hand performs what my mind
> conceives ... I attack my attacker ... The man who retreats is a vile coward; he
> who is defeated on his own land is no man. Thus is the Black. He falls down at
> a word of command, when attacked he runs away - when pursued he shows his
> back in flight. The Blacks have no courage, they are weak and timid, their
> hearts are contemptible. I have seen them, I am not mistaken about them.[55]

The inscription, quoted in Professor DeGraft-Johnson's classic *African
Glory,* clearly implied that the Egyptians considered themselves to be a distinct
race to the Blacks. After all why would they describe the Negroes in this way
and ban them from entering Egypt?

The solution to this puzzle was provided by Professors Yosef ben-Jochannan
and Cheikh Anta Diop, in their respective works.[56] The text, and many others
like it, had in fact been wrongly translated. The word mistranslated into
English as Blacks or Negroes, is *Nhsi,* generally given as Nehesi, Nahasi or
Nehusi in the transliterations. *Nhsi* has national not racial connotations, and
refers to Nubians. Dr Welsby, as we have seen, suggests that *Nhsi* is a
geographical term that identifies the Nubians who live along the Nile as
opposed to those of the Eastern Desert. Dr DeGraft-Johnson, an otherwise
reliable historian, was unaware of this. Equally unaware were Dr W. E. B.
DuBois and Dr Chancellor Williams. These writers believed that since the
Egyptians distinguished themselves from Negroes, the Egyptians had to have
been Mulattoes.[57]

The authentic Egyptian word for Blacks is Kemetiu, a name the Egyptians
used to describe themselves.[58] The text when correctly translated should have
read:

> I am the king; [my] word is performed. My hand performs what my mind
> conceives ... I attack my attacker ... The man who retreats is a vile coward; he
> who is defeated on his own land is no man. Thus is the Nubian. He falls down
> at a word of command, when attacked he runs away - when pursued he shows
> his back in flight. The Nubians have no courage, they are weak and timid, their
> hearts are contemptible. I have seen them, I am not mistaken about them.

The insults thrown at the Nubians by Senwosret III carry no racial
connotations. They are merely national or geographical insults. The
Egyptologists allowed the mistranslations to continue uncorrected since it
served their ideological and racist interests to do so.

We now review the question of the artistic depictions. The ancient Egyptians
used a particular artistic canon that could possibly deceive the modern scholar.
By convention, they represented men with a red skin colour and women with
a yellow skin colour.[59] There are paintings where some of the men are
represented with red and some with yellow skins, and in others, women are

painted with red skins. In some of these images, Nubians are depicted, but in the colours dark brown or jet-black. This has led scholars to speculate that the ancient Egyptians were a red-skinned (or perhaps yellow-skinned) race. Moreover, they were a different race to the Nubians. Dr Madden, cited earlier, held the queer view that these relatively light colours were themselves close approximations to the authentic colours of the modern Nubians. He wrote that:

> I was more struck here [at Philae] than elsewhere, by the different complexions given to the sexes, in their pictures; - the men are always painted red, the women yellow. The few colours known to the [Ancient] Egyptians enabled them to approach no nearer to the real complexions of their race. If a painter had now only the use of the primitive colours, he would find red would be the nearest approach to the swarthy complexion of the male Nubian, and yellow to the female, whose tint is so much lighter from the less exposure to the sun. But what struck me as the greatest proof I met with in Nubia, of the identity of the Nubian race and that of the [Ancient] Egyptians, is the strong resemblance of the former to the features of all the Egyptian statues.[60]

Despite Dr Madden's eloquence, we cannot agree with all of this. Dr Davidson shed far more light on this issue in a television programme entitled *Africa: Different but Equal*. He showed examples of Egyptian depictions of Nubians, one of which shows Nubian dancing girls depicted in the colour red (sic). Another Egyptian painting, this time showing Egyptian wrestlers from a tomb in Beni Hassan, depicted in red and yellow, were compared by Davidson with modern Nuba wrestlers (who are a jet-black Nubian people) who paint their skins red and yellow for ceremonial purposes.[61] The comparison strongly implied that the red and yellow colours merely represented skin-paint, or at the very least, ceremonial significance.

There are examples of Egyptian art that are definitely intended to be race specific as opposed to being merely ceremonial, such as the famous paintings from the Temple of Rameses III. In these images, Egyptians and Negroes are painted the same way using the same jet-black colour, contrasting with the colours of other races. Moreover, the Egyptians and Negroes are dressed the same. There are well-known jet-black images of Pharaohs Mentuhotep II, Thutmose I and Tutankhamen. In addition, there is a fresco of Thutmose III depicted jet-black in one scene and red in another. Clearly he could not have been both colours. The red has to be symbolic. Furthermore, there are plenty of New Kingdom paintings that depict Egyptian men and women in the same colour - namely chocolate brown. The paintings therefore show that the range of real skin tones among the Egyptians ranged from jet-black to chocolate brown. M. Champollion, the Father of Egyptology, directed attention to other such paintings that he saw in the early nineteenth century:

Right in the valley of Biban-el-Moluk, we admired, like all previous visitors, the astonishing freshness of the paintings and the fine sculptures on several tombs ... [T]hey wished to represent the inhabitants of Egypt and those of foreign lands. Thus we have before our eyes the image of the various races of man known to the Egyptians ... The first, the one closest to the god, has a dark red colour ... The legends designate this species as ... the Egyptians. There can be no uncertainty about the racial identity of the man who comes next: he belongs to the Black race ... The third [the Asian] presents a very different aspect; his skin colour borders on yellow or tan ... Finally, the last one [the European] is what we call flesh-coloured, a white skin of the most delicate shade ... I hastened to seek the tableau corresponding to this one in the other royal tombs and, as a matter of fact, I found it in several ... This manner of viewing the tableau is all the more accurate because, on the other tombs, the same generic names reappear, always in the same order. We find there Egyptians and Africans represented in the same way which could not be otherwise; but the *Namou* (the Asians) and the *Tamhou* (Europeans) present significant and curious variants.[62]

It is worth noting that the ancient Greeks had a tradition of painting men with black skins and women with white skins.[63] As in the Egyptian case, this is merely the artistic canon that they used. It does not prove that Greek men were black. Rather, it shows that a more sophisticated interpretation of the art is required.

Finally, we note that the Kushites of antiquity and the Igbos more recently, used the same red and yellow colour scheme as the Egyptians. In the Kushite Pyramid of Pharaoh Tanwetamani the female deities Isis and Nephthys are depicted in yellow. Hapi, a male deity said to have originated in Uganda, is depicted in red. The Kushite ruler, himself, is shown as chocolate brown.[64] This is probably the only natural colour in the picture and is well within the true Egyptian and modern Negro skin colour range. The Mbari art of Nigeria also depicts individuals as red or yellow. Nobody has yet claimed that the Igbos or Kushites belonged to a red or yellow race. Or at least not yet ...

Dr C. Loring Brace, a physical anthropologist, and his team, penned a very influential paper on the race-origins of the Ancient Egyptians called *Clines and Clusters Versus Race*. The document has been widely quoted and praised for its conclusion that the race concept is largely bogus and that the Ancient Egyptians cannot be classified as Black or White. In place of 'Race' Dr Brace *et al* propose to use the terms 'Cline' or 'Cluster'. These terms have the advantages of not being racist. How did Dr Brace *et al* arrive at this interesting conclusion?

They measured Egyptian crania using 24 measurement criteria. However, nearly all the measurements they selected to study were focused on the nasal regions of the skulls! In other words, Brace and colleagues read the paper of J. Michael Crichton, cited earlier. Mr Crichton demonstrated that the only significant difference on average between Egyptian crania and Negro crania was in the nasal region. We believe that this is the true reason Brace *et al* ignored other measurement criteria. Exploiting this fact allowed them to draw the following tentative conclusions:

> It is obvious that both the Predynastic and the Late Dynastic Egyptians are more closely related to the European cluster than they are to any other major regional clusters in the world. If South Asia - India - is discounted for the moment, the Somalis at the southernmost extent of this series show that there is a continuum of related groups which, given the Norwegians and Lapps in our European sample, runs all the way from the equator to the artic circle. When South Asia is separated into available constituents as is done on Figure 3, the Somalis change to show a tie with the Egypt-Europe spectrum.[65]

In their 'European cluster' Brace *et al* included the Indians, Nubians and Somalis. Since this is the case, why did they call this cluster 'European'? Why didn't they call it an 'East African cluster' or even an 'Indian cluster'? Falkenburger demonstrated that 36% of the crania had broad features, as discussed earlier. All that Brace *et al* had achieved was to dissolve this group into a statistical average to create the misleading impression that all of the Egyptians had narrow features. Falkenburger's study together with the royal sculptures proves that this could not possibly have been the case.

Brace *et al's* paper seems to be yet another piece of propaganda designed to create the impression that Europeans were responsible for building Egypt, East Africa and the Indian civilisations. Brace *et al* have presented little more than an update of the True Negro hypothesis as advanced by M. D. W. Jeffreys in 1951. In other words, all the arguments that Brace and his team presents are either taken directly or indirectly from Jefferys or from J. Michael Crichton. The only difference is that they avoid the term White Race. In its place, they substitute the less threatening European Cline or European Cluster. Furthermore, they present nothing that Professor Yosef ben-Jochannan did not publicly refute in 1971 with the publication *Africa! Mother of Western Civilization.*[66]

Due to the importance that the Egyptological mainstream has given this paper, we now discuss the key points raised in the Conclusion proper. This section opens with the following disclosure:

> The attempt to force the Egyptians into either a "black" or "white" category has no biological justification.[67]

Since Dr Brace and colleagues are not qualified to give biological opinions, this passage is wholly irrelevant. They are, however, qualified to give anthropological opinions. As we have seen, several anthropological studies clearly place the ancient Egyptians into the Black category. One study went as far as to argue that the two or three race model should be used "wherever possible". Classification by race is still central to physical anthropology. The interested reader should peruse the *American Journal of Physical Anthropology* to confirm this for him or herself:

> Egypt was basically Egyptian from the Neolithic right up to historic times.[68]

This is more irrelevance. What does "basically Egyptian" mean? Is it the Egyptian of Herodotus, the Father of History? Is it the Egyptian of De Volney, the Father of Orientalism? Is it the Egyptian of Champollion, the Father of Egyptology? Which is it?

> In 1989, the Dallas Museum of Natural History sponsored an exhibit at the Texas State Fair Grounds depicting Egyptian culture at the time of Ramses [sic] the Great. When the Blacology Speaking Committee in Dallas threatened to boycott the exhibit unless Ramses II was represented as "black," Mr. Aboul-Ela [the director of the cultural office of the Egyptian Embassy] justifiably complained that the point of the exhibit was being distorted by what we might call a peculiarly American form of "racial politics." As Mr. Aboul-Ela put it, "Ramses II was neither black nor white but Egyptian." When he referred to the scope of the exhibit, he stated, "This is an Egyptian heritage and an Egyptian civilization 100 percent." "Egypt of course is a country in Africa, but this doesn't mean that it belongs to Africa at large." "We cannot say by any means we are black or white. We are Egyptians."[69]

This is all irrelevant. Quoting an Arab or Turk as if he was descended from the ancient Egyptians is as inappropriate as quoting a European-American as if he was descended from the Aztecs:

> The ancient Egyptians "did not think in terms of race".[70]

This is fraudulent. The temple paintings of Rameses III and the paintings described by the Father of Egyptology makes it quite clear that the Egyptians did think in terms of race. In addition, they thought in terms of origins. The Egyptian term *Khentiu* means Lands of the South. It also means first, foremost, beginnings and chief. The Egyptian word *Yau*, a term for inner Africa, means old as in the Old Country. Moreover, the Egyptian word for west and their word for right is the same word. Similarly, the Egyptian word for east and their word for left is the same word. This shows that the Egyptians orientated themselves to the south - their place of origins.[71]

> The race concept ... is not mentioned in Herodotus, the Bible, or any other writings of classical antiquity.[72]

This is also fraudulent. Herodotus described the Egyptians as black and woolly haired. The classical writers Pliny, Vitruvius and Galen divided the regions known to them into Northern Europeans, Mediterraneans and Africans. The Book of *Genesis* divides the people of the region into the descendants of Ham (the Blacks), the descendants of Shem (the Semites), and the descendants of Japeth (the Europeans). This racial classification has proved so useful that anthropologists and linguistics continued to use it with major modifications until very recently. Concerning racial hatred, there are ancient Indian hymns dating to around 1000 BC known as the *Rg Veda*. Their apocalyptic anti-Black racism has been known about and discussed by European scholars since the nineteenth century. Finally, the Babylonian Talmud of the sixth century AD placed a most horrific racial spin on the *Genesis* classification by arguing that it is permissible to enslave the Children of Ham. This interpretation was used by Christian scholars to justify the enslavement of Black people and by the Dutch Reformed Church to justify *apartheid*. There is no way that Dr Brace and colleagues can be ignorant of any of this.

> Since it [i.e. the race concept] has neither biological nor social justification, we
> should strive to see that it is eliminated from both public and private usage. Its
> absence will be missed by no one, and we shall all be better off without it.
> R.I.P.[73]

We conclude that far from proving the death of the race concept, Dr Brace and colleagues have given it a new vitality. They have demonstrated a willingness to deceive their readers to suit racist and ideological agendas. Their paper continues to receive favourable reviews that are unjustified in view of its obvious methodological limitations. One cannot, for example, perform a comprehensive craniometric study by focusing the bulk of measurements on the nasal region. Nor can one classify disparate peoples such as East Africans, Indians and Europeans as belonging to the European Cluster. Furthermore, the concluding section of their paper is astonishingly weak, largely consisting of vacuous and fraudulent statements. Such obvious scholarly weaknesses would not have been tolerated from a Black scholar. Ordinarily, no journal would have published such substandard work. We believe that Brace and colleagues have only escaped academic criticism because they have played to the gallery. This sorry episode shows why the race concept is far from dead. Belonging to the right Cline still brings undeserved advantages.

Physical anthropology correctly understood has consistently supported the Negro identity of the Ancient Egyptians. This has always posed a dilemma for Egyptologists who wish to claim some other identity for the Nile Valley people. Adolf Erman, writing in 1894, made it quite clear what the ethnological (i.e. physical anthropological) position was at the time and the opposition to it.

The question of the race-origin of the Egyptians has long been a matter of dispute between ethnologists and philologists, the former maintaining the African theory of descent, the latter the Asiatic. Ethnologists assert that nothing exists in the physical structure of the Egyptian to distinguish him from the native African, and that from the Egyptian to the Negro population of tropical Africa, a series of links exist which do not admit of a break. The Egyptians, they maintain, cannot be separated from the Berbers, nor the latter from the Kelowi or the Tibbu, nor these again from the inhabitants round Lake Tsad [sic]; all form one race in the mind of the ethnologist, differentiated only by the influence of a dissimilar manner of life and climate.[74]

Dr Keith Crawford penned a fine review of a wide range of modern anthropological studies on the Egyptian skeletal remains. He drew the following conclusions on the peopling of Ancient Egypt, from prehistoric through to the Dynastic periods:

Egyptian populations from the Paleolithic period (35,000 B.C.) to the predynastic period ... display physical features common to Africoids with Broad Traits ("Negroid"). Features in African populations that were thought to indicate a Caucasoid influence may be attributable to natural selection and reflect the wide range of variability among "true" Africoid types. Morphometric analysis of crania, cephalometric studies (X-ray), estimates of stature, genetic analysis of both non-metric traits and blood groups, and studies of hair and pigmentation show that dynastic Egyptians are related to other Nile Valley and tropical African populations more closely than to any other population outside of Africa. Gene flow from outside of Africa may have introduced Caucasoid genes particularly during the First and Second Intermediate periods (dynasties 7-10 and 13-17, respectively) and the late dynastic period in Lower Egypt. Remains from Archaic/Old Kingdom, Middle Kingdom and New Kingdom rulers show affinities to Broad Africoid populations (Negroids).[75]

Our lengthy discussion of the ethnicity of the Ancient Egyptians was necessary because some scholars still claim that Negroes did not build any of Africa's important civilisations. Moreover, they use essentially the same arguments as those refuted here - endless variations on the True Negro hypothesis. "Indeed, if one must believe [some] western works", wrote Professor Diop:

it is useless to look into the interior of the African forest for a single civilization which, in the last analysis, might be the product of [B]lacks. The civilizations of Ethiopia and Egypt, the express testimony of the ancients notwithstanding, the civilizations of the Ife [i.e. Yoruba] and Benin, of the Chad Basin, of Ghana, all those referred to as neo-Sudanese (Mali, Gao [i.e. Songhai] etc.) those of Zimbabwe (Monomotapa), of the Congo on the Equator, etc. . . . according to the coteries of western scholars, were created by mythical whites who then vanished as in a dream, leaving the blacks to perpetuate the forms, organizations, techniques etc., which they had invented.

On an optimistic final note, Dr Diop opines that:

Such modes of thought obviously cannot persist forever … [76]

Notes

[1] Erik Hornung, *History of Ancient Egypt,* UK, Edinburgh University Press, 1999, p.90.

[2] Michael Rice, *Egypt's Making,* UK, Routledge, 1991, p.221.

[3] For an alternative view of the peopling of America see Ivan Van Sertima ed, *African Presence in Early America,* US, Transaction Publishers, 1992, pp.215-240.

[4] Cheikh Anta Diop, *Civilization or Barbarism,* US, Lawrence Hill Books, 1991, p.11.

[5] Basil Davidson, *Africa,* television series part 1: *Different but Equal,* UK, Michael Beazley, Rm Arts, Channel Four Television & Nigerian Television, 1984.

[6] Henri Lhote, *The Search for the Tassili Frescoes,* UK, Hutchinson of London, 1959, pp.12-3.

[7] Keith W. Crawford, *The Racial Identity of Ancient Egyptian Populations based on the Analysis of Physical Remains,* in *Egypt: Child of Africa,* ed Ivan Van Sertima, US, Transaction Publishers, 1994, p.61.

[8] Ibid., p.62.

[9] Cheikh Anta Diop, *The African Origin of Civilization: Myth or Reality?* US, Lawrence Hill Books, 1974, pp.78-83.

[10] Jacob Carruthers, *The Wisdom of Governance in Kemet,* in *Kemet and the African Worldview,* ed Jacob Carruthers & Maulana Karenga, US, University of Sankore Press, 1986, pp.24-5.

[11] There are many such images in Ivan Van Sertima ed, *Egypt Revisited,* US, Transaction Publishers, 1989.

[12] Pierre Montet, *Eternal Egypt,* quoted in Keith W. Crawford, *The Racial Identity of Ancient Egyptian Populations based on the Analysis of Physical Remains,* in *Egypt: Child of Africa,* p.64.

[13] Asa Hilliard, *Bringing Maat, Destroying Isfet,* in *Egypt: Child of Africa,* ed Ivan Van Sertima, US, Transaction Publishers, 1994, pp.139-140.

[14] Cf. ibid.

[15] Charles S. Finch, *Echoes of the Old Darkland,* US, Khenti, 1991, p.134.

[16] Ibid.

[17] Christopher Ehret, *The Civilizations of Africa,* UK, James Currey, 2002, p.57.

[18] J. Gardiner Wilkinson in George Rawlinson (translator), *History of Herodotus: Volume II, Third Edition,* UK, John Murray, 1875, p.170.

[19] W. W. How and J. Wells, *A Commentary on Herodotus, Volume 1,* UK, Clarendon Press, 1912, p.218.

[20] A. H. Sayce, *The Ancient Empires of the East: Herodotos I-III,* UK, Macmillan and Co., 1883, p.179.

[21] Martin Bernal, *Black Athena: Volume I,* UK, Free Association, 1987, p.241.

[22] Ibid., p.242.

[23] Wilhelm Spiegelberg, *The Credibility of Herodotus' Account of Egypt in the Light of the Egyptian Monuments,* US, ECA Associates, 1990 (originally 1927), p.37.

[24] Richard Poe, *Black Spark: White Fire,* US, Prima Publishing, 1997, p.355.

[25] Quoted in ibid., p.353.

[26] Ibid.

[27] D. E. L. Haynes, *Antiquities of Tripolitania,* Libya, The Antiquities Department of Tripolitania, 1959, p.19.

[28] Quoted in Serge Lancel, *Carthage: A History,* UK, Basil Blackwell, 1995, p.100.

[29] Serge Lancel, *Carthage: A History,* p.5.

[30] Quoted in Wayne Chandler, *The Moor: Light of Europe's Dark Age,* in *Golden Age of the Moor,* ed Ivan Van Sertima, US Transaction publishers, 1992, p.153.

[31] Cheikh Anta Diop, *The African Origin of Civilization: Myth or Reality?* p.278.

[32] Godfrey Higgins, *Anacalypsis, Volume I,* US, A & B Books, 1992, p.457.

[33] Quoted in Walter B. Emery, *Egypt in Nubia,* UK, Hutchinson, 1965, p.16

[34] Ivan Van Sertima, *Editorial,* in *Egypt: Child of Africa,* ed Ivan Van Sertima, US, Transaction Publishers, 1994, pp.4-6.

[35] Charles S. Finch, *Echoes of the Old Darkland,* p.42.

[36] See Ivan Van Sertima, *Editorial,* in *Egypt: Child of Africa,* pp.4-6.

[37] Keith W. Crawford, *The Racial Identity of Ancient Egyptian Populations based on the Analysis of Physical Remains,* in *Egypt: Child of Africa,* pp.59-60.

[38] Gordon Waterford, *Egypt,* UK, Thames & Hudson, 1967, pp.16-7.

[39] Quoted in Gerald Massey, *Ancient Egypt: The Light of the World, Volume I,* UK, T. Fisher Unwin, 1907, p.255.

[40] R. R. Madden, *Travels in Turkey, Egypt, Nubia and Palestine in 1824, 1825, 1826, and 1827, Volume II,* UK, Henry Colburn, 1829, pp.92-3.

[41] Cheikh Anta Diop, *Origin of the Ancient Egyptians,* in *Egypt Revisited,* ed Ivan Van Sertima, US, Transaction Publishers, 1989, pp.10-11.

[42] J. Michael Crichton, *A Multiple Discriminant Analysis of Egyptian and African Negro Crania,* US, The Peabody Museum, 1966, p.50.

[43] S. O. Y. Keita, *Further Analysis of Crania from Ancient Northern Africa,* in *American Journal of Physical Anthropology, Volume 87,* 1992, p.246.

[44] Dana Reynolds Marniche, *The Myth of the Mediterranean Race,* in *Egypt: Child of Africa,* ed Ivan Van Sertima, US, Transaction Publishers, 1994, p.109.

[45] Quoted in Keith W. Crawford, *The Racial Identity of Ancient Egyptian Populations based on the Analysis of Physical Remains,* in *Egypt: Child of Africa,* p.63

[46] J. Gardiner Wilkinson in George Rawlinson (translator), *History of Herodotus: Volume II, Third Edition,* p.170.

[47] Don Brothwell and Richard Spearman, *The Hair of the Earlier Peoples,* in *Science and Archaeology,* ed Don Brothwell and Eric Higgs, UK, Thames and Hudson, 1963, pp.432-3.

[48] Ibid, p.28.

[49] Martin Bernal, *Black Athena: Volume I,* p.242.

[50] Quoted in Mwalimu I. Mwadilifu, *European Scholars on the African Origins of the Africans of Antiquity,* US, ECA Associates, 1991, p.77.

[51] J. A. Rogers, *From "Superman" to Man,* US, Helga M. Rogers, 1990, p.19

[52] Duncan MacNaughton, *A Scheme of Egyptian Chronology,* UK, Luzac & Co., 1932, p.157.

[53] E. A. Wallis Budge, *Egypt in the Neolithic and Archaic Periods,* UK, Kegan Paul, Trench, Trübner & Co., 1902, pp.119-125.

[54] Quoted in John Jackson, *Introduction to African Civilizations,* US, Citadel Press, 1970, p.97.

[55] Quoted in J. C. DeGraft-Johnson, *African Glory,* UK, Watts & Co., 1954, pp.10-11.

[56] Yosef A. A. ben-Jochannan, *Africa! Mother of Western Civilization,* US, Black Classic Press, 1971, pp.102-4 and Cheikh Anta Diop, *The African Origin of Civilization: Myth or Reality?* pp.167-170.

[57] Dr W. E. B. DuBois, *The World and Africa,* US, International Publishers, 1965, pp.112 and Chancellor Williams, *The Destruction of Black Civilization,* US, Third World Press, 1987, pp.98-103.

[58] Jacob H. Carruthers, *Essays in Ancient Egyptian Studies,* US, Timbuktu Press, 1984, pp.22-3.

[59] James Brunson, *Ancient Egyptians: The Dark Red Race Myth,* in *Egypt Revisited,* ed Ivan Van Sertima, US, Transaction Publishers, 1989, p.53.

[60] R. R. Madden, *Travels in Turkey, Egypt, Nubia and Palestine in 1824, 1825, 1826, and 1827: Volume II,* p.117.

[61] Basil Davidson, *Africa,* television series part 1: *Different but Equal.*

[62] *Egypte Ancienne,* quoted in Cheikh Anta Diop, *The African Origin of Civilization: Myth or Reality?* pp.46-7.

[63] H. G. Spearing, *The Childhood of Art,* UK, Kegan Paul, Trench, Trubner & Co., 1912, pp.466-74.

[64] For a published photograph of the Pyramid of Qalhata see Timothy Kendall, *Kingdom of Kush,* in *National Geographic, Volume 178, Number 5,* ed William Graves, US, National Geographic Society, November 1990, pp.112-4.

[65] C. Loring Brace et al, *Clines and Clusters Versus Race, in Yearbook of Physical Anthropology, Volume 36,* 1993, p.10.

[66] Yosef A. A. ben-Jochannan, *Africa! Mother of Western Civilization.*

[67] C. Loring Brace et al, *Clines and Clusters Versus Race,* in *Yearbook of Physical Anthropology,* p.25.

[68] Ibid.

[69] Ibid.

[70] Ibid., p.26.

[71] Charles S. Finch, *Black Roots of Egypt's Glory,* in *Great Black Leaders: Ancient and Modern,* ed Ivan Van Sertima, US, Transaction Publishers, 1988, p.142.

[72] C. Loring Brace et al, *Clines and Clusters Versus Race,* in *Yearbook of Physical Anthropology,* p.26.

[73] Ibid.

[74] Adolf Erman, *Life in Ancient Egypt,* US, Dover, 1971 (original 1894), pp.29-30.

[75] Keith W. Crawford, *The Racial Identity of Ancient Egyptian Populations based on the Analysis of Physical Remains,* in *Egypt: Child of Africa,* p.68.

[76] Quoted in John G. Jackson, *Introduction to African Civilizations,* pp.7-8.

CHAPTER TEN: CARTHAGE AND NUMIDIA

Carthage

In the ninth century BC the city-state of Carthage was established. It was situated on the North African coast of modern Tunisia. Incoming Phœnicians, the early people of Palestine, founded it and called it Qart Hadasht (cf. Carthage) - their New Town, as opposed to Utica, also located in North Africa, their Old Town. Other influences in the culture came from different sources. The Libyans, the indigenous people of North Africa, played an important, and ultimately, the dominant role. Moreover, other peoples and cultural practices came from the Nile Valley. What was the resulting mix?

Anthropologists have studied skeletons from Carthaginian cemeteries. Professor Eugène Pittard, then at the University of Geneva, reported that: "Other bones discovered in Punic [cf. Phœnician] Carthage, and housed in the Lavigerie Museum, come from personages found in special sarcophagi and probably belonging to the Carthaginian elite. Almost all the skulls are dolichocephalic." Furthermore, the sarcophagus of the highly venerated Priestess of Tanit, "the most ornate" and "the most artistic yet found," is also housed in the Lavigerie Museum. Pittard says: "[T]he woman buried there had Negro features. She belonged to the African race!"[1] Professor Stéphane Gsell was the author of the voluminous *Histoire Ancienne de l'Afrique du Nord.* Also based on anthropological studies conducted on Carthaginian skeletons, he declared that: "The so-called Semitic type, characterised by the long, perfectly oval face, the thin aquiline nose and the lengthened cranium, enlarged over the nape of the neck has not [yet] been found in Carthage".[2]

Herodotus, the well-travelled Ancient Greek historian, discussed the origin of the Phœnicians. "This nation," said he, "according to their own account, dwelt anciently upon the Erythræan [i.e. Eritrean] sea; but, crossing thence, fixed themselves on the sea-coast of Syria [i.e. Palestine], where they still inhabit".[3] Lady Lugard, an outstanding authority on African antiquities, supports the view that the Phœnicians were of distant Eritrean origins. She declared that: "The Phœnicians are believed to have migrated from Erythrea on the coast of the Red Sea, about the year 2000 B.C., to the Mediterranean, where they were first established on a strip of Syria".[4]

The earliest known inhabitants of Palestine were the Natufians. Flourishing some 10,000 years ago, they were Negroes. Sir Arthur Keith, the great British

Carthage and Numidia (Map: Kieron Vital). Carthage was founded in 814 BC and lasted until 146 BC. Numidia was founded in the 5ᵗʰ century BC and lasted until 46 BC.

anthropologist, described them thus: "Mediterraneans with a distinct bias towards the African variety of that stock represented by the predynastic people of Egypt".[5] More recently, Donald Redford echoed the same point. He wrote: "this culture was a product of a human type of slight build with long heads (dolichocephalic) that can confidently be classified as *Homo sapiens.* Natufians, like the modern Bantus, practised evulsion of the incisors and apparently wore skins and at times headgear made of shells".[6] The *Bible* calls their descendants, several thousand years later, Canaanites. Canon Rawlinson says of the Canaanites:

> This people, a Hamitic race closely connected with the Egyptians, Ethiopians, and primitive Babylonians, spread itself at a remote date over the entire coast tract from the borders of Egypt to Casius, and formed the dominant population as far inland as the Cœle-Syrian valley, the lake of Gennesaret, and the deep cleft of the Jordan.[7]

In Greek accounts the people of this area were called Phœnicians. This name refers to a dark red or brown dye, which the Greeks later used to denote the colour of the Phœnicians.[8] This may imply that by the Greek period, the Phœnicians had become a mixed population having started out as black and ending up brown or dark red. Rawlinson, however, takes the view that the Phœnicians were *not* the same population as the Canaanites. Like Lugard, he accepts they migrated there in 2000 BC but believes instead that they came

Phœnicia (Israel/Palestine). Nimrud Ivory. 9th century BC. (Photo: Robin Walker). Reproduced by courtesy of the trustees of the British Museum.

"from the East". His evidence for this comes from the migration theory reported by Herodotus, but instead, Rawlinson identifies the Erythræan Sea as the Persian Gulf and not the Red Sea.[9] The problem here is that the people of Bahrain, even today, are Negroid. Moreover, the other peoples living along the coastline of the Persian Gulf are also dark skinned. Professor Van Sertima sensibly advises caution here because:

> I have found no authority in fact who could precisely define the Phoenicians [sic]. And that is because they are not a race but a nation, a conglomerate of peoples who became distinctive through nationhood as a separate entity. Even if they were originally Africans, that is not helpful when we come to deal with them in the first millenium B.C. To say that the American was originally Asian is not telling us anything about the American racial composition today, or even 300 years ago.[10]

There are, however, a series of ivories that depict the Phœnicians in the British Museum. Carved in the ninth century BC, the majority of the Nimrud Ivories depict the Phœnicians as Negroes.[11] Professor Lancel, an excellent modern authority, reports that the tradition of ivory carving was carried into Carthage and great efforts were made to preserve the Phœnician integrity of the style. Much of the art of Carthage shows Egyptianising or Hellenising (i.e. Greek) tendencies and thus fails to faithfully represent either the Phœnician or Libyan populations.[12] There are statues and depictions of people on coins that follow one or other tendencies. Mr Wayne Chandler, an African-American scholar, gives an example of this. He demonstrates that Hellenising portraits of

the Buddha depict him as a European.[13] Dr Lancel claims the Carthaginian ivories were different: "[T]he openwork ivories of Carthage appear to be in direct descent from the Nimrud pieces dated to the end of the eighth century [BC]". Professor Lancel shows two ivories recovered from the Byrsa cemetery at Carthage. One of them was in an Egyptianising style and shows two people. Lancel says of it: "The 'Cushitic' features are very noticeable in the way the two people are portrayed". The other ivory depicted an animal and was, according to Lancel, "in a Syro-Palestinian tradition". The problem here is that the two styles that Lancel identifies are both present in the Nimrud ivories of a century earlier. We therefore conclude that the Cushitic features depicted on the Byrsa cemetery ivory, also shows "great fidelity to Syrio-Palestinian models".[14] In closing the Phœnician question, we note that there is an official description of the sarcophagus of Esmunazar II, King of the Phœnician city of Sidon, and one of Phœnicia's most illustrious rulers. It reads as follows:

> The features are Egyptian, with large full almond shaped eyes, the nose flattened and the lips remarkably thick and somewhat after the Negro mould.

> The whole countenance is smiling, agreeable and expressive beyond anything
> I have ever seen in the disinterred monuments of Egypt or Ninevah.[15]

The Phœnicians were the great maritime traders of the ancient world. Mr R.
Bosworth Smith, author of the excellent *Carthage and the Carthaginians,* says
of them:

> It was they who learned to steer their ships by the sure help of the Pole Star,
> while the Greeks still depended on the [constellation of the] Great Bear; it was
> they who rounded the Cape of Storms [of South Africa], and earned the best
> right to call it the Cape of Good Hope, two thousand years before Vasco de
> Gama. Their ships returned to their native shores bringing with them sandal
> wood from Malabar [in India], spices from Arabia, fine linen from Egypt,
> ostrich plumes from the Sahara, ebony and ivory from the Soudan. Cyprus gave
> them its copper, Elba its iron, the coast of the Black Sea its manufactured steel.
> Silver they brought from Spain, gold from the Niger, tin from the Scilly Isles,
> and amber from the Baltic. Where they sailed, there they planted factories
> which opened a caravan route with the interior of vast continents hitherto
> regarded as inaccessible, and which became inaccessible for centuries when the
> Phœnicians disappeared from history.[16]

Among the colonies they founded were Lixus, Cadiz, Utica and Carthage.
Pliny the Elder reported that the Moroccan settlement of Lixus was founded at
an early date. Velleius Paterculus reports that Cadiz, located on the Spanish
coast, was established in 1110 BC. Pliny states that in Utica, on the North
African coast, wooden beams of Numidian cedar were placed in the Temple of
Apollo in 1101 BC. Does this date Utica to 1101 BC? No one seems to know
but this seems a fairly reasonable conjecture to make. Pseudo-Aristotle
claimed that Carthage followed Utica by 287 years. This seems to imply a date
of 814 BC for the founding of Carthage. The ancient writers Timaeus of
Taormina, Menander of Ephesus and Justin seem in general agreement with
this date. There were other Phœnician colonies. Sallust, a Latin historian,
echoing Phœnician sources, suggests that the North African settlements of
Hippo, Hadramentum and Leptis Magna were founded at an early date.
Menander of Ephesus names King Ithobaal of Tyre as founding the settlement
of Auza in North Africa in the first half of the ninth century BC.[17]

On the Mediterranean island of Sardinia archaeologists have discovered a
Phœnician stele at the site of Nora. It is the oldest known Phœnician inscription
in the western Mediterranean and is dated to the latter half of the ninth century
BC.[18] Professor Lancel of the University of Grenoble discusses other early
finds. Off the southern coast of Sicily was discovered a bronze statuette at the
site of Selinunte:

> At first it was seen as the god Melqart - the Greek Herakles, the Latin Hercules. In fact this figurine belongs in the series of representations of what Middle East archaeologists call a 'smiting god': the god striding towards the enemy and preparing to smite him with a weapon brandished in his right hand. If it is permissible to recognize it as a divinity of the Syrio-Palestinian world - a Baal or Reshef, rather than a Melqart - is it equally permissible to turn it into a testimony of Phoenician expansion in the west[?][19]

The statuette also wears a crown not unlike the White Crown of the pharaohs. In addition, he is wearing a kilt, again, not unlike those of the pharaohs.

At Cadiz was found "some problematic discoveries - such as the figure of what seems to be a Ptah".[20] Elsewhere in Spain near Almuñecar:

> There a cremation cemetery contains tombs dating from the end of the eighth century [BC], but with an Egypt aspect strongly indicated by alabaster jars bearing pharaonic cartouches belonging to the ninth century, while one of them shows, alongside pseudo-hieroglyphic inscriptions, a text in Phoenician.[21]

We note that the archaeological evidence of the smiting god, the Ptah, and the ninth century pharaonic cartouches, all show that Nile Valley culture was an important and largely inseparable element in some of the Phœnician colonies.

The founding of Carthage in 814 BC is associated with a moving story concerning events taking place in the Phœnician city of Tyre. There, King Pygmalion of Tyre murdered Acherbas, the husband of Elissa. She fled Tyre with some of its leading citizens and loyal followers. Her fleet landed on the island of Cyprus where she earned the name of Dido. Moreover, she rescued 80 virgins from the bondage of sacred prostitution from its Temple of Venus. On arriving on the North African coast of modern Tunisia, envoys from nearby Utica gave their blessings and brought gifts. From Tyre, Elissa brought liturgical artefacts for the worship of Melqart. This also preserved the memory of her murdered husband who was himself a priest of that deity. Hiarbas, King of the Libyans, wanted to marry Elissa but she refused remaining loyal to her dead husband. Instead she sacrificed herself on a funeral pyre that she had lit.[22] Is there any truth in this story? Mrs Erskine, an authority on North African history, seems to think so. She believes:

> We can accept Dido, whose real name was Eliza [sic], or something like it, as an historical personage; most writers do, and we must admit that if she fled from Tyre on account of a plebian rising against patricians, or for any other motive, the most likely place for her to choose as a new home would be the African coast. It was not only fertile and desirable as a country, it was a land already colonised by her compatriots.[23]

Virgil, the Roman writer, adds that Æneas and his followers fled a burning Troy and landed at Carthage. There, Elissa received them. She went further. She showered the visitors with presents and hospitality. Moreover, she fell madly in love with the somewhat indifferent Æneas. Sadly, he was called away from Carthage to fulfil other duties. It was at this point that Elissa commits suicide. Is this part of the story true? Mrs Erskine comments:

> St. Augustine [i.e. the African theologian of the fourth century AD] was exercised about this very point, as he tells us in his Confessions. When he was a young man, studying in Karthage [sic], he used to ask ignorant people if Æneas had ever visited Karthage, to which they would reply that they did not know; when he asked the learned the same question, they replied in the negative. The Saint's comment on tears that he had shed over a tragedy that never took place was that education is being conducted along the wrong lines.[24]

The tradition that links Dido/Elissa to Tyre certainly highlights the cultural link between Carthage and its parent city. It became a custom for the Carthaginians to send an embassy to Tyre to celebrate a sacrifice in the Temple of Melqart. They sent one tenth of the city's revenue. They also sent extraordinary gifts from time-to-time, such as booty seized in Sicily and a bronze statue of Apollo.[25]

In the seventh century BC, Carthage was a modest city of mud brick walling and beaten clay floors that:

> already occupied a sizable part of the littoral plain - hundreds of metres in both directions - not to mention the possible occupation of the heights of Byrsa. A suburban fringe of workshops (metalworkers, fullers, dyers, potters) ensured the production necessary for daily living, and already perhaps, as regards pottery for example, for export as well. The building alignments discovered show that at least in the central parts of the littoral plain (other orientations still seem questionable), in the seventh century [BC], the settlement was not established in a haphazard fashion, but followed a generalized layout roughly parallel to the shoreline.[26]

By the beginning of the seventh century BC, the Libyans had become the majority population in the city. Dr Lancel writes:

> [C]ertain ritual practices observable in the inhumation graves reflect the Libyan contribution which probably formed an important and surely even a majority component of Carthage's population at the beginning of the seventh century, some three or four generations after the city's foundation, assuming the tradition of date [of 814 BC for the founding of the city].[27]

The Libyan influence was not the only cultural factor, however. Professor Lancel reports that statues and tombs in a vaguely Egyptian style have been recovered dating to the middle seventh century BC.[28] Golden jewellery of Egyptian origin was found dating to the seventh or sixth centuries BC, as was locally made jewellery in an Egyptian style. Ivory was found where "again the influence of Egyptian iconography is revealed".[29] Moreover, thousands of scarabs and amulets dating to the seventh and sixth centuries BC were recovered. Among these were wadjet eyes, uraei, and images of Nile Valley deities. There were images of Ptah, Bes, Anubis, Ma'at, Bastet and Amen. More intriguing, were images of the specifically Nubian deity, Khnum. Twenty-Sixth Dynasty scarabs were also discovered.[30] Dr Lancel says of these: "The Saitic epoch [i.e. the Twenty Sixth Dynasty], with strong leanings towards the archaic, had tried hard to revive the golden age of Egyptian civilization, and it will be of no surprise to find the name of Mykerinos [i.e. Menkaura], the builder of one of the three great pyramids of Gizeh, on a blue-green paste scarab from the Douimès cemetery".[31] The Professor does not explore whether these archaic tendencies could not also have been brought to Carthage from the Twenty Fifth Dynasty since it is well known that it was they who started the archaicising process. In addition, being Kushites, they were more likely to have venerated Khnum. Finally, there is evidence that Taharqo, the great Twenty Fifth Dynast, conquered as far as Spain. Carthage must have therefore been within his sphere of influence.

By the end of the seventh century BC Carthage began to face the first of many challenges from Europe. The Greeks began to dispute the mastery of the western Mediterranean. Already by the eighth century BC they had colonies on Campania and the Island of Ischia. They sought to conquer markets and create trade routes. Moreover, they wanted the mineral wealth of the Isle of Elba and also Etruria. They occupied the Straits of Messina and gained control over the access to the Tyrrhenian Sea. Before long, they had colonies on the east coast of Sicily, particularly the cities of Syracuse and Gela. In the second half of the seventh century BC they founded Cyrene in Libya. This factor limited how far to the east the Phœnicians could expand in Africa. Finally, the Greeks established colonies in Marseilles and also Malaga.[32]

Carthage established a colony in Ibiza in 654 BC. From the sixth century BC, Carthage was in control of a variety of territories. Some of these were colonies it had established, but others originally belonged to the Phœnicians but passed into Carthaginian hands without conflict. The Phœnician city of Tyre fell in 573 BC. Carthage became the leading Phœnician city on losing its parent. Carthage is known to have controlled Malta from the sixth century until 218 BC. It controlled Gozo and Lampedusa from at least the sixth century BC. Phœnicians had already settled Sardinia in the ninth century BC. In addition, superb gold and silver jewellery were recovered, dating to the seventh and sixth centuries BC. Justin reports that the Carthaginian king Malchus defeated the restless natives of that island in the sixth century BC. Moreover, Hasdrubal and Hamilcar, two sons from the House of Mago, campaigned there.[33] Finally, beginning in the sixth century and certainly in the fifth century BC, Carthage extended its boundaries into Africa. This developed a Libyphœnician culture. By the second quarter of the fifth century BC the Carthaginians stopped paying annual tribute to the Libyans to lease the land.[34] Skulls identified as Phœnician were discovered west of Syracuse in Sicily. They were dolichocephalic, prognathous, and had distinctly Negroid affinities.[35] In one way or another, Carthage came to control Majorca, Minorca, Sardinia, western Sicily, the smaller Mediterranean islands, parts of Spain, and finally parts of North Africa.[36]

With a powerful people on the other side of the Mediterranean, rivalry with the Greeks soon gave way to conflict. Sicily became the combat zone from the fifth to the third centuries BC. Apparently, King Hamilcar, of the House of Mago, took three years to gather his naval forces of 200 warships, 3,000 troop transporters and an army of 300,000 men recruited from Africa, Spain, Sardinia, Corsica, Libya and Gaul.[37] They landed at Himera in Sicily and began to battle the Greeks. The conflict lasted all of one fateful day in 480 BC! The Carthaginians were utterly defeated. In 410 BC war erupted once more in Sicily but with greater successes. Hannibal, also of the House of Mago, commanded the conquest of the cities - Selinus, Himera and Syracuse. This was accompanied by a cruel destruction of those Greek colonial cities. He returned in 407 BC and destroyed Agrigentum, Gela and Camarina. After much bloodshed, a peace treaty was agreed between Carthage and the Greeks in 383 BC. Sicily was divided between them with an agreed boundary.[38]

The empire building had far reaching economic implications, especially for merchant shipping. The western part of the Mediterranean became, in effect, a Carthaginian lake. They controlled who may, or may not sail there, with the very real threat of severe penalties being imposed on foreign sailors.[39] Furthermore, there is a treaty, signed in 509 BC between Carthage and Rome, where the Romans and their allies agreed to "refrain from sailing beyond the Beautiful Promontory [wherever this is], unless storms or an enemy force compel them to do so". Moreover, "if a ship is driven, despite itself, beyond this headland, the crew are forbidden to buy or sell anything, except what may be necessary to render the said ship seaworthy again or to offer a sacrifice".[40]

Of the goods themselves, gold, precious stones, local manufactured products and slaves were shipped to Italy from Carthage. Malta, another of their colonies, had an industry in beautiful cotton cloths, known for their fineness and softness. These were carried to markets in Africa. Corsica produced wax and honey, and also exported slaves. One of the islands mined and smelted an unending supply of iron. Majorca and Minorca produced fruit and bred mules.

In Spain, Carthage found another market for its manufactured goods. Carthage also had a flourishing land trade with other countries in Africa, where they bought gold, salt, slaves and dates.[41] Herodotus specifically mentions that some of the gold came from, "a Libyan country" identified as Guinea, procured by dumb barter. This same method of trade continued in use for two thousand years.

There are accounts of Carthaginian exploration in the sixth or fifth centuries BC. Hanno, one of their admirals, commanded sixty ships that carried 30,000 Libyphœnicians along the north and west coast of Africa. The large numbers of people were transported to establish new colonies and the last of them were landed at Morocco as far south as Arguin. Hanno and the others continued their journey around the west coast of Africa and sailed past the Senegal River, noting that it abounded in crocodiles and hippopotami. There they encountered people but, as the document records it: "They drove us away by throwing stones at us". The expedition sailed on passing forests of odoriferous trees. Furthermore, they witnessed the locals clearing the forests using slash and burn techniques. At night, they overheard local music of pipes, cymbals, drums and shouts. Elsewhere, they saw a volcano. Finally, they encountered gorillas. They returned when their provisions failed them. Himilco, another sailor, led a maritime voyage to explore Western Europe and the British Isles.[42] The Reverend Michael Russell, a pioneering Africanist, informs us that:

> Historians and geographers have long disputed as to the extent of the navigation which the ships of Carthage accomplished in the Atlantic Ocean. Some are content with extending the limits of their voyages from the southern coast of Britain on the north to Cape Bojador on the south; while others, conferring upon them a share in the direct trade with the Baltic, conduct their ships to the mouth of the Vistula and the coast of Prussia, on the one hand, and on the other, to the estuary of the Gambia and the shores of Guinea. It is even maintained, that they crossed to America, and visited the borders of the New World.[43]

Reverend Russell, himself, did not share the view that Carthage visited America and dismisses the idea as conjecture being beyond fact and reasoning. He did, however, draw clear conclusions as to the extent of Carthaginian maritime activity: "Her commercial relations would thus have extended over nearly the whole of the known world, and would only have been surpassed by those of modern Europe since the discovery of America, and of the passage to the East by the Cape of Good Hope".[44]

Unfortunately, the costs of Carthaginian exploration and colonisation schemes were borne by her colonies, especially her conquered African neighbours. Carthage imposed a harsh tribute upon them. The value of this sometimes amounted to half of their annual produce. This made the Carthaginians a hated people elsewhere in Africa, and proved a decisive factor in their downfall.[45]

By the third century BC the city of Carthage was opulent and impressive. It had a population of 700,000 and may even have approached a million. The Greek and Roman accounts allow us to reconstruct a picture of the twenty-three mile circuit of towering walls that enclosed several imposing temples, a fortress, and many magnificent buildings. The city walls were of an extraordinary thickness and contained barracks for twenty thousand soldiers, magazines for war material, stalls for three hundred elephants, and stables for four thousand horses. Lining both sides of three streets were rows of tall houses, six storeys high. The streets lead on to the harbours. To the north and the west of the city lay the great suburb of Megara, full of gardens and villas, associated with the idle rich. The forum was probably situated in the lower town near to the two ports. The war harbour was circular and had docks all round. Before each dock stood columns, decorated with Ionic capitals. This formed part of a colonnade that surrounded the entire harbour. In the centre of the island stood the Admiralty buildings and palace, from which trumpeters would convey orders to the warships. The Carthaginian temples were lavish, decorated with metals, wood and marble. Herodotus described pillars of gold and lapis lazuli standing in front of them. The Temple of Eshmun (i.e. Imhotep) was the richest in the city and was approached by 60 steps. Finally, Carthage boasted public restaurants, theatres, libraries and baths.[46] Mr Bosworth Smith is emphatic in stating that:

> Carthage was, beyond doubt, the richest city of antiquity. Her ships were to be found on all known seas, and there was probably no important product, animal, vegetable, or mineral, of the ancient world, which did not find its way into her harbours and pass through the hands of her citizens.[47]

Archaeological finds indicate that the streets ran at right angles and were made of beaten earth typically five to seven metres wide. The houses had washing or shower rooms, with water cisterns, pipes, wastewater drains, and floors of mosaic tiles. They had living rooms with white marble tesserae mosaics, courtyards with mosaic floors, storerooms, and also staircases. The houses had impluvia. The porticoes had sloping roofs supported by stuccoed sandstone columns. In addition, there were residential blocks "exactly like ours today". Finally, the city had garbage collectors.[48]

Carthaginian control over the Mediterranean trade routes soon brought them into conflict with the newly rising power of Rome from the other side of the Mediterranean. The rivalry once more turned to conflict with the first of the Punic Wars. The confrontation began in 264 BC on the island of Sicily. At the request of the city of Messina, the Carthaginians attempted to set up a garrison there. For some reason, no one knows why, the people of Messina switched sides and appealed to the Romans against Carthage. The first important battle began in Agrigentum in the following year. In 256 BC the Romans struck against Africa itself. Using 330 vessels, they sailed from Sicily to Cap Bon and successfully ravaged the site. They were, however, recalled to Italy. Carthage, led by Hamilcar Barca, was forced to negotiate a peace settlement with the Romans in 255 BC, but the Roman demands were excessive. The hostilities continued.[49]

Xanthippus, a Greek mercenary, was instrumental in the Carthaginian campaigns. He organised cavalry, foot soldiers and elephants. They captured and imprisoned Regulus, the Roman consul. Rome suffered a series of naval disasters between 254 and 253 BC. Hannibal, Hamilcar's son, raided the coast of Italy for six years beginning in 247 BC. More successes came in Sicily. Hamilcar commanded a series of campaigns between 246 and 242 BC that almost drove the Romans off that island. Carthage, however, suffered an unexpected and fatal naval defeat in 241 BC. Hamilcar received full powers from the Carthaginians to negotiate with Rome to sue for peace. The victorious Romans forced Carthage to renounce its claim to the colony of Sicily.[50]

After the war, 20,000 of Carthage's mercenaries remained in western Sicily. They were a bizarre mix of nationalities including Iberians, Gauls, Balearics, Greeks and other Africans. Carthage refused to give them their full pay and this culminated in another war. Spendios, a half-Greek, and Matho, an African, led the rebellion. In addition, the mercenaries exploited the fact that other Africans in the surrounding territories hated Carthage, seeing it as an oppressive regional power. Those nations supported the rebels, seizing the opportunity to free themselves from Carthaginian overlordship. Many women of these nations surrendered their jewellery. Enough money from the jewellery was raised to pay the mercenaries their back pay and to finance the uprising. Hamilcar Barca raised a force of 10,000 men to engage the insurgents. In 238 BC he captured Spendios and had him crucified. Matho was taken prisoner and also crucified. By this period, a tired and weakened Carthage relinquished Sardinia to Rome.[51]

Carthage re-emerged but in a much reduced state. Hamilcar established a strong territorial presence in south east Spain and seized control of its rich mines. South of Alicante he built a new Carthage. Hasdrubal the Elder succeeded him in 229 BC and signed a treaty with the Romans, three years later. The provisions of the treaty are controversial, but it contained a clause that delimited the territorial boundaries separating that which belonged to Carthage, from that which belonged to Rome. Hasdrubal perished in 221 BC and was succeeded by Hannibal, his brother. A Celtiberian stabbed Hasdrubal to death.[52]

Carthage (Tunisia). Reconstruction of the brilliant city of Carthage at its height by M. Paul Auc

In 219 BC Hannibal, perhaps the best known personality in Carthaginian history (see also page 115), seized Saguntum in Spain. Polybius, the Roman historian, reported that this breached the treaty and was interpreted by the Romans as a declaration of war. A year later the second Punic War commenced. In May of that year, Hannibal raised an armed force of 90,000 men on foot and 12,000 men on horseback. By the summer, they reached Rhône. However, they were now a much-reduced force of 50,000 soldiers, 9,000 horsemen, and 37 elephants. Celts and Gauls flocked to his standard, however, and increased their numbers. They hated Roman imperial rule and saw the Carthaginian campaign as a way of getting back at the Romans. Hannibal's forces crossed

the Alpine passes at the end of the year. Being in winter, it was a difficult and costly crossing. Many people and animals, unfamilliar with such cold, died. From the north they marched on Italy, however. Penetrating deep into Italian territory, they seized Cannæ in 216 BC, killing 70,000 Roman soldiers. Carthage, on the other hand, lost 5,500 soldiers and 200 horsemen in the same campaign. Next they marched on Rome but were unable to breach the walls. They camped there for years.[53] Sir James Frazer, the author of *The Golden Bough* wrote, Hannibal "hung with his dusky army like a storm-cloud about to break, within sight of the sentinels of Rome". In 215 BC he sent two officers to Sicily to seduce the local rulers to break their loyalties to Rome.[54]

The Romans, however, made inroads. By 210 BC they destroyed Carthage's new allies in Sicily and the following year, Scipio, the Roman general, commanded an invasion of Spain. A year later the Roman army seized the gold and silver mines of that land which was the basis of Carthage's wealth. In around 206 BC a King of Numidia, an African state to the west of Carthage, changed alliances as Carthage began to lose. Allying himself with Rome, he persuaded Scipio to bring the war to Africa. In 204 Scipio invaded Africa causing Hannibal and Mago, his brother, to leave Italy and return home. The Romans engaged them at the Battle of Zama in 202 BC. Assisted by 10,000 horsemen, supplied by Numidia, the Romans triumphed. Scipio had planned for and frustrated Hannibal's secret weapon - the use of elephants.[55]

The terms of the peace treaty of 201 BC were harsh. Carthage was compelled to return lands that once belonged to Numidia. They were forbidden to make war on any people without the consent of Rome. They must hand over elephants and must not acquire others. They must abandon all ships except ten. Finally, they must pay a reparation of 10,000 talents over fifty years. Following the treaty, Scipio had the Carthaginian fleet burned.[56]

Carthage made some sort of recovery during this period with Hannibal still at the helm. "The business of that city was again as flourishing as it had ever been," says Mr Reade. "Again ships sailed to the coasts of Cornwall and Guinea; again the streets were lined with the workshops of industrious artisans".[57] The archaeological finds support the notion that the city recovered. Carthage even proposed to pay off the reparation due to Rome in 10 years. The Romans, however, refused. Eventually, the Romans demanded that the Carthaginians hand over Hannibal. Instead, he fled into exile in 196 BC.

The Romans began to have misgivings about the recovery the African city was making. A Roman senator was very public in expressing these concerns. Cato the Elder is reported to have ended each and every speech in the Senate between 152 and 150 BC with the phrase: "In any case I am of the opinion that Carthage must be destroyed." It did not matter what the issue was that the Senate discussed, Cato would always bring the argument back to his pet hate - Carthage. Moreover, in 151 BC the last of the fifty payments from Carthage was delivered. Rome now looked for a pretext to humiliate Carthage further. In 150 BC they got their chance. Carthage counter attacked Numidia who had abused Carthage for years while the Romans turned a blind eye. This allowed the Romans to claim that the treaty of 201 had been breached. In the following year Carthage sent an embassy to Rome to discuss the matter. The Romans demanded that Carthage hand over all weapons, catapults, cannonballs and engines of war. Carthage complied. They were delivered to Utica, who by now had gone over to the Roman side. The Romans then delivered their final terms to the Carthaginians. They demanded that the people of Carthage abandon their city and move inland from the sea to a distance of 15 kilometres. Carthage was about to be destroyed. Eventually, this news reached Africa with dramatic repercussions:[58]

> Karthage [sic] went mad [says Mrs Erskine]. People were torn to pieces in the streets; some Italians found there were tortured. And then the torrent was stemmed, and the Karthaginians rose to the full height of their greatness. They shut the gates and resolved to defend themselves to the last. But how was this to be done? There were no ships of war in the ports; the arsenals were empty; the stalls where the elephants and horses were stabled empty also. Without weapons, without any means of defence but the strong walls, the Senate of Karthage declared war on Rome. In a very short time the silent city was turned into a huge factory.[59]

Rome attacked in 149 BC. They besieged the city for three years. Eventually they breached the walls and began the genocide. At least 250,000 people were slaughtered in the atrocity and 50,000 were sold into slavery.[60] Some 500,000 volumes of the Carthaginian library disappeared.[61] Some texts were handed over to the Numidians. The destruction of a literature is always a setback to civilisation since accumulated knowledge dies with the destruction of each library. Mr Bosworth Smith discussed one Carthaginian text that survived that holocaust, penned by Mago. This work may indicate the standard of Carthaginian knowledge in general:

> What Aristotle was to the mediæval philosophers and theologians, that Mago seems to have been, in his measure, to the Italian agriculturists. Varro, the most learned of the Romans, and the author, among 489 other publications, of the most valuable treatise on ancient agriculture which we possess, quotes Mago as the highest authority on the subject, and other Roman writers have handed down to us with no less respect, various maxims on the breeding and management of cattle, the care of poultry and of bees, the planting of forest trees, and the treatment of the vine and the olive, the almond and the pomegranate, all drawn from the same fountain head. "We honour," says Columella, "above all other writers, Mago the Carthaginian, the father of husbandry".[62]

The final tragedy for the the great African city came with Scipio's last act. Mrs Erskine described the final humiliation with pathos:

> The smouldering fires in Karthage [sic] were relit, the marbles were hacked, the temples spoiled; so thorough was the work of destruction that hardly one stone remained on another. Then the plough was passed over the blackened soil, and the final curse was pronounced - that *Devotio* which dedicated the place to the Infernal Gods. The site of Karthage had stood for seven hundred years was cursed; the land was never to yield a harvest; no human habitation was to be raised on ground given over to the spirits of darkness.[63]

Numidia

Kingdoms have existed in Numidia since at least the fifth century BC. Diodorus Siculus reports that they were allies of the Carthaginians who also supplied troops for the Carthaginian army. Documents continue to mention kings and kingdoms for the next century and a half, but they all fail to give further details. The first Numidian ruler of which there is any detailed information is Navaras who assisted Carthage against Rome during the first Punic War. Navaras supplied a cavalry contingent of 2,000 men to the Carthaginian side. For this, Hamilcar Barca rewarded him with the hand of his daughter in marriage.[64]

Originally there were several Numidian kingdoms of which two became important. Both were located to the west of Carthage in the regions of Algeria and western Tunisia. The most westerly was of the Massaesylian Numidians, whose territory extended as far to the west as the river Moulouya. Their capital was the coastal city of Siga where a famous three-storey mausoleum stood. Its second capital was Cirta. King Syphax was an important figure during the second Punic War. He was probably the single most dominant figure in Numidian affairs, who also exercised power over lesser rivals. There are bronze coins struck during his time with the legend 'Syphax the King' written in Punic. He initially supported Rome during the War, but ended up allying with Carthage. In 206 BC his forces annexed the rival and more easterly kingdom of the Massylian Numidians. The following year he married Hasdrubal Barca's daughter.[65]

The easterly kingdom of the Massylian Numidians was much smaller than its rival. It possessed a famous third century BC tomb known as the Medracen. During the Second Punic War, Gaia, its king, supported Carthage with troops. In 206 BC Massinissa succeeded him to the throne. He initially supported Carthage but changed sides as Carthage began to lose. Syphax invaded his kingdom and exiled him. Massinissa successfully persuaded Scipio, the Roman commander, to bring the war to Africa. In this way he regained his throne in 203 BC and seized Cirta that year.[66] This conquest unified the two major Numidian kingdoms into one. Cirta became the capital of the unified kingdom.[67]

The terms of the peace treaty of 201 BC between Carthage and Rome required the Carthaginians to return to Massinissa "all the cities and territory held by him or his forefathers". In addition, over the next fifty years, Massinissa seized more and more of Carthaginian territory. His dream seems to have been the creation of a vast Numidian state from Morocco to Libya with Carthage as its capital. However, the Roman destruction of Carthage and their occupation of the site frustrated this grand ambition.[68] Despite this, Massinissa proved a dynamic ruler who had a long and brilliant career. The Roman

Numidia (Tunisia). The Mausoleum of Adeban in Dougga, 2nd century BC, as seen by Major Benton Fletcher. From Mrs Stuart Erskine, *Vanished Cities in Northern Africa* (UK, Hutchinson & Co., no date given for publication, opposite p.100).

historians credit him with an agricultural revolution that transformed the kingdom. Before his time, the territory was wild and uncultivated, peopled by robbers and marauders. During his reign the Numidians became one of the wealthiest people of the period, untroubled by "intrigue or domestic strife".[69] He received the elephants seized from Carthage and incorporated their use into standard Numidian warfare. He spread the use of coinage throughout the kingdom, which was a development of the use of bronze and silver coins issued only in limited numbers by Syphax and his successor in the west.[70] He patronised Greek and Roman scholars at his court and opened schools.[71] In addition, a new script developed in Numidia, with only five of its characters derived from the Phœnician, and is still used by the Tuaregs of today.[72] There are monuments in eastern Algeria and western Libya covered with these inscriptions. Punic, however, remained the language of the officials and scholars. After the fall of Carthage in 146 BC his sons collected what was left of its libraries. The Numidians were much interested in the religious literature of Carthage and adored Baal Hammon, perhaps its chief deity, and also the goddess Tanit. This became reflected in the fact that every important town in the kingdom had a sanctuary to Baal Hammon constructed at its gateway. The sanctuary near the royal residence of Cirta is the best-known surviving example. Finally, there are surviving stelae dedicated to Tanit.[73]

Cirta, Zama and Makthar became important cities. They were cosmopolitan and included Greek and Roman populations. After the fall of Carthage some of its survivors fled there, adding to the cultural melting pot. They were well received and found employment. The city dwellers typically wore long finely pleated robes of muslin that were gathered with a wide belt. Covering this, they wore cloaks with sleeves, open down the front. The women wore large collars and had pendulous earrings that almost touched their shoulders. Some wore large pointed bonnets. The clothing points to a luxurious and urban lifestyle.[74]

Great monuments survive from this period. There are stelae in Cirta that share features with those from Carthage. There are also three famous monuments that have received much scholarly attention. The so-called Tomb of the Christian Woman, located west of Algiers, and the Medracen, north of the Aurès, were enormous round towers. Step pyramids crowned both monuments. Columns with Doric capitals were built into the outer walls. The Mausoleum of Adeban, son of Yepmatath, stands at the foot of the hill at Dougga. Built on a podium of five steps, it had three storeys. The columns show Egyptian and Greek capitals. In addition, it had a bilingual Punic and Libyan inscription now housed in the British Museum.[75] In addition to the three cities of Cirta, Zama and Makthar, the Reverend Russell wrote that: "Even at the present day [i.e. in 1835 AD], there are found in Southern Numidia the remains of towns and castles, which present an air of great antiquity".[76]

Micipsa succeeded Massinissa to the throne in 148 BC and reigned for a lengthy 40 years. He abandoned the expansionism of his predecessor but continued his drive for agricultural expansion. It must be stressed that he ruled a vast territory. From the river Moulouya in the west to as far east as the Roman-controlled province surrounding Carthage, his authority was felt. Furthermore, he ruled various cities even further east of Carthage on the Tripolitanian coast, such as Leptis Magna. To the south, he ruled Capsa. He could raise a powerful army of infantry, cavalry, war elephants and even a small fleet. On the cultural front, he encouraged the spread of Punic literary culture and modelled various legal institutions of Numidia on those that existed in Carthage. He also encouraged the spread of Greek philosophy in Cirta.[77] The capital city itself reputedly grew to a population of 200,000 people.[78] He died in 118 BC and left his kingdom to his two sons, Adherbal and Hiempsal, and also Jugurtha, a nephew.[79]

Jugurtha seized the opportunity. He murdered the scholarly and bookish Hiempsal and drove Adherbal into exile. The exiled prince fled to Rome and requested their assistance in regaining his throne. Jugurtha, on the other hand, also had influential friends in the Roman hierarchy. The Roman Senate therefore proposed a compromise. They suggested the kingdom be divided between the two candidates. The western portion was offered to Jugurtha and the eastern portion was offered to Adherbal. Jurgurtha played along with it but quickly resumed the battle against Adherbal. He seized Cirta, the capital of the east, and killed Adherbal. Moreover, his troops massacred Italian residents in the city. The Romans were outraged. Bowing to public pressure, they attacked Numidia in 111 BC. Jugurtha initially gained the upper hand but was eventually defeated due to the treachery of his son-in-law. The Romans seized and imprisoned him in perhaps 105 BC and placed a puppet on the throne of a much-reduced Numidia.[80]

By 46 BC it was all over for the Numidians. The Romans under Julius Caesar annexed what was left of their territory and abolished their kingdom. In 30 BC the Romans seized Greek-ruled Egypt and were now the undisputed masters of all North Africa.[81] Waves of Germanic invaders called Vandals occupied North Africa in the fifth century AD, taking over from the Italian ruling class. Finally, the Arabians occupied North Africa in the seventh century AD. They still rule today and are the dominant population. The invasions transformed North Africa both culturally and racially. Negroes are now a minority in this part of Africa. In addition, their heritage and achievements were stolen by others and then distorted out of all recognition.

Notes

[1] Quoted in Cheikh Anta Diop, *The African Origin of Civilization: Myth or Reality?* US, Lawrence Hill, 1974, p.122.

[2] Quoted in Ivan Van Sertima, *The African Presence in Early Europe: The Definitional Problem,* in *African Presence in Early Europe,* ed Ivan Van Sertima, US, Transaction Publishers, 1985, p.137.

[3] George Rawlinson (translator), *History of Herodotus: Volume IV,* Third Edition, UK, John Murray, 1875, p.75.

[4] Lady Lugard, *A Tropical Dependency,* UK, James Nisbet & Co., 1906, p.10.

[5] Quoted in Dana Reynolds Marniche, *The Myth of the Mediterranean Race,* in *Egypt: Child of Africa,* ed Ivan Van Sertima, US, Transaction Publishers, 1994, p.117.

[6] Donald B. Redford, *Egypt, Canaan and Israel in Ancient Times,* US, Princetown University Press, 1992, p.6.

[7] George Rawlinson, *Phœnicia: The Story of the Nations,* UK, T. Fisher Unwin, 1889, p.20.

[8] Wayne B. Chandler, *Hannibal: Nemesis of Rome,* in *Great Black Leaders,* ed Ivan Van Sertima, US, Transaction Publishers, 1988, p.284.

[9] George Rawlinson, *Phœnicia: The Story of the Nations,* pp.20-2.

[10] Ivan Van Sertima, *The African Presence in Early Europe: The Definitional Problem,* in *African Presence in Early Europe,* p.137.

[11] There were nine such ivories on display at the time of our last visit. WA 134322 has a European type face. WA 118180 was damaged so badly as to preclude any judgement. WA 132919 did not depict any individuals. The other six ivories clearly depicted Negroes - WA 118147, WA 118148, WA 118120, WA 127412, WA 130487 and WA 118156.

[12] Serge Lancel, *Carthage: A History,* UK, Basil Blackwell, 1995, pp.330-50.

[13] Wayne B. Chandler, *Hannibal: Nemesis of Rome,* in *Great Black Leaders,* pp.313-8.

[14] Serge Lancel, *Carthage: A History,* p.76. See also p.75.

[15] Quoted in George Wells Parker, *The Children of the Sun,* US, Black Classic Press, 1981 (original 1918), p.18.

[16] R. Bosworth Smith, *Carthage and the Carthaginians, New Edition,* UK, Longmans, Green and Co., 1894, pp.2-3.

[17] Serge Lancel, *Carthage: A History,* pp.1-3 and 22-3.

[18] Ibid., pp.8-9.

[19] Ibid., pp.5-6.

[20] Ibid., p.12. See also p.13.

[21] Ibid., p.13.

[22] Ibid., pp.23-4, 35-6 and 38.

[23] Mrs Stuart Erskine, *Vanished Cities in Northern Africa,* UK, Hutchinson & Co., no date given for publication, p.38.

[24] Ibid., pp.40-1. See also p.39.

[25] Serge Lancel, *Carthage: A History,* pp.36-7.

[26] Ibid., p.45.

[27] Ibid., p.53.

[28] Ibid., pp.65-6.

[29] Ibid., pp.70-2.

[30] Ibid., pp.67-70.

[31] Ibid., p.69.

[32] Ibid., pp.78-9.

[33] Ibid., pp.81-4.

[34] Ibid., pp.93-4 and 134.

[35] Cheikh Anta Diop, *The African Origin of Civilization: Myth or Reality?* p.121.

[36] A. H. L. Heeren, *Historical Researches into the Politics, Intercourse, and Trade of the Carthaginians, Ethiopians, and Egyptians, Volume I,* UK, D. A. Talboys, 1832, pp.70-1 and 79-81.

[37] Serge Lancel, *Carthage: A History,* pp.88-90.

[38] R. Bosworth Smith, *Carthage and the Carthaginians, New Edition,* pp.47-54.

[39] Ibid., p.15.

[40] Serge Lancel, *Carthage: A History,* p.86. See also p.87.

[41] A. H. L. Heeren, *Historical Researches into the Politics, Intercourse, and Trade of the Carthaginians, Ethiopians, and Egyptians, Volume I,* pp.162-185.

[42] Ibid., pp.486-501.

[43] The Rev. Michael Russell, *History and Present Condition of the Barbary States,* UK, Oliver & Boyd, 1835, p.77.

[44] Ibid., pp.77-8.

[45] R. Bosworth Smith, *Carthage and the Carthaginians, New Edition,* pp.43-4.

[46] Mrs Stuart Erskine, *Vanished Cities in Northern Africa,* pp.44-7 and Sir J. A. Hammerton, *Carthage; Queen of the Seas,* in *Wonders of the Past: Second Volume,* ed Sir J. A. Hammerton, UK, The Amalgamated Press, no date given but probably 1937, pp.635-44.

[47] R. Bosworth Smith, *Carthage and the Carthaginians, New Edition,* p.30.

[48] Serge Lancel, *Carthage: A History,* pp.157-170.

[49] Ibid., pp.364-7.

[50] Ibid., pp.362 and 367-371.

[51] Ibid., pp.372-6.

[52] Ibid., pp.376-80.

[53] Ibid., pp.380-392.

[54] Quoted in J. A. Rogers, *World's Great Men of Color, Volume I,* US, Macmillan, 1972, p.106.

[55] Serge Lancel, *Carthage: A History,* pp.392-401.

[56] Ibid., p.402.

[57] Winwood Reade, *The Martyrdom of Man,* UK, Watts & Co., 1934 edition, p.111.

[58] Serge Lancel, *Carthage: A History,* pp.403-4 and 410-3.

[59] Mrs Stuart Erskine, *Vanished Cities in Northern Africa,* p.67.

[60] J. C. DeGraft-Johnson, *African Glory,* UK, Watts & Co., 1954, p.23.

[61] John G. Jackson, *Man, God, and Civilization,* US, Citadel Press, 1972, p.253.

[62] R. Bosworth Smith, *Carthage and the Carthaginians, New Edition,* pp.35-6.

[63] Mrs Stuart Erskine, *Vanished Cities in Northern Africa,* p.69.

[64] R. C. C. Law, *North Africa in the Hellenistic and Roman Periods,* in *The Cambridge History of Africa, Volume 2,* ed J. D. Fage, UK, Cambridge University Press, 1978, p.177 and p.179.

[65] Ibid, pp.179-180 and Serge Lancel, *Carthage: A History,* pp.396-7.

[66] Serge Lancel, *Carthage: A History,* pp.307-8 and 397-9.

[67] Roland Oliver & Brian M. Fagan, *Africa in the Iron Age,* UK, Cambridge University Press, 1975, pp.52-3.

[68] D. E. L. Haynes, *Antiquities of Tripolitania,* Libya, The Antiquities Department of Tripolitania, 1959, p.31.

[69] J. A. Rogers, *World's Great Men of Color, Volume I,* p.116.

[70] R. C. C. Law, *North Africa in the Hellenistic and Roman Periods,* in *The Cambridge History of Africa, Volume 2,* pp.181-3.

[71] Roland Oliver & Brian M. Fagan, *Africa in the Iron Age,* p.52.

[72] R. C. C. Law, *North Africa in the Hellenistic and Roman Periods,* in *The Cambridge History of Africa, Volume 2,* p.185

[73] Gilbert Picard, *Carthage,* UK, Elek Books, 1964, pp.170-2.

[74] Ibid., pp.170-1 and 173.

[75] Ibid., pp.173-4 and Serge Lancel, *Carthage: A History,* pp.307-9.

[76] The Rev. Michael Russell, *History and Present Condition of the Barbary States,* p.27.

[77] R. C. C. Law, *North Africa in the Hellenistic and Roman Periods,* in *The Cambridge History of Africa, Volume 2,* pp.183-4.

[78] B. H. Warmington, *The Carthaginian period,* in *UNESCO General History of Africa, Volume 2,* ed G. Mokhtar, UK, Heinemann, 1981, p.459.

[79] D. E. L. Haynes, *Antiquities of Tripolitania,* pp.32-3.

[80] Ibid., p.33.

[81] J. C. DeGraft-Johnson, *African Glory,* pp.25 and 27.

CHAPTER ELEVEN: THE WEST AFRICAN COAST

The Nok Civilisation

In central Nigeria a hitherto unsuspected culture bloomed between 1000 BC and 1000 AD.[1] Tin mining operations conducted in 1928 brought this civilisation out into the open. Lt-Colonel J. Dent Young, an Englishman, led mining operations in the Nigerian village of Nok, located in the Jos region. During these operations, one of the miners found a small terracotta of a monkey head. Other finds included a terracotta human head and a foot.[2] The Colonel, at a later date, had these artefacts placed in a museum in Jos.[3] In 1942 another artefact, clearly belonging to this same culture, was found, but this time in Jemaa, some distance away. This find was brought to the attention of Bernard Fagg, an English Cadet Administrative Officer. Mr Fagg had a background as an archaeologist and by the mid-forties he wrote on this and other finds in the region. The ancient culture was now called the Nok Civilisation, named after the village in which the small terracotta monkey head was discovered.[4]

Since then, around four hundred pieces of Nok art have been recovered.[5] Their peculiar style and fine finish characterised them. Contradictory dates for the Nok artefacts do appear in the literature, but Maurer and Langevin, two modern scholars, declare that "[a]fter calibration, the period of Nok art spans from 1000 BC until 300 BC".[6] The site itself is much older than this, however. There is evidence of human occupation as early as 4580 or 4290 BC.[7] For the birth of civilisation in the region, however, more conservative dates have been suggested. Maurer and Langevin believe that their dating of the art pieces indicate that "the entire chronology of some civilizations from West Africa need to be revised. These cultures may have begun earlier, at the beginning of the third millennium before Christ".[8] The view that the Nok Civilisation had its genesis around 3000 BC more than supports an earlier reflection made by Professor Ekpo Eyo, the former head of the Nigerian museums network. He noted that "the sculptures are so advanced that they must have had time to evolve … the question must be left open so that people will know there is a possibility Nok might be much older than is generally accepted today".[9]

The artefacts are mostly human statues made of terracotta. From a few inches in height to almost life size, they depict people wearing rows of bracelets,

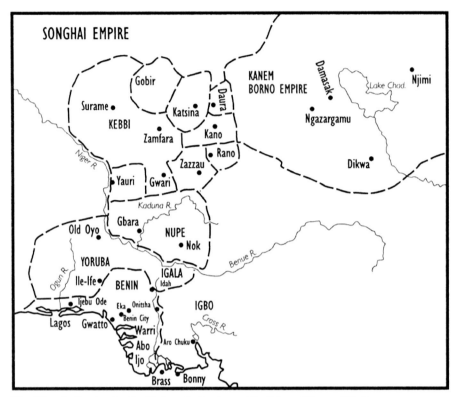

The Nigeria Region in the Sixteenth Century AD. (Map: Kieron Vital).

necklaces, skullcaps, and in at least one instance, a cape. Most show the hair exposed - the coiffeurs are inventive and bold with highly individual plaits, ridges, locks and buns.[10] Mr Fagg wrote that: "The Nok people must have taken just as many hours as the chic Lagos ladies of the twentieth century do arranging their coiffures, or, to put them into their own historical period, the Mediterranean ladies who were living in their villas north of the Sahara".[11]

The sculptors experimented with geometric shapes. Some of the heads are conical, but others are spherical or cylindrical. There are statues of elephants, monkeys, ticks and snakes, as well as human-animal combinations. There is a statue of a man amalgamated with a bird and also a statue of a sphinx. Moreover, there are statues of humans dominating wild animals showing their power over nature or possibly over their own animal instincts. These may represent priests.[12] Of the clothing depicted in the art were penis sheaths. Bernard de Grunne, an authority on the Nok, adds that:

> Without being diffusionist one can notice the following facts concerning the
> antiquity and distribution of penis-sheaths in Africa. The earliest

representations of this type of clothing appear on proto- and pre-dynastic Egyptian figures (around 3000 BC).[13] A famous example is the MacGregor statuette from the Ashmolean museum in Oxford, dated to 3100 BC. This type of Egyptian penis sheath called Bantu sheaths in the specialized literature appear to be "Libyan" in origin, probably from the paleonegritic cultural substratum.[14]

The Nok people wore heavy collars made of stone beads. In their ears, noses and lips, they wore quartz cylinders. Important personages wore cotton clothes whilst others wore small aprons of leather, bark-cloth, beads or basketwork ornaments over the pubis. It is likely that they also indulged in body decoration and used elaborate ornaments.[15]

Some of the statues are almost life size, being four or more feet in height. They show the oldest known examples of African proportion, an aesthetic where the statue's head is one-quarter or one-third the size of the body. Bernard de Grunne, mentioned earlier, suggests that this should be called the Nok Canon.[16] Professor Frank Willett, a very distinguished writer on Nigerian art, comments that:

> Making such large terracotta figures is a very unusual skill. The sculptors were able to fire them successfully, an extremely difficult task in an uncontrolled, open fire … They took great care to keep the thickness of the sculpture even."[17]

Elsewhere he adds that:

> The high degree of artistic skill of the sculptures suggest that the artists could have made naturalistic sculptures if they wished. Indeed, some of the animal sculptures represent their subject matter in a fairly realistic way."[18]

Dr Eyo, cited earlier, suspected that the commonality of style represented by the artefacts and their wide distribution may suggest that the Nok people lived in a hierarchically structured society that was:

> probably ruled by a class of noblemen, where there was a division of labour - iron-workers, farmers and so on - rich enough to support full time artists. Certain people must have stood out as eminent members of the community, and their existence and role were recorded by the artists who served under them.[19]

This idea of a stratified society is developed by de Grunne, who adds that: "The Nok statues are clearly images of dignitaries: kings, queens, priests, diviners. These images were surely worshipped in sacred shrines."[20] De Grunne, author of the valuable *The Birth of Art in Black Africa,* speculates that the shrines may have been domed, thatched buildings, built on a square base. Inside these buildings "were seated and standing Nok statues on the side walls

Nok (Nigeria).
Human head. 1000-300
BC. Teracotta. Height
24.5 cm. This is one of
400 known pieces of
art so far discovered
from the Nok Culture.
(Photo: National
Commission for
Museums and
Monuments, Lagos).

surrounding a central altar hypothetically with statues of a king, queen or other important cultural heroes".[21]

The Nok Civilisation was built on an agricultural basis. Grindstones have been found in Nok deposits that were used to pound grain. Among the statues are two clay figures each depicting a farmer carrying a tool, possibly an axe or a hoe slung over the shoulder. Oil bearing seeds called atili have also been found among the deposits. This suggests that the Nok farmers cultivated these plants to extract oil from them.[22] They are also thought to have cultivated yams and millet.[23] A statue of an individual wearing a patterned cape[24] indicates the existence of textile making of some skill. Mrs Euba, a Nigerian authority on textiles, wrote that: "[F]rom this early time the weaving of cotton on vertical looms probably existed, [but] the use of cloth was limited to a very few".[25]

Other evidence suggests that there was an iron smelting industry, one of the earliest in that part of the world. Professor Fred Anozie, former head of the University of Nigeria's Archaeology Department, noted that "as far back as at least 500 BC metal technology was already known".[26] Among the artefacts found at Nok were: "smelting tuyere, pieces of a furnace wall [and] iron slag". At Taruga, another site associated with the Nok Culture, the finds included "objects made from wrought iron, some slag, some tuyere fragments, pottery, terracotta fragments, and so on. The most interesting find consists of several concentrations of iron slag many of which contained the structure of the furnaces in their original positions".[27] Professor Eyo suspects that iron might have played an important part in the building of the kingdom. It would have given military and agricultural advantages to those familiar with iron, allowing them to dominate those without this technology. He asks:

> Could the uniformity of the Nok art tradition have been brought about, at least in part, by the sudden use of iron among a group of people within the area of the art? Such a people would first have improved their agriculture and weapons which would have enabled them to exercise considerable influence, such as exemplified by the art, over a wide area. The contact between the various groups might have been a mere interaction, but it could also have been common allegiance to one god or king.[28]

In answer to the Professor, we feel that the dates given for the use of iron (500 BC) are, perhaps, too late to account for the birth of a culture with widely distributed artefacts that date from 1000 BC. In support of the Professor, however, there is controversial evidence that Nok metallurgy may indeed predate 1000 BC. Dr Anozie was thus conservative in his dates. Dr Charles Finch, the distinguished African-American authority, informs us that:

> More recent work by C. A. Diop suggests that African iron smelting at ... an early date was not confined to the Nile Valley ... [A]t the Nok sites in Nigeria,

iron slag is present and several bits of charcoal found at the site have been
dated, respectively, at 3,500 B.C., 2,000 B.C., and 900 B.C. However, with
understandable caution, Diop hesitated to affirm straight out that iron smelting
(let alone steel-making) in West Africa could be attested back to the 4th
millennium B.C., though he did point out that no other valid explanation has
yet been forthcoming. Moreover, diggings near Kaolack, Senegal, reveal the
presence of copper and iron tools with associated charcoal debris dated back to
2,800 B.C. by two separate laboratories.[29]

There are distinguishing features of the Nok style. The eyes are often
depicted as triangular. In other pieces the lower lid of the eye form a circle
together with the eye lids. The nostrils, lips, pupils and ears are usually pierced
through with a hole. Finally, the hair and bracelets are depicted with unusual
care and attention.[30] Bernard de Grunne believes that it is possible to
distinguish five styles of Nok art. These were the Jemaa style, the Kuchamfa
style, the Katsina Ala style and two peripheral styles that may even suggest two
new and separate civilisations - the Sokoto style and the Katsina style.[31] If these
peripheral styles were indeed separate from the Nok Civilisation, then the
Sokoto culture has been tentatively dated at 200 BC to 200 AD. Similar dates
have been given for the Katsina culture.[32]

Igbo-Ukwu Civilisation

In 1938 another unsuspected culture was discovered, this time in Onitsa
Province of eastern Nigeria. This culture has since been called Igbo-Ukwu,
named after the village from which the artefacts were first encountered. Isaiah
Anozie, a Nigerian gentleman, stumbled across the treasures quite by accident.
At the time, he was digging a cistern to collect rainwater in his backyard. Two
feet below ground, he encountered a series of finely wrought bronze pieces.[33]
Subsequently, more bronzes were found by excavating the compounds of his
brothers, Richard Anozie and Jonah Anozie.[34] The objects recovered were
astonishing! As one writer put it: "Their superb workmanship and thousand-
year-old patina, with its green and purple lustre, are a wonder to behold".[35]
Radiocarbon dating for the finds established dates of the ninth and tenth
centuries AD. The artefacts were made of copper or leaded bronze - which is
an alloy of copper, tin and lead. They demonstrated geometric exactitude and
perfection of form.[36] The archaeologists were reduced to incoherent mumbling.
Primitive peoples do not produce metal work of anything like this quality. One
such scholar, Mr Peter Garlake, admitted that:

> Igbo Ukwu is probably the most enigmatic prehistoric site in Africa. It
> represents an almost unparalleled concentration of wealth - in bronze and beads
> - in the hands of one man. It is part of a sophisticated and idiosyncratic tradition

Igbo-Ukwu (Nigeria). Vessel in the shape of a shell surmounted by an animal. 9ᵗʰ/10ᵗʰ century AD. Leaded bronze. Length 20.6 cm. This masterful casting was made using the famous lost wax technique. (Photo: National Commission for Museums and Monuments, Lagos).

of craftsmanship and art that must have had a long history of development and is otherwise completely unknown. Yet, the present weight of the evidence indicates that it belongs to a period when the savanna states were still young. This is well before one would expect a concentration of power to have developed in forest polities … At present, Igbo Ukwu makes no economic sense.[37]

Among the finds were fine copper chains, wristlets, profusely elaborate staff ornaments - some decorated by coloured beads, vessels brilliantly cast in the shape of sea shells, drinking cups, pots, sword scabbards, a copper altar stand, pendants, and also flywhisks - a traditional symbol held by a person with authority.[38] The handle of the flywhisk depicts a horseman with his headdress, pouch and belt. Horses must have been utilised at that time as a means of transport.[39] One authority speculates that the horseman may have been a titled personage given the rarity of horses in the region and the need to import them.[40] Dr Charles Finch writes that: "Several of … the objects convey artistically the

Igbo-Ukwu
(Nigeria). Globular
waterpot on a stand.
9ᵗʰ/10ᵗʰ century AD.
Leaded bronze.
Height 32.3 cm.
(Photo:
National
Commission
for Museums
and Monuments,
Lagos).

impression of having lain at the bottom of the sea for eons of time collecting barnacles, corals, and other assorted marine life. This was an effect deliberately created by the caster".[41] The quality of the metal work was such that one scholar, Professor Willett, commented that: "One can only suppose that the smiths of Igbo-Ukwu enjoyed demonstrating their virtuosity".[42] The same writer comments that the:

> outstanding feature [of the treasures] is the great elaboration of the surface decoration: the objects have an encrusted appearance. Most conspicuous are the number of small animals, especially insects, which stand out from the surface. Tiny spirals are also commonly employed. Even repairs to faults in the castings were made in the form of spirals. Other decorations were formed of long fine threads, which may be run in straight lines or used to outline other shapes, particularly rectangles or lozenges, or to form networks of various types, either triangular or curvilinear.[43]

Historians and archaeologists have attempted to grapple with the significance of these finds:

> Such a concentration of wealth as the metalwork and the beads represent [says Professor Willett] has been thought to imply some sort of centralized government unlike the stateless societies that characterized Igboland at the time of the first European contacts.[44]

Some of the objects, especially those excavated at Richard Anozie's compound, were associated with a ritual burial of an important and probably titled personage. This is unusual, because Igbo society was supposed to have been one that did without kings:

> The site of Igbo Richard [says Professor Eyo] ... yielded much information about Igbo culture, its priest-king institution and its burial custom ... Here, the tomb of a priest king, lined possibly with carved wooden panels, was uncovered. The body of the inmate is believed to have been clothed in ceremonial regalia and sat on a stool with the two hands supported by copper brackets. The corpse wore a breast plate, copper anklets and strings of beads, a beaded head-dress and a bronze crown. In front of him a bronze leopard skull on a copper rod ... was stuck into the ground. The arrangement was then covered, first with wooden panels and then with earth.[45]

Also found in this tomb were three tusks of ivory, iron goods and pottery.[46] The important personage is now thought to have been a priest king or *Eze-Nri*. Many scholars believe that the copper and bronze artefacts were made exclusively for the household of this title-holder.[47] The Igbo-Ukwu region, however, is lacking in copper. Various scholars have thus theorised that trans-saharan trade caravans brought the copper in from the north. It is thought that the Igbos sold ivory, pepper, kola nuts and spices north to the Saharan states.[48] Horses could well have been used to conduct this trade.[49] Interestingly, well-preserved fabrics were found with the objects and this indicates the existence of an Igbo textile industry.[50] It is, however, possible that the source of the copper was the Kongo region, as Professor Eyo explains: "Perhaps the forest zone between Nigeria and the Congo, where copper is found in the Katanga District, was no barrier to the importation of copper into Nigeria".[51]

The Igbos are generally thought to have been the earliest workers of copper and its alloys in Mediæval West Africa by smithing. Their castings, by contrast, were of leaded bronze and show complete mastery of the lost wax technique.[52] Professor Fred Anozie explained this technique of manufacturing metal goods as follows:

(1) The first step is to obtain some plastic wax, which could be bees wax. The object to be cast was formed with the wax, inserting all the details and decorations. If for example a snake was to be cast, the [model] in wax should have the tail, the head, the eyes and the natural decorations of the snake.

(2) The model of the snake in wax is then covered with clay, leaving two openings "a" and "b". This became a mould with the model of the snake in wax.

(3) The mould was tilted a little and heated. The wax melted and flowed out through the lower hole 'b' and as nature does not allow for a vacuum, air goes in through the hole 'a' to take the space created by the wax lost through hole 'b'.

(4) The casting metal which could be copper or trash was cut into little pieces, put into the crucible and heated in a hearth.

(5) As soon as the metal melted, it was poured into the mould through the hole 'a', while the air in the mould was expelled through hole 'b' by the metal.

(6) Both the mould and its content were allowed to get cold and the mould broken to bring out the copper or brass snake.[53]

This technique, also called *cire perdue,* was later used by other Nigerian peoples in the manufacture of their art and crafts and is thus a legacy of the Igbo achievement. In closing, David Northrup penned a good summary of the Igbo-Ukwu finds and the industry and trade links implied by them:

Recent excavations have unearthed a spectacularly rich material culture dating from the ninth century A.D. . . . The Igbo-Ukwu finds showed evidence of metal working, weaving, and pottery making of unusual skill. The metal work included 110 major and 575 minor copper and bronze objects of very high quality and a very distinctive design ... Textiles of two types were found at Igbo-Ukwu: one of grass or leaf fibres in a previously unknown weave pattern, the other a kind of cloth remarkably similar to cotton. Both were of a high quality ... In addition over 20,000 pieces of pottery were recovered ... [Also recovered were] 165,000 beads ... of Indian manufacture with some perhaps from Venice.[54]

Yoruba Civilisation

By the eleventh century AD, the Yoruba, ruling from the city of Ife, were the leading cultural force in southern Nigeria. Their civilisation has been widely admired by many scholars. Professor Cheikh Anta Diop, for example, wrote that: "It is impossible to describe here all the riches of the civilization of Ife".[55] Herbert Wendt, a German science writer, was much more flattering:

> Modern ethnologists [says Wendt] have found the art of the Yorubas so astonishingly high in quality that they did not [at first] ascribe it to a Negro race ... It was Leo Frobenius who first ranked the culture of the Yorubas with that of the Mediterranean ... The Yoruba empire consisted of city states similar to those of ancient Greece ... [S]ome of these states had a hundred and fifty to two hundred and fifty thousand inhabitants. Art objects of the highest quality were found in their ruins - glazed urns, tiles with pictures of animals and gods on them, bronze implements, gigantic granite figures. The Yorubas introduced the cultivation of yams, the preparation of cheese and the breeding of horses into West Africa. They had outstanding artists in metal, gold-casters, cotton-weavers, wood-carvers and potters. Their professions formed themselves into guilds with their own laws, their children were brought up in educational camps, their public affairs were directed by a courtly aristocracy and an exuberantly expanding bureaucracy.[56]

Professor Leo Frobenius, a German scholar, was the pioneering authority on the Yoruba civilisation. When he first encountered this culture in the early twentieth century, he felt he had discovered remnants of the lost Greek civilisation of Atlantis. Unearthing beautiful statuary and old palaces, he heard, among the Yoruba, legends describing these ancient times. One such story alludes to an ancient royal metropolis with a palace of golden walls that had sunk beneath the waters of the Atlantic. In addition, Frobenius identified Olukun, the Yoruba sea god, with Poseidon, the ancient Greek deity.[57] While this analysis is all clearly in error, Mr Garlake explains why Frobenius could be forgiven for making these blunders:

> The calm repose and realism of the [Yoruba] sculptures were reminiscent of Classical Greece. The pantheon of Yoruba gods, their attributes, their vivid lives and complex responsibilities echoed Mount Olympus. The architecture of the houses and palaces, where rooms opened off enclosed courtyards, open to the sky, resembled the impluvia of early Mediterranean, particularly Etruscan [i.e. Roman], buildings. The Yoruba concept of the universe, their educational system, the organization of their society and their statecraft supported a Greek connection.[58]

Ile-Ife was the ancient capital city of the Yorubas (also known simply as Ife). Archaeological excavations showed that the site was inhabited by 600 AD.

Yoruba (Nigeria).
Superb mask of
Oni Obalufon II.
12th/15th century.
Copper. Height 29.5 cm.
(Photo: National Commission for
Museums and Monuments, Lagos).

Among its first residents were farmers who cultivated yams and oil palms.[59] "It is [also] clear", wrote Africanists Oliver and Fagan, "that from the earliest times the town had an important iron industry, and also that it engaged in the manufacture of glass".[60] According to William Fagg, an important authority, excavations of the Olukun grove site revealed coloured beads and also "glass in beautiful shades of deep red and blue, turquoise and several shades of green".[61] Professor Willett adds that: "Here evidently had been the centre of the great glass making industry which had spread blue glass *segi* beads across West Africa".[62]

Ile-Ife became a powerful city some time after 1000 AD. Home to the divine ruler, the Oni, it was also the centre of trade routes.[63] The Yoruba imported horses, salt, copper and brass from the Saharan states paid for by the exports of large crops of kola nuts and also cloth.[64] Textiles were an important industry. In the mid-nineteenth century, William Clarke, an English visitor, remarked that: "As good an article of cloth can be woven by the Yoruba weavers as by any people ... in durability, their cloths far excel the prints and home-spuns of Manchester".[65] But how far back in time does this industry go? Does it go back to the period under discussion? Mrs Euba, a textiles expert in the University of Ife, explains that:

> By the time of the ancient Ifes, weaving on the vertical loom was more extensive in the cotton-growing areas. From the bronzes [i.e. art pieces] of Ife and Benin ... we may picture a basic style of dress which makes use of draped cloths of various lengths, although even in earlier times the use of sewn garments was not unknown ... Everywhere in Nigeria weaving had reached a highly advanced stage by at least the end of the fourteenth century. Cotton was the yarn most frequently used ... A silk yarn ... called *anaphe,* was and still is used by the Yoruba to produce a cloth called sanyan, and was perhaps also used by the Hausa who today use the same silk ... to embroider costly robes.[66]

At the centre of Ife stood the Afin, which is the walled royal palace. It has been excavated "but little detail has been gleaned about the form of the medieval palace".[67] Despite this, Professor Frobenius learned enough to conclude that it "was a structure built of authentic enamelled bricks, decorated with artistic porcelain tiles and all sorts of ornaments".[68] Ile-Ife itself was walled and also paved. Excavations show that its walls were built in two concentric circles. As the population grew or the direct influence exerted by the Oni increased, new walls were taken under royal protection.[69]

Professor Ekpo Eyo narrates a curious oral tradition concerning Oni Oluwo, a distinguished Yoruba ruler. Apparently she was walking around the capital when her regalia got splashed with mud. Oluwo was so upset by this that she ordered the construction of pavements for all the public and religious places in the city.[70] Archaeology confirms that:

Pavements ... are widespread in Africa. Potsherd pavements are the most common types of pavements known in West Africa ... The most consistent reports about excavated pavements in West Africa have so far come from Ife, specifically the sites at: Oduduwa College, Lafogido, Ita Yemoo, Obalara's Land and Woye Asiri Land.[71]

The pavements embellished the courtyards and often had altars built at the ends against walls. Peter Garlake adds that:

Many [of the pavements] had regular and geometric patterns, often emphasized by the incorporation of white quartz pebbles in their surface. Such pavements have been found on prehistoric sites from Tchad [sic] in the northeast to Togo in the west.[72]

As early as 1913, Dr Frobenius speculated that there was a link between the Yoruba culture and the cultures of ancient America. He believed that this connection was forged at a date well before Christopher Columbus' so-called discovery of America:

I cannot finish [wrote Frobenius] without devoting a word or two to a certain symptomatic conformity of the Western Atlantic civilisation with its higher manifestations in America. Its cognate features are so striking that they cannot be overlooked, and as the region of Atlantic African culture is Yoruba ... it seems to be a present question, whether it might not be possible to bring the marvellous Maya monuments ... into some prehistoric connection with those of Yoruba.[73]

Strangely enough, recent archaeological evidence lends support to some of Frobenius' ideas. Scholars have discussed the validity of many pieces of evidence for ancient connections between Africa and America. Dr David Kelley is one such example. In his own words:

The kind of evidence field archaeologists like is the pavement of Île Ife [sic], a former Yoruba capital (Van Sertima 1976: 264-267). This is made from broken potsherds that were decorated by rolling corncobs over their surface before firing. Paul Mangelsdorf, who had seen some of the sherds assured me (about 1954) that they were indeed Zea mays [i.e. an American plant]. Another interpretation of Yoruba tradition is that the capital was moved from Île Ife to Old Oyo about A.D. 1100 or earlier (M. D. W. Jeffreys, 1953). If so, this site provides the hard evidence that archaeologists want for American plants in Africa in pre-Columbian times [i.e. before Columbus].[74]

No one knows whether Native Americans sailed across the Atlantic and visited Ile-Ife, bringing the maize with them. It is equally possible that Yorubas visited ancient America and returned with the maize. One thing is certain -

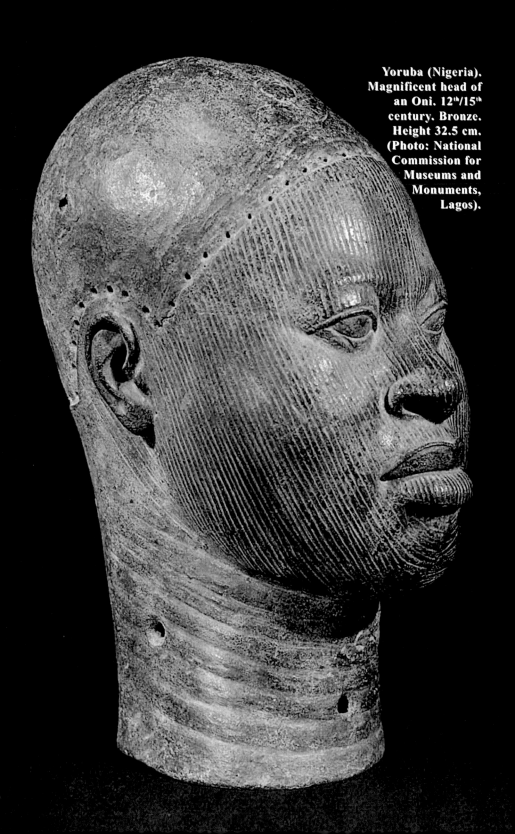

Yoruba (Nigeria).
Magnificent head of
an Oni. 12th/15th
century. Bronze.
Height 32.5 cm.
(Photo: National
Commission for
Museums and
Monuments,
Lagos).

contact between the two cultures occurred before 1100 AD or before whatever date is accepted for the paving of the city. Scholars today routinely speak of the Pre-Pavement period as between 800 and 1000 AD and the Post-Pavement period as after 1000 AD.[75] On this basis, contact between the two cultures, Yoruba and Native American, must therefore have taken place before 1000 AD.

According to the Reverend Samuel Johnson, himself a Yoruba and a pioneering Yoruba scholar, Ile-Ife had important sculptures:

> commonly known as the "Ife Marbles," several of which may be seen in Ile Ife to this day [i.e. 1921], said to be the handiwork of the early ancestors of the race. They are altogether Egyptian in form. The most notable of them is what is known as the "Opa Oranyan," (Oranyan's staff) an obelisk standing on the site of Oranyan's supposed grave, having characters cut in it ... Three or four of these sculptures may now be seen in the Egyptian Court of the British Museum, showing at a glance that they are among kindred works of art.[76]

The Ife Marbles are monoliths that date back before 800 AD. Of granite and iron, they range from one to eighteen feet in height and are associated with Ogun, the deity of iron.[77] The Reverend Johnson believes that the written characters on Opa Oranyan, the largest monolith, "suggest a Phoenician origin".[78] This raises all sorts of questions. Did the Yorubas have a script? Is the Reverend Johnson correct in saying that the script shows affinities to Phoenician? What happened to these British Museum exhibits since 1921?

One of the great achievements of the Yoruba is their urban culture. They had villages, hamlets and small market towns.[79] "By the year A.D. 1300," says a modern scholar, "the Yoruba people [also] built numerous walled cities surrounded by farms".[80] The other cities were Owu, Oyo, Ijebu, Ijesa, Ketu, Popo, Egba, Sabe, Dassa, Egbado, Igbomina, the sixteen Ekiti principalities, Owo and Ondo. The ruling dynasties of most, if not all, of these cities traced their origins to Ile-Ife.[81]

Supporting the populations of these city-states was agriculture. Practising crop rotation, the Yoruba in the Pre-Pavement periods, as we have seen, cultivated local crops of yam and oil palm. Originally Native American in origin, they cultivated maize. In later periods they grew potato, cotton, holchus sorgum, rice, cassava, melon, beans, groundnut, sugar cane, orange, okro, and various vegetables. This was in addition to yam, cocoyam, oil palm, kola and maize.[82]

The Owu city-state was the oldest daughter of Ife. Founded in the grassland area north of modern Orile-Owu, Oni Asunkungbada ruled as its first king. This state became a great military power in the region. Utilisation of cavalry forces led to its early importance. In addition, Owu exercised hegemony over both Oyo and Igbomina in their earlier years. Dynasts from Owu founded the cities of Owu-Ogbere and Owu-Ipole.[83]

Not long after, Oyo became a great city. It came to dominate the trade caravans. There were two such caravan routes that linked Yorubaland with the outside world. The first traversed the region in a north to southwest direction. Passing through Hausaland, it linked the Yorubas at Oyo to the trans-Saharan trade. From Oyo, it passed through Kisi, Saki, Iseyin, etc., ultimately reaching the coast at Ajase, the modern Porto Novo. The second caravan route traversed the region in a north to southeast direction. Again, it centred on Oyo, but this time it passed through Ilesa, Ekitiland, Owo, to the Kingdom of Benin, where it eventually reached the coast. Feeder routes linked these caravans from all directions within the Yoruba territories. Goods moved by head porterage or sometimes by the use of ferries if the routes crossed rivers. Nominal tolls were imposed on the movement of goods.[84]

The Afin (i.e. palace) at Oyo, over many generations, evolved into a great walled complex that enclosed buildings, courtyards, and large areas of forestland. Susan Denyer, an architectural authority, suggests that it may well have had over a hundred courtyards, each of an astonishing size, being far larger than a private house. One of them was as large as two football pitches. Each courtyard was used for a special function such as public assemblies, dancing at festivals, or for the Oba's private use. Denyer further suggests that the courtyards may well have been paved with quartz pebbles and potsherds. When Captain Clapperton, the English traveller, visited it in the 1820's, he reported that the palace complex covered an area of 260 hectares.[85]

Ile-Ife continued to exercise cultural and religious influence over the other walled cities, such as Owo. This religious influence, wrote Dr Davidson:

> was reflected ... by the beauty and excellence of Yoruba sculpture in wood and brass, clay and ivory ... Ife, has yielded many splendid things that were made long ago in honour of Yoruba beliefs and rulers ... Yoruba artists were called on to celebrate the *Oni* of Ife and his kinsman, and evolved one of the greatest schools of sculpture the world has known.[86]

The art, much of it in metal, was of great distinction. Dr Finch tells us that: "Such was the genius of the Ife metallurgical artists that nothing in the Renaissance surpassed their technique".[87] Professor Willett agrees. He feels that Yoruba art "would stand comparison with anything which Ancient Egypt, Classical Greece and Rome, or Renaissance Europe had to offer".[88] The development of Yoruba art is something of a puzzle, explains art historian Werner Gillon, because "the splendid artefacts found have all been masterpieces, and no traces of early beginnings by less accomplished artists have [ever] been discovered".[89]

The Yoruba civilisation flourished for many years, but it became a main target for slave traders and its vitality was gradually undermined. On the

African side, the city of Oyo in about 1600 took the lead in undermining the other city states and selling the captives to the Europeans. From the eighteenth century, the Dahomey Empire to the west continued the onslaught. Yoruba influence in the region gradually took a back seat to the newly rising power of Benin. This civilisation, in some ways a child of the Yoruba, became dominant by the fifteenth century where we take up the story.

Great Benin

From the fifteenth century onwards, West Africa began to face the rigours of the Slave Trade. The threat initially came from the Portuguese. Later it came from other Europeans. A few states survived this period, though in some of these, the leaderships failed to act decisively against the enslavers. A Portuguese ambassador could, however, record that:

> Twenty leagues from the coast there lives a monarch to whom his subjects show the same reverence as Catholics do the Pope. When foreign ambassadors come into his presence, they are never afforded a glimpse of his face. A curtain hides him from their sight: he only sticks out his foot, that they may kiss it when taking their departure.[90]

Great Benin, also known as Edo, was an important state that flourished in southern Nigeria. In the fifteenth century, it was an empire distinguished by the sumptuousness and comfort of its capital, Benin City, and by the refinement of its royal art. Oba (i.e. King) Ewuare the Great, founder of the empire, reigned between *c.*1440 and *c.*1473. Noted as a brilliant ruler, he is remembered for strong leadership and military prowess. Marching against 201 towns and villages over the southern Nigeria region, he captured their leaders and compelled the masses to pay tribute. Among the subdued regions were Eka, Ekiti, Ikare, Kukuruku, and the Igbo territories west of the Niger River. An able politician, he used religious authority and intimidation, as well as constitutional reforms, to strengthen his hand. These strategies fortified the Obaship against the power of over-ambitious ministers.[91]

The early history of Benin was a much more modest period associated with the Ogiso Dynasty. Igodo, first of its fifteen rulers, lived around 900 AD and enjoyed a long reign. Ogiso Ere, his son and successor, founded many villages such as Erua and Ego. He was a patron of craftsmen and, more significantly, he founded institutions. The guilds of weavers, carvers and potters, date back to his time. These craftsmen worked clay, wood and leather. Moreover, Ere established royal emblems and the ceremonies that accompanied them which continued into later times. These included the throne, the stool, ritual swords, the fan, the anklets, the collars and the crown.[92] Ogiso Orhorho, the eighth

Benin (Nigeria). Oba or War Chief and attendants. Early 17th century. Brass. Height 53.5 cm. (Photo: National Commission for Museums and Monuments, Lagos).

ruler, is remembered as an evil queen, who was assassinated in consequence of her tyranny. Ogiso Hennenden, the twelfth ruler, presided over a period of prosperity. The village of Benin grew in population as a result. Finally, Owodo was the last ruler of the Ogiso Dynasty. An ineffectual ruler, he was later banished for incompetence. He is primarily remembered as someone who never convened a meeting except in times of trouble or crisis.[93]

After his expulsion, two administrators, Evian and Ogiamve, ruled in the interregnum. The republican period, however, proved to be short lived. Evian attempted to install his son as the next Oba but the people revolted. Sending ambassadors to the Yoruba capital of Ife, the tradition goes, they begged for a ruler. The Yorubas responded and sent Prince Oranmiyan to Benin. The Prince founded the Second Dynasty in *c.*1170 AD after overcoming Ogiamve's resistance. Oranmiyan resided at a high walled palace built for him at Usama.[94] Concerning this monument, Professor Blier, an art historian, informs us that: "The construction of this building was considered so important that its creation has been ritually re-enacted at each royal enthronement".[95] Stride and Ifeka, authors of the well respected *People and Empires of West Africa,* place the Oranmiyan story in proper historical perspective:

> The main point about the Oranmiyan legend is that it links Benin to Yorubaland, emphasizing the influence of Yoruba methods of government on Bini institutions. Indeed tradition distinguishes most firmly between the Ogiso dynasty, which was apparently peculiar to Edo of Benin, and the second dynasty which shows marked Yoruba influences.[96]

Accompanying the Yoruba dynastic connection came the importation of state swords into Benin, stables of horses for ceremonial occasions, and later, a guild of royal brass casters.[97] A curious royal burial practice developed that reinforced this cultural link. When a king of Benin died, it became customary to send his head or other symbolic parts to Ife for a royal burial. A Yoruba artist was then commissioned to make a metal portrait of the head. The portrait was returned to Benin where it was placed on an altar. This practise continued until the time of Oba Ogolua, in the late thirteenth century. This king requested of the Oni of Ife that he might send a sculptor to Benin to teach Yoruba metallurgical art among the Bini. Complying with the request, the Oni of Ife sent Iguegha, a master sculptor, to Benin. Iguegha founded the Benin guild of bronzesmiths. Incidentally, to this day, there are shrines dedicated to him in Benin City.[98]

Developments in statecraft are associated with Oba Eweka I, Oranmiyan's son and successor. Ascending the throne in *c.*1200 AD, he reformed the government by introducing the Uzama Nihinron. They were a body of seven Counsellors of State, considered in some respects successors to the Ogiso

Dynasty. The seven titled positions were hereditary. As kingmakers, they ensured that each new Oba was installed according to precedent.[99] The most senior of these Counsellors presented the crown to the Oba at each new coronation. Considered guardians of tradition, they had rights similar to that of royalty. They had rights to have their own palaces and also their own priests.[100]

Ewedo succeeded Eweka I in *c.*1255. His accession to the throne was far from smooth, however. A military challenge came from yet another Ogiamve, an ambitious noble. Ewedo's army triumphed, however. The victorious Ewedo built a palace inside Benin City that became the new royal residence. Usama continued to maintain importance. Each new Oba was installed at a ceremony there to commemorate Ewedo's defeat of Ogiamve. The king asserted religious authority as well as the political. He appointed a Chief Priest to supervise public rituals and to strengthen his role as divine king. The Chief Priest's responsibility was to establish Earth Cult shrines.[101] Other reforms involved creating new titleholders and thus increasing the size of the bureaucracy. Finally, he passed good laws and commissioned the building of a prison. This institution continued to be in use right up until 1897. Chief Egharevba, the distinguished Benin historian, recorded that: "He was one of our greatest and most prudent Obas".[102]

Oba Ewuare of the fifteenth century ushered in another great wave of constitutional reforms. Like Ewedo before him, he used religious intimidation to buttress his authority as a sacred figure. Moreover, he appointed a new tier of bureaucrats creating a strongly centralised system to administer his empire. These bureaucrats, the Town Chiefs, were appointed to undermine the control of the hereditary Palace Chiefs. One of the Town Chiefs headed the newly created standing army.[103] Modern historians give different and conflicting explanations of how this worked but Stride and Ifeka explain it thus:

> Benin was apparently governed by the Oba, the Uzama and the palace chiefs. The palace chiefs were divided into three associations of title holders: the chamberlains, household officials and the harem-keepers. Palace chiefs both inherited and achieved their titles by paying fees to their association. What Ewuare found was that the palace chiefs were too powerful ... To strengthen the Obaship, Ewuare ... introduced another association of chiefs, the town chiefs ... They generally obtained their title on appointment by the Oba: only one title was hereditary. Ewuare appointed four town chiefs to increase his authority against the palace officials; later their number was much enlarged by Ewuare successors. Town chiefs played an important part in the government and the senior town chief, the Iyashere, became the commander-in-chief of the army. They sat with the palace chiefs and the Uzama on the State Council, which Ewuare was said to have set up.[104]

Benin (Nigeria). One of a delightful pair of leopards. Mid 16ᵗʰ century. Brass. Length 74 cm. The leopard is considered a royal symbol in Benin. (Photo: National Commission for Museums and Monuments, Lagos).

The Benin army contained divisions of knights that wore body armour. Dr Diop analysed Benin bronze art and noted that: "The appearance in bronzes of knights arrayed in all manner of cuirasses, armoured from head to toe, seems to prove that metallurgy was put to all kinds of uses, for all of this armour was, without doubt of local manufacture".[105]

Benin City began as an unwalled village. The first population expansion turning the village into a town began during the time of Ogiso Hennenden in around 1000 AD.

Oba Oguola raised the first walls in c.1283. For security reasons, he also had moats dug around the outskirts of the town and at other important towns and villages.

Oba Ewuare raised new walls in *c*.1460, building the great innermost walls and other ditches. Inside the city, he had good roads built such as Utantan Street and Akpakpava Street. Indeed, during his career, the city achieved great fame and importance.[106] It had a walled and moated inner city of nine gates called Ogbe. This part contained the Ogiso Dynasty and Second Dynasty palaces. Also there were the houses of the functionaries and the wards for the guilds. There were guilds of ivory carvers, iron and brass smiths, weavers and embroiderers, and finally drummers and sculptors. The Second Dynasty palace was located in the centre of the city at the terminus of three great avenues. Its central location and orientation reflected the temporal and cosmological power of the Oba. Surrounding this area was the Ore Nokua, the outer city. Also walled, it contained the compounds of residents previously associated with the Ogiso Dynasty. The Queen Mother and Crown Prince had their own palaces located outside both sets of walls. Ewuare popularised the impluvium architecture style of the Yorubas, creating for the first time in Benin a centrally planned metropolis built on a horizontal vertical grid.[107]

Mr Garlake suggested that the construction work of the walls and ditches were on "a scale comparable with the Great Wall of China".[108] Professors Oliver and Atmore, in a new work, add that:

> [E]xcavation has shown that the main city walls are but the nucleus of a vast system of defensive walling totalling perhaps 10,000 miles in all, which suggests that the city grew by encompassing a number of small, closely neighbouring towns, reflecting a growth in population around a successful industrial centre ... [109]

Even before the full extent of the city walling had become apparent, the *Guinness Book of Records* carried an entry in the 1974 edition that read as follows:

> The largest earthworks in the world carried out prior to the mechanical era were the Linear Earth Boundaries of the Benin Empire [i.e. Benin City] in the Mid Western state of Nigeria. They were first reported [by modern European scholars] in 1903 and partially surveyed in 1967. In April 1973 it was estimated by Mr Patrick Darling that the total length of the earthworks was probably between 5,000 and 8,000 miles *8,000-12,800 km* with the total amount of earth estimated at from 500 to 600 million yds³ *380-460 million m³*.[110]

Arts and crafts have always played an important role in this society. Ere of the tenth century patronised carvers and carpenters. In addition, he founded their guilds, later to become important institutions. The carvers produced goods of wood and ivory. Ere is also credited with introducing the use of wooden bowls and plates together with mortars and pestles.[111] During the Ogiso period, terracotta heads were made that surmounted the altars of the kings. There were also early manufactures in brass. Craftsmen made bracelets and bells.[112] Over three centuries later, we hear of Oba Oguola sending for a Yoruba artist to teach Yoruba-style metal art among the Binis. Iguegha, the Yoruba sculptor, founded the Benin guild of bronzesmiths.[113] Later still, Ewuare, the great Oba of the fifteenth century, was a patron of ivory carving.[114] Later still, arts and crafts would continue to develop.

Oba Ozolua, a successor of Ewuare the Great in *c*.1481, was another fine soldier who widened the boundaries of the empire. His campaigns saw Benin influence spread as far as the neighbouring kingdoms of Ekiti and Ijebu. In 1485 or 6, he received an ambassador from Portugal, Affonso d'Aveiro. Before long, diplomatic and commercial links between the two countries were forged.[115] A Portuguese chronicler recorded that Ozolua sent a priest and ambassador to Portugal "because he desired to learn more about these lands, the arrival of people from them in his country being regarded as an unusual novelty".[116] Ohen-Okun, "a man of good speech and natural wisdom", returned home laden with presents for himself, his wife and the Oba, all sent by the Portuguese.[117] To facilitate trade between the two countries, the priest established a trading factory at Ughoton.[118]

In an earlier period, Benin's trade links were with the Saharan states to the north. They exported ivory, pepper and cotton goods in exchange for Saharan copper and Sudanese horses. Oba Udagbedo (*c*.1299-*c*.1334), an industrious ruler, presided over a noteworthy period of agricultural expansion. Once trade links had been made with Portugal, and elsewhere in Europe, they exported dyed cotton cloth, wool, jasper, leopard skins, soap and later, palm oil. This was in addition to ivory and pepper.[119]

Some of the ivory had been beautifully and aesthetically carved into condiment sets and tableware that graced none but the highest tables. To this day, art historians marvel at their refined and exquisite beauty that also combines practical use. Werner Gillon, author of *A Short History of African Art,* informs us that:

> These objects depicted knights, sometimes on horseback, Portuguese coats of arms and Christian iconography … Apart from the many carvings made for Portuguese royalty and nobility, there were those acquired (possibly also through the Portuguese) by the Medici, who were the most avid collectors of these works. Among other royal collectors was Augustus, Duke of Saxonia, one of whose acquisitions in 1590 was recorded in 1595 by the Kunstkammer of Dresden. The Museum für Völkerkunde in Vienna has ivory spoons and a fork from the collection of the Castle of Ambrass in Tyrol, started by Archduke Ferdinand in the second half of the sixteenth century.[120]

Benin (Nigeria). Exquisite condiment bowl. 16th century. Ivory. 30.5 cm. (Photo: Werner Forman Archives).

The trade in soap is of particular interest since we are informed that: "By the seventeenth century, the production of soap was on such a scale that Portugal banned imports of West African soap in order to protect its own soap boiling industry".[121]

Oba Esigie ascended the throne in *c*.1504 and had a long and eventful reign of perhaps 46 years. He introduced a special post in the administration for his mother called the Iyoba, the Queen Mother. A Dutch chronicler would report a century later that the Oba "undertakes nothing of importance without having sought her counsel".[122] The art of the time reflects this reality. Esigie commissioned a highly improved metal art that has since achieved worldwide distinction. Of the best-known pieces are the famous Queen Mother Idia busts.[123] Professor Felix von Luschan, a former official of the Berlin Museum für Völkerkunde, stated that:

> These works from Benin are equal to the very finest examples of European casting technique. Benvenuto Cellini could not have cast them better, nor could anyone else before or after him … Technically, these bronzes represent the very highest possible achievement.[124]

Affonso d'Aveiro and other Portuguese agents returned to Benin. They aroused Esigie's interest in the possibility of acquiring firearms from Portugal for future campaigns. There was, however, a catch. Manuel, the Portuguese king wrote Esigie, explaining to him that:

> When we see that you have embraced the teachings of Christianity like a good and faithful Christian, there will be nothing within our realms which we shall not be glad to favour you, whether it be arms or cannon and all other weapons of war for use against your enemies; of such things we have a great store, as your ambassador Dom Jorge will inform you.[125]

It was not to be. In 1516 and without Portuguese arms, Esigie scored a crushing defeat on Igala to the north. They had attempted an invasion that posed a threat to the very existence of Benin. Esigie compelled the defeated Igala to pay reparations.[126] The Portuguese king did, however, send missionaries to Benin who successfully converted the Oba's son to the Christian faith. Bini Christians also established a few churches in Benin City at Ogbelaka, Idumwerie, and Akpakpava. The last church became the Holy Cross Cathedral. Christianity, however, remained distinctly a minority religion largely restricted to a few members of the court.[127] It seems that the indigenous religion was just too well organised to be undermined by this foreign threat.

By the latter half of the sixteenth century, the ancient village of Ughoton became transformed into the seaport of Gwatto. The Oba imposed a series of tolls and customs on goods that passed through here, some of which came via the Hausas from the Saharan Trade. Benin prospered greatly.[128] The markets were typically held in large public squares every three or four days. D. R., an anonymous Dutch source, tells us that: "These markets and traffikings are held and arranged in a very orderly manner".[129] The currency was cowrie shells.

On sale when James Welsh visited there in 1588, was soap that "smelleth like beaten violets", ivory spoons "very curiously wrought with divers portions of foules and beasts made upon them", cotton and woollen cloths "very curiously woven", bark cloth, pepper, ivory, palm oil, and mats that were "pretie [and] fine."[130] Incidentally, Welsh presented the Oba with the gift of a telescope.[131] Also for sale on a typical market day were foodstuffs such as fowls, dogs, monkeys, catfish, dried lizards, beans, fruit and vegetables. Other goods included dishes, drinking cups, and ironwork products. The iron products were fishing and agricultural tools, such as hoes. A variety of clothes were on sale. Dr Olfert Dapper, a Dutch geographer, listed Dutch textiles and other goods that were on sale in Benin, including gold and silver cloth, linen, red velvet, fine cotton stuffs, woollen stuffs, and Harlem stuffs with flower designs. Other Dutch goods included jugs, bangles, beads, red glass earrings, gilt-looking glasses and crystal.[132]

One trading product that the Bini had access to but refused to exploit was gold mining. Landolphe, an eighteenth century French writer, explained that: "[N]o one is allowed to touch them under pain of death, for fear lest Europeans in their avarice bring fire and sword as they did into Peru".[133]

The empire achieved its maximum expansion in the sixteenth century, ruling Ishan to the north, Isoko and Urhobo of the lower Niger delta, southern Yoruba territories, and western Igboland. Administering this territory were three tiers of imperial government. At the top was the Oba, an increasingly austere and sacred figure. Then came the State Council of Benin City. Beneath these were the tributary units. The units consisted of an overlord, royally appointed, who headed the unit. The overlord appointed a servant as his representative. Finally, there were the people of the village, town or dependency. Tradition dictated that the overlord lived in Benin City. His role was to transmit the interests of his constituents to the Oba. In addition, he had to organise the yearly or twice yearly collection of tribute in the form of yams, palm oil, meat, livestock and foodstuffs to be sent to the Oba's court. Tradition further dictated that the servant would live in the village, town or dependency to represent the overlord there.[134]

In the early 1600's other envoys from Europe visited Benin. Some of these left eye catching descriptions of what they saw. Samuel Blomert, a man who lived in Africa for several years, is one such example. In 1668 Dutch scholar, Dr Olfert Dapper, paraphrased his rich and full account in a famous book entitled *Description of Africa*. It is so engrossing that we have taken the liberty of reproducing portions from it that describe the splendour of Benin City:

The town, comprising the queen's court, is about five or six miles in circumference[135] … It is protected at one side by a wall ten feet high, made of double stockades of big trees, tied to each other by cross-beams fastened cross-wise, and stuffed up with red clay, solidly put together. This wall only surrounds the town on one side … The town possesses several gates, eight or nine feet in height and five in width, with doors made of a whole piece of wood, hanging or turning on a peg, like the peasant's fences here in this country [i.e. Holland]. The king's court is square, and stands at the right hand side when entering the town by the gate of Gotton [i.e. Gwatto], and is certainly as large as the town of Harlem [in Holland], and entirely surrounded by a special wall, like that which encircles the town. It is divided into many magnificent palaces, houses, and apartments of the courtiers, and comprises beautiful and long square galleries, about as large as the Exchange at Amsterdam, but one larger than another, resting on wooden pillars, from top to bottom covered with cast copper, on which are engraved the pictures of their war exploits and battles, and are kept very clean. Most palaces and the houses of the king are covered in palm leaves instead of square pieces of wood, and every roof is decorated with a small turret ending in a point, on which birds are standing, birds cast in copper with outstretched wings, cleverly made after living models. The town has thirty very straight and broad streets, every one of them about one hundred and twenty feet wide … from which branch out many side streets …

This indicates a planned city built on an enormous scale structured on a horizontal vertical grid. In colour, the buildings were terracotta red. Dapper compared the Exchange at Amsterdam with the palaces of the courtiers owing to the fact that it was the largest building in Holland.

The houses are built alongside the streets in good order [continues Dapper], the one close to the other … adorned with gables and steps, and roofs made of palm or banana leaves, or leaves from other trees; they are … usually broad with long galleries inside, especially so in the case of the houses of the nobility, and divided into many rooms which are separated by walls made of red clay, very well erected, and they can make and keep them as shiney and smooth by washing and rubbing as any wall in Holland can be made with chalk, and they are like mirrors. The upper storeys are made of the same sort of clay. Moreover, every house is provided with a well for the supply of fresh water.[136]

Benin's later history in the eighteenth and nineteenth centuries, however, show stagnation rather than cultural advance. The port of Gwatto silted up, leading to the merchants going elsewhere to trade. There were no great Obas after Orhogbua (*c.*1550-*c.*1578). Furthermore, the weaknesses of an over centralised government began to show itself in poor local representation and growing administerial corruption.[137] Even its metal art began to show a stiffness of concept and execution although the wood and ivory guild workers "maintained an extremely high artistic and technical standard right to the end".[138]

Benin history continued until 1897. In that year the British army invaded and plundered the country, exiling the Oba. The conquerors stole thousands of priceless artefacts that are still held by London institutions and private collections. Following this outrage, they burned the city. There are, however, descriptions by British writers that are worthy of discussion. Captain Richard Burton visited the Nigeria region in 1862. He was most puzzled by the architecture he witnessed because:

> It is impossible not to think that Yoruba [sic] in ancient times derived its architecture through the Romans, whose conquests in Northern Africa were as extensive as in North of Europe. We find in every house a Tuscan atrium, with a cavædium or gangway running round the rectangular impluvium, the tank or piscine, which catches the rain and drippings falling through the compluvium or central opening in the roof. Sometimes the atrium is a tetrastyle in which pillars at the four corners of the impluvium support girders or main beams of the roof.[139]

Burton further informs us that the royal palace "is supposed to contain not less that fifteen thousand souls."[140] This data corroborates both Blomert, who suggested that the palace was the same size as the Dutch city of Harlem, and another traveller called Utzheimer. Writing in 1603, Joshua Utzheimer suggested that the royal palace was "about the size of the [German] city of Tubingen".[141]

Burton was not alone in alleging Roman affinities in Benin architecture. Dr F. N. Roth, writing in the 1890s, gave the following description of a Benin house:

> The house (or compound) is about sixty by twenty-five feet ... it is furnished with a pent-roof all round. The roof ... is supported by heavy rafters, etc., much resembling the oak roofings of old houses in England. The rafters are carved, but most of them are covered with the figured brass sheetings which are so characteristic of the king's buildings, and are kept polished. The soil is banked up all round the walls to the height of about eighteen inches ... This embankment gives the centre of the house the look of a hollow, after the manner of the old Roman villas.[142]

Writing at the same time, Mr Cyril Punch noted that:

> There was usually an entrance court giving on to the street by a big door. There were two recesses ... In one were ranged the lares and penates, and the father of the household celebrated yearly [ancestral] rites in memory of his father. Through other recesses, by a door, entrance was gained to the first patio or reception room. The thatch sloped down to the centre and drained into the cistern, exactly as one sees in the houses of Pompeii. The drains were made very ingeniously.[143]

These days, scholars no longer claim Roman influence on Benin or Yoruba architecture. However, the fact that Benin City was compared to the Roman city of Pompeii does prove that they were comparable. This indicates the high standard of Benin architecture and shows that it was every bit as impressive as its art.

Kongo

As with Great Benin, much of our information on Kongo comes from reports and travelogues of European writers from the period. Professor Leo Frobenius, the pioneering German Africanist of the earlier twentieth century, wrote a splendid summary of what the earlier travellers saw five hundred years ago:

> When they arrived in the Gulf of Guinea and landed at Vaida [in West Africa] the captains were astonished to find streets well laid out, bordered on either side for several leagues by two rows of trees; for days they travelled through a country of magnificent fields, inhabited by men clad in richly coloured garments of their own weaving! Further south in the Kingdom of the Congo [sic], a swarming crowd dressed in 'silk' and 'velvet'; great States well-ordered, and down to the most minute details; powerful rulers, flourishing industries - civilized to the marrow of their bones. And the condition of the countries on the eastern coast - Mozambique, for example - was quite the same.[144]

One such report is the justly famous *History of the Kingdom of Congo* by slave trader Duarte Lopez and recorded by Filippo Pigafetta. Originally published in 1591, it has served as a basis for reconstructing Kongolese history. It is one of many useful Portuguese documents on Kongo history.[145] The Kingdom of Kongo was a flourishing state in the fifteenth century. It was situated in the region of northern Angola and western Congo. Its population was conservatively estimated at two or three million people. The country was divided into six administrative provinces and a number of dependencies. The provinces were Mbamba, Mbata, Mpangu, Mpemba, Nsundi and Soyo. The dependencies included Matari, Wando, Wembo and the province of Ambundu. All in turn were subject to the authority of the Mani Kongo (King). The capital of the country, Mbanza Kongo, was in the Mpemba province. From the province of Mbamba, the military stronghold, it was possible to put 400,000 soldiers into the field.[146]

The early history of the country is obscure, but it is believed to have been a vast empire in more exalted days. The Mani Kongo in the sixteenth century still held regal titles that alluded to these vanished glories.[147] The Mani Kongo once ruled Kongo, Loango (see page 47), Kakongo, Ngoyo, the Zaïre River region, the Ambundu, Angola, Aquisima, Musuru, Matamba, Mulilu, Musuku,

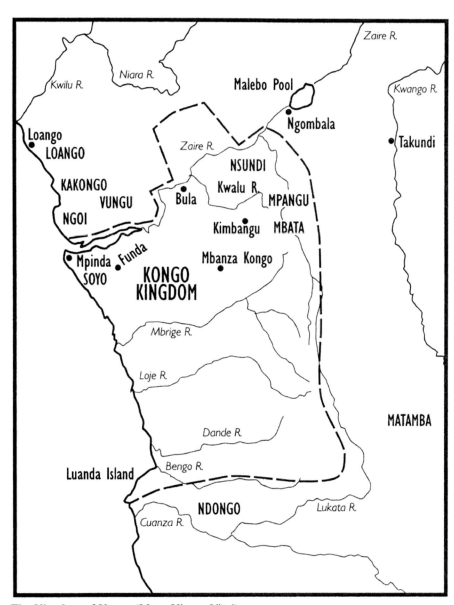

The Kingdom of Kongo (Map: Kieron Vital).

Anzico, Pangu-Alumbu, and other territories. The region covered stretches as far north as modern Gabon and as far south into Angola. In other words, the empire covered a vast region of 300,000 square kilometres. It is debatable whether one single law dominated the entire region. It is clear, however, that a single civilisation predominated. The Kikongo language is spoken the length of the coast as far north as Ogooué, from Stanley Pool to the Ocean. In the interior, it is spoken as far as the territory of the Bateke; also it is spoken as far east as the Kwango River. Throughout this large region are similar social structures, customs and religious beliefs.[148] By the late first and early second millennium period there is evidence from the region of copper mining and manufacture, iron smithing, ivory trading, and cloth manufacture - including bark and raffia textiles.[149]

The smallest political unit was the village, typically characterised by matrilineage. The head of each village seems to have been hereditary. Above the village level were the districts. Headed either by royally appointed officials or by provincial governors, they performed administrative duties and served as judges. All titleholders bore the title of *mani* (i.e. lord) followed by the name of their province, district, or their function. The government derived its income from taxation and labour. Tribute was paid in raffia cloth, ivory, hides, slaves and tolls. Brightly coloured *nzimbu* shells were the currency. These came from the island of Luanda and were typically mined and graded into size by women. Size dictated the relative value of each shell. Government income was used to grant gifts to the titleholders at court and also to the territorial rulers. The courts, royal and provincial, had officials, pages, musicians and soldiers. The taxes were paid once yearly at a ceremony in front of the king's palace. All territorial officials would come and bring their produce from their locality. They would also renew their oath of loyalty to the Mani Kongo. At this point, the king could remove incompetent officials if he so decided.[150]

In 1482 reports reached Nzinga a Kuwu, possibly the thirteenth Mani Kongo, that whales of a peculiar type had been spotted from the coast. These "whales" are thought to have been the boats of Portuguese sailors under the leadership of Diogo Cão. This marked their entry into Kongolese history. The Portuguese sailors returned in 1485 and envoys were exchanged between the two countries. The Portuguese left four Christian missionaries at the Kongo court while four Mpinda nobles accompanied Diogo Cão on his return voyage to Portugal.[151] According to Herbert Wendt, the Mpinda nobles were well treated in Portugal where they were taught Portuguese and laden with presents. They were also thoroughly questioned about their homeland. On the other hand, in the midst of the primeval forest, the Portuguese missionaries in Kongo:

> experienced a well-organized political system with taxes and rates, there was a brilliant court, [and] a great civil service. The state constructed roads, imposed tolls, supported a large army and had a monetary system - of … shells, of which the Mani Congo [sic] … had a monopoly. The Congo kingdom even had a few satellite states, for example the state of the Ngola [i.e. Ndongo] in present-day Angola. The original kingdom was about the size of France and Germany put together … [152]

In April 1491 on Cão's return, the Mani Soyo was baptised a Christian by the Portuguese missionaries. Taking the Portuguese name Dom Manuel, he had a church built in his province. Months later, the Mani Kongo received the Portuguese in Mbanza Kongo, laying on a celebration of music and dance for them. At this display, the Kongo nobles carried ironwood swords and shields. The lower orders carried bows and arrows. The King himself was seated on a throne inlaid with ivory raised on a platform. Trumpeters with instruments of ivory repeated their composition twelve times to represent the twelve generations of kings since the founding of the Kongo kingdom. During this meeting, the Mani Kongo converted to Christianity, taking the name Dom João I.[153] Mr Alan Scholefield, author of *The Dark Kingdoms,* suggests that:

> It was only then the Portuguese learnt the real reason for the quick conversion; the kingdom was on the point of civil war. Several [peoples] were rebelling against the central power and the Mani Congo [sic] was about to help his son Affonso put down the revolt. Naturally he wanted Portuguese aid. One must try to imagine the Portuguese at this moment; there were not many of them by comparison with their [B]lack hosts, they had come to this remote place to proselytise and begin a trading organization - and within a few weeks of their arrival, they were being asked to take part in a war which did not concern them in the least. But the request came from a brother in Christ and it was not possible to refuse. So, a [B]lack army marched out on to the central African field of battle under the banner of the Cross, accompanied by a number of white mercenaries carrying muskets. It is hardly surprising that they won the day and returned to the capital in triumph. In gratitude the Mani Congo settled the Portuguese in one section of the town not too far from his own palace and the two races lived in such amity that doors, it is said, were never closed and there was no need for guards. The co-existence had begun.[154]

Dr Chancellor Williams, the noted African-American social scientist, interprets the Christianisation of the Kongo as a cynical plot by the Portuguese to Europeanise the country. For example, Kongolese kings and nobles received European names on being baptised, they had their children educated in Portugal, they paid allegiance to the Roman Pope, Jesuits became counsellors to the royals, and a whole new class of people with European titles appeared such as dukes and infantes.[155] By 1512 the Portuguese *Regimento* appeared. Issued by their king, Manuel, it contained an outline for their Kongolese policy. The document begins with the assertion that all Catholic kings are brothers. It therefore follows that Manuel will help his brother, the king of Kongo, build Christianity in the kingdom. Moreover, the Portuguese ambassador is to act as an advisor to the Kongolese king in reforming the Kongo court along Christian lines. In particular, the Kongolese should receive European titles, carry European emblems and adopt Portuguese courtly etiquette. In addition, the

Kongolese should pay for the Christianisation programme by exporting copper, ivory, and slaves to Portugal. Finally, the ambassador should find out all that he could about the politics and geography of Kongo.[156] Dr Williams wrote an incisive analysis of the document:

> This is one of the most interesting and significant documents in the history of [B]lack people because it was the first detailed blue print for the conquest of the [B]lack man's mind (acculturation via Christianity), his body (slavery), and his country. This historic document, however, was couched in all the endearing words and phraseology of equality and brotherly love … [157]

Despite these negative undercurrents, the Portuguese sources give a bright picture of Kongo life. From them, we learn that the capital city, San Salvador (i.e. Mbanza Kongo), was advantageously situated on the highest mountain in the country. This offered a natural defence and gave a panoramic view of the kingdom.[158] Pigafetta gave its population as over 100,000 people. The king, Dom João I (i.e. Nzinga a Kuwu), raised thick walls, one mile in circumference around his palace and the royal houses. An area of similar size was reserved for the Portuguese and was also walled. The doors of the aristocratic homes faced the walls of the church, as did the homes of the Portuguese. Outside of the enclosures stood numerous buildings that belonged to various lords. Apparently it was not possible to determine the size of the town because all of the countryside was filled with palaces and rural houses. The habitation of each lord was a walled village.[159] Another source adds that the royal enclosure had several gates guarded by soldiers and trumpeters.[160] One source gives the population of Mbanza Soyo, the capital of the Soyo province, as 30,000 people.[161]

An abundance and variety of agricultural products were grown in Kongo. There were crops of bananas, cauliflower, coconuts, cola, citrus fruits, cucumber, palms of various varieties - including date palms, pineapples, plantains, rice, watermelons, yams, and many others. Other grains were imported from Egypt by an overland route. In addition, other agricultural produce of American origin were imported via the Portuguese. Built on their agricultural industries, the Kongolese produced oil, wine, vinegar and bread. From wild palms they made mats, baskets and other articles of everyday use.[162] Furthermore, their houses were typically made of tightly interlaced palm branches, divided into convenient rooms and were thatched. The impression conveyed by these buildings was more akin to that of weaving or basket making than of building in the traditional sense. The Kikongo word *tunga* means to build and to weave. Ornamental wooden palisades surrounded these habitations. Mats covered the floors.[163]

The most revered profession in Kongo was that of the ironsmith. They typically forged knives, weapons, axes and hoes. Moreover, they forged copper

DE RIEVIERE LELUNDA.

Kongo (Angola). View of the Kongolese capital city of Mbanza Kongo. Pigafetta gave its population as over 100,000 souls. Originally published in Olfert Dapper, *Description de l'Afrique,* 1668.

products and made bracelets using the celebrated lost wax technique.[164] Georges Balandier, author of the scholarly *Daily Life in the Kingdom of the Kongo,* made the following comment on the state of Kongo metallurgy:

> There is no doubting … the existence of an expert metallurgical art in the ancient Kongo; only the competition of objects from abroad and the slow deterioration brought about its decline. A further proof is provided by recent ethnographic documents. The Bakongo were aware of the toxicity of lead vapours. They devised preventative and curative methods, both pharmacological (massive doses of pawpaw and palm oil) and mechanical (exerting of pressure to free the digestive tract), for combatting lead poisoning. Technology and rational knowledge tried to keep in step.[165]

The European writers of the period, Pigafetta, Dapper and Ogilby, inform us of the delicate crafts of the peoples living in eastern Kongo and adjacent regions. They manufactured various textiles including, damasks, sarcenets, satins, taffeta, cloth of tissue and velvet - cut and uncut. They made the yarn from the leaves of palm trees from which threads of an extreme fineness and evenness were drawn. The products were light and waterproof. Professor DeGraft-Johnson made the curious observation that: "Their brocades, both high and low, were far more valuable than the Italian".[166] For comparison, we note that Italian brocade gained an important reputation in the fifteenth century. One reliable source informs us that during that century: "Leading Florentine merchants readily spent as much on a single outfit as on a large town-house; a set of brocade wall hangings could cost more than a country estate".[167] Although referring to an earlier century, this places Kongolese textiles within a context. Some of the Kongo treasures are still to be found in European museums. Professor Frobenius highlighted the importance of these collections:

> And what they told [says Frobenius] - those old captains, those chiefs of expeditions, the D'Elbées, the De Marchais, the Pigafettas, and all the others, what they told is true. It can be verified. In the old royal Kunstkammer of Dresden, in the Weydmann collection of Ulm, in many another European "curiosity cabinets" one still finds collections of objects from West Africa dating from that epoch: wonderful plush-velvets, of an extreme softness, made from the tenderest leaves of a certain banana tree; stuffs, soft and pliant, brilliant and delicate as silks, woven with well prepared raffia fibre, ceremonial javelins - their blades to the very points inlaid with the finest copper, bows so graceful, and ornamented so beautifully that they would do honour to any museum of arms whatsoever; calabashes decorated with the most perfect taste; sculpture in ivory and wood, the workmanship of which reveals skill and style.[168]

Dom João I died in 1506. His loyalty to the religion of the Portuguese, however, seems to have been merely opportunistic. Mr Scholefield narrates that:

> He had, in many ways, been a disappointment to the Portuguese. Quite soon after he had been baptized it became clear that he had become a Christian for reasons of state and that he had returned to [tradition] ... Traditional elements among the [B]lack nobility had never been happy about his baptism and spoke darkly of ancestors betrayed, of sorcery and vengeance. But what hastened John's [i.e. João's] apostasy was the uncompromising attitude of the Portuguese towards his marriages. They saw them as unchristian and tried to bring pressure on him to reject all his wives save one. What they did not realize was that the Mani Congo [sic] took on wives for precisely the same diplomatic reasons as European royalty: they represented power blocs. By many careful marriages the Mani Congo was able to make his position virtually unassailable. When the Portuguese remained intractably moral the Mani Congo reacted: he rejected their religion. About 1495 most of the missionaries and with them the [B]lack nobles who had been converted were obliged to leave the City of Congo.[169]

Dom Affonso I, a Christianised son, succeeded him. He was, however, met with vigorous opposition from his non-Christian brother Mpanzu a Kitima. Prince Mpanzu occupied the capital with the support of the Mani Kabunga, the traditional priest, and forces of nearly 200,000 men. They viewed the Christian

Kongo (Angola). The King of Kongo receiving European Ambassadors. This scene may represent an event that took place in 1642 when the Dutch arrived in Kongo. The King, however, was probably Garcia II and not Dom Alvaro. Incidentally, chandeliers were also reported to have hung from the ceiling of the Munhumutapan palace as well (see page 523). Originally published in Olfert Dapper, *Description de l'Afrique*, 1668.

influence as a threat to their power. Affonso, however, triumphed over Mpanzu in battle in spite of the fact that he had inferior numbers of perhaps 10,000 soldiers and 100 Christians, both Kongolese and Portuguese. Affonso attributed his victory to a religious miracle and thus strengthened his desire to spread Christianity in the land. After the battle, Affonso executed his brother but converted the Mani Kabunga. He gave the latter the position of Keeper of the Holy Water. Years later, he built the Church of the Holy Cross to commemorate the miracle.

Affonso I wrote to King Manuel of Portugal requesting that he send priests and technicians to spread Christianity further. Within three years, schools were established in which students were instructed in Portuguese and Christianity.[170] Furthermore, Affonso increased the flow of Kongo students to Portugal and he himself studied Portuguese laws. The Portuguese sent him a collection of these in five great volumes. His aim seems to have been the creation of a Renaissance style Christian state as then existed in Europe.[171] His achievements went beyond this, however. Dr Ehret reports that: "A local body of scribes was trained, able eventually to communicate in written Latin, Portuguese, and Kikongo".[172] By 1516, one source reports that the capital had one thousand students studying grammar, humanities and things of the faith. There were also schools for girls directed by the sister of the king. Finally, Affonso built churches. As well as the Church of the Holy Cross built in 1517, he built the Church of Our Lady of the Victories in 1526. By the close of the century, the capital had six churches.[173]

The relationship between Kongo and Portugal, however, eventually soured. In 1508 the first slaves from Kongo were sent as presents to King Manuel to pay for the Christianisation programme. The Portuguese workers sent to Kongo, in return, failed to deliver on the work that was agreed. In addition their shabby and arrogant conduct was a cause for concern. Nor was it long before their enslaving activities and abuses of Kongolese women got out of hand. Dr Williams wrote:

> The Portuguese Christianization of the Kongo created something more than chaos. It was a revolting mess, no matter from what angle it was viewed. To begin with, priests were not only among the leading slave traders, but they also owned slave ships to carry the "black cargoes" to distant lands. Priests also had their harems of [B]lack girls, some having as many as twenty each ... One of the main attractions that drew thousands of [W]hite men was their unlimited sexual freedom with all the [B]lack girls and women who were enslaved and helpless in the power of their masters. These "wholesale raids" on [B]lack womanhood continued to swell the mulatto population, the majority of which, as in the case of Egypt and the Sudan, became the faithful servants and loyal representatives of the conquering races to which their fathers belonged.[174]

These abuses prompted a series of letters from Affonso I to the Portuguese court. Mr Scholefield adds: "More than twenty of Affonso's letters to King Manuel and his successor, King John III, survive, and very bleak reading they make."[175] One such letter was dated 6 June 1526: "There are many traders in all corners of the country [wrote Affonso I]. They bring ruin to the country. Every day people are enslaved and kidnapped, even nobles, even members of the king's own family". The pleas fell on deaf ears and enslaving continued. Moreover, Affonso sent a gift of silver to Portugal in the 1520's. This convinced the Portuguese that silver mines existed within Kongo territory despite Affonso's assertions to the contrary. The Portuguese further believed that Kongo had an indigenous source of gold. These beliefs led Portugal to continue their actions in the region.[176] Professor Jan Vansina, the highly important authority on Kongo, comments that:

> Affonso's reign set a pattern in Kongo history for more than a century to come. The slave trade, the quest for mines, the Portuguese factions, and the half-

hearted efforts towards educating and converting the Kongolese would continue practically unchanged until the 1640's. Yet Kongo oral tradition sees Affonso as its greatest king.[177]

Dom Pedro I became the next ruler in 1545. Although supported by the local Portuguese, the people of the capital revolted and placed Diogo I on the throne in his place.[178] Of Diogo, DeGraft-Johnson says: "He was fond of valuable cloths of gold, tapestry, silk and lordly furniture".[179] A major crisis ensued in 1556, however. War broke out between slave dealing factions supported by the vassal king of Ndongo, to the south, against the Kongolese king's forces. Both sides were aided and abetted by rival Portuguese parties. The Ndongo and the slave dealers triumphed and their country became independent of Kongo overlordship.[180]

A second problem emerged for Kongo in 1569 during the reign of Dom Alvaro II, a successor. The Jaga, a semi-barbarian horde, invaded from lands to the east. They triggered a sudden and unprecedented collapse of social order in Kongo. Moreover they were slave traders. A famine and a six-year economic breakdown ensued. With the help of some of the Portuguese, Kongo expelled this element.[181] The Portuguese had other ideas, however. Beginning in 1575 and lasting for over a century, they launched a series of wars to capture Ndongo. Apparently they thought the country contained silver mines.[182] Kongo made some sort of recovery during this period. It entered the seventeenth century with its institutions and most of its infrastructure intact. In addition, it developed a newly created messenger system using runners. Marathoners were established at different posts along the main communication routes to quickly relay the messages from the capital and court to the distant provinces.[183]

In Ndongo, however, things were not going terribly well. After 1608, the Portuguese army commander-in-chief instituted a new policy of repression. Bento Cardoso devised a system where every Ndongo notable would be owned by a Portuguese official and was responsible for delivering a certain quantity of slaves to the Portuguese. Should the Ndongo notable fail therein, he too would be enslaved. Over a hundred notables were enslaved in a single year. Moreover, the Portuguese killed a further one hundred. Even the ruler of Ndongo, himself a slave trader, resisted the aggression. War dragged on for years but the Portuguese were forced to sue for peace.

In 1622 Ann Nzinga, the Ndongo royal sister, attended a peace conference with the Portuguese convened in the coastal city of Luanda. She demanded (1) that the Portuguese evacuate Kabasa, the Ndongo capital; (2) that the Portuguese wage war on the Jaga; (3) all Ndongo notables who had become vassals of the Portuguese must return to their former loyalty to the Ndongo crown. In return, Nzinga promised to hand over Portuguese prisoners of war. The provisions of the treaty were designed to end all fighting in the region, but

Ndongo (Angola). Ngola Ann Nzinga (ruled 1623-1663).

alas the Portuguese breached it almost immediately by invading Kongo. The following year, Ann Nzinga officially became the Ngola (which means King) (sic), and in this capacity made the regional alliances necessary to fight the Portuguese. She even made common cause with the Jaga. Ndongo was declared a free country the following year. All slaves entering the country were legally declared to be free. By 1629 her forces and allies captured Matamba, the neighbouring state to the east. Incidentally, this state had a tradition of being ruled by females. This too was declared a free country. In 1641 Garcia II, a vigorous king, emerged in Kongo. He made alliances with the Dutch (see also page 349) to fight Portuguese aggression. His death in 1661 ended the great era of Kongolese culture. In Ndongo, the death of Nzinga in 1663 marked a turning point. Her extraordinary and brilliant reign only delayed the inevitable.[184]

Towards the end of the seventeenth century, both Kongo, and the combined states of Ndongo and Matamba fell victim to European predator activities where "executions, treachery, robbery, and violence became the order of the day."[185] Before winding up this chapter, we note that one scholar, Professor W. E. B. DuBois, described the West African coastal culture in language far more glowing than we have. We give him the final word:

> Of all this West African cultural development our knowledge is fragmentary and incomplete, jumbled up with the African slave trade ... Nearly all has disappeared in the frantic effort to paint Negroes as apes fit only for slavery and then to forget the whole discreditable episode, wipe it out of history, and emphasize the glory and philanthropy of Europe ... Yet on the West Coast was perhaps the greatest attempt in human history before the twentieth century to build a culture based on peace and beauty, to establish a communism of industry and of distribution of goods and services according to human need. It was crucified by greed, and its very memory blasphemed by the modern historical method. There can be no doubt but that the level of culture among the masses of Negroes in West Africa in the fifteenth century was higher than that of northern Europe, by any standard of measurement - homes, clothes, artistic creation and appreciation, political organisation and religious consistency.[186]

Notes

1 Bernard de Grunne, *The Birth of Art in Black Africa,* France and Luxembourg, Adam Biro & Banque Generale du Luxembourg, 1998, p.15.
2 Werner Gillon, *A Short History of African Art,* UK, Penguin, 1984, p.75.
3 Ekpo Eyo and Frank Willett, *Treasures of Ancient Nigeria,* UK, William Collins & Sons, 1980, pp.3-4.
4 Bernard de Grunne, *The Birth of Art in Black Africa,* p.15.
5 Ibid., p.21.

[6] Francine Maurer and Olivier Langevin, *Dating of Ancient Civilizations from Nigeria,* in Bernard de Grunne, *The Birth of Art in Black Africa,* France and Luxembourg, Adam Biro & Banque Generale du Luxembourg, 1998, p.114.

[7] Bernard de Grunne, *The Birth of Art in Black Africa,* p.20.

[8] Francine Maurer and Olivier Langevin, *Dating of Ancient Civilizations from Nigeria,* in *The Birth of Art in Black Africa,* p.114.

[9] Ekpo Eyo and Frank Willett, *Treasures of Ancient Nigeria,* p.7.

[10] Bernard de Grunne, *The Birth of Art in Black Africa,* pp.26-28 and 90-97.

[11] Bernard Fagg, *Nok Terracottas,* UK & Nigeria, Ethnographica and The National Commission for Museums and Monuments, 1990, p.27

[12] Bernard de Grunne, *The Birth of Art in Black Africa,* pp.26-28 and 90-97.

[13] He is using the short chronology.

[14] Ibid., p.22.

[15] Titi Euba, *Dress,* in *The Living Culture of Nigeria,* ed Saburi O. Biobaku, Nigeria, Thomas Nelson & Sons, 1976, p.29.

[16] Bernard de Grunne, *The Birth of Art in Black Africa,* pp.28-9.

[17] Ekpo Eyo and Frank Willett, *Treasures of Ancient Nigeria,* p.27.

[18] Ibid., p.28.

[19] Ekpo Eyo, *Sculpture,* in *The Living Culture of Nigeria,* ed Saburi O. Biobaku, Nigeria, Thomas Nelson & Sons, 1976, p.12.

[20] Bernard de Grunne, *The Birth of Art in Black Africa,* p.24.

[21] Ibid.

[22] Ekpo Eyo and Frank Willett, *Treasures of Ancient Nigeria,* p.6.

[23] J. Desmond Clark, *The Spread of Food Production in Sub-Saharan Africa,* in *Papers in African Prehistory,* ed J. D. Fage & R. A. Oliver, UK, Cambridge University Press, 1970, pp.29-30.

[24] See Bernard de Grunne, *The Birth of Art in Black Africa,* p.50.

[25] Titi Euba, *Dress,* in *The Living Culture of Nigeria,* p.29.

[26] Fred Anozie, *Metal Technology in Precolonial Nigeria,* in *African Systems of Science, Technology & Art,* ed Gloria Thomas-Emeagwali, UK, Karnak House, 1993, p.84.

[27] Ibid., p.92.

[28] Ekpo Eyo, *Two Thousand Years of Nigerian Art,* UK & Nigeria, Ethnographica and The National Commission for Museums and Monuments, 1977, pp.52-4.

[29] Charles S. Finch, *The Star of Deep Beginnings,* US, Khenti, 1998, p.36.

[30] Bernard de Grunne, *The Birth of Art in Black Africa,* p.20.

[31] Ibid., pp.23-6.

[32] Ibid., p.26.

[33] Ekpo Eyo and Frank Willett, *Treasures of Ancient Nigeria,* p.7 and Ekpo Eyo, *Two Thousand Years of Nigerian Art,* p.72.

[34] Ekpo Eyo and Frank Willett, *Treasures of Ancient Nigeria,* pp.8-9.

[35] Laure Meyer, *Art and Craft in Africa,* France, Éditions Pierre Terrail, 1995, p.55.

[36] Ekpo Eyo, *Two Thousand Years of Nigerian Art,* pp.80-2.

[37] Peter Garlake, *The Kingdoms of Africa,* UK, Elsevier-Phaidon, 1978, pp.134-5.

[38] Ekpo Eyo and Frank Willett, *Treasures of Ancient Nigeria,* pp.9, 30-2, 66-86 and Ekpo Eyo, *Two Thousand Years of Nigerian Art,* pp.40 and 74.

[39] Ekpo Eyo and Frank Willett, *Treasures of Ancient Nigeria,* p.87.

[40] Herbert M. Cole, *The Lower Niger,* in *A History of Art in Africa,* by Monica Blackmun Visonà et al, UK, Thames and Hudson, 2000, p.276.

[41] Charles S. Finch, *The Star of Deep Beginnings,* p.32.

[42] Ibid., p.30.

[43] Ibid., pp.29-30.

[44] Ibid., p.29.

[45] Ekpo Eyo, *Two Thousand Years of Nigerian Art,* pp.76-8.

[46] Werner Gillon, *A Short History of African Art,* p.165.

[47] Ekpo Eyo, *Sculpture,* in *The Living Culture of Nigeria,* p.13.

[48] Ekpo Eyo and Frank Willett, *Treasures of Ancient Nigeria,* pp.9-10 and 29.

[49] Herbert M. Cole, *The Lower Niger,* in *A History of Art in Africa,* p.276.

[50] Ekpo Eyo and Frank Willett, *Treasures of Ancient Nigeria,* p.10.

[51] Ekpo Eyo, *Two Thousand Years of Nigerian Art,* p.88.

[52] Ekpo Eyo and Frank Willett, *Treasures of Ancient Nigeria,* 29.

[53] Fred Anozie, *Metal Technology in Precolonial Nigeria,* in *African Systems of Science, Technology & Art,* p.90.

[54] David Northrup, *The Growth of Trade among the Igbo before 1800,* in *Journal of African History, Volume XIII: No.2,* ed J. D. Fage et al, UK, Cambridge University Press, 1972, pp.217-9.

[55] Cheikh Anta Diop, *The African Origin of Civilization: Myth or Reality?* US, Lawrence Hill, 1974, p.158.

[56] Herbert Wendt, *It Began in Babel,* UK, Weidenfield and Nicholson, 1963, pp.213-4.

[57] Leo Frobenius, *The Voice of Africa: Volume I,* UK, Hutchinson & Co., 1913, p.345.

[58] Peter Garlake, *The Kingdoms of Africa,* p.39.

[59] Alastair Service, *Lost Worlds,* UK, Collins, 1981, p.137.

[60] Roland Oliver and Brian Fagan, *Africa in the Iron Age,* UK, Cambridge University Press, 1975, p.187.

[61] William Fagg ed, *The Living Arts of Nigeria,* UK, Studio Vista, 1971, *On Beads and Beadwork* (there are no page numbers in this book).

[62] Frank Willett, *Ife and its Archaeology,* in *Papers in African Prehistory,* ed J. D. Fage & R. A. Oliver, UK, Cambridge University Press, 1970, p.310.

[63] Alastair Service, *Lost Worlds,* p.137.

[64] Ibidem and Claudia Zaslavsky, *Africa Counts,* US, Lawrence Hill Books, 1973, p.201.

[65] Quoted in J. A. Atanda, *An Introduction to Yoruba History,* UK, Ibadan University Press, 1980, p.26.

[66] Titi Euba, *Dress,* in *The Living Culture of Nigeria,* pp.29-30.

[67] Alastair Service, *Lost Worlds,* p.137.

[68] Quoted in Cheikh Anta Diop, *Precolonial Black Africa,* US, Lawrence Hill, 1997, p.203.

[69] Peter Garlake, *The Kingdoms of Africa,* p.136.

[70] Ekpo Eyo and Frank Willett, *Treasures of Ancient Nigeria,* p.10.

[71] Nwanna Nzewunwa, *Prehistoric Pavements in West Africa,* in *West African Journal of Archaeology: Volume 19,* ed Bassey W. Andah and Ikechukwu Okpoko, Nigeria, Association Quest Africaine d'Archaeologie, 1989, pp.93-100.

[72] Peter Garlake, *The Kingdoms of Africa,* p.132.

[73] Leo Frobenius, *The Voice of Africa: Volume I,* p.348.

[74] David Kelley quoted in Ivan Van Sertima, *Early America Revisited,* US, Transaction Publishers, 1998, p.7.

[75] Robin Polynor, *The Yoruba and the Fon,* in *A History of Art in Africa,* by Monica Blackmun Visonà et al, UK, Thames and Hudson, 2000, p.229.

[76] Rev. Samuel Johnson, *The History of the Yorubas,* Nigeria, CSS Bookshops, 1921, p.6.

[77] Robin Polynor, *The Yoruba and the Fon*, in *A History of Art in Africa*, p.229.

[78] Rev. Samuel Johnson, *The History of the Yorubas*, p.6.

[79] Basil Davidson, *A History of West Africa 1000-1800*, UK, Longmans, 1977, p.120.

[80] Claudia Zaslavsky, *Africa Counts*, p.201.

[81] J. A. Atanda, *An Introduction to Yoruba History*, p.9.

[82] Ibid., p.25.

[83] Ibid., pp.10-1.

[84] Ibid., pp.27-8.

[85] Susan Denyer, *African Traditional Architecture*, UK, Heinemann, 1978, p.56.

[86] Basil Davidson, *A History of West Africa 1000-1800*, p.124.

[87] Charles S. Finch, *The Star of Deep Beginnings*, p.33.

[88] Frank Willett, *Ife and its Archaeology*, in *Papers in African Prehistory*, p.311

[89] Werner Gillon, *A Short History of African Art*, p.184.

[90] Affonso d'Alveiro quoted in Herbert Wendt, *It Began in Babel*, UK, Weidenfeld and Nicholson, 1963, pp.212-3.

[91] G. T. Stride & Caroline Ifeka, *Peoples and Empires of West Africa*, UK, Thomas Nelson and Sons, 1971, pp.311-3.

[92] Jacob Egharevba, *A Short History of Benin*, Nigeria, Ibadan University Press, 1968, p.1 and Rosemary Righter, *Great wonders from the wild heart of Africa*, in *The Times*, UK, 26 January 2002, p.21.

[93] Jacob Egharevba, *A Short History of Benin*, p.2.

[94] Ibid., pp.5-8 and Suzanne Preston Blier, *Royal Arts of Africa*, UK, Lawrence King, 1998, p.50.

[95] Suzanne Preston Blier, *Royal Arts of Africa*, p.50.

[96] G. T. Stride & Caroline Ifeka, *Peoples and Empires of West Africa*, p.310.

[97] Roland Oliver and Anthony Atmore, *Medieval Africa 1250 - 1800*, UK, Cambridge, 2001, p.89

[98] Werner Gillon, *A Short History of African Art*, p.253 and Ekpo Eyo, *Two Thousand Years of Nigerian Art*, pp.134-6.

[99] G. T. Stride & Caroline Ifeka, *Peoples and Empires of West Africa*, p.310.

[100] Suzanne Preston Blier, *Royal Arts of Africa*, p.50.

[101] G. T. Stride & Caroline Ifeka, *Peoples and Empires of West Africa*, pp.310-1.

[102] Jacob Egharevba, *A Short History of Benin*, p.10.

[103] Roland Oliver and Anthony Atmore, *Medieval Africa 1250 - 1800*, p.89 and G. T. Stride & Caroline Ifeka, *Peoples and Empires of West Africa*, pp.312-3.

[104] G. T. Stride & Caroline Ifeka, *Peoples and Empires of West Africa*, p.313.

[105] Cheikh Anta Diop, *Precolonial Black Africa*, p.204.

[106] Jacob Egharevba, *A Short History of Benin*, pp.2, 13-4, 83 and 90.

[107] Suzanne Preston Blier, *Royal Arts of Africa*, pp.50-1.

[108] Peter Garlake, *Great Zimbabwe Described and Explained*, Zimbabwe, Zimbabwe Publishing House, 1985, p.5.

[109] Roland Oliver and Anthony Atmore, *Medieval Africa 1250 - 1800*, p.91.

[110] Norris & Ross McWhirter, *Guinness Book of Records, 21st Edition*, UK, Guinness Superlatives Limited, October 1974, p.129.

[111] Jacob Egharevba, *A Short History of Benin*, p.1.

[112] Suzanne Preston Blier, *Royal Arts of Africa*, p.48.

[113] Jacob Egharevba, *A Short History of Benin*, p.11.

[114] Ibid., p.17.

[115] G. T. Stride & Caroline Ifeka, *Peoples and Empires of West Africa*, pp.313-4.

[116] Quoted in Basil Davidson, *Old Africa Rediscovered*, UK, Victor Gollanz, 1965, p.124.

[117] Basil Davidson, *African Kingdoms*, Netherlands, Time-Life Books, 1967, p.102.

[118] G. T. Stride & Caroline Ifeka, *Peoples and Empires of West Africa*, p.315.

[119] Ibid., pp.306-7 and 315-6, Basil Davidson, *Africa in History*, UK, Macmillan, 1991, p.78 and Jacob Egharevba, *A Short History of Benin*, p.11.

[120] Werner Gillon, *A Short History of African Art*, pp.30-2.

[121] G. T. Stride & Caroline Ifeka, *Peoples and Empires of West Africa*, p.159.

[122] Quoted in Suzanne Preston Blier, *Royal Arts of Africa*, p.51.

[123] Suzanne Preston Blier, *Royal Arts of Africa*, p.48.

[124] Quoted in *The Economist*, UK, 24 December 1994 - 6 January 1995, p.123.

[125] Quoted in Roland Oliver and Anthony Atmore, *Medieval Africa 1250 - 1800*, p.91.

[126] G. T. Stride & Caroline Ifeka, *Peoples and Empires of West Africa*, p.315 and Suzanne Preston Blier, *Royal Arts of Africa*, p.66.

[127] G. T. Stride & Caroline Ifeka, *Peoples and Empires of West Africa*, p.315 and Jacob Egharevba, *A Short History of Benin*, p.27.

[128] G. T. Stride & Caroline Ifeka, *Peoples and Empires of West Africa*, p.315.

[129] Quoted in H. Ling Roth, *Great Benin: Its Customs, Art and Horrors*, UK, F. King and Sons, 1903, p.132.

[130] Quoted in ibid., p.131.

[131] Jacob Egharevba, *A Short History of Benin*, p.31.

[132] H. Ling Roth, *Great Benin: Its Customs, Art and Horrors*, p.133.

[133] Quoted in ibid., p.143.

[134] G. T. Stride & Caroline Ifeka, *Peoples and Empires of West Africa*, pp.316-7.

[135] A Dutch mile is four times the length of an English mile.

[136] Quoted in H. Ling Roth, *Great Benin: Its Customs, Art and Horrors*, pp.160-1.

[137] G. T. Stride & Caroline Ifeka, *Peoples and Empires of West Africa*, pp.318-9.

[138] Werner Gillon, *A Short History of African Art*, p.268.

[139] Quoted in H. Ling Roth, *Great Benin: Its Customs, Art and Horrors*, p.167.

[140] Ibid., p.169. See also Susan Denyer, *African Traditional Architecture*, p.56.

[141] Quoted in Basil Davidson ed, *African Civilization Revisited*, US, Africa World Press, 1991, p.235.

[142] Quoted in H. Ling Roth, *Great Benin: Its Customs, Art and Horrors*, p.177.

[143] Quoted in ibid., p.187.

[144] Leo Frobenius, *Histoire de la Civilisation Africaine*, quoted in Anna Melissa Graves, *Africa, the Wonder and the Glory*, US, Black Classic Press, (originally 1942), p.4.

[145] J. C. DeGraft-Johnson, *African Glory*, UK, Watts & Co., 1954, p.134.

[146] Georges Balandier, *Daily Life in the Kingdom of the Kongo*, UK, George Allen & Unwin Ltd., 1968, pp.29-30 and J. C. DeGraft-Johnson, *African Glory*, p.135.

[147] J. C. DeGraft-Johnson, *African Glory*, p.135.

[148] Georges Balandier, *Daily Life in the Kingdom of the Kongo*, pp.29-30.

[149] Christopher Ehret, *The Civilizations of Africa*, UK, James Currey, 2002, p.269.

[150] Jan Vansina, *Kingdoms of the Savanna*, US, University of Wisconsin Press, 1966, pp.41-4. See also Alan Scholefield, *The Dark Kingdoms*, UK, Heinemann, 1975, pp.31-2.

[151] Jan Vansina, *Kingdoms of the Savanna*, p.45.

[152] Herbert Wendt, *It Began in Babel*, p.211.

[153] Georges Balandier, *Daily Life in the Kingdom of the Kongo*, pp.43-5, J. C. DeGraft-Johnson, *African Glory*, p.136, Alan Scholefield, *The Dark Kingdoms*, p.12 and Suzanne Preston Blier, *Royal Arts of Africa*, p.211.

[154] Alan Scholefield, *The Dark Kingdoms,* p.13.
[155] Chancellor Williams, *The Destruction of Black Civilization,* US, Third World Press, 1987, pp.246-9.
[156] Jan Vansina, *Kingdoms of the Savanna,* pp.48-9.
[157] Chancellor Williams, *The Destruction of Black Civilization,* p.251.
[158] Georges Balandier, *Daily Life in the Kingdom of the Kongo,* pp.30-1.
[159] See ibid., pp.146-7 and 151.
[160] Alan Scholefield, *The Dark Kingdoms,* p.12.
[161] Georges Balandier, *Daily Life in the Kingdom of the Kongo,* p.147.
[162] Ibid., pp.89-94 and J. C. DeGraft-Johnson, *African Glory,* pp.135-6.
[163] Georges Balandier, *Daily Life in the Kingdom of the Kongo,* pp.140-3 and 151, J. C. DeGraft-Johnson, *African Glory,* p.136 and Suzanne Preston Blier, *Royal Arts of Africa,* p.204.
[164] Georges Balandier, *Daily Life in the Kingdom of the Kongo,* pp.107-12.
[165] Ibid., pp.112-3.
[166] J. C. DeGraft-Johnson, *African Glory,* p.139. See also Suzanne Preston Blier, *Royal Arts of Africa,* p.216.
[167] Anthony Coleman ed, *Millennium: A Thousand Years of History,* UK, Bantam Press, 1999, p.126.
[168] Leo Frobenius, *Histoire de la Civilisation Africaine,* quoted in Anna Melissa Graves, *Africa, the Wonder and the Glory,* pp.4-5.
[169] Alan Scholefield, *The Dark Kingdoms,* p.18.
[170] Georges Balandier, *Daily Life in the Kingdom of the Kongo,* pp.48-56, J. C. DeGraft-Johnson, *African Glory,* p.137 and Jan Vansina, *Kingdoms of the Savanna,* pp.46-7.
[171] Roland Oliver and Anthony Atmore, *Medieval Africa: 1250-1800,* p.170.
[172] Christopher Ehret, *The Civilizations of Africa,* p.365.
[173] Alan Scholefield, *The Dark Kingdoms,* pp.22-3.
[174] Chancellor Williams, *The Destruction of Black Civilization,* p.253.
[175] Alan Scholefield, *The Dark Kingdoms,* p.27.
[176] See Jan Vansina, *Kingdoms of the Savanna,* pp.47-54.
[177] Ibid., p.57.
[178] Ibid.
[179] J. C. DeGraft-Johnson, *African Glory,* p.137.
[180] Chancellor Williams, *The Destruction of Black Civilization,* pp.258-60.
[181] Christopher Ehret, *The Civilizations of Africa,* pp.359-360.
[182] Basil Davidson, *Africa in History,* p.158.
[183] Christopher Ehret, *The Civilizations of Africa,* pp.365 and 367.
[184] Chancellor Williams, *The Destruction of Black Civilization,* pp.260-72 and Christopher Ehret, *The Civilizations of Africa,* p.368.
[185] J. C. DeGraft-Johnson, *African Glory,* p.143.
[186] W. E. B. DuBois, *The World and Africa,* US, International Publishers, 1965, pp.162-3.

CHAPTER TWELVE: WEST AFRICA'S GOLDEN AGE

Ancient Ghana

A Golden Age existed in West Africa dating from an early period. Ancient Ghana was situated in today's Mali and southern Mauritania region between the Senegal and Niger rivers. By the eleventh century, at the height of its power, the empire also included parts of Senegal and Guinea.[1] The capital was Kumbi-Saleh, but Nema, Walata, and Audoghast were important cities in the region.[2] The Soninkes were the main people that dominated this culture for most of its history, but there is some controversy here. The first kings of Ghana ruled from around 300 AD. One African scholar of the seventeenth century, As-Sadi, identified these early kings as relatively light complexioned Berbers.[3] Another African historian, Kati, discusses different theories of the origins of these early kings. He favours the view that they were Sanhaja Berbers and affirms that the early kings ruled from Qunbi (identified as Kumbi-Saleh).[4] The following statement by Kati indicates the antiquity of this city:

> I understand, on trustworthy evidence … that the Kaya-Magha were among the most ancient of rulers, of whom 20 reigned before the manifestation of the Prophet [Mahomet - He lived in the sixth century AD]. The name of his capital was Qunbi which was an important city. Their dynasty came to an end during the first century of the hijra.[5]

Modern scholars such as Professor Nehemia Levtzion and Professor J. S. Trimingham take a different view concerning the identity of these early dynasts. They favour the view that these rulers were Soninkes or some other dark-complexioned non-Berber people.[6] Returning to Mahmud Kati once more:

> One of the elders told me that the last of them [the Kaya-Magha Dynasty] was Kanisa'ay, who reigned at the time of the Prophet. He had a town called Kurunka, which was the residence of his mother. It is still inhabited. It is said that he had a thousand horses tied up at his residence … Then Allah brought their rule to an end. He gave the most ignoble of their people power over their nobles. They killed all the children of their kings, even ripping open the women to kill those in the womb.[7]

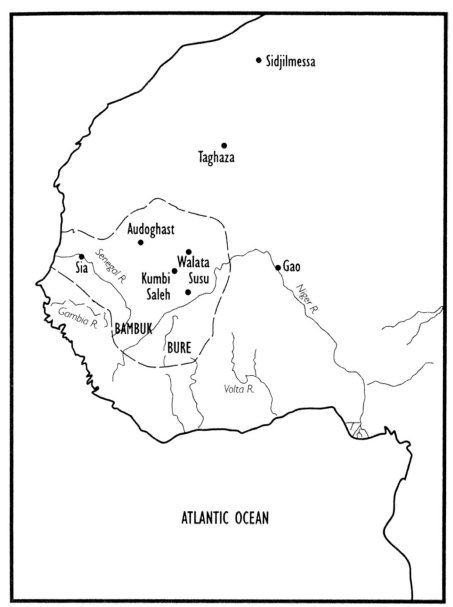

The Empire of Ancient Ghana. (Map: Kieron Vital). This was the first great empire in this part of Africa. Beginning as a kingdom in about 300 AD, it evolved into an empire in about 700 AD. The map shows the empire at its height in the eleventh century AD.

Professor Cheikh Anta Diop interprets this seventh century revolution as the overthrow of a "corrupt dynasty" by the masses.[8] Other scholars, such as Drs Davidson, Levtzion, and Oliver, fail to comment on this issue in their respective works but it seems clear that they would not differ significantly from this interpretation. Scholars following the lead given by Kati and As-Sadi, such as Daniel Chu and Elliott Skinner, interpret the revolution as the violent overthrow of the Sanhaja Berbers by the Soninke.

Following As-Sadi and Kati, it was thought that Ghanaian history began about 300 AD. At that time the capital city was founded and the first rulers took the dynastic title of Ghana (i.e. King) or Kaya Magha (i.e. King of Gold). According to Laure Meyer, author of two popular works on African arts and crafts, gold mines were opened in the region of Buré during this early period.[9] Even before 300 AD, however, other things were happening. Archaeological campaigns conducted in the late 1970s have revealed that well before the first kings of Ancient Ghana, there were early state-like communities and even early cities. Archaeological work completed in 1984 at 43 sites demonstrated that they belonged to an iron-using culture that dated back to 250 BC. The settlements grew into cities and towns of a considerable longevity and size.[10]

Old Djenné was just one of these early cities that dated back to 250 BC. By 500 AD it had a population of 20,000 people. London, for example, would wait another 700 years to reach this figure. Old Djenné was a centre of long distance trade in which they were the middlemen. Ceramics, copper, foodstuffs and iron exchanged hands. There was also a trade in gold and salt, two very important products in the ancient world. Encircling this early city by the year 800 AD was a clay brick wall 9 feet thick. Before long, settlements and workshops grew up around the city associated with craft specialities such as smiths, potters, sculptors, jewellers, brickmakers and builders, shipwrights, traders, fishermen and farmers.[11] The rise of the city was due to a number of factors. It was a trans-shipment point where goods were transferred from boat to donkey or from donkey to boat. Secondly, it was located near several channels of the Niger River and this gave it a natural moated defence from easy attack. Thirdly, it could control the movement of products carried along the Niger such as copper and gold. Copper entered Old Djenné from the east. Gold entered the city from the opposite direction. It was mined in the Bambuk and Buré regions 600 to 800 kilometres to the southwest. Fourthly, the city was close to overland routes accessed by donkey. Less than 100 kilometres to the east lay a major iron-producing area. Finally, Old Djenné lay between waterways, moist soils and dry savannah country. In the waterways and moist soils of the inland Niger Delta, fishing and rice growing took place. In the dry savannah country, crops of sorghum, pearl millet, and the like were grown.[12]

Even before 250 BC, evidence of a prehistoric Ghanaian culture exists. Large stone masonry villages were excavated in the Dhar Tichitt-Walata region, north of Kumbi-Saleh. These villages were built apparently "without major external influences". They flourished from around 1100 BC, giving a very early date for the culture, specifically identified by the excavators as Soninke. The villages consisted of roughly circular compounds connected by "well defined streets".[13] They were built near lakes for the accessibility of water, and made fishing a viable economic activity. There is also archaeological evidence of herding and agriculture.[14]

Between 1000 and 800 BC archaeological evidence indicates that four times as many villages flourished, accompanied by a greater development of agriculture. As before, the villages were large and of stone, but they were also walled. Each village was "encircled by a masonry wall over 2m high and 1m thick." Together with the fact that they were built on hills, this implies that the constructions were for defensive reasons. There is speculation, derived from the writings of the Greek historian Herodotus, that the Soninkes may have suffered sustained hostility from the Garamantes of the desert.[15] This early activity, building and trade, may support the ideas of the great German Africanist Professor Leo Frobenius, who reflected that:

> In the [nineteenth] century the superstition ruled that all high culture of Africa came from Islam. Since then we have learned much, and we now know today that the beautiful turbans and clothes of the Sudanese [i.e. West African] folk were already used in Africa before Mohammed was even born or before Ethiopian culture reached inner Africa. Since then we have learned that the peculiar organization of the Sudanese [i.e. West African] states existed long before Islam and that all the art of building and education, of city organization and handwork in Negro Africa, were thousands of years older than those of Middle Europe.[16]

Ancient Ghana began as a kingdom in the fourth century AD, but through territorial conquests, it developed into an empire by the eighth century AD. The empire builders were able to dominate their neighbours by their pre-eminence in iron technology. Exploiting this advantage for warfare, Soninke military supremacy was assured. They fought with lances and swords of iron against opponents who fought with bars of ebony. Iron also assisted in the development of agriculture. Iron farming tools were superior to alternatives.[17] An Arab writer of the eighth century, Ibn Fazari, called Ghana the land of gold and described its size as equal to that of the Idrisid state of Morocco.[18] Ghana first appears on a map drawn by Al-Kwarizmi before 833 AD.[19]

Ghana's wealth was based on an extensive trade network. The city of Kumbi-Saleh was the centre of major trade caravans carrying salt from the Sahara, and gold from the Wangara region.[20] Camel caravans came from the north, trekking across the Sahara and laden with salt. Donkey caravans were the most popular throughout the kingdom. From the south, goods were carried on the heads of porters. We speculate that the waterways were also important, especially in the later periods. Barges laden with goods sailed along the Senegal and Niger Rivers.[21] On the traffic, the Ghanaian authorities imposed a series of import and export taxes. Each merchant, for example, typically paid one dinar of gold (a golden coin) in taxes before being allowed to bring one donkey-load of salt into Kumbi. Moreover, each merchant had to pay another two dinars in gold for the privilege of taking that same donkey-load of salt out of Kumbi. Thus every time a donkey-load of salt passed through the capital, the Ghanaian treasury was three dinars richer. A dinar was equal to 72 grains of barley. Other goods were taxed. In Al-Bakri's time, the going tax rate on every camel- or donkey-load of copper was about five eights of an ounce of gold. General merchandise was taxed at the rate of one ounce of gold per load.[22] Ghana also produced or traded metal goods, cotton cloth, copper, and so-called 'Morocco' leather.[23] The Moroccans sold the leather into Europe, hence the name but perhaps 'Ghanaian' leather may have been a more appropriate term. Soninke society was divided into castes. Each caste specialised in a different area of economic or work activity. For example, the Kante clan formed the blacksmith caste, the Sissé clan were the government caste, etc. Other castes were cattle breeders, farmers, fishermen or weavers.[24]

Ibn Khaldun, the mighty historian of the fourteenth century, discussed the pre-eminence of Kumbi-Saleh as follows:

> At the time of the conquest of Northern Africa [by the Arabs between 639 and 708 AD], some merchants penetrated into the western part of the land of the Blacks and found among them no king more powerful than the king of Ghana. His states extended westwards to the shores of the Atlantic Ocean. Ghana [Kumbi-Saleh], the capital of this strong, populous nation, was made up of two towns … and formed one of the greatest and best populated cities in the world. The author of the *Book of Roger* makes special mention of it, as does the author of *Roads and Kingdoms*.[25]

Early in the ninth century, the Sanhaja Berbers, a relatively lighter coloured desert people, challenged Ghanaian power. They inhabited the northern frontier of Ghana and therefore controlled much of the Saharan trade between Ghana and North Africa. Audoghast was a key city in their possession. Under Tilutane, a great Berber leader, the Sanhaja unified. They established armies to raid Ghana's northern provinces to disrupt the gold trade to Kumbi-Saleh. Some 10,000 camel mounted soldiers made these raids. However, this display of Sanhaja unity did not outlive the passing of Tilutane. The Soninkes re-established control over their frontier areas, and a century later, they seized Audoghast from the Berbers.[26]

In the tenth century, an Arab geographer, Ibn Haukal, visited this region and saw for himself the size of the trans-Saharan trade. He was amazed at the

Ashanti (Modern Ghana). Hands and toga of Ashanti ruler Nana Owusu Sampa III. The Ashanti public rituals, with their lavish use of gold, share similarities with those of Ancient Ghana, one thousand years earlier. (Photo: Werner Forman Archives).

enormous transactions of merchants in the region. Writing in 951 AD, he told of a cheque for 42,000 golden dinars written to a merchant in Audoghast by his partner in Sidjilmessa.[27] He also informs us that the King of Ghana was "the richest king on the face of the earth" whose pre-eminence was due to the quantity of gold nuggets that had been amassed by the ruling Ghana and by his predecessors.[28] One of these golden nuggets was world famous, attracting the attention of the chroniclers of the time. Dr J. S. Trimingham informs us with considerable irony that: "The size of this nugget keeps on increasing. With al-Idrissi ... it reaches the size of a boulder of 30 rotls to which the king tethered his horse. Ibn Khaldun reports ... that this boulder, now in the possession of the king of Mali, weighed a ton".[29] There were economic reasons why the kings took the gold nuggets. Al-Bakri suggested that: "Without this precaution, gold would become so plentiful that it would practically lose its value".[30] If gold really did lose its value, a smaller quantity of goods could be imported from outside the empire and therefore standards of living would fall.[31]

Ibn Khaldun recommended *The Book of the Roads and Kingdoms,* as a reliable source on Ghana. This work was written in 1067 by Abu Ubaid Al-Bakri, a well respected geographer of the Middle Ages. The book contains a fine narrative on Ancient Ghana offering a picture of life in Kumbi-Saleh, a year after the Battle of Hastings. The royal town was called (by the Muslims) Al-Ghaba, meaning the forest of grove. Encircled by a wall, the king had a castle and domed buildings. There was a Royal Court of Justice. Near to the court stood a mosque built for visiting Muslims. Outside of Al-Ghaba was a guarded area of cottages and groves where the traditional priests kept their icons. The prisons and royal cemeteries were also there. The second town, originally six miles away from Al-Ghaba, was a Muslim quarter that included twelve mosques. Each institution had its own imams, muezzins and recitors. One mosque functioned as the Friday congregational mosque. Eventually, the space between the two towns became filled with suburbs creating a large city. Stone houses graced suburbia, standing in gardens. Other buildings were of stone with beams of acacia wood. Al Bakri alludes to the intellectual activity in the city. There were lawyers and scholars.[32] So enduring was its academic reputation that As-Sadi, the distinguished seventeenth century chronicler, described Kumbi, in retrospect, as not only a centre of trade caravans but it was also "the resort of the learned, the rich, and the pious of all nations".[33] Of metropolitan colour and fashions, Al-Bakri describes wrappers of cotton, silk, or brocade worn by the populace, incomes determining who could afford what.[34] We conjecture that the wrappers were draped around the wearers perhaps in the manner of a toga as the Ashantis of modern Ghana wear today.

There is a celebrated description of Emperor Tunka Menin's court showing a level of wealth that "was equalled only by that of the Aegean period".[35] The emperor, himself, succeeded his aged maternal uncle Bessi in 1063:[36]

> When he gives audience to his people [says Al-Bakri] … he sits in a pavilion
> around which stand his horses caparisoned in cloth of gold: behind him stand
> ten pages holding shields and gold-mounted swords: and on his right hand are
> the sons of the princes of his empire, splendidly clad and with gold plaited into
> their hair. The governor of the city is seated on the ground in front of the king,
> and all around him are his *vizirs* [i.e. ministers] in the same position. The gate
> of the chamber is guarded by dogs of an excellent breed, who never leave the
> king's seat: they wear collars of gold and silver.[37]

Another geographer informs us that it was the custom for the emperor to ride
around the poorest parts of the city on horseback each morning. He was
lavishly attired in jewels and silk and accompanying him was his entire court.
Before them marched a parade of giraffes, elephants and wild animals. Anyone
who had a grievance or a petition could address the emperor. The subject's case
would be dealt with on the spot. In the afternoon, the emperor rode alone
taking the same route but all were forbidden to speak to him.[38]

The city of Audoghast was originally independent of Ghana, but it was
captured in 990 AD. The Ghanaians exploited its internal problems for their
own advantages, particularly the strife between the Zanata Berbers and the
Arabs.[39] Ibn Haukal in the tenth century wrote that it was "a pleasant place
comparable with Mecca … in that it lies between two hills".[40] Al-Bakri informs
us that Audoghast was a prosperous caravan centre. It was large and densely
populated, with some its people coming from far-off Spain. A place of wealth
and comfort, it had very elegant houses, fine public buildings and several
mosques. Meat was plentiful. There were surrounding pastures, well stocked
with meat and cattle. The rich cultivated wheat as a garden crop, everybody
else grew dhurra, a rice-like substance.[41] At its markets, and also at Kumbi-
Saleh, it was possible to buy wheat imported from the north; cattle, sheep and
honey from the south; and various food products from elsewhere. Merchants
imported robes from Morocco and red and blue blouses from Moorish Spain.
Goods changed hands on the receipt of gold dust, gold coins, cowrie shells or
salt.[42]

Further west, in the region of the Senegal River, were the city-states of
Tekrur and Silla. The relationship of these cities to the Ghanaian Empire is
unclear, but it seems that these cities had a semi-independent status. Secondly,
Tekrur was more powerful than Silla and dominated the latter. Tekrur probably
dates back to around first century BC. By the time written records become
available, it ruled over a sizable portion of the Senegal River region.[43]
According to Al Bakri:

> [O]n the banks of the Nile [actually the Senegal River], is the town of Takrur
> [sic] inhabited by Negroes. These, like the rest of the Negroes, were once pagan
> [i.e. Traditionalists] and worshipped *dakakir* (*dakkur* in their language meaning

'idol' [i.e. icon]) until the reign of War-Jabi, son of Rabis. This king joined
Islam and introduced Islamic law. He enforced the religion upon his subjects ...
He died in ... A.D. 1040/1. Today (c.1067) the Takrur are Muslims. From
Takrur one travels to Silla, which likewise consists of two towns lying on both
banks of the Nile [i.e. Senegal River]. Its people are Muslims having been
converted by War-Jabi ... It is an extensive and populous kingdom almost equal
to that of Ghana. The means of exchange of the inhabitants of Silla are dura,
salt, brass rings, and fine cotton strips called *shakkiyya*.[44]

Another chronicler mentions the mode of dress of Tekrur and Silla: "The
ordinary people wear woollen *qadawir*, with woollen *karazi* on their heads,
whilst the upper class wear cotton clothing and head wraps".[45]

The Almoravides, a veil-wearing, hard-line Islamic movement posed the first
serious threat to the power of Ghana. The Ghanaian Emperor, after all, had a
standing army of 200,000 soldiers with 40,000 cavalry at his disposal.
(England in 1066, for example, had only 15,000 soldiers at its disposal).[46]
However, Ghanaian rule over Tekrur and the city of Audoghast made enemies
for the empire in these dependencies that would later rebound on Ghana.
Sometime around 1020, a Berber ruler of Audoghast converted to Islam.
Yahya, his successor, made a pilgrimage to Mecca and met the Islamic cleric
Ibn Yasin. Yahya invited the cleric to return to Africa with him to evangelise
among the Berbers. It didn't work. The Berbers exiled Ibn Yasin who was
forced to flee to Tekrur. In Tekrur, Ibn Yasin founded his Islamic movement -
the Almoravides. Berbers and Tekrur converts flocked to his standard fired up
by both Islam and revenge. The Berbers wanted the independence of
Audoghast from the non-Islamic rule of Ghana. They also wanted to Islamise,
by force if necessary, the Berbers of the desert. On the other hand, the Tekrur
wanted their independence from Ghana. A match had been made. By 1055 the
Almoravides wrested Audoghast from Ghanaian rule.[47] By 1062 they founded
the Moroccan city of Marrakesh.[48] In 1076 they declared Holy War on Ghana
and sacked Kumbi-Saleh. Finally, the Almoravides conquered Spain and
established a ruling dynasty.[49] Professor J. C. DeGraft-Johnson, author of the
classic *African Glory,* noted that the invasion of Ghana led to large numbers of
people fleeing further south such as the Akan (Ashantis, Fantis, etc.).[50] This is
possibly the reason for Ancient and Modern Ghana being in two different
places.

Almoravid rule over the empire, however, collapsed in 1087. Their
fanaticism lost its zeal. Ghana returned to Soninke leadership[51] who sparked a
brief renaissance, though some of the Empire's dependencies had become
independent. Al-Idrissi described this period in *The Book of Roger* written in
1153. The residence of the Ghanaian Emperor at this time, as paraphrased by
Lady Lugard, was: "A well-built castle, thoroughly fortified, decorated inside

Ancient Ghana (Mali, Mauritania, Guinea and Senegambia). Ruins of Kumbi-Saleh, the capital city, located in southern Mauritania. This house dates to the 13th or 14th century AD. Below it are buildings dating from the 7th century AD. (Photo: Serge Robert).

Camels were important in the moving of goods and people across the desert areas of West Africa. Originally published in Major Felix Dubois, *Timbuctoo the Mysterious* (UK, William Heinemann, 1897, p.256).

with sculptures and pictures, and having glass windows".[52] Al-Idrissi further informs us that Ghana was still a prosperous state that minted its own coins. In his own words:

> When the river returns to its bed, everyone sells his gold. The bulk of it is bought by the inhabitants of Wardjelan [in present day Libya] and by those from the tip of West Africa, whither this gold is transported to the mints, coined into dinars, and traded commercially for goods. This is how it happens each year. This is the principal product in the land of the Blacks ... In the country of [W]angara [i.e. in present day Guinea] there are flourishing cities and renowned fortresses, its inhabitants are wealthy; they possess gold in abundance, and receive the products brought to them from the other remotest portions of the earth. They attire themselves in robes and other kinds of raiment.[53]

We note, however, that the attempted Islamicisation by the Almoravides left a major mark on Ghanaian culture, and this became, and still is, a feature of West African politics. Traditional and Islamic culture was not always compatible and by the twelfth century, the empire broke up. Some kingdoms, such as the Mali and Tekrur, became independent of the empire. In 1180 some Soninkes established a rival kingdom to Ghana ruling from the city of Sosso. The Sosso launched raids on Kumbi-Saleh in the early thirteenth century. However, Kumbi-Saleh and Sosso faced a more menacing rival in the newly rising power of Mali. By 1240 the Malians had destroyed both the Sosso kingdom and the Ghanaian capital.[54] The fall of Kumbi-Saleh ended an era in history and the old capital, later abandoned, became a lost city. Dr Davidson narrates the story of its rediscovery in our times:

> As long ago as 1914 a French district officer, Bonnel de Mezières, dug into a site that was suggested by tradition ... De Mezières found enough to make him believe that this had probably been the capital of Ghana in El Bekri's [sic] day; and later excavation has gone far to vindicate him.[55]

De Mezières found sarcophagi, tombs of great dimensions, metallurgical workshops and ruins of towers.[56]

> Renewed work at this site of Kumbi Saleh [continues Davidson] ... began in 1939 ... Ten years later Thomassey and Mauny were at last able to undertake a systematic examination of these promising ruins in the light of a modern understanding of the matter. By 1951 they had tracked the remains of a large and elaborate Muslim city which had covered a square mile and may have had a population of about 30,000 people, very numerous for the world of 800 or 900 years ago.[57]

Dr Davidson gives no figure for the traditionalist city nearby, nor does he give a population figure for the six miles worth of suburbs that separated the two townships. Clearly the total city population was several times larger than 30,000 people. Archaeology has added yet another twist. Contrary to Al Bakri, the townships were not separated by 6 miles worth of suburbs, rather they were separated by 10 miles worth of suburbs. This makes the total city population even more difficult to calculate. This also shows that Ibn Khaldun was totally justified in referring to the Ghanaian capital as one of the best populated cities in the world. Of the city, itself, M. Denis-Pierre de Pédrals, the author of *Archeologie de l'Afrique Noire,* wrote that:

> We can still distinguish clearly the outline of an avenue, bordered by houses with walls more than one meter or one and a half meters above ground. The roofs have collapsed. Farther on, a strip of flat ground for a public square, with walls which seemed to have once supported upper floors. Sometimes the buildings are so well preserved that little would be needed to make them liveable again ... The other constructions are more complicated. One consists of five rooms four metres deep, with communicating halls. The masonry is perfect. The walls are thirty centimetres thick.[58]

Many objects were recovered from the city through excavation, including farming tools, fragments of pottery, glass weights for measuring gold, iron lances, knives, nails, painted stone bearing verses from the Koran, and "one of the finest pairs of scissors of that era ever to be found in any part of the world".[59]

Serge and Denise Roberts, two archaeologists, carried out excavations at Tegdaoust (i.e. Audoghast). They inform us that the city was occupied between the eighth and ninth centuries AD until the fourteenth century. In the eighth or ninth centuries, Audoghast was a village built of clay bricks. From the ninth century, stone-built houses made their appearance. They shared affinities with houses of the Mediterranean. At a later date, it appears that Audoghast was significantly rebuilt. The new city combined the layout of the stone houses but now constructed of clay bricks instead, producing a pleasing architectural marriage.[60] McIntosh and McIntosh, the archaeologists who excavated Old Djenné, inform us that: "Excavations at Tegdaoust and Koumbi [sic] Saleh revealed stone built mosques of considerable dimensions. The Koumbi Saleh mosque covers 2000 square metres and could have held over 2000 people".[61]

Before leaving ancient Ghana, we cannot fail to mention some recent intelligence concerning the city of Chinguetti. This city, still in existence today, lay to the north of the ancient Ghanaian empire. Professor Diop drew a map which implied that Chinguetti was fully a part of the Ghana Empire,[62] but its far northerly location makes this debatable. It is certain, however, that the city has architecture reminiscent in technique with that of Kumbi-Saleh.[63] Moreover, the same trade and cultural links that nourished Kumbi-Saleh, fed

Detail of the Grand Mosque of Djenné. The monument looks like a castle and may well reflect the designs of castles built during the Ancient Ghana era. Originally published in Susan Denyer, *African Traditional Architecture* (UK, Heinemann, 1978, p.170).

Chinguetti. With this in mind, an article recently appeared in *The Sunday Times Magazine* entitled *Writings in the Sand*. It concerned manuscripts in the Arabic language that were collected, written, and read by African Muslims from this region:

> The shadows lengthen, the Saharan sun begins to set, and the wise old men of Chinguetti settle down to their usual evening reading. In their sun-hardened hands they hold leather-bound tomes hundreds of years old. The fragile parchment pages are coming out of their binding, the edges are crinkly and torn, but the black ink of the flowing Arabic script stands out boldly as it did when it was first written. To western eyes this is Indiana Jones stuff: ancient texts holding secrets that have been lost over the centuries ... Though Chinguetti's importance as a commercial post diminished, it is still venerated as Islam's seventh holiest city ... Mohammed Habott, an amiable sexagenarian, willingly shows visitors into his house where his collection of books is stored. One of them dates from AD1087, and contains one of the earliest drawings of Makkah [i.e. Mecca], the city where the prophet Mohammed was born. And this is just one of about 3,450 books in the private libraries of Chinguetti and its neighbouring town, Oudane. There are other repositories, too - for example, Timbuktu, further east ... "The Arabic manuscript libraries remain one of the best-hidden treasures in Africa," says Professor Charles Stewart, a historian at Illinois university ... Though the exact content of the books kept at Chinguetti is not yet known, Stewart approximates that a quarter will be jurisprudence, 10% will be Sufism (mysticism), 10% Arabic language, 10% studies of the Koran, 10% literature, 10% biographies of the prophet Mohammed and Hadith (tradition), and 10% theology. The remaining 15% is likely to include works on history, logic, ethics, biography, mathematics, astronomy and astrology, medicine, encyclopedias, education and geography. They are stored in three libraries and 14 private collections.[64]

Mali

Ghana was basically a non-Muslim state. The Muslim sectors of its cities existed to house the growing number of African converts, and also to facilitate the trans-Saharan trade with North Africa.[65] The major state to survive the passing of Ghana was the Islamic state of Mali. In 1240 the Malians (also called Mandingas), led by Sundiata Keita, seized Ghana's capital, Kumbi-Saleh. They became the new masters of the gold and salt trade. At a later date, they opened the copper mines of Takedda as an additional source of revenue.[66] Chroniclers of the time attested to the importance of the trade. Ibn Khaldun, undisputed lord of the Mediæval historians, wrote that camel caravans trekked across the Sahara by way of the Hoggar mountains, one of half a dozen well-used trade roads. Each year, no fewer than 12,000 camels were counted on one of the routes.[67] Mali, at its height in the fourteenth century, included the lands

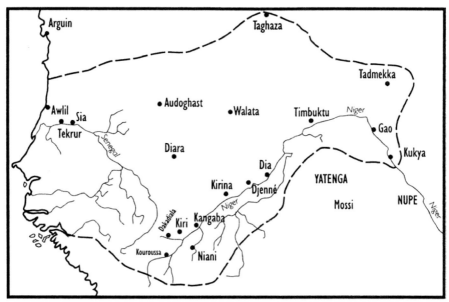

The Empire of Mali. (Map: Kieron Vital). This was the second great empire in this part of West Africa. It occupied approximately the same territory as Ancient Ghana, but was larger. The BBC described Mali as the richest state in the 14ᵗʰ century world.

now called Senegal, Gambia, Mauretania and Niger. In short, the second largest empire in the world of the fourteenth century, comparable in size to all of Western Europe combined.[68]

Ibn Battuta, the famous Muslim travel writer of the Middle Ages, favourably described the Malians, as follows:

> The [N]egroes … are seldom unjust, and have a greater abhorrence of injustice than any other people. Their sultan shows no mercy to anyone who is guilty of the least act of it. There is complete security in their country. Neither traveller nor inhabitant in it has anything to fear from robbers or men of violence.[69]

The early history of the Mandinga kingdom is traditionally said to date from *c*.1050 AD. This does not in fact date its beginnings, but rather the rule of Baramandanah, the first of its Islamic kings. He urged his successors to become Muslims.[70] One such king was Musa Keita (*c*.1100) who was said to have visited Mecca four times on religious pilgrimages.[71] Dr Trimingham believes that the Keita Dynasty had its origins earlier than the period of Baramandanah. He believes that the dynasty began as early as the ninth century. The founder of the line was Kabala Simbo Keita.[72] Herman Bell, in an insightful essay, had this to say on the pre Islamic religion of Mali:

Foremost among the traditional gods is Faro who bears a remarkable, though probably coincidental, resemblance to the ancient Egyptian god Osiris. Both these gods were associated with the river and fertility; both were dismembered, and where bits of their bodies were buried there arose centres devoted to their cult - in one case along the Niger and in the other along the Nile.[73]

This burgeoning kingdom, however, faced problems from rival powers. In 1224 Sumanguru led the Sosso in a devastating raid on the Malian capital of Djeriba. They razed the city and killed most of the ruling family. Eleven princes were put to death in the massacre, but Sumanguru spared one of them, a crippled boy called Sundiata.[74] Six years later, Sundiata triumphed over his disability and became the ruler of the Malians. He surrounded himself with a private guard made up of the thuggish element of the kingdom, and began a guerrilla campaign against Sosso dominance. Sundiata's first strike, however, was against Sangaran, a neighbouring kingdom. After this conquest, he campaigned against Labe and also the Niger Region. During these conquests he gathered an army recruited from among the defeated peoples to fight the Sosso. In 1235 he challenged the power of the Sosso at the Battle of Kirina. His armies defeated Sumanguru and destroyed the fortified and well-garrisoned capital of the Sosso. Five years later, Sundiata seized the city of Ghana and destroyed it. After these military actions, he returned to the ruins of his capital city, Djeriba, and received the sworn loyalty of the rulers of the conquered people at a triumphant and impressive ceremony. He allowed the Emperor of Ghana to retain the title of king. All the other former rulers were given new titles.[75]

Sundiata never again took to the battlefield. Devoting his time to economic and social development of the empire, he turned his armies into farmers and encouraged a programme of agricultural expansion. The soldiers grew cotton, peanuts and grains, and were also encouraged to raise poultry and cattle. He founded a new capital city called Niani. It was located on the confluence of the Upper Niger and Sankarini rivers. There were other military actions, however, but Sundiata's generals led them. They marched as far as the Atlantic, seized lands way to the east, subjugated the southern forest belt, and overpowered the desert regions of the north. These actions led to Malian control of the gold-fields of Wangara and created the trade route from there to the new capital of Niani.[76]

Mansa Wali succeeded Sundiata in 1255. He was the first ruler to take the royal title of Mansa. Wali's reign was largely tranquil, though there were conquests of Bambuk and Bondu. A devout Moslem, he made a pilgrimage to Mecca. He died in 1270 and four undistinguished rulers followed him. There were disputes, power struggles and many examples of poor management.[77] During this confusion, a freed slave proclaimed himself Mansa of Mali in

1285. This distinguished man, Mansa Sakura, campaigned against Tekrur, raided the Gao region, and may also have pacified Takedda, the famous copper-producing centre. The empire became prosperous under his reign, attracting merchants from the Middle East and elsewhere in Africa to trade. Unfortunately, Sakura was assassinated in Somalia after returning from a religious pilgrimage in 1300.[78] In 1999 the BBC produced an outstanding television series entitled *Millennium* based around the historical scholarship of the Oxford University historian Dr Felipe Fernandez-Armesto. The programme devoted to the fourteenth century opens with the following disclosure:

> In the fourteenth century, the century of the scythe, natural disasters threatened civilisations with extinction. The Black Death kills more people in Europe, Asia and North Africa than any catastrophe has before. Civilisations which avoid the plague, thrive. In West Africa the Empire of Mali becomes the richest in the world.[79]

Control over the gold mines was the most important source of this wealth. Dr Finch informs us that:

> Much alluvial gold was panned but most of the ore was obtained by sinking shafts sometimes 100 feet deep, often linked by side shafts and galleries. It is estimated that the total amount of gold mined in West Africa up to 1500 was 3,500 tons, worth more than $30 billion in today's market [i.e. in 1998].[80]

An Egyptian scholar, Ibn Fadl Al-Umari, published *Masalik ab Absar fi Mamalik al Amsar* in Cairo around 1342. In the tenth chapter of this work, there is an account of two large maritime voyages ordered by the predecessor of Mansa Musa, a king who inherited the Malian throne in 1312. This mariner king is not named by Al-Umari, but modern writers identify him as Mansa Abubakari II. According to Al-Umari, this king launched two hundred ships filled with men and a further two hundred ships amply stocked with food, gold and water to last for two years. The ruler sent them with a mission to explore the extremity of the Atlantic Ocean. In time, one ship returned. Its captain told the Malian king of his adventures. "Prince," he said, "we sailed for a long time, up to the moment when we encountered in mid-ocean something like a river with a violent current. My ship was last. The others sailed on, and gradually each of them entered this place, they disappeared and did not come back. We did not know what had happened to them. As for me, I returned to where I was and did not enter the current." The Mansa decided to see for himself. He had two thousand ships prepared, one thousand of which were equipped with provisions. They set sail across the Atlantic with a large party and never returned. Abubakari II left Mansa Musa I in charge of leading the empire.[81]

Mali. View of the city of Timbuktu. In the 14th century the city had an estimated population of 115,000 people. Typically 25,000 were at university and 20,000 were at school. London, by contrast, had a total 14th century population of 20,000 people. From Dr Henry Barth, *Travels and Discoveries in North and Central Africa, Volume III* (UK, Longman, Brown, Green, Longmans & Roberts, 1858).

Mali. Great Mosque of Timbuktu. Built by Mansa Musa I in 1326. Originally published in Susan Denyer, *African Traditional Architecture* (UK, Heinemann, 1978, p.171).

This account implies that Malians visited the Americas in 1311. This was 181 years before Christopher Columbus "discovered" the continent. It is, of course, well known that Columbus himself was fully aware of this important fact. Columbus, to give just one example, reported that he acquired metal goods of West African manufacture from the Native Americans.[82] Other evidence of this African voyage comes from an analysis of maps. Old maps of the Mexico region, drawn by Europeans, show that the Malians renamed places in the region after themselves. Names such as Mandinga Port, Mandinga Bay and Sierre de Mali exist as place names.[83] Moreover, two skeletons of Negro males have been recovered from a grave in Hull Bay near the Danish Virgin Islands. Dated at 1250 AD, this is only 61 years away from the period of the proposed Malian visit.[84] In addition, an old inscription was discovered at the bottom of a waterfall in the Reef Bay Valley, not too far from the African skeletons. This inscription was written in an old African script called Tifinagh. Originally of ancient Libyan origin, a Berber group in Mali used this script at that time. The inscription translates as follows: "Plunge in to cleanse yourself. This is water for purification before prayer."[85] Finally, the scholarly art historian, Count Alexander von Wuthenau, directed attention to fourteenth century carvings that were found in the Americas. These sculptures show men and women, clearly African, wearing turbans. Many have tattoo marks cut into their cheeks.[86] This art may well depict people from Mali.

Mansa Musa I ascended the throne in 1312. He was, perhaps, the most colourful personality in West African history. Of this monarch, Dr DeGraft-Johnson wrote that:

> It was in 1324 … that the world awoke to the splendour and grandeur of Mali. There across the African desert, and making its way to Mecca, was a caravan of a size which had never before been seen, a caravan consisting of 60,000 men. They were Mansa Musa's men, and Mansa Musa was with them. He was not going to war: he was merely going to worship at Mecca. The huge caravan included a personal retinue of 12,000 slaves, all dressed in brocade and Persian silk. Mansa Musa himself rode on horseback, and directly preceding him were 500 slaves, each carrying a staff of gold weighing about six pounds (500 mitkal). Then came Mansa Musa's baggage-train of eighty camels, each carrying 300 pounds (three kantar) weight of gold dust. This imposing caravan made its way from Niani on the Upper Niger to Walata, then to Tuat, and then on to Cairo. Mansa Musa's piety and open-handed generosity, the fine clothes and good behaviour of his followers, all quickly made a good impression. One might have thought that a pilgrimage to Mecca undertaken with such pomp and ceremony would have ulterior political motives, but no such motives have ever been adduced.[87]

In Egypt, Musa spent so much money in gold that he devastated that nation's economy.

> For years after Mansa Musa's visit [continues Professor DeGraft-Johnson], ordinary people in the streets of Cairo, Mecca, and Baghdad talked about this wonderful pilgrimage - a pilgrimage which led to the devaluation of gold in the Middle East for several years.[88]

In a recent book, Cynthia Crossen, senior editor of the prestigious financial newspaper *Wall Street Journal,* wrote: "You've heard about the extraordinary wealth of Bill Gates, J. P. Morgan, and the sultan of Brunei, but have you heard of Mansa Musa, one of the richest men who ever lived?"[89] Continuing this theme, Mrs Crossen comments that: "Neither producer nor inventor, Mansa Musa was an early broker, greasing the wheels of intercultural trade. He created wealth by making it possible for others to buy and sell".[90] Dr Davidson suggested that the rulers of Mali were "rumoured to have been the wealthiest m[e]n on the face of the earth".[91]

During his return journey from Mecca, Musa heard news that his army captured Gao in 1325. Sagmandia, one of his generals, led the victorious invasion. The captured city of Gao was a great prize. Al-Idrissi, the distinguished author mentioned earlier, described it as a "populous, unwalled, commercial and industrial town, in which were to be found the produce of all arts and trades necessary for its inhabitants".[92] Tim Insoll from St. John's College, Cambridge University, carried out important excavations in Gao. Some of his finds were on display at the British Museum at the time of one of our visits. Particularly intriguing was an exhibit entitled: "Fragments of alabaster window surrounds and a piece of pink window glass, Gao 10th - 14th century." Musa made a detour and visited the captured metropolis. In this city, he received the two sons of the Gao king as hostages, Ali Kolon and Suleiman Nar. He returned to Niani with the two boys and later educated them at his court.

Mali was divided into provinces governed by ferbers. The chief municipalities were ruled by inspectors, known as mocrifs. Law and order prevailed in the provinces, and merchants and their caravans travelled freely. They had little to fear from banditry. There were also vassal kingdoms not under direct imperial rule such as Djenné. During the time of Musa I, there were between 13 and 24 of these semi-independent kingdoms in alliance with the empire. The Mansa maintained a standing army of 100,000 men, of which ten percent were cavalrymen. They were mounted on camels and horses.[93]

Musa I embarked on a large building programme, raising mosques and universities in Timbuktu and Gao.[94] In Niani, he built the Hall of Audience, a building communicated by an interior door to the royal palace. It was "an admirable Monument" surmounted by a dome, adorned with arabesques of striking colours. The windows of an upper floor were plated with wood and framed in silver foil, those of a lower floor were plated with wood, framed in

Mali. Trade caravans approaching the city of Timbuktu. Salt entered the city from the north by camel caravan. Gold entered the city from the south by donkey caravan. Other goods arrived by barge or by head porter. From Dr Henry Barth, *Travels and Discoveries in North and Central Africa, Volume III* (UK, Longman, Brown, Green, Longmans & Roberts, 1858, opposite p.404).

gold. Like the Great Mosque, a splendid monument of Timbuktu, the Hall was built of cut stone.[95] During this period, there was an extraordinary level of urban living. Sergio Domian, an Italian art and architecture scholar, wrote the following about this period: "Thus was laid the foundation of an urban civilisation. At the height of its power, Mali had at least 400 cities, and the interior of the Niger Delta was very densely populated".[96]

Timbuktu rose from obscurity to great commercial and cultural importance. It had caravan connections to Angila, Dra'a, Egypt, Fez, Fezzan, Ghadamer, Sidjilmessa, Sus and Tuat. In addition, it became a centre of learning, one of the foremost centres of Islamic scholarship in world. The University of Sankore Mosque was highly distinguished for the teaching of Koranic theology and law, besides other subjects such as astronomy and mathematics.[97] Musa I promoted the spread of Islam and made the Eid celebrations at the end of Ramadan a national holiday.[98] Despite his religiosity, Musa was not fanatical. Professor Jackson wrote the following that demonstrates the Mansa's pragmatic attitude towards religion:

> On one occasion Mansa Musa sent a representative to the goldminers of
> Wangara, who were pagans [i.e. Traditionalists], for the purpose of converting

them to the Moslem faith. On the return of the special messenger, the monarch eagerly awaited his reply; and this is what he heard: "Your majesty, this is not the time to pursue the Wangara people to the south. They have refused to accept our faith. The miners of Wangara even threatened to stop producing gold if they were forced to become Moslems. It would not be wise to try to force them. The Wangara are skilled at forest fighting. They use poisoned arrows. The tsetse fly that brings the deadly sleeping sickness could destroy our army." This message did not please Mansa Musa ... but he had a genuine respect for the rights of all the people, and deemed it right to follow the advice of his courier.[99]

Towards the end of his reign, Musa initiated diplomatic links with Morocco, sending a deputation to the court of Al Sultan Aswad (i.e. the Black Sultan), Abu l-Hasan Ali. The Morrocan court responded, sending presents to Mali, typical of the finest of their kingdom and carefully chosen by their sultan. The honourable Ibn Ghanem led a deputation of the eminent to deliver the magnificent offering. Alas, Musa died in 1337, before the Moroccan envoy arrived. His successor, Mansa Maghan, received the gift. A tradition of exchanging presents between the two courts continued for many generations.[100]

Mansa Maghan became the ruler in 1337. The following year, the Mossi of Burkina Faso raided Timbuktu. They routed the Mali garrison and torched the city. Other problems emerged. The two Gao princes escaped. They fled to Gao and, at a later date, declared their independence from Mali.

Mansa Suleiman became the next ruler in 1341. His eighteen-year rule was one of stability, though he did have to contend with the Berbers of the desert. The desert dwellers seized Walata. They also raided Malian-controlled Tekrur.[101]

It was during the Suleiman period that Ibn Battuta, the most acclaimed traveller of the age, visited the country. Not only is Ibn Battuta's *Travels in Asia and Africa* a classic, it contains some of the best eye witness details of life in Mali during this period. For this reason, we feel justified in reproducing the following extracts from this precious work:

> I travelled [says Ibn Battuta] ... with travel companions whose leader was Abu Muhammad Yandakan al-Massufi, may God have mercy on him. In the company was a group of merchants of Sidjilmessa and others. We arrived after twenty five days at Taghaza. It is a village with no good in it. Amongst its curiosities is the fact that the construction of its houses and its mosques is of rock salt with camel skin roofing ... In it is a salt mine. It is dug out of the ground and is found there in huge slabs ... A camel can carry two slabs of salt. The [B]lacks [i.e. Malians] arrive from their country and carry away the salt. A camel load of it is sold in Iwalatan (Walata) for from eight to ten *mithqals,* and in the town of Malli [i.e. Niani] for twenty to thirty *mithqals* perhaps the price reaches up to forty. The [B]lacks exchange the salt as money as one would exchange gold and silver. They cut it up and trade with it in pieces.[102]

Mali. View of the houses in Djenné. Originally published in Major Felix Dubois, *Timbuctoo the Mysterious* **(UK, William Heinemann, 1897, p.92).**

Ibn Battuta witnessed various festivals while in the empire. On Fridays, the Mansa held festivals after the late afternoon prayers. Ibn Battuta tells us what happened:

> The sultan holds sessions during the days associated with the two festivals after the *'asr* (late afternoon) prayers on the *banbi* [i.e. platform]. The men-at-arms come with wonderful weaponry: quivers of silver and gold, swords covered with gold, their sheaths of the same, spears of silver and gold and wands of crystal. Four of the *amirs* stand behind him to drive off flies, with ornaments of silver in their hands which look like riding stirrups. The *farariyya* (commanders), the *qadi* [i.e. judge], and the preacher sit according to custom, the interpreter Dugha brings in his [i.e. the Mansa's] four wives and his concubines, who are about a hundred in number. On them are fine clothes and on their heads they have bands of silver and gold with silver and gold apples as pendants. A chair is set there for Dugha to sit on and he beats an instrument which is made of reeds with tiny calabashes below it, praising the sultan, recalling in his song his expeditions and deeds. The wives and the concubines sing with him and they play with bows. There are with them about thirty of his pages wearing red woollen robes and white caps on their heads. Each one of them has a drum tied to him and he beats it. Then come his retinue of young men who play and turn in the air as they do in Sind [i.e. India]. They have a wonderful gracefulness and lightness in this. They juggle with swords

beautifully and Dugha performs a marvellous game with a sword. At that point, the sultan orders that a gift be given him, they bring him a purse of two hundred *mithqals* of gold dust. An announcement of its contents is made to him over the heads of the people. The *farariyya* (commanders) get up and twang their bows, thanking the sultan. On the following day every one of them makes a gift to Dugha according to his means.[103]

After his visit to Walata, Ibn Battuta described the women as "extremely beautiful and are more important than the men". He continues in a like vein:

> The condition of these people is strange and their manners outlandish. As for their men, there is no sexual jealousy in them. And none of them derives his genealogy from his father but, on the contrary, from his maternal uncle. A man does not pass on inheritance except to the sons of his sister to the exclusion of his own sons. Now that is a thing I never saw in any part of the world except in the country of the unbelievers of the land of Mulaibar (Malabar) among the Indians.[104]

Some scholars believe that Ibn Battuta appears to be describing a matriarchal social order operating in Mali. Other evidence that supports this interpretation comes from an anecdote, again from Ibn Battuta's pen:

> It came about that in the days of my stay in Malli [sic] that the sultan [i.e. Mansa Suleiman] was angry with his senior wife, the daughter of his paternal uncle, who was called Qasa which signifies the queen among them. The queen is his partner in the kingship, following the custom of the [B]lacks. Her name is mentioned with his in the pulpit.[105]

Saïd Hamdun and Noël King, the translators of Ibn Battuta's narrative, comment on this passage as follows:

> The 'woman-king' is often important in African kingship. She was a sovereign in her own right. Often she was not in fact the king's spouse but a female monarch chosen from the princesses of the blood royal. We may be in this narrative witnessing the sultan's attempt to replace the African type of queen by the consort-type of queen, a person who owed her position to her husband.[106]

Civil war broke out on the death of Mansa Suleiman, lasting nine months. Mari Jata II became king in 1360 after defeating a rival. He cultivated the friendship of the court of Morocco. He sent them a giraffe, which created a stir after following a precarious journey across the Sahara. He also maintained friendly relations with Egypt. However, severe economic problems emerged during this reign. The king sold the largest golden nugget in the government's possession to Egyptian merchants for a knocked-down price. The sale bankrupted the treasury. Incidentally, this was the world famous nugget that was originally part of the Ghanaian emperor's treasury hundreds of years before. In 1374 Mansa Musa II succeeded him on paper, but in practise played very little political role. Keeping the Mansa in seclusion, the prime minister, yet another Mari Jata, ruled the empire. Mari Jata suppressed a Tuareg rebellion in Takedda and commanded raids on Gao. This prime minister was the last great ruler of Mali before things fell apart.[107] Stride and Ifeka inform us that:

> With Magan III's accession in 1390, our knowledge of Mali rulers ends and interest focuses on the disastrous results of Mali's disunity. The Soninke state of Diara threw off the Mali yoke and the Mossi, Tuareg and Songhai mounted increasingly successful pressure on the empire. In about 1400, the Mossi [of Burkina Faso] plundered deep into Masina, while the Songhai at last emerged from their long struggle to preserve the independence of Gao and began to occupy Mali territory. The Tuareg seized the commercial towns of Arawan, Walata and Timbuktu in about 1433 and ruined Mali's control of the trans-Saharan trade.[108]

Songhai

Songhai was the last of the vast West African empires. Originally a tributary state within the Malian Empire, it became independent as Mali declined. The Songhai Empire dominated West Africa in the fifteenth and sixteenth centuries, taking over from Mali. The Songhai, however, had a long and interesting early history that is well worth investigating.

The first Songhai dynasty was called the Dia, ruling from 690 AD until 1338.[109] Kukya was their capital city. It was very ancient. As-Sadi, the important African historian, informs us that it existed during the time of the Pharaohs. Louis Deplanges, a modern archaeologist, found vestiges of it in modern-day Mali.[110] By the ninth century, Gao, a rival Songhai city, had become much more powerful. It was a great trading city that attracted caravans and merchants from Morocco, Tunis and Egypt. Gao was divided into two main sections based on religion, just like the old Ghanaian capital, Kumbi-Saleh.[111] Gao, however, was more than just a city. It had become the centre of an early empire. One of the Arab writers of the ninth century wrote that:

> [Gao] is the greatest sovereignty of the Negroes, the most important and influential, to whom the other kingdoms pay allegiance ... Subject to this (king) are a number of kingdoms which pay him allegiance and acknowledge his overlordship ... Among them is the kingdom of Maraw which is extensive, whose king has a capital called al-Haya; and the kingdoms of Murdiya, al-Harbar, Sanhaja, Nadhkarir, Al-Zayanir, Arwar, Taqarut. All these are dependencies of the kingdom of [Gao].[112]

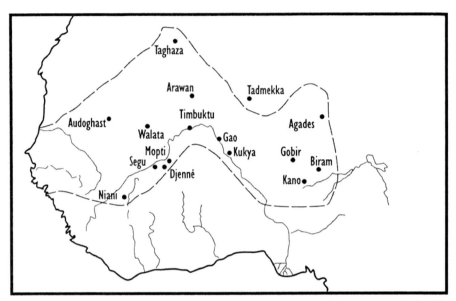

The Empire of Songhai. (Map: Kieron Vital). This was the third great empire in this part of West Africa. It occupied approximately the same territory as the Mali Empire, but was larger. At its height in the 16ᵗʰ century it was as large as all of Europe combined.

The fifteenth ruler of Kukya, Dia Kossoï moved his capital to Gao in the early 1000's, joining the two kingdoms. In 1009 Kossoï became Kukya's first Islamic king. He appointed Muslims to governmental positions.[113] Lady Lugard was very impressed with this era. "The Songhai Kingdom" wrote her Ladyship, "flourished exceedingly under the Mohammedan Zas [i.e. Dias]. Their capital was, of all the cities of the [B]lacks, that which had [the] most gold. It had also [an] abundance of cotton and rice".[114] During this period, the rulers received a sword, a seal and a Koran on their coronation. All came from Islamic dominated Spain.[115]

In 1325 the Malians captured Gao and absorbed it into their empire. In around 1338 Sonni Ali Kolon establishes of a new dynasty and, at a later date, declares independence from Mali.[116] In 1464 Sonni Ali, the eighteenth ruler of this line, became ruler of the Songhai kingdom. His first notable achievement was the capture of the city of Timbuktu in 1469, with its world famous University of Sankore Mosque. Djenné was the next city to fall after a siege lasting over seven years. An even bigger prize, it had international trading links, a university, and also the most brilliant architecture in the region. He took it in around 1473. To the south, lay the kingdoms of the Mossi, an enemy of the Songhai. In 1480 they launched a raid on the Songhai city of Walata. They besieged the city for a month leading Walata to capitulate. The victorious

Mossi seized people and booty. In 1483 Sonni Ali's army successfully drove this menace from the kingdom. Sonni Ali established the Songhai state as the third great West African Empire in this region. He became a world famous leader of this time, taking over most of the old Malian Empire. After a distinguished career, he died in November 1492, killed in a military campaign.[117] He was mummified after his death and thus followed very ancient African traditions.[118]

Sonni Baru Dao, the son of Sonni Ali, was also a follower of a traditional African religion. He rejected all attempts to convert him to Islam by Muslims in his empire. After several weeks of negotiations and no conversion, the Muslims resorted to battle. Backed by a large section of the army, the Muslims triumphed in April 1493. This brought Mohammed Touré, a former general, to lead the empire. He took the title 'Askia' and all those who followed him took the same dynastic title.[119] A devout Muslim, Askia Mohammed I made a pilgrimage to Mecca in 1496. One thousand infantry and a cavalry detachment of 500 horsemen accompanied him. He also took 300,000 gold pieces. In Mecca, Askia met the Caliph of Egypt, the Pope of the Islamic church. Askia requested that the Caliph appoint him as his religious representative in West Africa. The Caliph agreed. Askia Mohammed returned to Gao in 1497, with a new title. He was now the Caliph of the Western Sudan, spiritual ruler of all the West African Muslims.[120]

The empire Askia inherited from the Sonni Dynasty was already massive, yet he expanded north, east and west by conquest. Ultimately it would cover an area about the same size as all of Europe. By 1514 his armies captured the Hausa Confederation of northern Nigeria. Next to capitulate was the city of Agades in Niger, and finally the regions to the far west of the empire around the Atlantic.[121] As the kingdom grew into an empire, Askia Mohammed I came up with new methods of government, establishing a strongly centralised administration. Among the most important posts were the Minister of Treasury, the Minister of Tax Collection, the Minister of the Army and Navy, and the Minister of Trade and Industry.[122] In some territories, the Askia allowed the regional kings to rule as they had before, just as long as they paid tribute. In other territories, the Askia created a parallel post to the local governor called the *mondyo* (i.e. inspector), who formed the official link to the imperial Songhai government.[123] Askia Mohammed I died in 1538 and was buried in a Step Pyramid at Gao.[124] He is fondly remembered as Askia the Great.

Gao, at this time, housed a population of 100,000 people.[125] According to Leo Africanus, a Moorish visitor, it was unwalled. Its houses were ugly but a few such as the royal buildings and the like were impressive. The inhabitants were mostly wealthy merchants who always travelled here and there to trade gold and wares. Bread, meat, and in particular, rice, were greatly abundant.

Cucumbers, melons and fine pumpkins were plentiful, as were wells of fresh water. On market days, there was a place where a busy slave market flourished.[126]

Timbuktu had fairly spacious houses, built of clay bricks, wood and plaster. There were three famous mosques in the city. The great Malian king, Mansa Musa, built the Djinguerebere Mosque in the fourteenth century. It was an eerie nine-aisle building looking somewhat like a fortress.[127] There was the University Mosque in which 25,000 students studied[128] and the Oratory of Sidi Yayia.[129] There were over 150 Koran schools in which 20,000 children were instructed.[130] In addition, factories flourished, especially in the textile industry, which made goods of cotton cloth and linen. Some of these institutions employed up to 100 apprentices under the guidance of a master tailor.[131] The palace itself was enlarged and embellished by Askia Bengan, a successor of Askia Mohammed I, with courtiers employed in ever greater numbers:

> [Whose] habits of dress became sumptuous, and it would seem from incidental allusions that different functionaries had their different uniforms and insignia of office, to the wearing of which great value was attached. The dress and appointments of women became also extravagantly luxurious. They were served on gold. In full dress their persons were covered with jewels, and the wives of the rich when they went out were attended by well-dressed slaves.[132]

Leo Africanus provides the following information on the city:

> In Timbuctoo [sic] there are numerous judges, doctors [i.e. of letters], and clerics, all receiving good salaries from the king. He pays great respect to men of learning. There is a big demand for books in manuscript, imported from Barbary [i.e. North Africa]. More profit is made from the book trade than any other line of business.[133]

Djenné was an eight-gated city encircled by a rampart that could only be approached by crossing narrow streams and canals. Many of its buildings were attractive with houses of two storeys, often with indoor drainage systems. The Grand Mosque was outstanding. It was a huge monument then over two hundred years old. It was a castle-like building with obeliskoid pillars built into its walls. Trade flourished in Djenné. Merchants brought salt from mines in Taghaza and gold from Bitou to its markets.[134] Leo Africanus, after visiting Djenné, informs us of the continuing use of golden coins in the region: "The coinage used by these [B]lacks is unstamped gold. They also use pieces of iron for the purchase of items of low value, such as milk, bread and honey. These pieces weigh one pound, half a pound, and a quarter of a pound."[135]

Agades had an estimated population of 70,000 people.[136] Leo Africanus described it as a wealthy town boasting stately mansions in the Moorish style.

Mali. View of the University of Sankore Mosque in Timbuktu. National Geographic recently described Timbuktu as the Paris of the mediæval world, on account of its intellectual culture. According to Professor Henry Louis Gates, 25,000 students studied there. From Major Felix Dubois, *Timbuctoo the Mysterious* **(UK, William Heinemann, 1897, p.279).**

Its inhabitants were typically foreign merchants, artificers or government officials.[137] The city had one famous old mosque, whose minaret continues to dominate the city's skyline.

In 1529 Askia the Great was deposed by his son Musa. From that period until 1591 there was a great deal of political instability. Askia Musa (ruled 1529 to 1531) was a tyrant. He had many people assassinated, especially rivals to the throne. On one occasion a marabout approached the Askia and said the following to him: "We enjoyed prosperity and repose in the reign of thy father, the happy, the good; and we made prayers that God might accord him victory and a long life. We asked ourselves, Has he a son who shall be the hope of Islam? And we answered, Yes; so we offered prayers for thee as well as for thy father. Thou hast deceived our hopes, but we do not cease our prayers, only instead of invoking God in thy favour we pray against thee".[138] The army overthrew him in 1531. The military leaders, led by Muhammad Bengan, ruled until 1537. But they too were overthrown, this time by Askia Ishmail. Ishmail's two years in power were spent fighting rebels. Askia Ishak I, the next ruler, established some stability, but only after eliminating his rivals. He led the empire from 1539 until 1549.[139]

Askia Daud became emperor in 1549. His military victories restored Songhai control over trade routes to the north. There were battles with the Mossi, the Fulani, the Malians, Kebbi and Katsina. Daud was so sure of the bravery and fighting ability of his soldiers that he sent a raiding party of twenty-four horsemen to attack the Hausa city of Katsina. These resolute men hurled themselves at 400 Katsina cavalrymen who had come out to engage them.

Songhai (Niger). View of the city of Agades. This city may well have had 70,000 people in the 16th century. From Dr Henry Barth, *Travels and Discoveries in North and Central Africa, Volume I* (UK, Longman, Brown, Green, Longmans & Roberts, 1857, opposite p.408).

Needless to say, Daud's men were beaten. Fifteen of them were killed in this struggle, and the nine remaining were wounded and captured. The ruler of Katsina sent them back to Daud with the message: "Men of such incomparable bravery do not deserve to die."[140] In 1556 the Moroccans attacked Taghaza. They killed the Songhai governor of the city and a number of Tuaregs who were working in the salt caravans. The surviving traders petitioned Daud to abandon Taghaza for safer pastures. The Askia opened a new salt mine in 1557 where the old salt traders found work.[141]

Askia Daud was a fine administrator. He employed only trusted supporters to the key jobs in the government. Under his rule, trade and culture flourished. He repaired the University Mosque and enlarged the Djinguerebere Mosque, both in Timbuktu. The learned and dutiful Cadi, Al-Aquib, supervised these construction works. Scholarship also flourished and Daud was a scholar himself. He founded libraries and employed scribes to transcribe important manuscripts.[142] Following his victorious campaign against Mali in 1559, Askia Daud married a Malian princess. According to As-Sadi, the great Songhai historian of the seventeenth century:

> He [Askia Daud] caused the princess to be conducted to Songhai in a sumptuous equipage. She was covered with jewels, surrounded by numerous slaves, both men and women, and provided with an abundant baggage train. All of the utensils were of gold - dishes, pitchers, pestle and mortar, everything.[143]

As Professor Diop points out, the princess "then lived in a luxury comparable with that of Helen of Troy".[144]

In Morocco, there were a number of sinister developments. In 1577 Al Mansur was the sultan, having deposed the black ruler Sultan Mohammed XI. Al Mansur was seeking alliances to help build his kingdom. Queen Elizabeth I, the ruler of England, was looking for alliances to expand England into an empire. A match had been made. She secretly negotiated the supply of British timber to help build Morocco's navy. In return, the Queen had hoped that Morocco would help her to attack Spain. Al Mansur just wasn't interested. His interest for war lay to the south. His gaze landed on the prosperous Songhai Empire. Here was his chance to mark his achievements in the history of his kingdom.[145]

In Songhai, Askia Daud ruled until his death in 1582. Civil wars followed his death. During this period, the Moroccans sent a spying mission to the country. Major Dubois, author of the pioneering and scholarly *Timbuctoo the Mysterious,* tells us that:

> He sent an embassy in 1583, ostensibly charged with magnificent gifts, but in reality commissioned to reconnoitre the roads and principal towns of Songhois [sic], and make a study of its army. Askia El Hadj II [sic] received the embassy at Gao, and returned it laden with gifts of still greater splendour than those it had brought. This was fuel to the flames … [146]

Askia Al-Hajj Mohammed II, the victor of the civil war, ruled for four years. Mohammed Bano succeeded him and ruled for two years. Stability only returned in 1588 when Askia Ishak II became emperor.[147] West Africa's Golden Age was severely interrupted by an invasion from Morocco in 1591.

A Moroccan source informs us that Al Mansur spent many years convincing his Council of War of this massive project. Their main fear was the death toll in crossing the Sahara. "Prince" they replied, "there is an immense desert between our country and the Sudan [i.e. West Africa], which is devoid of water and vegetation, and so hard to traverse that the very birds lose their way there". "If these are all your objections," replied Al Mansur, "I see no reason why they should hinder my resolution … the conquest itself will be an easy one, for the Sudanese know neither powder nor cannon, nor are they acquainted with the muskets of terrifying sound. They are only armed with spears and sabres, and what can they avail against us? Why should we make war against the Turk, who gives much trouble and little profit, when the Sudan would be an easy conquest, and is richer than the whole of northern Africa?"[148] After persuading the Council of War and further years of planning, he wrote to Queen Elizabeth I on June 23 1590 requesting England's assistance. The Queen was more than happy to supply men and weapons. The possible rewards of looting the

Songhai (Mali). Mausoleum of Askia the Great in the city of Gao. 1538. This building resembles a step pyramid.

Songhai Empire for its gold proved too great an opportunity to miss. Queen Elizabeth supplied artillery, cannonballs, guns and soldiers.[149]

The lure of Songhai's wealth attracted other Europeans. In fact, of the 4,000 men in Al Mansur's first division of the army, 2,500 were Europeans. The artillerymen were mostly English and the commander of the army was a Spaniard named Judar Pasha. Professor DeGraft-Johnson tells us that: "So ready were Europeans to enlist in this Moroccan army that Spanish became its official language".[150]

In October 1590 the Moroccan army, under Judar Pasha - a eunuch, left to invade Songhai. The army consisted of 2,000 soldiers, 1,500 lancers, 500 cavalry, 1,000 camel-men, 8,000 camels, 1,000 packhorses and 600 scouts. Presumably the other 7,000 camels were laden with artillery and supplies. Guarding Judar Pasha was a personal unit of 70 trained bodyguards. The journey across the desert cost many lives. One-third of the army did not survive but they continued their surge towards Songhai. In February 1591 they reached the River Niger. Songhai scouts soon learned of the nature of the expedition and immediately raised the alarm. The Songhai War Council quickly assembled 18,000 cavalrymen and 9,700 soldiers who were led by Askia Ishak II. Songhai prepared to do battle. Judar Pasha, though vastly outnumbered, had the advantage. He had large stocks of guns, ammunition and cannons. Songhai had none of these weapons. As the war commenced, vast numbers were brutally slain.[151]

After his initial victory, Judar Pasha pressed on. He sacked, pillaged and burnt to the ground the cities of Djenné, Gao and Timbuktu. His army filled in water wells and destroyed fields of crops. As-Sadi tells us that after the invasion:

> The high cost of food ... was excessive; a great number of people died from hunger and the famine was such that people ate the corpses of draft animals and of human beings. The exchange rate fell to 500 cowries. Then the plague came in turn to decimate the population and killed many that the famine had spared. This high cost of food, which lasted two years, ruined the inhabitants, who were reduced to selling their furniture and utensils. All the elders were unanimous in saying that they had never seen such a calamity and that not one of the elders before then had ever told them about anything like it.[152]

In Morocco, by contrast, things were very different:

> '[Al Mansur] received so much gold-dust, musk, slaves, ebony, and other valuable objects,' says the [Moroccan] chronicle, 'that the envious are troubled and all spectators are stupefied. He now pays his functionaries in pure metal of good weight.' From which it would appear that he had not been above falsifying his coinage. 'There were fourteen [hundred] smiths in his palace employed in making the gold into coins, while other portions of the treasure were converted into necklaces and jewels, and the name of El Dékébi (the Golden) was given to the sultan.' Great public rejoicings continued at Marrakesh during three days, and deputations came from all parts to offer congratulations.[153]

After the Moroccan invasion of 1591, their first commander, Judar Pasha, was dismissed. Judar had become ill, affected by a tropical disease. Many in his army suffered the same ailment. The Moroccans replaced him as commander with another eunuch, Mahmud Ben Zergun.[154]

Mahmud led his troops to commit many brutal acts. One of these was the capture of the Sankore University professors. The arrests took place in late October 1593. The captured scholars were deported to Morocco in chains. Some of them were killed in a massacre along the way. Those that survived the journey were forced to serve the Moroccans. Others were imprisoned.[155] The Moroccan army confiscated the libraries of the scholars. Professor Ahmed Baba, the head of the University, lost 1600 books in this way. Other scholars with even larger libraries lost even more books. In the words of her Ladyship:

> [W]hile other forms of wealth were greedily appropriated, the contents of the libraries were destroyed. The sack of Timbuctoo [sic] was the signal for the letting loose of all the evils of lawless tyranny upon the country. From this time the history of the [region] becomes a mere record of riot, robbery and decadence.[156]

But that was not all. Professor Diop laments on the loss of "the judicial and administrative archives: assistants of cadis kept minutes of the sessions. But tons of documents have disappeared".[157] On a brighter note, however, Professor Henry Louis Gates, the noted African-American scholar, has recently shown that thousands of these old manuscripts still exist in the private libraries of leading Timbuktu families. The challenge is now to have the manuscripts catalogued and then translated.[158]

Professor Baba enjoyed a very high reputation in the Islamic world. Amongst the Songhai, he was known as "The Unique Pearl of his Time". In a Moroccan text from the period, the praise for him was even more gushing. He is described as "the imam, the erudite, the high-minded, the eminent among scholars, Abu l-Abbas Ahmed Baba."[159] In Morocco, the Arab scholars petitioned to have him released from jail. He was released a year after his arrival on May 9 1596. Major Dubois narrates that:

> All the believers were greatly pleased with his release, and he was conducted
> in triumph from his prison to the principal mosque of Marrakesh. A great many
> of the learned men urged him to open a course of instruction. His first thought
> was to refuse, but overcome by their persistence he accepted a post in the
> Mosque of the Kerifs and taught rhetoric, law, and theology. An extraordinary
> number of pupils attended his lectures, and questions of the gravest importance
> were submitted to him by the magristracy, his decision always being treated as
> final.[160]

Despite this adulation, Baba was careful to credit his learning to the Almighty and thus maintained his modesty. A Moroccan source tells of an audience he obtained with Al Mansur. It appears that the scholar gave the sultan something of a dressing down. Baba complained about the sultan's lack of manners, his ill treatment received during his original arrest, the sacking of his private library, and the destruction of Songhai. We are told by the Moroccan author that Al Mansur "being unable to reply to [any of] this, put an end to the audience."[161]

The professor was detained in Morocco for a total of 12 years. Eventually he received permission from Al Mansur's successor to return to Songhai. Just before his departure across the desert, he vowed in the presence of the leading scholars of Marrakesh who had gathered to give him a send off, "May God never bring me back to this meeting, nor make me return to this country!"[162] He returned to a devastated Timbuktu and died there in 1627.

In closing, we give the final word to Professor Ahmed Baba, who has left us the following sketch of his tutor, Professor Mohammed Abu Bekr of Sankore. Abu Bekr, the great master, would appear to have been a useful representative of the scholarly life of the University:

He taught his pupils to love science [wrote Baba], to follow its teachings, to devote their time to it [and] to associate with scholars ... He lavishly lent his most precious books, rare copies, and the volumes he most valued, and never asked for them again, no matter what was the subject of which they treated ... [Sometimes] a student would present himself at the door and ask for a book, and he would give it without even knowing who the man was ... He had a passion for books ... he collected them with ardour, both buying and causing them to be copied.[163]

Notes

[1] John G. Jackson, *Introduction to African Civilizations*, US, Citadel Press, 1970, p.199.
[2] Cheikh Anta Diop, *Precolonial Black Africa*, US, Lawrence Hill Books, 1987, pp.199-200.
[3] J. Spencer Trimingham, *A History of Islam in West Africa*, UK, Oxford University Press, 1962, p.48.
[4] Ibid.
[5] Quoted in ibid.
[6] Nehemia Levtzion, *Ancient Ghana and Mali*, UK, Methuen & Co., 1973, p.4 and J. Spencer Trimingham, *A History of Islam in West Africa*, p.26.
[7] Quoted in Nehemia Levtzion, *Ancient Ghana and Mali*, pp.18-9.
[8] Cheikh Anta Diop, *Precolonial Black Africa*, p.65.
[9] Laure Meyer, *Black Africa: Masks, Sculpture, Jewelry*, France, Éditions Pierre Terrail, 1992, p.179.
[10] Basil Davidson, *Africa in History*, UK, Macmillan, 1991, pp.87-8.
[11] Charles Finch, *The Star of Deep Beginnings*, US, Khenti, 1998, p.162 and Peter Garlake, *Early Art and Architecture of Africa*, UK, Oxford University Press, 2002, pp.97 and 99.
[12] Christopher Ehret, *The Civilizations of Africa*, UK, James Currey, 2002, pp.231-2.
[13] Patrick J. Munson, *Archaeology and the Prehistoric Origins of the Ghana Empire*, in *Journal of African History, Volume 21: No.4*, UK, Cambridge University Press, 1990, pp.459-60.
[14] Ibid.
[15] Ibid.
[16] Leo Frobenius, *History of African Civilization*, quoted in W. E. B. DuBois, *The World and Africa*, US, International Publishers, 1965, pp.201-2.
[17] Nehemia Levtzion, *Ancient Ghana and Mali*, p.14 and Daniel Chu and Elliott Skinner, *A Glorious Age in Africa*, US, Africa World Press, 1990, pp.19-20.
[18] J. Spencer Trimingham, *A History of Islam in West Africa*, p.48.
[19] Basil Davidson, *Old Africa Rediscovered*, UK, Victor Gollancz, 1959, p.84.
[20] J. C. DeGraft-Johnson, *African Glory*, UK, Watts & Co., 1954, p.80.
[21] Cf. Basil Davidson, *African Kingdoms*, Netherlands, Time-Life Books, 1967, pp.90-1.
[22] Daniel Chu and Elliott Skinner, *A Glorious Age in Africa*, p.38.
[23] John G. Jackson, *Introduction to African Civilizations*, p.202.
[24] Daniel Chu and Elliott Skinner, *A Glorious Age in Africa*, p.18.
[25] Quoted in Cheikh Anta Diop, *Precolonial Black Africa*, p.7.
[26] G. T. Stride & Caroline Ifeka, *Peoples and Empires of West Africa*, UK, Thomas Nelson and Sons, 1971, pp.38-40.

[27] J. Spencer Trimingham, *A History of Islam in West Africa*, p.51.

[28] Ibid., pp.51-2.

[29] Ibid., p.54.

[30] Daniel Chu and Elliott Skinner, *A Glorious Age in Africa*, p.28.

[31] G. T. Stride & Caroline Ifeka, *Peoples and Empires of West Africa*, p.37.

[32] Al-Bakri's writings are cited in J. Spencer Trimingham, *A History of Islam in West Africa*, pp.52-3 and Lady Lugard, *A Tropical Dependency*, UK, James Nisbet & Co., 1906, pp.96-7.

[33] Abdurrahman As-Sadi, *Tarikh es Sudan*, quoted in Lady Lugard, *A Tropical Dependency*, p.96.

[34] J. Spencer Trimingham, *A History of Islam in West Africa*, p.53 and Lady Lugard, *A Tropical Dependency*, p.96 and Daniel Chu and Elliott Skinner, *A Glorious Age in Africa*, p.40.

[35] Cheikh Anta Diop, *Precolonial Black Africa*, p.82.

[36] Ibid., p.48 and Nehemia Levtzion, *Ancient Ghana and Mali*, p.27.

[37] Quoted in Basil Davidson, *Old Africa Rediscovered*, p.86.

[38] Cheikh Anta Diop, *Precolonial Black Africa*, pp.63-4 and Lady Lugard, *A Tropical Dependency*, p.111.

[39] J. Spencer Trimingham, *A History of Islam in West Africa*, pp.51-2.

[40] Quoted in ibid.

[41] Lady Lugard, *A Tropical Dependency*, p.91.

[42] John G. Jackson, *Introduction to African Civilizations*, p.205 and Cheikh Anta Diop, *Precolonial Black Africa*, pp.134-5.

[43] G. T. Stride & Caroline Ifeka, *Peoples and Empires of West Africa*, pp.18-21.

[44] Quoted in J. Spencer Trimingham, *A History of Islam in West Africa*, pp.42-3.

[45] Quoted in ibid., p.44.

[46] Daniel Chu and Elliott Skinner, *A Glorious Age in Africa*, p.25.

[47] G. T. Stride & Caroline Ifeka, *Peoples and Empires of West Africa*, pp.20 and 41-2.

[48] Wayne Chandler, *The Moor: Light of Europe's Dark Age*, in *Golden Age of the Moor*, ed Ivan Van Sertima, US, Transaction Publishers, 1992, p.173.

[49] Ibid., pp.173-5.

[50] J. C. DeGraft-Johnson, *African Glory*, pp.83-5.

[51] John G. Jackson, *Introduction to African Civilizations*, p.207.

[52] Lady Lugard, *A Tropical Dependency*, p.96.

[53] Quoted in Cheikh Anta Diop, *Precolonial Black Africa*, pp.134-5.

[54] Daniel Chu and Elliott Skinner, *A Glorious Age in Africa*, pp.48-50 and Chancellor Williams, *The Destruction of Black Civilization*, US, Third World Press, 1987, pp.200-1.

[55] Basil Davidson, *Old Africa Rediscovered*, p.86.

[56] Cheikh Anta Diop, *The African Origin of Civilization: Myth or Reality?* US, Lawrence Hill Books, 1974, p.157.

[57] Basil Davidson, *Old Africa Rediscovered*, p.86. For more data see Daniel Chu and Elliott Skinner, *A Glorious Age in Africa*, pp.40-1.

[58] Quoted in Cheikh Anta Diop, *The African Origin of Civilization: Myth or Reality?* p.157.

[59] Daniel Chu and Elliott Skinner, *A Glorious Age in Africa*, p.41.

[60] Roland Oliver and Brian M. Fagan, *Africa in the Iron Age*, UK, Cambridge University Press, 1974, p.167.

[61] S. K. McIntosh and R. J. McIntosh, *The Early City in West Africa: towards an understanding,* in *The African Archaeological Review: Volume 2,* UK, Cambridge University Press, 1984, p.91.

[62] Cheikh Anta Diop, *Precolonial Black Africa,* p.97.

[63] Compare Allan Leary, *West Africa,* in *Architecture of the Islamic World,* ed George Michell, UK, Thames and Hudson, 1978, p.274 and Basil Davidson, *Old Africa Rediscovered,* plate 8, opposite p.65.

[64] Kathy Brewis, *Writings in the Sand,* in *The Sunday Times Magazine,* UK, 28 January 2001, pp.32-5.

[65] Implied in Chancellor Williams, *The Destruction of Black Civilization,* pp.202-4.

[66] John G. Jackson, *Introduction to African Civilizations,* pp.207 and 211.

[67] Basil Davidson, *Old Africa Rediscovered,* p.95.

[68] Basil Davidson, *African Kingdoms,* p.84.

[69] Ibn Battuta, *Travels in Asia and Africa,* (Translated by H. A. R. Gibb), UK, George Routeledge & Sons, 1929, p.329.

[70] Chancellor Williams, *The Destruction of Black Civilization,* p.202.

[71] J. Spencer Trimingham, *A History of Islam in West Africa,* p.64.

[72] Ibid., p.235.

[73] Herman Bell, *History and Religion,* in *Manding Art and Civilisation,* ed Guy Atkins, UK, Studio International, 1972, p.6.

[74] J. Spencer Trimingham, *A History of Islam in West Africa,* p.64.

[75] J. C. DeGraft-Johnson, *African Glory,* pp.93-5 and G. T. Stride & Caroline Ifeka, *Peoples and Empires of West Africa,* pp.47-50.

[76] J. C. DeGraft-Johnson, African Glory, p.95 and Daniel Chu and Elliott Skinner, *A Glorious Age in Africa,* pp.56-7.

[77] J. C. DeGraft-Johnson, *African Glory,* pp.95-6.

[78] Ibidem and G. T. Stride & Caroline Ifeka, *Peoples and Empires of West Africa,* pp.50-1.

[79] Jeremy Isaacs (producer), *Millennium: The 14th Century,* Television Series, UK, BBC Television, 1999.

[80] Charles Finch, *The Star of Deep Beginnings,* p.53.

[81] John G. Jackson, *Introduction to African Civilizations,* pp.234-5 and 261-3.

[82] Ivan Van Sertima, *Evidence for an African Presence,* in *African Presence in Early America,* ed Ivan Van Sertima, US, Transaction Publishers, 1992, pp.29-30.

[83] Harold G. Lawrence, *Mandinka Voyages across the Atlantic,* in *African Presence in Early America,* ed Ivan Van Sertima, US, Transaction Publishers, 1992, pp.185-194.

[84] Keith M. Jordan, *The African Presence in Ancient America: Evidence from the Physical Anthropology,* in *African Presence in Early America,* ed Ivan Van Sertima, US, Transaction Publishers, 1992, pp.112-3.

[85] Ivan Van Sertima, *Evidence for an African Presence,* in *African Presence in Early America,* p.51.

[86] Alexander von Wuthenau, *Unexpected African Faces in Pre-Columbian America,* in *African Presence in Early America,* pp.95-6 and Ivan Van Sertima, *They Came Before Columbus,* US, Random House, 1976, pp.138-9, Plate 5.

[87] J. C. DeGraft-Johnson, *African Glory,* p.97.

[88] Ibid.

[89] Cynthia Crossen, *The Rich and How They Got That Way,* UK, Nicholas Brealey, 2000, p.ix.

[90] Ibid., p.xi.

[91] Basil Davidson, *Africa,* television series part 3: *Caravans of Gold,* UK, Channel Four Television, 1984.
[92] Quoted in Lady Lugard, *A Tropical Dependency,* p.120.
[93] John G. Jackson, *Introduction to African Civilizations,* pp.210-1.
[94] J. C. DeGraft-Johnson, *African Glory,* p.98.
[95] Lady Lugard, *A Tropical Dependency,* pp.125-6 and Cheikh Anta Diop, *Precolonial Black Africa,* pp.84 and 200-1.
[96] Sergio Domian, *Architecture Soudanaise: Vitalite d'une tradition urbaine et monumentale,* France, Éditions L'Harmattan, 1989, p.15. Translated by this author.
[97] J. C. DeGraft-Johnson, *African Glory,* p.98.
[98] G. T. Stride & Caroline Ifeka, *Peoples and Empires of West Africa,* p.52.
[99] John G. Jackson, *Introduction to African Civilizations,* p.209.
[100] Lady Lugard, *A Tropical Dependency,* p.127.
[101] Cf. J. C. DeGraft-Johnson, *African Glory,* pp.99-100.
[102] Saïd Hamdun and Noël King, *Ibn Battuta in Black Africa,* US, Markus Wiener, 1994, p.30.
[103] Ibid., pp.52-3.
[104] Ibid., p.37.
[105] Ibid., p.55.
[106] Ibid., p.91.
[107] J. Spencer Trimingham, *A History of Islam in West Africa,* pp.72-3 and G. T. Stride & Caroline Ifeka, *Peoples and Empires of West Africa,* pp.54-5.
[108] G. T. Stride & Caroline Ifeka, *Peoples and Empires of West Africa,* p.55.
[109] J. Spencer Trimingham, *A History of Islam in West Africa,* pp.83-91.
[110] Cheikh Anta Diop, *The African Origin of Civilization: Myth or Reality?* p.157.
[111] Cheikh Anta Diop, *Precolonial Black Africa,* pp.81 and 91, and Daniel Chu and Eliott Skinner, *A Glorious Age in Africa,* pp.83-4.
[112] Al-Yaqubi, *Tarikh,* quoted in J. Spencer Trimingham, *A History of Islam in West Africa,* pp.85-6.
[113] Daniel Chu and Eliott Skinner, *A Glorious Age in Africa,* p.84.
[114] Lady Lugard, *A Tropical Dependency,* p.161.
[115] Cheikh Anta Diop, Precolonial Black Africa, p.81.
[116] Cf. J. C. DeGraft-Johnson, African Glory, pp.99-100.
[117] Cf. ibid., pp.101-3.
[118] Cheikh Anta Diop, *Precolonial Black Africa,* p.227.
[119] Ibid., pp.68-9 and 167.
[120] Ibid., pp.67-8.
[121] Lady Lugard, *A Tropical Dependency,* p.196.
[122] Cheikh Anta Diop, *Precolonial Black Africa,* pp.111-2.
[123] John O. Hunwick, *Timbuktu and the Songhay Empire: Al-Sadi's Tarikh al-Sudan down to 1613 and other Contemporary Documents,* Netherlands, Brill, 1999, p.xli.
[124] Cheikh Anta Diop, *The African Origin of Civilization: Myth or Reality?* p.178.
[125] Sergio Domian, *Architecture Soudanaise,* p.80.
[126] Leo Africanus is quoted in Basil Davidson, *African Kingdoms,* p.85.
[127] Sergio Domian, *Architecture Soudanaise,* pp.67-72.
[128] Henry Louis Gates, *Into Africa,* television series part 2: *The Road to Timbuktu,* UK, BBC Television, 1999.
[129] Major Felix Dubois, *Timbuctoo the Mysterious,* UK, William Heinemann, 1897, p.311. See also pp.286-7.

[130] Pierre Maas et al, *Djenné: Chef D'Oeuvre Architectural,* Netherlands, Universite de Technologie, Eindhoven, 1992, p.23.

[131] Cheikh Anta Diop, *Precolonial Black Africa,* pp.206-7.

[132] Lady Lugard, *A Tropical Dependency,* p.207.

[133] Quoted in Walter Rodney, *The Groundings with my Brothers,* UK, Bogle L'Ouverture publications, 1975, p.48.

[134] Sergio Domian, *Architecture Soudanaise,* pp.42-56 and Daniel Chu and Eliott Skinner, *A Glorious Age in Africa,* p.91.

[135] John O. Hunwick, *Timbuktu and the Songhay Empire: Al-Sadi's Tarikh al-Sudan down to 1613 and other Contemporary Documents,* pp.277-8.

[136] René Gardi, *Indigenous African Architecture,* US, Van Nostrand Reinhold Company, 1973, p.243.

[137] Lady Lugard, *A Tropical Dependency,* p.195.

[138] Major Felix Dubois, *Timbuctoo the Mysterious,* p.118.

[139] Cf. G. T. Stride & Caroline Ifeka, *Peoples and Empires of West Africa,* p.76.

[140] J. C. DeGraft-Johnson, *African Glory,* pp.110-1.

[141] Ibid., p.111.

[142] G. T. Stride & Caroline Ifeka, *Peoples and Empires of West Africa,* p.76.

[143] Quoted in Lady Lugard, *A Tropical Dependency,* p.142.

[144] Cheikh Anta Diop, *Precolonial Black Africa,* p.85.

[145] J. C. DeGraft-Johnson, *African Glory,* pp.111-2.

[146] Felix Dubois, *Timbuctoo the Mysterious,* p.124.

[147] G. T. Stride & Caroline Ifeka, *Peoples and Empires of West Africa,* p.76.

[148] Felix Dubois, *Timbuctoo the Mysterious,* p.124.

[149] J. C. DeGraft-Johnson, *African Glory,* p.113.

[150] Ibid.

[151] Ibid., pp.113-5.

[152] Quoted in Cheikh Anta Diop, *Precolonial Black Africa,* p.142.

[153] Felix Dubois, *Timbuctoo the Mysterious,* p.127. See also Laura Marshall (producer), *Timewatch: White Slaves, Pirate Gold,* UK, BBC Television, 2003. They give the number of smiths as 1,400.

[154] J. C. DeGraft-Johnson, *African Glory,* pp.115-6.

[155] Cheikh Anta Diop, *Precolonial Black Africa,* pp.193-4.

[156] Lady Lugard, *A Tropical Dependency,* p.310.

[157] Cheikh Anta Diop, *Precolonial Black Africa,* p.182.

[158] Henry Louis Gates, *Into Africa,* television series part 2: *The Road to Timbuktu.*

[159] John O. Hunwick, *Timbuktu and the Songhay Empire: Al-Sadi's Tarikh al-Sudan down to 1613 and other Contemporary Documents,* p.315 and Felix Dubois, *Timbuctoo the Mysterious,* p.306.

[160] Felix Dubois, *Timbuctoo the Mysterious,* p.307.

[161] Quoted in ibid., p.308.

[162] Quoted in ibid., p.309.

[163] Quoted in Anna Melissa Graves, *Africa, the Wonder and the Glory,* US, Black Classic Press, (original 1942), p.39.

CHAPTER THIRTEEN: THE CIVILISATION OF THE MOORS

The Caliphate of Cordova and the Empire of the Two Shores

By 500 AD the western part of the Roman Empire was in decline. This was of some importance since the Romans carried the flame of civilisation in Europe. Europe therefore entered an unhappy period known as the Dark Ages. This period lasted until 1100 AD. Often glossed over in the history books, Professor Robert Briffault, a keen student of the development of culture, wrote the following commentary on this part of world history:

> From the fifth to the tenth [sic] century Europe lay sunk in a night of barbarism ... more awful and horrible than that of the primitive savage, for it was the decomposing body of what had been a great civilization ... Cities had practically disappeared ... They were pulled down and used as quarries to build towers in which a bishop or a baron established himself who could afford some protection. In Nimes, for example, the remains of the population dwelt in huts built among the ruins of the amphitheatre. Other towns were completely abandoned ... Famines and plagues were chronic: there were ten devastating famines and thirteen plagues in the course of the tenth century alone. Cases of cannibalism were not uncommon; there were manhunts, not with a view to plunder but for food. It is on record that at Tournus on the Saône, human flesh was publicly put up for sale.[1]

Dr Briffault was not alone in holding this perspective. The historian, Joseph McCabe, wrote learnedly on medieval history. In his view:

> None of our modern sophistry redeems the squalor of Europe from the fifth to the eleventh century ... By the year 1,000 Europe was reduced to a condition which, if we were not Europeans, we should frankly call barbarism, yet at that time the Arabs had a splendid civilization in Spain, Sicily, Egypt, and Persia, and it linked on to those of India and China. We write manuals of the history of Europe or of the Middle Ages, and we confine ourselves to a small squalid area (Russia and Prussia were not yet civilized and Spain was Moorish) and ignore the brilliant civilization than ran from Portugal to the China Sea.[2]

The term 'Dark Ages' only applied to Europe. The rest of the world was not necessarily in a dark age. The Dark Age period of European Christendom actually corresponds to the Golden Age of Islamic civilisation. The Muslim city of Cordova in Spain was much like a modern city by at least 950 AD. It boasted paved streets drained by sewers, raised pavements and street lamps. Of this city, an old Muslim chronicler wrote the following:

> Cordova is the Bride of Andalusia [i.e. Spain]. To her belong all the beauty and all the ornaments that delight the eye or dazzle the sight. Her long line of Sultans form her crown of glory; her necklace is strung with the pearls her poets have gathered from the ocean of language; her dress is of the banners of learning, well knit together by her men of science; and the masters of every art and industry are the hem of her garments.[3]

This wonderful city had a population of at least one million, housed in 200,000 properties and 60,000 mansions and palaces. Of two storeys, the grander homes boasted latrines and running water. Fine gardens surrounded the larger buildings. There were 900 public baths and many private baths, not to mention 800 public schools and many colleges. Education was universal, being offered to girls as well as boys. Over 1,000 mosques flourished, of which one, the Great Mosque, is among the great buildings of the world. It had over 1,000 columns made of jasper, marble and porphyry that lifted a golden and scarlet roof. At night, lanterns by the thousand, of brass and silver, illuminated the monument. The burning oil was scented with perfume. Among its surprises are the striking glass mosaics, the ivory and wooden pulpit, the crossed arched sanctuary, the four fountains and the leafy courtyard. Other monuments were equally wonderful. The al-Zahra palace, almost a city by itself, had 15,000 [sic] doors of brass and iron. Of trade, the Cordovans had access to over 4,000 markets and 80,000 shops. They could buy Chinese tea, Indian spices, Russian furs, African ebony and ivory, and locally made goods. A massive wall measuring fourteen miles encircled this busy seven-gated city.[4]

The Arab invasion of North Africa was of great consequence. Many Africans fled south from North Africa to lands south of the Sahara. Those that remained were converted to Islam.[5] The Arabs occupied Egypt in 639 AD, Tripoli in 643, and south west Morocco by 681. In 698 they appointed the Yemeni, Musa ibn Nusair, Governor of North Africa.

Musa wanted to take control of Spain but feared that an invasion at this time would exhaust his armies. In Spain the Visigoths (Germans) had been in control for the previous 200 years. They had seized Spain from the rule of the ailing Roman Empire. Though Christians, the Visigoths had become as immoral and corrupt as the previous Roman administration.

The fortress of Ceuta, located on the northern tip of Morocco, posed another obstacle to Musa. Any campaign from Africa against Spain would have to bypass this fortress and the lands surrounding it. Count Julian, the master of the fortress, was an ally of King Roderick, the Visigothic ruler of Spain. Julian guarded the region from Arab attacks. Suddenly, however, Julian switched sides. Roderick apparently took advantage of Julian's daughter while she was at his Toledo court. In revenge, Count Julian threw in his lot with Musa. The Count offered Musa knowledge of Roderick's defences. Moreover, he offered ships that could be used to cross the Mediterranean for an invasion.[6]

In 710 Musa sent a reconnaissance mission of 500 African (i.e. Moorish/Berber) converts to Islam into Spain led by Tarif, a fellow African. Of the 500 troops, 400 of them were foot soldiers and the remainder were horsemen. Using four ships supplied by Musa, they landed at a port today called Tarifa and plundered Algericas. The expeditionary force confirmed that Julian's information on Roderick's weaknesses were true. Tarifa was not, of course, the original name of the port. The victorious expedition renamed the port in honour of Tarif. Incidentally, the Moors at a later date imposed a special tax at this port that today we call a tariff.[7]

The following year, Musa sent a second and more formidable African army into Spain. Tarik ibn Ziyad, the Berber/Moorish governor of Mauritania, led the expeditionary force of 6,700 African soldiers and 300 Arab translators and propagandists. On landing in Spain, they occupied Mons Calpe, a great cliff and the surrounding land, where they built a fortress. They renamed this region Gebel Tarik meaning Hill/Rock of Tarik. In more recent times, the Spanish have corrupted this name to produce 'Gibraltar'.[8]

Leaving this base, Tarik led his men in battles against the cities of Algericas and Carteya. During these campaigns, his armies grew. Thousands of native Spaniards flocked to his standard against the Visigothic rulers. On 18 July 711 AD, Tarik's 14,000 troops faced a force of 60,000 led by King Roderick at the Janda Lagoon. Tarik triumphed. He later seized Archidona, Cordova, Ecija, Elvira and Murcian Oribeula. Toledo, the capital, also fell. The Jews of the city handed control to Tarik.[9] According to Professor Edward Scobie, an African-American expert on Africans in European history, a European writer sympathetic to the Spaniards remembered the conquest in this way:

> [T]he reins of their (Moors) horses were as fire, their faces black as pitch, their eyes shone like burning candles, their horses were swift as leopards and the riders fiercer than a wolf in a sheepfold at night ... The noble Goths [the German rulers of Spain to whom Roderick belonged] were broken in an hour, quicker than tongue can tell. Oh luckless Spain![10]

In 712 AD Musa ibn Nusair mobilised an army of 18,000 Arabs and Africans. Professor C. P. Groves believes that Musa was "apparently taken by surprise at the speed of events, hastened across with an army the following year and completed the conquest, thus associating Arab arms with the final victory."[11] They seized Carmona, Cremona, Medina and Sidona. Abd-al-Aziz, Musa's son, commanded the conquest of Beja, Nieblu and Seville.

Roderick perished in 713 AD. Tarik's army, supplied with reinforcements by Musa, finally defeated him in battle on a mountain range of Segoyuela. The Visigoth king died in the campaign.[12] A consequence of the victory was that Africans entered Spain by the thousand. "So eager were they to come" says Brunson and Rashidi, "that some are said to have floated over on tree trunks".[13]

Eventually, Tarik and Musa met up in Toledo. "The meeting between the conqueror and his superior officer was not friendly", wrote Professor Lane-Poole, a venerable authority on the Moorish culture:

> Tarik went forth to receive the governor of the West with all honour, but Musa struck him with a whip, overwhelmed him with reprimands for exceeding his instructions, and, declaring that it was impossible to entrust the safety of the Moslems to such rash and impetuous leading, threw him into prison. When this act of jealous tyranny came to the ears of Khalif Welid he summoned Musa to Damascus, and restored Tarik to his command in Spain.[14]

The early years of Islamic rule in Spain were less than stable. From 716 to 747 AD a staggering nineteen governors ruled over Cordova. The Spaniards themselves remained turbulent throughout. Led by Count Pelayo, they engaged in guerrilla tactics. From the mountains of Murcia province, they attacked the Muslim invaders. In 722 AD the Spaniards scored an important victory at the Battle of Covandongo. They established Christian rule in Asturias and the northern regions of Spain, meanwhile, the Arabs and Africans controlled the southern regions.[15]

The Muslims took control of land vacated by the Spaniards who had fled north. The Arabs settled the most fertile land of the south and left the Africans poorer land in central Spain and areas closer to the north. This led to another conflict between Musa - the Arab overlord, and Tarik - the African subordinate. In time African and Arab conflict would escalate. Between 741 and 746 AD, civil war erupted between the two groups. The rebellion originated in North Africa and then spread to Spain.[16]

Stability emerged under the leadership of the Arab, Yusuf al-Fihri, who became ruler in 747 AD. Yusuf installed members of his family into key positions across the empire. He expanded roads and developed the cities. Able in battle, he won a border war against the Christian regime in the north. He also attempted to make Spain independent of the Umayyad Dynasty in the Middle East. Abd-al-Rahman, an Umayyad prince of mixed Arab and African (i.e. Moorish/Berber) ancestry, moved boldly to challenge this audacious strategy. In May 756 AD he defeated Yusuf outside the walls of Cordova. He became ruler of Islamic Spain and the first of the important Umayyad monarchs.[17]

Abd-al-Rahman I was an able ruler. He divided the country into military districts and administered it on this basis. Creating a standing army of 40,000 men, mostly Africans, he also began a navy. Attentive to security, he had fortifications built in many of the cities.

In agriculture, he made important developments that led to the growth of the farming industry. He introduced accurate land surveying, built granaries to combat food shortages, and established effective irrigation canals. From the Middle East, he imported cotton, fruits, rice, spices, sugarcane and vegetables.[18] In time, these policies stimulated Spanish farming and other industries. Sugarcane and cotton were planted near the Mediterranean coastal regions. Figs and olives were farmed in the south. Oranges and wine were cultivated in Granada and Malaga provinces. Oranges, rice, and palm trees sprouted in Valencia. This region, originally barren, benefited from Abd-al-Rahman's irrigation schemes. Other industries thrived. A silk industry grew up in Murcia. Leatherwork and dyeing flourished in Cordova. Ordnance developed in Toledo. Finally, a ceramics industry prospered in Almeria.[19]

The Umayyad Dynasty, despite being founded by an Arab-African, was in fact of such a mixed character that we should not assume that the rulers were Black. According to Mr J. A. Rogers, the great Jamaican researcher, an old Moorish chronicle described the earlier sultans of Spain as "blond, white, copper-colored, brown, reddish, dark, frizzly-haired, woolly-haired and the like."[20] Mr Wayne Chandler, an African-American writer, explained how this came about with great clarity:

> White slavery became widespread in Spain, [North] Africa, and the Mediterranean. The polygamous family structure common to many African cultures expedited the process of amalgamation and the consequences wrought havoc upon the inhabitants of Al-Andalus [i.e. Spain]. Licentiousness and immorality became more and more prevalent in the Moorish social structure. Predictably, there was a gradual eroding of virtues, philosophy and the pursuit of cultural excellence. Though Abdurrahman [sic] did not encourage or personally patronize the slave trade, its continued presence within his empire inevitably led to its collapse.[21]

Apart from the Umayyad sultans, who could have been of any ethnicity, the overwhelming majority of Muslims in the country were Africans. Professor Stanley Lane-Poole wrote that: "The Berbers were more numerous than the Arabs".[22] Sharing this view, Professor Jackson wrote that the Arabs "were always a minority in the so-called Arab culture of the Middle Ages".[23] Confirmation of this position has come from a somewhat surprising source. A 1992 edition of the journal *Human Biology* carried an intriguing article that was entitled *Importation Route of the Sickle Cell trait into Portugal: Contribution of Molecular Epidemiology*. The abstract to this valuable article reads as follows:

To elucidate the origin and spread of the sickle cell trait into the Portuguese population, we examined nine polymorphic DNA markers within the β globin gene cluster defining the haplotype. The population sample included 64 sickle-cell-gene-bearing individuals from defined Portuguese-speaking white, black, and Asian Indian populations. The nature and geographic distribution of the different βS haplotypes in Portugal suggest that the sickle cell trait has been imported twice: between the eighth and the thirteenth centuries from the Mediterranean basin (in association with the Benin haplotype) and after the fifteenth century from [B]lack Africa over an Atlantic route (Senegal and Bantu haplotypes).[24]

There are a number of different sickle-cell haplotypes. Among them are the Benin haplotype, the Senegalese haplotype, the Asian and Arab haplotype, etc. Had the Islamic culture been predominately Arab, it would have been the Asian/Arab haplotype that would have been introduced into the Portuguese population between the eighth and the thirteenth centuries and not the Benin haplotype. Furthermore, the researchers have been able to distinguish between the sickle-cell imported after the fifteenth century from the sickle-cell imported between the eighth and the thirteenth centuries. This separates the sickle-cell introduced by enslaved Africans from that introduced by African conquerors. This is strong evidence that the majority of Moors/Berbers were Negroes who carried the Benin haplotype into the Portuguese population. If they did this in Portugal, then they certainly did this in Spain.

According to Markus Hattstein, editor of an important modern work on Islamic culture, the Arabs in Spain were mostly "southern Arabs and Yemenites".[25] Even today, many of these people are Negroid. Taken with the Africans, we conclude that the Islamic culture of Spain was largely a Negro achievement. The Muslims that an ordinary Spaniard would have seen in charge of their destinies would have most likely been a Moor/Berber, or if not, a southern Arab. For this reason the culture is known as "The Moors in Spain". This is a reference to the Black colour of the conquering group whether from Africa or southern Arabia, even if the Umayyad rulers after Abd-al-Rahman I were of any ethnicity depending on the colour of their enslaved mothers. It is, of course, important to note that intermarriage was going on in the opposite direction too. For example, J. A. Rodgers informs us that: "Alphonso VI, white Christian king [of Spain] … took a Moorish wife, the lovely Zayda, who was the mother of his favourite son, Sancho".[26]

Hisham I succeeded his father in 788 AD, inheriting the throne aged 30. At the palace, he gathered poets, scholars and scientists, and created an intellectual culture in the land. In addition, the chroniclers remember him as "The Amiable" and "The Just", no doubt due to his numberless acts of piety. For example, he welcomed political refugees. In addition, he demonstrated compassion by personally visiting the sick and the disabled, even during stormy weather. On the practical side, he maintained order and security by having guards patrol the streets at night. In addition, he campaigned against the Christians of the north. He also displayed fortitude against the conspiracies of his uncles. To this effect, he had 1,000 Turkish guards protect his palace night and day. Finally, he rebuilt the bridge of Cordova, a not inconsiderable engineering feat.[27]

In 796 AD Al-Hakam became the next ruler. His reign was characterised by political instability and brutality. In 803 AD he faced a rebellion in Toledo. A number of newer Islamic converts rose up against him. At a feast, supposedly of reconciliation, he had 5,000 of these opponents killed. Two years later, he faced a conspiracy to unseat him. Suppressing this challenge, he had leading Cordovan nobles crucified. Following this, he gathered a force of 5,000 Slavic mercenaries to guard him. Years later new problems emerged. A Cordovan suburb revolted, blaming harsh taxes that Al-Hakam, himself, instituted. The sultan's response, brutal as ever, was to order the destruction of the suburb and the exiling of 25,000 people to Africa. Two thirds of these were sent to Alexandria, the remainder were sent to Fez.[28]

Abd-al-Rahman II ascended to the throne in 822 AD. This enterprising sultan converted the city of Cordova into a rival for Baghdad. He built palaces, laid out gardens, raised mosques, and constructed bridges. Professor Stanley Lane-Poole commented that:

> Four people ruled him throughout his career: one was a singer, the second a theologian, the third a woman, and the fourth a [B]lack slave. The most influential of these was the theologian Yahya, the same who had stirred up the students against Hakam, and who now acquired an absolute ascendancy over the mind of the new Sultan. The Queen Tarub and the slave Nasr, however, exercised no light authority in political matters.[29]

Apart from Yahya, Tarub and Nasr, the fourth influence of which Professor Lane-Poole wrote was Ziryab. This Black Middle-Eastern gentleman entered Spain in 822 AD. The leading musician and song stylist of his day, he founded the first conservatory of music in Cordova. An exquisite trendsetter, he revolutionised upper-class ideas of refinement and manners. He introduced the idea of changing one's wardrobe of clothes to follow the four seasons. Moreover, he popularised certain perfumes and the use of deodorant. Table manners did not go unaffected. Ziryab started the trend for the use of crystal tableware to replace goblets. Finally, he changed the custom of serving the different dishes of food all at once to the new style of beginning with a soup starter, followed by the main course, followed by desert.[30]

Sultan Abd-al-Rahman II and his successor, did however, face challenges from Christian fanatics.

Moors (Spain). Golden Tower of Seville. Built by the Almohad sultans. (Photo: Robin Walker).

> The very tolerance of the Moors only exasperated such fervent souls; they preferred to be persecuted, like the saints of old; they longed to be martyrs, and they were indignant with the Moslems, because they would not "persecute them for righteousness' sake" and ensure them the kingdom of heaven. Especially hateful to these earnest people was the open gaiety and sensuous refinement of the Moors; their enjoyment of life and all its pleasure, their music and singing, their very learning and science, were abhorrent to these ascetics. Life, to the true believer, meant only scourges and fasts, penances and confessions, purification through suffering, the mortifying of the flesh and sanctifying of the spirit. What happened was, in truth, nothing but the manifestation of the ascetic or monastic form of Christianity among the subject populations. A sudden and violent enthusiasm took the place of the indifference that had hitherto been the prevailing characteristic of Spanish Christianity, and a race for martyrdom began.[31]

The strategy these would-be martyrs adopted was to publicly blaspheme the Prophet Mahomet. The Islamic authorities begged these people to retract, not wishing to have them executed, but they persisted. This episode only came to an end during the time of Abd-al-Rahman II's successor. On 11 May 859 AD the Islamic authorities executed Eulogious, the spiritual leader of the Christian fanatics.[32]

Muhammad I followed Abd-al-Rahman II on to the throne. During his troubled reign, from 852 to 886 AD, much of the empire fell apart. Toledo became independent in 852 AD. Merida became independent thirteen years later. From the north, King Alfonso III of Leon, ruler of the Christians, seized Muslim territory. Muhammad was compelled to sue for peace with Alfonso in 883 AD. A year later, Umar ibn Hafsun, a ruler in the south, extended his power from Cordova to the Mediterranean. Umar's actions further weakened the hand of Muhammad.[33] During this confused period, some Moors seized other territories in southern Europe:

> Moorish domination [wrote Professor Scobie] extended to parts of Italy. In 846 A.D., they held the city of Rome in a state of siege while in 878 they captured Sicily from the Normans. Twenty years later the Moors took control of Southern Italy by defeating Otto II of Germany. As in Spain and Portugal, miscegenation took place on a wide scale between the Moors and the Italians … Like Portugal and Spain the blood of Africa permeated through all layers of Italian society and found its way into leading families, including the most illustrious royal families of the times - the Medicis.[34]

In 912 AD Abd-al-Rahman III became ruler of Spain, starting a second period of achievement. By the following year, he seized Seville. Years later he captured Merida, still under the rule of the Hafsun clan. In Africa he was proclaimed ruler of all Mauritania and Fez, thus establishing the Empire of the Two Shores with a court in Africa and one in Spain. To administrate these territories, he instituted a strongly centralised government founded on an efficient bureaucracy. He established good municipal administration, paid for by an effective tax system. Trade developed by the encouragement of agriculture through extensive irrigation, exploitation of the mineral resources of the land, and trade concessions for Jews. Finally, he built the palace-city of Medina al-Zahra and gathered poets and scholars at this residence.[35]

Al-Hakam II succeeded him in 961 AD and ruled for a creditable fifteen years. As crown prince, he was fond of books, scientists and scholars. On the throne, he sent agents across the Islamic world to procure books and compendia. He gave the agents large budgets to spend on scribes, scholars and copyists. In a Cordovan library, the sultan gathered 400,000 books accompanied by 44 volumes of indexes. In addition, he commissioned scholars to write books on ethics, statecraft and genealogy. He encouraged the study of geography, agriculture, astronomy, medicine, philosophy, and mathematics. Moreover, he established schools and centres of learning for people of all social classes.[36] Joseph McCabe wrote an excellent account of the intellectual culture of this period:

> Books were now in such demand that, Prof. Ribera estimates, Cordova alone produced 70,000 to 80,000 a year, all beautifully hand-written and very richly bound. The old parchment roll was discarded, and the manufacture of paper,

which the Persians had learned from the Chinese, occupied large mills at Xativa. The Caliph had a superbly housed collection of at least 400,000 - some writers say 600,000 - books, in rich bookcases … Courtiers and rich merchants followed his example, and libraries of 10,000 to 50,000 works were found in the mansions of the wealthy. "Even the humbler classes thirsted for books," says Ribera, and the servants or ladies of the harem were of higher price if they were well-read. "The wit of the learned is as precious as the blood of the martyr," a popular proverb ran. One copying shop at Cordova employed 170 women, and women authors were highly esteemed.[37]

At this time, a number of houses of learning were established in Christian Europe. There was one in Barcelona, Toulouse, Marseilles, Leon, Segovia, etc. They existed to translate Moorish and Arab texts from the original Arabic to Latin.[38]

In 978 AD Al-Mansur, a Yemenite noble, was elevated to power. Like the previous rulers, he was a patron of the arts and the sciences, but also able in warfare. Swelling the army with Africans, he is said to have won over 50 campaigns against the Christians of the north. Finally, he ordered a census of the city of Cordova. It revealed that the city had 213,077 houses for the working and middle classes, 60,300 palaces and mansions, 80,455 shops, 600 public baths, and 471 mosques.[39] Some scholars, who suggest that 1,000 mosques would have been nearer the mark, have considered this last figure of 471 too conservative.[40]

Cordova had become one of the greatest cities the world had yet seen. After much analysis of the old Islamic documents, Lady Lugard wrote an accurate and picturesque account of the city, its sophistication, and its scientific culture:

> The town in the time of the Ommeyades [sic] measured twenty-four miles by six, the greater part of which area was covered by mosques, palaces, and the houses of the great standing in beautiful gardens. These houses were palaces of luxury, magnificently decorated, cooled in summer by ingeniously arranged draughts of fresh air drawn from the garden over beds of flowers chosen for their perfume, warmed in winter by hot air conveyed through pipes bedded in the walls. There were bath-rooms supplied with hot and cold water. There were boudoirs, drawing-rooms, libraries, halls, corridors, and galleries lighted by windows of clear and coloured glass. Clusters of columns of marble, either plain or incrusted with more precious substances, supported roofs of mosaic and gold. The walls were decorated with mosaics, or covered with arabesque and floral paintings. The furniture was of the most precious and varied description. It was made of sandal and citron and other woods brought from the tropics, and curiously inlaid with mother-of-pearl, ivory, silver, and gold. There were tables of gold, set with emeralds, rubies, and pearls. In winter the walls were hung with tapestry, the floors were covered with thick Persian carpets, of which the most magnificent were embroidered with gold and pearls. There were luxurious couches piled with pillows. Vases of porcelain and crystal were

filled with flowers. Rare and curious objects from all over the world were brought together to satisfy the eye and taste. In the evening the rooms were lit by wax candles, which were distributed by groups of hundreds in chandeliers that hung from the ceilings. Great skill and taste were devoted to the design and workmanship of these chandeliers. They were often made from the metal found in the bells of Christian churches, and when this was the case, there seems to have been a special pleasure in designing them for use in the mosques. One famous chandelier is mentioned which held no less than 1804 [sic] candles. The gardens in which the great houses stood are described by every writer in terms of rapture. Bowers of roses; orange and pomegranate groves; shaded walks, over which lemon-trees were trained, so that the fruit when ripe "hung down like little lamps"; successions of colour and perfume, to procure which plants were brought from all parts of the world. Sometimes, to please a favourite wife, a whole hillside would be planted with her chosen colour. The use of water was thoroughly understood[.] Fountains, cascades, and lakes gave coolness and moisture to the air, and also provided opportunities for the keeping of fish and the special cultivation of water-plants. Garden fruits and vegetables were cultivated in rare perfection and variety. In the gardens there were labyrinths, and marble playing-courts. There were menageries of curious animals, and aviaries of foreign birds. Botany, horticulture, zoology, and ornithology were passions no less of the learned than of the rich.[41]

Al-Mansur died in 1002. Abd-al-Malik succeeded him and ruled until 1008. From this date until 1031, political unrest grew as less and less able men battled for the throne. Increasingly power fell into the hands of foreign mercenaries and military cadres. New threats came from secessionist groups. On 30 November 1031 Caliph Hisham III, the last legitimate monarch of the Umayyad line abdicated. "This marked the end of the caliphate of Cordoba [sic], and also of an important epoch in Islamic and European history."[42]

The Almoravid and Almohad Empires

The next part of the story concerns the Berbers of North and West Africa. In 1048 Yahya ibn Ibrahim, the ruler of the Berbers, made a pilgrimage to Mecca. He returned to North Africa with ibn Yasin, a religious leader. Ibn Yasin attempted to teach Islam among the Berbers but failed and was chased away. Ibn Yasin and his small band of devotees fled to an island in Tekrur on the Senegal River. There, they established a monastery and lived as recluses. In time, they became known as Al-Murabitun, or Morabites (meaning 'People of the ribat'). In Spain this name became Almoravides, the name generally used by historians. In Tekrur the movement grew. Large numbers of Tekrurians wanted their independence from Ancient Ghana and saw the new movement as a force that could win that independence.[43]

In 1052 the Almoravides, now 30,000 strong, invaded Sidjilmessa. Yahya served as General. After this success, they pressed on and took Morocco.

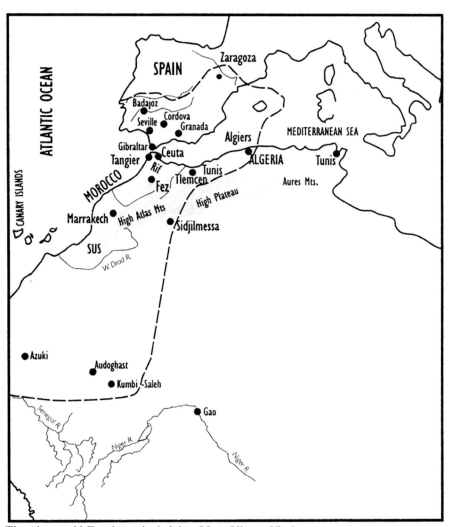

The Almoravid Empire at its height. (Map: Kieron Vital).

However, Yahya died in 1056 and the following year ibn Yasin died. Abu Bakar, brother of Yahya, assumed leadership of the movement. His conquests extended the empire from Senegal to Morocco. Sometime around 1061 Yusuf ibn Tashifin, a cousin of Abu Bakar, assumed control of the northern territories. In 1062 he founded Marrakech, the city of Morocco. This city became the African capital of the empire. By 1076 they conquered Ancient Ghana and held it until 1087. Tekrur became independent of Ghanaian imperial rule.[44]

Sometime in the latter half of 1082 hundreds of Moors and Arabs streamed into Africa, fleeing the campaigns of the Christians. In the following year, Al-Mutammed, the governor of Seville, joined them. Visiting Yusuf, he begged him to assist the Muslims in Spain against the Christian onslaught. Yusuf responded. He raised an army that was said to have included every ethnic group in the western desert and sent them across the sea into Spain. Armed with Indian swords and mounted on camels, the African army faced the Christians at Zalakah in 1086. They triumphed and pushed the Christians out of southern Spain.

In time Yusuf's forces seized Seville and dethroned its Islamic rulers. Apparently they had become "sunk in pleasure and sloth". The Almoravid Empire had a court in Africa centred in Marrakech and a court in Spain centred in Seville. This, according to Lady Lugard, "established once more a supreme sultan upon the throne of Andalusia". Furthermore, Yusuf's conquest and "the dynasty which he founded must be regarded as an African conquest and an African dynasty".[45] Incidentally, there is a "traditional" image of Yusuf that appears on the Catalan Atlas, a famous Spanish map of a slightly later period. Not only is he clearly depicted as a Negro but he is portrayed as darker in complexion than Mansa Musa, incongruously drawn on the same map.[46] The territory ruled by the Almoravides in Africa and Spain was extensive. Under their sway were the lands of Senegal, Morocco, Algeria and Spain. It was a larger area than that of Western Europe. Thirteen kings acknowledged the overlordship of Yusuf.[47]

In Africa Yusuf had great monuments built. Three great mosques date from his time, the mosque of Tlemcen, the mosque of Nedroma, and the mosque of Algiers. He also built an imposing stone fortress in Marrakech when other buildings at the time were of clay. Natascha Kubisch notes that:

> [He] founded the city of Marrakech in 1062 and laid out the great palm grove, but then handed over the further developments of the city to his son. Marrakech remained the capital of the empire under the Almohads and is one of the four royal cities of Morocco, alongside Rabat, Fez and Meknes. It is still a fascinating city today because of its African character and its surviving medieval buildings.[48]

The Almoravides probably introduced golden coinage into Europe. From the twelfth century, the Christian Spaniards minted golden coinage in imitation of Almoravid coins. The following century, mints in Florence, Genoa, Marseilles, and Venice turned out golden coinage in imitation of those of the Christian Spaniards. In the fourteenth century, golden coinage makes its appearance in parts of northern Europe.[49] According to Al-Idrissi, Wangaran (i.e. Guinean) gold was minted at some place "in the extreme west of Africa" in the twelfth century and put into circulation.[50] This may well have been the source of the Almoravid coins.

Ali ibn Yusuf, son of Yusuf ibn Tashifin, ruled from 1106. As ruler his thinking was very much guided by the ideas of the legal scholars of the time.

Moors (Spain). Highly decorated banner of the Almohades. From Stanley Lane-Poole, *The Story of the Moors in Spain* (US, Black Classic Press, 1990, p.215).

These scholars, however, had become very conservative and traditionally minded. They objected to the "new" ideas of Cordovan philosopher Al-Ghazzali. Following their lead, Ali had Al-Ghazzali's books publicly burned. As ever, challenges came from the Christians of the north. To fight them, Ali raised taxes to pay for military spending. The tax increase proved an unpopular policy and unrest spread in the cities. Despite this, Ali successfully countered the military actions of Christian King Afonso I of Aragon and Navarre. In July 1134 Ali defeated him at Frage. Challenges now came from the west. The earldom of Portugal became independent in 1139. This territory later expanded into a kingdom.[51]

Tashifin ibn Ali inherited his father's throne in 1143. He faced major challenges from the Almohades, a new religious movement spreading among the Berbers in Africa. They seized Oran (in Algeria) in 1145, and Marrakech in April 1147. In 1146 they crossed into Spain. The Almoravid Dynasty came quickly to an end.

The story of this new movement begins with a religious reformer called ibn Tumart. He was a Mesmuda Berber from the Atlas Mountain region of Morocco. Of these people, Brunson and Rashidi wrote that: "The Mesmuda Berbers were described as Blacks by Abu Shama in his *Kitab al-Ravdatayn*".[52] In 1106 ibn Tumart studied in Cordova and also travelled to the East to complete his religious education. On his return, he preached against the ideas dominant among the Almoravid establishment. The Almoravides tended to literalise the Koran and to anthropomorphise the idea of God. He also preached against their lax and luxurious lifestyle. In time, a small band of devotees gathered about him. Before long, a new movement was born with both a religious and a political programme. Ibn Tumart called them the Unitarians. In Spanish accounts, they are called the Almohades. Ibn Tumart, himself, was declared to be the Mahdi, the Messiah. Although the Mahdi died in 1130, the movement he founded grew.[53]

Abd-al-Mumin, another Mesmuda Berber, took control of the movement in 1133. A brilliant organiser, he unified the various Berber groups, not just the Mesmuda, into a cohesive force. In time, a power struggle took place between the Almoravid establishment and the newly rising Almohades. The newcomers triumphed. In 1147 they seized Marrakech and executed the last Almoravid monarch. Abd-al-Mumin commissioned the great Koutoubia mosque there as a symbol of his conquest over the Almoravides. By 1150 he became master of Spain. "Thus for a second time" wrote Lady Lugard, "a purely African dynasty reigned upon the most civilised throne of Europe". By 1160 his armies took control of Tunisia and penetrated Libya.[54] These actions gained control of trade routes. Dr Basil Davidson explained that: "the Magreb blossomed once again." Moreover, "cities like Fez and Tlemsen [sic] rivalled the urban beauty and

Moors (Morocco).
Koutoubiya Mosque of
Marrakech. Built by
Abd-al-Mumin in
*c.*1150 AD. (Photo:
Werner Forman
Archives).

learning of Granada and Cordova, unsurpassed by now throughout the western world".[55]

Abu Yakub Yusuf became the next ruler in 1163. Like his father, he ruled the Almohad Empire mostly from Marrakech in Morocco. Taking scholarship seriously, he funded the greatest Islamic thinker of the age - Ibn Rushd (also called Averroes). He appointed the great thinker to the post of High Court Judge in Cordova. Additionally, he appointed Ibn Tufail, another great scholar of the time, to be his personal doctor and prime-minister in Marrakech. He also began the transformation of the city of Seville into a great and prosperous city. This great ruler died in July 1184, following a campaign against the Christian ruler of Leon.[56]

Yusuf Yakub Al-Mansur, his son and successor, was an able and praiseworthy monarch but he faced great challenges. In Africa his armies became embroiled in a costly civil war with Berber rebels. For a while, Tunisia became independent of Almohad power. In Spain he tightened the screws on non-Muslims. Through high taxation, he forced many of them to leave Almohad controlled territory for the Christian regimes to the north.[57] In Africa and Spain, his government launched vast public works programmes, building mosques, schools, hospitals, and aqueducts. He founded the Moroccan city of Rabat, and also noted cities such as Alcassar and Mansura.[58] In Rabat some of the great buildings are still standing. Dr Nnamdi Elleh, the architectural scholar, wrote that:

> [T]he incomplete minaret of the Hassan Mosque remains a major landmark and dominates the city. Built in the Almohad style, its enormous base suggests that it would have been one of the tallest minarets if it had been completed. The gate of the Ouadiah Kasbah is another edifice that shows the Islamic style of the Almohads. The majestic gate symbolizes Ya'qub al-Mansur's [sic] desire to make Rabat his capital.[59]

Ali ibn Abd-Allah, a fourteenth century historian, made a valuable assessment of this ruler's career:

> His reign was remarkable for the tranquillity, the safety, the abundance, and the prosperity that reigned everywhere ... His government was excellent; he increased the treasury; his power was exalted; his actions that of a most noble ruler; his religion was sincere and deep; and he was a great benefactor of Islam.[60]

The Spanish city of Seville flourished exceedingly under the rule of the Almoravides and the Almohades. From 1086 to 1248 AD this city stood at the heart of the Moorish administrative machine. Even today the faint echo of the African presence is seen in the standing monuments of the city and is even marked on the complexions of the Seville population. Gary Younge, writing in *The Guardian,* observed that: "In terms of racial origin, local folk may define themselves in a number of different ways, but white they most definitely are not - you can see the rich, historical mix in their faces."[61]

Seville became a fine city of famous gardens, squares, and a suspension bridge. It had good streets lined with magnificent buildings and spacious houses. Their courtyards were planted with trees that bore oranges, lemons, and other fruits. The city boasted a population of perhaps half a million people, a massive number for a mediæval metropolis. In size, only Cordova, Baghdad, Eredo, and Cairo could compete. The river at Seville, its banks covered with over-arching trees, laced through a semi-urbanised district of farmhouses, high towers, castles, and clusters of buildings for a distance of thirty miles. A delightful boating river, it connected together what must have seemed like one large city. Pleasure boats and large trading vessels traversed its ports and quays.[62]

The Alcazar was the great palace of the Almohad sultans. They built it in 1181 on a site that dated back to Roman times. Walls surrounded the palace on one side that reached down to the river. Today only one of the great towers has survived intact. Later European kings have added to the rest of the structure, destroying its original integrity. Of the original features, however, Cecilia Hill, author of *Moorish Towns in Spain,* tells us that the Court of the Maidens was particularly impressive: "It is a study of delicate colouring and elaborate sculpture wrought by Moors." She further informs us that this court "is surrounded by a dado of azulejos that have the lustre of polished metal." The inner wall was "almost covered with stone arabesques, delicately and yet firmly cut on blue ground." The roof was of "carved wood, richly gilt and many coloured." Finally the throne was located "under the central, wider arch, with rich work in gold."[63]

More impressive, however, was the Giralda of Seville. Originally conceived as the minaret for the Great Mosque, Caliph Al-Mansur built it in 1196. The minaret itself is 350 feet high with each side measuring 50 feet. Most of its surface is smooth and unbroken. Only towards the summit of the tower were windows built. Some of these windows have simple horseshoe arches. Others on a higher tier have little columns of white marble. The whole impression given is one of grace and simple elegance. According to Cecilia Hill: "It is the highest ancient building made solely of brick." Today the minaret is adjoined to the Seville Cathedral apparently "the largest Gothic Cathedral in the world." Cecilia Hill informs us that: "It fills the exact site of the ancient Mosque" consequently "very little" is left of the old African-built monument. Of the little that remains today, however, is "the north wall of the Cathedral, the octagonal fountain in the forecourt, the hundred shafts of columns that

Moors (Spain). The Giralda of Seville. Built by Caliph Yusuf Yakub Al-Mansur in 1196 AD. It was the tallest ancient building made of brick. (Photo: Robin Walker).

surround the Cathedral precincts" and "its doors of bronze".[64] In other words a whole chunk of the "largest Gothic Cathedral in the world" *is* the Great Mosque of Seville as built by African sultan Al-Mansur.

Seville had an impressive reputation for science and art that was second only to that of Cordova. Even bishops of Christ flocked to its university to study. Of the great scholars of the city were Al Begi the Sage; Al Idrissi, author of an encyclopaedia of the sciences; and Averroes, the great philosopher.[65]

The Fall of Moorish Power

In the early thirteenth century, however, things fell apart. Again, there was African and Arab disunity, caused by Arab prejudice. Arab poet, Abu Ga'far, for example, refused the post of Secretary of Granada, because he did not wish to work alongside Sultan Abd-al-Mumin's son. Abu Ga'far felt that "the dark-skinned Berber seemed to him far below his own intellectual standards".[66]

Meanwhile, the European translation centres of Moorish and Arabic texts, established in the tenth century, had borne fruit. By the twelfth and thirteenth centuries there was the rise of the major European Universities. Bologna University (Italy) was established in 1158, Montpellier (France) in 1180, Oxford (England) in 1200, Toulouse (France) in 1223, Rome (Italy) in 1245 and Cambridge (England) in 1257.[67] Arguably, this process began the genesis of the European Renaissance.

In Africa various peoples began to cede from the empire beginning in 1216. By 1269 Almohad power in Africa had vanished. The Merinides became the new power in Morocco. Abu l-Hasan Ali (1335-1351), also called Al Sultan Aswad (i.e. the Black Sultan), was its greatest builder. He founded many of the cities in Morocco that exist today. In particular, he built great monuments in Fez such as madrassas and the like.[68] Moreover, Moroccan art and literature rose to its zenith under his patronage. His tomb is one of the architectural treasures of Morocco.[69]

In Spain the Christians seized Cordova in 1236, Vallencia in 1238, Murcia 1243, Jaen in 1245, and Seville in 1248. Additionally, the Almohades were overthrown in Spain to be replaced by new Islamic powers. The Nasrids established the city of Granada as the last stronghold of Moorish power in Spain.[70] Stanley Lane-Poole presented the relevant facts with typical accuracy:

> The kingdom of Granada was the last bulwark of the Moors in Spain. It was not much that was now left to them. Between 1238 and 1260, Fernando III. of Castille and Jayme I. of Aragon conquered Valencia, Cordova, Seville, and Murcia; and the rule of the Moors was now restricted to the present province of Granada, *i.e.,* the country about the Sierre Nevada and the sea coast from Almeria to Gibraltar. Within this limit, however, their kingdom was destined to

endure for another two centuries and a half. Though hemmed in on all sides, the Moors were well served by soldiers. The people of the conquered cities, the most valiant warriors of the vanquished Moslem states, came to place their swords at the disposal of the one remaining Mohammedan king. Fifty thousand Moors are recorded to have fled to his protection from Valencia, and three hundred thousand from Seville, Xeres, and Cadiz. Nevertheless, Granada was forced to become tributary to the Castillian crown. The founder of the dynasty of the Beny-Nasr [i.e. Nasrids], an Arab named Ibn-al-Ahmar, or the "Red man," because of his fair skin and hair, was a vigorous sovereign, but he could not withstand the power of the Christians, who now held nearly the whole of Spain. He paid homage and tribute to Fernando and his son Alfonso the Learned, not, however, without more than one struggle to free himself from their yolk; and from that time forward Granada with its surrounding territory was generally let alone by the Christian kings.[71]

Despite the light complexion of the ruling class, European writers remembered the masses of Moors of Granada as Negroes. In 1686 de Fontenelle, a French writer described the "Moors of Granada" as "a small [B]lack people, burned by the sun, full of wit and fire, always in love, writing verse, fond of music, arranging festivals, dances and tournaments every day".[72]

The greatest achievement of the Kingdom of Granada was the Alhambra Palace. Of this great monument, Cecilia Hill wrote the following:

In the Alhambra, we come to the perfection of Moorish art. Or let us say, to the greatest extant example of Moorish art in Spain. It has become one of the common heritages of the world. Even to the unlettered and untravelled, the word 'Moor' suggests, not Seville or Cordova, but Granada; and Granada means the Alhambra. In Granada we shall feel ourselves as wholly in Islam as, out of Africa, it is possible to feel, it is because of the Alhambra.[73]

Located on an outcrop of the Sierra Nevada, the palace was built on a site 720 metres by 220 metres. Surrounded by a wall, broken by twenty three towers, the complex consisted of seven palaces, houses for all social classes, offices, a mint, workshops, prisons, mosques, public baths, a Royal Necropolis, the Torres Bermeja, the Generalife, and a fortress.[74] Begun in 1377, the Court of the Lions is a particularly splendid part of the complex:

On entering [wrote Cecilia Hill], we stand amid a small labyrinth of columns, under a roof of stalactites in stone, amid which we must imagine suspended lamps with scented oil spreading a soft light. There is a forest of lovely columns, especially at the two ends, where the number is increased by a pavilion with a small dome on one of them, and coloured tiles as in the Court of Myrtles. The exquisite delicacy and seeming fragility of these columns, that seem to be made of pink ivory, and of stonework of the arcades above, worked like lace, is due to the fact that arches were never used by the Moors for structural purposes, but simply for ornament … In the bright sunshine of the centre, supporting a round, double fountain, stand the twelve famous lions sprouting water and watching us as they watched the Moors.[75]

After 1417, however, Muslim leadership in Granada became more and more unstable. There were short-lived reigns, factional fighting, and emirs achieving power by Christian backing. A more sinister threat came after 1469. The kingdoms of the Christians, Aragon and Castille, had become united by the marriage of Ferdinand and Isabella. From 1484 onwards they campaigned against the Moors and gradually closed in on the city of Granada. In 1491 they blockaded the city. The Moors finally capitulated.

On 2 January 1492 Ferdinand and Isabella entered Granada but as its masters.[76] They exiled Abu Abdallah, the last Moorish King, to Africa "where his descendants learned to beg their daily bread".[77] Four years later King Manuel of Portugal, the neighbouring country, ordered the expulsion of its African population. The expulsions from both lands continued up until the time of King Phillip III, who completed the policy in 1609. "It is stated", wrote Professor Lane-Poole, "that no less than three millions of Moors were banished between the fall of Granada and the first decade of the 17th century".[78] Some returned to North and West Africa, but others fled elsewhere in Europe where they were gradually absorbed. Professor Lane-Poole commented upon the sagaciousness of the expulsion policies:

In 1492 the last bulwark of the Moors gave way before the crusade of Ferdinand and Isabella, and with Granada fell all Spain's greatness. For a brief while, indeed, the reflection of the Moorish splendour cast a borrowed light upon the history of the land which it had warmed with its sunny radiance. The great epoch of Isabella, Charles V., and Philip II., of Columbus, Cortes, and Pizaro, shed a last halo about the dying moments of a mighty State. Then followed the abomination of desolation, the rule of the Inquisition, and the blackness of darkness in which Spain has been plunged ever since. In the land where science was once supreme, the Spanish doctors became noted for nothing but their ignorance and incapacity, and the discoveries of Newton and Harvey were condemned as pernicious to the faith. Where once seventy public libraries had fed the minds of scholars, and half a million books had been gathered together at Cordova for the benefit of the world, such indifference to learning afterwards prevailed, that the new capital, Madrid, possessed no public library in the eighteenth century, and even the manuscripts of the Escurial were denied in our own days [i.e. 1886] to the first scholarly historian of the Moors, though himself a Spaniard. The sixteen thousand looms of Seville soon dwindled to a fifth of their ancient number; the arts and industries of Toledo and Almeria faded into insignificance; the very baths - public buildings of equal ornament and use - were destroyed because cleanliness savoured too strongly of rank infidelity. The land, deprived of the skilful irrigation of the Moors, grew impoverished and neglected; the richest and most fertile valleys languished and were deserted; most of the populous cities which filled every district of Andalusia fell into ruinous decay; and beggars, friars, and bandits took the place of scholars, merchants, and knights. So low fell Spain after she had driven away the Moors. Such is the melancholy contrast offered by her history.[79]

Commenting on this passage, Professor Maulana Karenga, the rigorous African-American scholar, wrote that:

[I]t's interesting to note that after all the commentaries on and claims about the tragedy that would descend on Africans if and when Europeans left Africa, it was a major European state, Spain, that deteriorated after Africans left. Such is the irony and severe instruction of history.[80]

Notes

[1] Robert Briffault, *Rational Evolution*, US, The Macmillan Co., 1930, pp.109-111. Quoted in John G. Jackson, *Ages of Gold and Silver*, US, A. A. Press, 1990, pp.145-6.

[2] Joseph McCabe, *The New Science and the Story of Evolution*, UK, Hutchinson & Co., 1931, p.298. Quoted in John G. Jackson, *Introduction to African Civilizations*, US, Citadel Press, 1970, p.190.

[3] Stanley Lane-Poole, *The Story of the Moors in Spain*, US, Black Classic Press, 1990 (original 1886), p.129.

[4] John G. Jackson, *Introduction to African Civilizations*, pp.176 and Joseph McCabe, *The Golden Ages of History*, UK, Watts & Co., 1940, pp.153-4 and Stanley Lane-Poole, *The Story of the Moors in Spain*, pp.136-142 and Jose V. Pimienta-Bey, *Moorish Spain: Academic Source and Foundation for the Rise and Success of Western European Universities in the Middle Ages*, in *Golden Age of the Moor*, ed Ivan Van Sertima, US Transaction publishers, 1992, p.214.

[5] Chancellor Williams, *The Destruction of Black Civilization*, US, Black Classic Press, 1987, pp.50 and 56-7.

[6] Wayne Chandler, *The Moor: Light of Europe's Dark Age*, in *Golden Age of the Moor*, ed Ivan Van Sertima, US Transaction Publishers, 1992, pp.159-161.

[7] Ibidem and Stanley Lane-Poole, *The Story of the Moors in Spain*, pp.12-3 and John G. Jackson, *Introduction to African Civilizations*, pp.170-1 and James Brunson & Runoko Rashidi, *The Moors in Antiquity*, in *Golden Age of the Moor*, ed Ivan Van Sertima, US, Transaction Publishers, 1992, p.54.

[8] Ibidem and John G. Jackson, *Introduction to African Civilizations*, p.171.

[9] Wayne Chandler, *The Moor: Light of Europe's Dark Age*, in *Golden Age of the Moor*, pp.161-2.

[10] Quoted in Edward Scobie, *The Moors and Portugal's Global Expansion*, in *Golden Age of the Moor*, ed Ivan Van Sertima, US, Transaction Publishers, 1992, p.336.

[11] Quoted in J. C. DeGraft-Johnson, *African Glory*, UK, Watts and Co., 1954, p.70.

[12] Wayne Chandler, *The Moor: Light of Europe's Dark Age*, in *Golden Age of the Moor*, p.162.

[13] James Brunson & Runoko Rashidi, *The Moors in Antiquity*, in *Golden Age of the Moor*, p.55.

[14] Stanley Lane-Poole, *The Story of the Moors in Spain,* p.28.

[15] Markus Hattstein, *Spanish Umayyads: History,* in *Islam: Art and Architecture,* ed Markus Hattstein and Peter Delius, Germany, Konemann, 2000, p.208.

[16] Ibid.

[17] Ibid., p.209 and Wayne Chandler, *The Moor: Light of Europe's Dark Age,* in *Golden Age of the Moor,* pp.162-4.

[18] Markus Hattstein, *Spanish Umayyads: History,* in *Islam: Art and Architecture,* pp.210-1 and James Brunson & Runoko Rashidi, *The Moors in Antiquity,* in *Golden Age of the Moor,* p.57.

[19] Markus Hattstein, *Spanish Umayyads: History,* in *Islam: Art and Architecture,* pp.210-1.

[20] J. A. Rogers, *Nature Knows No Color-Line,* US, Helga M. Rogers, 1952, pp.57-8.

[21] Wayne Chandler, *The Moor: Light of Europe's Dark Age,* in *Golden Age of the Moor,* p.170.

[22] Stanley Lane-Poole, *The Story of the Moors in Spain,* p.101.

[23] John G. Jackson, *Introduction to African Civilizations,* p.189.

[24] Joao Lavinha et al, *Importation Route of the Sickle Cell trait into Portugal: Contribution of Molecular Epidemiology,* in *Human Biology: Volume 64, Number 6,* ed Michael H. Crawford, US, Wayne State University Press, December 1992, p.891.

[25] Markus Hattstein, *Spanish Umayyads: History,* in *Islam: Art and Architecture,* p.208.

[26] J. A. Rogers, *Nature Knows No Color-Line,* p.60.

[27] Stanley Lane-Poole, *The Story of the Moors in Spain,* pp.71-2.

[28] Ibid., pp.74-5 and Markus Hattstein, *Spanish Umayyads: History,* in *Islam: Art and Architecture,* p.212.

[29] Stanley Lane-Poole, *The Story of the Moors in Spain,* pp.78-81.

[30] Yusef Ali, *The Music of the Moors in Spain,* in *Golden Age of the Moor,* ed Ivan Van Sertima, US, Transaction Publishers, 1992, pp.308-314.

[31] Stanley Lane-Poole, *The Story of the Moors in Spain,* p.84.

[32] Ibid.

[33] Markus Hattstein, *Spanish Umayyads: History,* in *Islam: Art and Architecture,* p.213.

[34] Edward Scobie, *The Moors and Portugal's Global Expansion,* in *Golden Age of the Moor,* p.341.

[35] Markus Hattstein, *Spanish Umayyads: History,* in *Islam: Art and Architecture,* pp.214-5 and Lady Lugard, *A Tropical Dependency,* UK, James Nisbet & Co., 1906, pp.50-1.

[36] Markus Hattstein, *Spanish Umayyads: History,* in *Islam: Art and Architecture,* p.216.

[37] Joseph McCabe, *The Golden Ages of History,* p.163.

[38] Jose V. Pimienta-Bey, *Moorish Spain: Academic Source and Foundation for the Rise and Success of Western European Universities in the Middle Ages,* in *Golden Age of the Moor,* pp.217-8.

[39] Markus Hattstein, *Spanish Umayyads: History,* in *Islam: Art and Architecture,* pp.208, 216 and 218.

[40] For example Joseph McCabe, *The Golden Ages of History,* p.153.

[41] Lady Lugard, *A Tropical Dependency,* pp.40-2.

[42] Markus Hattstein, *Spanish Umayyads: History,* in *Islam: Art and Architecture,* p.217.

[43] Wayne Chandler, *The Moor: Light of Europe's Dark Age,* in *Golden Age of the Moor,* pp.171-3 and G. T. Stride and Caroline Ifeka, *Peoples and Empires in West Africa,* UK, Thomas Nelson and Sons, 1971, pp.41-2.

[44] Ibid.

[45] Lady Lugard, *A Tropical Dependency,* p.56.

[46] See Anthony Coleman ed, *Millennium: A Thousand Years of History,* UK, Bantam Press, 1999, pp.100-1.

[47] J. A. Rogers, *World's Great men of Color, Volume I,* US, Macmillan 1972, pp.217 and 222.

[48] Natascha Kubisch, *Almoravids and Almohads: Architecture,* in *Islam: Art and Architecture,* ed Markus Hattstein and Peter Delius, Germany, Konemann, 2000, pp.254-5.

[49] Roland Oliver & Brian M. Fagan, *Africa in the Iron Age,* UK, Cambridge University Press, 1975, p.172.

[50] Lady Lugard, *A Tropical Dependency,* p.112.

[51] Markus Hattstein, *Almoravids and Almohads: History,* in *Islam: Art and Architecture,* ed Markus Hattstein and Peter Delius, Germany, Konemann, 2000, p.247.

[52] James Brunson & Runoko Rashidi, *The Moors in Antiquity,* in *Golden Age of the Moor,* p.57.

[53] Markus Hattstein, *Almoravids and Almohads: History,* in *Islam: Art and Architecture,* pp.248-9.

[54] Lady Lugard, *A Tropical Dependency,* p.59 and Markus Hattstein, *Almoravids and Almohads: History,* in *Islam: Art and Architecture,* pp.249-250.

[55] Basil Davidson, *Africa in History,* Macmillan, UK, 1991, p.186.

[56] Markus Hattstein, *Almoravids and Almohads: History,* in *Islam: Art and Architecture,* pp.250-1.

[57] Ibid., p.251.

[58] J. A. Rogers, *World's Great men of Color, Volume I,* pp.228-9.

[59] Nnamdi Elleh, *African Architecture: Evolution and Transformation,* US, McGraw-Hill, 1997, p.96.

[60] J. A. Rogers, *World's Great men of Color, Volume I,* pp.228-9.

[61] Gary Younge, *Nights on the tiles,* in *The Guardian (Travel),* UK, 2 January 1999, p.15.

[62] Lady Lugard, *A Tropical Dependency,* pp.43 and 61-2 and Joseph McCabe, *The Golden Ages of History,* p.158.

[63] Cecilia Hill, *Moorish Towns in Spain,* UK, Methuen & Co., 1931, pp.78-84.

[64] Ibid., pp.75-7 and Lady Lugard, *A Tropical Dependency,* p.59.

[65] Cecilia Hill, *Moorish Towns in Spain,* pp.71-2.

[66] James Brunson & Runoko Rashidi, *The Moors in Antiquity,* in *Golden Age of the Moor,* pp.55-6.

[67] Jose V. Pimienta-Bey, *Moorish Spain: Academic Source and Foundation for the Rise and Success of Western European Universities in the Middle Ages,* in *Golden Age of the Moor,* p.225.

[68] Markus Hattstein, *The Magreb: History,* in *Islam: Art and Architecture,* ed Markus Hattstein and Peter Delius, Germany, Konemann, 2000, p.300.

[69] J. A. Rogers, *World's Great men of Color, Volume I,* pp.232-4.

[70] Markus Hattstein, *Almoravids and Almohads: History,* in *Islam: Art and Architecture,* pp.252-3.

[71] Stanley Lane-Poole, *The Story of the Moors in Spain,* pp.217-8.

[72] Quoted in John G. Jackson, *Man, God, and Civilization,* US, Citadel Press, 1972, p.276.

[73] Cecilia Hill, *Moorish Towns in Spain,* pp.134-5.

[74] Mariane Barucand and Achim Bednorz, *Moorish Architecture in Andalusia,* Germany, Tashen, 1992, pp.183-8.

[75] Cecilia Hill, *Moorish Towns in Spain,* pp.147-8.

[76] Markus Hattstein, *The Nasrids of Granada: History,* in *Islam: Art and Architecture,* ed Markus Hattstein and Peter Delius, Germany, Konemann, 2000, pp.276-7.

[77] Stanley Lane-Poole, *The Story of the Moors in Spain,* p.267.

[78] Ibid., p.279.

[79] Ibid., pp.viii-ix.

[80] Maulana Karenga, *Introduction to Black Studies,* US, University of Sankore Press, 1982, p.66.

CHAPTER FOURTEEN: THE CENTRAL SAHARA

Kanem-Borno

The Kanem-Borno Empire, at its height, flourished in the region of northeastern Nigeria, northern Cameroon, eastern Niger, western Chad, and southern Libya. Once horse-borne nomads, the Zaghawa built this Kanuri culture. They created a state renowned for its longevity and political stability. From the late eleventh century onwards its rulers came from the same family, the Sefuwa. The empire's known history takes us from the early ninth century AD to well into the nineteenth century.

The early monarchs ruled over Kanem, the eastern Niger and western Chad region. Dugu was the first of their kings, believed to have lived around 800 AD. The Dynasty, sometimes called the Dugawa, ruled until 1075.[1] This would appear to have begun as a very humble period. Al-Yaqubi, a noted Arab writer of the age (872 AD), informs us that the Zaghawa of Kanem had no use for towns and instead lived in "huts made of corn stalks":

> They have no kings of cities [continues Yaqubi]. Their ruler is called Karkur. Among the Zaghawa is a race called Hudin (Futin) who have a king who is a Zaghawi. Then there is the Kingdom of Malal which is at enmity with the [Zaghawi] ruler of Kanem. Their king is called Mai Umeyi.[2]

A century later the condition of culture had evolved greatly. Al-Muhallabi, writing in 985 AD, recorded that the Zaghawa kingdom had become important among the African kingdoms. Additionally, it was populous and could boast of two cities, Manan and Tarazaki. The government of this time was a divine kingship. In addition:

> Their houses are all of plastered clay [says Muhallabi], as is also the *kasr* [i.e. castle] of their king, whom they extol and worship as if he were God Most High. They pretend that the King does not eat any ordinary food. For his sustenance he has a secret body of persons, who take food to his compound, so that no one knows where his food comes from. If it so chances that any of his subjects meet the camel which carries the King's food, that man is at once killed on the spot. The King drinks with certain chosen companions. His drink is made from *dhurra* (millet) mixed with honey. As clothing, he wears trousers made of thin wool, and over them he is decked out in an upper garment of wool of poor quality, prickly and lousy, with silk over that. He is open-handed among his subjects ... [3]

For the common people, by contrast, things were much more modest. They wore animal skins and subsisted on their own farming produce supplemented with meat from their own animals. On their farmlands, millet, beans and wheat were cultivated.[4]

Al Idrissi, writing in the twelfth century, indicates that Manan was the capital. He further informs us that Njimi, another Kanuri town, was "very small" and "sparsely populated." Furthermore, there was another "town" of the Zaghawa (wherever this is), that "embrac[ed] many districts and was well populated".[5]

The Zaghawa, however, were conquerors. Oliver and Atmore, two modern historians, relate that:

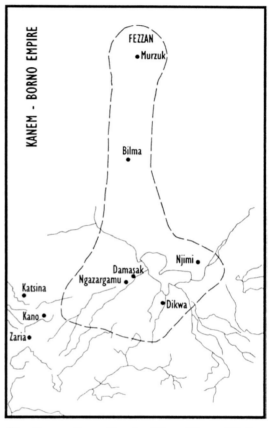

The Kanem-Borno Empire (Map: Kieron Vital).

> The northern Kanuri, like other pastoralists, were warlike and mobile, and since early Muslim times, if not before, they had been the main suppliers of slaves to Egypt and Ifriqiya [from this region]. The trade brought them in return the constantly developing weapons and accessories for successful conquest in Sudanese latitudes - the big Barbary horses, so essential to carry the armoured knight, the chain-mail for horse and rider, the harness and saddlery, the swords and shields, and heavy metal lances ... To monopolise such a golden road to wealth and power, and to guard it from rivals to the east and west, was an obvious incentive to empire.[6]

The So Culture (also called Sao) was an earlier and vastly superior civilisation that thrived in the same region. "Remains of Sao settlements to the southeast of Lake Chad" says a modern scholar, "have been traced back to the 4th century B.C."[7] Zaghawa nomads immigrated to the lands of the So and lived

Kanem-Borno. Royal Scene in Borno. From Major Dixon Denham et al, *Narrative of Travels and Discoveries in Northern and Central Africa*, (UK, John Murray, 1826, opposite p.79).

among them. Using trickery, the Zaghawa gradually took them over and later absorbed them into the Kanuri state. G. T. Stride and Caroline Ifeka presented the relevant facts about the So civilisation with characteristic accuracy:

> [T]he So people possessed considerable political and artistic genius. Although they never combined effectively to form an empire, they developed city-states which were the centres of intense local patriotism. Each city was surrounded by strong defensive walls and dominated the life of the surrounding countryside which it both protected and governed. Government was by an elaborate hierarchy, headed by a divine ruler ... Except on ceremonial occasions, the rulers made few public appearances and even then remained concealed from the common gaze by a screen. Women occupied a respected position in society and the Queen Mother and senior sister of the ruler exercised considerable political influence on the government of the state. The So people were mainly settled farmers but among them were craftsmen of considerable industrial and artistic merit. They were able to work in both clay and metals to manufacture household utensils, tools, and works of art for religious purposes. Impressive objects found by archaeologists include burial urns and ... figures of animals and human beings both in clay and bronze. All this had been achieved ... before about A.D. 700 ... The vigour of the government and civilization is best demonstrated by their long resistance to the empires of Kanem and Bornu [sic] and the fact that many cultural characteristics of the Kanuri [were later] adopted from the So.[8]

During the time of King Arku (1023-67), the Zaghawa extended their domain northwards into the Sahara. They established control over the trading activities of Muslims in the region. Islam came to have an influence in the royal court itself though it had little influence anywhere else in the kingdom. Queen Hawwa, Arku's successor, became the first Islamic sovereign of Kanem, ruling for four years. An equally short reign followed. During this confusion, Mai (i.e. King) Humé Jilmi took control of the kingdom in 1075. Ending the rule of the Dugawa, he founded the Sefuwa Dynasty.[9] How Islam spread into this region in the first place is not clear. Al-Bakri, that excellent Spanish geographer of the eleventh century, left a useful clue. Apparently, refugees from Arabia's Umayyads fled to Kanem to escape the persecution of their political rivals, the Abbasides.[10] We conjecture that Islam spread among the Kanemi from these refugees.

Jilmi's son, Mai Dunama I, ruled from 1086 until 1140. Dunama I made two pilgrimages to Mecca. He also commanded large cavalry forces in the region for the first time.[11] A subsequent ruler, Mai Salma ibn Bikur (1183-1210), seized control of the caravan routes to the north, especially to Fezzan. The Mai, also a devout Muslim, built a mosque of plaster in the town of Njimi replacing the older mosque constructed of reeds. His son, Mabradu, studied 150 books on Islam with the learned imam Abdullah Dili ibn Bikuru.[12]

These two factors, control of the trade routes and commonality of religion with the Islamic world, led to greater international contacts. In any case we hear of Abu Ishak Ibrahim Al-Kanemi, "a learned and celebrated poet" working at the Seville court of the great Almohad sultan, Al-Mansur.[13] Trade flourished across the Sahara. From the north came horses, fine metalware, glassware, fabrics and copper. From the west came kola nuts and ivory.[14] From the south came cotton goods. Merchants traded with Tripoli, Fezzan, and Egypt.[15] Kanem exported slaves, ivory, ostrich feathers, and live animals.[16]

In the thirteenth century Njimi became the new capital. From here, official and cultural contacts were established with the world at large.[17] Lady Lugard commented that: "The thirteenth century would seem to have been a brilliant period".[18] Mai Dunama ibn Salma (Dunama II) ruled from 1210 to 1248. He built Kanem into a great regional power. Commanding 30,000 cavalry and an even larger number of infantry, he conducted warfare in the desert. With camels instead of horses, his war machine campaigned against the entire Fezzan region of southern Libya. Crushed were the Bulala of the east. Pillaged were the Hausa cities of northern Nigeria. This latter group were compelled to pay tribute.[19] Dr Davidson reconstructs a scene of:

> Swinging tassels in the dust, harness brasses that glitter against quilted armour [see also page 432], long spears pennoned and pointed, brilliant cavaliers, all the creak and swing and clatter and pomp of an aristocratic army saddled for sack and loot: with the footsore *plebs* in goat-skin, armed with clubs and spears and small hope, trailing out behind - such were the warrior columns of the old Sudan [i.e. Africa], the feudal fire and challenge that were thrown, times without number, against the easy marts and watered villages of one imperial region after another, now with one side winning, now with the other.[20]

Mastery of the trade routes and the spoils of war built large state revenues. Kanemi Muslims established a school in Cairo that gained a considerable reputation. The institution had hostel facilities used by Kanem pilgrims going to or from Mecca or studying at Cairo's Al-Azhar University. Regularly they sent money for its upkeep.[21] In 1246 Dunama II exchanged embassies with Al-Mustansir, the king of Tunis. He sent the North African court a costly present, which apparently included a giraffe. An old chronicle noted that the rare animal "created a sensation in Tunis".[22] Professor Ronald Cohen penned a good summary of the achievements of this early period in his important study on Kanem-Borno culture:

> [B]y the twelfth and thirteenth centuries Kanem became a well-known state in the Islamic world. Trans-Saharan commerce was completely controlled, garrisons were built to protect the trade routes, and treaty relations were established with the Hafsid rulers of Tunis ... [A] travel[l]er's house ... was

constructed in Cairo … At the other extreme of the Islamic world, in Spain, a poet from Kanem was renowned … for his praise songs … This was a great period of Islamic civilization and Kanem played its part in that florescence.[23]

Sir Richmond Palmer, the pioneering and erudite authority on Kanem-Borno, seemed equally impressed. In his own words: "[T]he degree of civilisation achieved by its early [rulers] would appear to compare favourably with that of European monarchs of that day." Especially when it is understood that "the Christian West had remained ignorant, rude, and barbarous".[24]

However, the war against the Bulala highlighted internal problems. Dunama II was a strict Muslim. He converted many of the conquered peoples to Islam and instituted the Koran as the basis for law. Unfortunately, he went much further. He was determined to destroy Kanuri traditional religion by demonstrating that it was built on mere superstition. To demonstrate this, he opened the sacred *mune,* a sealed container said to hold the spirit of victory and of such importance that its secrets should never be divulged. Dunama, however, learned the hard way that the unity and power of the empire depended on harmony between the Muslims and the Traditionalists. His sacrilegious act of opening the container alienated a large section of the Kanuri. Even some of his own sons were appalled. They joined a serious rebellion against him, and the Bulala made a dangerous bid to seek independence from Kanem and to avenge the insult to a religion they shared with the non-Muslim Kanuri.[25] Dunama II inflicted a severe defeat on the Bulala but it highlights the problems associated with the imposition of Islam against the wishes of the followers of the older ancestral religions.[26] Other wars led to territorial expansion of the empire. The Kanemi conquered and absorbed the land of Gaga (i.e. Borno) in northeastern Nigeria after a *jihad*.[27] Henceforth, the Mais were known as Kings of Kanem and Lords of Borno.[28]

It is interesting to consider the administration of this vast territory. Dr Oliver and Dr Fagan's account of how it worked produced useful information that also throws light on old African matriarchy. Moreover, Oliver and Fagan's research demonstrates the extent to which Kanem-Borno copied its institutional structures from the conquered So:

> Despite the evident Muslim piety of many of the mais, the political structure which emerged in medieval Kanem retained strong traces of the pre-Islamic sacral kingship attributed by al-Muhallabi [sic] to the Zaghawa, and having many features in common with other states of the Sudanic belt [of West Africa]. The ruler led a ritually secluded existence, surrounded by titled office-holders and palace slaves. As in so many African kingdoms, the highest positions of all were held by two women, known as the Queen Mother and the Queen Sister, each of whom had her own court and officers. The highest male dignitaries were the provincial governors theoretically responsible for the north, the east,

Kanem-Borno. (Libya). View of the city of Murzuk. From Dr Henry Barth, *Travels and Discoveries in North and Central Africa, Volume I* (UK, Longman, Brown, Green, Longmans & Roberts, 1857, opposite p.168).

the south and the west. In practice these seem to have been central, privy council posts: the real administration of distant provinces was entrusted to military commanders, often princes of the royal house, each of whom surrounded himself with a court and officers on the same pattern as the central one.[29]

Sir Richmond Palmer alludes to two more important state officials. There was an Astronomer Royal and also a Reckoner of the Months.[30] We note that both positions require a high level of scholarly and scientific endeavour from its incumbents.

Problems with the Bulala emerged again in the fourteenth century. Jil ibn Sikuma, their king, challenged Mai Daud (1366-76) and subsequent Mai, Umar (1382-7). The Bulala campaign forced the latter to abandon Njimi, his ailing capital, and flee to Borno. This left the Bulala ruling in Kanem.[31]

Connected with these events, Lady Lugard narrates the story of a Kanem ruler who sought refuge in the Hausa city of Kano. He came accompanied by a great host of men with fifes, flags and drums on horseback. Accompanying the party were Mallams, the holy men. In Hausaland they received shelter as a guest of Sarki Daud, the king of Kano. Taking counsel with his Prime Minister, the Kano ruler inquired on how best to entertain the Kanem party. The Prime Minister warned: "If you allow this man to stay in one of the towns of your territory he will take possession of the whole place". They resolved to accommodate the Kanemi in houses built between Kano and a frontier town in an area shaded by locust trees. Fifty years later the same thing happened again. Another Kanem ruler fled to take refuge in Kano, again without negative consequences for Hausaland. However, by the late sixteenth century the Prime Minister's gloomy prophecy came true. The Kanemi, under Mai Idris Alooma, did indeed "take possession of the whole place".[32]

A century before that conquest, however, aspects of Kanuri courtly culture had already spread to Kano, perhaps brought there by the Kanem refugee prince. The Kano court came to adopt the use of the royal trumpet, the wearing of ostrich feather sandals, and the sporting of ostrich feather fans. Furthermore, the Kano court paraded the unmounted horses of the ruler, all following the Kanuri fashion.[33]

Borno (Gaga) was of great economic importance to the Kanemi. It was a source of animal products, foodstuffs, ivory, ostrich feathers and slaves - products that were used domestically and also exported north across the Sahara.[34] Glass was among the products sold to Borno. However, some of the indigenous people forged trade links with Kano, one of the city-states in northern Nigeria, instead. This created a web of trade links between Borno, Kano, Takedda (an important commercial and distribution centre), and North Africa. This attempt to divert trade away from Kanem was an important reason for Kanem's continued military actions in Borno.[35]

The ascension of Ali ibn Dunama (also known as Ali Ghaji) in 1465 ushered in a glorious epoch. He instituted governmental, military,[36] and religious reforms. He was also a great patron of scholars. Rather than risk further defeats at the hands of the Bulala, he consolidated power in Borno, where he established a new capital.[37] Founded around 1484, he built the city of Ngazargamu near the River Yobe.[38] Although in ruins today, it is still possible to distinguish a large complex of unique red brick construction. This was apparently the palace of the Mais. Other red brick ruins were the homes of the leading persons. An overwhelming seven metre high rampart, approached through five entrances, encircled this central area. It covered six square kilometres.[39] Lastly, Ali Ghaji, like his Songhai contemporary Sonni Ali, achieved world renown. His state, Borno, appears on a Portuguese map of 1489.[40]

The sixteenth century was associated with greater town and city life. Some of the towns (at Ali Gajiri, Damasak, Difa, Duji, Gashagar, Wudi, and Yo) developed into considerable urban centres, where pottery, weaving, leatherwork, and dyeing flourished. Borno leather paid for the importation of European manufactured goods, perfumes, armaments, etc.[41] Great luxury was associated with this period. According to Leo Africanus, the emperor's cavalry had golden "stirrups, spurs, bits and buckles." Even the ruler's dogs had "chains of the finest gold".[42] Raymond Michelet, author of an informative essay on African history, affirms that:

Kanem-Borno (Chad, Nigeria, Cameroon, Niger and Libya). Borno knight and horse equipped with quilted armour. This type of armour was also worn by soldiers and horses in Hausaland and Sudan. Originally drawn by Major Dixon Denham and published in Major Dixon Denham et al, *Narrative of Travels and Discoveries in Northern and Central Africa* (UK, John Murray, 1826, opposite p.278).

> The 16th century was one of immense prosperity. The northern country was opened up by irrigation and the Tuaregs driven back. So that, at this time, the kingdom of Songhay [sic], the Hausa states (or rather the Hausa-Kebbi kingdom) and the Bornu-Kanem [sic] kingdom formed a notable chain of empires along the same latitude, and all equally prosperous. This prosperity lasted [in Kanem-Borno] for two hundred years, until the beginning of the 19th century.[43]

In this period, the Sefuwa Dynasty reconquered Kanem,[44] exchanged embassies with Tripoli, and maintained trade and intercourse with the Turkish Empire, sending six ambassadors to Istanbul in 1574.[45]

Mai Idris Alooma (1564-96) was a most successful politician of the period who gained considerable international prestige. Mahmud Kati, the great Songhai historian, wrote that: "The mass of our contemporaries hold that there are four Sultans not counting the supreme Sultan [the Sultan of Constantinople] to wit - The Sultan of Baghdad, the Sultan of Cairo, the Sultan of Bornu [sic] and the Sultan of Melli [i.e. Mali]".[46] Dr Heinrich Barth, the nineteenth century German traveller, described Idris as "an excellent prince, uniting in himself the most opposite qualities: warlike energy, combined with mildness and intelligence; courage, with circumspection and patience; severity with pious feelings".[47]

His military prowess was outstanding with armies, possibly the first in Africa, to have muskets. Acquiring them from the Turkish Empire, "[n]orth, south, east, and west he carried his conquering arms", says Lady Lugard. "To give a list of the many [peoples] that he subdued could only weary the reader".[48] Imam Ahmad, the royal chronicler and aide, wrote a detailed account of Idris' campaigns. Part of his first hand report reads as follows:

> 'Abd ul Jalil ibn Bi fled and escaped, fearing our army. He had left his wife, the daughter of Yarima, in his house, turning from her when he saw the dust of our army, rising to the skies. For he was certain that the safety of a man himself is better for him than the safety of his wife. So he fled, deserting his wife, since personal necessity is more compelling than the lack of a wife, as the author of the book *Ifrikiya* has said.[49]

Idris reformed and standardised the judiciary by establishing a system of Islamic courts. He himself ruled according to Islamic political theory, taking a stand against, among other things, immorality in the capital. Oliver and Atmore wrote that: "[H]e presided over a court famous for the high standard of its legal and theological disputations".[50] Like his Songhai contemporaries, he was a patron of learning, encouraging scholars from many other African countries to take up residence in Borno. He improved navigation on the Yobe River. He commissioned the building of longer, flat-bottomed boats initially for his navy.

For land transportation, he imported a much greater number of camels replacing the dependence on mules, oxen and donkeys. The great Mai was also a builder, raising new brick mosques in the cities that replaced the older buildings. He also founded a hostel in Mecca for Borno pilgrims. Following the fall of Songhai in 1591, the great Mai became the undisputed champion of the Muslims in the region. The empire became the Borno Caliphate.[51] Phillip Koslow, a modern historian, declared that:

> His contemporary, Elizabeth I of England, a shrewd and strong-willed monarch who gave her name to an age and has been repeatedly celebrated in books and films, could hardly have claimed greater achievements in war, administration or diplomacy.[52]

The achievements of Idris, however, like that of other Kanem rulers, owed much to the advice and direction given by the Queen Mother. Idris' mother, Queen Amsa, ruled a short while before her son's succession. Of this Queen, Lady Lugard says:

> She was a very distinguished woman, to whose advice it is believed that her son owed much of the wisdom of his conduct. Under her influence an important embassy was sent to Tripoli, and the policy of maintaining intercourse and trade with the outer world by the medium of the Turkish Empire, which had always been the policy of prosperous Bornu [sic], was actively developed.[53]

The Caliphate in the seventeenth century presented an image of strength and power to the outside world, repulsing invaders from all sides. The Kanuri ruled as far north as Murzuk, to the hills of Darfur in the east, as well as Borno to the southwest. Their monarchs are remembered as pious Muslims and patrons of Islamic scholarship.[54] Mai Muhammad and his two successors, Ibrahim and Umar, ruled over half a century of internal peace and security.[55] The Mai was largely a secluded religious figure, as in pre-Islamic times. In practice, day-to-day government lay in the hands of twelve key dignitaries. As before, these included the commander of the armed forces, the commanders of the various provinces, the heir apparent, the Queen Mother and the Queen Sister.[56]

Ngazargamu, the capital city, burst its shell, becoming one of the largest cities on earth at the time. By 1658 the metropolis, according to architectural scholar Susan Denyer, housed "about quarter of a million people".[57] It had 660 streets. Many were wide and unbending, reflective of town planning. The dendal, or high streets, were lined on both sides by trees that offered shade. Four Friday mosques, each used by 12,000 worshippers at a time, served religious needs.[58] These buildings must have been erected on an impressive scale. Moreover, the construction techniques in general were sophisticated: "Heinrich Barth, who inspected the remains of these walls during the 19th

Kanem-Borno (Niger). Elaborate robe worn by royal women at the Borno Court. Cotton and silk. Length 99 cm. Collected by Gustav Nachtigel and housed in the Museum für Völkerkunde in 1876. Real date believed to be early 19th century. (Photo: Werner Forman Archives).

century [says a modern scholar], declared that their workmanship was equal in quality to the finest masonry he had seen in Europe".[59]

Dr Davidson calls this the "harvest time of Kanem-Bornu [sic] civilisation". He notes that though little is known about the way of life for ordinary people during this period:

> [W]e may well imagine that they made the best of these peaceful years. Farmers could work their fields in safety. Travellers and pilgrims could follow the roads without fear. Those who lived in towns and market-villages could prosper with the spread of trade that came both from everyday security and from unified rule over a wide country. There was growth of learning in the towns, and of schools in the villages. There was regular traffic between Kanem-Bornu [sic] and the Egyptian and Tunisian provinces of the Turkish empire in North Africa.[60]

This tranquillity was challenged by two serious invasions in 1667. Mai Ali successfully fought off both the Tuaregs of the desert, and the Junkun from the eastern Nigeria region. Both groups raided the capital in search of booty. Dan Marina, a contemporary at the Hausa University of Katsina, composed a poem dedicated to the Borno Caliph. This literary offering shows, for good or ill, how African Muslims came to view Traditionalist enemies:

> 'Ali has triumphed over the heathen [i.e. Junkun], a matchless triumph in the path of God.
> No sultan like him; A Laith among Laiths, ever stout of heart.
> Has he not brought us [i.e. Muslims] succour? Verily but for him
> Our hearts had never ceased from dread of the unbelievers.
> Narrow had become to us the earth pressed by the foe,
> Till 'Ali saved our children and their children yet unborn.
> O people! Say with one accord 'May God grant him recompense for our deliverance.'
> He drove back to the furthest borders the army of the Junkon [sic],
> And God scattered their host disheartened.[61]

Though the empire survived the invasions, there was a great famine that took place towards the end of the seventeenth century[62] - the first of a series.

The terminal decline and break up of the empire began towards the very end of the eighteenth century, possibly prompted by economic factors. The Caliphate lost control of an important desert trade in salt to the Tuaregs. The Tuareg interruption of the trade routes caused a series of famines in the southern part of the empire. The Fulanis, another people in the region whose power was ascending, occupied the capital in 1808 and destroyed it in 1812.[63] All of this led to both the decline of the Caliphate and the break down of its internal cohesion.

The Hausa Confederation

The Hausa Confederation consisted of seven independent cities and their surrounding territories (see page 314). Known as the Hausa Bakwai, or "pure" Hausa States, the cities were Gobir, Biram, Katsina, Kano, Daura, Rano and Zazzau. Gobir was the most northerly and Zazzau the most southerly. They flourished in the region of northern Nigeria from the eleventh or twelfth centuries[64] to the early twentieth century. Though linked by language, for most of their history the Hausa never formed a unified territory. Scholars thus describe them as a confederacy of independent states. Hausa historians also claim kinship with other states in the Nigeria region known as the Banzai Bakwai, or "impure" Hausa States. These were Zamfara, Kebbi, Gwari, Nupe, Yoruba and Kwararafa. In truth, the other cities were not part of the Hausa territories, but their histories are linked with those of the Hausa.[65]

What is known about the early history of the Hausa Bakwai, however, is very uneven. In particular, little of the history seems to be currently known of Biram, Daura and Rano. Canon Robinson, the pioneering Hausa scholar, wrote that: "According to the mythical genealogy of the Hausas, their original ancestor was Biram".[66] Lady Lugard confirms this. She related a tradition that Biram was "the father of the states":

> [He] had six children, of whom Zaria [i.e. Zazzau] and Katsena [sic] were first born as twins, then Kano and Rano, another pair of twins, and after them Gober [sic] and Daura. To each of his children the progenitor of the Haussa [sic] States is said to have assigned certain duties. Gober, the most northerly of the states, which in historic times served as a military rampart between peaceful Haussaland and the warlike tribes of the desert, was appointed war chief, with the special duty of defending his brethren. Kano and Rano, safe behind this rampart, were appointed ministers of industry - dyeing, weaving, &c. Katsena and Daura were ministers of intercourse and trade, and Zaria, which is a province of great extent to the south of the others, and dividing their fruitful plains from the hilly country of Bautchi, was appointed chief of slaves, with the special duty of supplying labour for the industry of his brothers.[67]

Was Biram really the first of the Hausa States? Did it really direct the culture of the others cities? Historians do not know. Concerning Daura and Rano, Lady Lugard wrote:

> Daura would seem to have been one of the most ancient of the Haussa [sic] States, and references to it are frequent in the Kano chronicle; but like its sister Rano, it does not appear to have played a very important public part in the history known to us of Hausaland.[68]

The *birni,* or walled village, was the original basis of each state. Distinguished from an ordinary village or hamlet, the walls enclosed a large self-sufficient community where trade, industry and agriculture took place. Moreover, villagers from the surrounding rural areas could enter the *birni* in times of emergency caused by threats from enemy armies. Each *birni* was designed to withstand blockades.[69] Within the walls, exchange took place between farmers and craftsmen.[70] The Hausas unified the different *birni* and hamlets into towns, and the most important became capital cities. The capitals governed the hundreds of other walled villages and held the seat of government. In each capital, an elaborate hierarchy and administration evolved.[71] To give some context, Lord Lugard, the husband of Lady Lugard, estimated in 1904 that there were 170 walled towns still in existence in the whole of just the Kano province alone.[72]

Bagauda became the first Hausa Sarki (i.e. king). Ruling Kano from 999 AD to 1063, the *Kano Chronicle* portrays him as a conqueror who seized power

Hausa (Nigeria). Modern view of the mediæval city of Kano. (Photo: Michael Crowder).

over the settlement of Dala. At this settlement, a culture flourished among the Abagayawa. Rock paintings were found at Birnin-Kudu. Additionally, iron working was found dating to 700 AD. Other evidence indicates the existence of mining. In addition, the Abagayawa established settlements around Dala, such as Gazarawa, Zadawa, Fangon-Zaura, Dunduzawa, Shariya, Sheme, Gande-giji and Tokarawa. Some of these settlements were towns. Worshippers of Tsumburburai, their priest made once yearly sacrifices of black animals in the grove of Jakara. In Dala there was an important shrine to this deity which was a sacred tree called Shamuz.[73] Professor J. Spencer Trimingham claims this early culture belonged to the So civilisation and says they were "characterised by matrilineal succession in the ruling class and [also] walled towns".[74] Professor Moughtin, an architectural scholar, wrote that urbanism in the region was stimulated by trade and iron smelting which dates back to "the earlier part of the first millennium AD".[75] Sarki Bagauda fired the first shot against the religion of the Abagayawa, however. He destroyed the sacred grove of Tsumburburai.[76]

The third Sarki of this line, Bagauda's grandson Gijimasu, raised the first great walls of Kano City in the late eleventh or early twelfth century.[77] Subsequent rulers asserted authority, not just in the city, but also in the localities. During the reign of Tsaraki, the fifth Sarki (1136-63), the first walls of Kano were completed. He also armed his soldiers with shields made of sturdy hides. This allowed Kano to both govern and protect the people of the surrounding rural communities.[78] Sarki Naguji, a successor, had a long reign of 53 years (1194-1247). He imposed an annual land tax equal to one eighth of each worker's produce. Stride and Ifeka contextualised these developments as follows: "Thus, there developed an administrative system capable of dealing with the affairs of a political unit larger than a village community".[79]

Conflicts sometimes arose between the city dwellers and the rural communities. The *Kano Chronicle,* the important Hausa history, tells of counsellors coming to Sarki Shekkerau in 1290 to warn him of rising tensions in the countryside. The counsellors thought stern measures should be taken against the peasants but Shekkerau had other ideas. He received a delegation from the peasants at the royal palace, and listened patiently to their eloquent arguments for local autonomy. According to the *Chronicle,* the Sarki "left them with their power and their own religious customs".[80]

Barandamasu became the next ruler in 1307. Of this ruler, the *Kano Chronicle* recorded that he "excelled all men in courage, dignity, impetuosity in war, vindictiveness and strength". The Chronicle relates that the anthem 'Stand firm, Kano is your city' was composed during this time. Moreover, three-foot long trumpets were introduced into state rituals.[81]

Islam began to make its presence felt during the time of his successor, introduced by Wangarans from Mali. Sarki Yaji (1349-85) enlisted Wangaran support in an attack upon Santolo, a neighbouring city. The Malians promised their support but only on one condition. They demanded that the Sarki adopt Islam and appoint Islamic officials. Yaji complied. Following his conquest of Santolo and the surrounding rural areas, he converted and built the first mosque in Kano, beneath the Shamuz shrine. The Abagayawa were insulted. They contemptuously used the mosque as a lavatory. Yaji was forced to establish a patrol to guard the building.[82] Elsewhere in Hausaland, Islam was introduced. In Katsina of the fifteenth century, the minaret of Muhammad Korau is still a landmark in the city. In Zaria, by contrast, Islam made no progress until the nineteenth century.[83]

The fifteenth century was eventful with brilliant reforms - some inspired by Kanem-Borno.[84] Abdullah Burja, the eighteenth ruler of Kano, was the architect of great prosperity. In 1438 he was crowned Sarki of Kano on the death of Sarki Daud. Within a few years, he became the most powerful sarkuna in the Hausa Confederation. His general led military campaigns for seven years in the regions to the south. The campaigns attempted to open the trade route to Gwanja on the edge of the forest belt. The Kano cavalry, typical of the time, were equipped with plumed iron helmets and chainmail. Their horses were protected with *lifidi* - a thick quilted armour made of cloth. Burja's raids proved successful. Twenty one thousand prisoners were captured. The General dispatched the captives to twenty-one settlements in Kano City. From Gwanja, through this newly opened trade route, kola nuts and gold dust flowed into Kano.[85]

Meanwhile, serious diplomatic problems had emerged with Borno. The *Kano Chronicle* attempts to put a brave face on it but admits that after the conflict "many towns were given to Borno." This indicates that Burja was defeated in whatever-it-was the authors of the *Chronicle* were trying to conceal. The city of Kano remained independent and surprisingly, direct trade was established with Borno despite the conflict.[86] Moreover, the sarki sent gifts to the ruler of Borno, acknowledging the Bono Mai's supremacy as an Islamic leader. This started a tradition that continued late into the eighteenth century.[87]

Of the Hausa rulers, Abdullah Burja was the first to encourage the use of camels as beasts of burden. Previously, Kano businessmen and traders waited on camel caravans controlled by the Tuaregs to arrive from the north. Under Burja's new policy, Kano merchants could transport their own goods across the desert. In the footsteps of these merchants followed the Hausa language and culture. Hausa became the biggest indigenous language spoken in Africa after Swahili. In reputation, Hausa merchants came to rival the legendary Wangaran merchants of Guinea,[88] the economic powerhouse behind Mali. It is worth remembering that the BBC in the *Millennium* series described Mali as the richest empire in the fourteenth century world. In Kano Burja established the Kurmi Market. A veritable magnet, it attracted goods from all over the world.[89]

Yakubu succeeded Burja in 1452. Pursuing a policy of peace and commerce, large numbers of Malian immigrants settled in Kano. Developing the intellectual culture of the city, these Fulani intellectuals introduced the Islamic teachings of dogmatics and grammar. This added to the already established teachings of jurisprudence and the hadith.[90] Yakubu set the stage for his brilliant successor, Sarki Muhammad Rumfa.

Rumfa became ruler of Kano in 1463. He greatly extended the walls of the city and built an imposing new palace, the Gidan Rumfa, with courtly attendants adopting fashions from Borno. They wore extravagant sandals of ostrich feathers and sported fans from the same bird. His principal officers built palaces of their own. Reforming the government, he appointed a nine-member council of advisors and promoted slaves to important positions. Slaves managed the treasury, staffed the palace, attended to the harem, and policed the city. He enforced Islamic law. Humiliating the Abagayawa, he compelled leading citizens to become Muslims and built a Friday Mosque on the sacred Shamuz site. Women were kept in purdah. Additionally, Eid al-Fir, the great Islamic festival after Ramadan, was celebrated for the first time. He offered active support to scholars. One famous scholar, Sheikh Muhammad Al-

Maghili, taught Koranic studies in Katsina and law at Kano.[91] He wrote a treatise on government called *On The Obligations of Princes*. One excerpt from this great work reads as follows:

> The sojourn of a prince in the city breeds all manner of trouble and harm. The bird of prey abides in open and wild places. Vigorous is the cock as he struts round his domains. The eagle can only win his realm by firm resolve, and the cock's voice is strong as he masters the hens. Ride, then, the horses of resolution upon the saddles of prudence. Cherish the land from the spoiling drought, from the raging wind, the dust-laden storm, the raucous thunder, the gleaming lightning, the shattering fireball and the beating rain. Kingdoms are held by the sword, not by delays. Can fear be thrust back except by causing fear? Allow only the nearest of your friends to bring you food and drink and bed and clothes. Do not part with your coat of mail and weapons and let no one approach you save men of trust and virtue. Never sleep in a place of peril. Have near to guard you at all times a band of faithful and gallant men, sentries, bowmen, horse and foot. Times of alarm are not like times of safety. Conceal your secrets from other people until you are master of your undertaking.[92]

In this work, Rumfa was advised to install an Ombudsman to receive complaints against the government. Rumfa put the advice into practice[93] and Al-Maghili left for the Songhai city of Gao in 1502. The only significant failure of his career was an inconclusive eleven year war conducted against Katsina. The *Kano Chronicle* says of him: "He can have no equal in might, from the time of the founding of Kano, until it shall end".[94] From this period on, Lady Lugard says: "Kano may be reckoned with the civilised native powers of the Sudan [i.e. Africa]".[95]

Skirmishes with Katsina continued intermittently until a truce was agreed in 1706. Though all these battles were ultimately inconclusive, Katsina emerged supreme. Songhai, under Askia the Great, seized Kano in around 1512. Sarki Muhammad Kisoki gave one of his daughters in marriage to the Askia. Like the rest of Hausaland, Kano became part of the Songhai Empire for the greater part of the sixteenth century. For most of the eighteenth century Kano fell under the hegemony of Borno.[96]

Birnin Katsina was established in the fifteenth century under Muhammad Korau (*c*.1444-94). The Durbis were the original masters of the Katsina territories. They were Ancestralists and their domination began in the twelfth century. Controlling the markets and fairs of the region, they established hegemony over Birnin Samri, Tsagero, and Yandaka. In the fifteenth century, however, new iron working in what became Birnin Katsina undermined the economic stranglehold of the Durbis. Moreover, new populations migrated into the area with a foreign religious ideology. The Barebari entered from Borno, the Wangara and Fulanis came from the west, and the Absenawa came from the

Hausa (Nigeria). Two elegantly decorated pages of a miniature Koran showing the beauty and elegance of Hausa calligraphy. Late 17ᵗʰ or early 18ᵗʰ century. Size 3" x 3". (Photo: Werner Forman Archives).

north. They brought Islam. Thus when Muhammad Korau gained mastery of the region, Katsina was already a cosmopolitan Islamic city with a flourishing iron working industry. In around 1493 the scholarly and brilliant Sheikh Muhammad Al-Maghili visited the city. He converted Korau, the ruler, and also helped him to establish Islam on a more solid basis.[97]

The independence of the city, however, was undermined in the early sixteenth century. The Songhai, under Askia the Great, conquered Katsina. During this period, however, trade with Tunis brought great prosperity. In 1554 Katsina became independent of Songhai. Ali Murabus, one of the greater Katsina rulers, built the powerful outer walls in around 1560.[98]

Zazzau in the fifteenth century had various fortified places, such as Turunku and Kufena.[99] Zaria city, however, dates back to 1536. Bakwa Turunku founded it after conquering Kufena. Apparently Turunku, her previous capital, lacked sufficient sources of water to support the growing needs of her commercial centre. On her death in c.1566, Karama, a soldier, succeeded her. Princess Amina, Turunku's daughter, accompanied him on campaigns. In 1576 Amina became the undisputed ruler of Zazzau. Distinguished as a soldier and an empire builder, she led campaigns. She had walled forts built as area garrisons to consolidate the territory conquered after each campaign. Some of these forts still stand today. Amina subdued the whole area between Zazzau and the Niger and Benue rivers, absorbing the Nupe and Kwararafa states. The *Kano Chronicle* says: "Every town paid her tribute. The Sarkin Nupe [i.e. king of Nupe] sent her forty eunuchs and ten thousand kolas … In her time all the products of the west came to Hausaland". The southern expansion provided large supplies of slave labour. Additionally, Zazzau came to control the trade route from Gwanja and began to benefit from the trade previously enjoyed only by Kano and Katsina.[100]

Nupe, to the south of Zazzau, had some distant cultural relationship with the Hausa. They enjoyed a high reputation for the quality of their craftsmanship in brass, silver, and glass manufacture. They were also skilled as boat builders, for war and trade. Sarki Tsoede welded the Nupe peoples into a state in the early fifteenth century. He built large forces of cavalry and led the Nupe on a programme of territorial expansion. They subdued the Yagba, Bunu, and Kakanda, and may have driven the Yoruba from their second capital of Old Oyo. Moving north they conquered the Ebe, Kamberi, and Kamuku areas. Tsoede founded the city of Gbara on the lower Kaduna River. On the opposite side, he founded the city of Dokomba. Originally a stable for his 1,000 horses, Dokomba became the main city after Gbara outgrew itself. Gbara could no longer serve the requirements of the court, the army, and the cavalry.[101]

Unique among the "Hausa" states, there are nine surviving bronze masterpieces of controversial origins, but associated with Sarki Tsoede (see page 447). They are comparable in style and quality to the brilliant metal art of the Yoruba and Benin.[102] Moreover, both the Leipzig and British Museums continue to house elaborate brass vessels, urns, daggers, hilts, etc., of Nupe manufacture and several centuries old. Some date to the fifteenth century.[103]

Kebbi was located to the west of the other cities. It was another of the Banzai Bakwai, an "impure" Hausa State. Muhammad Kanta founded it in the early sixteenth century. The son of a Katsina princess, he had an extraordinary career. A brilliant soldier, his army was the only one to withstand the hegemony of Songhai. Some accounts, accepted by Trimingham, and Stride and Ifeka, claim he overthrew Songhai imperial power in Hausaland and imposed tribute on these captured territories himself. Less controversially, he founded imposing cities, the ruins of which are still in existence. Surame, the capital of Kebbi, proved almost impregnable. Surrounded by a moat, it had seven concentric stone and clay walls.[104] Philip Koslow, a modern historian, suggests that the wall construction involved a work force of 10,000 people.[105] Gungu, another of Kanta's constructions, was a garrison town. Finally, Leka was the holiday residence for the royal family.[106]

By the fifteenth or sixteenth centuries, according to Philip Koslow, all of the Hausa cities had emerged with the customary walls and also trade links with the north.[107] Of the walls themselves, we are told that:

> At Kano, for example, there is a great mud wall, some eleven miles in length
> with thirteen gates in all … Lord Lugard, writing in 1902, described it as about
> forty feet in height … Even in its present ruined state it is a noble monument.
> At Zaria a similar wall has practically disappeared, except for some short
> lengths near a few of the gates.[108]

Each city was divided into wards and subdivided into family compounds. An
elder headed each compound. Typically he supervised repairs to the walls of
the city that became necessary after the rainy seasons.[109]

Kano and Katsina were bustling industrial centres of activity associated with
cotton goods, leather manufacture, agriculture, iron smelting, weaving and
dyeing. Nupe specialised in brass, silver, and glass manufacture. The royalty of
Nupe and Kebbi boasted copper-sheathed boats of local manufacture. The
Hausa Confederation traded with the Yoruba to the south, bought Akan gold
from the west and traded with Egypt and the rest of North Africa.[110] Some of
these commercial activities were given a new impetus caused by the break up
and fall of Songhai in 1591.[111] Although referring to a later period, a modern
scholar noted that: "It has been estimated that in 1851, the City of Kano
exported 10 million pairs of sandals, 5 million hides and sheepskins, each year
to North Africa".[112] Additionally, "for several centuries" says another scholar
"the best [leather] bindings for European books came from Nigeria; for
Morocco leather (so-called because Europe imported it via Morocco) is made
from Nigerian goat skin".[113] The Kano market was the most important venue
for the buying and selling of these products. Canon Charles Robinson, a
Cambridge University authority on Hausa Studies, definitively described this
institution. Writing in 1900, he declared the following:

> Kano may claim to possess the largest market place, not merely in Africa, but
> in the world. The French traveller, Colonel Monteuil, estimated its average
> daily attendance at thirty thousand; and though I should not have ventured on
> quite so large as one myself, I do not think that his estimate is very extravagant.
> Size, moreover, is the least interesting feature of the Kano market. In the first
> place its antiquity is deserving of notice. The market has probably been held on
> the exact site where we now find it for at least a thousand years. At the time of
> the Norman conquest of England [i.e. 1066 AD] trade was being conducted in
> the Kano market amidst surroundings closely resembling those that we now
> see. Kano would then have furnished better-made cloth than any to be found in
> England at that time.[114]

Each state was typically governed by a Council, composed of the great
ministers. Apart from the Sarki, there was the Galadima (his deputy or heir
apparent), the Madawaki (the commander-in-chief), the Magaji (the minister of
finance), the Yari (the chief of prisons), the Sarkin Dogarai (the head of the
royal bodyguard) and the Sarkin Yan Doka (the chief of police). The Madawaki

Nigerian stamp depicting Queen Amina (*c.*1533-1610) issued in 1975 to commemorate International Women's Year.

was the second most important official on the Council. Apart from the ceremonial functions, he advised the king on appointments to high office. He was also on the panel of kingmakers. Local government was in the hands of the village heads. Some of these were royally appointed. Justice was administered by the Alkali who administered Maliki law in the light of local traditions. Appeals could be made up to the Chief Alkali. In the villages, however, the village head decided upon minor issues. Taxes were imposed on movable property, livestock, annual production, and as tribute on conquered states. Citizens paid in kind. Tribute was sometimes paid by the supplying of slaves.[115]

Kano was as large as the Songhai capital of Gao.[116] A survey of 1585 suggested that Gao had a population of at least 100,000 people.[117] Kano had a planning policy to keep only half the city as residential. This may indicate a Kano population of between 50,000 and 100,000. We are informed by Leo Africanus, a Moorish contemporary, that: "The inhabitants are rich merchants and [are] most civil people. Their king was in times past of great puissance, and had mighty troops of horseman at his command".[118]

Katsina of the mid sixteenth century was more imposing with a circuit of thirteen or fourteen miles. Divided into a hundred residential quarters, it was a cosmopolitan city. It had quarters for the Bornoese, the Malians, the Songhai, the Asben, the Arabs, and people from Gobir. It boasted industrial quarters for saddlers, shoemakers and dyers, and workshops for smiths and tailors. There were warehouses of textiles, salt and lead, and great halls for the conduct of business. There was an official or government quarter. The Sarki's palace itself developed into a complex of stores, halls, stables, and houses. Elsewhere, there were schools and mosques,[119] and, "as in all great towns", there was a student's quarter.[120] The outlying region could grow tobacco, indigo, yam, melons, pomegranates, and many other foodstuffs.[121]

Surame, even in ruin, was an impressive sight, built on a horizontal vertical grid. Mr E. J. Arnett, a modern scholar, describes it thus:

> The walls of Surame are about 10 miles in circumference and include many large bastions or walled suburbs running out at right angles to the main wall. The large compound at Kanta is still visible in the centre, with ruins of many buildings, one of which is said to have been two-storied. The striking feature of the walls and whole ruins is the extensive use of stone and *tsokuwa* (laterite gravel) or very hard red building mud, evidently brought from a distance. There is a big mound of this near the north gate about 8 feet in height. The walls show regular courses of masonry to a height of 20 feet and more in several places. The best preserved portion is that known as *sirati* (the bridge) a little north of the eastern gate … The main city walls here appear to have provided a very strongly guarded entrance about 30 feet wide, approached from left and right by a passage deepening to the point of entrance and sloping up from there into the town. The entrance, however, is filled in with a solid masonry wall in

Nupe (Nigeria). Seated figure. 12ᵗʰ/15ᵗʰ century. Copper. Height 53.7 cm. One of the nine remarkable Tsoede Bronzes. Probably casted at Ile-Ife for Nupe patrons. (Photo: National Commission for Museums and Monuments, Lagos).

remarkable preservation. It stands from 25 to 30 feet high ... From its name, *sirati*, or bridge ... [it is probable that] the entrance gateway of the town was surmounted by an archway, or bridge ... Surame is said to have been abandoned by the successors of Kanta about 1715 A.D.[122]

The fall of Timbuktu in 1591 left Katsina the leading intellectual centre of West Africa.[123] Lady Lugard suggests that it "seems to have been regarded as a sort of university town".[124] Abu Abdullah Mohammed ibn Mohammed (1595-1667), also called Dan Masani, was its most celebrated scholar. He wrote on law, theology, poetry, politics, and even on the wonders of Yorubaland. Furthermore, he wrote a 500-page commentary on the ishiriniya of al-Fazzai, he also wrote a treatise on rebellion, and one on Maliki law.[125] Mohammed ibn Mohammed, an astronomer and mathematician, wrote an interesting paper on the theory of mathematical chronograms, also known as magic squares.[126] Moreover the city itself flourished as a trading centre. An account from the eighteenth century describes Katsina as follows:

> The rich men boasted of their houses full of gold and silver. Every rich man had a square house which they filled with gold and silver. And the result was that it was a city of vainglory. It had seven gates and in it were seven places of treasure. One of them was the store of gold from the Guga gate to Yandaka gate. And the ma'adanawa [warehouses] of salt from the gate of Guga to the gate of Marusa. And outside the town, kwalli (antimony), silver, tin and lead. And the place is from the market of Darama to inside Albaba.[127]

Lady Lugard even noticed that: "the manners of Katsena [sic] were distinguished by superior politeness over those of the other towns".[128]

Gobir in the eighteenth and nineteenth centuries became the most powerful state of the Hausa Confederation. Early in the eighteenth century, Gobir began to exploit the power vacuum left by a failing Kebbi. Sarki Barbari ruled from 1742 to 1770. His armies marched against Zamfara, Maradi, Katsina, Yauri, and Nupe. They extracted tribute from Kano.[129] However, Gobir itself faced a far more powerful threat from the Fulanis. Austere and fanatical in their religion, they no longer tolerated the laxness and growing corruption of the Hausa rulers. In 1804 they revolted against these regimes declaring *jihad* on the rulers. William Winwood Reade, author of *The Martyrdom of Man,* gave an account of the relevant facts:

> Othman [sic] Dan Fodio, the Black Prophet ... went out of Mecca, his soul burning with zeal. He determined to reform the Sudan [i.e. that part of Africa] ... Dan Fodio sent letters to the great kings of Timbuktu, Haoussa [sic], and Bornu [sic], commanding them to reform their own lives and those of their subjects, or he would chastise them in the name of God ... Dan Fodio united the Fulah [i.e. Fulani] tribes into an army which he inspired with his own spirit.

> Thirsting for plunder and paradise, the Fulahs swept over the Sudan; they marched into battle with shouts of frenzied joy, singing hymns and waving their green flags on which texts of the Koran were embroidered in letters of gold.[130]

Many ordinary Hausas joined the Fulani campaigns. They empathised with the Fulani attack on the luxury, injustice, and high taxation associated with the Hausa Sarkunas (i.e. Kings). Moreover, the government officials were not above confiscating livestock and other goods of ordinary people. Nor were they above capturing young women to serve in the harem.[131]

In 1812 the Shehu (meaning 'teacher'), Uthman Dan Fodio triumphed over the Hausa kings. Ruling from Gobir, he changed the name of the city to Sokoto. The empire he built became the Sokoto Caliphate. Establishing a centralised government, he began a stability in the region that ultimately created an economic boom. Hausaland had seen nothing like it since the fifteenth and sixteenth centuries.[132] Kano cotton, for example, clothed half of West Africa.[133] Furthermore, the Shehu and his descendants were scholars of impressive intellects. Dr Davidson wrote that: "To Uthman, his brother Abdullah and his son Muhammad Bello are attributed some 258 books and essays on a variety of theoretical and practical subjects".[134] Between 1822 and 1830 two English travellers, Dixon Denham and Hugh Clapperton, visited the Caliphate and also Borno. They recorded that the palace of Kano possessed a mosque and "several towers three or four stories high".[135] Dr Barth visited there in 1854 and estimated the population of Hausaland at 50 million people.[136] The best concise description of the Caliphate and also Borno, however, comes again from the pen of William Winwood Reade. He wrote a splendid summary of what the Englishmen witnessed on their travels:

> Denham and Clapperton … were astonished to find among the [N]egroes magnificent courts; regiments of cavalry, the horses caparisoned in silk for gala days and clad in coats of mail for war; long trains of camels laden with salt and natron and corn and cloth and cowrie shells - which form the currency - and kola nuts, which Arabs call "the coffee of the [N]egroes." They attended with wonder the gigantic fairs at which the cotton goods of Manchester, the red cloth of Saxony, double-barrelled guns, razors, tea and sugar, Nuremberg ware and writing-paper were exhibited for sale. They also found merchants who offered to cash their bills upon houses at Tripoli; and scholars acquainted with Avicenna, Averroes, and the Greek philosophers.[137]

Things were falling apart, however. Canon Robinson paints a picture of great instability due to the different cities slave raiding each other. Although Robinson himself suggests otherwise, this could only have severely disrupted the social and economic life in our opinion. Slaves were sold in markets at Kano and elsewhere.[138]

The fall of this culture is associated with the military activities of the British. In 1903 their armies overthrew the Sokoto Caliphate. They incorporated the captured territory with the conquered lands of Benin, Igbo and Yoruba to form the modern state of Nigeria.[139]

Note on the Role of Islam in African Culture

Dr Leo Frobenius, the great German Africanist, was among the first to refute the notion that the civilisations of West Africa and the Central Sahara were of Arab inspiration (see page 362). Nevertheless, misconceptions continue to persist. What is less well known is that the Arabic script, used in many of these civilisations, was in fact of African origin. Ibn Khallikan, the great biographer of the Middle Ages, claimed that Abul Aswan, an African, invented the Arabic script.[140] Furthermore, the greatest literature of the Arabs was penned by Blacks including Luqman, Antar, Ibrahim Al-Mahdi, and the greatest intellect of them all, Al-Jahiz.[141] On the genesis of Islam, one cannot overlook the outstanding contribution of Bilal, an Ethiopian, who was considered one third of the origin of that religion, where Al'lah was the first part, and Mahomet was the second.[142] In addition, the Ka'aba of Mecca, the only substantial piece of early Islamic architecture in the entire Saudi Arabian region, was rebuilt in its present form by Ethiopian architects (see page 466). It should also be acknowledged that Christianity, like Islam, is also partly of African origin. Among those outstanding Africans who brought glory to the early church were Tertullian, Perpetua, St Cyprian, and the venerable St Augustine.[143]

In conclusion, the presence of Christianity in early Europe, despite its non-European origins, does not de-Europeanise European historical achievements any more than the presence of Islam in early West and Central Africa de-Africanises African historical achievements.

Notes

[1] J. Spencer Trimingham, *A History of Islam in West Africa*, UK, Oxford University Press, 1962, pp.114-5 and Philip Koslow, *Kanem-Borno: 1,000 Years of Splendor*, US, Chelsea House, 1995, p.20.

[2] Quoted in Sir Richmond Palmer, *The Bornu Sahara and Sudan*, UK, John Murray, 1936, p.127.

[3] Quoted in ibid., p.156.

[4] Ibid.

[5] Quoted in J. Spencer Trimingham, *A History of Islam in West Africa*, p.114.

[6] Roland Oliver and Anthony Atmore, *Medieval Africa: 1250-1800*, UK, Cambridge University Press, 2001, p.80.

[7] Philip Koslow, *Kanem-Borno: 1,000 Years of Splendor*, p.13.

[8] G. T. Stride & Caroline Ifeka, *Peoples and Empires of West Africa*, UK, Thomas Nelson and Sons, 1971, pp.113-5.

[9] Philip Koslow, *Kanem-Borno: 1,000 Years of Splendor,* pp.21-2.

[10] J. Spencer Trimingham, *A History of Islam in West Africa,* pp.114-5

[11] G. T. Stride & Caroline Ifeka, *Peoples and Empires of West Africa,* p.116.

[12] Ibid., pp.116-7 and J. Spencer Trimingham, *A History of Islam in West Africa,* p.116.

[13] Lady Lugard, *A Tropical Dependency,* UK, James Nisbet & Co., 1906, p.65.

[14] John G. Jackson, *Introduction to African Civilizations,* US, Citadel Press, 1970, p.220 and Philip Koslow, *Kanem-Borno: 1,000 Years of Splendor,* p.23.

[15] Basil Davidson, *Africa in History,* UK, Macmillan, 1991, pp. 94-5.

[16] Philip Koslow, *Kanem-Borno: 1,000 Years of Splendor,* p.23.

[17] J. Spencer Trimingham, *A History of Islam in West Africa,* p.117.

[18] Lady Lugard, *A Tropical Dependency,* p.270.

[19] G. T. Stride & Caroline Ifeka, *Peoples and Empires of West Africa,* pp.116-7 and Philip Koslow, *Kanem-Borno: 1,000 Years of Splendor,* pp.23-4.

[20] Basil Davidson, *Old Africa Rediscovered,* UK, Victor Gollancz, 1959, p.82.

[21] Muhammad Al-Hajj, *Some Diplomatic Correspondence of the Seifuwa Mais of Borno with Egypt, Turkey and Morocco,* in *Studies in the History of Pre-Colonial Borno,* ed Bala Usman & Nur Alkali, Nigeria, Northern Nigeria Publishing Company, 1983, pp.156-7 and Roland Oliver and Anthony Atmore, *Medieval Africa: 1250-1800,* pp.8-9.

[22] Quoted in Sir Richmond Palmer, *The Bornu Sahara and Sudan,* pp.185-6.

[23] Ronald Cohen, *The Kanuri of Bornu,* US, Holt, Rinehart and Winston, 1967, p.14.

[24] Quoted in Basil Davidson, *Old Africa Rediscovered,* pp.81-2.

[25] G. T. Stride & Caroline Ifeka, *Peoples and Empires of West Africa,* p.117.

[26] J. Spencer Trimingham, *A History of Islam in West Africa,* pp.117-8 and G. T. Stride & Caroline Ifeka, *Peoples and Empires of West Africa,* p.117-8.

[27] J. Spencer Trimingham, *A History of Islam in West Africa,* pp.118-9.

[28] Lady Lugard, *A Tropical Dependency,* p.270.

[29] Roland Oliver & Brian M. Fagan, *Africa in the Iron Age,* UK, Cambridge University Press, 1975, p.153.

[30] Sir Richmond Palmer, *The Bornu Sahara and Sudan,* pp.51 and 119.

[31] J. Spencer Trimingham, *A History of Islam in West Africa,* pp.120-1.

[32] Lady Lugard, *A Tropical Dependency,* pp.272-4.

[33] Bawuro M. Barkindo, *Kano Relations with Borno Early Times to c.1800,* in *Kano and Some of Her Neighbours,* ed Bawuro M. Barkindo, Nigeria, Ahmadu Bello University Press, 1989, p.155.

[34] Ibid., p.148.

[35] Ibid., pp.148-9.

[36] Lady Lugard, *A Tropical Dependency,* pp.274-6 and J. Spencer Trimingham, *A History of Islam in West Africa,* p.121.

[37] G. T. Stride & Caroline Ifeka, *Peoples and Empires of West Africa,* pp.118-9.

[38] J. Spencer Trimingham, *A History of Islam in West Africa,* p.121.

[39] A. Mahadi, *The Cities of Borno,* in *Cities of the Savannah,* ed Garba Ashiwaju, Nigeria, The Nigeria Magazine, no date given for publication, pp.13-4.

[40] Lady Lugard, *A Tropical Dependency,* p.274.

[41] Muhammad Nur Alkali, *Economic Factors in the History of Borno under the Seifuwa,* in *Studies in the History of Pre-Colonial Borno,* ed Bala Usman & Nur Alkali, Nigeria, Northern Nigeria Publishing Company, 1983, pp.62-4.

[42] Quoted in Basil Davidson, *A History of West Africa 1000 - 1800,* UK, Longmans, 1977, p.157.

[43] Raymond Michelet, *African Empires and Civilisations*, in *Negro: An Anthology*, ed Nancy Cunard, US, Frederick Ungar Publishing Co., 1970, p.368.

[44] J. Spencer Trimingham, *A History of Islam in West Africa*, p.122.

[45] Muhammad Al-Hajj, *Some Diplomatic Correspondence of the Seifuwa Mais of Borno with Egypt, Turkey and Morocco*, in *Studies in the History of Pre-Colonial Borno*, pp.158-161 and Philip Koslow, *Kanem-Borno: 1,000 Years of Splendor*, p.41.

[46] Quoted in Sir Richmond Palmer, *The Bornu Sahara and Sudan*, p.6.

[47] Quoted in Philip Koslow, *Kanem-Borno: 1,000 Years of Splendor*, p.33.

[48] Lady Lugard, *A Tropical Dependency*, pp.280-1.

[49] Quoted in Sir Richmond Palmer, *The Bornu Sahara and Sudan*, p.236.

[50] Roland Oliver and Anthony Atmore, *Medieval Africa: 1250-1800*, p.84.

[51] Bawuro M. Barkindo, *Kano Relations with Borno Early Times to c.1800*, in *Kano and Some of Her Neighbours*, pp.158-161, G. T. Stride & Caroline Ifeka, *Peoples and Empires of West Africa*, pp.123-4 and Philip Koslow, *Kanem-Borno: 1,000 Years of Splendor*, pp.33-41.

[52] Philip Koslow, *Kanem-Borno: 1,000 Years of Splendor*, p.41.

[53] Lady Lugard, *A Tropical Dependency*, p.279.

[54] G. T. Stride & Caroline Ifeka, *Peoples and Empires of West Africa*, p.124 and Philip Koslow, *Kanem-Borno: 1,000 Years of Splendor*, p.43.

[55] Basil Davidson, *A History of West Africa 1000 - 1800*, p.277.

[56] Philip Koslow, *Kanem-Borno: 1,000 Years of Splendor*, p.44-5.

[57] Susan Denyer, *African Traditional Architecture*, UK, Heinemann, 1978, p.35.

[58] Ibidem and A. Mahadi, *The Cities of Borno*, in *Cities of the Savannah*, pp.9 and 14.

[59] Philip Koslow, *Kanem-Borno: 1,000 Years of Splendor*, p.44.

[60] Basil Davidson, *A History of West Africa 1000 - 1800*, p.277.

[61] Quoted in Sir Richmond Palmer, *The Bornu Sahara and Sudan*, pp.85 and 246-7.

[62] Basil Davidson, *A History of West Africa 1000 - 1800*, p.277.

[63] G. T. Stride & Caroline Ifeka, *Peoples and Empires of West Africa*, p.125 and A. Mahadi, *The Cities of Borno*, in *Cities of the Savannah*, p.17.

[64] J. Spencer Trimingham, *A History of Islam in West Africa*, p.126.

[65] G. T. Stride & Caroline Ifeka, *Peoples and Empires of West Africa*, pp.86-7.

[66] Charles Henry Robinson, *Nigeria: Our Latest Protectorate*, UK, Horace Marshall & Son, 1900, p.13.

[67] Lady Lugard, *A Tropical Dependency*, p.239.

[68] Ibid., p.248.

[69] J. Spencer Trimingham, *A History of Islam in West Africa*, p.127.

[70] John G. Jackson, *Introduction to African Civilizations*, p.221.

[71] J. Spencer Trimingham, *A History of Islam in West Africa*, p.127.

[72] See Susan Denyer, *African Traditional Architecture*, p.70.

[73] J. Spencer Trimingham, *A History of Islam in West Africa*, p.127, G. T. Stride & Caroline Ifeka, *Peoples and Empires of West Africa*, pp.89-90 and Sule Bello, *The Birnin Kano and the Kasar Kano to 1804 A.D.*, in *Cities of the Savannah*, ed Garba Ashiwaju, Nigeria, The Nigeria Magazine, no date given, pp.27-9.

[74] J. Spencer Trimingham, *A History of Islam in West Africa*, p.126.

[75] J. C. Moughtin, *Hausa Architecture*, UK, Ethnographica, 1985, p.20.

[76] Philip Koslow, *Hausaland: The Fortress Kingdoms*, US, Chelsea House, 1995, p.17.

[77] Sule Bello, *The Birnin Kano and the Kasar Kano to 1804 A.D.*, in *Cities of the Savannah*, p.29.

[78] G. T. Stride & Caroline Ifeka, *Peoples and Empires of West Africa,* p.90 and Philip Koslow, *Hausaland: The Fortress Kingdoms,* p.17

[79] G. T. Stride & Caroline Ifeka, *Peoples and Empires of West Africa,* p.80.

[80] John G. Jackson, *Introduction to African Civilizations,* p.221.

[81] G. T. Stride & Caroline Ifeka, *Peoples and Empires of West Africa,* p.91 and Philip Koslow, *Hausaland: The Fortress Kingdoms,* p.17.

[82] J. Spencer Trimingham, *A History of Islam in West Africa,* p.131 and Philip Koslow, *Hausaland: The Fortress Kingdoms,* p.21.

[83] J. Spencer Trimingham, *A History of Islam in West Africa,* pp.131-2.

[84] Bawuro M. Barkindo, *Kano Relations with Borno Early Times to c.1800,* in *Kano and Some of Her Neighbours,* pp.151 and 154-5.

[85] Philip Koslow, *Hausaland: The Fortress Kingdoms,* p.29.

[86] Lady Lugard, *A Tropical Dependency,* p.252.

[87] Bawuro M. Barkindo, *Kano Relations with Borno Early Times to c.1800,* in *Kano and Some of Her Neighbours,* p.153.

[88] Philip Koslow, *Hausaland: The Fortress Kingdoms,* p.29.

[89] Ibidem and Jeremy Isaacs producer, *Millennium: The 14th Century,* Television Series, UK, BBC Television, 1999.

[90] J. Spencer Trimingham, *A History of Islam in West Africa,* p.132.

[91] Lady Lugard, *A Tropical Dependency,* pp.253-4, J. Spencer Trimingham, *A History of Islam in West Africa,* pp.131-3 and Sule Bello, *The Birnin Kano and the Kasar Kano to 1804 A.D.,* in *Cities of the Savannah,* p.30.

[92] Quoted in Sir Richmond Palmer, *The Bornu Sahara and Sudan,* frontispiece.

[93] Basil Davidson, *Africa,* television series part 4: *The King and the City,* UK, Michael Beazley, Rm Arts, Channel Four Television & Nigerian Television, 1984.

[94] Quoted in G. T. Stride & Caroline Ifeka, *Peoples and Empires of West Africa,* p.93.

[95] Lady Lugard, *A Tropical Dependency,* p.253.

[96] G. T. Stride & Caroline Ifeka, *Peoples and Empires of West Africa,* pp.93-4.

[97] Y. B. Usman, *The Birne of Katsina,* in *Cities of the Savannah,* ed Garba Ashiwaju, Nigeria, The Nigeria Magazine, no date given, pp.37-9 and G. T. Stride & Caroline Ifeka, *Peoples and Empires of West Africa,* p.95.

[98] G. T. Stride & Caroline Ifeka, *Peoples and Empires of West Africa,* p.95.

[99] Sule Bello, *Birnin Zaria,* in *Cities of the Savannah,* ed Garba Ashiwaju, Nigeria, The Nigeria Magazine, no date given, p.77.

[100] G. T. Stride & Caroline Ifeka, *Peoples and Empires of West Africa,* p.97 and J. Spencer Trimingham, *A History of Islam in West Africa,* p.129.

[101] G. T. Stride & Caroline Ifeka, *Peoples and Empires of West Africa,* p.100.

[102] Ekpo Eyo, *Two Thousand Years of Nigerian Art,* UK & Nigeria, Ethnographica and The National Commission for Museums and Monuments, 1977, pp.150 and 160-5.

[103] William Fagg ed, *The Living Arts of Nigeria,* UK, Studio Vista, 1971, *On Brass-Casting and Brass-Working* (there are no page numbers in this book, but see plates 4-6) and Werner Gillon, *A Short History of African Art,* UK, Penguin, 1984, pp.233-5.

[104] G. T. Stride & Caroline Ifeka, *Peoples and Empires of West Africa,* pp.101-3, J. Spencer Trimingham, *A History of Islam in West Africa,* pp.134-5 and Daniel Chu and Elliott Skinner, *A Glorious Age in Africa,* US, Africa World Press, 1990, pp.101-8.

[105] Philip Koslow, *Hausaland: The Fortress Kingdoms,* p.45.

[106] G. T. Stride & Caroline Ifeka, *Peoples and Empires of West Africa,* p.103.

[107] Philip Koslow, *Hausaland: The Fortress Kingdoms,* pp.23-4.

[108] Arthur M. Foyle, *Nigerian Architecture,* in *The Geographical Magazine, Volume XXII: Number 5,* ed Michael Huxley, UK, January 1951, p.180.

[109] Philip Koslow, *Hausaland: The Fortress Kingdoms,* p.24.

[110] John G. Jackson, *Introduction to African Civilizations,* p.222, Basil Davidson, *Africa in History,* p.97, W. E. B. DuBois, *The World and Africa,* pp.212-3 and G. T. Stride & Caroline Ifeka, *Peoples and Empires of West Africa,* p.161.

[111] Implied in Lady Lugard, *A Tropical Dependency,* p.264.

[112] Benaebi Benatari, *The Document of African Civilisation,* UK, Unpublished Paper, 1999, p.40.

[113] S. Irein Wangboje, *Art and Crafts,* in *The Living Culture of Nigeria,* ed Saburi O. Biobaku, Nigeria, Thomas Nelson & Sons, 1976, p.18.

[114] Charles Henry Robinson, *Nigeria: Our Latest Protectorate,* pp.138-9.

[115] G. T. Stride & Caroline Ifeka, *Peoples and Empires of West Africa,* pp.109-11.

[116] J. Spencer Trimingham, *A History of Islam in West Africa,* p.136.

[117] Sergio Domian, *Architecture Soudanaise: Vitalite d'une tradition urbaine et monumentale,* France, Éditions L'Harmattan, 1989, p.80 and cf. R. W. Morris, *Our Commonwealth in the Old World,* UK, George Allen and Unwin, no date given, p.35.

[118] Quoted in Lady Lugard, *A Tropical Dependency,* p.254.

[119] Y. B. Usman, *The Birne of Katsina,* in *Cities of the Savannah,* pp.39-40 and Lady Lugard, A Tropical Dependency, pp.262-3.

[120] Lady Lugard, *A Tropical Dependency,* p.263.

[121] Ibid., pp.263-4.

[122] Quoted in Sir Richmond Palmer, *The Bornu Sahara and Sudan,* pp.229-30.

[123] Claudia Zaslavsky, *Africa Counts,* US, Lawrence Hill & Co., 1973, p.275.

[124] Lady Lugard, *A Tropical Dependency,* p.265.

[125] Y. B. Usman, *The Birne of Katsina,* in *Cities of the Savannah,* p.41.

[126] Claudia Zaslavsky, *Africa Counts,* pp.138-151.

[127] Quoted in Y. B. Usman, *The Birne of Katsina,* in *Cities of the Savannah,* p.40.

[128] Lady Lugard, *A Tropical Dependency,* p.265

[129] G. T. Stride & Caroline Ifeka, *Peoples and Empires of West Africa,* p.108.

[130] Winwood Reade, *The Martyrdom of Man,* UK, Watts & Co., 1934 edition, pp.235-6.

[131] Philip Koslow, *Hausaland: The Fortress Kingdoms,* pp.41-4.

[132] Ibid., pp.44-9.

[133] Winwood Reade, *The Martyrdom of Man,* p.230.

[134] Basil Davidson, *Africa in History,* pp.251-2.

[135] Quoted in Susan Denyer, *African Traditional Architecture,* p.57.

[136] Lady Lugard, *A Tropical Dependency,* p.416.

[137] Winwood Reade, *The Martyrdom of Man,* p.230.

[138] Charles Henry Robinson, *Nigeria: Our Latest Protectorate,* pp.16-8 and 160-4.

[139] Philip Koslow, *Hausaland: The Fortress Kingdoms,* pp.51-2.

[140] Ivan Van Sertima, *The Lost Sciences of Africa: An Overview,* in *Blacks in Science: Ancient and Modern,* ed Ivan Van Sertima, US, Transaction Publishers, 1983, p.26.

[141] J. A. Rogers, *World's Great Men of Color, Volume I,* US, Macmillan, 1972, pp.67-72, 138-42 and 148-171.

[142] Ibid., pp.143-7.

[143] Yosef A. A. ben-Jochannan, *African Origins of the Major Western Religions,* US, Black Classic Press, 1971, pp.73-137.

CHAPTER FIFTEEN: EAST AFRICAN ANTIQUITIES

Ethiopia

In Ethiopia,[1] in the Tigre region, stands the ruined Temple of Almaqah. The pride of the city of Yeha, it is one of the oldest monuments in the country. Some think it was built before the fifth century BC.[2] The Temple is a two-storey structure, raised on a stepped plinth. It is 25 metres long and rectangular in plan. The walls are of huge limestone blocks, finely dressed and polished with two small windows.[3] Francisco Alvarez, a Portuguese visitor, saw it in about 1520 and described its "exquisite masonry". He also wrote that the monument showed a "royal grandeur such as I have never seen."[4] Graham Hancock, an authority on Ethiopian history, writes "little or nothing is known about the people who built this great edifice".[5] Dr David Phillipson, another modern authority, reports archaeological speculation that Yeha had a population of 10,000 inhabitants.[6]

Other settlements belonging to this state were located at Kaskase, Matara and Hawilti-Malazo. In these places ruins of temples and water reservoirs have been found.[7] Excavations at Yeha and at other early Ethiopian sites revealed an exquisite throne, statues, religious artefacts, altars and censers bearing fifth and fourth century BC inscriptions. Other artefacts of a more mundane nature were also excavated. These include pottery, lamps, spears, axes, sickles, chisels and daggers, all made of bronze.[8] David Buxton of Cambridge University wrote that: "These finds have revealed a comparatively advanced culture which, though strongly influenced by southern Arabia, is yet different from anything known to have existed there."[9]

In truth, there is little hard evidence that this early Ethiopian culture was of South Arabian origins. Mr Hancock and Mr Buxton claim that Almaqah was originally a South Arabian deity, and they may be correct. But since little is known of the people who built the Temple of Almaqah we can hardly conclude that they were Arabs. The other artefacts that have been excavated are too different from Arabian models to suggest an Arabian origin, as we have seen. The only argument that Hancock and Buxton have left is that the written inscriptions associated with the Yeha culture show affinities with the languages spoken at that time in South Arabia. Again, they are correct, but again this too is inconclusive. Ethiopia is generally accepted to be the place of origin of both

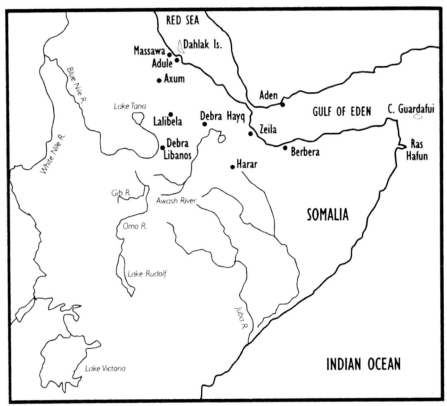

The Empire of Axum. (Map: Kieron Vital).

the Semitic and Cushitic language groups/families. Semitic and Cushitic speakers migrated from here to populate North and East Africa and also Arabia.[10] Therefore, similarities between the languages of Ethiopia and Arabia are to be expected. This also shows that the very first Arabians (and Semitic speakers in general) were Africans anyway. Moreover, genuine cultural links between the Southern Arabs (the Yemenis) and the Ethiopians really did exist and flourished from the ancient periods, symbolised by the Queen of Sheba period, up till the seventh century AD.[11] A modern scholar comments that:

> [I]t would seem possible to adopt a[nother] ... position, in which Ethiopia and South Arabia are seen as comprising parts of a single Red Sea cultural area, without either side assuming a dominant position ... Furthermore, while objects indicating a relationship with South Arabia were once thought to demonstrate the presence of a superior colonial power, it is now recognized that most of them were likely to have been created by Ethiopians themselves, and a more careful or more subtle analysis of their significance is therefore required.[12]

Axum (Ethiopia). Fallen Stele in Axum. *c*.100 AD. Originally carved as a single block of granite, this is the largest obelisk in the world. It has details carved into it that represent a doorway and 13 storeys worth of windows. Furthermore, it weighs a staggering 500 tons. (Photo: Werner Forman Archives).

Some writers go further than this. Mr Garlake reports that: "An argument has even been put forward that the direction of influence flowed not from Arabia to Africa but in the other direction: that south Arabia derived its early arts from Aksumite [sic] territories and not vice versa".[13]

The early inscriptions were in a script variously called Proto-Ethiopic, Himyaritic or Sabaean. What is in a name? The writers who believe that this culture originated in Yemen are likely to call both the Yemeni and the African inscriptions 'Himyaritic' or 'Sabaean'. Those who believe the culture originated in Africa are likely to call both the African and Yemeni inscriptions 'Proto-Ethiopic'.[14]

In and around Axum, another great city, there are over 50 stelae, many of them undecorated. Some are believed to be very old, but firm dates have not been established.[15] Near to some of these obelisks, one kilometre from Axum on the road to the city of Gondar, is a massive building containing a drainage system with "finely-mortared stone walls, deep foundations and an impressive throne room".[16] Ethiopian tradition establishes this building as the palace of Empress Makeda, the fabled Queen of Sheba (1005-955 BC). Tradition also establishes one of the obelisks, carved with four horizontal bands, each topped with a row of circles in relief, as the marker of the Queen's grave.[17] It was probably due to this evidence that J. A. Rogers, the famous Jamaican historian, declared that: "A few years ago her tomb, as well as the ruins of a great temple and twenty-two obelisks of her period, were excavated at Axum".[18] Finally, there are obelisks that seem to be intermediate in date and style between those of the Makeda period and those of the early Christian era.

Even before the Yeha and Makeda periods, a number of historians have suggested that Ethiopia "was part of a vast stretch of land on both sides of the southern Red Sea, part of which the ancient Egyptians knew as the Land of

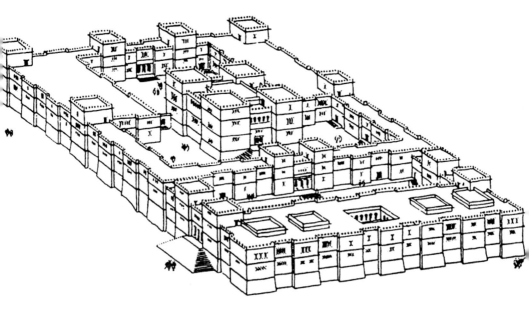

Axum (Ethiopia). Reconstructon of the castle complex of Ta'akha Maryam at Axum. *c.*300 AD or earlier. The overall dimensions are 80 m x 120 m. From D. Krencker et al, *Deutsche Aksum-Expedition, Book II* (Germany, Georg Reimer, 1913, p.113).

Punt".[19] This region exported a key product in the ancient world - incense. The priestly classes of many ancient civilisations used it as part of their religious rituals. Huge quantities of this product were consumed, since it was a "fuel for the machinery of the gods".[20] Dr Roderick Grierson, an English historian, is the editor of a valuable work on Ethiopian antiquities called *African Zion*. In a fascinating essay, he informs us that:

> As early as 1500 B.C., the reliefs carved in the great [Egyptian] temple of Deir el Bahri near Thebes [i.e. Waset] record the most famous of all ancient expeditions, the mission sent by the Eighteenth Dynasty queen Hatshepsut to the land of Punt. The reliefs depict the delight of the ancient Egyptian explorers in their discoveries: ivory, ebony, gold, date palms, giraffes, lions, cheetahs held on leashes, and baboons clambering over the rigging of the five ships as they loaded with treasure for the queen … For centuries, legends of Punt had fascinated Egyptian mariners, and expeditions had set out as early as 2800 B.C. in the reign of the Fifth Dynasty pharaoh Sahure. The inscriptions of Hatshepsut maintain that Punt was known only "from mouth to mouth by hearsay of ancestors" and then make the claim "but I have led them on water and on land, to explore the waters of inaccessible channels, and I have reached the terraces of incense". . . . The precise location of Punt remained a mystery. Frankincense and myrrh grew on both sides of the Red Sea [Ethiopia/Somalia and Yemen], although in later centuries it was South Arabia that was most associated with the luxury trade of the desert … However, the reliefs at Deir el Bahri depict giraffes, and the inscriptions refer to heavy rains in Punt causing the Nile to flood, suggesting that it must have lain on the African side, in the region of Ethiopia.[21]

Dr Richard Pankhurst, another contributor to the same work, believes that trade between Egypt and this region dates to an even earlier period than the Fifth Egyptian Dynasty, but like Dr Grierson, he uses the short Egyptian chronology: "Egyptian vessels probably reached the area as early as the first or second dynasty (3400-2980 B.C.). Such contacts continued for several millennia".[22] We note, however, that Ta-Seti emerged several generations before the Egyptian First Dynasty and pioneered many of the same religious rituals. It is therefore possible that the trade of which Dr Pankhurst speaks dates back to this very early period. Some scholars of earlier generations, such as Lady Lugard and Arnold Heeren, speculated that trade between Egypt, Kush, and the Red Sea took place in very early times but both assumed, probably in error, that this early trade passed through Meroë. We believe their ideas were basically correct but instead the trade passed directly from Nekheb in Egypt to the Red Sea coast, and indirectly through Qustul in Nubia.

From this early period, archaeologists recovered evidence of early food production. Referring to a site near the city of Axum, Dr David Phillipson reported that:

[S]eeds of cultivated *finger millet,* dating probably to between the mid-fifth and the third millennium BCE, were found at the same level as was the tooth of a camel. If these objects are correctly associated, they are of major significance, for the finger millet would be the earliest actual remains of any of the putatively Ethiopian crops, and the camel would be shown to have a much greater antiquity in this part of Africa than had previously been believed.[23]

The Ancient Kushites of the Sudan, at a much later date, became famous for the production of very high quality iron. This led a modern writer to describe the Kushite city of Meroë as the "Birmingham of Africa".[24] The Kushites, at this date, traded through a road that led to two ports on the Eritrean coast called Azab and Adule,[25] the latter became a centre of world trade with contacts with the Far East, Greek-ruled Egypt and India.[26] In 100 BC the city of Axum became the new capital for the Ethiopians, taking over from Yeha. According to Mr Hancock, it was noted for:

> a written language, *Ge'ez,* and [they] created a new imperial power and political cohesion. They also gave Ethiopia a new religion - Christianity, in the fourth century AD. Their sophisticated and prosperous culture mobilised large groups of labour and enough wealth to build great edifices - monumental architecture that survives to the present day. These massive buildings and towering stone sculptures are eloquent witness to a high level of artistic ability and engineering and mathematical skills.[27]

By 50 AD Zoscales was the first of its line of rulers to take the imposing title *Negus Negaste* (King of Kings).[28] The names of over twenty of his successors are preserved by gold, silver and bronze coins struck during their lifetimes at mints in Axum, and probably also Adule and Yemen.[29] Other rulers left behind massive granite obelisks of precise construction that adorn the city. These mock multi-storey structures, aligned to the sun but dedicated to Almaqah, towered over "cyclopean" walls of the royal burial chambers.[30] Power in this region was probably conferred on these rulers through election rather than inheritance. The rulers headed a confederation of subsidiary, tributary and vassal kings.[31] A good overview of Axum's status in the world of that time is provided by the following excerpt:

> Axum remained the chief power in the region washed by the southern Red Sea until the eighth century ... Merchants of Axum [the capital city] and Adulis [i.e. Adule], wrote an Alexandrian merchant in about 523 ... and sold their ivory in Persia, Arabia, India, and Byzantium. Their merchant vessels were so famous that a Mesopotamian poet used them to describe the progress of a royal caravan: it forged ahead, he said, like one of the ships of Adulis, whose "prow cuts through the foam of the water as a gambler divides the dust with his hand".[32]

Abyssinia (Ethiopia). Exterior and interior of the Cave Church of Yemrehanna Krestos in Lasta. 12ᵗʰ century AD. From Allessandro Augusto Monti Della Corte, *Lalibelà* (Italy, Società Italiana Arti Grafiche, 1940, plate XXXVII).

As well as ivory, the Axumites traded gold, rhinoceros-horn, hippopotamus hides and teeth, exotic animals, frankincense, emeralds (originally from Nubia), and slaves. These exports paid for the importation of silks, cotton, swords, wine, and glass drinking vessels. They also imported metals. Gold and silver became transformed into plates. Gold and bronze were fashioned into statuary, some to a towering height of 15 feet. They fashioned weapons of steel. They also made lacquerware, military cloaks for the elite and olive oil. They had trading links with Kush, Egypt, the Roman provinces, the Mediterranean, Arabia, India, Sri Lanka and China.[33] Through these trading links, foreign influences entered the country. Some of the coins struck in Axum and Adule show affinities to those of the Greeks and the Romans. Some coins show Greek inscriptions and the Greek language was widely understood in the region.[34] Foreign influences in African societies should, of course, be placed within a proper framework, as Professor Chancellor Williams explains in a very different context (also relevant to Chapter 16):

> Egyptian, Asian, Greek and Roman influence was marked on African institutions in Nobadae [i.e. Nobadia] as it was on the complexion of most of the people living in this fringe kingdom … It is an influence that could be praised to high heaven as the eclectic process of civilization itself had not the Caucasians resorted to thefts and lies in their vain and ignoble attempts to preempt the whole field of human progress as being theirs and theirs alone.[35]

Dr Munro-Hay placed the Ethiopian coinage in a proper historical perspective. In his view:

> An exceptional feature of the Aksumite [sic] kingdom was its coinage ... Almost no other contemporary state anywhere in the world could issue in gold, a statement of sovereignty achieved only by Rome, Persia, and the Kushan kingdom in northern India at the time of Aksumite power. The simple fact of Aksum's coin production over several centuries bears witness to the cultural and economic development of the state.[36]

In 150 AD the *Adulis Inscription* was written. It paints a picture of a diverse and multi-ethnic society brought together under the common law and order of the *Negus Negaste*. It calls for peace among the nations under his rule, freedom of movement, safety along the caravan routes, and uninterrupted import and export of goods by land or sea. Among the peoples governed were those "in the interior of the frankincense country." The peoples near the sea are given "instructions to guard the coast." Unfortunately for us moderns, the king's name has been lost,[37] but the name of another second century empire builder, Gadara, has come down to us.

In 183 AD Gadara was a politically dominant figure in Yemenite affairs across the Red Sea. His son and successor was equally dominant in this territory until 213 AD. Less than a century later, Azbah, a later Axumite king, sent military forces to Yemen and settled troops there. Between 335 and 370 AD Axum occupied Yemen once more under Ezana.[38] He also led victorious campaigns against Kush, the peoples of Lake Tana, and the peoples of the desert. In this way, Ezana seized the trade routes linking Egypt and Syria with the countries of the Indian Ocean. The Straits of Bab-al-Mandeb, now under Axumite control, was one of the three main shipping highways in the ancient world.[39]

Ezana proclaimed the country to be a Christian state, one of the oldest surviving Christian nations in the world. An inscription of the period recorded a prayer of the *Negus Negaste:*

> May the Lord of Heaven make strong my kingdom! And as He has this day conquered for me my enemy may he conquer for me wheresoever I go ... (I will rule) the people with righteousness and justice, and will not oppress them.[40]

A Byzantine writer called Rufinus related the story of how Christianity spread to Ethiopia, though other writers, Socrates and Sozemius, corroborate the particulars.[41] Rufinus tells of Meropus, a Phœnician philosopher, who sailed to India accompanied by two Syrian boys. Frumentius was the older of the two boys. Aedesius was the younger. On their return journey, their vessel, a Greco-Roman ship, was attacked as they tried to moor at an Ethiopian port.

Abyssinia (Ethiopia). The building on the left is the House (or Church) of Emmanuel. From Susan Denyer, *African Traditional Architecture* (UK, Heinemann, 1978, p.200). The building on the right is the House of Abba Libanos. From Allessandro Augusto Monti Della Corte, *Lalibelà* (Italy, Società Italiana Arti Grafiche, 1940, plate XX). Emperor Lalibela built both of them between 1180 and 1220 AD. Both were carved out by chiselling and hollowing the living rock of the mountainside to a depth of 11 or more metres! Is Lalibela the Eighth Wonder of the World?

All on board were killed, except the two boys. Their age spared them. Apparently relations between the inhabitants of the port and Greco-Roman sailors had recently become strained due to earlier abuses of Ethiopian hospitality. The Ethiopians sought revenge on all who could be identified as kinsfolk of the Greco-Roman merchants, hence their storming of the ship. Eventually, the two young Syrians were taken to King Ella Amida, Ezana's predecessor. The king saw potential in the boys and later installed Frumentius as his treasurer and secretary, and made Aedesius his cup-bearer. Frumentius rose to great influence within the country. When King Ella Amida died, Ezana, his young son, succeeded him. The Queen-Regent invited Frumentius to assist in governing the country until the young Ezana became of age. The Syrian encouraged the spread of Christianity throughout Ethiopia, building churches and encouraging trade. Christianity already existed in Ethiopia, however, but it was not then the state religion. In time, Ezana assumed full control and Frumentius became Ethiopia's first bishop. The coins and inscriptions illustrate the reality of this. The early coins of Ezana's time show the crescent-and-disk emblem of the old deity Mahrem. The later coins issued just after 330 AD show the Christian cross with the motto: "May the country be satisfied" - the first coins in the world to carry this Christian design.[42]

Another feature attributed to Ezana's reign was the introduction of a new written script - the vocalised Ethiopic. A refinement of the Proto-Ethiopic/Sabaean script of the Yeha period, vocalised Ethiopic influenced the Armenian and Georgian scripts of Eastern Europe. A Russian historian, Y. M. Khobishanov noted that: "Soon after its creation, the Ethiopic vocalised script began to influence the scripts of Armenia and Georgia. D. A. Olderogge suggested that Mesrop Mashtotz used the vocalised Ethiopic script when he invented the Armenian alphabet".[43]

Several monuments date back to Ezana's time such as the Ta'akha Maryam, the Cathedral of Saint Mary of Zion, several other churches, and also convents. Scholars have attempted to reconstruct the Axumite castle complex of Ta'akha Maryam, now in ruins, using evidence provided by the obelisks and other monuments (see page 458). The palace was a massive four-towered structure of stone and timber with windows of timber frames. It rose to a lofty height, being of four storeys.[44] Axum also contained the Cathedral of Saint Mary of Zion, one of the oldest Christian cathedrals on Earth. Francisco Alvarez described this monument in around 1520 AD as follows:

> In this town, we found a noble church; it is very large, and has five naves of a good width and of great length, vaulted above, and all the vaults are covered up, and the ceiling and sides are all painted; it also has a choir after our fashion. This church has a very large circuit, paved with flagstones like gravestones, and it has also a large enclosure, and is surrounded by another large enclosure like the wall of a large town or city.[45]

There was, however, a flourishing Israelite tradition in the country among the Falasha Jews.[46] Ezana left a Christian imprint in Yemen, but the Axumites were expelled from there in 370 AD.[47] Whichever be the case, the achievements of the Axumites were outstanding. They had a maritime trade from the Roman provinces on the one hand, to China on the other. They minted gold, silver and bronze coins. They had a literature and scripts of their own. Their cultural influences spread far and wide. Finally: "In the first half of the first millennium CE," says a modern scholar, "Aksum [sic] was ranked as one of the world's greatest empires".[48] A Persian cleric of the third century AD identified Axum as the third most important state in the world after Persia and Rome.[49]

Emperor Kaleb was an important monarch on the sixth century AD world stage. Remembered as a passionate defender of the new faith, he commissioned the magnificent chapel of Debre Damo. He built it of dry stone and timber.[50] In later life, he became a monk devoted to studying the divine word. He was buried in a tomb/chapel in Axum on a local hilltop.[51] In earlier years, however, he presented at court in white linen garments, embroidered with gold and set with pearls. The royal throne was a gilded chariot drawn by four elephants. Flute music accompanied the proceedings.[52]

Abyssinia (Ethiopia).
Startling interior of
the House of Mary in
Lalibela. Built by
Emperor Lalibela
between 1180 and
1220 AD. From
Allessandro Augusto
Monti Della Corte,
Lalibelà (Italy, Società
Italiana Arti Grafiche
1940, plate X).

Like previous monarchs, Kaleb was much preoccupied with Yemenite affairs. In that land, a civil war had erupted between Christians and Israelites. The Axumites were invited to help the Christian effort. Emperor Kaleb sent across 70,000 men and an armada of 150 ships. General Abraha headed the campaign.[53] The Axumites triumphed, but the General had ideas of his own, proclaiming himself ruler of Yemen.[54] Abraha raised a fine cathedral at Sana, "the like of which existed nowhere else in the world", containing marble, mosaics, and decorated with gold.[55] Its purpose was to win converts to the Christian faith. Abraha's religious zeal was his undoing. He attempted to challenge the pre-Islamic religion of the Holy city of Mecca and thus inflamed the anti-Christians. They in turn appealed to the Persian King Chosroes for an armed intervention. The Axumites were beaten in 572 AD and Yemen became a territory of the Persian Shah.[56] Edward Gibbon, the venerable historian, wondered that "if a Christian power had been maintained in Arabia, Mohammed must have been crushed in his cradle, and Abyssinia [i.e. Axum] would have prevented a revolution which has changed the civil and religious state of the world".[57]

Emperor Armah was a noteworthy king of the seventh century AD. He lived during the period that Islam came into existence in Arabia, founded by the Arabian prophet Mahomet. Armah offered sanctuary to some of the first converts to the new religion fleeing from persecution in Arabia.[58] Of course, Bilal, one of the founders of Islam, was himself an Ethiopian. Caliph Omar of Damascus, the first spiritual ruler of the Muslims, described him as "the third part of Islam".[59] In addition Mr Garlake, in a recent text, made the extraordinary assertion that: "It is probable that the Ka'aba of Mecca, rebuilt in 609 [AD], is, behind its veils, a classic Aksumite [sic] building."[60]

Unfortunately for Ethiopia, however, Islam was adopted by the Yemenites and also by nomads who lived on Ethiopia's Red Sea coast. This meant that Ethiopia, as a Christian state, found itself surrounded by Islamic states. Their key port of Adule was destroyed towards the end of the century and this effectively barred them from trade with the rest of the world.[61] Ethiopia went into a period of decline as Gibbon poetically put it: "Encompassed on all sides by the enemies of their religion, the Aethiopians slept near a thousand years, forgetful of the world by whom they were forgotten".[62] Mr Buxton explains:

> The declining years of the Axum kingdom share something of the obscurity prevailing in contemporary Europe, when the Carolingian Empire was breaking up and King Alfred was fighting the Danes in southern England. The fortunes of the kingdom fluctuated. For a brief period it was able to re-assert its authority over the Red Sea coasts and even to extend it to the Dahlak Islands and the distant port of Zeila on the Gulf of Aden. But these were the flickerings of a candle about to be extinguished. The kingdom, finally deprived of its outlet to the sea, stagnated culturally ... [63]

In 940 AD Judith, a Falasha conqueror, seized the throne and proclaimed herself Queen. Inspiring dread in many Christian minds, she destroyed the churches, killing thousands in the process.[64] Her campaigns ended both the thousand-year supremacy of the city of Axum, and also an era of Ethiopian history. Succeeding her were the Zagwe Dynasty, who ushered in a Golden Age. They ruled from Roha, their new capital in the south, later renamed Lalibela. Their empire controlled a vast territory, much of it mountainous, but still larger than that controlled by Axum.[65] They also welcomed Egyptian migrants fleeing the oppressive rule of the Arabs, to cite Mr Buxton once more:

> [T]he Christian Copts [i.e. Egyptians] were sometimes compelled by persecution to flee to other countries. Under Al-Hakim, before and after the year 1000, many of them reached Abyssinia [i.e. Ethiopia], and it is likely that the artistic links with Coptic Egypt ... resulted from this migration.[66]

Some authorities have suggested a Falasha origin for the Zagwes,[67] but among the splendours of their building programmes, are a series of eleven rock-hewn *churches* in their new capital. Emperor Lalibela (*c.*1150-1220) built these strikingly impressive engineering marvels in the late twelfth and early thirteenth centuries.[68] His dream seems to have been the creation of a New Jerusalem in Ethiopia. There is a "River Jordan" in the region, a "Calvary", a "Mount of Transfiguration", a church called "Golgotha" and another called "Bethlehem."[69] Sir Wallis Budge, the great Egyptologist, was the English translator of the *Kebra Negaste (The Glory of the Kings)* and other important Axumite documents. He commented on the architectural significance of the eleven churches:

> Abyssinia [i.e. Ethiopia] contains the most remarkable churches in the world ... which certainly deserve to be reckoned with the Seven Wonders of the world. All who have seen them marvel, not at their beauty, but at the mind of the man who conceived their design, and the colossal labour which was expended in their making ... The rock-hewn temples of Rameses II at Kalabshah and Abu Simbel cannot be compared with the churches at Lalibala, because no attempt was made to alter the shape of the hills of sandstone out of which the temples were hewn, and to make the temples resemble independent buildings.[70]

Mr Buxton calls this construction programme "an achievement almost unparalleled in history".[71] In 1209 Lalibela sent an embassy to Cairo bringing the sultan unusual gifts including an elephant, a hyena, a zebra, and, of course, a giraffe. He sent the Coptic Patriarch a crown of pure gold. Finally, the *Kebra Negaste,* the Ethiopian epic, was begun during his time.[72]

The Swahili States

The Swahili States were a number of major cities that flourished on the East African coast between the ninth and the sixteenth centuries. They were renowned for sophisticated and tasteful architecture. Their mosques were "as grand as the medieval cathedrals of Europe" and Lamu, one of their cities, was "as sophisticated as medieval Venice". The region "was the setting for the legendary adventures of Sinbad and the Arabian Nights".[73] Indeed, even in ruin, these sites are quite rightly tourist attractions in Kenya and Tanzania. The various cities were spread over a region of 2500 miles from Somalia to Mozambique.[74] The major city-states were Mogadishu and Brava in Somalia, Lamu, Mombasa and Malindi/Gedi in Kenya, Kilwa and Mafia on islands just off the coast of Tanzania, the islands of Pemba and Zanzibar, and finally Sofala in Mozambique. There was another major city in Mozambique called Sinna.

Unlike the other cities just mentioned, Sinna was not actually on or near the coast.[75] The ruins of some 50 other Swahili towns and cities have come to light,[76] but these were less important than the ones just mentioned. These states flourished due to their important role in the Indian Ocean trade. They imposed taxes and duties on merchant ships that arrived at their ports.[77]

The seasonal monsoon winds shaped the trading patterns between East Africa and Asia. The northeast monsoon started in November and reached its full strength in January. It blew from India and the Persian Gulf towards East Africa and down its coastline. The monsoon generated a current that

The Swahili Confederation (Map: Kieron Vital). This culture flourished from about 700 to 1505 AD.

flowed along the East African coast as far south as Lamu in Kenya. The winds would reliably carry ships even further south to Kilwa in Tanzania. The Arab and Asian sailors generally traded in the Gulf and Red Sea at the start of the season and accumulated cargo. They would then set sail and carry their cargo to markets in East Africa. In April the southwest monsoon starts. By June or July it created a strong northerly current that flows up the Somali coast towards India. The dhows (i.e. Arab ships) usually set sail from East Africa towards Asia as soon as this monsoon was strong enough.[78]

Of course, not all the merchant shipping came from the Arab or Asian worlds. East African ships were on the Indian Ocean too. The East African vessels without sails were called *mtepe* and those with sails were called *dua la mtepe*.[79] There is a model of a 70 ton Swahili vessel in the Fort Jesus museum of Mombasa.[80] Vessels of this type have a long history. They date back at least as far as the first century AD. A first century AD guidebook, *Periplus Maris Eryhthraei*, records that the East Africans made "sewn" boats. This is probably an early reference to the *mtepe*.[81] Like the Arab sailors, East African mariners used the monsoon winds, this time to sail to and from Asia. Just as Arab sailors stopped off in East Africa between January and June in between the monsoons, African mariners stopped off in Asia between July and November for the same reason. Finally it must be noted that some scholars give Swahili sailors a much bigger role on the Indian Ocean. One modern source claims that: "The Swahilis [also] built and sailed the dhows and navigated the treacherous channels to the main trading ports. By controlling the sea, they maintained firm control over all commerce in the region".[82]

Some historians claim that the East African culture was partly, if not entirely, of Arab or Persian origins, established by merchant sailors from these distant lands. Captain Stigand, author of the pioneering *The Land of Zinj,* was of this view.[83] The Swahili language today has a number of Arabic words mixed up in it, and it was at one time argued that this demonstrates an important Arab element in the formation of Swahili culture. "What is less well understood however," wrote Dr Sutton, an excellent English authority on East African history: "is that the bulk of these borrowings are not ancient in (Ki)Swahili, but belong to the last two hundred years or so (the period of the "new" Arabs and the Zanzibari state)".[84] In the eighteenth century AD, well after the great East African culture had declined, Arab sultans in fact controlled East Africa.[85] It was during this late period, and not before, that the partial Arabicisation of the Swahili language, architecture, and culture had begun. Reinforcing this point, our scholarly friend Dr Sutton, informs us that:

> Despite popular thinking … [Swahili architecture and towns] are not 'Arab'. Both in the styles and in the building techniques and materials, Swahili Islamic

Swahili (Kenya). View of the enchanting mediæval city of Lamu. Typically Swahili cities had multi storey buildings of up to five storeys. From R. F. Mayer, *Kenya Camera Studies* (Kenya, The East African Standard, 1934, p.24).

architecture is distinct from that of Arabia (just as Turkish and Indian and West African Islamic is distinct and not to be described as 'Arab'). The misapprehension that the Swahilis and their cultural history are Arab or 'half-Arab' is based on a shallow historical understanding.[86]

Dr Mark Horton, an English archaeologist, is a prominent scholar in the study of Swahili antiquities. His excavations have shown that the very earliest mosques on the East African coast date from the eighth century AD. They were flimsy timber-thatched buildings and were much like temporary mosques built even now from time to time by East Africans. Swahili fishermen build fishing villages, including a mosque, to serve them only during the fishing seasons. The wooden mosques excavated by Dr Horton indicate that the first Muslims on the coast were Africans and not Arabs. From there, the Africans evolved mud and timber mosques, which were much larger. Finally, they progressed to building stone-built mosques.[87]

The first writer to mention the East African culture of which we are aware was Ibn Hordadbeh, writing in 886 AD. He wrote that, "whoever goes to the land of the Zanj [i.e. the East African coast], surely catches the itch".[88] Of considerably more substance is the account by Al-Masudi. This distinguished

Arab historian visited the East African coast in 916 AD. He documented his extensive travels in a book called *Meadows of Gold and Mines of Gems.*[89] He described the "Zanj" (i.e. East Africans) as having an empire spread over a large territory divided by valleys, mountains and deserts.[90] Their capital was in the land of Sofala. Controversially, Basil Davidson thinks this is Sinna, a town located 150 miles inland from the coast of today's Mozambique.[91] "It is a land abounding in gold, rich in wonderful things and very fertile", says Al-Masudi. The King of kings took the dynastic title "Waqlimi", meaning Son of the Great God or Master. He could command an army of 300,000 cavaliers mounted on cows since "they have neither horses nor mules".[92] The Zanj had a trade in ivory with India and China with the traffic passing through Oman. The ivory was used to make the handles of daggers in India, and royal chairs in China. It was also used to make chess pieces.[93] The Zanj were skilled workers in metal and were distinguished as traders.[94]

Other evidence indicates that ambergris and rhino-horn were also exported from the coast at this time. Ambergris was a perfume made from whales. Rhino-horn had medicinal properties and was particularly popular in the Far Eastern markets.[95]

Interestingly, Al-Masudi described the religion of the Zanj, but he wrote from an unenlightened Muslim standpoint: "Everyone worships what he pleases," says he, "a plant an animal [or] a metal".[96] His comments are instructive in refuting fashionable theories that the Swahili States, as they were later called, were founded by Arabs, Persians or other Islamised elements. There were, however, Muslims among them, and Islam became a popular religion in the region.[97] This was the case when Ibn Battuta visited the coast in the early fourteenth century. He described the more northerly people of the coast as Berbers - "a people of the Blacks". The more southerly people he calls Zanj - "of very black complexion".[98] Marco Polo, writing some years earlier, describes the Zanzibari as Blacks, but adds that they were "idolaters".[99] This may imply that Islam made little progress there at that time, but the religion spread later. Dr Gervaise Mathew, a noted archaeologist who excavated the East Africa region, concluded that: "Some time in the thirteenth and fourteenth centuries the culture of the coast became integrally Islamic. But even if the culture had become Islamic, still it would seem to be [N]egro".[100]

As the cities developed, the mosques and the graveyards became the focal points around which the houses were grouped. As the towns became larger and the graveyards filled, new mosques and graveyards were built, followed by new houses being grouped around them.[101] In this way, aspects of ancestor reverence were preserved, even under Islam. Between 800 and 1000 AD, Shanga and Manda became major cities of between 15,000 and 18,000 people. Dr Ehret wrote that they were "far larger, in fact, than any contemporary town

Swahili (Kenya). Ruined palace in Gedi. (Photo: Robin Walker). Dr Finch gives a date of *c.*1000 AD for its construction in *The Star of Deep Beginnings* (US, Khenti, 1998, plate 17). Other authorities give dates of the fourteenth or fifteenth centuries. This building had perhaps 54 rooms, 11 courtyards, 7 burial areas and 6 indoor toilets.

in Europe north of the Pyrenees".[102] The houses themselves were grouped close together with narrow walkways separating them to accommodate donkey traffic.[103] In the fourteenth and fifteenth centuries, pillar tombs were built. These structures, a uniquely Swahili construction, were tall pillars, inlaid with Chinese porcelain bowls, connected to one end of a tomb.[104]

Dr Mark Horton and also Dr John Sutton, another authority on Swahili culture, addressed the supposed role of the Persians in East African history.[105] Both scholars argue that many East Africans were schooled in Persia in the eleventh century AD and became learned in the Kufic style of the Arabic script, a script popular in Persia. This explains why so-called "Persian" writing is inscribed on many old Swahili monuments built at this time, but does not prove that the Persians built the East African monuments. Many Zanj boasted of their Persian education, and in time, this created the myth that the first great Swahili dynasty, the Shirazi, was of Persian origins.[106]

Ali ibn Al Hasan, the founder of the dynasty, lived around 1070 AD. He had a number of silver and copper coins of Kilwa and Mafia struck during his time. The coins have rhyming couplets on them that read as follows: "The majestic sultan Ali ibn Al Hasan" and on the other side, "In the name of God, the compassionate, the merciful." The Shirazi Dynasty ruled from around 1070 until around 1300.[107] This period saw the break up of the Zanj Empire, described by Al-Masudi, to its transformation into a number of independent city-states - the Swahili Confederation.

Earlier in the text, we cited a valuable work by the Moorish scholar Al-Idrissi. In *The Book of Roger,* we are informed that by the twelfth century AD, the Zanj traded iron on the Indian Ocean. It was of a superior quality that was used to make the famous Damascus Blades of the Middle Ages.[108] This proved profitable and the proceeds could be linked to the early development of the Kenyan city of Malindi. Other towns that depended on the iron trade were Manisa, Dendema and Djentema (identified as Mombasa, Quilemane and Chindi respectively). Dr Charles Finch, one of our best scholars, identified the superior iron described by Al-Idrissi as wootz steel.[109] Evidence discovered in 1978 showed that East Africans were making steel for more than 1,500 years, fully 600 years before Al Idrissi documented the trade:

> In the September 22 issue of *Science* [says a modern writer], two [Brown University] professors announced what for those interested in the history of technology is a rather startling discovery. Assistant Professor of Anthropology Peter Schmidt and Professor of Engineering Donald H. Avery have found as long as 2,000 years ago Africans living on the western shores of Lake Victoria had produced carbon steel in preheated forced draft furnaces, a method that was technologically more sophisticated than any developed in Europe until the mid-nineteenth century.[110]

Schmidt and Avery found 13 ancient iron furnaces in the Lake Victoria region of Tanzania.[111] The furnaces made use of blowpipes and bellows to inject oxygen into the base of the furnace and saved fuel. When smelting steel, it is important to keep the temperature above 1150°C to melt the impurities and separate the iron from the ore. It is also important to keep the temperature below 1540°C, the melting point of iron. The ancient metallurgists of this region worked at around 1450°C.[112]

In Idrissi's time, leopard skins were another key trading product of the Zanj.[113] Also important was timber. Mangrove-poles in particular were sold to the building industries of Oman and Persia.[114] Of the iron and ivory trades described by Al-Masudi and Al-Idrissi, it was highly probable that at least some of these products came from the Zimbabwe region in the interior. Zimbabwe gold was a major item of Indian Ocean trade from the tenth century AD.[115] Dr Davidson presented some interesting information on the trading links and envoys to China:

> [Chinese annals from the Sung Dynasty] of 1083 speak of a second visit to the imperial court [of China] of a foreign envoy with a name whose last three

characters may reasonably be read as "the Zanj". This ambassador had come
from so far away that the Emperor Shön-tsung, "besides giving him the same
presents which he formerly bestowed on him, added thereto 2,000 ounces of
silver".[116]

In 1414 the city of Malindi sent ambassadors to China, carrying a gift of a
giraffe. The gift created a sensation at the imperial court.[117] The size and scale
of the Indian Ocean trade from the twelfth century was astonishing. Dr
Davidson commented that: "To those who read of it in Sicily, or heard [I]drisi
talk of it, this eastern trade must have seemed rich beyond dreams, a strange
and glittering El Dorado".[118] A Time-Life documentary on the Swahili culture
entitled *Africa: A History Denied* offered a similar view. They described the
commerce as "on a scale not seen since the Greek and Roman times".[119]
Mogadishu, the Somali port, rose to prominence at this time. By the thirteenth
century, great monuments were built there such as the Mosque of Fakhr al
Din.[120]

Just before 1300 the Abu al-Mawahib, a new dynasty, overthrew the older
Shirazi Dynasty. Al Hasan ibn Suleiman, one of its great sultans, ruled the
Tanzanian city of Kilwa. The *Kilwa Chronicle,* an old Swahili history,
describes him as "renowned for his generosity and courage" who also
"excelled in all branches of knowledge."[121] During the time of this great sultan
(in 1331), Ibn Battuta visited the region. Battuta's book, *Travels in Asia and
Africa,* contains much that is useful including the following account of his visit
to Mogadishu:

> One of the customs of the people of this city is that when a ship arrives at
> anchorage, the *sunbugs* (these are small boats) come out to it. In every *sunbug*
> is a group of young people of the town, and every one of them brings a covered
> dish with food in it. He offers it to one of the merchants of the ship and says,
> 'This is my guest.' Each one of them does similarly. When the merchant
> disembarks from the ship he goes nowhere but to the house of his host from
> among these young people. But a man who has frequented the place a good deal
> and obtained a knowledge of its people may lodge where he wishes.[122]

Ibn Battuta gives further details of old African hospitality. He left an
interesting account of Swahili cuisine:

> The *qadi* [i.e. judge] took my hand and we came to that house which is near the
> shaikh's house. And it was bedded out and set up with what is necessary. Then
> he came with food from the shaikh's house. With him was one of his *wazirs*
> who was in charge of guests. He said, '*Maulana* gives you *al-salamu 'alaikum*
> [i.e. peace be unto you] and he says to you, you are most welcome.' Then he
> put down the food and we ate. Their food is rice cooked with ghee placed on a
> large wooded dish. They put on top dishes of *kushan* - this is the relish, of

chicken and meat and fish and vegetables. They cook banana before it is ripe in fresh milk and they put it on a dish, and they put sour milk in a dish [i.e. yogurt] with pickled lemon on it and bunches of pickled chillies, vinegared and salted, and green ginger and mangoes. These are like apples and they have a stone, and when they ripen they are very sweet and are eaten like fruit. But before they ripen they are bitter like lemons and they pickle them in vinegar. When they eat a ball of rice, they eat after it something from these salted and vinegared foods. Now one of the people in [Mogadishu] habitually eats as much as a group of us would. They are extremely large and fat of body.[123]

Days later, he visited the Tanzanian city of Kilwa:

We spent a night on the island of [Mombasa], and then set sail for Kilwa, the principal city on the coast the greater part of whose inhabitants are Zanj of very black complexion. They have tattoo marks on their faces, like the Limiyyin of Janada [i.e. in West Africa]. A merchant told me that a fortnight's sail beyond Kilwa lies Sofala, where powdered gold is bought from a place a month's journey inland called Yufi. Kilwa is one of the most beautiful and well-constructed cities in the world. The whole of it is elegantly built.[124]

Ibn Battuta described the Kenyan city of Mombasa as "a large island," and the Somali city of Mogadishu as "a town endless in its size".[125] The opulence that was evident at Kilwa was to be found all along the coast at numerous sites including Kua, Songo Mnara, Mombasa and Malindi. In their palaces and town houses were the striking pottery of Nishapur and Sultanabad, the celadon of Sung China, Ming ornaments and bowls of great elaboration, beads and precious stones of India, artefacts and figurines in ivory and gold, jewellery of copper and jade, and carpets of the Middle East and Mecca.[126] Dr Gervaise Mathew adds that:

We can reconstruct much of the life in such towns from Swahili poems. It seems clear that though dependant for their wealth on Indian Ocean trade they still remained integrally African. Pate was perhaps the wealthiest among them - it became a proverb that the nobles there climbed by silver ladders into ivory beds".[127]

Chinese records of the fifteenth century mention the Somali city of Brava and note that Mogadishu had houses of "four or five storeys high".[128] However, one of the best descriptions of a Swahili city in its heyday was an account of Kilwa by Gaspar Correa, a Portuguese writer of the early sixteenth century. He documented that:

The city is large and is of good buildings of stone and mortar with terraces, and the houses have much woodwork. The city comes down to the shore, and is entirely surrounded by a wall and towers, within which there may be 12,000 inhabitants ... The streets of the city are very narrow, as the houses are very high, of three and four storeys, and one can run along the tops of them upon the terraces, as the houses are very close together.[129]

Visitors commented on the craftsmanship of the doors, the excellent joinery and the surrounding streams, orchards and fruit gardens.[130] One of these, Duarte Barbosa, also left favourable descriptions of the other seaport cities. Mombasa was apparently "a very fair [i.e. beautiful] place, with lofty stone and mortar houses, well aligned in streets after the fashion of Kilwa". Malindi had "many fair stone and mortar houses of many stories, with great plenty of windows and flat roofs ... The place was well laid out in streets." Pate and Lamu were "well walled with stone and mortar". Brava, "a great town", had "very fine stone and mortar houses". Mogadishu, the most northerly of the ports, was "a very great Moorish [i.e. African] town ... a place of great wealth".[131] The attire of the people, to cite Barbosa, also demonstrates the allusions to "great wealth":

> The Moors of Sofala [in the Mozambique region] ... clothe themselves from the waist down with cotton and silk cloths, and other cloths they wear over their shoulders like capes, and turbans on their heads. Some wear small caps dyed in grain in chequers [sic] and other woollen clothes in many tints, also camlets and other silks.[132]

In Kilwa, the level of luxury reached was astonishing: "[T]hey are finely clad in many rich garments of gold and silk and cotton, and the women as well; also with much gold and silver chains and bracelets, which they wear on their legs and arms, and many jewelled earrings in their ears".[133] The people of the island cities of Pemba, Mafia and Zanzibar dressed in the same style as described for Kilwa, also with the associated opulence. The coastal wealth was based on trading a vast number of products principally gold, ivory and wax. Barbosa further informs us that the cities had become very cosmopolitan with large and integrated immigrant populations from the golden East, probably Arabs and Indians.[134]

This splendid culture came to an unfortunate end. Early in the sixteenth century, the Portuguese sent their fleets and armies into this region causing great ruin. Dr Davidson narrated this unfortunate episode:

> It was at Mozambique, during his first voyage, that da Gama [a Portuguese captain] exchanged the first shots. Back again on the coast in 1502, this time with a score of ships from home (the largest but one of all fleets that Portugal would send to the golden East), da Gama threatens to burn Kilwa unless its ruler will acknowledge the supremacy of the king of Portugal and pay him yearly tribute in gold. Ravasio does the same at Zanzibar and Brava. Meeting resistance, Almeida storms Kilwa and Mombasa, burning and destroying. Saldanha ravages Berbera. Soares destroys Zeila. D'Acunha attacks Brava.[135]

Swahili (Kenya). The Great Mosque in Gedi. (Photo: Robin Walker). Scholars give different dates for this monument. The official data in the Kenyan museums date this monument to the 13th century AD.

Hans Mayr, a German eyewitness, described the catastrophic results of the Portuguese policy in Mombasa:

> The Grand-Captain ordered that Mombassa [sic] should be sacked, and that each man should carry off to his ship what ever he found: so that at the end there would be a division of the spoil, each man to receive a twentieth of what he found. The same rule was made for gold, silver and pearls. Then everyone started to plunder the town and to search the houses, forcing open the doors with axes and iron bars. There was a large quantity of cotton cloth for Sofala in the town, for the whole coast gets its cotton cloth from here. So the Grand-Captain got a good share of the trade of Sofala for himself. A large quantity of rich silk and gold embroidered clothes were seized, and carpets also; one of these which was without equal for beauty, was sent to the King of Portugal, together with many other valuables.[136]

In 1961 Mr Neville Chittick, a British archaeologist, found the ruins of Husuni Kubwa, the royal palace of Kilwa.[137] It was a marvellous building with over a hundred rooms, including a reception hall, galleries, courtyards, terraces and an octagonal swimming pool [sic]. The rooms were elaborately decorated and had vaulted roofs. The private quarters, believed to be that of the sultan, was at one end of the building. The *diwan,* where the sultan sat, and the public reception halls were in the centre. There was a great forecourt on the opposite side from the harbour. The second floor of the building was imaginatively roofed with barrels, domes and conical designs, all made of concrete. At night, oil lanterns, numbering thousands, illuminated this wonderful monument.[138]

In Gedi, a recent visitor to its ruined houses saw what were once indoor toilets and bathrooms. Running piped water also existed and was controlled by taps.[139]

Notes

[1] By "Ethiopia" in this chapter, we mean the region covered by the modern country of the same name and also Eritrea. Other writers call this region Axum or Abyssinia.
[2] Graham Hancock, *The Beauty of Historic Ethiopia,* Kenya, Camerapix, 1996, pp.26-7.
[3] David Buxton, *The Abyssinians,* UK, Thames and Hudson, 1970, pp.86-9.
[4] Quoted in Peter Garlake, *Early Art and Architecture of Africa,* UK, Oxford University Press, 2002, p.14.
[5] Graham Hancock, *The Beauty of Historic Ethiopia,* p.26.
[6] David W. Phillipson, *Ancient Ethiopia,* UK, The British Museum Press, 1998, p.47.
[7] Taddesse Tamrat, *Church and State in Ethiopia: The Early Centuries,* in *African Zion,* ed Roderick Grierson, US, InterCultura, 1993, p.33.
[8] David Buxton, *The Abyssinians,* p.36.
[9] Ibid., p.37.
[10] Charles S. Finch, *Echoes of the Old Darkland,* US, Khenti, 1991, p.134.
[11] Cheikh Anta Diop, *The Cultural Unity of Black Africa,* UK, Karnak House, 1989, pp.48 and 84-9.

[12] Roderick Grierson, *Dreaming of Jerusalem,* in *African Zion,* ed Roderick Grierson, US, InterCultura, 1993, p.7.

[13] Peter Garlake, *Early Art and Architecture of Africa,* p.76.

[14] Ayele Bekerie, *Ethiopic: An African Writing System,* US, Red Sea Press, 1997, pp.18-22, 31-60.

[15] Graham Hancock, *The Beauty of Historic Ethiopia,* p.43.

[16] Ibid.

[17] Camerapix, *Ethiopia: A Tourist Paradise,* Ethiopia, Ethiopian Tourist Commission, 1996, p.28.

[18] J. A. Rogers, *World's Great Men of Color, Volume 1,* US, Macmillan, 1972, p.86.

[19] Richard Pankhurst, *Ethiopia Revealed: Merchants, Travelers, and Scholars,* in *African Zion,* ed Roderick Grierson, US, InterCultura, 1993, p.19.

[20] Roderick Grierson, *Dreaming of Jerusalem,* in *African Zion,* p.6.

[21] Ibid.

[22] Richard Pankhurst, *Ethiopia Revealed: Merchants, Travelers, and Scholars,* in *African Zion,* p.19.

[23] Quoted in Ayele Bekerie, *Ethiopic: An African Writing System,* pp.46-7.

[24] Mentioned in A. J. Arkell, *The Valley of the Nile,* in *The Dawn of African History,* ed Roland Oliver, UK, Oxford University Press, 1961, p.10.

[25] A. H. L. Heeren, *Historical Researches into the Politics, Intercourse, and Trade of the Carthaginians, Ethiopians, and Egyptians, Volume I,* US, ECA Associates, 1991 (original 1832), pp.453-68.

[26] Basil Davidson, *Africa in History,* UK, Macmillan, 1991, p.44.

[27] Graham Hancock, *The Beauty of Historic Ethiopia,* p.19.

[28] Basil Davidson, *Africa in History,* p.44 and R. A. Caulk, *North-East Africa before the rise of Islam,* in *The Cambridge Encyclopedia of Africa,* ed Roland Oliver and Michael Crowder, UK, Cambridge University Press, 1981, p.107.

[29] Graham Hancock, *The Beauty of Historic Ethiopia,* p.30.

[30] Ibid., pp.42-3 and R. A. Caulk, *North-East Africa before the rise of Islam,* in *The Cambridge Encyclopedia of Africa,* p.108.

[31] Peter Garlake, *Early Art and Architecture of Africa,* p.73.

[32] Basil Davidson, *African Kingdoms,* Netherlands, Time-Life Books, 1967, p.42.

[33] Graham Hancock, *The Beauty of Historic Ethiopia,* p.27, Charles Finch, *The Star of Deep Beginnings,* US, Khenti, 1998, pp.31-2, 50, David Buxton, *The Abyssinians,* p.38 and Peter Garlake, *Early Art and Architecture of Africa,* pp.73-4.

[34] Graham Hancock, *The Beauty of Historic Ethiopia,* p.30 and David Buxton, The Abyssinians, p.38.

[35] Chancellor Williams, *The Destruction of Black Civilization,* US, Third World Press, 1987, p.140.

[36] Stuart C. Munro-Hay, *Aksumite Coinage,* in *African Zion,* ed Roderick Grierson, US, InterCultura, 1993, p.101.

[37] Taddesse Tamrat, *Church and State in Ethiopia: The Early Centuries,* in *African Zion,* pp.33-4.

[38] Cf. Runoko Rashidi, *Africans in Early Asian Civilizations: An Overview,* in *African Presence in Early Asia,* ed Runoko Rashidi, US, Transaction Publishers, 1995, p.34.

[39] Anu M'Bantu & Fari Supiya, *Ethiopia's First Christian Emperor: Ezana of Axum,* in *West Africa, Issue 4303,* UK, Afrimedia International, 26 November - 2 December 2001, p.43.

[40] Quoted in E. A. Wallis Budge, *A History of Ethiopia, Nubia & Abyssinia, Volume I-B,* US, ECA Associates, 1991 (original 1928), p.257. See also pp.251-8.

[41] David Buxton, *The Abyssinians,* p.39-41, Joseph E. Harris ed, *Pillars in Ethiopian History: The William Leo Hansberry African History Notebook, Volume 1,* US, Howard University Press, 1974, pp.64-70 and Anu M'Bantu & Fari Supiya, *Ethiopia's First Christian Emperor: Ezana of Axum,* in *West Africa, Issue 4303,* p.43.

[42] Stuart C. Munro-Hay, *Aksumite Coinage,* in *African Zion,* p.102.

[43] Quoted in Anu M'Bantu & Fari Supiya, *Ethiopia's First Christian Emperor: Ezana of Axum,* in *West Africa, Issue 4303,* p.43.

[44] David Buxton, *The Abyssinians,* pp.93-6.

[45] Quoted in Graham Hancock, *The Beauty of Historic Ethiopia,* p.39.

[46] Yosef A. A. ben-Jochannan, *We the Black Jews,* US, Black Classic Press, 1993, pp.90-100.

[47] Runoko Rashidi, *Africans in Early Asian Civilizations: An Overview,* in *African Presence in Early Asia,* p.34.

[48] Peter Garlake, *Early Art and Architecture of Africa,* p.73.

[49] Ayele Bekerie, *Ethiopic: An African Writing System,* p.70.

[50] R. A. Caulk, *North-East Africa before the rise of Islam,* in *The Cambridge Encyclopedia of Africa,* p.109.

[51] Joseph E. Harris ed, *Pillars in Ethiopian History: The William Leo Hansberry African History Notebook, Volume 1,* p.107 and David Buxton, *The Abyssinians,* pp.93-6.

[52] Basil Davidson, *African Kingdoms,* p.42.

[53] John G. Jackson, *Introduction to African Civilizations,* US, Citadel Press, 1970, p.272.

[54] R. A. Caulk, *North-East Africa before the rise of Islam,* in *The Cambridge Encyclopedia of Africa,* p.110.

[55] E. A. Wallis Budge, *A History of Ethiopia, Nubia & Abyssinia, Volume I-B,* p.266.

[56] R. A. Caulk, *North-East Africa before the rise of Islam,* in *The Cambridge Encyclopedia of Africa,* p.110.

[57] Quoted in Joseph E. Harris ed, *Pillars in Ethiopian History: The William Leo Hansberry African History Notebook, Volume 1,* p.108.

[58] Richard Pankhurst, *Ethiopia Revealed: Merchants, Travelers, and Scholars,* in *African Zion,* pp.20-1.

[59] J. A. Rogers, *World's Great Men of Color, Volume 1,* p.146.

[60] Peter Garlake, *Early Art and Architecture of Africa,* p.75.

[61] David Buxton, *The Abyssinians,* p.43 and Graham Hancock, *The Beauty of Historic Ethiopia,* p.50.

[62] Quoted in David Buxton, *The Abyssinians,* p.43.

[63] David Buxton, *The Abyssinians,* p.43.

[64] Larry Williams & Charles S. Finch, *The Great Queens of Ethiopia,* in *Black Women in Antiquity,* ed Ivan Van Sertima, US, Transaction Publishers, 1988, p.33.

[65] David Buxton, *The Abyssinians,* pp.44-6.

[66] Ibid., p.45.

[67] For example Larry Williams & Charles S. Finch, see above.

[68] Basil Davidson, *Africa in History,* p.122 and David Buxton, *The Abyssinians,* p.45.

[69] Roderick Grierson, *Dreaming of Jerusalem,* in *African Zion,* pp.12-3.

[70] E. A. Wallis Budge, *A History of Ethiopia, Nubia & Abyssinia, Volume I-B,* pp.164-5.

[71] David Buxton, *The Abyssinians,* p.45.

[72] Bernard Hamilton, *Spreading the Gospel in the Middle Ages,* in *History Today, Volume 53 (1),* ed Peter Furtado, UK, History Today Limited, January 2003, p.45.

[73] David Dugan, *Time Life's Lost Civilizations,* video series, *Africa: A History Denied,* Holland, Time Life Video, 1995.

[74] John G. Jackson, *Introduction to African Civilizations,* p.273.

[75] Ibid., pp.273-4.

[76] Basil Davidson, *Africa,* television series part 3: *Caravans of Gold,* UK, Channel Four Television, 1984.

[77] Basil Davidson, *African Kingdoms,* p.88.

[78] Peter Garlake, *The Kingdoms of Africa,* UK, Elsevier-Phaidon, 1978, p.96.

[79] Charles Finch, *The Star of Deep Beginnings,* pp.220-1.

[80] Ivan Van Sertima, *The Lost Sciences of Africa: An Overview,* in *Blacks in Science: Ancient and Modern,* ed Ivan Van Sertima, US, Transaction Publishers, 1983, p.18.

[81] Christopher Ehret, *The Civilizations of Africa,* UK, James Currey, 2002, p.187.

[82] David Dugan, *Time Life's Lost Civilizations,* video series, *Africa: A History Denied.*

[83] Captain C. H. Stigand, *The Land of Zinj,* UK, Constable & Company, 1913, pp.116-7.

[84] John E. G. Sutton, *A Thousand Years of East Africa,* Kenya, British Institute in Eastern Africa, 1990, p.60.

[85] David Dugan, *Time Life's Lost Civilizations,* video series, *Africa: A History Denied.*

[86] John E. G. Sutton, A Thousand Years of East Africa, Kenya, p.60.

[87] David Dugan, *Time Life's Lost Civilizations,* video series, *Africa: A History Denied.*

[88] Quoted in Basil Davidson, *Old Africa Rediscovered,* UK, Victor Gollancz, 1959, p.134.

[89] John G. Jackson, *Introduction to African Civilizations,* p.272.

[90] Basil Davidson, *Old Africa Rediscovered,* p.135.

[91] John G. Jackson, *Introduction to African Civilizations,* pp.273-4.

[92] Al Masudi, *The Country of the Zanj,* in *African Civilization Revisited,* ed Basil Davidson, US, Africa World Press, 1991, pp.133-4 also quoted in The Hon. A. Wilmot, *Monomotapa: Its Monuments and its History,* UK, T. Fisher Unwin, 1896, pp.106-7.

[93] Al Masudi, *The Country of the Zanj,* in *African Civilization Revisited,* p.134.

[94] Basil Davidson, *Old Africa Rediscovered,* p.137.

[95] John E. G. Sutton, *A Thousand Years of East Africa,* p.65.

[96] John G. Jackson, *Introduction to African Civilizations,* p.274.

[97] Basil Davidson, *Africa in History,* p.80.

[98] Cf. Saïd Hamdun & Noël King, *Ibn Battuta in Black Africa,* US, Markus Wiener Publishers, 1993, pp.15 and 22 and Ibn Battuta, *Kilwa in 1331,* in *African Civilization Revisited,* ed Basil Davidson, US, Africa World Press, 1991, p.143.

[99] Marco Polo, *The Travels,* UK, Penguin, 1958, pp.300-1.

[100] Quoted in Basil Davidson, *Old Africa Rediscovered,* p.177.

[101] Ronal Lewcock, *Zanj, The East African Coast,* in *Shelter in Africa,* ed Paul Oliver, UK, Barrie & Jenkins, 1971, p.81.

[102] Christopher Ehret, *The Civilizations of Africa,* p.249.

[103] David Dugan, *Time Life's Lost Civilizations,* video series, *Africa: A History Denied.*

[104] Ronal Lewcock, *Zanj, The East African Coast,* in *Shelter in Africa,* p.81.

[105] John E. G. Sutton, *A Thousand Years of East Africa,* Kenya, pp.77-80.

[106] Ibid.

[107] Ibid., pp.67 and 79.

[108] John G. Jackson, *Introduction to African Civilizations,* pp.278-9.

[109] Charles Finch, *Africa and the Birth of Science and Technology,* US, Khenti, 1992, pp.20-1.

[110] Debra Shore, *Steel-Making in Ancient Africa,* in *Blacks in Science,* ed Ivan Van Sertima, US, Transaction Publishers, 1983, p.157.

[111] Ivan Van Sertima, *The Lost Sciences of Africa: An Overview,* in *Blacks in Science,* p.9.

[112] Charles Finch, *Africa and the Birth of Science and Technology,* US, Khenti, 1992, pp.20-1.

[113] Basil Davidson, *Old Africa Rediscovered,* pp.143-4.

[114] John E. G. Sutton, *A Thousand Years of East Africa,* p.65.

[115] John G. Jackson, *Introduction to African Civilizations,* p.281.

[116] Basil Davidson, *Old Africa Rediscovered,* pp.158-9.

[117] Ibidem and Jeremy Isaacs producer, *Millennium: The 15th Century,* Television Series, UK, BBC Television, 1999.

[118] Basil Davidson, *Old Africa Rediscovered,* p.143.

[119] David Dugan, *Time Life's Lost Civilizations,* video series, *Africa: A History Denied.*

[120] Peter Garlake, *The Kingdoms of Africa,* pp.105-6.

[121] Quoted in John E. G. Sutton, *A Thousand Years of East Africa,* pp.80-2.

[122] Saïd Hamdun & Noel King, *Ibn Battuta in Black Africa,* p.16

[123] Ibid., p.18.

[124] Cf. Quoted in John E. G. Sutton, *A Thousand Years of East Africa,* p.81 and Ibn Battuta, *Kilwa in 1331,* in *African Civilization Revisited,* p.143.

[125] Saïd Hamdun & Noël King, *Ibn Battuta in Black Africa,* pp.16 and 21.

[126] Basil Davidson, *Old Africa Rediscovered,* pp.172-3.

[127] Gervaise Mathew, *The Land of Zanj,* in *The Dawn of African History,* ed Roland Oliver, UK, Oxford University Press, 1951, p.51.

[128] Quoted in Basil Davidson, *Old Africa Rediscovered,* p.161.

[129] Gaspar Correa, *Lendas da India,* quoted in John E. G. Sutton, *A Thousand Years of East Africa,* p.77.

[130] Duarte Barbosa, *Swahili Civilization,* in *African Civilization Revisited,* ed Basil Davidson, US, Africa World Press, 1991, p.159.

[131] Ibid., pp.160-3.

[132] Ibid., p.156.

[133] Ibid., p.159.

[134] Ibid., pp.159-163.

[135] Basil Davidson, *Old Africa Rediscovered,* p.169.

[136] Quoted in John G. Jackson, *Introduction to African Civilizations,* p.304.

[137] Basil Davidson, *African Kingdoms,* p.88.

[138] H. N. Chittick, *A Guide to the Ruins of Kilwa,* Tanzania, Ministry of Community Development and Culture, 1965.

[139] Charles Finch, *The Star of Deep Beginnings,* p.160.

CHAPTER SIXTEEN: MEDIÆVAL NUBIA

The Early History

Despite the fall of Kush in 350 AD, the mediæval and late history of the region continued to shimmer in brilliance. The archaeology shows that it remained rich and cultured. There was a population explosion, at least in Lower Nubia. Rulers could erect large architectural projects as skilled as those of the Kushites, such as massive fortifications. Furthermore, pottery vessels were plentiful and seem to have been discarded even when in fine condition.[1]

Al-Yaqubi, writing in the ninth century AD, wrote that the Nubians were divided into two kingdoms, Makuria and Alwa. Al-Masudi recorded that one group of Nubians had their capital at Dongola and the other group had their capital at Soba. These kingdoms occupied the Nile Valley from the First Cataract to the district of Sennar on the Blue Nile. From the sixth century AD, a common religion and language united the region. From at least the sixth century AD, however, there were three Nubian kingdoms; Nobadia to the north whose capital lay at Faras, Makuria in the middle whose capital lay at Old Dongola, and Alwa to the south whose capital lay at Soba East.[2] The story of these kingdoms follows the fall of the pharaonic state of Kush (discussed earlier in Chapter Seven).

On the history of these kingdoms, a range of materials is available including graffiti, etched on pottery and the walls of buildings, inscriptions, funerary stelae and also archival material. The Nubians kept archives and from the site of Qasr Ibrim legal texts, documents and correspondence were discovered.[3] Dr Welsby is the author of a highly informative book on Mediæval Nubia. He informs us that: "On the site are preserved thousands of documents in Meroitic, Latin, Greek, Coptic, Old Nubian, Arabic and Turkish."[4] The majority of the source material was in Greek, Coptic and Old Nubian. Dr Welsby notes that: "The level of at least some degree of literacy in these three languages appears to have been high."[5] However, Dr Welsby takes a disparaging view of the Nubians' use of Greek. He notes that the Greek used in certain inscriptions were mixed with Old Nubian. Moreover: "An examination of the various inscriptions and documents in Greek indicates that there is no linear progression from a sound knowledge of Greek in the early medieval period to the use of appalling ungrammatical Greek towards the end".[6] Dr Welsby,

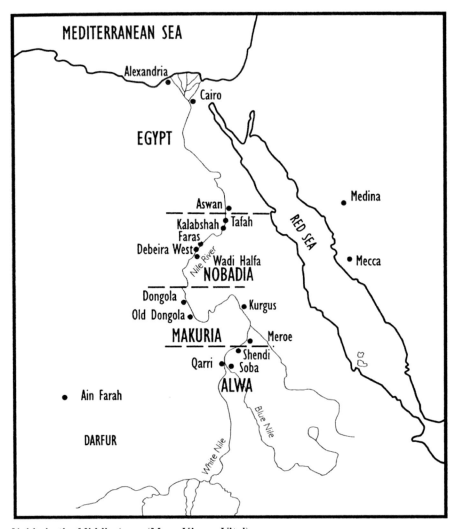

Nubia in the Middle Ages. (Map: Kieron Vital).

though unaware of it, is actually describing Greek Creole. This demonstrates that the Mediæval Nubians had a high degree of literacy in at least Old Nubian, Coptic, Greek, and at a later date, Greek Creole. Furthermore, some of them had facility in Meroitic, Latin, Arabic and Turkish. Objectively speaking, this is an astounding educational achievement that ought to humble many modern peoples and nations - including Welsby's own.

Strabo describes the Nubae (cf. Noba and Nobadae) as "a large tribe, who, beginning at Meroe, extend as far as the bends of the river, and are not subject to the Aethiopians [i.e. Kushites] but are divided into separate kingdoms".

They gradually infiltrated the Kushite state over many years. As Kush faltered, they became increasingly powerful and gradually emerged as the new ruling class. In the last days of the Kushite state, there was a decline in fine pottery, art, literacy and architecture. Moreover, there was the demise of its religious and state institutions. By the fourth century AD, the Noba to the south, by contrast, dwelt in masonry towns, had temples and images, possessed gold and silver vessels, and practised agriculture.[7]

Another people challenged the authority of Kush. These were the Blemmyes, a people of the eastern desert. By the late fourth century AD, they became embroiled in a struggle with the Nobadae for regional supremacy. Epiphanius, a Palestinian monk, reported that the Blemmyes had occupied the emerald mines of the eastern desert near Kalabsha. Other evidence would date this event to somewhere between 392 or 394 AD. By 423 AD they were masters of five towns, el-Laqeita, Kalabsha, Khiris, Taifa and Qirta. Kalabsha had an important temple dedicated to Mandulis and may well have been the Blemmyan capital. The temple walls contain the names of four Blemmyan kings, Tamal, Isemne, Degou and Phonen.[8]

Both the Blemmyes and the Nobadae took an aggressive position against Egypt, then under Roman rule. John of Ephesus wrote that the Nobadae "who are not only not subject to the authority of the Roman Empire, but even receive a subsidy [from the Romans] that they do not enter nor pillage Egypt". Around 423 AD Olympiodorus, a Roman diplomat, visited the Blemmyan country to persuade them to accept federate status within the Roman Empire. His mission was successful. However, both the Blemmyes and the Nobadae, despite the treaty obligations and annual subsidies paid to them, continued to raid Roman occupied Egypt. In 452 AD the Romans felt compelled to react with force. They battled both the Nobadae and the Blemmyes and expelled them from Roman occupied territory. The peace treaty, ratified at Philae, called on the Africans to return prisoners and livestock captured in Egypt, pay war damages, and surrender the children of their elite families as hostages to the Romans. In return the Romans would allow the Africans to worship at the Temple of Isis at Philae, which was in Roman occupied territory. In addition, they agreed to allow the statue of the Goddess Isis to be sent to Lower Nubia during the annual ancient celebration. However, at a later date, the Africans overran Egypt and released the hostages.[9]

In the early fifth century AD, Nobadae became increasingly dominant over the Blemmyes. Kharamadoye, a Nobadae king, records that he campaigned against the Blemmyes and thus controlled the territories from Philae to Soleb, near the Third Cataract. The Blemmyes regained the northern territories for a short while only to lose it again.[10] One of the inscriptions on the Temple of Mandulis is of a king called Silko. Dated before 450 AD, he describes himself

Nubia. Interior of the Church opposite Debeira. *c.*650-800 AD. From Geoffrey S. Mileham, *Churches in Lower Nubia* (US, University of Philadelphia, 1910, plate 6c).

as "King of the Noubades and all the Aithiopians". The inscription recounts his three campaigns against the Blemmyes. Apparently he "came to Talmis (Kalabshah) and Taphis (Taifa). On two occasions I fought with the Blemmyes; and God gave me the victory. On the third occasion I was again victorious and took control of their cities." Moreover, Silko battled the Blemmyes at Qasr Ibrim to the First Cataract. This campaign ended Blemmyan dominance of Lower Nubia. The identity of the "God" mentioned in the inscription is controversial. Some writers believe that it is the God of the Christians. We, however, keep an open mind. A letter was discovered in 1976 at Qasr Ibrim written by Phonen, the last Blemmyan king and also his son, to Aburni, the king of the Nobadae and his sons. The letter demonstrates that Phonen was an enemy of Silko. Phonen tells of negotiations he had opened with Silko, with the aim of recovering lost Blemmyan lands. Phonen offered Silko sheep, cattle and camels in return for the land. Silko, however, broke the agreement soon after receiving the livestock. In addition, he killed the Blemmyan envoy and imprisoned some Blemmyan prophets.[11]

The Silko inscription is in the Greek language, which was also the official language of Roman occupied Egypt. Next to the inscription are two images, thought to represent Silko. In one of the representations, the king is on horseback spearing an enemy. The other looks slightly pharaonic. Silko was buried at Ballana, where seven generations of rulers have been discovered dating before 500 AD. Buried with them were crowns that were heavily influenced by pharaonic designs. The crowns were much like those worn by the royal princes of Kush and the viceroys rather than those of the Kushite pharaohs themselves. The crowns probably show that the Nobadian kings saw themselves as the descendants of the Kushites. Other evidence comes from the graveyards at el-Hobagi. Among the artefacts recovered were bottles and cups, lances, swords, and archery equipment. Also buried with the dead were horses, some with silver trappings, donkeys and camels.[12]

The Three Nubian Kingdoms

By the middle of the sixth century AD, the documents identify three Nubian kingdoms, Nobadia (also called Nobadae) to the north whose capital lay at Faras, Makuria in the middle whose capital lay at Old Dongola and Alwa to the south, whose capital lay at Soba East. The archaeology, however, shows two distinct cultures, one belonging to Nobadia and the other belonging to Makuria and Alwa. Nobadia ruled from the First to the Third Cataract of the Nile. Makuria ruled from the Third to some location between the Fourth and Fifth Cataracts. Alwa ruled south of this boundary. Of the little specifically known of this period, it seems that Nobadia and Alwa shared good political relations.

However, there was much conflict between Nobadia and Makuria. Ibn Selim says they were often at war.[13] Furthermore, throughout these kingdoms cultural continuities from Kush were of great significance. Not only did the Nubians continue to venerate the Goddess Isis, they built Kushite style temples at Qasr Ibrim, Jebel Adda and Soba East.[14]

The Nubian kingdoms became Christian in the sixth century AD. In 531 AD Emperor Justinian of Byzantium (i.e. the Late Roman Empire) apparently "got the idea of making the Aithiopians and Homeritae his allies with a view to damage the Persians".[15] Professor C. P. Groves suggests that Justinian's reasons were much more sinister:

> [T]he Church was recognized as a pillar of the State, so that to propagate the Christian faith was at the same time to consolidate the imperial power. Justinian pursued the policy in Africa of encouraging to become Christians all those chiefs and kings who sought his goodwill. He gave it as a definite instruction to his administrators that they should do all they could to incline the people to Christianity ... Religious propaganda for imperial expansion was the policy. As Mesnage drily remarks, it was found more economical to make use of the Gospel than military power for the security of distant territories![16]

The early Roman church, however, was divided between two dogmas. The Melkites believed that Christ had separate human and divine natures, while the Monophysites believed that Christ had a single nature - both human and divine. Among the Romans this manifested itself as rivalry between the Melkite Emperor Justinian and the Monophysite Empress Theodora. Both sent separate missions to Nobadia. Theodora's Monophysite mission reached Nobadia first, around 543 AD, and was able to influence the Nobadian king. Julian headed the Monophysite mission. He was an Egyptian monk described as "an old man of great worth". During his stay, he baptised the king, his nobles, and many other people. The Nobadian converts were entrusted to the care of Theodore, the Bishop of Philae. The conversion of Makuria is recorded in 568 AD thus: "[A]bout this time, the people of the Maccurritae [sic] received the faith of Christ". They probably converted to Melkite Christianity. In 573 AD a delegation arrived in Byzantium from Makuria bearing gifts for the Emperor Justin "of elephant tusks and a giraffe". Finally, according to John of Ephesus: "[W]hen the people of Alodia [i.e. Alwa] knew that the Nobades [sic] had been converted, their king sent a letter to the king of the Nobades, asking to send him (the bishop) who had taught and baptised the Nobades, that he might instruct and baptise also the Alodaei". Although Makuria would later dominate and then absorb Nobadia, Monophysitism became the dominant dogma. When Islam arrived on the scene in the seventh century AD, the Nubians retained close ties with the Monophysite church at Alexandria.[17]

One of the missionaries built a church in Nobadia at some point between 569 and 575 AD. Since the previous churches began life as temples renovated from Ancient Kush, this was the first new church in the region to have been constructed. The Temple of Isis at Philae was put to church use by around 535 to 537 AD. Among the other Kushite buildings that became churches were the Temple of Taharqo at Qasr Ibrim, the Temple at Taifa, and a Twenty Fifth Dynasty temple at Tabo.[18]

A Coptic language inscription has survived that commemorates the conversion of the Temple at Dendur into a church dating to the time of the Nobadian king Eirpanome. The date is given as either 559 or 574 AD. It records that:

> By [the w]ill of god and the decree
> Of King Eirpanome and the [man] zealous
> In the word of god, Joseph, the *exarch* of
> Talmis, and by our receiving the cross
> From Theodore, the bish[op] of Philae,
> I, Abraham, the most hum[ble] priest,
> [it is] who set up the cross on the day
> they founded this church … [19]

Archaeological data suggests that Christianity entered Nobadia before the official conversion. In Lower Nubia and Ballana, for example, Christian symbols were found carved on pottery, after firing, presumably by the owners. At Jebel Adda leather quivers were found in fifth century AD graves that had the cross as a decorative motif. At Qasr Ibrim a cross motif was found on the wall of a rock cut tomb, dating from the late fourth or fifth centuries AD.[20] There is also, of course, the controversial inscription of King Silko already mentioned.

With the introduction of Christianity, the Nubians began building monuments that echoed the basilica, a type of church architecture popular in the Roman Empire. Dr Welsby, that excellent authority on Nubia, explains how this came about:

> Within the Roman Empire the early church builders had turned to the secular basilica as the model for church architecture, with its axial plan, a long central nave flanked by aisles. It was this basic concept which was introduced into Nubia along with Christianity. Churches are typically rectangular with all the rooms contained within the rectangle. Externally the walls appear to have been provided with little in the way of embellishment. Windows were small and doorways were usually, although not invariably, narrow openings. The most impressive feature of many churches may have been their roofs. Although many, particularly the earlier ones, had flat roofs supported on timbers presumably covered with a layer of mud or mud brick, others were commonly

vaulted or covered with domes. Some of these domes were very prominent and representations of churches on wall paintings, graffiti and actual buildings surviving until recently at several sites, show them as impressive and striking monuments.[21]

Archaeology tells us interesting things about early Christian Nubia. One individual was buried at the Monastery of the Holy Trinity at Old Dongola, clad in an extremely elaborate garb consisting of costly textiles of various fabrics, including gold thread. Seventeen others were buried in coarse shrouds. The burials were probably of a king of Makuria buried alongside seventeen monks. At Soba East there were individuals buried in fine clothing, also including items with gold thread. They were probably kings of Alwa. Leather sandals and shoes survived. One individual was buried with a particularly fine pair of sandals. In the graves near Church A at Soba, were found a range of exquisite textiles - some also with gold thread. Another noteworthy burial was that of a child. The body was placed in a wooden chest which had the corners strengthened with iron brackets and was closed by an elaborate lock.[22] There is a grave near the eastern room in the Cruciform Church at Old Dongola, known as the grave of the Nubian Queen. In the burial there is evidence of mummification and the Egyptian custom of tying the limbs together.[23]

Underground crypts have been found in a small number of Nubian churches. The earliest were in Building X at Old Dongola constructed in the mid-sixth century AD. Building X may well have been an important memorial church constructed in honour of the people buried within it.[24]

Of the royal burials at Soba East, the only royal tombstone found in Nubia, the inscription reads as follows:

O God of the spirits and all flesh, Thou who hast rendered death ineffectual and has trodden down Hades, and hast given life to the world, rest the soul of (Thy) servant David, the King, in the bosom of Abraham and Isaac and Jacob, in a place of light, in a place of verdure, in a place of refreshment, whence pain and grief and mourning hath fled. Pardon [every sin committed] by him in word or deed [or thought; remit and annul] because [there is no man who will live] and will not sin. For [Thou only, O God, art without] sin, and Thy justice [is justice for] ever. O Lord, Thy word [is truth] for Thou art the rest and resurrection of Thy servant and to Thee we sign the glory of the Father and the Son and the Holy Ghost, now and always and forever Amen. The years from his birth when he was not a king (were) [..] whereas he was king 16 years 3 months. After the Martyrs 732 he completed (his life) in the month of Hathor the 2nd; Thursday.[25]

The Archangel Michael was extremely popular throughout Nubia, and for that matter, Axum. His name is found carved on walls and pottery, written out as a monogram or as a cryptogram. Cryptograms are based on the idea that Greek letters have numerical equivalents. In the case of those forming the name Michael, the numbers add up to 689. For example, MIXAEΛ = 40 (M) +10 (I) + 600 (X) + 1 (A) + 8 (E) + 30 (Λ) = 689 = ΧΠΘ. The monks in the Monastery of the Holy Trinity at Old Dongola decorated their eating vessels with both a cross and also cryptograms of Michael. They probably did this to protect themselves from negative powers.[26]

In the early seventh century AD relations between Nubia and the Byzantine Empire seems to have been friendly. In 619 AD, however, that all changed. That year the Persians, under King Chosroes, occupied Byzantine controlled Egypt for nine years until ejected by the Byzantines. The Nubians sent the Persian invaders a gift of a giraffe. Meanwhile, a new contender, the Arabs, emerged onto the world stage. Islam stimulated the meteoric rise of the Arabians as a military force. Their armies marched into Egypt in December 639 AD, ending over 600 years of Roman occupation. After this conquest, they marched beyond Egypt's borders to the west and the south. To the west they overran Byzantine-ruled Libya, Tunisia and Algeria and pressed on to Morocco.[27] Today, they are still the dominant power in North Africa.

The Byzantine governor of Egypt solicited assistance from the Beja and the Nubians against the Arab invasion. Unfortunately, hostilities broke out between these two allies, leading to no assistance being sent. This sealed the fate of the Byzantine garrison, who were forced to withdraw from Egypt under the terms of a treaty. They left Alexandria in September 642 AD. In 641 or 642 AD the Arabs sent an army of 20,000 men into Nubia, killing and plundering. The Nubians amassed a large army of 100,000 and struck back at the Arabs with such force that "the Muslims had never suffered a loss like the one they had in Nubia". Hostilities were brought to a close without significant Arab gains. A peace treaty was signed call the *Baqt*.[28]

Zacharias, King of Nobadia, however, broke the *Baqt* and raided Upper Egypt, taking Aswan and Philae. This led to a second Arab campaign against Nubia in 652 AD. With an army of 5,000 horsemen, the Arabs marched further south to the Makurian capital of Old Dongola. They laid siege to the walled city and battered away with catapults. In the process they destroyed the Church of the Stone Pavement. However, not everything appears to have gone to plan.[29] An Arab sheikh who participated in both of these invasions reported:

> I never saw a people who were sharper in war than they [i.e. the Nubians]. I heard one of them say to the Muslims: 'Where do you want me to hit you with my arrows?' and in case the Muslim would disdainfully say: 'In such a spot', the Nubian would never miss it. They were fond of fighting with arrows: but their arrows would scarcely ever hit on the ground. One day, they arrayed themselves against us and we were desirous to carry the conflict with the sword: but they were too quick for us and shot their arrows, putting out our eyes.[30]

The Nubian archers had a major impact on the invaders. They nicknamed the Nubians, "pupil smiters" and "archers of the eyes".[31]

The Makurians put up a determined resistance under King Qalidurut and fought the Arabs to a stalemate. Eventually another *Baqt* was drawn up. This *Baqt* was mentioned in detail by many Arab authors, who described it as an exchange of goods of equal value. According to Al-Masudi, the *Baqt* stipulated that the Makurians should supply annually to the Arab rulers of Egypt:

> 365 slaves to the treasury of the Muslims
> 40 slaves to the emir of Egypt
> 20 slaves to his delegate who resides in Aswan who is in charge of overseeing the *Baqt*
> 5 slaves to the judge of Aswan, who together with the emir of Aswan presides over the delivery of the *Baqt*
> 1 slave to each of the 12 court witnesses chosen from among the people of Aswan to supervise the delivery of the *Baqt*.

In return, the Arabs agreed to provide Makuria with the following:

> 1000 *ardeb* of wheat
> 300 *ardeb* of wheat to the delegates of the Makurian king
> 1000 *ardeb* of barley
> 1000 jugs for the king
> 300 jugs for the king's delegates
> 2 horses of the breed used by the emir
> 4 pieces of *qabati* cloth for the king
> 3 pieces of *qabati* cloth for his delegates
> 8 pieces of *buqturiyyah* cloth
> 5 pieces of *mu'lama* cloth
> a mantle of *mukhmala* silk (velvet or wool)
> 10 pieces of *Abu Buqtor* cloth
> 10 pieces of *Ahasi* cloth.[32]

The *Baqt* also stipulated freedom of travel for Nubians in Arab-ruled Egypt and vice versa. Actual settlement by either people in each others' territories, however, was forbidden. In addition, any slaves who sought refuge in Nubia were to be handed back to the Arabs. Finally, the Arabs were allowed the privilege of building a mosque in Old Dongola and that Muslims must be allowed free access to it to pray and to stay within its vicinity.[33]

During this period, Nobadia disappears from the records. It appears to have become the northern part of Makuria. As Professor Chancellor Williams put it: "[T]he Blacks had achieved a major goal by incorporating Nobadae [sic] with Makuria and thus reestablishing what had become the recognized boundary between Ethiopia [i.e. Nubia] and Egypt at the First Cataract. The precise manner of this amazing achievement is unknown".[34]

In the following centuries, there was much friction between Makuria and Egypt, often caused by infringements of the *Baqt* by one side or the other, usually by Makuria. Several writers up to the twelfth century recorded Arab complaints about non-payment of the *Baqt*. One such document is a letter dated November 758 AD. In this source, the Governor of Egypt complained to the ruler of Makuria that Makuria had granted asylum to runaway slaves against the stipulation of the *Baqt*. Moreover, the slaves sent to the Arabs from Makuria were often the disabled and weak, or consisted of old men or young boys. The Governor further complained that Arabs in Makuria had been prevented in their movement around the country and that Arab merchants had been robbed.[35]

Between the eighth and the twelfth centuries AD there were several battles between Egypt and Makuria. Both sides were the aggressors on occasion. These were, however, mere skirmishes and should only be seen as such. Between 723 and 742 AD, the Arabs raided Nubia. One "battle of pillage" was fought and the Arabs seized a number of people. By the middle of the eighth century AD the balance of power had swung in favour of Makuria. Around 748 AD Cyriacus, their emperor, invaded Egypt. The story concerns Abba Michael, head of the Christians at Alexandria, who had been imprisoned by Abd el-Malik, the Egyptian ruler. Emperor Cyriacus demanded the patriarch's release from jail but Abd el-Malik refused to comply. Cyriacus promptly marched into Egypt "with a great army, including a hundred thousand horsemen, with a hundred thousand horses and a hundred thousand camels." He campaigned as far as Cairo where he encamped outside the city. During the campaign, he sent the *eparch* (see page 495) to go on ahead and demand the release of the patriarch. The Arabs, however, seized the *eparch* and had him imprisoned also. On the arrival of Cyriacus' army at Cairo, Abd el-Malik released the patriarch. The victorious Makurians withdrew and went back to Nubia.[36]

More aggression followed from the north with raids into Nubian territory commanded by Abd al A'la ibn Hamid between 762 and 770 AD.[37]

In 833 AD Emperor Zakaria sent a delegation headed by his nephew to the Caliph of Baghdad, to protest at the great number of Arab incursions into Makurian territory. Furthermore, he denounced the *Baqt* and was quite prepared to fight the Arabs over it. In the end it was agreed that the *Baqt* could be paid triannually instead.[38]

Hostilities resumed between 854 and 855 AD. Al-Omari, an Egyptian, moved into the eastern desert beyond Aswan with a group of slaves to excavate a gold mine. Some of his men entered the Nile Valley in search of water, but were arrested by the Makurians who subsequently had them executed. Al-Omari resorted to battle. The Makurian Emperor Giorgios appointed his nephew, Nyuti, to head an elite force against the Egyptians. After some

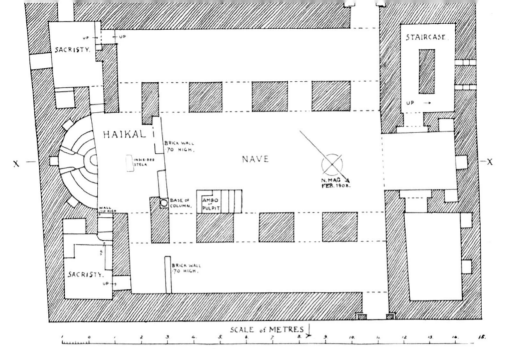

Nubia. Plan of the Church opposite Debeira. From Geoffrey S. Mileham, *Churches in Lower Nubia* (US, University of Philadelphia, 1910, plate 8).

skirmishes, a treaty was agreed between the two sides. The agreement that Nyuti negotiated allowed Al-Omari to settle with his men in a designated area of Makuria against the wishes of Giorgios, the Makurian Emperor. This caused a crisis. The Emperor sent his eldest son to continue the battle against both Al-Omari, and his nephew, Nyuti, but he was defeated several times. Giorgios then appointed another of his sons, Zacharias, to command the army. Zacharias succeeded in persuading Al-Omari to remain neutral in the Makurian civil war. He won Al-Omari's support by bribing him with money and promised the hand of Nyuti's soon-to-be-widowed wife. Zacharias succeeded in capturing Nyuti. Following this, his army fell upon the unsuspecting Egyptian force. They failed to catch Al-Omari, who was forced to abandon his position and return to Egypt.[39]

In the middle of the tenth century AD, the Makurians raided the Oases, followed in 956 AD, by a forceful attack on Aswan, the Egyptian frontier town. The campaign did not end well for Makuria, however. The Egyptian army, advancing by both land and river, counter-attacked. They entered Nubia and defeated the Makurian Emperor in battle. Pressing on, they captured the citadel of Ibrim and seized its cathedral. Following this, they ransacked then burned the cathedral's library. In 1969, however, a number of ecclesiastical manuscripts in Coptic were discovered that survived the flames. The Muslims made little attempt to occupy the newly conquered territory but returned to Egypt a few months later with 150 captives and a number of decapitated heads.[40]

In 1066 Nasir ed-Dawla raided Nubia "but the Sudan crushed him, plundered his army and took all his equipment". In 1172 the Makurians were again on the offensive. They marched towards Aswan. In response Salah ed-Din, ruler of Egypt, ordered his men to march against Nubia. The Egyptians captured Qasr Ibrim in 1173, and took booty and prisoners.[41]

Trade and Culture

Despite the many raids and skirmishes, the *Baqt* of 652 AD established peaceful relations with the Arab and other Muslim rulers of Egypt. In the 600 years of relative peace, the Nubian kingdoms attained great wealth. They developed a rich culture that stretched from the First Cataract at least as far south as Soba East. The northern kingdom of Makuria is the better known because of the large quantity of Arab sources and the archaeology. It is likely, however, that Alwa was even more significant. Ibn Selim Al-Aswani, in the tenth century, recorded that: "The King of Alwa is more powerful than the king of Maqurra [sic], has a larger army and more horses than the Maqurran: his country is more fertile and larger." Another eyewitness, Ibn Haukal, wrote about the same time. He considered Alwa to be the most prosperous part of the whole of Nubia. Abu Salih tells us that Alwa had 400 churches.[42]

With the rulers of Makuria, Nobadia and Alwa, the succession was passed through the matrilineal line. The monarch was the undisputed head of state holding, at least in theory, absolute authority over all his subjects. For example, the subjects had no automatic right of land ownership. Thirteen crowns from the early period were found. Four crowns belonged to kings, six to queens and three to princes. They were of five types. Two were clearly derived from Kushite models. All were made from a simple band of two sheets of silver over a plaster core. They typically had decorative embellishments, embossed decoration, precious stones or glass and/or with the circlet topped by ram's head, uraei and plumbed crests.[43]

Abu Salih and John the Deacon refer to the Makurian emperor, Cyriacus, as Lord of the Nubians under whom thirteen priest kings ruled. The most important of these kings was the *eparch,* equivalent to the Latin *praefectus.* Arab sources call him the 'Lord of the Mountain' or the 'Lord of the Horses'. The *eparch* typically resided in the north of Makuria and concerned himself with relations between Makuria and Egypt. The *domesticos* was a deputy and we find *domesticoi* of the king and of the *eparch.* Also important was the *Nauarchos.* Originally a Byzantine title meaning admiral, there is a Nubian inscription where the word means "the admiral, supreme on the water".[44]

After the monarchy, the Church was the next most important institution. The Nubian Church became firmly under the leadership of the patriarch of

Nubia. Capital from Church opposite Debeira. From Geoffrey S. Mileham, *Churches in Lower Nubia* (US, University of Philadelphia, 1910, plate 6a).

Nubia. Lintel above a door from Church opposite Debeira. From Geoffrey S. Mileham, *Churches in Lower Nubia* (US, University of Philadelphia, 1910, plate 6b).

Alexandria. Among the Makurian bishoprics were those at Faras, Kallama, Merka, Old Dongola, Sai, Shanqir, Taifa, Qasr Ibrim and Qurta. In Vansleb's *Histoire de l'église d'Alexandrie* published in 1677, are recorded six bishoprics in the Kingdom of Alwa. These were at Arodias, Banazi, Borra, Gagara, Martin and Menkesa. At Faras, Qasr Ibrim (see page 500), Old Dongola and Soba East, the cathedrals of those bishoprics were located. It is believed that the large number of Coptic documents at Qasr Ibrim, particularly from the eighth and ninth centuries AD, might be related to that site being a refuge for Copts fleeing persecution in Egypt, following revolts against their Arab rulers that took place in 725, 739 and 750 AD.[45] It is also on record that many Copts fled to Ethiopia for the same reasons.

Dr Welsby informs us that:

> The large numbers of churches known and the large numbers of monasteries referred to in the sources testify to the wealth of the Nubian Church ... [T]he destruction of a church at Sus in the later thirteenth century when the Muslims carried off golden crosses and other objects of gold, the whole of which was valued at 4,640½ dinars, the silver vases also taken were valued at 8,660 dinars.[46]

The Church were land owners. Along with the monks, the church also provided legal, medical and secretarial services to the rest of society. They helped in the civil administration and had their own scribes. The monastic institutions were also involved in manufacturing, especially of pottery.[47]

Military strength was a major factor in the survival of the Nubian kingdoms. Cavalry appears to have been important and was a major component of Cyriacus' army along with troops mounted on camels. The Alwan army, in the later tenth century AD at least, was probably larger. Ibn Selim informs us that the king of Alwa had a larger army with more horses than the king of Makuria. It was, however, the military prowess of Makuria that ensured the survival of the Nubian kingdoms since it acted as a buffer that protected Alwa.[48]

The inhabitants of Makuria were technically the slaves of the emperor (i.e. the state). In theory, this meant that all produce legally belonged to the state. This system of redistribution maintained the religious elite and the civil elite. In Lower Nubia, however, Islamic coinage did circulate. From Qasr Ibrim were found several Islamic coins and a few coin weights. One of these has an Old Nubian inscription *'Eparch of Nobadia'*. Goods moved by boats, donkeys and camels.[49]

Agriculture was the mainstay of the Nubian domestic economy. It was supplemented by animal husbandry and also by hunting and fishing. Agriculture was much enhanced by the introduction of the *saqia*. The *saqia* was a wooden wheel that carried two parallel ropes to which pots were attached. It was rotated through a series of gears by a draught animal. As this

Nubia (Sudan). Capital from the Cathedral of the Granite Columns in Old Dongola. Late 7th century AD. (Photo: Louis Buckley, Black Nine Films).

happened, the pots filled with water as they were submerged and emptied that water at a higher level into an aqueduct.[50] Ibn Haukal recorded that:

> The most prosperous part of the country [i.e. Nubia] is the territory of Alwa, which has a continuous chain of villages and a continuous strip of cultivated lands, so that a traveller may in one day pass through many villages, one joining the next, supplied with waters drawn from the Nile by means of *saqias*.[51]

Of the products grown were bananas, barley, big citrus, dhurra/sorghum, dom palm, palm trees, vines and wheat. In the northern region cotton was grown. One of the uses of dhurra was to make beer. At Soba East a number of crops were cultivated. Among these were bulrush millet, foxtail millet, cowpea, cucumber seeds, dates, dom palm, fig seeds, hulled barley, lentils, nuts, peas, pulses, sesame and termis bean. Vineyards flourished in the region around Old Dongola. The impetus for the local wine industry was a response to the interruption of the supply of Egyptian wine in the middle of the eighth century AD due to Islam. Twelve grape-pressing plants have been identified between the regions of Ikhmindi and Meinarti.[52]

At Debeira bones of sheep, goats, cattle and pigs were found in domestic contexts. In addition, the inhabitants ate camel meat and domestic chicken. Al-Masudi recorded that Nubia had fine camels, sheep and cattle. Their kings rode on purebred horses.[53]

Throughout Nubia, pottery decoration was an art form. Pottery was produced at Faras, Old Dongola, and Soba East, among other sites. The ceramics made in Nobadia during the fifth and sixth centuries AD were particularly fine. Soba Ware decoration was highly distinctive in being very different from that found in the rest of Nubia. There was a very wide range of motifs applied to the pottery. Almost 500 motifs have been published. They show the use of geometric or curvilinear patterns in Nubian pottery. Chinese porcelain also made an appearance from time to time.

Iron was used extensively for weaponry and large numbers of arrows, in particular, have been found in post-Meriotic graves. Tools of iron including adzes, axes and hammerheads, blades from a bow saw, chisels, knives, hoes, metal cutters and tongs were found in the royal tombs at Ballana. Iron was also used to make bindings for strengthening boxes and chests. Copper alloy was widely used to make needles, vessels of various types, and also weaponry. However, from a few sites, among them Debeira West and Soba East, large lumps of glass have been recovered. At Ibrim the most common types of beads were made of glass.[54]

Nubian shoes were of light construction, not entirely unlike a modern slipper. Typically they had one or two ply soles with uppers of soft and fine leather. The most commonly worn footwear at Ibrim was the leather sandal. There were also palm rope sandals and palm leaf sandals. A particularly fine pair of leather sandals was found on the feet of a woman buried at Soba East. At Ibrim was also found a knee-length riding boot made of fine leather or pigskin. Superlative examples of shoes with patterns in gilt can be seen on wall paintings at Faras mostly on the feet of women. Leather was also used for belts.[55]

Cloth manufacture was probably conducted on a large scale at Qasr Ibrim. At the site was found a large collection of equipment associated with sewing, spinning and weaving. Also found was a vast quantity of textiles made of cotton, wool, silk, and linen. The silk was imported from Egypt, the Middle East or China. The other textiles were locally manufactured and were coloured with four dyes. Madder was used for shades of red and orange, indigo was used for shades of blue, weld was used for shades of yellow, and Persian berries were also used for shades of yellow.[56]

The church paintings depict the nobility of Makurian society wearing rich robes. The burial of a dignitary at Jebel Adda in the late thirteenth century confirms this opulence. He was interned with a long coat of red and yellow patterned damask of Egyptian origin folded over his body. Underneath, he wore a pair of plain cotton trousers of long and baggy cut. A pair of red leather slippers with turned up toes lay at the foot of the coffin. The body was wrapped in enormous pieces of gold brocaded striped silk, bearing stamps of the

Nubia (Sudan). Cathedral of Qasr Ibrim. Late 7th century AD. From Geoffrey S. Mileham, *Churches in Lower Nubia* (US, University of Philadelphia, 1910, plate 2).

Egyptian government. Timotheos, the Bishop of Pachoras, was buried at Qasr Ibrim, again, with some distinction. His outer garment was a large bell shaped hooded cloak of fine navy wool, embellished with silk and with a lining of red-brown cotton. Around the head was wrapped a turquoise veil of fine cotton. His main garments were of the *jellabiya* type and trousers. Beneath this was a narrow cotton body belt with white silk stitching. A fine linen mappa was tucked into the front of his cloak. Exquisite clothing has also been recovered from Soba East. Individuals buried to the east of Church A wore various fabrics, including some with gold thread interwoven among flax fibres. Both flax and cotton were found, and also a knitted cap.[57]

Philae was the major place where river trade between the Nubians and Arabs was conducted. Qasr Ibrim was probably an important centre of trade through the port of Aidhab on the Red Sea. Ibn Selim records that at Soba East there was a large colony of Muslims. These may well have been merchants. He further mentions trade routes, probably from the kingdom of Alwa, to the Red Sea ports of Badi, Dahlak and Sawakin. Al-Idrissi described how Bilaq, a town of the Nuba, lying between two branches of the Nile, is the point where merchants from Nubia and Ethiopia met with those from Egypt to trade.[58] Finally, there was a land trade from Nubia to West Africa along the caravan routes.[59]

At Old Dongola ceramic materials and locally manufactured amphorae were found. Faras also had a dominant role in the supply of ceramics. Throughout Nubia the fine Islamic glazed wares were sold. Ceramics played an important role in transporting and storing foodstuffs. Trade in certain food items was extensive. From the evidence of the amphorae used to transport wine, it would appear that the heyday of the wine trade from Egypt to Nubia occurred in the

Early Christian period via the Red Sea. After Islam became fully dominant in Egypt, the Nubian wine industry received a boost. From Alwa came hard woods, ebony, frankincense, and various timbers. Cotton was exported to the North. Probably the most important international trade good, however, was gold. Though available in northern Nubia, Ibn Selim tells us that gold was plentiful in Alwa. Ibn Haukal concers and specified that the "Alwans control the gold mines." Goods from the Islamic world certainly reached as far south as Soba. Excavations have recovered fine glassware from there, including tableware and containers for perfume and other products. Also recovered were glazed wares. Finally, Chinese porcelain of twelfth to thirteenth century dates have also been recovered.

In early Nobadia a number of fortified sites were found at Faras, Ikhmindi, Kalabsha, Sabaqura and Sheikh Daud. They had many features in common, both in their plan, and style of construction. Within the defences at Ikhmindi and Sheikh Daud, the layout of the buildings were remarkably regular and well planned. They had two roomed apartments that back onto the inner face of the defensive wall and are separated by a narrow street. The church occupied the central position.[60]

Faras was the capital of Nobadia. It had a very long history dating back to the Egyptian Middle Kingdom period. The Egyptians built a fortress there. By the tenth century AD it had become the capital of Maris. Abu Salih, writing in the twelfth century, says that it is a well-populated city and also the dwelling place of the *eparch*. Faras had defence walls that enclosed an area of 4.6 hectares. These walls were the largest building projects achieved in medieval Nubia. The curtain wall was nearly 4m thick and 11.6m high. At the angles were substantial square external towers projecting 10m, while spaced at regular intervals along the curtain were slightly smaller towers. Two main gates survive in the centre of the south and west walls. Within these walls, there was a church of clay bricks constructed in the middle of the sixth century AD. Eventually, a cathedral was built on its site in 707 AD. The cathedral was a large five-aisle building covering 564 square metres and had Coptic and Greek inscriptions. In the tenth century AD the cathedral seems to have been damaged by fire. Two modern scholars, however, P. L. Shinnie and M. Shinnie, consider this building "the superior of many buildings of medieval Africa and the Near East." Also within the defensive circuit were three churches, two palatial structures, a monastery and an industrial complex that produced pottery. The two palaces date back to the seventh century AD and were linked by a narrow alleyway. They were certainly at least two storeys in height. Although built of mud brick, they had carved stone portals and the ground floor rooms were decorated with murals. Another monument of curious interest was a large wooden cross that was publicly erected to commemorate the conversion

Nubia. South Domed Church of Serra East. Built somewhere between 1150 and 1400. From Geoffrey S. Mileham, *Churches in Lower Nubia* (US, University of Philadelphia, 1910, plate 33c).

of the city to Christianity. Faras, had, however suffered extensively from wind blown sand. In the thirteenth century the Old Monastery and the palaces were engulfed by it. The city centre may have been abandoned at this time. Later in the century there was a renaissance. The Nubians built the north monastery with a church at first floor level over the sanded remains of its predecessor. They also rebuilt and renovated the cathedral. In the later period, however, when the sand had built up against the cathedral to the level of its windows, a flight of steps was constructed from ground level down to the north corridor. The cathedral at this time, like other churches in late Nubia, had become a largely underground structure.[61]

Qasr Ibrim was a great Nobadian city. It had a long history stretching from at least the Kushite period of the tenth century BC. From the X-Group period, a number of large houses were constructed there. The site was densely built over, with houses that were well constructed and substantial. In the early Christian period, the old temples were destroyed or modified with churches and a cathedral taking their place. Showing official town planning, a number of the earlier houses were demolished and a piazza on two levels was laid out over their remains. In the Classic Christian Period, the hilltop contained churches, large areas of open piazza, a cemetery, and residences of the *eparch* and church officials. Abu Salih describes the city, with its defensive wall and a "large and beautiful church, finely planned and named after Our Lady the pure Virgin Mary. Above it is a high dome upon which rises a large cross." This monument was probably built in the later half of the seventh century AD. It was a five-aisled basilica with a wide nave and apse. In size it measured 596 square metres. Beneath this building were crypts with barrel-vaults, 2m high, entered down two flights of stairs from the north and south outer aisles. The nave and aisles were paved with well-fitted stone slabs.[62]

Arminna West and Debeira West were Nobadian villages. Arminna West dates back to Kushite times. During the Christian period, the village experienced a revival. A clay-brick church was constructed as were finely built houses. The clustering together of the buildings may well demonstrate a highly integrated society. On the north western side of the settlements was a public building whose function is not yet known.[63] Jakobielski, a Polish specialist in Christian archaeology, provided further data: "Settlements investigated, such as Debeya [sic] West or Arminna, present a picture of a prosperous and at the same time surprisingly free and egalitarian society, where differences in social status were not reflected in material culture."[64] Specifically concerning the village of Debeira West, Professors Oliver and Fagan report that: "The University of Ghana … [found that a]ll the buildings were of sun-dried brick, with vaulted ceilings. Two storeys were usual, with a stairway leading to the roof. The village shared a common sanitary and drainage system. There was a communal oil-press and an irrigation wheel."[65]

In early Makuria there were many walled fortifications. The most notable of these were at Bakhit, Diffar, Estabel, Jebel Deiga, Old Dongola, Selib and Sinada.[66]

Old Dongola was the capital of Makuria. Its earliest houses date to the early sixth century AD. However, the city rapidly began to spread beyond its walls. By the late sixth century AD, two large churches, the Old Church and Building X, were constructed. In the aftermath of the siege of Old Dongola in 652 AD, the clay brick wall was strengthened by at least two rectangular towers. From the seventh to ninth centuries AD, high status houses were built to the north of the ecclesiastical complex.[67] Jakobielski provided further data on these houses:

> Further northwards extend a[n] … eighth to … ninth century housing complex. The houses discovered here differ in their hitherto unencountered spatial layout as well as their functional programme (water supply installation, bathroom with heating system) [sic] and interiors decorated with murals.[68]

Over the whole of this area churches and monasteries were found together with pottery kilns. Abu Salih wrote the following about the city: "[I]t is a large city on the banks of the blessed Nile, and contains many churches and large houses and wide streets. The king's house is lofty." The Throne Hall of the Kings was probably built in the ninth or tenth century AD. It was constructed almost exclusively of clay bricks with walls 1.1m thick. The ground floor

Nubia (Sudan and Southern Egypt). Typical interior of a mediæval Nubian church as reconstructed by Somers Clarke. From Somers Clarke, *Christian Antiquities in the Nile Valley* (UK, Clarendon Press, 1912, p.93).

consisted of long and narrow barrel-vaulted rooms of a lofty height. On entering the building, the doorway led to a monumental staircase winding around a square newel. On the first floor was a square hall, surrounded by an arcaded loggia on three sides and with additional rooms to the west, flanking the stairway. The throne hall had a timber roof supported by four columns. Another writer, Ar-Rumi, mentions the "high, insuperable stone walls." Ibn el-Faqih, writing around 900 AD, describes the city as encircled by seven walls, the lower parts of which were made of stone. At a later date, the earliest houses were demolished and replaced by newer houses of two storeys or more. Many of these houses still survive to a height of 3.7m with large arched windows in the upper storey or storeys. A feature of these houses, which is common to the houses excavated beyond the defences, is the presence of a narrow toilet unit by the external wall at the end of one room. Eventually the Old Church was rebuilt as the Cathedral of the Granite Columns. The new monument covered 697 square metres. Building X was built over to become the Church of the Stone Pavement and, in the late seventh century AD, the Cruciform Church.[69] The Monasteries were also important. They were among the largest building complexes to be constructed in Nubia and typically contained a church, a refectory and accommodation for the monks.[70] The Monastery of the Holy Trinity in Old Dongola had particularly fine mural paintings. Dr Welsby described them as follows:

> Among these paintings are some of the greatest masterpieces known from Nubian mural art. One of these is a painting of a king under the protection of the Holy Trinity . . . The king wears a robe decorated with medallions each containing an eagle. His raised right hand supports a cross, while in his left hand he holds a tiara-shaped crown topped by a cross against his chest. In the clouds above him sufficient remains to indicate that the three busts of the Holy Trinity were depicted, the central figure *en face,* the flanking figures turned inwards. The figure on the right rests one hand on the king's shoulder, the central one crowns the ruler with the heavenly crown and the figure on the left holds the cross of the king's earthly crown. Each holds a book in the left hand. This painting is also of particular interest from a technical point of view as it clearly demonstrates that the artist made use of a stencil. The heads and halos of the Trinity are identical in regard to shape and size apart from the changes necessary to allow the flanking figures to look towards the centre of the composition.[71]

Soba was the capital of Alwa. Of this city, Ibn Selim described "fine buildings and large monasteries, churches rich with gold and gardens: there is also a great suburb where many Muslims live." Its Throne Hall was a clay brick building 46.1m by 18.6m. It had long narrow rooms at ground floor level. Like the rooms in the Throne Hall at Old Dongola, its function was probably

Nubia. Manuscript of the *Miracle of St Menas* in the Old Nubian script. 1053 AD.
(Photo: Robin Walker).

to elevate the palatial apartments mirroring the arrangement in the old Kushite palace of Queen Amanishakheto. Archaeology has recovered fragments of ceramic grilles for windows. The window glass panes were also found close by. Evidence of window glass was also found at the Makurian cities of Old Dongola and Hambukol.[72]

Jebel Adda first rose to prominence in the late Kushite period. During the early mediæval period, a defensive wall of mud brick and stone was built. In the late medieval period Adda became the capital of the kingdom of Dotawo. Much of the hilltop appears to have been redesigned in the thirteenth century AD. It had an impressive complex of buildings, including a church, a mansion, and a palace. The palatial structure was enlarged in the fourteenth century. It had a large monumental entrance and consisted of several interconnected buildings constructed over a long period of time. The old Kushite defences were modernised and a new stone-lined gate was added.[73]

In the later periods, a special house type was developed between Qasr Ibrim and the Third Cataract. The castle house was designed primarily as a fortified residence. Usually constructed of clay bricks, some had stone-built ground floors. A key feature was the physical separation of the ground floor vaulted rooms from the domestic quarters on the first floor. Typically, the entry to the building was only at first floor level and it probably had a removable ladder. Trap doors gave access from the first floor to the ground floor storage chambers. Even at the first floor level many doorways were extremely low and would be difficult for an intruder to breach.[74]

The Fall of Mediæval Nubia

By the thirteenth century, however, Makuria faced grave challenges from Egypt. Moreover, the northern parts of the Empire had become Arabicised. This process began in the ninth century AD when Muslims were able to buy land in Maris, a province in northern Makuria. Makurian law decreed that all land was the property of the emperor (i.e. the state). However, a number of Muslim residents of Aswan, who had bought land in northern Makuria, successfully challenged this in Egyptian courts. The Makurian king, however, claimed that his land had been sold illegally. As a result of this ruling, the status of Maris province was different from that of the rest of Makuria. In Maris estates could be passed on by inheritance, while elsewhere, the inhabitants remained technically the slaves of the emperor (i.e. the state). Thus Arabs were able to own land in Maris and pass it on to their descendants through generations.[75] According to Al-Masudi, the Makurians of the north began losing ground with the infiltration of the Arabs and the Beja into their land. Moreover, there was much intermarriage between Muslim men and Beja women. Dr Welsby says: "Over the next several hundred years the racial and cultural composition of Nubia was gradually modified by the arrival of Muslims from the north and east and by the conversion of certain sectors of the Christian population to Islam."[76]

In 1265 the ruler of Qoz (from Egypt) attacked Makuria "killed many people, took prisoners and then returned". Makuria also faced threats from the Arabs of the eastern desert as well as Egypt. The Egyptians gained control of Aidhab, the port on the Red Sea. This threatened to isolate Makuria from access to the Red Sea trade and place control of Nubian trade in the hands of Egypt. Around 1275 Emperor David of Makuria seized the initiative. He marched on Aidhab on the Red Sea and "committed hideous actions." Following this, he advanced on Aswan where he burned the *saqias*.[77]

However, the following year Shekanda, a younger and impatient relative of David, went to Cairo to seek the sultan's help against David in a plan to secure the Makurian throne for himself. Dr Williams narrates that: "The Sultan had every reason to grasp this wonderful opportunity handed to him through the Blacks themselves. Not only would he be able to settle scores with them, but he would also be able to create conditions for [Egyptian] hegemony over their land."[78] The invading party left for Makuria on 20 January 1276 but the Makurians attacked them on camels before they could cross the boundary. The invaders pressed on and took the fortress at Daw. They captured many prisoners, among them the *eparch*. He was sent to Cairo and executed in a particularly gruesome manner. He was sawn in two. The ruler of Egypt brought up the rear guard. His forces wrought destruction and massacred anyone who survived the initial slaughter. The invaders finally caught up with Emperor David at Old Dongola and defeated him. David sought refuge in northern Alwa but was handed over to the Muslims and later sent to the Sultan's court. During the occupation of Old Dongola, the invaders burned the churches. They also carried off everything of value found in them. Shekanda paid a heavy price for involving Egypt. After he was installed on the throne, they offered Makuria the choice of (i) embracing Islam, (ii) paying the tax on the infidel or (iii) being killed. Shekanda agreed to the only sensible option and chose to pay the tax on the infidel of one dinar per head. The Makurian king was now a puppet of the ruler of Egypt. One half of all the revenues of Makuria now belonged to the Sultan and Shekanda was obliged to provide him every year with 3 elephants, 3 giraffes, 5 female panthers, 100 camels and 400 oxen. Moreover, the districts of el-Ali and el-Jabal were placed directly in the hands of the Sultan. In those provinces all the dates and cotton produced were to be handed over as well as any other goods that had traditionally been reserved for the Makurian rulers.[79]

Some years later, the King of el-Abwab, northern Alwa, complained to the Egyptian Sultan about the mistreatment of envoys between them by the ruler of Makuria. In 1286 the Egyptians attacked, sending two armies into Makuria. Semamun, the Makurian Emperor, ordered the evacuation of the country. In his absence, the invaders placed the son of the royal sister on the throne and also appointed a new *eparch*. The Egyptian armies returned home arriving at their court in August 1288. As they withdrew, Semamun returned to Old Dongola, seized the city, and regained power. The Muslim royal puppet and the *eparch* fled to the Egyptian court. The Egyptians assembled another large army to battle the Makurians. They set off from Cairo in October 1289. Semamun again ordered evacuations. He himself fled upstream to the island of Mograt, fifteen days journey from Old Dongola, accompanied by his court. The Makurian Emperor, after refusing to swear allegiance to the Sultan and fearing the arrival of an Egyptian fleet, fled even further upstream to the Kingdom of el-Abwab. However, the royal princes, officials and priests were left abandoned on Mograt. They made their peace with the invaders and swore allegiance to them. Furthermore, they handed over the Makurian crown and other royal regalia. Following this, a great banquet was held in the largest of Old Dongola's churches, where the new royal appointee by the Sultan's court was enthroned. This puppet swore loyalty to the Egyptian Sultan and was required to pay the *Baqt*. Leaving a garrison behind in the capital, the Egyptians again withdrew, arriving in Cairo in May 1290. Once again Semamum returned to Old Dongola and, with the support of the army and some of the princes, arrested the puppet ruler at the palace. He gave safe passage to the Muslim garrison who then withdrew to Qoz. Moreover, he ordered the execution of the puppet ruler and the puppet *eparch*. Following this, he wrote to the Egyptians and offered to pay the *Baqt* every year. This brought some peace.[80]

"In 1304", narrates Dr Williams, "still another self-seeking [B]lack leader journeyed to Cairo to have himself crowned as the servant-king of the Blacks by the Sultan al Nasir. The Sultan sent an expedition to Dongola - a task now easier than before - and his new servant was crowned as King Amai."[81] In 1316 yet another puppet was placed on the throne, Abdallah Barshanbu, this time a Black Muslim. The Arab chief, Kanz ed-Dawla, quickly vanquished him from his throne. Makuria was now under direct Arab rule.[82] More problems followed in 1365. The Egyptians assembled an army of 3,000 cavalry and marched on Makuria on 8 December. Ibn Khaldun suggests that the spread of the Juhanya Arabs throughout Makuria spread pillage and disorder. The Nubian kings were then forced to make alliances with the invaders and the whole area eventually disintegrated into anarchy. The Makurian Empire was no more. Dr Welsby adds: "Once Old Dongola ceased to be the seat of the Makurian kings it disappears from the historical record."[83]

The kingdom of Alwa held on until the late fifteenth century. However, in the accounts of the invasions of Makuria in 1276, documents allude, for the first time, to an independent kingdom of el-Abwab, the earlier northern province of Alwa. The el-Abwab king usually sided with the Egyptians in conflicts between Egypt and Makuria. One of its kings, Adur, sent an embassy to the Egyptian court in 1286 with presents of an elephant and a giraffe. He also handed over David, the fleeing Makurian Emperor, to the Muslims. In the light of what transpired in Makuria, this cannot be seen positively. Whichever be the case, by the late fifteenth century, Alwa collapsed. The desert Arabs from the east occupied the country. They seized Soba, its capital, and reduced it to ruins. When the traveller David Reubeni arrived there in 1523, it was a shambles.[84]

Before winding up this chapter, we give the last word to Professor Chancellor Williams. He was among the first of the historians to put the Mediæval Nubian culture into the proper historical context. He demonstrated its real relevance to world history in general and to the African heritage in particular. According to him:

> The prosperity in this center of the [B]lack world represented one of the last great epochs in the history of the Blacks … [I]t was also one of their finest hours on the stage of human progress. Here the measure of a people's genius could be taken without speculation. Here the message of who Blacks were was wrought in stone and iron for the succeeding generations of Blacks who were to lose their very identity in blood and tears of unbroken oppression. The Arab scholars were properly amazed at a way of life so superior to that of their own homeland. It was something to be amazed about. For there were not only public baths but public latrines, drainage and central water systems, but the most remarkable evidence of prosperity and progress was reflected in the advanced standard of living among the masses. The[re were] … homes of brick and stone in cities, towns and villages - brick houses, and larger houses for the great common people … [T]his was something for the visiting Arab scholars to write home about. (It would be something to write about anywhere in this last part of the twentieth century.)[85]

Notes

[1] Derek A. Welsby, *The Medieval Kingdoms of Nubia*, UK, The British Museum Press, 2002, p.13.
[2] Ibid., pp.7-8 and 28.
[3] Ibid., p.9.
[4] Ibid., p.241.
[5] Ibid., p.237.
[6] Ibid., p.238.
[7] See ibid., pp.14-5.
[8] Ibid., pp.16-7.
[9] See ibid., pp.18-9.
[10] Ibid., p.20.

[11] See ibid., pp.17-8.

[12] Ibid., pp.20-2 and 41.

[13] Ibid., pp.24-8.

[14] Ibid., p.23.

[15] Quoted in ibid., p.32.

[16] C. P. Groves, *The Planting of Christianity on Africa,* quoted in J. C. DeGraft-Johnson, *African Glory,* UK, Watts & Co., 1954, p.49.

[17] See Derek A. Welsby, *The Medieval Kingdoms of Nubia,* pp.32-3 and 35.

[18] See ibid., pp.35-6.

[19] Quoted in ibid., p.37.

[20] Ibid., p.38.

[21] Ibid., p.139.

[22] Ibid., pp.39 and 50.

[23] Ibid., p.66.

[24] Ibid., p.52.

[25] Quoted in ibid., p.62.

[26] Ibid., pp.65-6.

[27] Ibid., p.68.

[28] Ibid., pp.68-9.

[29] Ibid., p.69.

[30] Quoted in ibid.

[31] Ibid., p.69.

[32] Ibid., pp.70-1.

[33] Ibid., p.71.

[34] Chancellor Williams, *The Destruction of Black Civilization,* US, Third World Press, 1987, p.141.

[35] Derek A. Welsby, *The Medieval Kingdoms of Nubia,* p.70.

[36] Ibid., p.73.

[37] Ibid.

[38] Chancellor Williams, *The Destruction of Black Civilization,* p.150 and Sir E. A. Wallis Budge, *A History of Ethiopia, Nubia & Abyssinia: Volume I,* US, ECA Associates, 1991 (originally 1928) p.104.

[39] Derek A. Welsby, *The Medieval Kingdoms of Nubia,* pp.74-5.

[40] Ibid., p.75.

[41] See ibid., pp.75-6.

[42] See ibid., p.83, John Lewis Burckhardt, *Travels in Nubia,* UK, John Murray, 1819, p.500 and L. Kropácek, *Nubia from the late 12th century to the Funj conquest in the early 15th century,* in *UNESCO General History of Africa: Volume IV,* ed D. T. Niane, UK, Heinemann, 1984, p.406.

[43] Derek A. Welsby, *The Medieval Kingdoms of Nubia,* pp.88 and 92.

[44] Ibid., pp.92-3 and 96, and Chancellor Williams, *The Destruction of Black Civilization,* p.151.

[45] Derek A. Welsby, *The Medieval Kingdoms of Nubia,* pp.97, 99 and 101.

[46] Ibid., p.102.

[47] Ibid., pp.102-3.

[48] Ibid., pp.81-2 and John Lewis Burckhardt, *Travels in Nubia,* p.500.

[49] Derek A. Welsby, *The Medieval Kingdoms of Nubia,* pp.203-4.

[50] Ibid., pp.183-5.

[51] Quoted in ibid., p.185.

[52] Ibid., pp.185-7.

[53] See ibid., pp.187-8.

[54] Ibid., pp.128, 194-7, 216 and 234-5.

[55] Ibid., pp.199-200.

[56] Ibid., p.189.

[57] Ibid., p.200.

[58] Ibid., pp.205, 208-11, 213 and 215.

[59] Chancellor Williams, *The Destruction of Black Civilization*, p.140.

[60] Derek A. Welsby, *The Medieval Kingdoms of Nubia*, p.129.

[61] Ibid., pp.117-8, 156, 159, 161, and P. L. Shinnie and M. Shinnie, *New Light on Medieval Nubia*, in *Papers in African Prehistory*, ed J. D. Fage and R. A. Oliver, UK, Cambridge University Press, 1970, pp.283-4.

[62] See Derek A. Welsby, *The Medieval Kingdoms of Nubia*, pp.121-2, 145-6 and 156.

[63] Ibid., p.123.

[64] S. Jakobielski, *Christian Nubia at the height of its civilization*, in *UNESCO General History of Africa: Volume III*, ed M. Al Fasi, UK, Heinemann, 1988, p.204.

[65] Roland Oliver and Brian M. Fagan, *Africa in the Iron Age*, UK, Cambridge University Press, 1975, p.125.

[66] Derek A. Welsby, *The Medieval Kingdoms of Nubia*, p.130.

[67] Ibid., p.118.

[68] S. Jakobielski, *Christian Nubia at the height of its civilization*, in *General History of Africa: Volume III*, p.200.

[69] See Derek A. Welsby, *The Medieval Kingdoms of Nubia*, pp.118-9, 130, 150, 156-7, 160-1 and 166.

[70] Ibid., p.164.

[71] Ibid., p.230.

[72] Ibid., pp.120-1, 162, 180 and John Lewis Burckhardt, *Travels in Nubia*, p.500.

[73] Derek A. Welsby, *The Medieval Kingdoms of Nubia*, pp.122-3 and 162-3.

[74] Ibid., p.169.

[75] Ibid., p.75.

[76] Ibid., pp.78-9 and 106.

[77] See ibid., pp.242-4.

[78] Chancellor Williams, *The Destruction of Black Civilization*, p.151.

[79] Derek A. Welsby, *The Medieval Kingdoms of Nubia*, pp.244-5 and Sir E. A. Wallis Budge, *A History of Ethiopia, Nubia & Abyssinia: Volume I*, p.105.

[80] Derek A. Welsby, *The Medieval Kingdoms of Nubia*, pp.245-6.

[81] Chancellor Williams, *The Destruction of Black Civilization*, p.152.

[82] Ibid., pp.152-3 and Derek A. Welsby, *The Medieval Kingdoms of Nubia*, pp.246-7.

[83] Derek A. Welsby, *The Medieval Kingdoms of Nubia*, pp.248-9.

[84] Ibid., pp.254-5 and Y. F. Hasan and B.A. Ogot, *The Sudan, 1500-1800*, in *UNESCO General History of Africa: Volume V*, ed B. A. Ogot, US, Heinemann, 1992, p.172.

[85] Chancellor Williams, *The Destruction of Black Civilization*, pp.149-50.

CHAPTER SEVENTEEN: SOUTHERN AFRICA

Great Zimbabwe

Great Zimbabwe is an important ruined city in southern Africa. Its megalithic fortress-like ruins, twelve buildings spread over three square miles, are impressive. Built of granite bricks that lock together without mortar, some of the walls are 35 feet high and 17 feet thick in places. Their floors were constructed from cement made of crushed granite. There were numerous drains and dadoes.[1] At its height in the fourteenth century AD, the city "was as big as mediaeval London" accommodating 18,000 people.[2] The name Zimbabwe is derived from the Shona *Zimba Oye* meaning Great Revered House.[3]

Historians and Archaeologists traditionally designate the most notable of the twelve buildings as the 'Temple' - famous for its conical tower in the lower valley, and the 'Acropolis' - the turreted castle structure on the overlooking hill. Mr J. Theodore Bent, an English scholar, was an early excavator of the site, working there in 1891. His *The Ruined Cities of Mashonaland* recount his impressions on visiting this city. Clearly overwhelmed by the experience, he described the "labyrinthine character of the interior" referring to the Temple:

> Entering from the northern portal, we at once plunge into its intricacies. The great and astounding feature is the long narrow passage leading direct from the main entrance to the sacred enclosure, so narrow in parts that two people cannot walk abreast, whilst on either side of you rise the stupendous walls, thirty feet in height, and built with such evenness of courses and symmetry that as a specimen of the dry builder's art it is without a parallel.[4]

The use of dry stone walling and crushed granite cement has proved to be an excellent choice "vindicated by the fact that many of its walls still stand while elsewhere, cemented masonry has succumbed to the fear of time".[5] Reconstructing the early history of this city has been difficult though, as Mr Bent clearly explained:

> Vainly one tries to realise what it must have been like in the days before ruin fell upon it, with its tortuous and well-guarded approaches, its walls bristling with monoliths and round towers, its temple decorated with tall, weird-looking birds, its huge decorated bowls, and in the innermost recesses its busy gold producing-furnace. What was this life like?[6]

Shona (Zimbabwe). The outer wall of the Temple at Great Zimbabwe. *c.*1335 AD. The outer wall was made from 100,000 tons of granite bricks held together without any use of mortar. (Photo: Ku-Amka Productions).

The cottages within the walls and elsewhere were circular in shape with thatched roofs. Their walls, 12 to 18 inches thick, were made of *daga*. This material was derived from an admixture of clay and gravel. Peter Garlake, a former Senior Inspector of (the) Monuments, described these dwellings in a carefully researched study called *Great Zimbabwe*. We are pleased to quote the following extract from this work:

> The elaborate plans and lavish construction, necessitating abundant material and labour, also exhibited considerable technical proficiency and a virtuosity that achieved almost sculptural effects. The *daga* structures in the Ruins were in fact structural accomplishments of the same order as the masonry walls …
> [Y]et fundamentally they are only developments and refinements of traditions that were almost ubiquitous in the cultures of this area and time. Both reflect a concern for appearance, ostentation, even luxury, achieved regardless of the cost in labour or material.[7]

Unlike many cities, however, Great Zimbabwe did not have standard streets, public squares, or commercial and industrial areas. It was laid out for private domestic purposes to shelter people and livestock. Furthermore, it contained warehouses and shrines. A footpath approached the entrance to each cottage.[8]

In 1902 European treasure hunters discovered a horde of goods from just outside the Temple. The goods were of a startling quantity and variety. Of local manufacture were fifty pounds of iron hoes, golden beads, and a huge quantity of coiled wire of bronze, copper, gold and iron (some were twisted into bracelets). Also found were numerous copper ingots, copper jewellery, iron gongs, stone moulds for copper ingots and large quantities of ivory. In short, the locally made goods were luxury products and insignia of power. Of foreign origins were a Persian bowl, Chinese celadon, Syrian glass, an iron spoon, iron lamp stands, copper chains, bronze hawk bells, cowrie shells, glass beads and a chain of coral.[9] What were these goods doing there? Were they tribute received by the ruler of Great Zimbabwe?

Mr Garlake wrote the following summary of the economic and craft activities at Great Zimbabwe:

> Great Zimbabwe was a centre of crafts and industry. Gold, copper and iron were worked. Crucibles and the tools used in drawing metal into thin wire needed for bangles and bracelets have been found in deposits in the Hill Ruin and in the Elliptical Building. Gold beads, gold wire and thin sheets of gold, used to cover wooden carvings, were found in abundance. Nodules of iron ore were found on the floor of a cave in the Hill Ruin. There were remains of smelting furnaces close by. Soapstone was carved to make flat, wide dishes. Their sides were decorated with carved interwoven cable patterns or friezes of long-horned cattle, zebras or baboons. Monoliths were surmounted by carvings of stylized birds. They represent a sculptural style in the process of formation. It had no apparent antecedents and no issue. Terracotta figurines of cattle are like those from Leopard's Kopje sites. Cotton was spun and presumably woven, to judge from the many spindle whorls cut from potsherds.[10]

Evolution of Southern African Culture

Great Zimbabwe emerged out of cultural developments in south central Africa that date back more than seventeen centuries. At that time, early Iron Age villages flourished in the region. These settlements, typically of one acre or more, were located near to deep soils, probably to pursue agriculture. Archaeologists have recovered pottery, bone fragments and traces of houses. The bone fragments show evidence of hunting wild game. In sites of later date, the fragments tend to show evidence of domesticated cattle. The houses were built of mud and stick with thatched roofs supported by a central pole. They had hardened floors.[11]

The types of skeletons recovered show a gradual population change from the Khoisan type of Negro, typical of Southern Africa, to Negroes more typical of Central or West Africa. The archaeological evidence shows the "slow and

Shona (Zimbabwe). Soapstone carvings of birds. These sculptures decorated Great Zimbabwe's Eastern Temple. From Michael Huxley ed, *The Geographical Magazine, Volume II: No.2* (UK, The Geographical Magazine, December 1935, p.156).

progressive assimilation"[12] of the northerners into the population. The evidence refutes the oft-made charge that the migrating "Bantus" from Central and West Africa exterminated the "Bushmen" of the South - typical of White South African pseudo-historical writing. Professors Oliver and Fagan show that the evidence requires a much more subtle explanation:

> In South Africa, the very evidence of this interaction between hunters and food producers has fostered the illusion that the Bantu, at least, were recent immigrants who arrived in wave upon wave of massive, conquering migrations from the [B]lack north - migrations which were stopped only by the guns of the white commandoes as they approached the eastern frontiers of the Cape Colony during the eighteenth century. It comforted the white colonist of South Africa to think of the Bantu as a migrant warrior, with no more right to the land than the European who had conquered and subjugated him. This, however, is not the picture which emerges … The first lesson that we have to bring to the study of the South African Iron Age is that learned in the regions further north, namely that the beginnings of food production and metallurgy represented, in human terms, an infiltration rather than a conquest. The farmers [i.e. Bantus] came in search of deep, well-watered soils, which were in general not the places favoured by the hunters [i.e. Khoisan]. They established their dominance not by fighting with the hunters, but by living a more settled life in denser communities, so that in any contacts it was the hunters who came to the farmers, and not vice versa. This symbiosis lasted for centuries before the hunters were finally absorbed.[13]

J. Desmond Clark, former Director of the Rhodes-Livingston Museum, uncovered evidence of the earliest known iron-using communities in southern Africa. At Lusu and Machili, two sites in Zambia, Dr Clark conducted systematic excavations. He sent the charcoal samples to Professor W. F. Libby at the University of Chicago, the pioneer of radiocarbon dating. The results, though not perfect (see an earlier chapter) showed that Lusu dated back to 186 BC ± 180 years. Furthermore, Machili dated back to 96 AD ± 212 years. Iron was therefore a part of village life in parts of south central Africa two thousand years ago.[14]

Though not a perfect example, Dr Brian Fagan excavated Isamu Pati, a southern African site that flourished from the seventh through to the thirteenth centuries AD. While Isamu Pati used iron in only the later periods of its history, Fagan's evidence is still instructive in recreating the life of a typical village from this early era:

> The people of Isamu Pati lived in pole and mud houses, which may have been arranged around a central cattle enclosure. They certainly grew sorgum, the carbonised remains of which have been found in the deposit. The presence of grain bins makes it likely that they also grew millet, for sorgum does not store well, whereas millet does. The implements of tillage included iron hoes and light axes, but there was a noticeable scarcity of iron tools, except for the smallest items like arrow-heads and razors. Bush clearing may have been severely restricted by the lack of really strong tools, and cultivation may have been limited to the natural clearings. Even so, gardens may have been more often cultivated with wooden digging-sticks than with iron hoes. Cattle, small stock, dogs and chickens were present from the first, but what is really striking is the persistence of hunting and gathering into the Iron Age economy. A wide range of wild vegetables and fruit was gathered. Hunting was practiced throughout the occupation, the favoured game being small antelope such as the orbi and duiker. In the lowest levels of the site the bones of game animals predominate in the middens. It is only in the later stages that the bones of domestic cattle appear in large numbers.[15]

N. J. van der Merwe excavated sites around Phalaborwa, in the northeast Transvaal. He found abundant evidence of iron and copper mining shafts and furnaces dating from the eighth century AD, at the earliest, through to the nineteenth century.[16]

Other archaeologists excavated Ziwa and Leopard's Kopje - southern African sites associated with gold mining. At Ziwa a distinctive style of pottery flourished that dated to the fourth, ninth and tenth centuries AD. At Leopard's Kopje an early style of pottery (Leopard's Kopje I) was discovered, again, associated with gold mining activities. This pottery dated to the eighth and ninth centuries AD. Professors Oliver and Fagan argue that the fourth century Ziwa date was probably erroneous. They therefore conclude that the same communities that made the Ziwa and Leopard's Kopje I pottery also mined gold between the eighth and tenth centuries AD.[17]

At Leopard's Kopje evidence of a new culture was discovered associated with a new style of pottery (Leopard's Kopje II). The new culture, dating to the tenth and eleventh centuries AD, emerged in south west Zimbabwe and the northern part of South Africa. Bambandyanalo, in South Africa, is the best known site belonging to this culture. The Leopard's Kopje II villages were built near rocky hills and were walled using rough stone walling. The culture produced clay figurines of women, domestic animals and cattle. The human figurines depict features typical of Khoisan women, showing that the Khoisan were a powerful element within this culture. Moreover, the culture was strongly pastoral. Cattle became the currency. Finally, there is evidence of trade links to the Indian Ocean. Among the artefacts recovered were glass beads, thought to have come from the Indian Ocean trade with East Africa.[18] Mr Garlake explained the importance of cattle to this culture:

> [Cattle] would have reinforced and ratified group identity and cohesion. They were probably exchanged as bridewealth. They demonstrated prestige and were a means of creating patronage and obligation. Anthropologists have often speculated that cattle herding can be associated with the start of centralized forms of government. Cattle need wide grazing lands. Often herds are cared for by children and receive little supervision. Inevitably disputes over grazing arise and there are pressures on grazing lands. From these come a need for arbitration and hence for an authority with the power to adjudicate and to enforce its decisions.[19]

In the Transvaal and Orange Free State of South Africa ancient stone buildings "widely occur".[20] A good example is the Uitkomst Culture in the Transvaal, which "had roots in the first millennium A.D."[21] Hundreds of stone-built forts were found in and around the region of Johannesburg. The sheer scale of the evidence may indicate that this region was already a regional capital. Also discovered were eleventh century AD iron smelting furnaces and ancient pottery. Robert Moffat visited the Transvaal in 1829 and noted that the South Africans cultivated kidney beans, millet, pumpkins, sweet reed and watermelons. Of the stone architecture, Moffat informs us that:

> The ruined towns exhibited signs of immense labour and perseverance, every fence being composed of stones, averaging five or six feet high, raised apparently without either mortar, lime or hammer. Everything is circular, from the inner fences which surround each house, to the walls which sometimes encompass the town. The remains of some of the houses ... were large ... the walls of clay with a small mixture of cow-dung, and so well polished that they had the appearance of being varnished. The walls and doorways were neatly ornamented with architraves and cornices. The pillars supporting the roof, in the form of pilasters projecting from the wall and fluted, showed much taste.[22]

Shona (Zimbabwe). The Cone Tower in the Temple at Great Zimbabwe. c.1335 AD. (Photo: Popperfoto).

Stone buildings of this type date back to about 1000 AD. "As one would expect," writes Drs Oliver and Fagan, "the Transvaal building styles resemble those of the early Leopard's Kopje tradition of Rhodesia [i.e. Zimbabwe], and this is believed to be true of the pottery also". Stressing this point, they believe that: "[I]t could well be that the elements of the practice [of stone architecture] were introduced into South Africa from Rhodesia [i.e. Zimbabwe]".[23]

The tradition of stone building in the Zimbabwe region may itself date to any period from the first to the seventh centuries AD. Mr Bent reported that a second century AD Roman coin was found in an abandoned mine in the region.

Other coins from Persia, Rome and Greek-ruled Egypt dating from the second century BC through the sixth century AD, have been recovered from Pemba, on the East African coast. Since life in the Zambesi region is not separable from life on the coast, it implies the birth of a culture in the Zambesi region too. Archaeologists have discovered three pole and *daga* structures built on a stone podium in the Zambesi region. In addition, they found dry stone walling in the same archaeological context. These dated to within the first two-thirds of the first millennium AD. On this evidence, M'Bantu and Supiya conclude that: "[E]ither the Elliptical Building dates from between the 1st and the 7th centuries [AD], or the tradition of stone masonry that created it is that old".[24]

At Manikwene, near the East African coast of Mozambique, there is a stone-built capital site made of limestone bricks. Carbon dates establish that the court flourished from about 1150 to 1600. The products found there included iron gongs, a symbol of power; Chinese blue and white porcelain; glass; golden pellets; and ceramics showing local originality. A key economic mainstay of this site was cattle. Prime beef was highly valued by the dwellers of the site.[25]

The Empire of Munhumutapa

Around the twelfth and thirteenth centuries, an empire emerged - the first in southern Africa. The empire unified the territories associated with the Ziwa culture, Leopard's Kopje I, and also Leopard's Kopje II cultures. Furthermore, the empire managed the commerce of the region. Controlling access to the gold producing regions, they produced a larger array of metal objects, exported gold and ivory to the Indian Ocean and imported glass beads. Zimbabwe was the capital of the empire.[26] By 1085 the Shona built the mighty stone castle on the hilltop. Known today as the Acropolis, this structure gave a panoramic view of the vast plateau.[27] In the valley below, they built the first stone walls of the Temple. Also built were larger and more substantial houses. Finally, archaeologists have found spindle whorls, sure evidence of a textiles industry.[28]

What was the name of this empire? Later sources would call it Munhumutapa (also called Mwenemutapa*)*. Traditions name its first ruler as Mutota and another early ruler as Matope. Each took the imposing title Mutapa (i.e. Emperor). Before the imperial rule of the Mutapas, the kings were just rulers of Great Zimbabwe. One of these was remembered as Chimubatamatosi. Historians usually place all of these men in the fifteenth century AD, but this is certainly a shallow interpretation of the traditions. Dr Stan Mudenge, author of a scholarly work on Munhumutapa, made the following significant point:

> The history of the Mutapa empire from its foundation until about 1490 suffers
> from a lack of accurate dating … It seems that the names of six Mutapas said
> to have succeeded before 1490 are most probably a telescoped version of the

reality. Therefore the achievements often ascribed to such legendary figures as Mutota and Matope may well represent processes of state formation to which a number of other, as yet unknown, Mutapa rulers contributed.[29]

On this basis, we place Mutota in the twelfth or thirteenth centuries AD. Furthermore, we date Chimubatamatosi to an even earlier period but later than 1085. Of Mutota, one traditional story presents him as a Prince of Great Zimbabwe. From there, he led a conquering army through the Shangwe region into Dande to secure a reliable source of salt. Before his death, he imposed authority over the lands of Guruuswa.[30]

Matope, a successor, was the greatest conqueror of the early Mutapas. In a series of campaigns, he conquered the Tavara and Tonga. In addition, he seized the Barwe kingdom. Economic considerations seem to have been paramount. Swahili traders used to sail to the mouth of the Zambezi. Six leagues up stream was the town of King Mongalo. There the Swahili hired *almadias* (i.e. barges) to carry their merchandise along the channel to a trading bazaar. This was located in a large village in Tonga country. There, Swahili and Shona traders met and exchanged goods. In the interior, another famous trading centre was in the land of the Mambara. Here large quantities of copper were traded. The overland trade route with Sofala through Manyika had its own bazaars. In addition to the bazaars, individual Swahilis who travelled throughout the land selling their merchandise facilitated trade. Matope, in imposing a political empire over this network, offered the peace and security that allowed the gold and ivory trade to flourish. The next important phase in the growth of the Mutapa Empire was the inclusion of the lands of Uteve and also Manyika.[31]

Gold ornaments were found buried with important personages at Mapungubwe in South Africa, which could have been a religious centre of the empire. There are reasons to believe that this site was a trading capital in its own right. It was rich in cattle and trade goods. From one of the graves, a golden rhinoceros was recovered, as was a wooden bowl and staff, both covered with sheets of beaten gold. Also found were golden necklaces and fourteenth century AD Chinese celadon dishes.[32] Gold was also buried with important personages at Ingombe Illede in Zambia, which was a trading settlement that specialised in copper production. According to Oliver and Fagan, it is "certain" that both sites have "Zimbabwe-type ruins".[33]

Since there are stone-built forts in the Johannesburg region, Ingombe Illede, and Manikwene, we conclude that the Mutapas held sway from Ingombe Illede in Zambia, to the north, to Johannesburg in South Africa, to the south. The empire ruled as far east as Manikwene in Mozambique, near to the coast of the Indian Ocean. It was already one of the largest empires in Mediæval Africa. Dr Mudenge draws conclusions that are not entirely dissimilar to those that we have drawn. He wrote that:

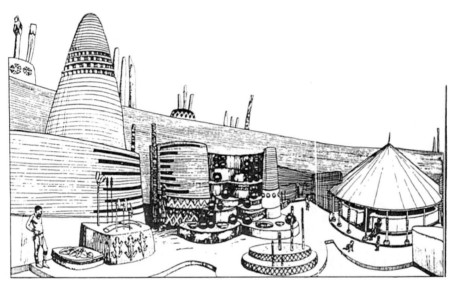

Shona (Zimbabwe). Reconstruction of the interior of the Temple at Great Zimbabwe. Perhaps a total of 18,000 people lived in and around these walls in the 14th century. Incidentally, London, at this time, housed 20,000 people. The only criticism to note here is that the person depicted on the left would appear to have been somewhat underdressed, judging from the old documents (see pages 530-531). Originally published in Peter Garlake, *Life at Great Zimbabwe* (Zimbabwe, Mambo Press, 1982, there are no page numbers in this book). (Sketch: Reproduced with the generous permission of Mambo Press).

Besides the well known Mutapa-related states of Uteve, Barwe and Danda found in Mozambique, there are also less known but equally interesting Shona-related states of the Vhenda, Lobedu and Phalaborwa in the northern Transvaal as well as Gambe's (Manekweni?) [sic] kingdom of Mozambique. In southern Mozambique and north east Transvaal are found the Tsonga-speaking peoples, some of whom not only claim to have Shona origin in their traditions but whose adelphic collateral system of succession demonstrates clearly that they are more related to the Shona than to any other Bantu-speaking people south of the Zambezi or the Limpopo rivers. In the Republic of Botswana are found the Kalanga speaking people whose dialect is accepted as part of Shona and whose history and culture are closely tied to the historic Shona. North of the Zambezi are found people collectively known as Gova who claim and show clear evidence of being related to the Shona. Furthermore, it has been argued that the Zimba of the sixteenth century were in fact a section of the Shona people who crossed north of the Zambezi … [T]here are other ruins clearly related to the Zimbabwe stone culture found outside the country, like Mapungubwe in the northern Transvaal and Manekweni [sic] in southern Mozambique.[34]

Between 1335 and 1450, the city of Zimbabwe was at the height of its wealth and prestige. Much of the capital was rebuilt in a new and highly improved masonry style, following a devastating fire. The walls were built of dressed stones and regular coursing.[35] The walls themselves probably looked as they do now but it must be remembered that there would have been houses within and without of *daga*. Moreover, floors, walkways, and walls were laid in beautiful and polished *daga*. Dr Finch notes that the visual effect of this "must have been dazzling".[36]

Other courts emerged during this period at Chipadze, Lekkerwater, Nhunguza and Ruanga. Like Great Zimbabwe, they were built of stone. They contained the same mix of luxury products and locally produced goods. Cattle continued to be an important part of their economies. Dr Oliver and Atmore tell us that: "It looks very much as if they were the provincial outposts of a Great Zimbabwe kingdom that was expanding its territory northwards during this period".[37]

From the period of Mutapa Mutota, Great Zimbabwe stopped being the administrative capital of the region. The new capital of Munhumutapa was at Mount Fura, much further north. Great Zimbabwe held significance as a cultural and religious centre. Portuguese sources from the seventeenth century AD describe the new capital, but it was then in ruins. Manuel de Faria e Sousa wrote: "In the mountain Afur [i.e. Fura] near Masapa are seen the ruins of stately buildings supposed to be palaces and castles".[38] Dos Santos wrote that: "[O]n the summit of this mountain some fragments of old walls and ancient ruins of stone and mortar are still standing, which clearly show that once there were houses here and strong dwellings".[39] What did the palace look like before ruin came? An eighteenth century geography book provided the following data, which had already been discussed by Dr Olfert Dapper in 1668:

> The inside consists of a great variety of sumptuous apartments, spacious and lofty halls, all adorned with a magnificent cotton tapestry, the manufacture of the country. The floors, cielings [sic], beams and rafters are all either gilt or plated with gold curiously wrought, as are also the chairs of state, tables, benches &c. The candle-sticks and branches are made of ivory inlaid with gold, and hang from the cieling by chains of the same metal, or of silver gilt. The plates; dishes, and bowls belonging to the Emperor's table, are made of a sort of porcelain, curiously wrought on the edges with sprigs of gold resembling those of coral. In short, so rich and magnificent is this palace, that it may be said to vie with that which distinguishes a monarch of the East.[40]

X shaped ingots became the currency of the region. Valuable imports passed through the empire such as Chinese celadon porcelain, Persian glazed wares, fine Indian textiles, and a larger quantity of glass. To pay for this, the empire made luxury products in the form of ornaments and jewellery in gold and

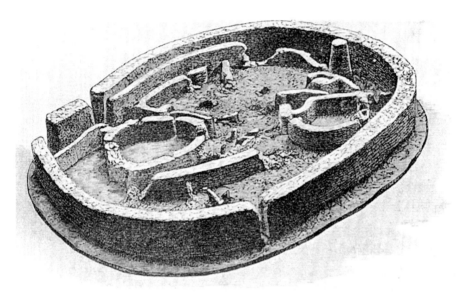

Shona (Zimbabwe). Model of the Great Zimbabwe Temple. _c._1335 AD. From R. N. Hall and W. G. Neal, _Ancient Ruins of Rhodesia: Second Edition_ (UK, Methuen & Co., 1904, opposite p.166).

copper.[41] The early miners of the gold belts displayed great efficiency and industriousness. They exhausted the empire's 4,000 gold mines. A modern scholar wrote that:

> Ancient gold mines greater than 4,000 feet in length and 150 feet deep have been discovered in [the country of] Zimbabwe. The presence of numerous adits driven into the sides of hills testify to the volume of extraction work done. The estimated amount of gold ore mined from the entire region by the ancients was staggering, exceeding 43 million tons. The ore yielded nearly 700 tons of pure gold which today [i.e. 1998] would be valued at over $7.5 billion.[42]

Ian D. Colvin made an equally astonishing observation many years ago:

> The bygone miners must have been industrious beyond belief, since they worked in rock so obdurate that the same sort of reef is nowadays blasted with dynamite, and yet they removed many million tons of ore. It is a practical testimony to their skill that the modern engineers follow to this day the lines of their ancient workings.[43]

The gold workers produced gold thread to weave into cloth, golden chains, golden wire of various gauges, golden beads with fine microscopic chevron decorations, and gold plating to cover objects. They covered statues, arrowheads and battleaxes with beaten gold.[44] At the time of our last visit, the Horniman Museum in London, had exhibits of headrests with the caption: "Headrests have been used in Africa since the time of the Egyptian pharaohs. Remains of some headrests, once covered in gold foil, have been found in the ruins of Great Zimbabwe and burial sites like Mapungubwe dating to the twelfth century after Christ."

In addition, their industries included iron smelting, copper and bronze production, and an ivory trade.[45] The traffic took place on the Indian Ocean, through the Swahili states, particularly though Sofala.[46] Furthermore, they produced ceramics of exceptional quality, distinguished by absolute accuracy and geometric designs. One archaeological find was apparently "worthy of a good period of classic Greek ware".[47] Their soapstone bowls were equally noteworthy and exacting. Bent noted that:

> The work displayed in executing these bowls, the careful rounding of the edges, the exact execution of the circle, the fine pointed tool-marks, and the subjects they chose to depict, point to the race having been far advanced in artistic skill … Seven of these bowls were of exactly the same size, and were 19.2 inches in diameter.[48]

There are enigmatic allusions here and there to the use of a written script among the southern Africans of antiquity. Joao de Barros, a distinguished Portuguese annalist of the mid-sixteenth century, wrote an important description of the southern African culture. He informs us of a fortress in the vassal kingdom of Butua, ruled by a prince called Burrom: "Over the gate of the building is an inscription, which neither the Moorish [i.e. Swahili] traders who were there, nor others learned in inscriptions, could read, nor does anyone know in what character it is written."[49] Another fleeting glimpse suggestive of a script includes the discovery of a hieroglyphic inscription on some rocks at Tete in Mozambique, beside the Zambezi River. It was discovered in 1896 and the text of the inscription was published at the time.[50] Finally, Dr Albert Churchward, author of that profound work *Signs and Symbols of Primordial Man,* drew attention to some important personal communication on this topic:

> Brother Lt.-Col. E. L. de Cordes, 30°, who was in South Africa for three years, informed the writer [i.e. Dr Churchward] that in one of the "Ruins" there is a "stone-chamber," with a vast quantity of Papyri, covered with old Egyptian hieroglyphics. A Boer hunter discovered this, and a large quantity was used to light a fire with, and yet still a larger quantity remained there now.[51]

Scholars have debated the possibility that the builders of Great Zimbabwe possessed highly sophisticated mathematical and astronomical knowledge, in addition to their better known engineering skills. Some writers suggest that the

Temple contains structural features that display mathematical and/or astronomical alignments - as has been claimed for the Great Pyramid of Giza, for example.

Robert M. W. Swan, a mining engineer, began this debate in 1891 with a controversial paper entitled *On the Orientation and Measurements of Zimbabwe Ruins.* Mr J. Theodore Bent included this paper as Chapter V of his *Ruined Cities of Mashonaland.* In the paper, Swan presented measurements and calculations that implied that π was built into the very structure of the Temple.[52] Eighty years later, Peter Garlake rubbished Swan's claims. Garlake reported that nearly all of Swan's measurements were simply wrong or taken from arbitrary places in the ruins.[53] More recently, however, Laurance Doyle in *Encyclopaedia of the History of Science, Technology and Medicine in Non-Western Cultures,* has shown that Garlake's refutation may not be entirely conclusive. Doyle's research has shown that:

> [B]y comparing the oldest maps and photographs it was found that the original ruins have been significantly tampered with [i.e. since Swan's time] - certain smaller towers or pillars having been removed with one, at least, having been added. In addition, some of the internal monoliths have been reseated recently.[54]

For this reason Doyle maintains an open mind on the mathematical question. He does, however, believe that Great Zimbabwe was astronomically aligned. In his view:

> [P]reliminary investigations do reveal that the native African peoples that built Great Zimbabwe were aware of the sky and may indeed have marked important astronomical seasonal events. For example, in a preliminary survey, a "chevron" pattern on the southeast corner of the large outer wall is bisected by the rising position of the Sun on the summer solstice from inside the enclosure, and aligns with what has been called the "altar" as well as an original pillar inside the enclosure. As this large patterning does not appear at any other place on the outer wall it would appear to be a conspicuous candidate for a summer solstice marker built into the Great Enclosure. In addition, a large passageway within the Great Enclosure - about 2 meters in width, 30 or so meters in (curving) length, with 10 meter high brick walls on either side, would allow a limited view of the sky with an angular extent and curvature matching the position and angular extent of the Milky Way overhead on the summer solstice. While the Milky Way was a very important calendrical marker for the Karanga people of this area [who are a part of the Shona] (Sicard 1969, McKosh 1979) this observation too must be confirmed with further research. Finally, from a cleared platform at the top of the Hill Complex, two large stones (approximately 5 meters in height) in close proximity to each other can be seen to form a slit directed precisely east which could have served as a solar marker for the equinoxes.[55]

Doyle does, however, stress that further scholarly verification is required before a definitive conclusion can be made:

> These and other observations are, however, preliminary and a better understanding of the calendrical systems of the early inhabitants of this region would substantially improve further investigations into any astronomical features that may have been built into the ruins at Great Zimbabwe.[56]

Doyle's position receives additional support from an artefact reported in 1906. A recovered platter shows that the Munhumutapans had a zodiac, apparently derived from a West African original. Dr David Randall-Maciver, an early British excavator, speaks of "the wooden platter with bungled figures of the zodiac ... belongs to a class well known to ethnographers as coming from the west coast of Africa".[57] We believe that the zodiac described here, contrary to Dr Maciver, was probably not bungled. It was merely different to the one used by Europeans.

The Portuguese sailed to this region in about 1499. Their chroniclers recorded events from the late fifteenth century AD. In the 1480's Mukombero was on the Munhumutapan throne. The best remembered event during his reign was the revolt of the Changamire of Guruuswa. Changamire Togwa I was originally a chief justice or governor of the Mutapa Empire who owned vast lands. In time, he increased his wealth to such an extent that even Mukombero began to feel threatened. Other favourites of the Emperor also became fearful. They spread rumours that Togwa had ambitions to the imperial throne. Mukombero decided to act. A custom existed whereby if a Mutapa wanted to eliminate a vassal he would send him a bowl of poison. If the vassal wished to comply with the sentence, he was offered time to dress himself in his best attire and then publicly drink the poison. If he refused, however, he would be executed for high treason. Changamire Togwa I refused to comply and instead sent word to the Mutapa that he would be prepared to fight him in war but he preferred a peaceful solution. As a sign of goodwill, he also sent the emperor 4,000 cows and a vast quantity of gold that could fill four water barrels. However, Mukombero would not change his mind and so a battle ensued. Togwa stormed the royal zimbabwe (probably at Mount Fura) and slew the Emperor. Declaring himself the new Mutapa, Togwa ruled peacefully for four years.[58]

In 1493 or 1494 Chikuyo, eldest son of Mukombero, ascended the throne after defeating Togwa I. Chikuyo re-established control over most of the empire. There was, however, intermittent warfare between him and Changamire Togwa II that lasted until the early sixteenth century. By 1515 more problems emerged. The Portuguese Captain of Sofala received an embassy from "a local lord whom they call Ynhamunda [i.e. Nyamunda] and

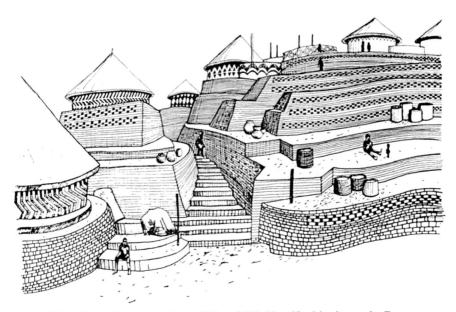

Shona (Zimbabwe). Reconstruction of Khami. We identify this city as the Benemaraxa of the European documents. Again, the people depicted here are somewhat underdressed (see pages 530-531). Originally published in Peter Garlake, *Life at Great Zimbabwe* (Zimbabwe, Mambo Press, 1982, there are no page numbers in this book). (Sketch: Reproduced with the generous permission of Mambo Press).

who has risen against the king of Bonapotapa [i.e. Munhumutapa]." During the wars against Nyamunda, Mutapa Chikuyo faced further revolts from other rulers, Osono and Omboyro. Another Portuguese source says: "The king of Butua [i.e. Guruuswa] … is as great as the king of Menomotapa [i.e. Munhumutapa] and is always at war with him." Besides this picture of turmoil, António Fernandes wrote an account of his journey through the empire that indicates that peace and order prevailed in most of the regions.[59]

Most authorities present the conflict between the Changamires and the Mutapas as a civil war that resulted in the empire forever being split into two. In *Classical Splendour: Roots of Black History,* we assented to this point of view. We now think this is entirely erroneous. To begin with, Changamire Togwa I was a close relative of the Mutapas. Donald Abraham, an important authority, claims that Changamire was a son of Matope and a half brother of Mukombero. Pachecho, another important authority, claims that Mutota himself was of the same family as Changamire. Da Silva suggests that Changamire was a grandee of the court of Mutapa Nembire, who did such outstanding service that he was highly rewarded. The Mutapa gave him his first daughter as wife, some lands in the western part of the kingdom, some nobles and other subjects, as well as "the title of Xangamire [sic]".[60] In addition, both the Portuguese and the Mutapans believed that the Munhumutapa Empire controlled the disputed south western territories of Guruuswa. For example, Dr Mudenge wrote: "Barreto asked [the Mutapa's permission] to be allowed to proceed to the mines of Manyika and Guruuswa". And again: "[T]he Mutapa was not opposed to have Barreto march to the mines of Guruuswa".[61] In addition, all contemporary maps and accounts claim that Munhumutapa controlled nearly as far south as the Cape of Good Hope in South Africa. Duarte Barbosa, for example, reported that: "These Moors of Benematapa say that there is much gold in a country very far situated in the direction of the Cape of Good Hope, in another kingdom which is subjected to this King of Benematapa".[62] Furthermore, one account also indicates that the empire had two great cities - Zimbabwe and Benemaraxa (see pages 52-54). We identify Benemaraxa as the Changamire city of Khami.

Neshangwe became emperor in about 1530. He was faced with the growing menace of the Portuguese. They had replaced the Swahili bazaars along the Zambezi with their own. Additionally, they seized control over the Swahili cities of Quelimane, Sena and Tete. In 1542, however, hostilities had reduced to such an extent that the Mutapa's ambassador could visit Sofala. The lands around Sofala, however, had been devastated by war.[63]

The Portuguese sources provide useful data on the Mutapa Empire. João Dos Santos wrote: "It is common among these [people] to live to ninety and a hundred years of age." Moreover: "Most of these [people] are as black as jet with woolly hair; they are handsome men, especially the Macarangas, who dwell in the lands of Quiteve."[64] Father de Monclaro wrote a valuable decription on the typical modes of dress and hairstyles:

> All of them commonly wear loosely woven cotton cloth … called *machiras* … They wear horn-like headgear as an adornment, being made of their own hair turned back in a strange manner; these horns are in general use in [the region], and provide a good shade. In the middle of the head they make one which draws the hair in a most orderly well-arranged fashion, first making the hair long by means of small pieces of copper or tin which they tie at the end of a few hairs brought together, so that the weight gradually makes them long and not crisp, and thus they go about with their heads covered with these small pieces. Once the hair has grown long, they bring it together in the middle of the head in a fair amount to make a bigger horn, the hair being tied with a certain grass with which they make a very comely thread of a certain length; the tapering end is left untied. Then in most regular fashion they do make other small horns, being very skilful in this; and the women wear many copper rings in their arms and legs, being drawn very fine, and the same they make with gold, which is extremely fine and with this thread they make these rings.[65]

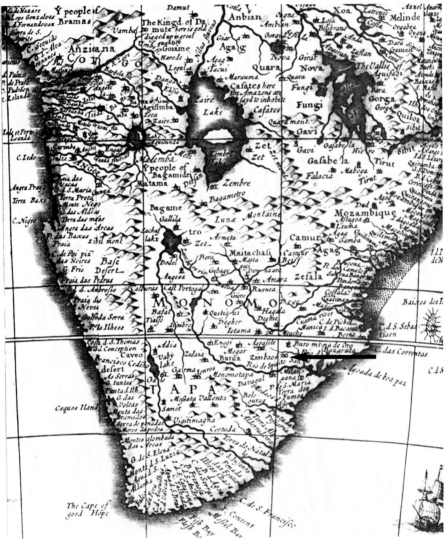

John Speed drew this map of Africa in 1627. It was the first map of Africa published in England. Notice the huge territory assigned to the Empire of Monomotapa (i.e. Munhumutapa). Notice also that *Zimbaos* (see arrow) is Great Zimbabwe.

Father Gomes, another of the Portuguese archival sources, tells us that:

> The people dress in various ways: at court and *Zimboôe* [sic] of the Kings their grandees wear cloths of rich silk, damask, satin, gold and silk cloth; these are three widths of satin, each width four *covados* [2.64m], each sewn to the next, sometimes with gold lace in between, trimmed on two sides, like a carpet, with

a gold and silk fringe, sewn in place with a two fingers' wide ribbon, woven with gold roses on silk - a very well made thing manufactured by the [people] themselves ... These cloths are worn from the waist down the right side trailing along the floor and the left just down to the knee. Others dress in cotton cloth with coloured stripes, black being their favourite colour. Of all the women, the Mocranga [sic] are the ones who dress best, the cloth coming down to one *palmo* above the feet; that part of the leg showing is covered with bright copper bands. At some other places where they do not have so much cloth, the men wear skins, one in front, one at the back, and the women dress in a very short cloth and those who do not have one wear a piece of threshed bark that becomes cinnamon coloured and is as soft as cloth and woven by nature as if it were cloth. In other places the men wear skins and the women a little net made of coloured beads and nothing else ... Elephant hunters and their wives dress in the stomachs of the animals they kill, very nice grey cloth which, divided in two, is enough for two people and is so soft that it feels like satin.[66]

The smallest social unit was the *imba* or nuclear family. Each family owned and worked its own gardens and lived in its own distinct compound of a village. The man, or father of the house, owned the largest garden where he grew the major crops of millet, rice, beans and, after the sixteenth century, maize. In addition, there were other gardens belonging to the wife (sometimes wives) and older unmarried children, both males and females. These were smaller in size and could only be tended to after the family garden had been done. The wife usually grew groundnuts, peanuts, pumpkins, beans, cucumbers, yams and some grain crops.[67]

Above this was the village. The village head was the most senior male member of the family that founded the village. If a man wanted help in weeding his gardens, threshing his grain or building a house, his wife would brew beer and then invite the village to a work party. Hunting and fishing were often done as co-operative efforts. Elephants were hunted for their flesh and ivory. Each night the men of the village would meet at the *dare* or village assembly. Every mature man had this right but women were excluded. The *dare* was both a village assembly and a village court and it could impose fines but only for minor offences.[68]

A number of villages formed a ward under a *sadunhu*. The boundaries of a ward were clearly defined. The headquarters of a *sadunhu* was normally a fairly large village or town. At this *dare,* the procedures were more formal.[69]

Above the *sadunhus* were the *madzishe* or kings. Some of these kings preferred to be addressed as *Madzimbabwe* (i.e. He that dwelleth in a zimbabwe). The *madzishe* were the *reis* (kings) of the Portuguese documents. The headquarters and residence of such a ruler were sizeable settlements called *muzinda*. The sizes of kingdoms varied greatly from 30 kilometres to 90 kilometres in length and width. A king had legislative as well as judicial powers which he exercised in consultation with his *dare*. A *madzishe* was chosen, invested and crowned in accordance with the practices of his kingdom by the emperor. He derived his income from a number of sources, such as judicial fees, labour, and tribute. These could be paid either in cattle, grain, gold, hoes or other such valuables. Any hunter who killed an elephant had to pay the tusk if it touched the ground. Skins of royal animals such as lions, leopards and similar animals had to be handed over to the king. The provincial kings built courts for themselves and maintained their own bodyguards and musicians.[70]

At the imperial court, routine matters of state were dealt with by the council (*dare*) made up of the immediate advisors of the Mutapa. He personally chose these men on his accession. Counted among them were the Governor of the Provinces, Captain General of the Armies, Chief Major domo, Chief Musician, Captain of the Vanguard in times of war, Deputy of Mutapa, Chief Doorkeeper, Chief Wizard and also the Emperor's Apothecary. In addition, there were many other officers of lower rank. Some of the wives had specific duties related to foreign relations. The most important posts included Chief Minister and Governor of the Provinces. He was the contact point at court for provincial rulers when they or their representatives visited the imperial court. There were also bodyguards, musicians, dancers and jesters, pages, valets, cooks, and the royal wives. Damiac de Goes says: "The said king [i.e. Mutapa] uses two insignia, one being a small hoe with an ivory point [i.e. handle], which he always wears in his girdle to show his subjects that they should cultivate and profit by the land, so that they may live in peace on what they obtain from it, without taking another's property; the other consist of two assegais, showing that with one the king administers justice and with the other defends his people".[71]

The Mutapa had a standing army of 100,000 men but he could mobilise 300,000 should the need arise. Additionally, he had 5,000 or 6,000 Amazons (i.e. female soldiers). Munhumutapa, while not militaristic in character, possessed a strong military structure to defend itself and also to enforce authority over a vast area. Demonstrating this is the fact that houses of ordinary people needed no doors, because: "They say that houses are built with doors for fear of thieves and malefactors, from whom it is the king's duty to protect his people, and above all the poor". Putting of doors at the entrance of houses was a privilege granted by the Mutapa to a few nobles.[72]

The wealth enjoyed at the imperial court was derived from agriculture, pastoral activities, trade, mining, hunting, tribute, taxation, presents, craft specialisms and industries. The dominant economic activity was, of course, agriculture. The second source of economic power was pastoralism - especially cattle. For trading purposes gold continued to be of importance. According to the Portuguese, the Shona could tell where gold was to be found by observing soil types and vegetation. Elephant hunting, according to de Barros and Goes, resulted in 4,000 or 5,000 elephants being slaughtered each year, producing 10,000 to 25,000 tonnes of meat. Tolls and tariffs were imposed and collected from foreign traders. In addition to the above sources of income, the Mutapas received presents from traders as well as from their subjects who visited their zimbabwes. Textiles were an important craft industry. They weaved threads of imported cloth together with locally produced cotton so as to produce cloths of rich silk, damask, and satin laced with gold. Finally, boat building increased as more *almadias* were needed to carry trade goods up and down the river.[73] Tribute, taxation, judicial fees and presents were other sources of royal income. "Every year", says a Portuguese source, "the vassal kings of the Emperor are obliged to send their sons to him as ambassadors with presents of gold, ivory, slaves, cattle, sheep and small livestock." But "The Emperor ... also sends the latter a present of some items of cloth of high quality and orders the ambassador to be given some clothes for him to wear".[74]

What did they do with the money? Most of this went to the Mutapa and his immediate family. Some of it also went to social security. According to Bocarro:

> [The Mutapa] shows great charity to the blind and maimed, for these are called the king's poor, and have land and revenues for their subsistence, and when they wish to pass through the kingdoms, wherever they come food and drinks are given to them at the public cost as long as they remain there, and when they leave that place to go to another they are provided with what is necessary for their journey, and a guide, and some one to carry their wallet to the next village. In every place where they come there is the same obligation, under penalty that those who fail therein shall be punished by the king.[75]

Father da Silveira was a Portuguese zealot belonging to the Society of Jesus. In his writings, he lamented about some Africans being "corrupted by the infernal sect of Mohamed [sic] and even mixed with the pestilential Jews." Da Silveira saw his chief mission as converting the Mutapa. Moreover, if he converted the Mutapa and his people, then the Christians would dominate the trade of lower Zambezia. He arrived at the zimbabwe of Mutapa Negomo on 1 January 1561. Negomo received him well and offered him gold, land, cattle, and women as presents. Da Silveira, however, politely turned these down, explaining that what he sought was the conversion of the Mutapa himself. Within a month of his arrival at the Mutapa's court, da Silveira baptised Negomo, giving him the name Dom Sebastião. The Queen Mother was given the name Doña Maria. Very soon he converted and baptised between 250 and 300 people of high rank.[76]

The Swahili, especially Mingame, an Islamic teacher, probably watched all of this with misgivings. Some of the court dignitaries who refused to be baptised felt equally threatened by da Silveira's religious influence. On 15 March 1561 the Portuguese zealot was killed. He died at the Mutapan court. This raised the question: Who did it? Professor Chancellor Williams, as usual, seemed to have glimpsed the bigger picture:

> [It] was just what the Portuguese needed as a reason for open intervention with eventual Portuguese sovereignty over the entire region. It was an old trick, well known and practised by the secret agents of great powers: To sacrifice one's own fellow citizens in a foreign land, if by so doing, the larger ends of the state might be served. The Portuguese version that the priest's death was "engineered by the Muhammadans of Mozambique" may or may not have been true. The Portuguese themselves may have done it.[77]

Two or three days after da Silveira's death, Portuguese traders came to Negomo and warned him that Portugal was bound to send an army to avenge his death. They even had the audacity to claim that as da Silveira was a servant of God, Negomo should expect that God should punish him for ordering da Silveira's death.[78]

The Jesuit Society sent two more members to continue da Silveira's work, but they were hindered from proceeding to Munhumutapa and had to return to Goa in India. Meanwhile in Portugal, the Jesuit lobby began to campaign for more activist policies in Angola and Munhumutapa. Many were now advocating evangelisation through sword and fire. The King of Portugal agreed. He appointed Francisco Barreto, a former governor of India and friend of da Silveira, to lead the invasion. The chief motive behind the expedition was to seize "the abundance of the wealth" in Munhumutapa. Da Silveira's death was merely the excuse given. Sousa, a Portuguese writer, recorded that: "The great inducement to this conquest was the information and experience of the vast quantity of gold found, particularly at Manyika in the kingdom of Makaranga".[79]

The invading fleet arrived at Sena on 17 December 1571. They bought native cattle as provisions and also to draw their carts. However, many of these animals died soon after they arrived. Father Monclaro, a Portuguese clergyman in the invading party, felt the Swahili must have poisoned them. In addition, some horses and also soldiers died. Monclaro ascribed these deaths to poison. The clergyman had a young Swahili stable hand beaten and tortured until he confessed to the existence of a poison plot. The Portuguese response was swift as it was brutal. They massacred the Swahilis at Sena and confiscated 15,000 *maticals* of gold.[80] The Portuguese slaughtered the Swahilis in the most gruesome of ways. Monclaro recorded that some were:

slain with strange inventions. Some were impaled alive, others tied to trees in the extreme branches thereof, the branches being forcibly brought together and then released, the victim being thus rent asunder. Others still were cut up with axes from the back, others with bombards ... others were delivered up to the soldiers, who had their sport by shooting them with arquebuses.[81]

On 19 July 1572 Barreto's army left Sena for the interior, while over 20 canoes sailed up the river loaded with provisions, merchandise and ammunition. Barreto's first target was the Samungazi Tonga, who were accused of having maltreated Portuguese traders in the past. The Portuguese won an indecisive victory over them. The Samungazi lost between 4,000 and 6,000 men and many others were injured. They promised to be vassals of the Portuguese in future if Barreto refrained from burning their land. After Barreto returned to Sena, Mutapa Negomo sent a powerful embassy to negotiate with him. The embassy stated its mission as being that (i) Mutapa Negomo wanted to be a friend of the king of Portugal, (ii) he intended to clear the "thorns" between his people and the Portuguese, and (iii) he wanted continuation of trade with the Portuguese. Barreto replied by asking Negomo to expel the remaining Swahili and to allow Portuguese priests to return to his Empire. In addition, he required that the Emperor promise that he himself would keep the faith as well as to hand over the gold mines to the Portuguese. The two sides then exchanged presents. The Mutapa sent eight arm and leg bracelets of gold, of very fine thread weighing less than 10 *maticals*. In return, Barreto sent the Mutapa goods worth 6,000 *cruzados,* which was equivalent to Barreto's yearly salary.[82]

Barreto died in May 1573 and was succeeded by Vasco Homem. Homem started to recruit new men for the conquest of the gold mines. In 1574 he commenced his expeditions through Uteve to Manyika kingdom. In the next few years, he made significant inroads in Muhumutapa. Initially, kingdom after kingdom fell and pledged their loyalty to the Portuguese crown. Eventually however, Mutapa Negomo dispatched a force of 100,000 men to engage Homem. Faced with such an overwhelming force, the Portuguese withdrew. The Barreto-Homem debacle came to an end on 13 March 1577.[83]

Surprisingly, trade between the Portuguese and Munhumutapa continued peacefully after the Barreto-Homem expedition. In the 1580's, the Portuguese established market places on the Zimbabwe highlands at Masapa, Ruhanje and Bukutu. Commercial intercourse between the Portuguese and the Mutapa Empire increased considerably.[84]

Gatsi Rusere ascended the imperial throne between 1586 and 1589. During his 34 or so years, much of the Empire fell apart. In 1597 he was faced with the problems of the Zimba and Mumbo. They invaded south of the Zambezi and started occupying lands in the gold producing regions. The Mutapa responded. He mobilised his forces and chose the Governor of the Provinces to be its commanding officer. On hearing of these preparations, the invaders retreated but practised a scorched earth policy. This forced the imperial army to give up the chase for want of provisions. Gatsi Rusere, when he was told of how the invaders escaped, ordered the Governor of the Provinces to be put to death. This act triggered a civil war which led to him being deposed. To regain his throne, he was forced to rely on Portuguese support. The Mutapa rewarded his Portuguese allies well on 1 August 1607. He offered them all the mines of gold, silver, copper, iron, lead and pewter to be found in his Empire. After signing the above document, the composite Gatsi Rusere-Portuguese forces successfully crushed the rebellion. Following this, many provincial rulers pledged their loyalty to Gatsi Rusere. Portuguese relations with Gatsi, however, deteriorated. On 10 August 1613 Madeira left Sena with an army to go and occupy the silver mines of Chikova. Gatsi mobilised 9,000 or 10,000 men and ambushed Madeira. However, much of the empire fell apart during these battles. By far the biggest loss was the breakaway of the kingdom of Barwe, which drastically reduced the size of the Mutapa Empire. The Manyika Kingdom, closely related to Barwe in origin, also ceded from the empire. From 1618 until his death around 1623 Gatsi Rusere was merely the ruler of the kingdom of Mukaranga rather than ruler of an empire.[85]

By 1624 Kapararidze inherited the throne of a much-diminished Munuhumutapa. His rise to power was not uncontroversial. Many thought the throne should have gone to the rival house of Mavhura. During his time, the Portuguese introduced the *prazo* system whereby significant quantities of land were handed over to individual Portuguese officials. Meanwhile, Mavhura, the rival, became close to the Portuguese Dominicans. The Emperor was alarmed at this development and moved to nip it in the bud. On 17 November 1628 he ordered the death of the Portuguese ambassador. When reports of this death reached Portuguese controlled Tete and Sena, the Portuguese mobilised an army. Other anti-Kapararidze forces mobilised and declared Mavhura to be the rightful Mutapa. At Masapa, however, Kapararidze's army awaited Mavhura and his allies. During the battle, the Mutapa was defeated and was forced to withdraw with heavy losses. The Mavhura-Portuguese forces stormed the imperial zimbabwe and looted it. The victors held a victory mass at a little church dedicated to Our Lady of the Rosary. Mavhura was declared Emperor of Munhumutapa in May 1629.[86]

The Portuguese, however, required the new ruler to sign a treaty of vassalage to the Portuguese crown. The treaty made it clear that (i) Mavhura received the throne in the name of the King of Portugal; (ii) the Portuguese were to be allowed complete freedom to convert any Munhumutapan to Christianity; (iii) expel all the Swahili from his dominions within one year and to allow all those who remain to be killed and their property confiscated by the Portuguese; (iv) to allow Portuguese ambassadors to enter his zimbabwe in full armour and speak to him seated on a chair without clapping their hands; (v) to treat all other Portuguese as if they were ambassadors; (vi) to consult with the Captain of Masapa, a Portuguese official, on matters of war and peace; (vii) to search and reveal the existence of silver mines to the Captain of Masapa. Finally, (viii) he was to allow Tete to annex the lands surrounding it so that they could be used by the Portuguese crown. Moreover, Mavhura, his queen and four or five nobles were baptised by the Portuguese. Mavhura was given the name Dom Filippe and his Queen that of Doña Giovanna.[87]

The Treaty of 1629 represented the death of the Munhumutapa Empire. Through the rest of the seventeenth century, the Portuguese gained control over more and more land. With this control came increased political power and the spread of mass enslavement. The Portuguese enslaved many of the Mutapa's subjects without a just cause, an act regarded as a great outrage. Compounding the problem, the Portuguese not only enslaved ordinary people but even the sons and daughters of the nobility.[88]

Let us close this section by giving the final word to Professor Cheikh Anta Diop. He provided a brilliant overview of thousands of years of African continuity:

> African history proceeded without interruption. The first Nubian dynasties were prolonged by the Egyptian dynasties until the occupation of Egypt by the Indo-Europeans, starting in the fifth century BC. Nubia remained the sole source of culture and civilisation until about the sixth century AD., and then Ghana seized the torch from the sixth century until 1240, when its capital was destroyed by Sundiata Keita. This heralded the launching of the Mandingo Empire [i.e. Mali] ... Next came the empire of Gao [i.e. Songhai], the empire of Yatenga [in today's Burkina Faso] ... and the kingdoms of the Djoloff and Cayor [in Senegal] destroyed by Faidherbe under Napoleon III. In listing this chronology, we wanted to show that there was no interruption in African history. It is evident that, if starting from Nubia and Egypt, we had followed a continental geographical direction, such as Nubia - Gulf of Benin, Nubia - Congo, Nubia - Mozambique, the course of African history would still have appeared to be uninterrupted. This is the perspective in which the African past should be viewed.[89]

Notes

[1] F. M. C. Stokes, *Zimbabwe,* in *The Geographical Magazine, Volume II: No.2,* ed Michael Huxley, UK, The Geographical Magazine, December 1935, p.143.
[2] David Dugan, *Time Life's Lost Civilizations,* video series, *Africa, A History Denied,* Holland, Time Life Video, 1995.

[3] Anu M'Bantu and Fari Supiya, *The Elliptical Building: Master builders of Zimbabwe*, in *West Africa, Issue No. 4300*, UK, 5-11 November 2001, p.43.

[4] J. Theodore Bent, *The Ruined Cities of Mashonaland*, UK, Longmans, Green and Co., 1902, pp.110-1.

[5] Anu M'Bantu and Fari Supiya, *The Elliptical Building: Master builders of Zimbabwe*, in *West Africa, Issue No. 4300*, p.43.

[6] J. Theodore Bent, *The Ruined Cities of Mashonaland*, p.132.

[7] Peter Garlake, *Great Zimbabwe*, UK, Thames and Hudson, 1973, p.119.

[8] Peter Garlake, *The Kingdoms of Africa*, UK, Elsevier Phaidon, 1978, p.77 and Nnamdi Elleh, *African Architecture: Evolution and Transformation*, US, McGraw-Hill, 1997, p.209.

[9] Peter Garlake, *The Kingdoms of Africa*, pp.78-9 and Molefi Asante and Kariamu Asante, *Great Zimbabwe: An Ancient African City-State*, in *Blacks in Science*, ed Ivan Van Sertima, US, Transaction Publishers, 1983, pp.90-1.

[10] Peter Garlake, *The Kingdoms of Africa*, p.78.

[11] Roland Oliver and Brian Fagan, *Africa in the Iron Age*, UK, Cambridge University Press, 1975, p.94.

[12] Ibid., p.94.

[13] Ibid., pp.106-7.

[14] Ibid., pp.94-5.

[15] Ibid., p.99.

[16] Ibid., p.109.

[17] Ibid., pp.102-3.

[18] Ibid., pp.103 and 204.

[19] Peter Garlake, *The Kingdoms of Africa*, p.71.

[20] Roland Oliver and Brian Fagan, *Africa in the Iron Age*, p.110.

[21] Ibid.

[22] Quoted in ibid., pp.110-12.

[23] Roland Oliver and Brian Fagan, *Africa in the Iron Age*, p.112.

[24] Anu M'Bantu and Fari Supiya, *The Elliptical Building: Master builders of Zimbabwe*, in *West Africa, Issue No. 4300*, p.43.

[25] Roland Oliver and Anthony Atmore, *Medieval Africa: 1250 - 1800*, UK, Cambridge University Press, 2001, pp.199-200 and Peter Garlake, *The Kingdoms of Africa*, pp.81-2.

[26] Roland Oliver and Brian Fagan, *Africa in the Iron Age*, pp.204-5.

[27] Charles Finch, *The Star of Deep Beginnings*, US, Khenti, 1998, p.149.

[28] Roland Oliver and Brian Fagan, *Africa in the Iron Age*, pp.204-5.

[29] S. I. G. Mudenge, *A Political History of Munhumutapa c1400-1902*, Zimbabwe, Zimbabwe Publishing House, 1988, pp.37-8.

[30] Ibid., p.38.

[31] Ibid., pp.40-5.

[32] Roland Oliver and Brian Fagan, *Africa in the Iron Age*, pp.205-7, Roland Oliver and Anthony Atmore, *Medieval Africa: 1250 - 1800*, pp.200 and 202, Peter Garlake, *The Kingdoms of Africa*, p.72 and Werner Gillon, *A Short History of African Art*, UK, Penguin, 1984, p.343.

[33] Roland Oliver and Brian Fagan, *Africa in the Iron Age*, pp.205-7 and Roland Oliver and Anthony Atmore, *Medieval Africa: 1250 - 1800*, pp.200 and 202.

[34] S. I. G. Mudenge, *A Political History of Munhumutapa c1400-1902*, pp.23-5.

[35] Roland Oliver and Brian Fagan, *Africa in the Iron Age*, pp.205-6.

[36] Charles Finch, *The Star of Deep Beginnings*, p.151.

[37] Roland Oliver and Anthony Atmore, *Medieval Africa: 1250 - 1800*, pp.202-3.

[38] Quoted in David Randall-Maciver, *Mediæval Rhodesia*, US, Negro Universities Press, 1969 (original 1906), p.92

[39] Quoted in ibid.

[40] Quoted in K. M. Keynon, *Sketch of the Exploration and Settlement of the East Coast of Africa*, in *The Zimbabwe Culture*, G. Caton-Thompson, UK, The Clarendon Press, 1931, pp.271-2.

[41] Roland Oliver and Brian Fagan, *Africa in the Iron Age*, p.206, and Roland Oliver and Anthony Atmore, *Medieval Africa: 1250 - 1800*, pp.202 and 206.

[42] Charles Finch, *The Star of Deep Beginnings*, p.50.

[43] Ian D. Colvin, *Zimbabwe's Ruins of Mystery*, in *Wonders of the Past, Volume 2*, ed Sir J. A. Hammerton, UK, Amalgamated Press, 1937, p.969.

[44] Charles Finch, *The Star of Deep Beginnings*, p.51.

[45] Peter Garlake, *Great Zimbabwe*, pp.113-7 and P. C. Mazikana & I. J. Johnstone, Zimbabwe Epic, Zimbabwe, National Archives of Zimbabwe, 1982, pp.28-9.

[46] Cheikh Anta Diop, *Precolonial Black Africa*, US, Lawrence Hill Books, 1987, p.136.

[47] J. Theodore Bent, *The Ruined Cities of Mashonaland*, p.206.

[48] Ibid., p.196.

[49] Joao De Barros, *Da Asia*, quoted in *The Ruined Cities of Mashonaland, 3rd Edition*, by J. Theodore Bent, p.238.

[50] P. Diagne, *History and Linguistics*, in *UNESCO General History of Africa, Volume I*, ed J. Ki-Zerbo, UK, Heinemann, 1981, p.252.

[51] Albert Churchward, *The Signs and Symbols of Primordial Man*, 2nd Edition, UK, George Allen & Co., 1913, p.75.

[52] J. Theodore Bent, *The Ruined Cities of Mashonaland*, pp.141-178.

[53] Peter Garlake, *Great Zimbabwe*, pp.68-9.

[54] Laurance R. Doyle, *Astronomy of Africa in Encyclopaedia of the History of Science, Technology and Medicine in Non-Western Cultures*, internet article, http://www.safaris.cc/8art.encyclo.htm.

[55] Ibid.

[56] Ibid.

[57] David Randall-Maciver, *Mediæval Rhodesia*, pp.93-4.

[58] S. I. G. Mudenge, *A Political History of Munhumutapa c1400-1902*, pp.47-9.

[59] Ibid., pp.49-55.

[60] Ibid., p.72.

[61] Ibid., pp.209 and 212.

[62] Quoted in The Hon. A. Wilmot, *Monomotapa*, UK, T. Fisher Unwin, 1896, p.138

[63] S. I. G. Mudenge, *A Political History of Munhumutapa c1400-1902*, pp.55-6.

[64] João Dos Santos, *Ethiopia Oriental*, quoted in S. I. G. Mudenge, *A Political History of Munhumutapa c1400-1902*, pp.30 and 36.

[65] Quoted in S. I. G. Mudenge, *A Political History of Munhumutapa c1400-1902*, p.29.

[66] Quoted in ibid., pp.199-200.

[67] S. I. G. Mudenge, *A Political History of Munhumutapa c1400-1902*, pp.9-10.

[68] Ibid., pp.12-4.

[69] Ibid., pp.14-5.

[70] Ibid., pp.18-20.

[71] Ibid., pp.85-113.

[72] Ibid., pp.134 and 154.

[73] Ibid., pp.161-187.

[74] Ibid., pp.188-9.

[75] Quoted in ibid., p.192.

[76] S. I. G. Mudenge, *A Political History of Munhumutapa c1400-1902*, pp.63-5.

[77] Chancellor Williams, *The Destruction of Black Civilization*, US, Third World Press, 1987, pp.285-6.

[78] S. I. G. Mudenge, *A Political History of Munhumutapa c1400-1902*, pp.65-8.

[79] Ibid., pp.201 and 203.

[80] Ibid., pp.203-8.

[81] Quoted in ibid., p.209.

[82] S. I. G. Mudenge, *A Political History of Munhumutapa c1400-1902*, pp.209-217.

[83] Ibid., pp.217-221.

[84] Ibid., pp.222-3.

[85] Ibid., pp.224-243.

[86] Ibid., pp.245 and 253-8.

[87] Ibid., pp.258-262.

[88] Ibid., pp.266-275.

[89] Cheikh Anta Diop, *The African Origin of Civilization: Myth or Reality?* US, Lawrence Hill Books, 1974, pp.147-8.

CHAPTER EIGHTEEN: THE FALL OF AFRICA AND THE RESISTANCE

The Migrations

We have made frequent allusions to the research of Professor Chancellor Williams, author of *The Destruction of Black Civilization.*[1] In this work he presented a theory that much of African culture had spread across the continent from a single source. According to Dr Williams, the Nile region of Ancient Egypt and Nubia were once the most densely populated parts of Africa. When Caucasians invaded these countries, the indigenous peoples fled to avoid being captured, colonised or enslaved. They left their homelands and fled south to safer pastures. This is why Negroes are a minority in North Africa today. The Professor suggests that many themes in African history, past and present, happy and sad, are to be found in an analysis of the invasions and the subsequent migrations of peoples.[2] It should be noted that Africans had suffered slavery and destruction even before the West African experience of the last five hundred years. Following Dr Williams, it is possible to show that the twin themes of the spread of African culture from its ancient source, and the tragic destruction and degeneration of that culture are linked.

We have mentioned the Roman, Vandal (i.e. German), and Arabian invasions of North Africa. All three groups treated the indigenous Africans with a cruel hostility, destroying and enslaving many. The Africans had three main options: they could resist, and be destroyed by superior arms; they could submit, and be absorbed and possibly enslaved; or they could migrate elsewhere, creating refugee problems.

Professor Williams describes the migrations as a great human tragedy. People in retreat before the slave traders often fled to some of the most inhospitable places they could find. Some took to the hills, others to the swamps, and others to the caves. Under these extreme circumstances, their culture degenerated, often to the level of savagery. If organised enslavement and violence continued over generations, whole communities would know no other life other than the hills, the caves, or the swamps. There were other consequences. Small communities, cut off from all others for generations, soon developed their own dialects and languages. This is the root cause of the hundreds of dialects spoken today, even over small geographical areas. Moreover, a mentality of distrust of others developed among these fragmented and isolated communities, often caused by Blacks and people of mixed ancestry being used by the invaders to do the slave raids. As communities saw their own people acting against them, they increasingly saw other Black groups as 'traditional enemies' to be blamed and mistrusted for generations. Thus the combination of the migrations, communities being raided by Black and Mixed-Race groups, the birth of new dialects and languages, a mentality of distrust and exclusivity, and the cultural decline of millions into savagery, are the basic reasons for the tribalism and political instability of modern Africa.

North Africa was the first region of the continent to suffer in this way. The Persian invasion of Egypt in 525 BC was particularly fateful. From that date until the present, Egypt has never been free of foreign control. The Romans enslaved 50,000 Africans following their conquest of Carthage in 146 BC.[3] The Vandal conquest of the region in the fifth century of our era was one of the worst. Their destructiveness is difficult to believe. Far more devastating, however, in terms of the scale of the genocide against the Africans, was the Roman re-conquest of 533 AD. Emperor Justinian reasoned that: "God has given us … to subdue the Vandals, Alans, and Moors and to recover the whole of [Roman] Africa and Sicily, and we have good hope that the Lord will grant us the rest of the Empire." With 500 ships and a force of 10,000 infantry and 5,000 cavalry, his forces marched on the Carthage region. Procopius, an official chronicler on the staff of the invading general, recorded that: "In estimating the territory that he [i.e. Emperor Justinian] depopulated, I should say that millions perished. For Libya … was so thoroughly ruined that for a traveller who makes a long journey there it is no easy matter to meet a human being."[4]

By the eighth century AD the Arabs were the new masters of North Africa and their enslavement activities are continuing. Even today, the enslavement of Africans continues in Mauritania and the Sudan at the hands of the White Berbers and the Arabs.[5] Iraq was a slave state in the Middle Ages. Africans that were captured and deported there were compelled to dig salt marshes in and around Basra. Between the seventh and the ninth centuries AD, they rebelled 3 times. In 868-883 AD there was the famous Revolt of the Zanj. Thousands on both sides were killed in the rebellion. During this period, the Zanj built a capital of their own called Moktara, meaning the Elect City. In the early ninth century AD, a highly distinguished Black Arab scholar, called Al-Jahiz, felt compelled to write *The Book of the Glory of the Blacks Over the Whites* to counter rising anti-Black prejudices by the light-skinned Arabs. Of the notable Africans captured by the Arabs were Dhu 'l-Nun al-Misri, an Upper Egyptian who founded Sufism (i.e. mystical Islam). Another famous captive was Malik Ambar. This great man became Prime Minister of Ahmadnagar in India between 1607 and 1626.[6]

The Kanem-Borno Empire was much engaged in the trans-Saharan slave trade. They sold the captives to the Arabs in North Africa. Why did they do this? One possible answer was debt. Lady Lugard noted that in sixteenth century Songhai:

> Systems of banking and credit, which seem to have existed under the earlier kings of [Mali], were improved. Banking remained chiefly in the hands of the Arabs, from whom letters of credit could be procured, which were operative throughout the Soudan [i.e. West Africa], and were used by the [B]lack travelling merchants as well as by Arab traders.[7]

When Denham and Clapperton visited the Hausa and Borno regions in the early nineteenth century, banking was still largely in the hands of the Arabs, as we have seen (see page 449). Richardson, another travel writer, visited one of the tributary states within Borno and reported that:

> The Arabs here are either purveyors to the court or bankers; they sell goods to the "Sultan" at exorbitant prices or lend money for the tax which he has to pay annually to the kings of Bornu [sic] ... Purveyors and bankers are infamous usurers who take pitiless and ruthless advantage of this poor potentiates's straits. On one occasion of my farewell visit, the latter was sadly calculating how many more [slave] raids he would have to organise in order to satisfy his creditors.[8]

Clapperton visited Fezzan (in southern Libya) in 1822. According to him, the result of the trade meant that: "It is hardly possible to go one mile of the whole journey without coming across the skeletons of Africans".[9] Major Denham, his colleague, reported that "after a long day during which these human remains had never been out of sight," he "counted over a hundred skeletons near a well". The Arab response to the suffering of the Africans was not encouraging: "The Arabs laughed: Peuh! ... A curse on their fathers!"[10]

Enslavement by Europeans

Professor Williams noted that the migrations became an even greater problem with the European enslavement of Africans. This activity began in 1441 with the Portuguese expeditions to North and West Africa. The rule of the Moors and Yemenis in the Iberian peninsular, and the transfer of high science and technology into that region, resulted in Spain and Portugal becoming the most advanced nations in Europe. In 1230 the Moors had lost most of Spain and by 1492, they lost it altogether. The Moors and Yemenis introduced nautical skills into the region. In addition, they introduced gunpowder technology.[11] Thus the Moorish and Yemeni culture in Spain and Portugal of the Middle Ages would eventually rebound on Africa in a serious and negative way.

The enslavement of Africans by Europeans is traditionally held to have started in 1441. Antam Gonçalves, a young Portuguese mariner, sailed to Rio de Oro on the coast of southern Morocco. "O how fair a thing it would be" said Gonçalves to his crew, "if we, who have come to this land for a cargo of such petty merchandise, were to meet with the good luck to bring the first captives before the face of our Prince." Later joined on the coast by Nuño Tristão, "a youthful knight very valiant and ardent", they kidnapped twelve Africans and gave them as a present to Prince Henry of Portugal. One of the captives, of noble birth, revealed particulars of the land from which he came to the Portuguese. With this intelligence, the Prince sent an embassy to Pope Martin V to state his plans for more conquests and enslavement. Welcoming the new crusade, the Pope offered to grant "to all of those who shall be engaged in the said war, complete forgiveness of all their sins". The African noble requested his freedom in exchange for five or six Africans. Gonçalves sailed south once more and ransomed the captive and one other for ten more captives.[12]

In 1443-4 Nuño Tristão sailed once more down the West African coast. His crew seized 29 men and women from canoes they were paddling near the shore. In Lisbon, the cargo of captives silenced critics who saw the expeditions as a waste of resources. A Portuguese account suggests: "their covetousness now began to wax greater. And as they saw the houses of others full to overflowing of male and female slaves, and their property increasing, they thought about the whole matter and began to talk among themselves". The Portuguese agreed to fund six ships under Gil Eanes and Lançarote. Their campaign led to the initial capture of 165 men, women and children "besides those that perished and were killed." Eventually they sailed home with 235 captives. Dr Davidson notes that: "With this pathetic triumph the oversea slave trade may really said to have begun."[13] One modern writer wrote:

> Hunting people often say they hunt the fox and deer in order to save these poor animals from being exterminated by the cruel farmers. Dom Henry's [of Portugal] motive for kidnapping black folk at the estuaries of the Senegal and Gambia may have been similarly unselfish.[14]

"Within thirty years of the development of the trade by the Portuguese" comments F. George Kay, an English journalist:

> mulattoes were in responsible positions as interpreters, brokers, and guards. These were children of liaisons that were voluntary for both partners and semi-permanent ... Inevitably rape and force were the origins of many of these children. The sadism aroused by the trade could not but direct itself into sexual assault. It is noteworthy how often the contraband slaves smuggled on board [the slave ships] by members of the crew were women ... Almost as quickly as Columbus's sailors spread syphilis in Europe, the crews of the slavers took the

disease to Africa. The great and small poxes were soon rampant along the coast.[15]

In 1482 the Portuguese built Elmina Castle on the coast of modern Ghana. The first of many fortified dungeons, the local ruler, Kwame Ansa, initially opposed the building. Arguing that friends who see each other only occasionally are better friends than those who live in close proximity, Ansa refused the Portuguese request to build there. Diogo de Azambuja, the Portuguese agent, refused to take "no" for an answer, however. Kwame Ansa appeared to concede and warned that peace and truth must be maintained. The following day as the Portuguese began to build "the [N]egroes ... briskly attacked the men at work". The Portuguese response was to bribe the Negroes with gifts. Modern European apologists (a.k.a. "historians") present these bribes as evidence that the Portuguese paid to lease the land! Clearly the Africans were not satisfied. They apparently "committed so many thefts and evil deeds [against the Portuguese] that Diogo de Azambuja decided to burn their village".[16]

William Winwood Reade, an English historian, placed the Portuguese actions into a more global context:

> The achievements of the Portuguese were stupendous - for a time. They established a chain of forts all down the western coast of Africa and up the east coast to the Red Sea; then round the Persian Gulf, down the coast of Malabar, up the coast of Coromandel, among the islands of the Archipelago, along the shores of Siam [i.e. Thailand] and Burma to Canton and Shanghai. With handfuls of men they defeated gigantic armies; with petty forts they governed empires. But from first to last they were murderers and robbers, without foresight, without passion. Our eyes are at first blinded to their vices, but as the light fades their nakedness and horror are revealed.[17]

The voyage of Christopher Columbus to the American continent in 1492 opened up this part of the world to European predatory activities. The indigenous peoples (the so-called Red Indians) were genocided by the million and enslaved Africans were sent to the Americas to replace them. Previously all such captives were sent to Europe.[18] The Spanish conquerors found great demand for labour in the West Indies and also the mines of Central America. At first they enslaved the Native Americans but the high death rates robbed the conquerors of this labour force. This created a need for indentured labour from other sources. In 1501 Black and White slaves were deported to Hispaniola, the island of Haiti and Dominican Republic. Ovando, the Spanish governor, did not initially approve of the presence of Blacks because they were making the Native Americans too disobedient. Four years later, however, he changed his mind.[19]

In the year 1510 Royal Orders were given to transport large numbers of Africans for sale. Fifty Africans were transported, followed by two hundred Africans. A licensing system was established that year, followed by the imposition of taxes three years later. The result was both an official trade and unofficial smuggling to avoid paying the taxes. The deportees became chattel slaves as opposed to domestic servants. Great cruelty was therefore associated with the trade from this period. The King of Spain wrote to Sampier in Hispaniola, claiming: "I cannot understand why so many Negroes die".[20]

In 1515 the first batch of slave-grown West Indian sugar was shipped to Europe. Three years later the first Africans were shipped directly to the Caribbean and the Americas. These developments marked the beginning of the Triangular Trade. The credit for this system was in no small part due to the activities of the Reverend Las Casas, a Portuguese humanitarian priest. His *The Tears of the Indians* was written as a plea to other Europeans to stop the genocide of the Native Americans. One historian reported that:

> In 1517, Bartholomé de las Casas, Bishop of Chiapa, proposed, it is suggested out of good nature and in the hope of benefiting the natives [of the Americas], that each Spanish gentleman should be permitted to import twelve Negro slaves. The advice of the Bishop was adopted. The King gave a patent to one of his favourites, authorizing him to import 4,000 [N]egroes annually to Hispaniola, Cuba, Jamaica and Porto Rica [sic]. This patent was sold to the Genoese, who shared it with the Portuguese … And all the nations of Europe were soon engaged in the traffic.[21]

Captured Africans were deported directly to the Americas. This was the first leg in a ship's journey and the first part of the triangle from Africa. From the Americas, slave produced minerals and foodstuffs were sent to Europe. This was the second leg in a ship's journey. Finally, from Europe, cheap manufactured goods were exported for sale to enslavers in Africa. This was the final leg in a ship's journey. Money was made (1) by selling Africans to planters and mineworkers in the Americas, (2) by selling minerals and foodstuffs in Europe, and finally, (3) by selling consumer goods to enslavers in Africa.[22]

The Africans resisted. They rebelled in Hispaniola in 1522. They rebelled again in Porto Rico in 1527, then Santa Maria in 1529 and also Panama in 1531. The following year the Spanish established a special police force to catch runaways.[23]

In 1562 England entered the trade through the person of Sir John Hawkins. Merchants in London backed Hawkins with the supply of three ships, the Salamon, the Swallow and the Jonas. The English accounts claim that he procured 300 Africans "by sword and partly by other means". Portuguese accounts reveal Hawkins' piracy. He intercepted five Portuguese ships and took over 900 Africans.[24] A year later, Hawkins was again in West Africa, this time with four ships. George Kay, an English journalist, reports that Hawkins "had 'great pleasure to behold' the Africans fleeing from them, crying out and leaping in the air, mystified when pellets from the pursuers' arquebuses [i.e. firearms] caused almost invisible but crippling wounds."[25] This was the same John Hawkins who commanded his crew to "serve God daily and love one another".[26] Sir John led other campaigns with the ships, the William and John, the Minion, the Swallow, the Angel, the Judith and the Jesus of Lubeck. Mr Kay, however, believes that historians should not judge Hawkins too harshly, after all:

> He was born in an England whose Queen had no compunction in having enemies beheaded. Death by hanging, drawing and quartering was the legal penalty for treason. Poisoners could be boiled to death. Minor crimes were punishable by mutilation - nose slitting, ear removal, hand amputation, and branding. It is in this context that Hawkins of the transatlantic slave trade has to be regarded.[27]

The latter sixteenth century was characterised by increasing violence against Africans in both Africa and Europe. The atrocities were fast approaching the scale of the genocide then waged against the Native Americans. Professor Lane-Poole narrates the tragic story of the expulsions of Africans from Spain and Portugal culminating in the shameful Day of All Saints atrocity:

> The late wars, it was said, had carried off more than twenty thousand Moors, and perhaps fifty thousand remained in the district on that famous Day of All Saints, 1570, when the honour of the apostles and martyrs of Christendom was celebrated by the virtual martyrdom of the poor remnant of the Moors.[28]

In Africa, by this time, the Portuguese had already burned the Swahili cities, undermined Kongo, and had attempted an invasion of Munhumutapa. In the 1590's the Arabs, in conjunction with their English and Spanish backers, destroyed the Songhai Empire. In addition to burning the cities of Gao, Timbuktu and Djenné, they seized the intelligentsia and confiscated much of their literature. The trade routes through all these territories were severely disrupted.

By the end of the sixteenth century, the Portuguese and the Spaniards did most of the enslavement activities. By the beginning of the seventeenth century, other European nations became involved such as Holland, England, France, Denmark, Sweden and Prussia.

The Dutch took military actions to reduce the Portuguese role and to increase their own. By 1612 they built Fort Nassau at Mowree on the coast of modern

Ghana. In around 1617 they obtained an island of Cape Verde called Gorée where they built two forts. In 1637 they seized Elmina Castle from the Portuguese, and five years later, they seized Axim, the last of the Portuguese forts.[29] They allied themselves with the coastal peoples in this campaign. "The Africans had no objection", reports George Kay, "to the Dutch increasing Elmina's defences and building more forts because the newcomers made it clear that the defences were against rival Europeans and not to intimidate the African". It was the Portuguese that the coastal people hated. Anyone who opposed them was seen as potential friends at that time.[30] The Africans proved shortsighted in this view. In 1621 the Dutch set up the Dutch West India Company. Controlling 27 lists of slave buyers, the company linked the enslavement of Africans to the colonisations in the Western Hemisphere. In the 1630's the Dutch colonized Curacao, St Eustatius and Tobago. Moreover, they possessed another important territory in North America called New Amsterdam (later called New York).[31]

The English made a number of moves. In 1609 they colonised Bermuda. In 1625 they colonised Barbados. In North America, they conquered territories in New England, Maryland and Virginia. In the year 1618 King James I gave a charter of monopoly to 30 London merchants to deal in enslaved people.[32]

In 1626 the French began the colonisation of Guadaloupe. They colonised Martinique in 1635. In North America, they possessed Nova Scotia and St Lawrence. In 1671 the Danes began the colonisation of St Thomas. Finally, the Spanish had St Augustine in Florida.[33]

From the 1640 period there was a major economic revolution in the Americas. Multicrop cultivation of coffee, cocoa, indigo, etc. was shifted to the cultivation of tobacco, coffee, cotton and more importantly sugar. This led to a massive demand for labour to cut cane, to grind cane, to transform the output into sugar and to make molasses and rum. Tobacco was also labour intensive. Dr Davidson suggests that the scale of enslavement exploded. He described it as "at first a trickle … and then a flood". England and France dominated this new system.[34]

From around 1654, the English changed their laws to 'barbadoe' their convicts. Given as a punishment for a crime or for debt, the convicts were sent to Barbados and Virginia. Those who were barbadoe'd were condemned to hard labour for a period of time.[35] This resulted in Whites joining Blacks on a few of the plantations.

Incidentally, two enslavers of Quaker origins, David and Alexander Barclay, were prominent in 1756. Both had connections in London. David owned a large plantation in Jamaica and was a prominent merchant in American and West Indian commerce. Both men married into the banking families of Gurney and Freame. As they say, the result made history … (i.e. Barclays Bank).[36]

The impact of enslavement on Africa devastated more than just the west coast. There were even captives deported from Malagasy (Madagascar) and East Africa to the American continent.[37] Again, Blacks and Mixed-Race groups were seduced into this process, causing crisis migrations, degeneration of huge numbers of Africans into savagery, and fuelling the tribalism of today. "For this indeed was the age of the gangster", says Professor DeGraft-Johnson:

> Violence, brutality, and ferocity became the necessities of survival, for generosity and good neighbourliness had lost their meaning. The stockades of grinning skulls, the selling of one's own children as slaves, the unprecedented human sacrifices, were all the sequel to this grand finale, the rape of African culture and civilization. The African could not understand what he had done to the gods to merit such horrors and cruelties, and his attempts to propitiate them became more and more extreme.[38]

There was also a major loss of scientific knowledge and technological skills, a key factor in modern Africa's technological backwardness. Professor Ivan Van Sertima, editor of that pioneering work on ancient African science and technology, *Blacks in Science: Ancient and Modern,* brilliantly explained how this came about. The Professor notes that throughout the world before the industrial revolution, knowledge of science and high technologies were restricted to those at the "centers" of a civilisation such as the priest-castes, the city dwellers and the like. At the "peripheries" of those same civilisations (the villages, forest areas or desert outposts), the situation was quite different:

> Thus, a skilled African surgeon could be performing delicate eye-cataract surgery in the city of Jenné [sic] in medieval Mali while a villager would be going blind with cataracts a few hundred miles away on the edges of the same empire, for lack of his fine medical instrumentation and expertise.[39]

"It is important to understand this", continues Dr Van Sertima:

> if we are to understand how a science or technology may rise and fall with a civilization, why the destruction of a center could lead to the almost instant evaporation or disappearance of centuries of knowledge and technical skills. Thus a nuclear war could shatter the primary centers of twentieth-century technology in a matter of days. The survivors on the periphery, although they would remember the aeroplanes and the television sets, the robots and the computers, the space machines now circling our solar system, would not be able for centuries to reproduce that technology. Apart from the almost wholesale slaughter of the technocratic class, the interconnection between those shattered centers and the equally critical interdependency between the centres and their peripheries, would be gone forever ... A dark age would certainly follow. Centuries afterwards, the technological brilliance of the twentieth century would seem dream-like and unreal. Until archaeology began

to pick up the pieces, those of us who follow in the centuries to come will obviously doubt what had been achieved in the centuries preceding the disaster. This has happened before in the world. Not in the same way, of course, but with the same catastrophic effect. It happened in Africa ... We are all familiar with the slave trade and the traumatic effect of this on the transplanted [B]lack but few of us realize what horrors were wrought on Africa itself. Vast populations were uprooted and displaced, whole generations disappeared, European diseases descended like the plague, decimating both cattle and people, cities and towns were abandoned, family networks disintegrated, kingdoms crumbled, the threads of cultural and historical continuity were so savagely torn asunder that henceforward one would have to think of two Africas: the one before and the one after the Holocaust. Anthropologists have said that eighty percent of traditional African culture survived. What they mean by traditional is the only kind of culture we have come to accept as African - that of the primitive on the periphery, the stunned survivor.[40]

As in North Africa, the enslavers used religion to pacify the enslaved. The Arabians used Islam and the Europeans used Christianity. Unfortunately, this is a major problem for modern Black scholars to analyse, because most Blacks today are Muslims or Christians. Consequently, merely pointing out that Islam and Christianity have been used in this way has caused consternation among the faithful. Many have considered criticism of the invaders who have used religion for wicked purposes, as equivalent to an attack on their religious beliefs. Unable to distinguish one from the other, many Blacks today dislike analysing the migrations, their causes, or the tribalism that has resulted from it. This is because their religion may be negatively exposed by such analysis.[41]

To demonstrate the role of religion, we have already discussed the 1526 letter of King Affonso I of Kongo to the Portuguese (on page 350) begging them to stop the slave raids. However, elsewhere in the same letter Affonso asks the Portuguese to continue the Christianisation programme! Why didn't he respond more aggressively by declaring war? Clearly Affonso was blinded to the Portuguese threat because he erroneously believed that they shared his commitment to the religious faith. He thought they and he were Christian brothers. Black Muslims made the same mistake. Their responses when faced with similar challenges were equally unsatisfactory. When confronted by Arab slave raids in the late fourteenth century, Mai Uthman of Kanem-Borno wrote an equally pathetic letter to the Sultan of Egypt saying:

> [W]e have sent to you our envoy, my cousin Idris b. Muhammad, in connection with a problem which we encountered. The Arabs called Judhama, and others, have enslaved our free subjects - women, children, weak men, our relatives and other Muslims. Some of these Arabs are polytheists, apostates outside the fold of the Faith. They raided the Muslims and killed a great number of them during a war which broke out between us and our enemies [i.e. the Bulala]. In the

course of that war they killed our king Amr b. Idris, the Martyr ... These Arabs have ruined all our land, the country of Borno, and have taken our free subjects and our Muslim relatives as captives; some they sell to the traders from Egypt, Syria and other places, and some to keep for themselves as domestic slaves. Verily, God has placed in your hands the Government of Egypt from the Sea (i.e. Mediterranean) to Aswan, but your dominions have become a market-place. Send forth messengers to all your lands, to your emirs, your vezirs [sic], your qadis [i.e. judges], your governors, your ulama [i.e. savants] and your market-supervisors; let them conduct an investigation and inquiry into this affair. If they find our people let them release them, from the hands of those who hold them captives, and put them to the test. If they say: "We are free men - we are Muslims", believe them and do not regard them as liars. And after you have ascertained this, release them and allow them to return to their liberty and their Faith. Some of the Arabs, indeed, spread corruption in our land and are good for nothing. They are ignorant of the Book of God and the Sunna of our Messenger, and they regard wickedness an attractive occupation. Fear God, therefore, and do not let them enslave and sell our people.[42]

A war of propaganda began back then, and dominates now. Dr Davidson noted that up until the late seventeenth century: "Nobody talked as yet of any 'civilizing mission'."[43] Nor was the slave trade based around ideas of Negro inferiority. Professor DuBois noted that: "[D]uring these days the Mohammedan rulers of Egypt were buying [W]hite slaves by the tens of thousands in Europe and Asia and bringing them to Syria, Palestine and the Valley of the Nile".[44] As the violence against Negroes increased to the levels unleashed against the Native Americans, however, there was a growing attempt to specifically undermine their status in the eyes of the world. Writers began fabricating a literature for the general public that portrayed Africa as a land of savages to give the impression that the transatlantic enslavement system was beneficial to the enslaved. In addition, enslavement became explicitly linked to a civilizing mission. Works like *Some Years Travels into Divers Parts of Asia and Afrique* were produced (1634). Even then, the author of that book claimed that the people of the West African coast were nothing but plunderers and villains.[45] Three hundred years later, Professor Arnold Toynbee of Oxford University wrote a very famous work, *A Study of History,* where he informed his readers that the Black race had never built a single civilisation![46] In the seventeenth century, however, the literature written for traders, government officials, and geographers contained little of the dishonest nonsense aimed at the masses. Similarly, in the twentieth century, a few scholars tried to keep the truth alive in around the same period as Toynbee such as Professors Frobenius and Churchward, but they were shouted down and drowned out by a powerful mass media and an 'educational' system. Even in our times, plenty of left-wing and liberal scholars have continued the character assassinations of Frobenius and Churchward. This is how the absurd notion that Africa had no history became the dominant view. Images of jungle savages eating missionaries in cooking pots were also fabricated to make the propaganda stick, but as Lady Lugard, that excellent authority on West African history, pointed out:

> [Two slave] traders [Barbot and Bosman], were much disturbed by a widespread belief among the natives [of Africa] that "we buy them only to fatten and afterwards eat them as a delicacy." Barbot tells us that "natives infected with this belief will fall into a deep melancholy and despair, and refuse all sustenance, though never so much compelled and even beaten to oblige them to take some nourishment, notwithstanding all which they will starve to death … And, though I must say I am naturally compassionate, yet have I been necessitated sometimes to cause the teeth of those wretches to be broken, because they would not open their mouths or be prevailed upon by any entreaties to feed themselves, and thus have forced some sustenance into their throats".[47]

Consequences for the West Africa Coast

The consequences of the trade for each region varied greatly. Kongo and Ndongo were largely destroyed by it. Great Benin sold captives from time to time but a policy was enforced to prevent the trade from dominating its activities with outsiders. Cloth remained its largest export in the sixteenth and seventeenth centuries. Dr Ehret, author of an impressive work on African history, provided a good overview of the situation:

> When the Benin kingdom resisted the growing demand for slaves … Oyo [in Yorubaland] responded to it. With their fast-striking cavalry forces, the Oyo military leaders launched a series of wars that between 1600 and 1750 brought most of the Yoruba city-states under its sway. These wars produced slaves directly in the form of war captives. Oyo's conquests gained for it as well new wealth in the form of duties and tribute … A second notable state, Dahomey, became even more intimately bound up with the slave trade than Oyo. Dahomey, founded in about the 1620's, started out as a small interior kingdom [in present day Benin] … Competition over the proceeds of the growing slave trade led its rulers to attack and finally defeat the equally small coastal states of Popo and Whydah in 1727. The Dahomey kings then appointed their own officials at Whydah, maintaining through those officials a direct royal control over the trade with Europeans the coast and restricting the access of Europeans to the interior of the country.[48]

In the region today called Ghana the Portuguese built Elmina Castle in 1482, and not without local opposition. William Towerson, an English navigator and trader, visited the region in 1556. He reported that the Portuguese traders made life for the local people somewhat trying:

> [W]e judged that the Portugals had spoiled their boats, because we saw half of
> their towne destroyed ... a young fellow ... tolde us that the Portugales were
> bad men, and that they made them slaves if they could take them, and would
> put yrons upon their legges.[49]

Furthermore, some locals put up resistance to the Portuguese actions.
Towerson wrote "Don John [a chief] had warres with the Portugals". We may
conjecture that Don John had even been converted by the Portuguese, hence
his European name. Note that even he is battling against them! In addition:

> This town of John de Viso standeth upon an hill, like the towne of don John,
> but it hath been burned, so that there are not passing six houses in it; the most
> part of the golde that comes thither comes out of the countrey, and no doubt if
> the people durst for feare of the Portugals bring forth their gold, there would be
> had good store; but they dare not sell anything, their subjection is so great to
> the Portugales ... [50]

Towerson's impressions tend to refute the notion that enslavement was
conducted as fair trade between equally armed participants.

John Barbot, a French enslaver, visited the region in 1683. He presented a
mixed and complex picture of life in the region, but the Dutch were now
dominant, having swept away Portuguese power:

> The better to curb the [B]lacks along the coast, and to engross the whole trade,
> [the Dutch] erected small forts at Butri, Shama, Cape Coast, Anomabu,
> Koromantin, and Accra, pretending to the [B]lacks, they did it to protect and
> defend them against the outrages and insults of their neighbouring enemies of
> the inland country, who used often to attack them. Being thus grown powerful,
> the more to keep down the [B]lacks and prevent their attempting any thing
> against them, they laid duties on their fishery at Axim, Elmina, and Mori,
> forbidding them, under severe penalties, to hold any correspondence, or trade
> with other Europeans, as has been observ'd before.[51]

Clearly life had not improved very much for the dwellers of this unhappy
region. Barbot explains that:

> The kingdom of Accra is tributary to and dependant on the king of Akwamu;
> [there are] ... three villages ... each of them under the cannon of an European
> fort, viz ... the English fort of James ... the Dutch fort of Crèvecoeur; and ...
> that of St. Francis Xaverius.[52]

Barbot claims to be baffled why the Blacks "ever permitted Europeans to
build three such good forts so close together." Nevertheless, Barbot answers
his own question: "[S]o great is the power of money ... that the late king of
Accra, about forty years since, being gained by considerable presents the

Danes and Dutch made him ... granted the liberty at first asked of him, for each of them to build a stone house [i.e. fort] ... under the obligation of seven marks of gold yearly, for each house".[53] Thus the answer appears to have been bribery.

Moreover, Barbot informs us that the European settlements "increased the plenty of goods, and consequently lessened their prices." Thus some Africans would have approved of the European presence and would have wanted to trade with them. On the other hand, Barbot describes the wars between the Akwamus and the Akim. They sold their war captives to the Europeans residing at Nungwa and Accra, and thus "a ship is often furnish'd with four or five hundred [B]lacks in a fortnight or three weeks."[54]

William Bosman, of the Dutch West India Company, described the story as it was in 1700. Like Barbot, he presented a complex and mixed picture. For example, Axim flourished exceedingly under European influence. It would not have been difficult to see why they would have encouraged trade with the Europeans:

> This country called Axim, is cultivated, and abounds with numerous large and beautiful villages, all extraordinary populous; some of which are situate on the sea-shore, and others farther on the main land; the most considerable amongst the former lie under the Brandenburgian and Dutch forts, of which the latter is by much the best. The [N]egro inhabitants are generally very rich, driving a great trade with the Europeans for gold ... [and] industriously employ'd either in trade, fishing, or agriculture, and that is chiefly exercised in the culture of rice, which grows here above all other places in an incredible abundance and is transported hence all the Gold Coast over.[55]

Unfortunately there were other consequences:

> But the last fatal war betwixt the Ahantas and the Adomians hath reduced [Sekondi] to a miserable condition and stript it of most of its inhabitants ... 'Tis indeed deplorable to see it at present and reflect on its former flourishing condition in the years 1690 and 1691.[56]

In addition:

> The English fortress [at Sekondi] was burnt and destroy'd by the Ahanta [N]egroes; its chief commander and some of the English being killed, and the rest being plunder'd of all their own and the company's goods ... Sekondi was one of the finest as richest villages, as well in money as in people, upon the whole coast. But the Adomese conquerors entirely burnt and destroy'd it ... The village or town of Takoradi ... 'tis now so ruined, that no visible remnants of it are left ... The town of Sharma is moderately large and well peopled, but its inhabitants so miserably poor that I do not believe they have any like them on the Gold Coast ... About 15 or 16 years past [Elmina] was very populous ... but about 15 years past the small-pox swept away so many, and since by the

Komenda wars together with the tyrannical government of some of their generals, they have been so miserably depopulated and impoverished, that 'tis hardly to be believed how weak it is at present ... Under the English fort [at Cape Coast, the town] ... was formerly well-peopled; but this, as well as all the other[s], has suffered very much in the Komenda war; besides that the multiplicity of English interlopers hath continually stript it of its inhabitants.[57]

Freda Wolfson, of the University of Exeter, concludes:

From the records it is clear that while the white traders were welcomed for the fascinating array of goods they offered for sale, Europeans who intended to settle in the country were not ... Only in the face of great opposition did the Portuguese build their fort; and once established there, they were hard put to it to protect themselves and their property. It was by force alone that they were able to keep their hold over the local people, whose favour they were obliged to seek with frequent presents and by paying regularly for the lease of the land on which the buildings stood. The pattern was set for all the Europeans who followed the Portuguese pioneers. Right down to the beginning of the nineteenth century, the European hold was precarious. The English trader Henry Meredith, writing about 1810, noted that Europeans could only assert their authority over the inhabitants by terrorizing them.[58]

Inland from the coast, the Ashanti Union was established after the year 1700. They came to rule over most of the modern Ghana region for the next two hundred years. Osei-Tutu founded the union by encouraging a common citizenship based on loyalty to a national symbol - the Golden Stool. According to tradition, the stool fell from heaven and landed gently into the lap of Osei-Tutu. The basis of the empire was, of course, trade. Crops of transatlantic maize, sweet potatoes and pineapples were grown. Gold was still an important mainstay for the region. However, slave trading their conquered enemies also proved to be a profitable enterprise. The Ashanti army were armed with muskets supplied from Birmingham, England.

Opoko Ware (1720-50) established the Ashanti Empire as the most important power in the central forestlands. During his time, and the time of his successors, the empire grew larger than modern Ghana. They traded with other states in West Africa, also with the Dutch at Elmina, and with the English at Cape Coast. Osei Kwado (1764-77) made administrative innovations that led to the growth of a civil service. In this bureaucracy, appointments to its commercial, financial and political posts were on the basis of efficient service and not on hereditary factors. Furthermore, the Empire had an efficient network of couriers that carried the emperor's (i.e. the Asantehene's) orders in all directions. By the early nineteenth century, Kumasi, the capital city, boasted two storey buildings and arcades. It had a population of 40,000 people.[59] Thomas Bowditch describes the capital as follows:

Ashanti (Ghana). The Oldest House in Kumasi. 18th century.

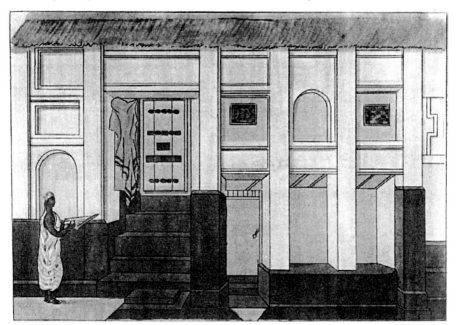

Ashanti (Ghana). Odumata's Sleeping Room.

These two-storey Kumasi houses were sketched and published in T. Edward Bowditch, *Mission from Cape Coast Castle to Ashantee* (UK, John Murray, 1819).

> Four of the principal streets [of Kumasi] are half a mile long, and from fifty to one hundred yards wide. I observed them building one, and a line was stretched on each side to make it regular. The streets were all named, and a superior captain in charge of each ... What surprised me most ... was the discovery that every house had its cloacae [i.e. toilet], besides the common ones for the lower orders without the town. They were generally situated under a small archway in the most retired angle of the building, but not unfrequently [sic] upstairs, within a separate room like a small closet ... the holes are of a small circumference, but dug to a surprising depth, and boiling water is daily poured down, which effectually prevents the least offence [i.e. odour]. The rubbish and offal of each house was burnt every morning at the back of the street, and they were as nice and cleanly in their dwellings as in their persons.[60]

Mr William Winwood Reade visited the Ashanti Empire. His 1874 work *The Story of the Ashantee Campaign* gave the following picture of the Asantehene's palace:

> [A prisoner] ... showed me the sights of Kumasi ... [and] we went to the king's palace, which consists of many courtyards, each surrounded with alcoves and verandahs, and having two gates or doors, so that each yard was a thoroughfare. These doors were secured by padlocks. An ordinary house has one court-yard; a large house three or four; the king's palace had ten or twelve. But the part of the palace fronting the street was a stone house, Moorish in its style ... with a flat roof and a parapet, and suites of apartments on the first floor. It was built by Fanti masons many years ago. The rooms upstairs remind me of Wardour Street. Each was a perfect Old Curiosity Shop. Books in many languages, Bohemian glass, clocks, silver plate, old furniture, Persian rugs, Kidderminster carpets, pictures and engravings, numberless chests and coffers. A sword bearing the inscription *From Queen Victoria to the King of Ashantee* [sic]. A copy of the *Times*, 17 October 1843. With these were many specimens of Moorish and Ashanti handicraft, gold-studded sandals such as only the king and a few great chiefs may wear, with, strange to say, Arabic writing on the soles; leopard-skin caps lined with yellow velvet and adorned outside with beaten gold like that of Kashmir, and a plume of the same precious metal; saddles of red leather, magnificent canopies or state umbrellas of velvet and satin, baskets or cradles in which Ashanti chiefs are accustomed to be carried on the heads of slaves, with other curious and tasteful things too numerous for me to describe or even catalogue.[61]

The British eventually overran the Ashanti Empire in 1896. They changed the name of the conquered territory to the Gold Coast. After independence in 1957 Dr Kwame Nkrumah, the first president, renamed it Ghana - the name it has today. It is, however, appropriate to point out that the real period of African independence was *before* the European conquests and mass enslavement and not after 1957.

Black History in the Atlantic Age

Much of the information reported in this chapter is not Black history. Our colleague Amittai Lumumba long taught that Black history during this period must also conform to the Karenga definition, previously discussed on pages 6 and 7. Black history in the Atlantic Age is therefore composed of the rebellions and the Maroon societies. Dr W. E. B. Dubois provided a list of important rebellions by enslaved Africans that "show that the docility of Negro slaves in America is a myth:"

1522: Revolt in San Domingo
1530: Revolt in Mexico
1550: Revolt in Peru
1550: Appearance of the Maroons
1560: Byano Revolt in Central America
1600: Revolt of Maroons
1655: Revolt of 1500 Maroons in Jamaica
1663: Land given [to] Jamaican Maroons
1664-1738: Maroons fight British in Jamaica
1674: Revolt in Barbados
1679: Revolt in Haiti
1679-1782: Maroons in Haiti organized
1691: Revolt in Haiti
1692: Revolt in Barbados
1695: Palmares; revolt in Brazil
1702: Revolt in Barbados
1711: Negroes fight French in Brazil
1715-1763: Revolt in Surinam
1718: Revolt in Haiti
1719: Revolt in Brazil
1738: Treaty with Maroons
1763: Black Caribs revolt
1779: Haitians help the United States Revolution
1780: French Treaty with Maroons
1791: Dominican Revolt
1791-1803: Haitian Revolution
1794: Cuban revolt
1794: Dominican revolt
1795: Maroons revolt
1796: St. Lucian revolt
1816: Barbados revolt
1828-1837: Revolts in Brazil
1840-1845: Haiti helps Bolivar
1844: Cuban revolt
1844-1893: Dominican revolt
1861: Revolt in Jamaica
1895: War in Cuba[62]

There were various 'Maroon' societies in the Americas and the Caribbean. The Maroons were Africans who escaped from enslavement. Some of them revived African traditions, languages, religions, etc. A few of these societies included Native Americans. The most impressive of these mini-Africas was Palmares, located in Brazil. Professor Abdias Do Nascimento, a Brazilian historian, narrates that:

> In early 1595, some of the enslaved Africans in Brazil broke the shackles of slavery and fled to the jungle between the states of Pernambuco and Alagoas. Initially it was a small band of escapees. But this group grew little by little until it became a community of nearly thirty thousand "rebel" Africans. They established the first government of free Africans in the New World, indisputably a true African State, known as the Republic of Palmares.[63]

Palmares, under King Zumbi, could mobilise a royal guard of 5,000 men. The capital, Macaco, had a reputation for invincibility. Zumbi had the palace, guards, officials, and ceremonies, typically associated with an important ruler.[64] Dr Nascimento continues:

> The Republic of Palmares, with its immense population by the standards of the epoch, dominated a territorial area more or less one third the size of Portugal. This land was the property of all. The fruits of collective labor were the property of all. The free Africans planted and harvested a wide variety of products and bartered with their white and indigenous Brazilian neighbors. They were very effectively organized, both socially and politically, in their African manner and tradition, and were highly skilled in the art of war. Palmares put into question the entire colonial structure: the army, the land tenure system of the Portuguese patriarchs - the *latifundio* - and the Catholic Church. It withstood some twenty-seven wars of destruction, waged by both the Portuguese and the Dutch colonial military structures established in Pernambuco. Palmares resisted for more than half a century: from 1634 to 1694.[65]

Maroon communities existed on the Caribbean island of Jamaica. Professor Barrett, a Jamaican scholar, provided an admirable summary of the most important events:

> The story of the Jamaican Maroons begins with the English defeat of Spain in 1655. The Spaniards, finding themselves outclassed by the British, sailed from the north coast of Jamaica to Cuba and left their slaves to the British. But the slaves had ideas of their own. Although we have no true records of the treatment of Spanish slaves in Jamaica up to 1655, we may assume from the behaviour of the Spanish slaves that they were discontent with slavery, for they soon sought freedom in the hill country where they fought a gruelling war to the death.[66]

Juan de Bolas was the first leader of the Maroons. A village named after him still flourishes near the borders of Clarendon and St Catherine in Jamaica. In 1663, after eight years of raiding the British, an attempt was made to pacify the Maroons. The British made Juan de Bolas a colonel and sent him back to his followers to sue for peace. The Maroons correctly saw the whole matter as a trap to re-enslave them. They ambushed their leader and, according to one writer: "He was cut to pieces."[67]

Other pockets of escapees flourished in the northern and eastern territories of the island. The majority of these were deported from the Koromantyn slave dungeon, located in present day Ghana. Since most were originally captured prisoners of war when they were in Africa, they were skilled in guerrilla warfare. Edward Long, a planter historian, states: "With the importation of slaves by the English, almost from the start irrepressible spirits among the Koromantyn fled to the mountains and found refuge with the Maroons in such numbers that they soon gained control of the entire body."[68]

The "irrepressible spirits among the Koromantyn" included an Ashanti family deported to Jamaica. The family members were Cudjoe (cf. Ashanti name Kojo), Accompong (cf. Acheampong), Cuffee (cf. Kofi), Quaco (cf. Kwaku) and Johnny.

> Cudjoe, on assuming his command, appointed his brothers Accompong and Johnny to be leaders under him, and named Cuffee and Quaco subordinate captains. The brunt of the Maroon campaign was carried on under these five men and were assisted by others, mainly in the northern and southern parts of Jamaica. On the east side of the island, another sizable group of Maroons formed under the leadership of the legendary Acheampong Nanny who was said to be either the wife or the sister of Cudjoe. Not much is known of her, but there is a town named in her honor in that point of the island, and her fame has been so great in Jamaican folk tradition that the legislature has posthumously named her the first woman to receive the distinction of National Hero in the year 1975. But if nothing is known of Nanny, much is known of her colleague in command, Captain Quaco, who later supervised the signing of the treaty with the English for that group of Maroons in 1739.[69]

The treaty signed with the British was a retrograde step, however. It guaranteed the security and independence for the Maroons but only on the condition that they returned other escapees. This turned the Maroons into an unofficial police force serving British interests. After the treaty, they became an obstacle to the freedom and independence of other Blacks in Jamaica.[70]

In South America, a Maroon kingdom in Colombia established a treaty with the Spanish signed in 1599.[71] Other Maroon communities flourished in the Guyana/Surinam region. The historian, James Rodway, one of the early writers on Caribbean history, reported that:

> Towards the end of the [eighteenth] century a number of ... communities of bush Negroes had been formed in Demerara, and their depredations became so common that regular expeditions were sent against them, guided by Indian trackers. In 1795 they joined with the slaves to raise a general insurrection, but special measures were taken so that they were almost suppressed for a time. Before this they had formed a line of stations for seventy miles from the river Demerara to the Berbice. Every camp was naturally surrounded by water, and by driving pointed stakes in a circle, and leaving the entrance to wind through a double line under water, they were made almost impregnable.

The Maroons of Surinam, like the Maroons of Jamaica, were never conquered. The British signed treaties with them in 1749 and 1761, but disputes continually occurred. The European colonists were always more or less in fear of their raids.[72]

In Barbados the Africans attempted to take over on more than one occasion. In 1649 a plot was discovered to eliminate all of the Europeans from the island. Unfortunately, a treacherous slave informed on the conspirators and frustrated the plan. Eight of the leading activists were condemned to death.[73] As Edmund D'Auvergne put it:

> The shorter cut to freedom was tried over and over again by the ill-used people ... The fears of the earlier planters were justified by repeated servile insurrections. These revolts of the damned against the fiends were all unsuccessful, either suppressed with hideous cruelty or nipped in the bud through the treachery generally of some soft-hearted servant who did not wish her master or mistress to be "murdered." The Koromantees were almost always the prime movers in these conspiracies. In 1676, according to a contemporary account published in London, their design "was to choose them a king, an ancient Gold Coast Negro; one Coffee [cf. Kofi], who should have been crowned in a chair of State exquisitely wrought ... Trumpets to be made of elephant's teeth and gourds were to be sounded, with a fell intention to fire the sugar canes and so run in and cut their masters' - the planters' throats in the respective plantations whereunto they did belong. Hearing a young Koromantee tell another that he would have no hand in murdering white folk, a house-wench belonging to Justice Hall, informed her master, "thinking it a pity such good people as her master and mistress should be destroyed." The plot was frustrated and the ringleaders apprehended. Six were burnt alive.[74]

In addition, eleven were beheaded and five committed suicide. Other frustrated conspiracies were planned for 1693 and 1702.[75]

In the United States, some enslaved Africans established communities of their own. According to Professor Maulana Karenga:

> There is evidence of the establishment of at least fifty [such] Maroon communities between 1672-1864 with varying life-spans. These communities

The aftermath of the Battle for Haiti, as depicted in an old nineteenth century print. The successful conclusion of this battle led to the dismantling of the system of mass enslavement of Black people.

existed in the forest, mountain and swampy regions of several states, i.e., Virginia, North Carolina, South Carolina, Georgia, Louisiana, Mississippi, Alabama and Florida. However, the most notable and largest communities existed in the Dismal Swamp, along the Virginia-North Carolina border and in Florida in union with the Seminole Indians [i.e. Native Americans] ... These Maroons sought in varying ways to duplicate the African societies from which they came. They built communal agricultural societies, raised crops and animals and fowl, maintained families with African kinship patterns and even engaged in trade with whites in certain areas.[76]

There were many examples of armed resistance. Over 250 revolts were recorded in the United States alone. Some of these were joint campaigns by Africans and Native Americans. One of the earliest known examples of such joint campaigns was in Hartford, Connecticut in 1657. From this date, there were a series of conspiracies and insurrections against the Europeans by such joint action. In the New York City rebellion of 1712, Native Americans campaigned jointly with the Africans. The alliances were due to the two groups sharing a common experience of being enslaved, their common mistreatment by the Europeans, their intermixture, and finally the need to defend themselves from the threat of conquest or re-enslavement.[77]

On a more mundane level, enslaved Africans rebelled in more subtle ways. Too subtle as it turned out for Dr Samuel Cartwright of the University of Louisiana. He theorised that the rebellious Africans were suffering from a peculiar disease that only affects Negroes! Called *Dysthesia Aethiopica,* he gave the symptoms as follows:

From the careless movements of the individuals affected with this complaint they are apt to do much mischief, which appears as if intentional, but is mostly owing to the stupidness of mind and insensibility of the nerves induced by the disease. Thus they break, waste, and destroy everything they handle; abuse horses and cattle; tear, burn, or rend their own clothing ... They wander about at night, and keep in a half nodding state by day. They slight their work - cut up corn, cane, cotton, and tobacco, when hoeing it ... They raise disturbances with their overseers ... When driven to labour by the compulsive power of the [W]hite man, he performs the task assigned to him in a headlong manner, treading down with his feet or cutting with his hoe the plants he is put to cultivate; breaking the tools he works with, and spoiling everything he touches that can be injured by careless handling. Hence the overseers call it "rascality," supposing that the mischief is intentionally done.[78]

In Haiti the Africans staged a revolution that led to the complete independence of the people for the first time in the western hemisphere. Bookman Dutty began the struggle on 22 August 1791. Leadership of the revolution then passed to General Toussaint L'Ouverture. The revolution was

Emperor Jean-Jacques Dessalines (1758-1806) as depicted in an old nineteenth century print. He was the first ruler of an independent Haiti in 1804.

completed in late 1803 under the leadership of Jean-Jacques Dessalines. In the process, the Haitians destroyed two French invasions, a Spanish invasion and an English invasion. After the victory, Dessalines tried and then executed thousands of Europeans for high crimes against the Blacks of Haiti. On 22 February 1804 Dessalines gave the relevant orders to dispense justice on the criminals.[79]

The first result was that Napoleon, the French ruler, abandoned his political ambitions in the Western hemisphere. He sold the colony of Louisiana to the United States:

> A second effect of the revolution [says a modern authority] was the decision by Britain to end the slave trade and the eventual dismantling of the chattel slave system entirely [by the late nineteenth century]. Actually, abolition was part of a larger plan designed to prevent the Black take-over of the rest of the West Indies and portions of Central and South America. Britain, the United States and perhaps other European powers began covertly supporting white Creole revolutions to offset the possibility of a repetition of Haiti. Indeed, in less than 20 years after the Black nation gained its independence, all of South America and Mexico became independent under white Creole leadership. The willingness of the United States to recognize and support these newly independent countries was not merely to prevent Europeans from coming back, but also to guarantee that incipient Black revolts were stamped out before they became torrents.[80]

The Colonial Conquests

The Haitian Revolution demonstrated to the world that European enslavement of Africans could not continue indefinitely in the way that it had. By the late nineteenth century it was over, with millions deported and many more killed. All serious scholarship places the losses as upwards of fifty million.[81] As Basil Davidson put it: "So far as the Atlantic trade is concerned, it appears reasonable to suggest that in one way or another, before and after embarkation, it cost Africa at least fifty million souls. This estimate may be about one fourth of [B]lack Africa's approximate population today and is certainly on the low side".[82] Africa, however, was not allowed the space to recover from this. Mass enslavement was quickly followed by the conquest and colonisation of Africa, following the 1884-5 Berlin Conference. The Conference itself marked the climax of the "Scramble for Africa". Involving Great Britain, France, Portugal and Germany, it legitimised and formalised a process of conquest.[83] The European powers decided to carve up the entire continent between them, later using extreme brutality to seize and rule the conquered lands. For example, at least eleven million Africans disappeared between 1885 and 1900 in the Belgian controlled Congo.[84]

Again, this was accompanied by migrations, and as usual, the degeneration of culture. During this period Benin, the Hausa Confederation and Borno fell to the British, and Kanem fell to the French. The national boundaries that exist today were established by these European conquests. Consequently the boundaries bear no resemblance to any of the civilisations described in this book. For example, some territories seized by the British in West Africa were renamed Nigeria. Composed of Great Benin, the Yoruba States, the Hausa Confederation, the Igbo territories, a part of Borno, and other smaller states, Nigeria is a patchwork of ethnic groups. Some groups were linked by culture or religious outlook. This was the case with the Hausa Confederation and Borno. Other links existed between Great Benin and Yorubaland. Trade linked them all. The point is, however, that at no time were these states ever one political unit since the cultural differences that separated them were too large. Only during the time of Queen Amina (1576-1610) did anything approaching a modern Nigeria exist in the mediæval world. Yet today, modern Nigerians are expected to cope with the after effects of British Colonialism as one large happy territory.

Other peoples were split across colonial boundaries. This was the case with Munhumutapa. The Portuguese seized one part of its territory and renamed it Mozambique. The British seized another part and called it Rhodesia. Finally, the Dutch seized the southern portion and called it South Africa. The Shona of today are therefore divided into Portuguese speakers and English speakers. The imposition of colonial culture has therefore divided the Shona, and they are likely to become increasingly different from each other as time passes. For the former Munhumutapans of South Africa, racist and colonial propaganda masquerading as "historical scholarship" has successfully convinced them that the Empire of Munhumutapa had nothing to do with them. Thus the colonial programme set the scene for civil wars, instability, and of course, more migrations and an even greater degeneration of culture. Colonial and post-colonial controlled education and mass media also added to the problems since these too undermined African culture.

During the Colonial Era, Black history, in the Karenga sense, emerged in Europe and the Americas. In 1900 Henry Sylvester Williams, a Trinidadian lawyer, called the first of six historic Pan-African meetings. Held in London, the First Pan-African *Conference* interested Black people in England but also had delegates from the United States. Bishop Alexander Walters of the African Methodist Episcopal Church was in attendance, as was another African-American, the scholarly Dr W. E. B. DuBois. At the conference, Dr DuBois predicted that the central problem of the twentieth century was going to be "the problem of the colour line". In other words, the race politics of European domination was likely to inform the relationship of Europe to the non-White world.[85] He was, of course, completely correct in this prediction.

The Honourable Marcus Garvey (1887-1940). Founder and president of the U.N.I.A. and African Communities League. Consisting of six million people, it was the largest organisation of Black people of all time.

Dr DuBois led the First Pan-African *Congress*. Convened in Paris in 1919, they resolved that laws should be passed by the European Colonial powers to protect the colonised "natives [of Africa]" from foreign exploitation, slavery and capital punishment. Moreover, they called for education for the natives and for their participation in the running of their own countries.[86] This Congress, like all the others, however, did not have any real power to change the repression under which Black folk lived, but they represented a movement of ideas where Black people could protest and develop strategies where something of value could eventually emerge.

The next three Congresses were equally weak in their demands. At the Second Pan-African Congress in London and Brussels in 1921, the delegates resolved that Africans should be allowed local self-government. At the Third Pan-African Congress in London and Lisbon in 1923, they resolved that "[B]lack folk be treated as men". The Fourth Pan-African Congress in New York in 1927 was the last one led directly by Dr DuBois.[87]

The Honourable Marcus Garvey, DuBois' rival, led another wing of the struggle. Born in Jamaica into a Maroon family, he went on to become the greatest Black leader of the twentieth century. In 1914 he founded the Universal Negro Improvement Association and its coordinating body, the African Communities League. In 1920 the organisation held its first convention in New York. In a short time, the Association boasted 1,100 branches in more than 40 countries, such as Cuba, Panama, Costa Rica, Ecuador, Venezuela, Ghana, Sierra Leone, Liberia, Namibia and South Africa.

Aimed at independence from European domination, the Honourable Garvey was an institution builder. His movement had their own militias, the Black Cross nurses, barbershops, bakeries, tailors, newspapers, steamships, and most impressive of all, six million paid up members. In addition, the movement had an uncompromising ideology to address economic, cultural, and religious transformation and reconstruction, in addition to its political and military programme.[88]

By the late 1920's however, the Garvey Movement was falling apart. American secret service agents infiltrated the Association and wreaked internal chaos. Eventually, the baton was passed to Mrs Garvey and to an ageing Dr DuBois. They called the Fifth Pan-African Congress in Manchester, England, in 1945. For the first time, Africans directly from Africa were in large numbers. Among these were Dr Kwame Nkrumah, Jomo Kenyatta, Dr J. C. DeGraft-Johnson, Nnamdi Azikiwe. Also there were Trinidadians George Padmore and C. L. R. James. For the first time, the Congress resolved to call for African independence. At a much later date ... they get it. The Africans that attended the Conference became major players in the Post-Colonial Africa.[89] Dr Nkrumah became the first president of an independent Ghana in 1957 with

George Padmore as a close advisor. Other African states followed suit. Thus was born the Independence Period.

Migrations and the Nile Valley

There was another side to the migrations. Many migrants held onto aspects of their civilisations and were able to rebuild them after fleeing elsewhere. Therefore people in one part of Africa may have originated elsewhere on the continent. This is sufficient to destroy any notion of a true Negro originating in West Africa only, because Negroes from all over Africa are likely to be mixed with Negroes from elsewhere on the continent. Returning to Professor Williams, his view that Ancient Egypt and Sudan were once the most densely populated parts of Africa implies that some of the people living elsewhere in Africa are in fact partly of distant Nile Valley origins. This may seem a novel view, but many scholars have expressed ideas that are remarkably similar.

Al-Masudi, the highly regarded Arab geographer of the tenth century AD, wrote of a great migration of Africans, possibly from the region of Kush:

> When the descendants of Noah spread across the earth, the sons of Kush, the son of Canaan, travelled toward the west and crossed the Nile. There they separated: Some of them, the Nubians and the Beja and the Zanj, turned to the rightward, between the east and the west; but the others, very numerous, marched toward the setting sun ... [90]

While this is written in biblical analogy, it appears to suggest that many peoples in western and eastern Africa are in fact migrants of *Kushite* origins. Professor Abbé Amélineau, the pioneering French archaeologist of the nineteenth century, advanced a related, but slightly contrasting view. He relates much of present African culture to prehistoric *Egyptian* origins:

> Egyptian civilization is not of Asiatic, but of African origin, of Negroid origin, however paradoxical this may seem. We are not accustomed, in fact, to endow the Black or related races with too much intelligence, or even with enough intelligence to make the first discoveries necessary for civilization. Yet, there is not a single tribe inhabiting the African interior that has not possessed and does not still possess at least one of those first discoveries. [91]

The father of Egyptology, M. Jean Francois Champollion, suggested that the Nubians of today are direct descendants of the ancient Egyptians as we have already noted. There are aspects of the Ancient Egyptian culture that seem to have been preserved by the Nubians. Dr Georg Gerster, a Swiss explorer, described some of these similarities in an interesting article in *National Geographic* entitled *Threatened Treasures of the Nile*. In one part of the article, he states that the Copts are direct descendants of the Ancient Egyptians, but elsewhere under the section heading *Nubians Retain Old Egyptian Ways,* he tells us that:

> An Egyptian from the time of the Pharaohs would feel more at home among Nubians than anywhere else in today's United Arab Republic [i.e. Egypt]. He would recognise their flat-bottomed boats, almost as broad as they are long … He would recognise the tunnel-vaulted architecture and the furniture in Nubian dwellings, the wooden locks on the doors, and the receptacles made of Nile mud for the storage of grain and lentils. And the tiny braids of Nubian women, shining with pomade - wasn't that the ancient Egyptian fashion?[92]

The article (pages 616-7) has a brief discussion of domestic architecture under the section heading *Nile Dwellers Build With Adobe As Egyptians Did 6,000 Years Ago.* Here, Dr Gerster demonstrates striking similarities between Ancient Egyptian, modern Coptic and modern Nubian domestic architecture.

Sir Harry Johnston, a distinguished writer on Africa, wrote that many peoples today living in East Africa and the Sahara are Hamites and related to the Egyptians from ancient times. In his view the Hamites were: "[T]hat [N]egroid race which was the main stock of the ancient Egyptian, and is represented at the present day by the Somali, the Gal[l]a, and some of the blood of Abyssinia and of Nubia, and perhaps by the peoples of the Sahara Desert."[93]

Professor J. Spencer-Trimingham, a notable British scholar, argued that key elements in the Kanem-Borno Empire and some of the Hausa States were migrants from Kush:

> A[n] influence is that of the central Saharan nomadic Zaghawa often mentioned by Arabic writers. They may be classified as [N]egroid Kushites and were spread over a vast area of central Sahara and northern Sahil from Fezzan to Nubia. They facilitated the diffusion of Nubian culture into central … [Africa] and influenced the history of the region since they founded, or at least provided dynasties for, Kanem and certain Hausa states … [94]

Dr J. C. Moughtin, an Irish architectural scholar, was one of the foremost authorities on the Hausa monuments. He convincingly argued that Hausa architecture of the Middle Ages bore a strong, and possibly even genetic, relationship with that of Ancient Egypt:

> The roots of Hausa architecture are lost in antiquity, but it is possible that it shares a common ancestry with the great buildings of Pharaonic Egypt. Some of the early pre-dynastic hieroglyphics depict houses with small pinnacles similar to the Zankwaye that decorate Hausa buildings. The whole character of the Egyptian house drawings resembles that of the architecture of both present day Nubia and Hausaland.[95]

The Frenchman, Major Felix Dubois, was the pioneering authority on Songhai. He suggested that migrants originally from Egypt founded Djenné, the great West African city. He asks:

> What is this town, then, with its wide, straight roads, its houses of two stories (some with a sketch of a third) built in a style that instantly arrests the eye? ... What is this civilisation, sufficiently assured to possess a manner and style of its own? My thoughts naturally turn to the culture of the Khalifs ... [b]ut ... there is nothing Arabic in this style ... This style is not Byzantine, Roman, nor Greek; still less is it Gothic or Western ... At last I recall these majestically solid forms; and the memory is wafted to me from the other extremity of Africa. Their prototypes rise upon the banks of another great river ... [I]t is in the ruins of ancient Egypt in the valley of the Nile, that I have witnessed this art before.[96]

Professor Roland Oliver and Professor Fagan, both contemporary Africanists, think that the ruling classes and some of the populations of the Hausa Confederation, Great Benin, Mali and the Akan States (modern Ghana region), were conquerors originally from, or influenced by "a common source, probably [from] outside the region".[97] While they offer no evidence that conquest actually took place, their opinions are interesting nonetheless:

> We do not know precisely when or from where the horse-borne conquerors came. It could be that in some sense they were the descendants of the Saharan charioteers. It could be that they came from the kingdom of Meroë [i.e. Kush], or from the savannas to the east. It could be that some of the later and more powerful waves of migrants were in origin connected with the X-Group horsemen of post-Meroitic Nubia ... [98]

Dr Davidson notes that: "There is practically no well-known people in West Africa without its legend of an eastern or a northern origin in the remote past. Sometimes these traditions are complete enough to enable an intelligent guess at their approximate date." Moreover, "they 'marched' most precisely from the middle Nile to the middle Niger; along a trans-African route, that is, which migrating peoples had undoubtedly used from times exceedingly remote, and of whose existence the Arabs were well aware."[99]

Professor Kurt Mendelssohn, author of *The Riddle of the Pyramids,* claimed that the Ashanti and the Sudanese may well have been of Ancient Egyptian ancestry. He noted that:

> [A] curious similarity exists between the habits and customs of the Akan tribes of today with those of Ancient Egypt. The Ashanti migrated into West Africa only a few centuries ago. Until then they had lived in the Sudan, the only place in which the traditions of ancient Egypt had been preserved intact until about fifteen hundred years ago.[100]

Professor Frank Willett, an authority on Yoruba antiquities, feels that the Yoruba ruling class were originally "a small but influential group of people" who "established themselves as rulers over an indigenous iron-using population". Dr Willett seems unsure who these conquerors were but feels they could have come from Kush "which collapsed in the early fourth century [AD], or a few centuries later from Zaghawa or from Christian Nubia." Like Oliver and Fagan, Willett offers no evidence that such a conquest ever took place. Whichever be the case:

> Yoruba civilization appears therefore to result from the fusion of a small intrusive ruling class, bringing ideas from outside, with a highly artistic indigenous population. The resulting social pattern seems to have borne some resemblance to that of the City States of Ancient Greece.[101]

Professor Leo Frobenius, the great German savant, believed that many of the Kisra (i.e. Nupe) were of Kushite origins:

> Hence the Kisra traditions most brilliantly stand the test of comparison with more ancient written and historical material. They prove that this strong current of influence, the power of establishing empire and the institutions of state primacies came from Nubia from ancient Napata. Individual events further teach us that this union of Central Sudan with Nubia never entirely ceased and also that the consciousness of the actuality of such an old-time bond has since its inception never been quite dead ... Islamic immigrants and scribes knew it to have been so, and consequently, translated it in the manner with which they were most familiar ... What however fills us with profound astonishment is the perception we have gained of the marvellous power of the expansive culture which enabled these ancient Nubians to become the directors of the stream of civilisation flowing from the East through the central Soudan as far as the Upper Niger.[102]

The Englishman, J. Theodore Bent, was a prominent authority on Zimbabwean antiquities. He suggested that the people of that nation were of Egyptian origin although his reasoning left a lot to be desired:

> Some of them [the Zimbabweans] are decidedly handsome, and not at all like [N]egroes except in skin[!]; many of them have a distinctly Arab cast of countenance, and with their peculiar rows of tufts on the top of their heads looked en profil like the figures one sees on Egyptian tombs.[103]

Mr Carl Engel, the author of the incomparable and erudite work, *The Music of the Most Ancient Nations,* opened another area of research as early as 1864, though few, if any scholars seem to have followed up on his ideas. Essentially, his view is that musical instruments and techniques have diffused across the ancient world, accompanying the spread of culture across the world. Giving the example of the harp, he noted that:

> The [N]egroes in Western Africa and in Soudan possess, however, an instrument which bears a strong resemblance ... to some of the harps which we see represented on Egyptian monuments. The [N]egroes in Senegambia and Guinea call it *boulou,* or *ombi,* and use strings made from a kind of creeping plant, or from the fibrous root of a tree.[104]

He informs us that the sistrum, now used by the priests of Ethiopia, was originally an ancient Egyptian musical instrument. In addition, the talking drum, thought to have been a West African instrument, existed in ancient Egypt.[105] Finally, J. Theodore Bent noted that the thumb piano, an ancient instrument associated with Zimbabwe, was also of Egyptian origins:

> One finds instruments of a similar nature amongst the natives north of the Zambesi. Specimens in the British Museum of almost exactly the same construction come from Southern Egypt and the Congo, pointing to the common and northern origin of most of these African races.[106]

Oliver and Fagan feel that the Zimbabwe kingdoms show some connections to Kush. In their own words:

> The social institutions of the Mwenemutapa's [sic] kingdom, and doubtless those of the ancestral dynasty which had ruled from the stone-built Great Zimbabwe three hundred miles to the south, were pagan African institutions of the same general character as those which are known to have existed at different times all the way from Mero[ë] to Takrur and from Ethiopia to the Transvaal.[107]

Moustafa Gadalla, a contemporary 'Egyptian' Egyptologist, wrote an unusual book entitled *Exiled Egyptians: The Heart of Africa.* In this work, he claims that the people of Kush, pre-Islamic Kanem, Nok, Jukun, early Hausaland, Wagadu (i.e. Ancient Ghana), Yoruba, the city of Djenné, and Benin were partly of Ancient Egyptian origins. The following is representative of his ideas:

> This book deals in some detail with the migration throughout West Africa only. This is not to underestimate and/or neglect the dispersion of Egyptians and/or Egypt model society, to east, central and southern Africa. Such dispersion was caused by foreign invasions and the Islamic onslaughts on Western Africa in the 11th century. Substantial archaeological evidence shows that there was a significant population growth between 750 and 1110 CE [i.e. AD], accompanied by the emergence of a dozen or so stable and distinct regional traditions, which flourished in central and eastern Africa. These new societies

had the same features of the ancient Egyptian model government, beliefs, and building technologies. The dispersion to central and southern Africa in the 11th century, began from near the Upper Bennu River, to the Congo and Southern Africa. Academia and records tell us that this was the largest migration in Africa's history. These people, who are called *Bantu,* created states that emerged in Africa's interior without any reference to events at the coast.[108]

We give the final word on this topic to Dr Mendelssohn. He urges some caution in the use of this type of data:

> It is, of course, dangerous to rely too much on this similarity between African customs which have been retained to this day and a civilisation [Ancient Egypt] that flourished thousands of years ago. On the other hand it is equally unrealistic to disregard completely the undoubtedly existing parallels. If nothing else, we can look upon some of the customs and beliefs which have survived in Africa as a possible pointer to the thoughts and motives of the people of Ancient Egypt which have been lost to us.[109]

Notes

[1] Chancellor Williams, *The Destruction of Black Civilization,* US, Third World Press, 1987.
[2] Ibid., pp.176-194.
[3] J. C. DeGraft-Johnson, *African Glory,* UK, Watts & Co, 1954, p.23.
[4] Quoted in John G. Jackson, *Ages of Gold and Silver,* US, A. A. Press, 1990, p.245.
[5] Cf. Michael Butcher, *Mauritania's Slavery Shame,* in *The Voice,* UK, Voice Communications, 10 January 1995, p.13 and *Sudan Human Rights Voice,* UK, Sudan Human Rights Organisation, October 1993.
[6] Runoko Rashidi, *Commentary: Black Bondage in Asian Lands,* in *African Presence in Early Asia,* ed Runoko Rashidi, US, Transaction Publishers, 1995, pp.138-9 and Graham W. Irwin, *African Bondage in Asian Lands,* in *African Presence in Early Asia,* ed Runoko Rashidi, US, Transaction Publishers, 1995, pp.140-5.
[7] Lady Lugard, *A Tropical Dependency,* UK, James Nisbet & Co, 1906, p.201.
[8] Quoted in Raymond Michelet, *African Empires and Civilisations,* in *Negro: An Anthology,* ed Nancy Cunard, US, Frederick Ungar Publishing Co., 1970, p.369.
[9] Quoted in ibid.
[10] Quoted in ibid.
[11] Maulana Karenga, *Introduction to Black Studies,* US, University of Sankore Press, 1982, p.69.
[12] Basil Davidson, *The African Slave Trade,* US, Little, Brown and Company, 1980, pp.53-5.
[13] Ibid., p.57.
[14] Edmund B. D'Auvergne, *Human Livestock,* quoted in J. C. DeGraft-Johnson, African Glory, p.157.
[15] F. George Kay, *The Shameful Trade,* UK, Frederick Muller, 1967, p.64.
[16] Barros, *The Portuguese Land at Elmina,* in *Pageant of Ghana,* ed Freda Wolfson, UK, Oxford University Press, 1958, pp.39-44.

[17] Winwood Reade, *The Martyrdom of Man,* UK, Watts & Co., 1934 edition, p.272.

[18] Cf. John G. Jackson, *Introduction to African Civilizations,* US, Citadel Press, 1970, pp.304-5.

[19] Basil Davidson, *The African Slave Trade,* pp.63-4.

[20] Ibid., pp.64-5.

[21] Chapman Cohen, *Christianity, Slavery and Labour,* quoted in John G. Jackson, *Ages of Gold and Silver,* p.222.

[22] Basil Davidson, *The African Slave Trade,* pp.65 and 68.

[23] Ibid., p.65.

[24] Ibid., p.67.

[25] F. George Kay, *The Shameful Trade,* p.30.

[26] Quoted in John G. Jackson, *Ages of Gold and Silver,* p.223.

[27] F. George Kay, *The Shameful Trade,* p.41.

[28] Stanley Lane-Poole, *The Story of the Moors in Spain,* US, Black Classic Press, 1990 (original 1886), p.279.

[29] Basil Davidson, *The African Slave Trade,* p.71.

[30] F. George Kay, *The Shameful Trade,* p.44.

[31] Basil Davidson, *The African Slave Trade,* pp.71 and 74.

[32] Ibid.

[33] Ibid., p.74.

[34] Ibid., pp.75-6.

[35] Ibid., pp.64-5.

[36] Eric Williams, *Capitalism and Slavery,* UK, Andre Deutsch, 1944, p.101.

[37] Cf. Frederic G. Cassidy, *Jamaica Talk,* UK, Macmillan, 1961, p.17.

[38] J. C. DeGraft-Johnson, *African Glory,* p.153.

[39] Ivan Van Sertima, *Blacks in Science: Ancient and Modern,* US, Transaction Publishers, 1983, pp.7-8.

[40] Ibid., pp.8-9.

[41] Chancellor Williams, *The Destruction of Black Civilization,* pp.56-7.

[42] Quoted in Muhammad Al-Hajj, *Some Diplomatic Correspondence of the Seifuwa Mais of Borno with Egypt, Turkey and Morocco,* in *Studies in the History of Pre-Colonial Borno,* ed Bala Usman & Nur Alkali, Nigeria, Northern Nigeria Publishing Company, 1983, p.165.

[43] Basil Davidson, *The African Slave Trade,* p.73.

[44] W. E. B. Du Bois, *The World and Africa,* US, International Publishers, 1965, p.52.

[45] J. C. DeGraft-Johnson, *African Glory,* p.105.

[46] Arnold Toynbee, *A Study of History,* quoted in *Man, God, and Civilization,* John G. Jackson, US, Citadel Press, 1972, p.184.

[47] Lady Lugard, *A Tropical Dependency,* p.339.

[48] Christopher Ehret, *The Civilizations of Africa,* UK, James Currey, 2002, pp.413-4.

[49] Towerson, *English Impressions,* in *Pageant of Ghana,* ed Freda Wolfson, UK, Oxford University Press, 1958, pp.47 and 49.

[50] Ibid., pp.49-50.

[51] Barbot, *French Views,* in *Pageant of Ghana,* ed Freda Wolfson, UK, Oxford University Press, 1958, p.63.

[52] Ibid., p.70.

[53] Ibid., pp.70-1.

[54] Ibid., p.72.

[55] Bosman, *The Coast, 1700,* in *Pageant of Ghana,* ed Freda Wolfson, UK, Oxford University Press, 1958, pp.80-1.

[56] Ibid., pp.82-3.

[57] Ibid., pp.83-4.

[58] Freda Wolfson ed, *Pageant of Ghana,* pp.2-3.

[59] Basil Davidson, *Africa in History,* UK, Macmillan, 1991, pp.237-240 and Basil Davidson, *African Kingdoms,* Netherlands, Time-Life Books, 1967, pp.107-8.

[60] Thomas Bowditch, *At Kumasi,* in *African Civilization Revisited,* ed Basil Davidson, US, Africa World Press, 1991, p.385.

[61] Reade, *The Palace, Kumasi, 1874,* in *Pageant of Ghana,* ed Freda Wolfson, UK, Oxford University Press, 1958, pp.161-2.

[62] W. E. B. Du Bois, *The World and Africa,* pp.61-2.

[63] Abdias Do Nascimento, *Brazil: Mixture or Massacre?* US, The Majority Press, 1989, p.28.

[64] Anthony Coleman ed, *Millennium: A Thousand Years of History,* UK, Bantam Press, 1999, p.186.

[65] Abdias Do Nascimento, *Brazil: Mixture or Massacre?* p.29.

[66] Leonard Barrett, *The Rastafarians,* US, Beacon, 1988, p.30.

[67] Ibid., p.31.

[68] Quoted in ibid., p.31.

[69] Ibid., p.32.

[70] Ibid., pp.36-7.

[71] Anthony Coleman ed, *Millennium: A Thousand Years of History,* p.186.

[72] James Rodway, *The West Indies and the Spanish Main,* UK, T. Fisher Unwin, 1896, pp.225-7.

[73] Ibid., p.213.

[74] Edmund B. D'Auvergne, *Human Livestock,* quoted in J. C. DeGraft-Johnson, *African Glory,* p.160.

[75] James Rodway, *The West Indies and the Spanish Main,* p.214.

[76] Maulana Karenga, *Introduction to Black Studies,* pp.98-9.

[77] Ibid., pp.100-1.

[78] Julius Lester, *To Be a Slave,* UK, Longman Group, 1968, p.99.

[79] Jacob Carruthers, *The Irritated Genie,* US, The Kemetic Institute, 1985.

[80] Ibid., pp.110-1.

[81] Siaf Millar, *Afrikan Enslavement: The Numbers Game,* UK, Unpublished Paper, 1995.

[82] Quoted in Alan Scholefield, *The Dark Kingdoms,* UK, Heinemann, 1975, pp.29-30.

[83] Basil Davidson, *Africa in History,* p.284.

[84] John G. Jackson, *Introduction to African Civilizations,* pp.310-12. The eleven million figure is very conservative see also Siaf Millar, *In The Name of Civilisation,* in *The Alarm: Issue 18,* ed Pascoe Sawyers, UK, Alarm Promotions, May-June 1996, pp.16-8.

[85] Colin Legum, *Pan-Africanism: A Short Political Guide,* UK, Pal Mall Press, 1962, pp.24-5.

[86] Ibid., pp.28-9 and 133-4.

[87] Ibid., pp.29-30.

[88] Maulana Karenga, *Introduction to Black Studies,* pp.116-120 and see also James G. Spady, *Marcus Mosiah Garvey,* in *Great Black Leaders,* ed Ivan Van Sertima, US, Transaction Publishers, 1988, pp.370-408.

[89] Colin Legum, *Pan-Africanism: A Short Political Guide,* pp.31-3 and 135-7.

[90] John G. Jackson, *Introduction to African Civilizations*, p.198.

[91] Abbé Amélineau, *Prolegomenes a l'etude de la religion Egyptienne*, 1916, quoted in *European Scholars on the African Origins of the Africans of Antiquity*, Mwalimu I. Mwadilifu, US, ECA Associates, 1991, p.18.

[92] Georg Gerster, *Threatened Treasures of the Nile*, in *National Geographic, Volume 124: Number 4*, ed Melville Bell Grosvenor, US, National Geographic Society, October 1963, p.602. See also pp.586-621.

[93] Sir Harry Johnston, *The Uganda Protectorate, Volume II*, UK, Hutchinson & Co., 1902, p.473.

[94] J. Spencer Trimingham, *A History of Islam in West Africa*, UK, Oxford University Press, 1962, pp.104-5.

[95] Quoted in Nnamdi Elleh, *African Architecture: Evolution and Transformation*, US, McGraw-Hill, 1997, p.25.

[96] Felix Dubois, *Timbuctoo the Mysterious*, UK, William Heinemann, 1897, pp.84-6.

[97] Roland Oliver & Brian M. Fagan, *Africa in the Iron Age*, UK, Cambridge University Press, 1975, p.69. See also pp.67-8.

[98] Ibid., p.68.

[99] Basil Davidson, *Old Africa Rediscovered*, UK, Victor Gollancz, 1959, p.67.

[100] Kurt Mendelssohn, *The Riddle of the Pyramids*, UK, Thames and Hudson, 1974, p.24.

[101] Frank Willett, *Ife and its Archaeology*, in *Papers in African Prehistory*, ed J. D. Fage & R. A. Oliver, UK, Cambridge University Press, 1970, p.324.

[102] Leo Frobenius, *The Voice of Africa: Volume II*, UK, Hutchinson & Co., 1913, pp.626-7.

[103] J. Theodore Bent, *The Ruined Cities of Mashonaland, 3rd Edition*, UK, Longmans, Green and Co., 1902, p.56.

[104] Carl Engel, *The Music of the Most Ancient Nations*, UK, John Murray, 1864, p.34. See also pp.210-1.

[105] Ibid., pp.219 and 223-5.

[106] J. Theodore Bent, *The Ruined Cities of Mashonaland, 3rd Edition*, pp.81-2.

[107] Roland Oliver & Brian M. Fagan, *Africa in the Iron Age*, p.208.

[108] Moustafa Gadalla, *Exiled Egyptians: The Heart of Africa*, US, Tehuti Research Foundation, 1999, p.301.

[109] Kurt Mendelssohn, *The Riddle of the Pyramids*, p.24.

CHAPTER NINETEEN: THE PEOPLING OF THE ANCIENT EAST

A splendid era of black seems to have preceded all the later races! There must once have been a tremendous Negro expansion, since the original masters of all the lands between Iberia [i.e. Spain] and the Cape of Good Hope [i.e. South Africa] and East India were primitive and probably dwarfed [B]lack men. We have long had proof that a primitive Negroid race of pigmies [sic] once lived around the Mediterranean. Blacks were the first to plow the mud of the Nile, they were the dark skinned, curly haired Kushites. Blacks were masters of Sumeria and Babylon [i.e. Iraq] before it became the country of the four tongues. And in India, the kingdom of the Dravidian Monarchs, the [B]lack and godless enemies existed until the period of written history.[1]

So wrote German historian Herr Eugen Georg. The Greek writers of antiquity designated a considerable portion of the ancient Near East and southern Asia as Ethiopia. These very regions were associated with the earliest civilisations ever to have existed in Asia. But who built them? Sir Wallis Budge informs us that:

> It seems certain that classical historians and geographers called the whole region from India to Egypt, both countries inclusive, by the name of "Ethiopia," and in consequence they regarded all the dark-skinned and [B]lack peoples who inhabited it as "Ethiopians."[2]

Good examples are Homer, the eighth century BC author of *The Iliad* and *The Odyssey,* and Herodotus, the learned historian of the fifth century BC. They classified the populations of Sudan, Egypt, Palestine, Arabia, Mesopotamia (i.e. Iraq and Syria), and India, as Ethiopians.[3]

Lady Lugard tells us that: "The fame of the Ethiopians was widespread in ancient history". Continuing this theme, she adds:

> The annals of all the great early nations of Asia Minor are full of them. The Mosaic [i.e. Biblical] records allude to them frequently; but while they are described as the most powerful, the most just, and the most beautiful of the human race, they are constantly spoken of as black, and there seems to be no other conclusion to be drawn, than that at that remote period of history the leading race of the Western world was a [B]lack race.[4]

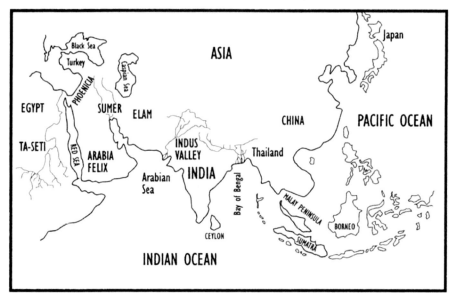

The Ancient East. (Map: Kieron Vital).

If Budge and Lugard are correct, there appears to be strong agreement between the Greek historians and geographers, the Mosaic records, and the annals of "all the great early nations of Asia Minor" concerning the original peopling of the ancient Near East and southern Asia.

Sir Richmond Palmer, the astonishingly erudite English Africanist, described the early distribution of the Sudanese, as stated by Mediæval Arabic documents. "The word Sudan", says Sir Richmond:

> comes from an Arabic root which means swarthy or black. The Sudanese were to the Arabs, at the time of their political ascendancy which extended to mediæval Europe, the people of swarthy or dark appearance whose habitat lay nearest to Syria, North Africa and Europe. The races of the Sudan [i.e. Negroes] were, however, separated from the Mediterranean and the Caucasian races and the main centres of Arab civilization by the great stretches of desert which extended from the Persian Gulf to the shores of the Atlantic in the region of Cape Verde and Cape Blanco. As a geographical term therefore the word Sudan, properly speaking, always implied or connoted all the regions which subtended on the south or lay adjacent to the deserts which extend from Oman and Hadramaut [in Arabia] through Nubia to Lake Chad and the Bight of Benin.[5]

Writing in the ninth century AD, Al-Jahiz, the brilliant Black Arab scholar, stated that:

As we said the Blacks are more numerous than the Whites since they are made
up of the Ethiopians, the Fezzans, Berbers, Copts, Nubians, Fagwans, the
people of Mero[ë], Ceylon, India, Quamar and Indo-China … The isles
between Africa and China are all peopled with Blacks; that is Ceylon, Kalah,
Zabig. Most of the Arabs also are as black as we, the Negroes are, and cannot
be counted amongst the Whites."[6]

The Arabic sources, although written in the mediæval period, corroborate the
Classical sources. Can other evidence be brought to bear on this question?
   Edward Balfour, writing in 1885, gave a clear statement of the ethnological
or physical anthropological position as the evidence then appeared:

Ethnologists are of the opinion that Africa has had an important influence in the
colonization of Southern Asia, of India, and of the Easter Islands in times prior
to authentic history or tradition. The marked African features of some of the
people in the extreme south of the Peninsula of India, the Negro and Negrito
[i.e. Pygmy] races of the Andamans and Great Nicobar, the Semang, Bila, and
Jakun of the Malay Peninsula, and the Negrito and Negro, Papuan and
Malagasi races of the islands of the Indian Archipelago, Australia, and
Polynesia, indicate the extent of the colonization.

Mr Balfour draws a clear conclusion from the evidence.

[I]t becomes highly probable that the African element in the population of the
Peninsula [i.e. India] has been transmitted from an archaic period before the
Semitic, Turanian [i.e. Mongolian], and Iranian races entered India and when
the Indian Ocean had Negro tribes along its northern as well as its eastern and
western shores … Perhaps all the original population of southern Arabia, and
even of the Semitic lands was once African.[7]

Later anthropological scholarship would corroborate this view. Sir Arthur
Keith was a highly distinguished scholar, soon to become master of the British
physical anthropologists. Writing in 1932, he discussed this prehistoric
distribution of the Black race:

The enigma of modern anthropology [says Sir Arthur] is the Black Belt of
mankind. It commences in Africa and peters out among the natives of the
Melanesian Islands of the Pacific. At each extremity of the belt, in Africa as in
Melanesia, we find peoples with black skins, woolly hair, more or less
beardless, prognathous and long-headed. We cannot suppose these [N]egro
peoples, although now widely separated, have been evolved independently of
each other. We therefore suppose that at one time a proto-[N]egroid belt crossed
the ancient world, occupying all intermediate lands, Arabia, Baluchistan, India,
Further India, the Philippines and Malay Archipelago. We further suppose that
intermediate parts of the proto-[N]egroid belt became transformed, giving rise
to the hamitic peoples of Africa and to their cousins the Dravidian and brown-
skinned peoples of India.

Sir Arthur explained in general terms what happened to some of these Negro populations:

> Then, at an uncertain date, the great Black belt was broken into by two great eruptions from the north. The Mongolian [i.e. Yellow] stock, evolved to the north of the Himalayas, broke southwards into Further India, the Malay Archipelago, and reached the islands of the Pacific, obliterating, except in isolated areas, the people of the proto-[N]egroid belt, thus isolating the people of India from those of Melanesia. There was another racial break-through which separated - in a racial sense - India from Africa … The Caucasian stock broke southwards into the Arabian peninsula and the lands which link Mesopotamia to the Punjab, Persia, Baluchistan and Afghanistan.[8]

We cannot entirely agree with the position taken by Balfour and Georg. They have unwittingly given the impression that Africans colonised Asia just before the Semites and Aryans got there. It is much more likely that the early Negro populations in Asia were descended from much earlier dispersals of Black people from that hoary age when early man populated the globe. As previously discussed, some of these early peoples evolved into Caucasians and others into Mongolians. In southern and western Asia, however, due to the similarity of climatic conditions to those prevailing in Africa, these early peoples maintained their African appearance.

Canon George Rawlinson was a celebrated scholar in the nineteenth century. Holding the position of Camden Professor of Ancient History at the University of Oxford, he was also the Canon of Canterbury. He translated the writings of Herodotus and included many supplementary essays to contextualise the Greek historian's findings in the light of modern, that is, nineteenth century scholarship. One such essay, *On the Ethnic Affinities of the Nations of Western Asia,* was particularly impressive. Rawlinson wrote an instructive discussion of the peopling of the ancient East and the Caucasianisation that later followed:

> Recent linguistic discovery [i.e. in 1862] tends to show that a Cushite or Ethiopian race did in the earliest times extend itself … from Abyssinia [i.e. Modern Ethiopia] to India. The whole Peninsula of India was peopled by a race of this character before the influx of the Arians [i.e. Aryans]: it extended from the Indus along the seacoast through modern Beloochistan [sic] and Kerman, which was the proper country of the Asiatic Ethiopians; the cities on the northern shores of the Persian Gulf are shown by the brick inscriptions found among their ruins to have belonged to this race; it was dominant in Susiana [i.e. Iran] and Babylonia [i.e. Iraq], until over-powered in the one country by Arian [sic], in the other by Semitic intrusion; it can be traced, both by dialect and tradition, throughout the whole south coast of the Arabian peninsula, and it still exists in Abyssinia, where the language of the principle tribe (the Galla) furnishes, it is thought, a clue to the cuneiform inscriptions of Susiana and Elymais.[9]

The Asiatic Ethiopians, to which the professor alludes, are generally thought to have been the Dravidians, the first inhabitants of India and Pakistan.[10] Founders of the ancient civilisation of the Indus Valley, there are some 100 million Dravidian speakers in southern India today. Many, though by no means all, are of very black complexions with straight, wavy or curly hair. Some are indistinguishable from Africans,[11] but the vast majority resemble the indigenous Australians. Mr Godfrey Higgins, author of *Anacalypsis,* discussed this. We have reproduced the following from this great work:

> Mr. [Wilford] … informs us that many very ancient statues of the God Buddha in India have crisp, curly hair, with flat noses and thick lips; and adds, "nor can it be reasonably doubted, that a race of Negroes formerly had power and pre-eminence in India." This is confirmed by Mr. Maurice, who says, "The figures in the Hindoo [sic] caverns are of a very different character from the present race of Hindoos: their countenances are broad and full, the nose flat, and the lips, particularly the under lip, remarkably thick …" [The] testimony of the Rev. Mr. Maurice is fully confirmed by Sir W. Jones, who says, "The remains of architecture and sculpture in India … seem to prove an early connexion between this country and Africa … the ancient Hindus, according to Strabo, differed in nothing from the Africans but in the straightness and smoothness of their hair, while that of the others was crisp and woolly; a difference proceeding chiefly, if not entirely, from the respective humidity or dryness of their atmospheres."[12]

Later scholarship corroborates this. Professor Lynn Thorndike, author of *A Short History of Civilisation,* described the Ancient Indians as "short black men with almost Negro noses".[13] Dr Will Durant in *Our Oriental Heritage* described them as "a dark skinned, broad nosed people whom, without knowing the origin of the word, we call Dravidians."[14]

Recent South Indian scholarship continues to show an awareness of the facts. Professor Uthaya Naidu, author of *The Bible of Aryan Invasions, Volume II,* wrote the following data:

> The Aryan invasions [of India] which led to the collapse of the Semito-Negroid Indus Valley civilization plunged India into 2500 years of darkness lasting from 1500 BC to 1000 AD. It may sound cruel but the Vedic religion does prescribe that the Aryan race is superior to other races and is hence justified in massacring, looting and ruling over all others. These Brahmanic Dark Ages were the darkest ever experienced in the history of mankind. The initial 1000 years, comprising the Vedic Dark Ages (1500 BC - 500 BC) of this episode were the darkest of all. The Early Vedic Dark Ages were marked by two major devastating Aryan invasions.[15]

There is a website called *Statement of Aims and Objectives [Mughalstan Nation].* It exists to promote the cause "of a sovereign and independ[e]nt

Mughalstan homeland for the South Asian Muslims and a restoration of the fabulous 1000-year Mughal Caliphate." On the web page is a section called *Historical Justice* where we read the following:

> Although the land originally belonged to Sudroid [cf. Sudra] Negroes, these peoples were exterminated by blood-thirsty Aryan invaders in the cataclysmic Sudra [in Hinduism this means low caste] Holocaust. The glorious Indus Valley Civilization was completely wiped out by the Vedic Aryans. Moreover, the Buddhists and Jains were subsequently annihilated by the Brahminists [i.e. Aryans], and it is to free the oppressed peoples of South Asia, who were enslaved to the most terrible tyranny of Brahminism, that Mahmud-e-Ghazni and the Islamic heroes decided to liberate South Asia. Mughalstan thus meant liberation for millions of South Asians, who welcomed the establishment of Mughalstan in the regions depopulated by Brahminist Genocides.[16]

Khshatrapa Gandasa, wrote *Four-Nation Theory: Sakastan, Dalitstan, Mughalstan and Hindu Rashtra.* In this essay we read the following data:

> Study of South Asian history reveals that the subcontinent was a collection of several distinct nations, each with its own distinctive race, language, culture and independ[e]nt history ... History reveals that the following historically distinct and separate nations have existed for the last several centuries in South Asia before being illegally occupied by the Brahminists [i.e. Aryans]: Dalitstan and Dravidistan - The aboriginal Sudroid populations of Africoid descent have formed the historically distinct nations of Dalitstan and Dravidistan (both being lumped together as 'Sudrastan') for more than 4000 years. Dalitstan is a modern term comprising the historically Adivasi dominated regions of Gondwana, Jharkhand, Baghelkhand and Bundelkhand (all attested in 18th-century Mughal chronicles), whilst Dravidistan comprises the historically separate Dravidian-speaking regions of Tamil Nadu, Kerala, Karnataka and Telingana. The Chola empire, Gondwana kingdom and Cera kingdom were only some of the more glorious Sudroid empires of yore before the Brahminists destroyed these states![17]

Professor Rawlinson's allusion to the invasions of earliest India and Iran by Aryans (Caucasians speaking Indo-European languages), and the invasion of early Iraq by Semites, are of considerable importance in understanding the racial picture of the Middle East and southern Asia of today. 'Ethiopians' (a Greek term) or 'Kushites/Cushites' (the Hebrew equivalent) were the first and at one time the *only* inhabitants of western and southern Asia. Descendants of the early dispersals of Africans across the globe, these were the Blacks described by Georg, Budge, Lugard, Palmer, Al-Jahiz, Balfour, Keith and Rawlinson. Skeletal remains of them date back 95,000 years or more. By 10,000 BC, the Natufian Culture was established in the region, primarily in Palestine. Dr Charles Finch[18] suggests that it was the parent of the later civilisations that followed, such as Sumer (Iraq), Elam (Iran), Arabia Felix (Yemen), and the Indus Valley (India/Pakistan).

The Elamites flourished in the region now designated as Iran. Many of the earlier authorities classified them as Cushites. Professor Rawlinson, writing in 1862, described them based on their depictions in the art of Assyria, a Semitic culture that flourished in today's Syria region:

> In Susiana [i.e. the capital of Elam], where the Cushite blood was maintained in tolerable purity ... there was, if we may trust the Assyrian remains, a very decided prevalency of a [N]egro type of countenance, as the accompanying specimens, carefully copied from the sculptures, will render evident [Professor Rawlinson reproduces two sketches here from the art of Assyria of an Elamite and also a Kushite for comparison]. The head was covered with short crisp curls, the eye was large, nose and mouth in the same line, the lips thick.[19]

Mr Philip Smith, author of an outstanding student history, corroborated the findings of Rawlinson a few years later, though his source material was different. From an analysis of old Persian accounts, he concluded that:

> The Iranian branch [of the Aryan invaders] ... overran Media, eastern Susiana, Persia [i.e. Elam], and the fertile parts of Carmania; expelling from those countries or reducing the old Cushite inhabitants, whom the Iranian legends describe as men of a black complexion, with short and woolly hair.[20]

In a journal article dated 1887, Reginald Poole, of the British Museum staff, informs us that: "There is one portrait of an Elamite (Cushitic) king on a vase found at Susa [i.e. the Elamite capital]; he is painted black and thus belongs to the Cushite race."[21]

The French archaeologist, M. Marcel Dieulafoy, conducted a systematic excavation of Elam for the first time. In 1894 he published the findings in a pioneering study entitled *L'Acropole de Susa*. Unfortunately this is a very rare book but Professor Diop has quoted portions from it that we have reproduced:

> On removing a tomb placed across a raw-brick wall which was part of the fortifications of the Elamite gate [says Dieulafoy], the workers uncovered a funeral urn. The urn was encased in a masonry covering composed of enamelled bricks. These came from a panel depicting a personage superbly dressed in a green robe with yellow, blue, and white embroidery. He wore a tiger skin and carried a cane or a golden spear. Most surprising of all, the personage whose lower jaw, beard, neck, and hand I found was [B]lack. His lips were thin, the beard thick; the embroidery, of archaic style, seemed to be the work of Babylonian artisans ... Only powerful personages had the right to carry long canes and wear bracelets. Only the governor of a fortified post could have his image embroidered on his tunic. Yet, the owner of the cane, the master of the citadel was [B]lack. It is therefore highly probable that Elam was ruled by

a [B]lack dynasty and, judging by the features of the face already described, an Ethiopian dynasty … [22]

Sir Gaston Maspero, the distinguished French scholar of the early twentieth century, described the Elamites thus: "a short robust people of well-knit figure with brown skins, black hair and eyes, who belonged to that Negritic race which inhabited a considerable part of Asia".[23]

Dr Roland Dixon, Professor of Anthropology at Harvard University, showed that descendants of the Elamites continue to exist in Iran. Published in 1923, *The Racial History of Man* contains the following information:

> In the south, along the shores of the Persian Gulf, there was a narrow fringe of dark-skinned, frizzly-haired folk of simple culture, blends perhaps of the Proto-Negroid and the Proto-Australoid types [i.e. similar to Australian Aborigines], comparable with a large part of the population of southern India to-day.[24]

More recent scholarship has provided additional data. Professor Walther Hinz, author of *The Lost World of Elam,* says the following, based on an analysis of Persian artefacts:

> In the glazed relief of his bodyguards with which Darius, king of Persians, decorated the Palace at Susa in 500 B.C., the artist clearly depicts three different races. Some guards are white-skinned, and are obviously intended to represent Persians, although in Elamite garb. A second group is brown-skinned and a third is very dark, almost black. These must be the Elamites from the hinterland.[25]

Dr Richard Frye, the Aga Khan Professor of Iranian History at Harvard University, edited a useful work entitled *The History of Iran.* Published in 1984, we read the following intelligence:

> We may summarize the recent work on the ethnology and anthropology of Iranian areas briefly. In the realm of physical anthropology and the study of crania, the presence of Negrito [i.e. Pygmy] elements in southern Iran and Baluchistan, as well as Dravidian types in Central Asia in ancient times leads to the supposition that the pre-Aryan inhabitants of the Iranian plateau [i.e. Elamites] did leave clues to their identity, but work in this domain has only begun.[26]

John Baldwin, an American Orientalist, wrote an important work on Arabian antiquities in 1869, called *Pre-Historic Nations.* This work traces the earliest civilisations of Arabia. Baldwin informs us that:

> At the present time [i.e. 1869] Arabia is inhabited by two distinct races, namely descendants of the old Adite [i.e. a descendant of Ham], Kushite, or Ethiopian

race, known under various appellations, and dwelling chiefly at the south, the east, and in central parts of the country, but formerly supreme throughout the whole peninsula; and the Semitic Arabians - Mahomet's race - found chiefly in the Hejaz and at the north. In some districts of the country these races are more or less mixed, and since the rise of Mahometanism [i.e. Islam] the language of the Semites, known to us as Arabic, has almost wholly superseded the old Ethiopian or Kushite tongue ... To the Kushite belongs the purest Arabian blood.[27]

Mr Baldwin cannot be completely correct. He suggests that the oldest known languages of Arabia belonged to the Kushite group. While these languages are indeed different to Arabic and share affinities to languages spoken in Ethiopia, they actually belong to the Semitic group. He is correct, however, to suggest that the earliest Arabs belonged to an "Adite, Kushite, or Ethiopian race". Sir John Gardiner Wilkinson, cited in an earlier chapter, noted that both Pliny the Elder, and Hebrew sources, depict the early Arabs as Black. Physical anthropologists in Mr Balfour's time, shared this view. An old *Encyclopaedia Britannica* had this to say about the early Arabs:

The inhabitants of Yemen, Hadramaut, Oman and the adjoining districts, in shape of head, color, length and slenderness of limbs and scantiness of hair, point to an African origin.[28]

Dr Bertram Thomas, an authority on Arabian antiquities and a former Prime Minister to the Sultan of Muscat and Oman, was particularly well informed on this issue. He declared that:

The original inhabitants of Arabia then, according to Sir Arthur Keith, one of the world's greatest living anthropologists, who has made a study of Arab skeletal remains, ancient and modern, were not the familiar Arabs of our own time but a very much darker people. A proto-[N]egroid belt of mankind stretched across the ancient world from Africa to Malaya. This belt, by environmental and other evolutionary processes, became in parts transformed, giving rise to the Hamitic peoples of Africa, to the Dravidian peoples of India, and to an intermediate dark people inhabiting the Arabian peninsula. In the course of time two big migrations of fair-skinned peoples came from the north, one of them, the Mongoloids, to break through and transform the dark belt of man beyond India; the other, the Caucusoids [sic], to drive a belt between India and Africa.[29]

More recent findings by Russian anthropologists corroborate the earlier research. They found that Equatorial (i.e. African) types originally peopled Arabia and the surrounding regions.[30] Other evidence shows that these Black populations are still there:

> Non Mediterranean Veddoids [i.e. Pygmies] live as a minority in parts of the southern Yemen and the Western Aden Protectorate; in the Hadramaut they become numerically important, while still farther east they are the chief factor in the tribes of Mahra-land [i.e. the Mahras], at the extreme end of the Aden Protectorate, and the Shahara, Qara, and other tribes in the Sultanate of Oman. All these tribes speak pre-Arabic Semitic languages.[31]

According to Professor Diop, between 5000 and 4000 BC, Caucasian people speaking Indo-European languages invaded Western Asia from the north. The intermarriage between the invading peoples and the early Black populations created a Mulatto population speaking Semitic languages. Prior to this period, the Semites did not exist.[32] Where there was little or no intermarriage, the Blacks retained their languages and the Whites retained theirs. Sir Henry Rawlinson, the decipherer of cuneiform, classifies the languages of the early Blacks as Cushitic. The languages spoken by the invading Whites were, of course, Indo-European.

There is another theory, first advanced by Joseph Greenberg. He claimed that both Cushitic and Semitic originated in the region now designated Ethiopia and later spread to Arabia and elsewhere by migration.[33] According to this view, the Semites of Arabia and the Middle East were originally Africans. In later periods they became modified in appearance by intermixture with other peoples invading from the north. In contemporary academic circles, this latter theory appears to be gaining the upper hand.

The Semites became dominant for the first time in history when the Akkadians, led by Sargon I, overthrew the Sumerians in Mesopotamia. The date for this event, however, is controversial. Duncan MacNaughton gives it as 2895 BC. The Caucasian migration into Arabia, alluded to by Dr Thomas, is believed to have taken place in the eighteenth century BC for the first time.[34] The Blacks were pushed into the southern region of the peninsular (Arabia Felix), where they established a splendid civilisation. The rest of Arabia gradually took on a Mulatto character.[35] The Aryans invaded the Indus Valley, beginning in the third millennium BC. After much struggle, the Dravidians were pushed into the southern and central regions of India where the majority live today.[36]

To reiterate, the indigenous Negro populations were displaced, destroyed, or absorbed, by invading light-skinned peoples speaking (or adopting) Semitic or Indo-European languages. Western and southern Asia today is consequently a very mixed population but the Caucasian type greatly predominates. The Semitic language is dominant in Arabia, Syria, Iraq and Lebanon. Indo-European is dominant in Iran and India. Negro populations have survived in all of these regions. Among these are the Mahras of the Arabian peninsular, the dark populations of Iran, and some of the Dravidians of southern India. In all such cases, however, they have been submerged and are now marginalized. Of the distribution of these modern Black populations, Professor George Dorsey, one time curator of the Field Museum of Natural History, wrote the following:

> Open your atlas to a map of the world. Look at the Indian Ocean - on the west, Africa, on the north, the three great southern peninsulas of Asia [i.e. Arabia, India, Malay]; on the east, a chain of great islands terminating in Australia. Wherever that Indian Ocean touches land, it finds dark-skinned people with strongly developed jaws, relatively long arms and kinky or frizzled hair. Call that the Indian Ocean or Negroid division of the human race.[37]

Notes

[1] Eugen Georg, *The Adventure of Mankind*, US, E. P. Dutton & Co., 1931, pp.44-5. Quoted in John G. Jackson, *Man, God, and Civilization*, US, Citadel Press, 1972, pp.184-5.

[2] E. A. Wallis Budge, *A History of Ethiopia, Nubia & Abyssinia, Volume I-A*, US, ECA Associates, 1991 (original 1928), p.vii. See also and pp.1-2.

[3] John G. Jackson, *Man, God, and Civilization*, pp.188-190.

[4] Lady Lugard, *A Tropical Dependency*, UK, James Nisbet, 1905, p.221.

[5] Sir Richmond Palmer, *The Bornu Sahara and Sudan*, UK, John Murray, 1936, p.1.

[6] Abu 'Ulthman 'Amr Ibn Bahr Al-Jahiz, *The Book of the Glory of the Blacks Over the Whites*, quoted in J. A. Rogers, *World's Great Men of Color, Volume I*, US, Macmillan, 1972, p.169.

[7] Edward G. Balfour ed, *Negro Races*, in *Cyclopaedia of India, Third Edition, Volume II*, UK, Quaritch, 1885, p.1073. Quoted in W. E. B. DuBois, *The World and Africa*, US, International Publishers, 1965, pp.178-9.

[8] Sir Arthur Keith, *Appendix*, to *Arabia Felix*, by Bertram Thomas, UK, Jonathan Cape, 1932, pp.320-1.

[9] George Rawlinson (Translator), *History of Herodotus, 3rd Edition, Volume I*, UK, John Murray, 1875, p.675.

[10] Indus Khamit-Kush, *What They Never Told You in History Class*, US, Luxorr Publications, 1983, pp.173-201.

[11] Charles Finch, *Echoes of the Old Darkland*, US, Khenti, 1991, p.20.

[12] Godfrey Higgins, *Anacalypsis, Volume I*, US, A & B Publishers, 1992 (original 1836), pp.57-8.

[13] Quoted in John G. Jackson, *Man, God, and Civilization*, p.247.

[14] Ibid.

[15] Uthaya Naidu, *The Bible of Aryan Invasions, Volume II*, see http://www.light1998.com/The-Bible-of-Aryan-Invasions/ bibai2.html

[16] *Statement of Aims and Objectives [Mughalstan Nation]*, see http://www.geocities.com/mughalstan/mn/aimobjec.html

[17] Khshatrapa Gandasa, *Four-Nation Theory: Sakastan, Dalitstan, Mughalstan and Hindu Rashtra*, see http://www.dalitstan.org/books/gandasa/gandasa8.html

[18] Charles Finch, *Echoes of the Old Darkland*, pp.130-4.

[19] George Rawlinson, *Five Great Monarchies of the Ancient Eastern World, Fourth Edition, Volume III,* UK, John Murray, 1879, pp.325-6.

[20] Philip Smith, *The Ancient History of the East,* UK, John Murray, 1871, p.395.

[21] Reginald Stuart Poole, *The Egyptian Classification of the Races of Man,* in *The Journal of the Anthropological Institute, Volume xvi,* UK, Trübner & Co., 1887, p.371.

[22] Quoted in Cheikh Anta Diop, *The African Origin of Civilization: Myth or Reality?* US, Lawrence Hill Books, 1974, pp.103-4.

[23] Quoted in Runoko Rashidi, *Africans in Early Asian Civilizations: An Overview,* in *African Presence in Early Asia,* ed Runoko Rashidi, US, Transaction Publishers, 1995, p.26.

[24] Roland B. Dixon, *The Racial History of Man,* US, Charles Scribners' Sons, 1923, p.307.

[25] Walther Hinz, *The Lost World of Elam,* UK, Sidgwick & Jackson, 1972, pp.21-2.

[26] Richard N. Frye ed, *The History of Iran,* Germany, Verlagsbachhandlung München, 1984, p.41.

[27] Quoted in John G. Jackson, *Introduction to African Civilizations,* US, Citadel Press, 1970, p.70.

[28] Quoted in Drusilla Dunjee Houston, *Wonderful Ethiopians of the Ancient Cushite Empire,* US, Black Classic Press, 1985 (original 1926), pp.113-4.

[29] Bertram Thomas, *The Arabs,* UK, Thornton Butterworth, 1937, p.355.

[30] M. Nesturkh, *The Races of Mankind,* U.S.S.R., Foreign Languages Publishing, 1966, p.75.

[31] Naval Intelligence Division, *Western Arabia And The Red Sea,* June 1946, pp.368-9. Quoted in Runoko Rashidi, *Africans in Early Asian Civilizations: An Overview,* in *African Presence in Early Asia,* p.55.

[32] Charles Finch, *Echoes of the Old Darkland,* pp.130-1, and 135.

[33] For an example, see Martin Bernal, *Black Athena: Volume II,* UK, Free Association, 1991, p.531.

[34] Cheikh Anta Diop, *The African Origin of Civilization: Myth or Reality?* p.124.

[35] Ishakamusa Barashango, *Afrikan Genesis, Volume I,* US, IVth Dynasty Publishing Co., 1991, pp.54-5.

[36] Wayne Chandler, *The Jewel in the Lotus: The Ethiopian Presence in the Indus Valley Civilization,* in *African Presence in Early Asia,* ed Runoko Rashidi, US, Transaction Publishers, 1995, pp.102-4.

[37] George A. Dorsey, *Why We Behave Like Human Beings,* US, Harper and Bros., 1925, pp.44-5. Quoted in John G. Jackson, *Man, God, and Civilization,* pp.186-7.

CHAPTER TWENTY: SUMER AND ELAM

The Sumerian Problem

Sumer was the first civilisation to emerge in Asia. Called Chaldæa in some of
the literature and Primitive or Proto-Babylonia elsewhere,[1] it was situated
between the Tigris and the Euphrates valleys of southern Iraq. The rivers
played an important part in the evolution of culture, much as it did in Africa's
Nile Valley. The Greeks called the region 'Mesopotamia', meaning (the land)
between the rivers. From the earliest times the Tigris and the Euphrates
deposited their alluvium on a bed of rocks between Arabia and Iran.[2] Eighteen
ancient city-states emerged in the region including Eridu, Kish, Lagash,
Nippur, Umma, Ur, Uruk and Shurrupak. The Sumerians were succeeded by
Semitic cultures in approximately the same region, but centred towards the
north. Chief among these were Akkadia, Babylonia and Assyria. These cultures
were not contemporaneous but followed each other in chronological fashion
with long periods of overlap.

The origin and ethnicity of the Sumerians, the oldest culture, has become the
subject of a lengthy and unresolved debate. To begin, we discuss the ideas of
Dr Georges Roux. He is author of *Ancient Iraq;* currently the best popular
work on Mesopotamia. He asks:

> Who are these Sumerians, whose name can now be pronounced for the first
> time and who are going to occupy the state of history for the next thousand
> years? Do they represent a very ancient layer of population in prehistoric
> Mesopotamia, or did they come from some other country, and if so, when did
> they come and whence? This important problem has been debated again and
> again ever since the first relics of the Sumerian civilisation were brought to
> light more than a century ago, and is still with us.[3]

Before 1920, however, there was little real controversy. All important
authorities classified the Sumerians as Blacks, or else portrayed them as a
mixture of Black and Yellow. In addition, all authorities today are agreed that
they were not Semites. As Dr Roux admits: "The whole of the Early Dynastic
period (*c.* 2900-2334 BC) was to elapse before the first written [Semitic]
documents appeared in the north in the wake of the Akkadian conquerors."[4]

In 1836 Godfrey Higgins' superb *Anacalypsis* was published. This two-
volume work was a most interesting and scholarly attempt to reconstruct the

earliest pages of human history. With respect to the Sumerians, he wrote the following:

> In consequence of the prejudice (for it is really prejudice) against the Negro ...
> being learned and scientific, arising from an acquaintance with the present
> Negro character, I admit with *great difficulty* the theory of all the early
> astronomical knowledge of the Chaldees having been acquired or invented by
> his race, and that the Chaldees [i.e. Sumerians] were originally Negroes.[5]

Similar ideas were widely expressed. In 1857 Count Adam Gurowski, a Polish aristocrat, wrote that "around the mouth of the Tigris, of the Euphrates, down to that of the Indus, originally dwelt the [B]lack, or, as now called the African brotherhood."[6]

With the birth of Assyriology, in the middle of the nineteenth century, the position of Higgins and Gurowski found continued support. Sir Henry Rawlinson was the Father of Assyriology. An authority of considerable erudition, his reputation was based on his pioneering decipherment of the cuneiform scripts of Mesopotamia and Persia. In this respect, Dr Roux calls him "that extraordinary army officer, sportsman, explorer and philologist, undoubtedly the greatest of all".[7] In a foundation essay, *On the Early History of Babylonia,* Sir Henry related that:

> In regard to the language of the primitive Babylonians, although in its
> grammatical structure it resembles dialects of the Turanian family, the
> vocabulary is rather Cushite or Ethiopian, belonging to that stock of tongues
> which in the sequel were everywhere more or less mixed up with the Semitic
> languages, but of which we have probably the purest modern specimins [sic] in
> the Mahra of Southern Arabia and the Galla of Abyssinia [i.e. modern
> Ethiopia].[8]

George Rawlinson, the brother of Sir Henry, was the Canon of Canterbury and also Camden Professor of Ancient History at the University of Oxford. He is, perhaps, best known for a superb set of volumes entitled *Five Great Monarchies of the Ancient Eastern World.* Originally published in 1862, this great work went through many later editions. Concerning the Sumerians, or as he prefers to call them, the "Proto-Chaldæan element", he notes that:

> [T]he primitive or Proto-Chaldæan element, [exerted] an influence which
> appears to have been considerable. This element, as has been already observed,
> was predominantly Cushite; and there is reason to believe that the Cushite race
> was connected not very remotely with the [N]egro.[9]

Zénaïde Ragozin was a member of the Société Ethnologique of Paris and also the American Oriental Society. He wrote the popular text *Chaldea: The*

Story of the Nations. In this book, he presented a colourful theory of the origin of the Sumerians. He designates the earliest inhabitants of Iraq as Turanians. They were a Yellow people akin to the Chinese or Japanese. He believed that Cushites conquered them, invading from the east. The invaders introduced what we now identify as Sumerian culture. These Cushites were part of the race of Ham. According to Ragozin, however, they were dark coloured but definitely not Black. Moreover, they originated in Central Asia. Some of these brown skinned Cushites migrated into India [sic] where they encountered Black people for the first time where:

> Hundreds of years spent under a tropical clime and intermarriage with the Negro natives altered not only the colour of the skin, but also their features. So that when Cushite tribes, with the restless migratory spirit so characteristic of all early ages, began to work their way back again to the north, then to the west, along the shores of the Indian Ocean and the Persian Gulf [i.e. to Sumer], they were both dark-skinned and thick-lipped, with a decided tendency towards the Negro type.[10]

In 1887 Gerald Massey, an English scholar, wrote a fascinating and incisive essay entitled *The Hebrew and Other Creations Fundamentally Explained.* In this lecture, Massey emphasises the following point:

> But Cush is the [B]lack. The Cushites were the Black race; and the aborigines [i.e. original inhabitants] of Babylonia [i.e. Sumer] were the Black men of the monuments, the "black heads" of the Akkadian Texts.[11]

In 1907 Professor Charles Seignobos of the University of Paris issued *History of Ancient Civilization.* Written as a school text, it demonstrated what ideas were in the French mainstream at that time. He suggested that the Cushites or Hamites started civilisation but at a later date the White races penetrated their lands:

> It is within the limits of Asia and Africa that the first civilized peoples had their development - the Egyptians in the Nile Valley, the Chaldeans [i.e. Sumerians] in the plain of the Euphrates. They were peoples of sedentary and peaceful pursuits. Their skin was dark, the hair short and thick, the lips strong. Nobody knows their origin with exactness [i.e. in 1907] and scholars are not agreed on the name to give them (some terming them Cushites, others Hamites). Later, between the twentieth and twenty-fifth centuries B.C. came bands of martial shepherds who had spread over all Europe and the west of Asia - the Aryans and the Semites ... There is no clearly marked external difference between the Aryans and the Semites. Both are of the [W]hite race, having the oval face, regular features, clear skin, abundant hair, large eyes, thin lips, and straight nose. Both peoples were originally nomad shepherds, fond of war.[12]

In 1912 H. G. Spearing of the University of Oxford wrote *The Childhood of Art*. In this valuable work, he presented a discussion of the earliest Chaldean art. Professor Spearing wrote the following on the Sumerians:

> These people (in later times called Sumerians) had reached a fairly high stage of civilisation long before their independence was threatened by outsiders. This discovery was very disconcerting to literary historians and philologists, for that race was proved to be - not a branch of the civilising Aryans nor of the gifted Semitics, but of a [N]egroid people having affinities with the Mongols.

Emphasising this point, Spearing says:

> The conclusion arrived at scandalised the philological world, which, as Professor Sayce says, "was comfortably convinced that none but a Semitic or Aryan people could have been the originators of civilisation," and was "little able to understand what is meant by scientific evidence."[13]

Berosus was a priest of Belus during the time of Antiochus II (261-246 BC). He was the Mesopotamian equivalent of Manetho in that he compiled a history of Mesopotamia for a Greek audience. Like Manetho, his book is now lost. What we know of it comes from the quotations of Josephus, Polyhistor, and the Christian fathers. Interestingly, modern scholars do not like his chronology of Mesopotamia any more than Egyptologists like the chronology of Manetho. Concerning the origins of Sumerian culture, Berosus recounted a traditional story to the effect that:

> There was originally at Babylon [i.e. Sumer] a multitude of men of foreign race who had colonized Chaldea, and they lived without order, like animals. But in the first year there appeared, from out of the Erythrean Sea where it borders upon Babylonia, an animal endowed with reason, who was called Oannes. The whole body of the animal was that of a fish, but under the fish's head he had another head, and also feet below, growing out of the fish's tail, similar to those of a man; also human speech, and his image is preserved to this day. This being used to spend the whole day amidst men, without taking any food, and he gave them an insight into letters, and sciences, and every kind of art; he taught them how to found cities, to construct temples, to introduce laws and to measure land; in short, he instructed them in everything that softens manners and makes up civilization, so that from that time no one has invented anything new. Then, when the sun went down, this monstrous Oannes used to plunge back into the sea and spend the night in the midst of the boundless waves, for he was amphibious.[14]

Clearly this story needs to be interpreted. Those scholars who portray Sumer as a mixture of Black and Yellow interpret the "multitude of men of foreign race who had colonized Chaldea" as the Yellows. Furthermore, they interpret the fish-man "from out of the Erythrean Sea" as the conquering Blacks.

Sir Leonard Woolley was an Oxford educated archaeologist. He directed excavations in Iraq for many years. In his writings, he makes dubious and contradictory claims about the ethnic origins of the Sumerians.[15] However, he had read the above tradition by Berosus and agreed that Sumerian culture was not indigenous to Iraq, having been brought in from the sea. He commented that:

> [A]s our excavations seem to show, there is a good deal of truth in that tradition ... [I]t was not in the Euphrates valley that the arts were born, and although it is not likely to have been the Indus Valley [of India and Pakistan] either, later research may well discover some site between those two extremes where the ancestors of our Sumerians developed the first real civilisation of which we have any knowledge.[16]

This raises the question, where did the Sumerians come from? Logic would dictate that they came from either Nubia and/or Egypt, on the simple grounds that no other civilisations existed at that time. No other cultures had introduced writing, the sciences, the arts or city building. In addition, Sumerian texts mention the important place names Magan, Meluhha and Dilmun. They are said to give clues to where the Sumerians came from. Professor William J. Perry, an English scholar with a strong interest in the origin and spread of culture, attempted to identify these places:

> Since the culture of Sumer ... came from elsewhere, whence came it? The answer usually given is that it came from the mountainous regions of central Asia ... The Sumerian stories of origins tell a very different tale ... Dilmun has been identified with some place or other in the Persian Gulf, perhaps the Bahrein Islands, perhaps a land on the eastern shore of the Gulf; in any case, it was situated in the Gulf itself. With regard to Meluhha and Magan there is some dispute. In a late inscription of the Assyrians it is said that Magan and Meluhha were archaic names for Egypt and Ethiopia.[17]

Professor Perry, himself, identifies Meluhha as Yemen and Somalia. This may indicate that the ancestors of the Sumerians originally lived in Yemen, Somalia and also Egypt before migrating to Bahrain. From there, they migrated to Iraq.[18] Since Meluhha does mean 'Ethiopia', as Professor Perry admits, this may suggest that some of the ancestors of the Sumerians migrated from Nubia instead of Yemen or Somalia. The rest came from Egypt.

Sir Norman Lockyer, the brilliant English astronomer, took a different position. He suggested that the entire culture may have originated in Tanzania instead. In his own words:

> The colony who founded Eridu [i.e. the oldest of the Sumerian cities] were originally inhabitants of some country where the chief agricultural operations

> were carried on about the time of the Autumnal Equinox in the northern
> hemisphere. This country might lie south of the equator, and indeed we find one
> which answers the requirements in the region of the great lakes and on the coast
> opposite Zanzibar ... [T]hey would naturally have brought not only their
> southern stars, but their southern seasons with them; but their springtime was
> the northern autumn, their summer solstice the northern winter. This could have
> gone on for a time, and we see that their sun-god was the god of the winter
> solstice, Tammuz=Nergal.[19]

Modern Assyriologists are generally happier with theories that make no
mention of African origins. They prefer to claim that (i) they don't know where
the Sumerians originated from, or (ii) the Sumerians originated in India, or
finally (iii) the Sumerians originated in Persia. We believe that options two or
three aren't much of an improvement on the African theory. We have already
discussed solid evidence that the original inhabitants of India (i.e. the Indus
Valley) and Persia (i.e. Elam) were Black. Moreover, their descendants,
Negroes, Pygmies and Proto-Australoids, have survived to the present day.

Just as Black populations have survived in India and Iran, Herbert Wendt, a
German writer, informs us that: "the Sumerians did not disappear. Even to-day
[i.e. in 1963] their descendants live on, a dark-skinned group in the populations
of Hither Asia."[20] Dr Roux informs us that "the Ma'dan, or marsh-Arabs,
appear to have preserved to some extent the way of life of the early Sumerians
established on the fringe of the swamps more than five thousand years ago."[21]
Concerning the Marsh Arabs, an interesting article appeared in *The Sunday
Times Magazine* of 27 July 2003 entitled *The Eden Project.* In this report,
Christina Lamb, its author, told of the sorry fate of the Marsh Arabs. They face
discrimination in modern Iraq, instigated by the once ruling Ba'ath Party.
Lamb informs us that:

> The Marsh Arabs are a heavily built people of medium height, with light skins
> darkened by years in the sun. The official Ba'ath party newspaper, Al-Thawra,
> described them as 'monkey-faced people' who were not real Iraqis but
> descendants of [B]lack slaves brought to the south in the Middle Ages.[22]

Bringing all of this data together, we believe that populations descended
from the Sumerians survive today among the Marsh Arabs and other
populations in Hither Asia. They have preserved some of the ways of life of the
Sumerians of old. Moreover, some of these Marsh Arabs are Negroid enough
to prompt the once ruling Ba'athist establishment to erroneously claim that
they were descended from mediæval African captives.

Concerning the physical anthropology of the Sumerians, the Field Museum
and Oxford University carried out excavations in 1926 and 1928. Many of the
skulls were found to be hyperdolichocephalic (i.e. very long skulled). At the

time, however, the Field Museum published hazy and dubious conclusions from the data. This did not prevent Mrs Houston, the pioneering African-American Orientalist, from drawing her own conclusions. She wrote that: "Recent investigations of Oxford University [i.e. in 1926] at Kish in Mesopotamia reveal that the Sumerians were a [B]lack people".[23] Years later, Henry Field, the sponsor of the early excavations after whom the Field Museum was named, cited the following data in *Papers of the Peabody Museum, Volume 48:* "[T]he original inhabitants of the Caucasus probably consisted of very dark-skinned people … This would imply kinship with the hypothetically Negroid first inhabitants of Babylonia".[24]

These ideas are still relevant. Physical anthropology in recent times has undergone a new twist due to the pioneering work of Professor Richard Jantz and Stephen Ousley. Based at the Forensic Anthropology Center at the University of Tennessee, they provide a human identification service to the US government, as well as for local and national police forces. Jantz and Ousely developed these ideas into Fordisc 2.0, a computer programme that can identify decomposed human remains by race and sex using skull measurement data.[25] In 1997 Fari Supiya, our colleague, applied the Jantz/Ousely programme to all the Kish remains housed at the Natural History Museum in London. The Fordisc 2.0 programme classified the Kish remains amongst other southern populations, such as the Ancient Egyptians and the Dogon (West Africa).[26] Subsequent craniometric research by Mr Supiya allowed him to draw the following conclusions:

> Skulls … have been recovered from the ancient cemeteries … from the cities of Kish, Nippur and Eridu. All these skulls have long narrow crania like indigenous people from hot climates. When compared with skulls from the world's largest data base [by W. W. Howells], they resemble the sub-Saharan Africans in this respect and people from the Andaman Islands off the coast of India also the Australo-Melanesians who stretch into the Pacific Ocean. The narrow nasal areas of most Kish skulls made them resemble people from Sahelian West Africa and the Horn of Africa. Those from Nippur had wider nasal areas that made the face similar to Melanesians, the Black people of the Pacific. Those from Eridu have protruding jaw areas that make them resemble Australian indigenous people.[27]

Concerning the long bone proportions, Herbert Wendt reports that: "Skeletons of ancient Indian-Dravidian and Vedda [i.e. Pygmy] types have been found at Ur and Kish."[28] In a 1956 paper, Daris Swindler, a physical anthropologist, reported long bone measurements of Nippur skeletons. In a 1975 paper, Professor Ted Rathbun, another physical anthropologist, reported long bone measurements of Kish skeletons. Fari Supiya compared the long bone ratios suggested by the data against the ratios of Black, White and Yellow populations. The figures were arrived at by dividing the upper long bone by the lower long bone, multiplied by 100. Supiya presented his findings thus:

White Americans	82.0
Black Americans	84.5
Black South Africans	86.0
Chinese	81.0
Ancient Egypt	84.5
Ancient Nippur	84.2
Ancient Kish	85.5[29]

The data suggests that the Sumerian samples were tropically adapted and thus had Negro body proportions.

Concerning Sumerian art, Mr Wendt wrote that: "Ancient Sumerian statuettes resemble statuettes of the Indus civilization."[30] The popular examples of Sumerian art known to us, however, suggests a different conclusion. Some representations show individuals with long hair and beards with Caucasoid facial features. Others show long hair and broad features, possibly depicting a mixed origin.[31] There are seemingly Negro images of rulers Gudea, Lugal-kisalsi, and Ur-Nammu, but there are also seemingly Caucasoid images of Eanatum I and Ur-Nina. A. H. Sayce, a former Professor of Assyriology at Oxford University, was the first scholar to decipher and publish original translations of monolingual Sumerian texts. He made important comments on Sumerian art that are worthy of consideration:

> The physical characteristics of this race cannot as yet be fully determined. The oldest sculptures yielded by Babylonian excavation belong to a time when the Semite was already in the land. It might be supposed that the early monuments of Tello, which were erected by Sumerian princes and go back to Sumerian times, would give us the necessary materials; but not only are they too rude and infantile to be of scientific use, they also indicate the existence of two ethnological types, one heavily bearded, the other beardless, with oblique eyes and [N]egrito-like face.

He also informs us that:

> The excavations of Dieulafoy and de Morgan at Susa [in Elam] have shown … that a beardless and short-nosed [N]egrito type with round heads was aboriginal [i.e. the original inhabitants] in Elam … M. de Morgan has pointed out that similar brachycephalic and beardless [N]egritos are represented on the monuments of Naram-Sin as serving in the army of Akkad.[32]

Finally, the Sumerians called themselves the "Sag Gigga" (i.e. Black heads) in their literature.[33] This is possibly indicative of their racial origins.[34]

In conclusion, whatever else can be said about the Sumerians, none of the evidence supports a Semitic or Indo-European origin for them. It is clear that the bulk of evidence points the other way. The only point that we need add is that more recent linguistic research suggests that the Sumerians did not speak Cushitic but instead spoke a language more closely alligned to Niger-Congo. Fari Supiya presents this evidence in the *Afterword*. We therefore draw the conclusion that Sumer had, at the very least, an important and formative Negroid component. On this basis, we feel totally justified in including it as a part of Black history, fully aware that no contrary data exists to refute our view.

Mesopotamian Chronology

The chronology of Mesopotamia is a controversial issue. We open this brief discussion with a statement by Walther Hinz, the author of *The Lost World of Elam*. This book is the only important text devoted to this civilisation produced in years:

> Over a thousand years later, Assurbanipal [i.e. in 646 BC] reported the terrible attack which the Elamites launched on Mesopotamia: 'Kuter-Nahhunte of the Elamite, careless of his oath to the great gods, and full of misplaced confidence in his own strength, laid hand on the shrines of Akkad, and levelled Akkad to the ground'. At the same time, Kuter-Nahhunte took the statue of *Nanaja,* the Mesopotamian goddess of victory and fertility, to Susa. The Assyrian king adds: 'Nanaia [sic], who had been angry for one thousand, six hundred and thirty five years' - this must be a scribal error, for the period between this report in 646 BC and Kuter-Nahhunte's attack was certainly no more than 1075 years.[35]

This invites a number of questions. How did Professor Hinz know that the figure of 1635 years was a scribal error? Why is he so sure that the correct figure was no more than 1075 years? On what basis was this arrived at?

The Mesopotamian chronologies that are fashionable today have no more credibility than the Meyer-Breasted nonsense used for Egypt. To illustrate this, in a previous chapter we made mention of the clay cylinder of King Nabonidus.[36] On this document is the statement that King Sharaktishuriyash ruled in Mesopotamia 800 years before Nabonidus' time. Since Nabonidus lived in 552 BC, this implies that Sharaktishuriyash flourished before 1352 BC. It is generally agreed among historians that a certain Burnaburiash lived over 120 years before Sharaktishuriyash. This places King Burnaburiash around 1475-1448 BC. However, Burnaburiash corresponded with Akhenaten of Egypt and his letters have come down to us. Akhenaten obviously must have lived at the same time as Burnaburiash. Duncan MacNaughton, the Scottish chronologist, places Akhenaten between 1501 and 1474 BC and this harmonises well with the Nabonidus data. Professor Breasted and all the other short chronologists for Egypt place Akhenaten over a hundred years later. To appease the short chronologists, specialists in Mesopotamian chronology customarily claim an error in the Nabonidus document. In other words the scribe should have said that Sharaktishuriyash lived 680 years before Nabonidus's time instead of the 800 years specified.[37]

We present a third example of this silliness. In another inscription, Nabonidus stated that King Hammurabi rebuilt Ebbar, the temple of the Sun God in Larsa, 700 years before the time of Burnaburiash.[38] We do not know which Burnaburiash this is since more than one king had this name.[39] Dr Roux dates Hammurabi to 1792-1750 BC. Moreover, his king list contains two Burnaburiash kings. He dates Burnaburiash I to c.1530 BC and Burnaburiash II to 1375-1347 BC.[40] In neither case is the interval between these kings and Hammurabi 700 years. No doubt if we asked Dr Roux to justify this, he too would claim the Nabonidus document contains scribal errors.

In 1926 Mrs Houston presented a useful Mesopotamian chronology in *Wonderful Ethiopians of the Ancient Cushite Empire.* She dates the earliest kings of Sumer to 4500 BC, the time of Sargon to 3800 BC, Hammurabi to 2500 BC, and the Kassite invasion to 1750 BC.[41] The advantage of this chronology is that it fits many of the known facts about Mesopotamia. In addition, it allows for some synchronisms between Mesopotamia and Egypt. For example, Professor Hornung reported that cylinder seals from the Third Ur Dynasty were found in an archaeological context dateable to the time of Amenemhet II (3331-3299 BC) of Egypt.[42] The chronology used by Mrs Houston would place Ur III at around 3500 BC. This is just before the start of the Twelfth Dynasty of Egypt and thus harmonises tolerably well.

In 1929 Duncan MacNaughton wrote *A Scheme of Babylonian Chronology.* He dates the earliest kings of Sumer to 3189 BC, the time of Sargon to 2895 BC, Hammurabi to 2406 BC, and the Kassite conquest to 1984 BC. As with his work on Egyptian chronology, he presented an exquisite synthesis of the available data. For example, Reverend Baikie noticed that some of the jewellery from the time of Amenemhet II matches in style the jewellery from the burial of Chieftess Shubad of Ur.[43] Modern historians now prefer to call this distinguished lady Puabi. Dr Roux reports that her grave "belongs to the dawn of history, to the period immediately preceding the First Dynasty of Ur". Moreover, it was one of "seventeen royal tombs".[44] This dates the chieftess to anywhere between one and seventeen generations before Ur I. MacNaughton dates the commencement of Ur I to 3006 BC. This too harmonises well with the dates given for Amenemhet II.

We are aware of the strengths of two chronologies but what of their differences? Nearly 800 years separates the dating of King Sargon on the reckoning of Houston compared with the reckoning of MacNaughton. Why is this? The controversy is, again, due to the clay cylinder of Nabonidus. This document dates Naram Sin, Sargon's grandson, to around 3750 BC.[45] This places Sargon at 3800 BC. Mrs Houston implicitly accepted this data. MacNaughton explicitly rejects it. He has attempted to make his chronology tie in as closely as possible with the reckoning of Berosus. Berosus' chronology is hard to interpret, however. While we accept that MacNaughton's date of 3189 BC for the first kings of Sumer is a valid interpretation of Berosus, it is not necessarily the only interpretation. A second and far more devastating problem concerns the dating of pre-Ur I and Ur III. Obviously both of them cannot be contemporaneous with Amenemhet II!

We draw the conclusion that the short chronologies fashionable among mainstream Assyriologists are invalid. However, more research needs to be done to clean up the longer chronologies used by MacNaughton and Houston. In the interim, we shall date Mesopotamian history following MacNaughton closely. We do at times disagree with this great scholar, but this will be made clear to the reader as the issues arise.

Sumer

Archaeology has proved invaluable in tracing the earliest history of Iraq. Scholars view its earliest pages as a sequence of proto-historical cultures that preceded classical Sumerian civilisation.[46] Dr Roux presents a tentative chronological table but warns us that: "radiocarbon dates must be taken with caution".[47]

The Hassuna period	c.5800-5500 BC
The Samarra period	c.5600-5000 BC
The Halaf period	c.5500-4500 BC
The Ubaid period	c.5000-3750 BC
The Uruk period	c.3750-3150 BC
The Jemdat Nasr period	c.3150-2900 BC

The only comment that needs to be made here is that we would, perhaps, be tempted to move some of these dates back 200 years or so to arrive at a consistent chronology.

Trade was always a key factor in Sumerian history and proto-history. Copper was imported from Anatolia, Cyprus, Iran and Magan. Tin entered the land from the Caucasus, Iran, and possibly Afghanistan. Silver was imported from the Taurus Mountains. Gold came in from various deposits between Egypt and India. Hard stones and semi-precious stones came in from Iran. Diorite came from Magan. Ordinary timber was obtained in the Zagros Mountains. The more valuable cedar was brought in from the Amanus or Lebanon. Other varieties of wood came in by sea from Meluhha.[48] It is important to note, however, that Dr Roux does not identify Magan with Egypt and Meluhha with "Ethiopia" despite the evidence of the "late inscription of the Assyrians" cited by Dr Perry. We, however, agree with Perry on this issue and also George Rawlinson. He wrote:

> Hur or Ur, the most important of the early capitals, was situated on the Euphrates, probably at no great distance from its mouth. It was probably the chief commercial emporium in the early times; as in the bilingual vocabularies its ships are mentioned in connexion with those of Ethiopia.[49]

How did the goods move? The only pack animal available was the ass. Outside Mesopotamia, two great roads led west to Syria and the Mediterranean. To the east things were much more difficult. The people of the Zagros were generally hostile, and the mountain itself was hard to negotiate. Goods also moved by waterways. The Persian Gulf was another great trade route. Merchant ships sailed on it from Ur to Dilmun, Magan and also Meluhha. Excavations conducted in Bahrain, Kuwait, Oman, Qatar, Saudi Arabia and the United Arab Emirates, brought to light physical evidence of cultural and commercial links with Mesopotamia and Elam. These connections date back to the fifth millennium BC.[50]

The Hassuna culture is the oldest in Iraq, dating back to perhaps 5800 BC. The Iraqi Directorate of Antiquities found six layers of houses that were progressively larger and better built. In size, plan and building materials, these houses share features with those in present day northern Iraqi villages. Six or seven rooms were built in two blocks around a courtyard. One block was the living quarters and the other was the kitchen and storage area. They had domed ovens where bread was baked. The walls were typically of clay with floors of clay mixed with straw. Of the goods found were mortars, sickle-blades of flint, stone hoes, clay spindle-whorls and clay figurines of women. The skulls found, like those from Byblos and Jericho, belonged to a "large-toothed variety of the long-headed Mediterranean race". Dr Roux says this "suggests a unity of population throughout the Fertile Crescent in late Neolithic times." The data also supports the view that they were Natufians or at least akin to the Natufians (see pages 290-1). At one site was found tools and weapons of flint and obsidian, pieces of copper ore, and a few copper and lead ornaments. Of greater significance was found the earliest examples of the stamp-seal, the forerunner of the cylinder seal. The site of Umm Dabaghiya was sophisticated where the floors of the houses were made of large clay slabs. In addition, the floors and walls were carefully plastered with gypsum. Finally, several houses boasted beautifully carved and polished alabaster bowls.[51]

The Samarra culture dated back to around 5600 BC. Samarra houses were large, regular in plan and had multiple rooms and courtyards. Unlike the Hassuna houses built of pressed mud, these were built of large, cigar-shaped clay bricks. Walls and floors were typically covered with thin plaster. Some houses contained exquisite vessels of translucent marble. The culture produced attractive pottery decorated in red, dark-brown and purple. The pottery contained geometric designs, representations of human beings, antelopes, birds, fishes, scorpions and other animals. The potters decorated the rims of bowls, the surface of plates, and the neck and shoulders of pots. The makers of these vessels were undoubtedly inventive artists. Of great importance, the Samarra culture was the first to practice a primitive form of irrigation using the Tigris floods to water their fields. They grew crops of barley, linseed and wheat.[52]

The Halaf culture dated back to around 5500 BC. It had a number of new and highly distinctive features. Like the earlier cultures, the settlements were still villages. However, some Halaf villages now had cobbled streets and the rectangular houses gave way to the roundhouse. These were simple, beehive-shaped buildings, sharing affinities with those of Aleppo in northern Syria. This culture produced a superb pottery, the most beautiful ever seen in Mesopotamia. Finally, they grew crops of barley, einkorn, emmer, flax, lentils, wheat and other vegetables. Moreover, they bred cattle, dogs, goats, pigs and sheep.[53]

The Ubaid culture dated back to around 5000 BC. During this period, great monuments were built at Eridu. In its ruins were unearthed an impressive series of seventeen temples built one above the other. The lowest and earliest of these temples were small, one roomed buildings. However, even these contained altars, offering tables, and a fine quality pottery that was decorated with elaborate and elegant geometric designs. Some of the Ubaid houses were frail structures of reed matting supported by wooden poles and sometimes plastered with clay. These share affinities with buildings that can be seen around Basra today. More substantial buildings were of pressed mud or mud bricks. The Ubaid period temples of Eridu were made of large mud bricks set in clay mortar. They were raised on mud-brick platforms that may have been the inspiration for the ziggurats of later times. Inside they had a long rectangular nave surrounded by small rooms. At one end of the nave, against the wall, was a low podium that once supported a religious statue. At the other end of the nave stood the brick altar. The external walls were adorned with shallow buttresses and niches that gave an interplay of light and shade.[54] Incidentally, Eridu Temple VII, as reconstructed by Dr Roux, shares many affinities with certain First Dynasty Egyptian monuments such as the Abydos tomb of Queen Neith-Hotep.[55]

During the fourth millennium BC, classical Sumerian civilisation blossomed in the southern half of Iraq. The northern half followed a somewhat different course and lagged behind in many respects. Sumer emerged with its city-states whose great walls were inhabited by architects, artists, factory workers, merchants, overseers, peasants, priests, scribes and soldiers. Scholars describe this change as the progression from the Uruk Period (3750-3150 BC) to the Jemdat Nasr Period (3150-2900 BC). The Ubaidian Culture was the parent of this progression.[56]

The site of Uruk was large and impressive, covering four hundred hectares. It was born of the coalescence of two towns half a mile apart - Kullaba, devoted to the sky-god An, and E-Anna - dedicated to the love goddess Inanna. Towards the end of the Uruk period, perhaps 3300 BC, writing appears for the first time in Asia. Pictographic tablets were discovered in the archaic temple of E-Anna. The tablets were economic documents showing lists of workmen, the goods produced, and receipts.[57] The Jemdat Nasr period differed little compared to the Uruk period that preceded it. There are only minor differences in style and quality of artefacts. Dr Roux, however, believes that the Elamites of Iran invented the Proto-Elamite script during this period.[58]

With the birth of writing, we move to a more secure understanding of Sumerian history. The Sumerian King List contains an uninterrupted list of kings from the very beginnings of the monarchy. The earliest data contained in it is, however, mythical. These myths may well have a clear meaning, but at present they are difficult to interpret and lead to many contradictory theories. According to the Sumerian King List, kingship was first "lowered from heaven" into the city of Eridu. In that city two kings reigned for a total of 64,800 years. After the Eridu period, kingship was "carried" to Badtibira where three kings reigned for a total of 108,000 years. From Badtibira, kingship was passed on to Larak where one king reigned 28,800 years, to Sippar (one king, 21,000 years), and finally to Shuruppak (one king, 18,600 years).[59] What does any of this mean? Most Assyriologists simply have no idea.

The Flood allegedly ended this first Golden Age but the same question is raised: Was the flood historical? Archaeology confirms that a flood of limited and localised proportions did in fact happen. On three Mesopotamian sites, Ur, Kish and Shuruppak, were found sizeable deposits of water-borne clay and sand associated with flooding. Dr Roux dates this to around 2900 or 2800-2600 BC.[60] Professor Stephen Langdon, an important authority, dates the Flood to 3300 BC. Duncan MacNaughton dates it to 3189 BC.[61] We suggest that Langdon's date is more consistent with the chronology that follows here.

After the Flood, claims the Sumerian King List, kingship was again "lowered from heaven", but this time into the northern city of Kish. The first four dynasties of Kish probably correspond with the First Chaldæan Dynasty of

Berosus. The First Dynasty of Kish consisted of 23 kings who reigned for a combined total of 24,510 years. Berosus is equally extravagant. His First Dynasty lasted 34,080 years. Of the kings listed on the Sumerian King List, twelve have Semitic names, six have Sumerian names, and four have names of unknown origin. This may well indicate a mixture of ethnic elements in Kish at that period. Dr Roux believes this dynasty was at least partly historical and should be placed shortly after 2800 BC.[62] Duncan MacNaughton, however, regards this period as fully historical. He believes that the extraordinarily long reigns do not in reality refer to years but should be divided by 50 to have any real meaning. On this basis, he dates the First Dynasty of Kish from 3189 to 2699 BC, a time period of 490 years. Moreover, he dates the first four dynasties of Kish, which is the same as the First Dynasty of Berosus, to between 3189 and 2508 BC, a time period of 681 years.[63] We accept the First Dynasty of Kish as fully historical but we cannot accept MacNaughton's dating of it. Phillip Smith, in our view, presented a more elegant explanation of the Berosus data. He wrote that:

> From the Deluge of Xisuthrus to the capture of Babylon by Cyrus and the fall of the Babylonian empire, Berosus reckons *Eight Dynasties,* which, though the numbers assigned to them are imperfect, were evidently intended to fill up the cycle of 10 *sars,* or 36,000 years. The *First Dynasty* is obviously mythical, consisting of 86 demigods, whom he calls *Chaldæans,* and who reigned at Babylon for 34,080 years; a number doubtless assigned so as to complete, with the length of the period which Berosus regarded as historical, the above total of 36,000 years. Thus the so-called historical period would consist of 1920 years; and, reckoning backwards from the fall of Babylon, it would begin in B.C. 2458.[64]

The Second Dynasty of Berosus, according to MacNaughton, consisted of eleven kings. According to Mr Smith, they began to reign in 2458 BC. This is not too different to MacNaughton who offers a date of 2508 BC. Hammurabi was sixth of these eleven kings. As we have seen, there are documents that independently date him against the reign of one of the Burnaburiash kings. Also, there are documents that date one of the Burnaburiash kings against Nabonidus on the one hand, and Akhenaten on the other. In addition, MacNaughton synthesised all of this data. On this basis, we follow MacNaughton's dating of the Second Dynasty and all subsequent dates in Mesopotamian history. For the earlier dynasties, however, we follow MacNaughton's dates for most of the Sumerian cities except those of Kish.

For the earliest kings of Sumer, we believe that the First Dynasty of Kish reigned from 3300 BC. For reasons already explained, no firmer dates can be established. At this early date, they were the first kings on the whole continent of Asia. The Sumerian King List mentions 23 rulers of this dynasty.

Archaeology confirms the existence of one of them. In 1959 was found a fragment of a large alabaster vase. On it was engraved in a very archaic script "Me-bárag-si, King of Kish". On the Sumerian King List is the similar-sounding Enmebaragesi, twenty second king of the First Dynasty of Kish. It also mentions the interesting data that "he carried away as spoil the weapons of Elam". Agga, his son, succeeded him. However, by this time, kings had already emerged in Uruk who would challenge the supremacy of Kish. Gilgamesh, the fifth king of Uruk was a contemporary of Agga. By 3146 BC, at the latest, he dethroned Agga and ended the First Dynasty of Kish. For the next 140 years, Gilgamesh's seven successors dominated Uruk and Kish.[65]

Dynastic Sumer was a relatively small country of 30,000 square kilometres. This is comparable in size to Belgium or perhaps four or five English counties. Linguistically it was divided between the Semitic-speaking people of the north, who became the Akkaddians, and the Sumerian-speaking south. In the late fourth millennium BC, both Sumer and Akkad were divided into city-states. Each of the 18 city-states typically consisted of the metropolis, its satellite towns and villages, and its gardens and farms. Here they grew crops of barley and wheat. Many of these cities were walled and reinforced by towers. Lagash was one of the larger city-states. Covering a total area of 2,880 square kilometres, it had a population of perhaps 30 or 35,000 people. From the time of Gilgamesh's successors, Uruk became a huge metropolis covering more than 400 hectares. It housed 40 or 50,000 people. At the same time, urban centres appeared in the north at places like Mari and Assur. Also built in the early period was the Oval Temple of Khafaje. It was a splendid building of two enclosures. Its nave was raised on a platform.[66]

The Sumerian rulers took the title of *lugal* (king) or *ensi* (governor). His wife was known as *nin* (lady or queen). The rulers and their families lived in palaces rather than temples. Palaces have been excavated at Eridu, Kish and Mari. The layout of each building shared common features. They had square central courtyards surrounded by chambers on three sides. On the fourth side was located the audience hall. Surrounding the building were two parallel thick walls, separated by a narrow corridor. Throughout Sumerian history, the rulers aspired to the title 'King of Kish'. This signified being ruler of the whole of Sumer and Akkad and therefore master of the whole region. Another goal worthy of any prince was to control the city-state of Nippur.[67] Nippur was the seat of Enlil, the supreme deity of the Sumerians.[68]

The city-state of Ur, in the fourth millennium BC, had been greatly enriched by maritime and land trade. The treasures buried with the rulers were superb. They include a dagger and sheath of pure gold, decorated with lapis lazuli. There was a ram in a thicket made of gold, silver, lapis lazuli, shell and red limestone. Meskalamdug, one of the chiefs, was buried with a helmet made of a single piece of 15-carat electrum. There was a bull's head made of gold leaf, wood and lapis lazuli.[69] Finally, the jewellery of Chieftess Puabi was impressive. It was comparable in style and quality with those of Twelfth Dynasty Egypt.

In 3006 BC Mesannepadda founded the First Dynasty of Ur (also called Ur I). He overthrew the last king of Uruk as well as his contemporary, Mesalim of Kish. After this, Sumer experienced a tranquillity that lasted about a century with Ur in the driving seat. Meanwhile in the city-state of Lagash, Ur-Nanshe was busy building temples, digging canals and importing wood from Dilmun. There is a famous wall plaque where he is shown with his wife, seven sons and three officials.[70]

In Lagash around 2960 BC Eanatum became the *ensi*. Like Ur-Nanshe, his grandfather, Eannatum was a builder of temples and canals. On a more practical level, he was a soldier. He battled the Elamites of Iran, and purged their influence from Sumer. Additionally, he protected the eastern flank of the kingdom by conquering several towns on Elam's border. He overthrew Ur and Uruk and "added to the princeship of Lagash and the kingship of Kish". He also battled against Umma. This began as a territorial dispute over a certain field situated at the border between the two states but claimed by both. War erupted leading to victory for Eanatum. He apparently "marked off the boundary with Enakalli, the *ensi* of Umma; he restored Mesalim's stele to its former place" and levied on Umma a heavy tax in barley. Eannatum's victory was commemorated by a masterpiece of Sumerian sculpture, *The Stele of the Vultures*.[71]

Urukinimgina (2903-2895 BC) was the last ruler of Lagash. An inscription tells of how he, as champion of the gods, put an end to the corruption and abuses that existed before his reign. There were inspectors who were busybodies who meddled in all affairs. Huge taxes were levied on burials and weddings. Rich officials bought houses below their true price. As ever, the poor suffered greatly. Moreover, the previous *ensi* had built vast estates of land by encroaching on sacred land. Urukinimgina responded. He deleted many official posts, reduced taxation, and reinstated respect for the deity Ningirsu. An inscription claims: "He freed the citizens of Lagash from usury, monopoly, hunger, theft and assault; he established their freedom."[72] The Reverend James Baikie, a populariser of archaeology and ancient history, assessed the likely impact of his policies:

> One can imagine the indignation of the ruling families of the state, who found
> half of the offices on which they had depended for the support of their younger
> sons abolished by the stroke of Urukagina's [i.e. Urukinimgina's] stylus, the
> disaffection of the army of tax-gatherers who found their occupation gone, the
> disgust of the priestly robbers who could no longer claim half the estate of a

man in return for the mumbling over his dead body of a few prayers, the spite of the diviners who found themselves obliged to live on their salaries, and the general conviction of the bureaucracy that things would never be right until this upsetting usurper [Urukinimgina] was got out the way.[73]

Meanwhile, Lugalzagesi (2906-2881 BC), a vigorous *ensi,* had emerged in Umma. He seized the city-state of Girsu and then marched on Lagash, dethroning Urukunimgina. One unhappy scribe penned an account of what happened:

> The men of Umma have set fire to the (temple) Antasurra [i.e. in Girsu], they have carried away the silver and the precious stones … They have shed blood in the temple E-engur of the goddess Nanshe; they have carried away the silver and the precious stones … The men of Umma, by the despoiling of Lagash, have committed a sin against the god Ningirsu … As for Lugal-zagge-si, ensi of Umma, may his goddess Nidaba make him bear his mortal sin upon his head![74]

After Lagash, Lugalzagesi seized Uruk. In time he conquered the rest of Sumer, becoming the first empire builder in the region. His Sumerian Empire lasted until his death in 2881 BC.[75]

Sargon (2895-2839 BC) became the next important figure in Sumerian affairs. He was a Semitic speaking northerner whose armies defeated the Empire of Lugalzagesi. He started a dynasty of Akkadian rulers that dominated Sumer for two hundred years. We believe that the Semites, on average, were lighter in complexion than the Sumerians, but not by much. There are artefacts from the northern regions that indicate the continued presence of Negroes. Originally from a humble background, Sargon became the cup-bearer of Ur-Zababa, King of Kish. In time he overthrew his master and marched against Uruk. After this, he seized Ur, Lagash and Umma. On the Euphrates he founded a new capital, Agade, where he built a palace and also temples for Ishtar and Zababa. Appointing Akkadian governors in all the main city-states, he promoted Akkadian, a Semitic language as much as Sumerian, to be the language of officialdom. These conquests seemed huge to the people of those times leading to the Akkadian rulers styling themselves as rulers of 'the Four Regions of the World'. Having consolidated his political power in Sumer, Sargon launched several military campaigns against Elam and Syria. The Elamites put up a strong resistance, but were eventually defeated. Sargon had several of Elam's cities sacked, and made vassals of the kings of Elam and the neighbouring districts. The Elamite city of Susa was transformed by Sargon's viceroy from the rank of a modest marketplace to that of a great city. Additionally, Akkadian was imposed as the official language of Elam. "In his old age", says a late Babylonian chronicle, "all the lands revolted against him and they besieged him in Agade". But "he went forth to battle and defeated them".[76] The early period of Sumerian and Akkadian culture was important for the whole of western and southern Asia. Dr Roux says:

> The Sumero-Akkadian culture and its support, the cuneiform writing, were adopted not only by the people of northern Mesopotamia, but the Hurrians, the Lullubi and the Elamites. Conversely, Mesopotamia was immensely enriched by the introduction of bronze, silver, wood and stone in large quantities, while numerous prisoners of war working as slaves provided cheap and abundant labour. Elam, Bahrain (Dilmun), Oman ... and the whole Gulf came under Mesopotamian influence, while Proto-Indian seals, vases and ornaments found in Iraq testify to commercial relations with the Indus Valley ... where flourished the brilliant civilisation of Harappa and Mohenjo-Daro. In art the new tendencies were towards realism, and true portraits replaced the more or less conventional figures of Early Dynastic times.[77]

Rimush, Sargon's son and successor, repressed a revolt in Sumer and Elam with vigour, but his authority was challenged even in his own palace. After nine years on the throne (2839-2830 BC), "his servants", says a Babylonian source, "killed him with their *kunukku*", whatever they are. Manishtusu followed Rimush as ruler. An inscription claims the following: "Manishtusu, King of Kish, when he had subjugated Anshan and Shirikum [i.e. Elam], he crossed the Lower Sea in ships ... He defeated them and subjugated their cities; he overthrew their lords and seized the whole country as far as the silver mines." Naram-Sin, a successor, had a long reign (2814-2777 BC) and was much preoccupied with military operations at the periphery of Mesopotamia. Under Sharkalisharri, his successor, however, the king of Elam declared his country independent. To make matters worse, the Elamite king abandoned the Akkadian language for his own tongue, and even dared take the supreme title 'King of the Universe'. In 2753 BC Sharkalisharri, like the previous rulers, was overthrown in a coup leading to the collapse of the Akkadian Empire.[78] The state of anarchy was such that the Sumerian King List asks:

> Who was king? Who was not king?
> Was Igigi King?
> Was Nanum King?
> Was Imi king?
> Was Elulu king?
> Their tetrad was king, and reigned 3 years![79]

Into this vacuum stepped the Gutians. According to Josef Ben-Levi of the Kemetic Institute of Chicago: "They were Caucasian tribesmen from the Zagros Mountains and related to another group of Zagros tribesmen known as the Kassites".[80]

The Sumerians rose against them in 2724 BC. Utuhegal, *ensi* of Uruk, gathered an army and led the revolt. Several princes joined him and together they defeated the invaders. Tiriqan, the Gutian king, fled, but was captured and handed to the Sumerian leader. An inscription reads: "Utu-hegal [sic] sat down; Tiriqan lay at his feet. Upon his neck he set his foot, and the sovereignty of Sumer he restored into his (own) hands." After seven years on the throne, however, Utuhegal was overthrown by one of his own officers. Ur-Nammu, the distinguished official, took the titles 'King of Ur, King of Sumer and Akkad' and founded the Third Dynasty of Ur.

The Third Dynasty of Ur (2717-2609 BC) was one of the most brilliant periods in the history of Sumer. Sir Leonard Woolley wrote:

> At no time in its long history was the City of Ur so important as in the days of the Third Dynasty … when it was the capital of the Sumerian empire. The founder of the dynasty was Ur-Nammu … and he founded a royal house of which four generations after him were to sit upon the throne; he was a great conqueror and a great ruler, famous for his justice and his good works, whose dominions extended from the Persian Gulf to the Mediterranean, and his monuments were broadcast throughout the cities of Mesopotamia.[81]

Ur-Nammu and his successors restored centralised authority throughout the length and breadth of the region. They also created a century of relative peace, and with it, prosperity. The consequence of this was a renaissance in all areas of Sumerian art and literature. Ur-Nammu "freed the land from thieves, robbers and rebels" and either he or his son dictated the earliest known collection of laws on earth. For some crimes, such as physical injury, the offender was no longer punished by death or mutilation. Instead he was fined in silver, the quantity of which varied according to the gravity of the offence. Ur-Nammu also revived agriculture and improved communications by digging canals. He had towns fortified against future wars, and in Ur, Uruk, Eridu and Nippur, he built ziggurats. Even today they are still the most impressive monuments on these sites. The Ziggurat of Ur measured 60.5 by 43 metres at its base and had at least three tiers. Against the north-eastern side of the tower, three long flights of steps converge towards a landing half way between the first and the second platforms. From this point, other steps led to the second and third storeys and finally to the shrine.[82]

The building of temples was traditionally considered to be a royal privilege but there is a distinguished exception. Gudea (*c.*2700-2674 BC), *ensi* of Lagash, carried out an ambitious and magnificent building programme. Gudea left behind numerous portraits and inscriptions that were amongst the most impressive examples of Sumerian art. Ernest Babelon, author of *A History of Mesopotamia,* described some of these masterpieces:

To the number of ten, they are of a blackish diorite with a tinge of blue; All are
headless and bear inscriptions in the name of Gudea or Ur-Bau ... The man's
head found in the great courtyard is of lifesize, the hair and beard completely
shaven, as in certain Egyptian statues. The eyebrows form an exaggerated
projection above enormous eyes; the skull is elongated remarkably; the
mutilated nose alone prevents us from having the complete type of the
Chaldean race, with its hard features and thick sensual lips.[83]

In Lagash Gudea built or restored at least fifteen temples. In Girsu he
devoted particular care to the E-ninnu, the temple of Ningirsu. About the
craftsmen themselves, an inscription says: "From Elam came the Elamites,
from Susa the Susiana. Magan and Meluhha collected timber from their
mountains ... and Gudea brought them together in his town Girsu."[84]

In Ur King Shulgi succeeded Ur-Nammu in 2699 BC. The first half of his
long reign was spent in peaceful activities. He completed the temples and
ziggurats begun by his father. Furthermore, he raised new monuments. During
his time the calendar was reformed and a new measure of grain superseded the
local measures formerly in use. It is possible that he conducted a thorough
political, economic and administrative reorganisation of the kingdom. He also
established two great schools at Ur and Nippur. The scholars here wrote many
extant masterpieces of Sumerian literature. In 2675 BC Shulgi embarked upon
a long series of annual military campaigns against Kurdistan and eventually
succeeded in turning it into a Sumerian province. In Elam, the Guti caused a
state of anarchy worse than in Sumer. Shulgi seized the advantage and captured
Elam. In Susa he installed a Sumerian governor and built a temple to
Inshushinak, Elam's supreme deity. Finally, he enlisted Elamite soldiers into a
kind of 'foreign legion' entrusted with the defence of Sumer's south eastern
border. Shulgi called himself 'King of the Four Quarters' and was worshipped
as a deity during and after his time.[85]

Amar-Sin, son of Shulgi, reigned for nine years (2653-2644 BC). Like his
father, he divided his time between building temples and conducting
campaigns. He too was deified. During the reigns of Shulgi and Amar-Sin, the
Sumerian Empire reached the pinnacle of its power. At the periphery were
independent states drawn into Sumerian influence by political marriages. Then
came conquered countries transformed into provinces and placed under the
care of a governor. Finally, in the heart of the kingdom, the former 18 city-
states became provinces. A network of roads connected the different parts of
this vast territory. Moreover, there were fixed halting places, one day's walk
apart, where the officials, escorted by soldiers and policemen, received a
government ration.[86]

The Ur rulers introduced an institution called rotation. This was a taxation
system whereby each *ensi* of Sumer and Akkad in turn paid the state a monthly

tax in cattle or sheep. The state also received tribute in silver, cattle, hides and various objects, as well as gifts sent by foreign rulers. The scribes noted all incoming and out-going goods and stored the data in archives. The archives found at Ur, Nippur, Girsu, and Umma, held a huge number of administrative documents. To date 40,000 of them have been published but as many, if not more, are still lying in the drawers of museums, universities and private collections.[87]

Throughout Sumer were large factories producing flour, leather and textiles. They employed thousands of workers, most of them female. In the region of Girsu, for example, 15,000 women were employed in the local textile industry. In the same area a cereal factory was found that produced 1,100 tons of flour per year. Moreover, this same factory made beer, bread, clay pots, grindstones, leather, linseed oil, mortars and woven reeds. Employed by the factory were 134 specialists and 858 skilled workers, including 669 women, 86 men and 103 teenagers.[88]

As well as industrial advances, a great scientific culture developed in the land. Professor George Rawlinson, one of the great pioneers in Assyriology, wrote that:

> The "Chaldæan learning" of a later age appears to have been originated, in all its branches, by the primitive people [i.e. the Sumerians]; in whose language it continued to be written even in Semitic times.

He continues:

> We are informed by Simplicius that Callisthenes, who accompanied Alexander to Babylon, sent to Aristotle from that capital a series of astronomical observations, which he had found preserved there, extending back to a period of 1903 years from Alexander's conquest of the city. Epigenes related that these observations were recorded upon tablets of baked clay, which is quite in accordance with all that we know of the literary habits of the people ... [Moreover:] There is nothing fanciful, or (so to speak) astrological, in the early astronomy of the Babylonians ... It was only in later times that the Chaldæans were fairly taxed with imposture and charlatanism.[89]

Mrs Houston agrees, but she provides further data. According to her:

> The astronomy of the early Chaldeans was without the astrological principles of later times. Diodorus Siculus said that the Chaldeans could attribute comets to their natural causes and could foretell their reappearance. Seneca estimated that their theory of comets was as exact and intelligent as that of moderns. Ideler of Berlin, has shown that in their ancient calculations of the eclipse of the moon, quoted by Ptolemy, they differed from modern calculations only in minute degree. Observatories were set up in all the chief towns and royal

astronomers sent regular reports to the king ... The Chaldeans must have understood the manufacture of the telescope, for Layard reported the discovery of a lens of power in the ruins of Babylon.[90]

On the political front, however, there were problems. Soldiers and guards became aware that the nomads were on the move. The first indication that things were not as quiet as they had been occurs during the reign of Shu-Sin, the brother and successor of Amar-Sin. In 2640 BC the king built a fortress to keep these nomads at bay. Who were these nomads? A Sumerian inscription says:

> The MAR.TU who know no grain ... The MAR.TU who know no house nor town, the boors of the mountains ... The MAR.TU who digs up truffles ... who does not bend his knees (to cultivate the land), who eats raw meat, who has no house during his lifetime, who is not buried after his death ... [91]

Many writers, such as Rashidi, feel that the MAR.TU were light skinned Indo-Europeans or Semites who later became the Amorites.[92] In any case, the programme of building protective fortresses must have proved effective against the MAR.TU, since we do not hear about them in the records over the next ten years. Meanwhile, Shu-Sin died and was succeeded in 2635 BC by his son, Ibbi-Sin. During his time, the empire quickly fell apart. One by one, various provinces declared themselves independent. The eastern provinces went their own way and Susa did the same. Additionally, the Amorites were pressing in on the borders. In the fifth year of Ibbi-Sin, they broke through the defences and ravaged the country, cutting off all roads to Ur. Ibbi-Sin defeated them but was faced with famine and internal challenges to his authority. In 2616 BC Ishbi-Irra broke away and proclaimed himself king of the city-state of Isin. To make matters worse, the Elamites took advantage of the situation to invade Sumer. Facing a famine, attacked by both the Amorites and the Elamites, and reduced to a mere city-state, the Sumerian Empire collapsed.[93]

In 2609 BC the Elamites surrounded the walls of Ur. Storming the city and burning it, they seized Ibbi-Sin as prisoner and marched him to Elam - where he later died. A Sumerian inscription records the folowing:

> O Father Nanna, that city into ruins was made
> Its people, not potsherds, filled its sides
> Its walls were breached; the people groan.
> In its lofty gates, where they were wont to promenade, dead bodies were lying about;
> In its boulevards, where the feasts were celebrated, scattered they lay.
> In all its streets, where they were wont to promenade, dead bodies were lying about
> In its places, where the festivities of the land took place, the people lay in heaps

Ur - its weak and its strong perished through hunger
Mothers and fathers who did not leave their houses were overcome by fire;
The young lying on their mothers' laps, like fish were carried off by the waters;
In the city, the wife was abandoned, the son was abandoned, the possessions
were scattered about
O Nanna, Ur has been destroyed, its people have been dispersed![94]

Elam

Elam was an ancient federal state located in Iran. The major cities were Awan,
Simashki, and Susa, the capital city. It was a very hot country. Strabo, the
famous geographer, claimed that any snake or lizard brave enough to cross a
Susian street during a summer noon, would be roasted alive. Moreover, M.
Dieulafoy, the pioneering excavator of Susa, recorded temperatures up to 72°C.
The federation included Susiana, consisting of meadows and farmland and also
Anshan, the high valleys and mountain chains. The plain of Elam owed its
fertility to the rivers. Three rivers flowed through Susiana, the Karkheh, the
Diz, and the Karun. The Elamites themselves wrote the name of their country
as *hal-ta-am-ti*, which might mean 'Land of the Lord', or 'Land of God'.[95]

The highest authority in the federation was the king. He held the title 'King
of Anshan and Susa' and exercised power over a whole host of vassal-princes.
There was also a viceroy. He held the title 'Regent of Elam and Simashki' and
was the younger brother of the king and also his successor. Next was the ruler
of Susiana or the 'Prince of Susa'. He was the eldest son of the king. Typically,
the Viceroy would make regular tours through the individual states - a practice
that enhanced the unity of the federation. However, the King and Regent both
remained in Susa, the federal capital.[96]

Information on everyday life for the most ancient Elamites is to be found in
seal impressions from the third or fourth millennium BC. Professor Walther
Hinz is the leading authority on Elamite culture. We deem it proper to cite his
analysis of these scenes:

> [T]he landscape of Susiana is depicted by winding rivers, where fish swim
> between rushy banks. Up on the plateau among pines, cedars, and terebinths,
> buffalo, chamois and mountain goats can be seen moving about. All kinds of
> animal[s] inhabit the open ground or the undergrowth, graze peacefully or flee
> from lions. Then the Elamite hunter appears on the scene. He is quite naked or
> clad only in a loin cloth, and his weapons are bow and arrow, spear or pike.
> Accompanied by his dogs, he hunts the red deer, the antelope, the wild boar or
> even the wild cat. While in one place naked fishermen drag giant tortoises to
> land, in another an Elamite poles his boat, with its gracefully curved prow, to
> the bank. The captain of the boat, who has already disembarked, is carrying the
> prize fish, two large barbel, while his assistant follows him bearing a basket of

smaller fish on his head. Not far from the town, cattle are grazing; milk jars stand ready near the cows. Shepherds drive goats back to their crude brick stall; the entrance is flanked by a huge tower, and so the stall will probably belong to a palace or a temple. Whole armies of men are at work in the fields; they are preparing them for the sowing, using three pronged hoes ... Women also help with the farming; we see them, clothed in wide smocks, working on the date palm plantation. In the town, all is bustle and activity. In the pottery workshop, stone vessels are being produced; while one man polishes the handle of a jar, other craftsmen smooth plates by rubbing them together. Women are also to be found in the workshops; they are seated on low wooden stools or on level ground, and are mostly occupied in preparing wool. The granaries are particularly busy. According to the seals, the silos are constructed of mud bricks and are surmounted by a long series of domes. The exterior is provided with niches; between them and the flat roof stretches a row of narrow ventilation holes. Workers come and go with sacks or jars, bearing their burdens on head or shoulder, reaching the domes by ladders or by steps built on at the side. A terraced foundation raised the granaries above ground level; but there were also silos that were built partly underground, as is attested by a mathematical text found at Susa. Scribes squat near the granaries to record on their clay tables each bushel of corn as it is delivered. Wine stewards adopt the same position to fill their measures or to cork their jars.[97]

In the fourth millennium BC the Elamites began to write in pictographs following the Sumerian example. The Proto-Elamite script contained more than 150 basic logograms and was used largely for business purposes. They wrote inventories, records of entry, receipts, and also delivery notes. One of these tablets shows the earliest known occurrence of the horse. Later in the fourth millennium BC, evolved a syllabic script that again mirrored Sumerian developments. Eventually a linear script evolved that contained around eighty symbols. This allowed for the wider expression of personal, political, historical and religious matters.[98]

As we have already seen, the oldest firmly historical information on Elam dates back to c.3150 BC when Enmebaraggesi, of the First Dynasty of Kish, carried off its weapons as booty. Additionally, the Elamites had to continually defend themselves against the Mesopotamians who envied their resources only to be found in the Elamite mountains. Chief among these were timber, stone, iron, and horses. The Elamites did take an aggressive position from time to time. The Sumerian King List informs us that later, probably between 3100 and 3050 BC, Ur was "struck with weapons and its kingship transferred to Awan". This shows that the kings of Awan were very powerful and managed to sustain a position of supremacy over Mesopotamia. In about 3050 BC, however, a king of Kish succeeded in ending Elamite supremacy.[99]

Following a period of probable confusion, a new dynasty of twelve kings emerged. Peli was the founder of this house. Following him on the throne were

Tata, Ukkutahesh, Hishur, Shushuntarana, Napilhush and Kikku-siwe-tempt. Beyond knowing their names, very little else can be confidently stated about these rulers. In 2848 BC King Luh-ishshan, the eighth ruler of the dynasty, had to contend with the ambitions of Sargon of Akkad. Sargon defeated him and took the title 'King of Kish, conqueror of Elam and of Warahshi'. Having plundered Susa and Awan, Sargon allowed the Elamite king to remain on the throne, but only as his vassal.[100] Under Akaddian rule, the Elamites began to adopt Akkadian culture. Akkadian became the official language of inscriptions, replacing Elamite. After nearly a hundred years of dominance, however, problems surfaced in Akkad with the Gutians. This encouraged the Elamites to break free from Akkadian control.[101]

Kutik-Inshushinak was the last of the twelve kings of Awan. He was able to reassert Elam's independence and to inaugurate a period of national prosperity. Leading a resurgence in patriotism, he employed the Elamite linear script for inscriptions on monuments, as well as Akkadian. He began his career as 'Governor of Susiana' as an Akkadian vassal. At a later date, however, he led a series of campaigns against Mesopotamia. An Akkadian inscription lists over seventy places that were "thrown under his feet at one blow". The inscription concludes that even the King of Simashki came of his own free will and "seized the feet" of Kutik-Inshushinak, i.e. sought his protection and forgiveness. In 2763 BC Kutik-Inshushinak finally became King of Elam. In two of his Akkadian inscriptions he describes himself as "Mighty king of Awan". In Elamite linear inscriptions, he describes himself as "King of the land, a chosen one, a victor". He boasts on one stele that god Inshushinak "looked mercifully on him and [gave] him the four quarters of the earth". He dedicated a great new temple in Susa to the deity Inshushinak, offering many and varied sacrificial gifts. One of its monuments depicts the king giving the deity a bolt of bronze and cedar-wood. One last testimony to his many and varied activities, the king commissioned great feats of engineering. He had a canal dug at Sidari.[102]

After this period of achievement, things fell apart. In 2743 BC the Dynasty of Awan fell. There are no more inscriptions in the Elamite linear script. Moreover, it seems that the Gutians, Caucasian hordes from the Zagros, were causing confusion in Elam just as they did in Akkadia.[103]

The next rulers to arise in Elam were of the Dynasty of Simashki. Originating in the mountains of the north, they were initially subject to the Gutians and the Sumerians. Elam reappears in the inscriptions of Gudea of Lagash (c.2700-2674 BC). Apparently, he seized "with weapons the town of Anshan in Elam". He also asserted that Elamites came from Elam and Susians came from Susa to help him reconstruct temples in Sumer. However, the Elamites would soon turn the tables on the Sumerians. We previously mentioned that King Shulgi of the Third Dynasty of Ur created an Elamite 'foreign legion' in Mesopotamia.[104]

After 2635 BC King Lurak-luhhan of Simashki launched an attack on Susiana from the mountains and freed Awan, Adamdun and Susa from Sumerian control. The Sumerian ruler Ibbi-Sin responded to the challenge and marched on Elam, regaining the towns previously lost. He seized Lurak-luhhan and dragged him to Ur in triumph. However, in 2628 BC Ibbi-Sin had once again to march against the rebellious Elamites. This time, however, his power had been undermined by famine, the Amorites, and by internal treachery. While this was going on, Hutran-tempt, the new king of Simashki, seized the initiative and marched on Sumer. In 2609 BC his armies crushed Sumer in a single invasion. The Elamites reduced Ur to "hills of ruin and places of desolation". The King of Simashki, may have been helped in Sumeria by the Elamite 'foreign legion' troops created by Shulgi. The Elamites seized Ibbi-Sin and also statues of Sumerian deities. All were carried to Elam. Nearly twenty years later, Elam was completely free of Sumerian power.[105]

Indattu-Inshushinak (2568-2523 BC) was an outstanding ruler. He had already been governor of Susiana and Viceroy of Elam. Even before he was king, he encouraged a policy of reconstruction in Susa. He repaired the fortifications of the city and built a new city wall. He repaired the Temple of Inshushinak and dedicated a limestone basin.[106]

Indattu II, his grandson, ascended to the throne in 2503 BC. He inspired a burst of architectural activity. According to the inscriptions, he refused to repair the old walls in Susa that surrounded the temple grounds, but instead had them replaced by new walls of brick. There is a splendid seal impression where he is shown seated on a simple throne, wearing a turban and costly garments. With his right hand, he presents a curved staff to his chancellor. The third figure, a goddess, witnesses the nomination of the chancellor. Dr Hinz explained that the chancellors were judges and were also responsible for the 'tablet house' or scribal schools where young officials of the future were instructed in the cuneiform script.[107]

This period came to an end at the hands of the Mesopotamians. Gungunum (2516-2489 BC), fifth ruler of Larsa, marched against Anshan in two successful campaigns. Professor Hinz says that beyond this: "The details of the downfall of the kingdom of Simashki are no more discoverable than the case of the collapse of Awan. Only the names of the last two kings of Simashki are extant: *Indattu-napir* and *Indattu-tempt*."[108]

In about 2450 BC a new and powerful line of kings emerged in Elam. Its founder was Epart. He was apparently an upstart who seized the throne by force. He added to the Temple of Inshushinak and started a Temple to the Moon.[109] Meanwhile, to the west in Mesopotamia, the dominant people were now the Babylonians. They would prove to be just as much of a challenge to the Elamites as the Sumerians and Akkadians were.

Silhaha succeeded Epart as king and enjoyed a comparatively long reign. Silhaha installed his sister's son Attahushu as Regent of Susa. The Regent embarked on a policy of extensive innovation in Susa. As Epart and Silhaha had done before him, he added to the Temple of Inshushinak and completed the Temple of the Moon. One of his Akkadian inscriptions states that he, as "shepherd of the people of Susa" and concerned for the safety of their life, dedicated a temple to the "great mistress Ninegal (Pinikir)." In a shrine, he commemorated Narunte, the Elamite goddess of victory, and Anunitum, her Akkadian equivalent. To the west of Susa, he built a fortified palace, linking it to the capital by a bridge. Finally, he erected the *Stele of Righteousness* in the market place at Susa. It acted as an official price index.[110]

Sirktuh I and Siwe-palar-huhpak were the next two kings of Elam. They actively opposed Babylonian power and battled against their great ruler Hammurabi. Both were unsuccessful but Siwe-palar-huhpak did extend Elamite territory towards the highlands. He gave himself the title 'Increaser of the kingdom.' This compensated for his losses against Hammurabi.[111]

Kuduzulush I became the next ruler of Elam. He elevated his nephew Kuter-Nahhunte to Prince of Susa. The Prince left an impression not only on the kings of Elam but also on Assyrian rulers of a much later period. In 2281 BC, during the time of Hammurabi's successor, he launched a daring attack on Babylonia and took the statue of Nanaja, the deity of victory and fertility. He thus avenged the submission forced on his uncle Siwe-palar-huhpak by Hammurabi. In a later era, scribes reported the attack which the Elamites launched on Mesopotamia: "Kuter-Nahhunte of the Elamite, careless of his oath to the great gods, and full of misplaced confidence in his own strength, laid hand on the shrines of Akkad, and levelled Akkad to the ground". Additionally, Kuter-Nahhunte took the statue of the goddess Nanaja to Susa. It was further reported that: "Nanaia [sic], who had been angry for one thousand, six hundred and thirty five years who had left us and established herself in Elam, a place unworthy of her". The Elamites, however, were greatly inspired by this victory. Shihak-Inshushinak, a later king, wrote that he would like to "prove the honour of Kuter-Nahhunte and his [son and prince of Susa] Tempt-agun". Moreover, King Shutruk-nahhunte named his eldest son after this distinguished ancestor.[112]

After this period, however, there are severe gaps in our knowledge. Dr Hinz, our scholarly friend, says: "Subsequent Grand Regents form a dynasty that embraces twelve generations, but due to the absence of further source material, they remain for the most part mere names". It seems that the Kassites, a new and rising power in the Near-East, conquered Elam and "sounded the knell of the Eparti dynasty".[113]

In about 1500 BC a new ruling house had arisen in Elam - the Igehalkids. Ige-haliki started a dynasty that would lead Elam through its Classical Period. Humban-numena, the fourth king of the dynasty, ascended the throne around 1425 BC. He erected a temple to the 'great goddess' possibly Pinikir, in the city of Liyan. The inscription calls upon not only the deities Humban and Kiririsha but also the "benevolent gods of Liyan". It also says: "I am Humban-numena, son of Attar-kittah, expander of my kingdom, monarch of Elam, ruler of Elam, governor of Elam, King of Anshan and Susa". Furthermore: "A healthy life was granted to me. God Inshushinak preserved the monarchy for me". These inscriptions were not mere idle boasts. Humban-numena's rule was long and stable. He also laid a foundation in peace and prosperity. The country thrived and wealth flooded into the national treasury.[114]

Untash-napirisha came to the throne in about 1381 BC. Under his rule Elam enjoyed a Golden Age. In fact, the country bloomed more under him than at any other period. During his rule, four Kassite kings succeeded each other in neighbouring but hostile Mesopotamia, while he quietly observed the continuing collapse of Babylonia. However, when the time seemed ripe, he seized the opportunity. He launched a surprise and wholly successful attack on Mesopotamia.[115]

At Choga Zambil Untash-napirisha built a new and carefully planned city. Called Dur-Untash, it contained a huge ziggurat and an extensive sacred precinct called the Siyankuk. Everything here was on a grand scale. An inner wall surrounded the ziggurat, with its five steps. It was perfectly square with each side measuring 105 metres. The corners of the basic square were aligned to the four compass points. The city had thirteen temples. Statues of lions, bulls or gryphons guarded their entrances. The bulls were of terracotta encrusted with lapis lazuli. Considered symbols of divinity, horns formed an important part of every temple. Inside these monuments were numerous royal statues, cast in gold, silver, bronze, and even alabaster. Each temple had its own sacred groves. Surrounding the sacred precinct was an outer wall, over four thousand metres long. Its bricks were inscribed with threats, mostly in Elamite. They warn: "he who takes in a charge [?] the walls of the sacred precinct, who makes a breach in them, steals the inscribed bricks, burns the door beams, and opens the gates to the approaching foes, may he be struck by the punishing sceptre of Humban, Inshushinak and Kiririsha. May he have no descendants under the sun".[116]

The king must have encountered great difficulty in providing Dur-Untash with water. He had water diverted from the Karkheh River by building a 50 kilometre canal. Naturally, the canal served to irrigate farms along its course before reaching the city. Dur-Untash, however, was still higher than the surface of the canal, posing a difficult technological challenge. The builders solved this by constructing a large tidal basin. The fissures in the brick-work of the walls were filled with bitumen, and nine ducts on the bottom of the basin connected it with a smaller basin inside the town wall. To feed it, the builders made use of the principle of communicating tubes.[117] Professor Hinz comments as follows:

> For years, King Untash-napirisha was forced to mobilise a whole army of tens of thousands of tile-makers, brick-bakers, masons, navvies, handymen and donkey-drivers - and he also had to provide for them. He needed experts for the ingenious drainage and irrigation schemes of Dur-Untash; for the plans for the decoration of the walls in brightly painted mosaic; and for the countless sacred offerings in metal, marble, frit or glass. He needed a whole school of industrious scribes to letter the thousands of tiles, for all were written by hand: no stamps were used. We must admit a certain admiration for the organizational capacity of the Elamites.[118]

Kiten-Hutran, the next ruler, was the nephew of Untash-napirisha. He seems to have been more interested in military glory than building temples or writing inscriptions. Seizing the initiative, in 1318 BC, he launched a campaign into Mesopotamia. The Elamite army crossed the Tigris and conquered Nippur. After five years on the throne, Dr Hinz says "We do not know what happened next; it is only certain that Kiten-Hutran vanished abruptly from the historical scene, and with him the dynasty of the Igehalkids. In any case a new dynasty soon appeared".[119]

Hallutush-Inshushinak was the father of the new ruling house, the Shutrukids. Shutruk-nahhunte, his son and successor had a distinguished career. A text from his time revealed that the Temple of Kiririsha (built by Humban) in Liyan was already ruined but fortunately Shutruk-nahhunte was on hand to repair it. On a practical front, the king launched campaigns. In 1179 BC, accompanied by his eldest son, Kutir-nahhunte, the king marched out from Susa, crossed the Karkheh River and attacked Mesopotamia. The Babylonian accounts dramatise how the Elamites "rushed down from the mountains with horses and chariots" and defeated the princes of Babylon. They seized the famous obelisk that bore the Code of Hammurabi and imposed a vast tribute on Babylonia. The Babylonians were compelled to pay 120 talents of gold (about 2,600 kilograms), and 480 talents of silver (about 14,400 kilograms). The Babylonians struggled for three years against Elamite domination but eventually capitulated. Their ruler was captured and exiled in Elam.[120]

In around 1165 BC Shilhak-Inshushinak became the next ruler of Elam. Professor Hinz believes that he was "the last of the great kings of Elam". Shilhak-Inshushinak left by far the largest number of inscriptions that have come down to the modern period. He continued the aggressive policy towards

Babylonia favoured by his predecessors. He plagued their rulers by repeated campaigns.[121]

Hutelutush-Inshushinak became king in 1131 BC. Unfortunately, he faced a powerful and brilliant rival in Babylonia known as Nebuchadnezzar I. The Babylonian king launched an attack on Elam in 1126 BC. However, some of the priests of Susa and also a regional prince threw their lot in with Nebuchadnezzar I. Five years later, the Babylonians renewed their attacks on Elam. We read that: "Hutelutush-Inshushinak, King of Elam, hid himself in his mountain". In addition, "King Nebuchadnezzar was victorious, he overcame the land of Elam and plundered its treasures". Dr Hinz narrates that:

> Although this Babylonian domination was not to be permanent for Elam. Many centuries later, this decisive victory was still not forgotten. It appears that at this period … Susa was so severely damaged that for some time it forfeited its position as the capital of Elam; at any rate, for nearly four centuries no texts survive from the city. The final years of the Shutrukids are hidden in an obscurity no less profound than that which shrouded the end of the kingdoms of Awan, Simashki and the Eparti. Elam's great classical period comes to an abrupt end, and "the rest is silence".[122]

In the ninth century BC that silence was broken. Elam appears in an inscription as an enemy battling the Assyrians. In the middle of the eighth century BC, Humban-tahrah founded a new kingdom in Elam and thus began the final chapter in the federation's history. The kingdom lasted little more than a century and its history was characterised by Elam's struggle against Assyria - a near White Semitic speaking people, and also the threat posed by the emerging Medes and Persians - both Aryan peoples. The Assyrians were a particularly barbarous lot. Dr Rashidi says of them:

> The Assyrians elevated warfare to an exact science. They were not content to merely conquer peoples; they must completely destroy them. Around the smoking ruins that had been cities would stretch lines of tall stakes, on which were impaled the bodies of the defeated community leaders, flayed alive. Scattered about were huge mounds of the viciously mutilated bodies of the dead and dying. Those who survived the holocaust were deported to other regions of Assyrian control.[123]

The beginnings of the Aryan migration into Iran dates back to around 1000 BC. The Medes and Persians first occupied Persian Kurdestan, the area once held by the Guti. During the early seventh century BC, the Persians separated from the Medes, and migrated east along the Zagros to Shiraz. From this base they gradually moved east under their kings, Teispes and Cyrus I. As they advanced from Persepolis to Susa, they appropriated more and more of Elamite territory.[124]

King Humban-nikash (742-717 BC) was the second ruler of the new kingdom of Elam. In 720 BC he battled the famous Assyrian King Sargon near Dêr. A Babylonian chronicle mentions that: "He inflicted a crushing defeat on Assyria".[125]

Shutruk-nahhunte II, his successor, no longer referred to himself as 'King of Anshan and Susa' but as 'Expander of my kingdom'. In 710 BC King Sargon of Assyria attacked Babylonia. The Babylonian king fled to Elam, where he was granted asylum. In return, Shutruk-nahhunte II expected Babylonian help in a later joint campaign against Assyria. They seized their opportunity in 703 BC, during the time of Sargon's successor. The combined campaign was successful, but internal problems emerged in Elam. In 699 BC Shutruk-nahhunte II fell victim to a palace coup. His younger brother, Hallushu-Inshushinak, had him jailed and then usurped his throne. Six years later the Assyrians returned as a regional power and defeated the allied Elamite and Babylonian forces at Nippur. The vanquished Hallushu-Inshushinak made his way back to Susa, but "the people of Susa", says a Babylonian chronicle, "shut the gates before him and slew him".[126]

His successor did not last even one year on the throne. In July 692 BC apparently "Kudar, King of Elam was captured and killed during an uprising". Dr Hinz comments that: "The violent overthrow of three successive kings of the same house: such a thing had never before happened in Elam. There could be no clearer sign of the collapse of the kingdom."[127]

The Assyrians continued to battle Elam. They launched two fateful but successful campaigns, in 647 and 646 BC. The conquerors wrought awful destruction on the Elamites. In the autumn of 646 BC Susa fell. The Assyrian king boasted that he "opened their treasure-houses, where there were piles of silver and gold, of treasures and riches which had been amassed by earlier kings of Elam right up to the most recent; apart from me, no other conqueror had laid hand upon them". Among the treasures were garments, ornaments, royal insignia, weapons, "and all the palace furniture on which the king sat or lay, the bowls which he used for meals, washing and anointing, the chariots of triumph and of war decorated with gold and electron, the horses and mules with their gold and silver trappings - all this I took back to Assyria". The Assyrian king continued:

> In the course of a march which lasted fifty five days, I transformed the land into a wilderness. I scattered salt and thistle on its meadows. The wives and daughters of the kings of Elam, of old and new family, the town governors, the commanders, the whole corps of officers including the engineers, all the inhabitants, whether male or female, old or young, the horses, the mules, the donkeys, the cattle both large and small, more numerous than a swarm of locusts - all this I dragged back to Assyria.[128]

In 629 BC the Medes had risen to a position of regional influence. Their king formed an alliance with the king of Babylonia. In 612 BC they jointly seized Assyria and with it, control of Susiana. The mountains of Anshan, however, remained in Persian hands, but they were now the subjects of the Medes. In the time of Cyrus II, Persia overthrew Mede supremacy and then defeated Babylonia. Susiana then became a Persian possession taken from the Medes and the Babylonians. In this way, the whole of Elam was brought under Persian rule in 539 BC.[129] This led to the dominance of the Aryan people and Indo-European language in Iran that has continued up until the present time. Independent Black rule in this region was now over. Before winding up this chapter, we give the final word to Dr Rashidi, the world's leading authority on the role of Blacks in Asian history. He comments that:

> Albeit in a severely diminished capacity, after the devastation of Susa, the Blacks of Elam remained an important regional factor. Herodotus finds them represented as Persian auxilaries in the Greco-Persian wars. During the same period southern Balchustan, extreme eastern Iran and western Pakistan, was known as Gedrosia, "the country of the dark folk" ... In spite of the early and continued incursions of the new peoples in the north, and the decisive defeat at the hands of the Assyrians, the ancient Susian Elamites distinguished themselves as a highly advanced and aggressive people who developed their land, and defended it from conquest again and again. Like the Sumerians of Mesopotamia they established a standard for civilization that the kingdoms and empires that followed could only imitate. 2500 years after its last national defense, reports of the remnants of this Kushite colony called Elam, with its Susian heartland, persist.[130]

Notes

[1] Runoko Rashidi, *Africans in Early Asian Civilizations: An Overview,* in *African Presence in Early Asia,* ed Runoko Rashidi, US, Transaction Publishers, 1995, p.21.

[2] Indus Khamit Kush, *What they never told you in history class,* US, Luxorr Publications, 1983, p.193 and George Roux, *Ancient Iraq, Third Edition,* UK, Penguin Books, 1992, pp.2-4.

[3] George Roux, *Ancient Iraq, Third Edition,* p.80.

[4] Ibid., p.79.

[5] Godfrey Higgins, *Anacalypsis, Volume II,* US, A & B Books, 1992 (originally 1836), p.364.

[6] Count Adam Gurowski, *America and Europe,* US, D. Appleton & Co, 1857, p.175.

[7] George Roux, *Ancient Iraq, Third Edition,* p.28.

[8] Henry C. Rawlinson, *On the Early History of Babylonia,* in *History of Herodotus, 3rd Edition, Volume I,* (Translated by George Rawlinson), UK, John Murray, 1875, p.433.

[9] George Rawlinson, *Five Great Monarchies of the Ancient Eastern World, Volume II,* UK, John Murray, 1879, p.500.

[10] Zénaïde Ragozin, *Chaldea: The Story of the Nations,* US, G. P. Putnam's Sons, 1886, p.188.

[11] Gerald Massey, *The Hebrew and Other Creations Fundamentally Explained,* in *Gerald Massey's Lectures,* US, Samuel Weiser, 1974, p.134.

[12] Charles Seignobos, *History of Ancient Civilization,* UK, T. Fisher Unwin, 1907, p.17.

[13] H. G. Spearing, *The Childhood of Art,* UK, Kegan Paul, Trench, Trübner & Co., 1912, pp.255-6.

[14] Quoted in Zénaïde Ragozin, *Chaldea: The Story of the Nations,* p.185.

[15] Leonard Woolley, *Ur of the Chaldees,* UK, Pelican Books, 1938, compare pp.41and plate 4 (a) against 83-4.

[16] Ibid., p.17.

[17] W. J. Perry, *The Growth of Civilisation, 2nd Edition,* UK, Penguin Books, 1937, pp.59-61.

[18] Ibid., p.61.

[19] J. Norman Lockyer, *The Dawn of Astronomy,* UK, Cassell & Co., 1894, pp.373-4.

[20] Herbert Wendt, *It Began in Babel,* UK, Weidenfeld and Nicholson, 1963, p.85.

[21] George Roux, *Ancient Iraq, Third Edition,* pp.11-2.

[22] Christina Lamb, *The Eden Project,* in *The Sunday Times Magazine,* UK, 27 July 2003, p.26.

[23] Drusilla Dunjee Houston, *Wonderful Ethiopians of the Ancient Cushite Empire,* US, Black Classic Press, 1985 (original 1926), p.206. See also Runoko Rashidi, *Africans in Early Asian Civilizations: An Overview,* in *African Presence in Early Asia,* pp.21 and 23.

[24] Henry Field, *Papers of the Peabody Museum, Volume 48,* US, Harvard University Press, 1953, p.53.

[25] S. D. Ousely and R. L. Jantz, *FORDISC 2.0, Personal Computer Forensic Discriminant Functions,* US, University of Tennessee, 1996.

[26] Personal communication. Write to historicalwalker@yahoo.com for details.

[27] See Anu M'Bantu, *The Blackheads: A History of Mesopotamia,* UK, Anu-Enlil-Enki Publishing, 2001, pp.4-5.

[28] Herbert Wendt, *It Began in Babel,* p.83.

[29] See Anu M'Bantu, *The Blackheads: A History of Mesopotamia,* p.5.

[30] Herbert Wendt, *It Began in Babel,* p.83.

[31] Professor John G. Jackson stated that the Sumerians "are shown on the monuments as beardless and with shaven heads. The later Semitic Babylonians are depicted … with beards and long hair". See John G. Jackson, *Man, God, and Civilization,* US, Citadel Press, 1972, p.242.

[32] A. H. Sayce, *The Archæology of the Cuneiform Inscriptions,* UK, S. P. C. K., 1907, pp.72-3.

[33] See Hunter Havelin Adams III, *African Observers of the Universe,* in *Blacks in Science,* ed Ivan Van Sertima, US, Transaction Publishers, 1983, p.34.

[34] Runoko Rashidi, *More Light on Sumer, Elam and India,* in *African Presence in Early Asia,* ed Runoko Rashidi, US, Transaction Publishers, 1995, p.163.

[35] Walther Hinz, *The Lost World of Elam,* UK, Sidgwick & Jackson, 1972, p.97-8.

[36] *Inscription on a Clay Cylinder of Nabonidus,* in *Light from the East,* by Rev. C. J. Ball, UK, Eyre and Spottiswoode, 1899, pp.208-11.

[37] Duncan MacNaughton, *A Scheme of Egyptian Chronology,* UK, Luzac & Co., 1932, pp.8-9 and 371-2.

[38] See Rev. C. J. Ball, *Light from the East,* p.211.

[39] Duncan MacNaughton, *A Scheme of Babylonian Chronology*, UK, Luzac & Co., 1929, p.53.
[40] George Roux, *Ancient Iraq, Third Edition*, see the *Chronological Tables* in the back of the book (there are no page numbers here).
[41] Drusilla Dunjee Houston, *Wonderful Ethiopians of the Ancient Cushite Empire*, pp.172-3.
[42] Erik Hornung, *History of Ancient Egypt*, UK, Edinburgh University Press, 1999, p.61.
[43] See Duncan MacNaughton, *A Scheme of Egyptian Chronology*, pp.142-3.
[44] George Roux, *Ancient Iraq, Third Edition*, p.136.
[45] *Inscription on a Clay Cylinder of Nabonidus*, in *Light from the East*, pp.208-11.
[46] George Roux, *Ancient Iraq, Third Edition*, pp.33 and 48.
[47] Ibid., p.26.
[48] Ibid., pp.12-3.
[49] George Rawlinson, *Five Great Monarchies of the Ancient Eastern World, Volume I*, pp.15-6.
[50] George Roux, *Ancient Iraq, Third Edition*, pp.13-5.
[51] Ibid., pp.49-51.
[52] Ibid., pp.53-4.
[53] Ibid., pp.55-8.
[54] Ibid., pp.59-60 and 62-3.
[55] Compare ibid., p.52 and Michael Rice, *Egypt's Making*, UK, Routledge, 1991, p.160, plate 60.
[56] George Roux, *Ancient Iraq, Third Edition*, pp.66-8.
[57] Ibid., pp.68, 73 and 75.
[58] Ibid., pp.76-7.
[59] See ibid., pp.108-9.
[60] Ibid., pp.111-3.
[61] See Duncan MacNaughton, *A Scheme of Egyptian Chronology*, pp.342-6.
[62] George Roux, *Ancient Iraq, Third Edition*, pp.114-6.
[63] Duncan MacNaughton, *A Scheme of Babylonian Chronology*, pp.12-3 and 21-3.
[64] Philip Smith, *The Ancient History of the East*, UK, John Murray, 1871, p.204.
[65] George Roux, *Ancient Iraq, Third Edition*, pp.123 and 139-40.
[66] Ibid., pp.124-7 and 130.
[67] Ibid., pp.134 and 139.
[68] Runoko Rashidi, *More Light on Sumer, Elam and India*, in African Presence in Early Asia, p.167.
[69] Alastair Service, *Lost Worlds*, UK, Marshall Cavendish, 1981, pp.96-7 and 100.
[70] George Roux, *Ancient Iraq, Third Edition*, pp.140-1.
[71] Ibid., pp.141-2.
[72] Ibid., p.138.
[73] James Baikie, *The Life of the Ancient East*, UK, A. & C. Black, 1923, p.214.
[74] Quoted in George Roux, *Ancient Iraq, Third Edition*, p.144.
[75] Ibid., pp.144-5.
[76] See ibid., pp.145-6 and 52-5.
[77] Ibid., pp.160-1.
[78] Ibid., p.155.
[79] Quoted in ibid., p.158. See also pp.156-7.

[80] A. Josef Ben-Levi, *The First and Second Intermediate Periods in Kemetic History,* in *Kemet and the African Worldview,* ed Maulana Karenga and Jacob Carruthers, US, University of Sankore Press, 1986, p.57.

[81] Leonard Woolley, *Ur of the Chaldees,* p.80.

[82] George Roux, *Ancient Iraq, Third Edition,* pp.161-4.

[83] Quoted in Anu M'Bantu, *The Blackheads: A History of Mesopotamia,* p.6.

[84] George Roux, *Ancient Iraq, Third Edition,* pp.165-7.

[85] Ibid., pp.168-9.

[86] Ibid., pp.170-1.

[87] Ibid., p.171.

[88] Ibid., pp.172-3.

[89] George Rawlinson, *Five Great Monarchies of the Ancient Eastern World, Volume I,* pp.100-1.

[90] Drusilla Dunjee Houston, *Wonderful Ethiopians of the Ancient Cushite Empire,* pp.198-9.

[91] Quoted in George Roux, *Ancient Iraq, Third Edition,* p.176. See also p.175.

[92] Runoko Rashidi, *Africans in Early Asian Civilizations: An Overview,* in *African Presence in Early Asia,* p.25.

[93] George Roux, *Ancient Iraq, Third Edition,* pp.176-7.

[94] Quoted in ibid., p.179. See also pp.178-9.

[95] See Walther Hinz, *The Lost World of Elam,* pp.17-21 and 68.

[96] Ibid., pp.88-9.

[97] Ibid., pp.23-4.

[98] Ibid., pp.28-31.

[99] Ibid., p.69.

[100] Ibid., pp.69-73 and 180.

[101] Ibid., pp.36-9 and 74.7.

[102] See ibid., pp.77-8.

[103] Ibid., p.79.

[104] Ibid., pp.79-83.

[105] Ibid., pp.83-5.

[106] Ibid., p.85.

[107] Ibid., pp.85-7.

[108] Ibid., p.87.

[109] Ibid., pp.87, 92 and 94.

[110] Ibid., pp.92-4.

[111] Ibid., pp.94-7.

[112] See ibid., pp.97-8.

[113] Ibid., p.99.

[114] See ibid., pp.112-3.

[115] Ibid., p.114.

[116] See ibid., pp.55-7, 115-6 and 169-170.

[117] Ibid., pp.116-7.

[118] Ibid., pp.168-9.

[119] Ibid., pp.119-121.

[120] Ibid., pp.121-2 and 124-6.

[121] Ibid., pp.127-8.

[122] Ibid., pp.133 and 135-7.

[123] Runoko Rashidi, *Africans in Early Asian Civilizations: An Overview,* in *African Presence in Early Asia,* p.27.

[124] Walther Hinz, *The Lost World of Elam,* pp.138-9.

[125] Ibid., p.139.

[126] Ibid., pp.147-9.

[127] Ibid., p.149.

[128] Quoted in ibid., p.159. See also pp.157-8.

[129] Ibid., pp.159-60.

[130] Runoko Rashidi, *Africans in Early Asian Civilizations: An Overview,* in *African Presence in Early Asia,* p.28.

CHAPTER TWENTY ONE: INDUS VALLEY AND ARABIA

Indus Valley Civilisation

The Indus Valley Civilisation was located in the region of Pakistan and western India. The empire ruled a huge territory, larger than the combined areas of Egypt and Mesopotamia. Its western border was near the modern Iran/Pakistan border. The territory stretched as far east as the modern city of Mumbai. Northwards it stretched to the western elbow of the Ganges River and thus formed a rough triangle. Encompassed within this region was the Indus River. The Indus River fed the Indus Valley Civilisation in much the same way the Nile fed the Pharaonic culture and the Two Rivers fed the Sumerian and Akkadian cultures. The Indus and its tributaries cover almost 100 miles of the Pakistan and northwest India region. The great city of Mohenjo-Daro was located on the Indus but the city of Harappa was on one of its tributaries.[1]

Beginning in 1856 British engineers took notice of an ancient Indian city, then called Brahminabad. Among the ruins were bricks of such exceptional quality that the British used them to lay a railway. In 1892 General Sir Alexander Cunningham, Director General of the Indian Archaeological Survey, began to take a more systematic interest in the ancient city and other ruined sites belonging to the same culture.[2] In the 1920's other archaeologists, such as Marshall and Mackay, followed in the wake of Cunningham:

> But Aryan pride of race [wrote Englishman S. G. Blaxland Stubbs] … received something of a shock from archaeological investigations carried out by Sir John Marshall and, more recently by Dr. E. Mackay in the valley of the Indus. Here ample evidence has been found of a race whose complex civilization and high culture were equal, and in some respects superior, to those of early Mesopotamia and Egypt.[3]

Within this vast territory, more recent archaeological excavations have found 1,000 settlements. Most of these were villages of 2 to 5 acres located near to rivers or streams. Of the important settlements were Kalibangan, Quetta and Lothal. Chanu Daro was a medium sized town that has attracted curious attention. Far more important, however, were the two capitals, Mohenjo-Daro and Harappa. Due to the importance of Harappa, some scholars call this civilisation the 'Harappan Culture' and the Indus Valley people 'Harappans.'[4]

The earliest villages emerged between 6000 and 7000 BC. According to Wayne Chandler, the noted African-American historian, some of these villages evolved into the planned cities of Mohenjo-Daro and Harappa sometime between 3000 and 2500 BC.⁵ Sir Mortimer Wheeler was at one time the Director General of Archaeology in India and was also Archaeological Adviser to the Government of Pakistan. His influence has led many scholars to agree a general date of 2300 BC for the mature period of the Indus Valley Civilisation. He gave his reasoning surrounding this date as follows:

> Both from archaeological and from epigraphical evidence, it is known that in the time of the great Sargon of Agade and his successors contact between southern Mesopotamia and the Indus was at its liveliest. And within a mere handful of years the date of Sargon is now securely established: as nearly as may be 2370-2344 BC; or, to take the Sargonid period as a whole, let us say 2370-2284 BC. Thereafter a second wave of Mesopotamian trade began with King Ur-Nammu, about 2100 BC, and continued until the Larsa period, about 1900 BC ... Here is near-historical precision of a kind by which new material evidence from the Indus and Mesopotamia ... may be expected in the fullness of time to lend a fresh exactness to the dating of our Indus Civilization.

Sir Mortimer considered the following pieces of evidence:

> [T]he occurrence of Indus seals in Sargonid associations at Ur, Kish and Tell Asmar; of etched beads, as used by the Harappans, from similar levels at Tell Asmar; of gold disk-beads with axial tube at Mohenjo-daro [sic] at Early Dynastic III - Sargonid dates in Mesopotamia, and in Troy IIG about 2300 BC; and bone inlays and knobbed pottery, of distinctly Indus types in Sargonid deposits at Tell Asmar; all these and their like are assured evidence that the Indus Civilization was mature by the time of the Sargon Dynasty.⁶

The problem with all of this is that the Sargonid period is far from being "securely established". Reverend Baikie, author of *The Life of the Ancient East,* informs us that at one time scholars accepted that Sargon I ruled from 3800 BC. They derived this date from the Cylinder of Nabonidus, a primary source document in the British Museum. Baikie further explains that many scholars had since rejected this early date in favour of a lower date of 2650 BC.⁷ This more conservative date for Sargon I is still 280 years earlier than Sir Mortimer Wheeler's "securely established" date of 2370 BC. Moreover, Sir John Marshall, also using "the evidence of Mohenjo-Daro seals found at Kish and Ur", concludes that the Indus civilisation flourished between "3250 B.C. and 2750 B.C."⁸ Where does this leave us? Our position is much more in line with that of Sir John Marshall. We date the mature period (i.e. the time contemporaneous with Sargon I) to around 2895 BC in line with our chronologies for Egypt and Mesopotamia.

Mohenjo-Daro and Harappa each had an estimated population of 40,000 people according to the excavations:

> The most striking aspect of these city ruins [says Mr Chandler] is their undisputable evidence of sophisticated city planning … The two major cities are similarly laid out, again demonstrating deliberate city planning. As one author put it, the city was "Built in a gridlike fashion with a large main street; it seems almost a minute version of Manhattan Island" … A few thousand years transpired before the Romans began to construct towns along similar patterns and then another millennium passed before municipal planning would be seen on the earth again.[9]

The thoroughfares were laid out on a mathematical pattern. Avenues ran north to south and east to west. The main boulevards were 35 feet wide. Shops and restaurants lined them but the most important public buildings were the Granary, the Citadel and the Great Bath.[10] In addition, one excavator described another important building (230 x 78 feet) as "the residence of a very high official, possibly the high priest or a college of priests." Whatever this building was it was certainly no ordinary house.[11] Concerning the Granary, Sir Mortimer Wheeler believed that it "may be equated with a modern State Bank".[12]

The Great Bath at Mohenjo-Daro and its surrounding complex were 185 feet long and 100 feet broad. Surrounding the building was a wall 6 or 7 feet thick with six entrances. The bath itself was a 20 by 40 foot structure built to a depth of eight feet. It was accurately constructed with bricks held with gypsum mortar and covered with bitumen. This ensured that it was watertight. Also built were drains that allowed the bathing water to be changed at regular intervals.[13] Of the quality of the construction, Mr Stubbs, in a fine essay, tells us that: "Sir John Marshall and Dr Mackay consider that both on excellence and solidity of construction, it could not be improved upon by any modern [i.e. in 1937] builder. After 5,000 years it still holds water".[14]

The houses were entered through a main doorway on a side street. They were often two or more storeys high and built around a central square courtyard. The windows of each room faced the courtyard rather than the street. This ensured privacy and may also have kept out the debris from the dusty and unpaved streets. Most houses, large and small, had chutes to dispose of rubbish and waste. Filtering into tunnels, the waste emptied into central sewers. Also built were sumps or drainage pits to collect the heaviest waste in order that the main channels would be unobstructed.[15] Mr Chandler, in an impressive essay, tells us that:

> Virtually every household was equipped with what much of the modern western world still thinks of as "modern conveniences." In addition to the trash chutes, each household had bathrooms with drains which carried waste to the

sewers under the main streets. Almost every dwelling had its own private well from which fresh water was drawn. Apparently, prosperity was not as elusive to the Harappans as it was to their contemporaries in Egypt and Sumer.[16]

The quality of these conveniences were high. Mr Stubbs informs us that: "From the bathroom ran earthenware drain pipes laid in gypsum mortar and brickwork". Furthermore the construction was "in a style that, like all the drainage work found in this most ancient city, would probably pass inspection by a modern sanitary inspector".[17] Further support for this position comes from Sir Mortimer Wheeler. In his view: "The high quality of the sanitary arrangements at Mohenjo-daro [sic] could well be envied in many parts of the world today. They reflect decent standards of living coupled with an obviously zealous municipal supervision".[18]

"A further aspect of Harappan life" according to anthropologist Professor Walter Faiservis:

> is its standardization. In architecture, building bricks were standard in size and were laid in standard ways. Drainage and sewer systems were standard in pattern. Dwellings were standard in dimensions and special structures (possibly public) were positioned with respect to private ones according to standard plans. Other aspects of the same phenomenon included standard weights and measures, pottery that was standard in shape and ornamentation and standardized artefacts such as ladles, loom weights and even toy carts.[19]

Basing his research on the excavations of Sir John Marshall, Mr Stubbs was also impressed by the standards of the brickwork. He wrote that the bricks "have perfectly flat faces and sharp edges and would do credit to the best modern brickmaker and bricklayers". Moreover:

> The effect of the wide expanse of bare, red brick buildings is such that Sir John Marshall likens it to "the ruins of some present-day working town of Lancashire." Stark utilitarianism is the feature of every building. The plainness of the buildings is, however, atoned for by the excellence of their construction.[20]

The Harappans grew crops of barley, corn, cotton, peas, sesame, wheat and other garden vegetables. They domesticated cats, dogs, cattle and buffaloes and may have domesticated pigs, camels, horses, asses and elephants. They traded vigorously with Mesopotamia. The presence of Indian pottery and seals discovered in Mesopotamia suggests that Indus traders settled there. Far to the southeast, the port of Lothal became important. The dock was controlled by a sluice gate that enabled the ships to load or unload during high or low tide. Cotton was their main trading commodity, but they also handled copper, gold, lapis lazuli, timber and turquoise. The gold came from southern India and

Afghanistan. The copper came from Rajasthan, Afghanistan or some even more exotic location. The lapis came from Afghanistan and the turquoise came from Elam. In addition, they made jewellery of gold, silver, and rare and precious stones, such as agate, carnelian and lapis. Most of their artefacts, however, were of wood, bone, clay, flint and shell. Facilitating trade, they had a system of standard weights and measures.[21] The *Rg Veda,* a collection of Aryan traditions, describes the Indus people as "rich in cattle and dwell in fortified places called Pur".[22]

The Harappans had a written script. Scholars know of 2,290 surviving texts, but reading the documents is still a challenge. The script made use of 419 signs, of which 200 were in general use. The script is logo-syllabic where some signs represent words but other signs are of syllabic value. "Earnest attempts" says Dr Faiservis "have been made to relate Harappan to Minoan, Canaanite, Hittite and even to the peculiar 'writing' of Easter Island".[23] According to Sir Mortimer Wheeler "a fair measure of literacy is to be inferred ... from the recurrence of the script as graffiti on pots and potsherds".[24] In other words literacy was widespread. This is a very important cultural achievement.

In terms of material culture, some great statuary has been recovered. From the city of Harappa, two sculptures were found of such quality that Sir Marshall felt even a "Greek [sculptor] of the 4th century B.C. might well have been proud".[25] Mention has already been made of toys. The Indus Valley people made model animals that nod, rattles made in the shape of elephants, clay whistles in the shape of birds, toy carts pulled by model oxen, balls, and even marbles.[26]

"So much for a broad summary of what is known" writes Professor Fairservis:

> What is not known may be of equal significance. There is no evidence of rivalry between the different Harappan states, of warfare ... or of the kings and courts and great temple complexes so characteristic of the other ancient civilizations of the Old World ... The Harappans cultivated cotton and perhaps rice, domesticated the chicken and may have invented the game of chess and one of the two great early sources of nonmuscle power: the windmill. (The other was the water wheel.)[27]

Excavations of artefacts from the late third millennium BC indicate that horse-riding invaders raided villages in Baluchistan to the west of the Indus. The Aryan incursion had begun. By 1800 BC more invaders from the Western Steppes streamed in. Indus villagers and townsfolk crowded into the cities for their own safety. Excavations from Mohenjo-Daro show that increased population density led to mansions becoming transformed into tenements where large rooms were divided into smaller ones. Moreover, the city's defences were strengthened. The inhabitants blocked one of the 4 gateways to the city.[28]

Ultimately, however, the Aryan invaders engulfed the land and slaughtered many. The *Rg Veda,* the Aryan traditional account, claims that Indra, their war deity, destroyed hundreds of the Dasas' [i.e. Harappans'] fortified places. Professor W. E. B. DuBois, the venerable African-American social scientist, provided an admirable summary of the *Rg Veda:*

> The *Rig [sic] Veda,* ancient sacred hymns of India, tells of the fierce struggles between these [W]hites and [B]lacks for the mastery of India. It sings of Aryan deities who rushed furiously into battle against the [B]lack foe. The hymns praise Indra, the [W]hite deity, for having killed fifty thousand [B]lacks, "piercing the citadel of the enemy" and forcing the [B]lacks to run out in distress, leaving all their food and belongings.[29]

Mr Chandler describes the archaeological evidence surrounding the Aryan campaigns:

> The position of the skeletons found in cities leaves little doubt as to the violent manner of their deaths. The archaeologist Mackay discovered two skeletons lying on a short flight of brick steps and two more just outside the steps. He recorded that "There seems no doubt that these four people were murdered ... It can be regarded as almost certain that these skeletal remains date from the latter end of the occupation of Mohenjo-Daro and not later intrusions." Mackay describes another group of nine skeletons, five of them children, lying "in strangely contorted attitudes and crowded together," as though "thrown pell-mell into a hurriedly made pit." It appears, comments Mackay, that this group "tried to escape with their belongings at the time of the raid but were stopped and slaughtered by the raiders".[30]

The conquest, however, was no mere walkover. The Harappans amassed armies, some numbering 10,000 people, to battle the invaders. Their resistance resulted in a thousand year struggle for supremacy that culminated in the battle of the Mahabharata in the fifth century BC. Meanwhile more and more indigenous people migrated eastwards. Fleeing Aryan repression, they rebuilt their arts and sciences. Ultimately, many of them ended up in central and south India where they are concentrated today.[31]

Where the Aryans conquered, they imposed the Hindu caste system on the indigenous people - an early form of *apartheid.* This system divided the population into Brahmins, Khyshatriyas, Vaishas, Sudras and Outcastes. The Aryans became the Brahmins, the top caste, and the Indus Valley people became the Sudras and the Outcastes. Also among the Outcastes were some peoples of Aryan-Black admixture. This system, with modifications, is still in operation today. Colour and shade prejudice is still a feature of life in the modern Indian subcontinent. The Aryans seized most of Pakistan and northwest India by 800 BC and have gradually taken control of the entire subcontinent.[32] V. T. Rajshekar, the noted South Indian journalist, wrote an admirable summary of the main facts:

> The original inhabitants of India were dark-skinned and closely resembled the Africans in physical features. They founded the Indus Valley Civilization which, according to historians, was one of the world's first and most glorious. Aryan tribes invaded India, destroyed the Indus Valley Civilization, and employed a cunning, deceptive religious ideology to enslave the indigenous people. Those who fled to India's forests and hills later came to be called "tribals." As these native Indians were gradually overcome, captured and enslaved they were kept outside village limits and "untouchability" was enforced upon them ... The native people of India (currently known as "Untouchables, Tribals and Backward Castes") were not Hindus. They were Animists - Nature Worshippers. Since India's Dalits were once autonomous tribal groups, each group was known by its own tribal name. The Aryans created "caste" out of these tribal divisions by hierarchically arranging them in ascending degrees of reverence and descending degrees of contempt ... Aryans based their whole philosophy on color (varna). The four-fold caste system is based on skin (varna) color. The natives are dark-skinned and the Aryans light.[33]

Arabia Felix

Negro populations have inhabited Arabia since at least 6000 BC. Called Veddoids by the anthropologists, they make up a significant proportion of the present day Mahra ethnic group. Labelled Cushites by Sir Henry Rawlinson,[34] the Mahra are of light to dark brown complexions with wavy to curly hair.[35] Sir Richmond Palmer describes this period as: "The first dawn of history in the Sudan".[36] Dr Rashidi, editor of the important *African Presence in Early Asia,* tells us that: "These were the first Arabians. They were black in the beginning and remain so to this day".[37] John Baldwin, the nineteenth century European-American Orientalist, noted that:

> To the Kushite belongs the purest Arabian blood, and also that great and very ancient civilization whose ruins abound in almost every district of the country.[38]

The first civilisation in Arabia was Saba, located in Yemen and western Oman. Greek and Roman writers called this territory "Arabia Felix" (i.e. Happy Arabia). Consisting of the most fertile land in the region, it possessed great advantages in climate. The Greeks and Romans further divided Arabia into Arabia Petrae (i.e. Stony Arabia) - the northwestern region, and Arabia Deserta (i.e. Desert Arabia) - the central regions.[39] Our focus is on the Arabia Felix region.

Dr Rashidi reports evidence that there were population movements of nomads from northern and central Arabia into the south that took place in 1500 BC. Further movements took place in 1100 BC. Dr Diop dates this same movement to the eighteenth century BC. Unlike Rashidi, Diop describes these people as Caucasians and identifies them as Jocktanides, an ethnic group mentioned in the *Bible*. Diop's view harmonises well with the anthropological research of Sir Arthur Keith, previously cited, but we keep an open mind on this question. The Sabaean civilisation became influenced by the cultural admixture of northern and central Arabian elements with the southerners of Yemen and Oman. Diop informs us that the southerners regained their dominance and absorbed the northern peoples.[40]

In the tenth century BC, a mysterious stateswoman known as the Queen of Sheba (cf. Saba) ruled Yemen. Called Bilqis in the Koran or Makeda in the *Kebra Negaste,* she was very likely an Ethiopian, basing this on the location of her tomb. Yemen was part of her sphere of influence. There are, however, different accounts of her origins. Professor William Hansberry, master of the African-American historians, draws attention to a mediæval manuscript of Al-Hamdani. This Muslim scholar died in the Arabian city of Sana in the mid tenth century AD. His account portrays Bilqis as the daughter of Shar Habil, the king of Yemen, and Ekeye Azeb, an Ethiopian princess. Furthermore, she was born in Marib, but spent her youth in Ethiopia. She returned to Marib just before her father's death.[41] Professor Hansberry informs us of other Arabian traditions of her parentage that contradict the Hamdani account. "Another tradition" says Hansberry, "maintains that Belkis's [sic] father was the vizier or prime minister of King Shar Habil, an alleged tyrant, and her mother was a jinni (a supernatural being that could take human or animal form and influence human affairs)".[42] The Al-Hamdani account is clearly the more reliable and allows us to conclude, contrary to the recent claims of the British Museum's *Behind the Myth* exhibition, that the Queen of Sheba was undoubtedly a Negress. She was either fully Ethiopian, or else half Ethiopian and half Yemeni. We have already discussed evidence that the Yemenis of this period were Negroes.

Unlike some other personages in African history, there are an abundance of documents surrounding this ruler.[43] It is, however, difficult separating fact from legend. Josephus, for example, portrays her as Queen of Ethiopia and Egypt. Other sources give her sovereignty over parts of Syria, Armenia, India and Indonesia. Larry Williams and Charles Finch conclude: "We can at least say that she ruled over a substantial nation-state and may have exercised control over more far-flung lands that gave her dominions the status of an empire".[44] Believed to have ruled from 1005 to 955 BC, she established trading networks carried by 520 camels and 370 ships. Tamrin, her chief merchant, headed this operation.[45]

Saba was a highly developed country, even then. Women had a high status, frequently appearing as rulers in their own right. Moreover, some female deities were venerated such as Al'lat, the Goddess of Mecca. However, Almaqah, the chief deity venerated in the capital city of Marib, was a male deity. Other evidence suggests the existence of sophisticated irrigation systems and also trade.[46] An old *Encyclopaedia Britannica* gave the following account of the early history of the region based on the traditions that have been handed down:

> The first dawning that deserve to be called historic find[s] Arabia under the rule of a southern race. They claimed descent from Khatan. They were divided anciently into several aristocratic monarchies. These Yemanite [sic] kings descendants of Khatan and Himyar 'the dusky,' a name denoting African origin, whose rulers were called 'Tobba,' of Hamitic etymology, reigned with a few dynastic interruptions for about 2500 years. They demanded the obedience of the entire southern half of the peninsula and the northern by tribute collectors. The general characteristics of the institutions of Yemen bore considerable resemblance to the neighboring one of the Nile Valley.[47]

The Sabaeans domesticated the camel. They were used for transportation and trade, later earning the nickname "the ships of Persia." For centuries, the region became a mart. Its location made it accessible for merchant shipping from both the East and West, and also camel caravans. Sabaean merchants handled luxury items such as ebony and ivory, fine jewels, precious metals, silk and also spices.[48] Their most important products, however, were frankincense and myrrh. Frankincense was used for religious, ritualistic, and medical purposes. It was burned at religious offerings and funerary rites. It was also carried in royal processions. In addition, it was an antidote to poisons and was used to stop bleeding. Myrrh was a cosmetic and an ointment. It was also used for mummification.[49] Herbert Wendt, a German historian, informs us that the Sabaeans:

> were not only excellent horsemen and camel-drivers, but also exceptionally fine seamen … From India they brought cinnamon and nard, from [Sri Lanka] magnificent textiles, from Malaya indigo and pepper. And in return the Indian vessels put into the Arab harbours, acquired products from the Mediterranean and paid with precious stones and woods. As early as the middle of the second millennium BC there must have been a lively seagoing trade between India and southern Arabia. It is possible that there was even, in 985 BC, a Chinese expedition to the land of Sheba [i.e. Saba]. More reliable than these rather legendary accounts are the business relationships between the Sabaeans and the classical spice-lands of Further India and Indonesia. Grecian explorers in Alexander's days found numerous Arabian bases along the Coast of Spices, with names like Zabae, Sabana and Sabara which indicates that these harbours were founded by Sabaeans.[50]

An eighth century BC Assyrian inscription of King Sargon II gives information on the products traded through Saba:

> Piru, the king of Musru, Samsi, the queen of Arabia, It'amra, the Sabean. The(se) are the kings of the seashore and from the desert. I received as their presents gold in the form of dust, precious stones, ivory, ebony-seeds, all kinds of aromatic substances, horses (and) camels.[51]

The Biblical prophet Ezekiel also alludes to the Sabaean trading activities:

> The merchants of Sheba and Raamah were thy merchants; they traded in thy fairs with the best of all spices, and with all precious stones, and gold. Haran, and Calneh, and Eden, the merchants of Sheba, Asshur, and Chilmad were thy merchants. These were thy merchants in all sorts of things, in blue clothes, and embroidered work, and in chests of rich apparel, bound with cords, and made of cedar, among thy merchandise.[52]

An important aspect of the spice trade, however, was secrecy. Sir Richmond Palmer explained the significance of this:

> The secrecy of the trade was further augmented and strengthened by the exclusiveness of the religious ideas and rites attached to it. The control of the Arabian incense trade was thus one of the leading planks in the foreign policy of all the great empires of the ancient world, such as Babylonia, Assyria and Egypt. It was probably due initially to the jealousies surrounding the incense trade, its sanctity and its prestige, that Arabia remained, and has remained until the present day, almost a *terra incognita* to the rest of the world.[53]

As early as 1500 BC, although some authorities give much later dates like 700 BC, the Sabaeans undertook substantial building projects of basalt, granite and limestone. Chief among these was the Awwam Temple also called the Mahram-Bilquis. Dedicated to Almaqah, it was the largest shrine in Arabia. An elliptical wall surrounded the structure, enclosing a vast area of 60,000 square feet. On the northern wall lay the entrance, guarded by eight stone rectangular pillars that were forty feet high. Through these pillars lay the peristyle hall. The hall was a large building, containing a paved court surrounded by rooms. Through there, a passage led to the open enclosure. Wall inscriptions show that some of the pilgrims "came from distant lands".[54] Peter Garlake, the noted archaeologist, described the temple as follows:

> [It] has an open enclosure of much the same shape and size as the Elliptical Building [in Great Zimbabwe]. Its walls have carefully constructed faces built of stone blocks laid in courses without mortar, battered back and containing a loose internal fill ... The limestone blocks ... were cut to perfect rectangles and their faces pecked to a smooth finish ... The faces of the walls were bonded

together with a sophisticated system of cross walls. An integral part of the temple was a series of rectangular pillared and roofed entrances ... [where the] carved capitals, cornices and friezes [show a rigid linear geometry].[55]

The open enclosure contained sculptures of gleaming bronze. The largest was a 30 foot image of Almaqah portrayed as a bull.[56]

The Marib Dam was another of the very early constructions. It too dated back to 1500 BC (but again some authorities give a much later date of 700 BC). Begun by Sumuhu'alay Yanaf and Yithi'amara Bayyim, two early mukkaribs (priest kings), legend has it that Lockman, the great sage of Arabian tradition, designed the building.[57] Stretching 3,000 feet across a wadi, it was "twice the width of Colorado's Hoover Dam".[58] The earthen ridge divided the onrushing waters into two channels that irrigated some 24,000 acres of land, sustaining at least 50,000 people. One authority on Sabaean antiquities, described it as an agricultural scheme on a vast scale that has "not been equalled to our day".[59] Rashidi says that the construction "was Saba's greatest achievement, and served its builders and their descendants for more than a thousand years". Today, "the huge sluice gates built into the rocky walls of the wadi are very well preserved and stand as silent witnesses to the creative genius of the South Arabian people".[60]

Mrs Drusilla Houston, the pioneering and brilliant African-American Orientalist, provides further evidence of Sabaean large-scale building and irrigation activities:

> In one district the whole mountainside was terraced from top to bottom. Gen. Haig saw in this district everywhere above below and around, endless flights of terraced walls. One can hardly realize the enormous amount of labor, toil and perseverance, these represent. These walls were usually four or five feet in height, but toward the top, they were sometimes as high as fifteen to eighteen feet. Agriculture among these indefatigable people was brought to the highest degree of perfection. They constructed immense dikes, forming permanent reservoirs, which irrigated the lowlands in dry weather.[61]

Marib, the ancient multi storey capital, still exists today. An astonishing city of clay brick and timber, it had tower blocks that rose to a height of 80 feet. In the Queen of Sheba's time, it probably contained 20,000 people. Furthermore, a processional walkway linked the city to the Awwam Temple.[62]

Dr Rashidi informs us that Ubar and Saffara, two other ancient cities, were rediscovered by the modern world in 1992. Ubar, the "Queen of the Frankincense Trade," was a fortress city of crenulated towers. Claimed to have been built five thousand years ago, it was discovered in a barren area of modern Oman. Saffara was fifty percent larger. It too was important in trade and boasted eleven crenulated towers.[63]

Accounts from the time of Alexander the Great, Diodorus, Pliny and Agatharchides give favourable impressions of the wealth of Saba or southern Arabia. Alexander the Great said: "Taking them all in all, they are the richest nation in the world".[64] Diodorus Siculus corroborates this view. He informs us that:

> The perfumes of Arabia ravished the senses and were conveyed by the winds to those who sailed near the coast. Having never been conquered, by the largeness of their country, they flow in gold and silver; and likewise their beds, chairs, and stools have their feet of silver; and all their house stuff is so sumptuous and magnificent that it is incredible. The porticoes of their homes and temples, in some cases are overlaid with gold. They have enjoyed a constant uninterrupted peace for many ages and generations.[65]

Agatharchides, another Classical writer, recorded that:

> The Sabaeans surpass in wealth and magnificence not only the neighboring barbarians but all the nations whatsoever. As their distant situation protects them from foreign plunderers, immense stores of precious metals have been accumulated among them, especially in the capital. They have curiously wrought gold and silver drinking vessels in great variety, couches and tripods with silver feet; an incredible profusion of costly furniture in general; porticoes with large columns partly gilt and capitals [of columns] ornamented with gold fretwork set with precious stones; besides an extraordinary magnificence reigning in the decorations of their houses, where they use silver, gold, ivory and the most precious stones and all other things men deem valuable.[66]

Al Hamdani wrote that in the city of Sana:

> The smallest house has at least one or two cisterns; the cesspools are deep, built at a distance from another, and, because of the hard gypsum tiles, the spotless plaster and the clean floors, are free of any stench or obnoxious odour. A lavatory remains in use from one century to another without needing to be drained or cleansed.[67]

Such wealth encouraged the Romans to attempt an invasion of Saba. In 25 AD Roman Emperor Augustus sent an army into Arabia led by Aelius Gallus. The invasion failed miserably. Weakened by bad roads, hardship, hunger, illness and toil, the invaders were severely defeated by the Sabaeans. The Roman army were crushed just two days march away from Marib. As a warning, the Sabaeans sent the remaining soldiers back to Rome.[68]

Scholars have alluded to the continuities in culture between Yemen and Ethiopia on the other side of the Red Sea. Both cultures claim the Queen of Sheba as a founding ruler. Moreover, parallels between the early religion, language, agricultural practices, and scripts of both peoples have led to the speculation, already discussed in a previous chapter, that Yemenites founded aspects of Ethiopian culture in around the fifth or sixth century BC. Whichever be the case, in the early Christian era, Ethiopia maintained an aggressive interventionism in Yemenite affairs that maintained the cultural links.

In 183 AD for example, Gadara, king of Axum, was a politically dominant figure in Yemenite affairs. His son and successor was equally dominant in the region until 213 AD. Less than a century later, Azbah, a later Axumite king, sent military forces to Yemen and settled troops there. Between 335 and 370 AD, Axum occupied Saba once more. There were other military actions and occupations in the sixth century AD.[69]

In the fourth century AD Christianity began to have an impact in the region, but also Judaism. In 325 AD six Arabian bishops attended the Council of Nicae, a cornerstone in the birth of Christianity. The Axumite invasion of 335 AD continued the spread of Christianity. Members of the Yemeni ruling class adopted the new religion. But the Christians tried to undermine the use of incense burning in cremations. They dubbed it a pagan ritual and substituted burials instead. This belief undermined the incense trade passing through Yemen. Moreover, direct sea routes were established between Asia with the west. Both factors weakened Yemen's economic position. The leadership of Malikkarib Yuhad'in, who briefly asserted Sabaean power, halted the decline. However relations between Yemenite Jews and Christians began to worsen.[70]

In the sixth century AD a civil war erupted between Christians and Jews. Yemenite king Dhu Nuwas, a Jew, battled his Christian enemies and burned churches. The Axumites were invited to help the Christian effort. Emperor Kaleb of Axum sent across 70,000 men and 150 ships under the leadership of General Abraha.[71] They triumphed over Dhu Nuwas, but the General had ideas of his own, proclaiming himself ruler of Yemen.[72] Abraha raised a fine cathedral at Sana, "the like of which existed nowhere else in the world", containing marble, mosaics, and decorated with gold.[73] Its purpose was to win converts to the Christian faith. He also made substantial repairs to the Marib Dam. Abraha's religious zeal, however, was his undoing. He attempted to challenge the religion of the Holy city of Mecca, the worship of the Goddess Al'lat. This inflamed the anti-Christian coalition who appealed to the Persian King Chosroes for an armed intervention. The Axumites were beaten in 572 AD and Yemen became a territory of the Persian Shah.[74]

During the wars with Axum and Persia, and also the later Islamic jihads, the older Sabaean monuments became damaged or were destroyed. One such building was the Castle of Ghumdan. Twenty storeys high, the upper floors of this skyscraper contained polished marble. Crowning the building were 4 bronze lions.[75] The *Guinness Book of Records* notes that: "The oldest [castle] in the world" excluding the Egyptian fortresses and the like, "is that at Gomdan

[sic], in the Yemen, which originally had 20 storeys and dates from before A.D. 100".[76]

When Islam came on the scene in the seventh century AD the Yemenis adopted it. Axum was cut off from the rest of the world, surrounded by its religious enemies. This broke the cultural link between Ethiopia and Yemen that had existed for the previous 1,600 years. During the Islamic period the northern Arabs became dominant ending the supremacy of the southern Arabs. According to Mrs Houston: "The conquering Mohammedan tribes of the north in idol-destroying mood have effaced all the pagan temples that once covered Arabia".[77] Professor Thompson, author of *Economic and Social History of the Middle Ages,* presented an admirable summary of the achievements of the Sabaean civilization and the emigration of people that took place after it declined:

> Evidences of a former great prosperity in southern Arabia (Yemen) are not lacking. All the classical writers, Herodotus, Pliny, and Strabo frequently allude to it under the name of Saba or Sheba as the richest country on the globe. Dependent on a vast hydraulic system, massive walls of masonry confined its streams. One reservoir was eighteen miles in circuit and 120 feet deep. An innumerable population in this territory, in hundreds of cities and villages, carried agriculture to its highest perfection. Merchants of great wealth sent their fleets to China and their caravans across the Syrian and African deserts. They both purchased on their own account and bought and sold on commission. Their warehouses were filled with stores from all climes - silver vessels, ingots of copper, tin, iron, lead, honey, wax, silks, ivory, ebony, coral, agates, civet, musk, myrrh, camphor and other aromatics. Grain was raised extensively and could be stored for thirty years. The cotton plant, the sugar cane, and the coco palm flourished. The balsam of Mecca, the gum arabic, the sap of the acacia tree, the famed frankincense, were important articles of export as were salt, gold and pearls. For an unknown period, embracing, however, many centuries, the prosperity of Sheba continued. Then it declined and a general emigration took place. The former paradise was transformed into an uninhabited desert. The time of the decline and the causes are hidden in obscurity.[78]

In closing our discussion of the Asian civilisations, we are pleased to give the penultimate word to Mrs Houston, an authority whose work should be better known and discussed:

> A distinctive race ... colonised the first civilized centers of the primitive world. The ancients called this pioneer race, Cushite Ethiopians, the founders of primeval cities and civilized life. The wonders of India, to which Europe sought a passage in the age of Columbus, the costly products and coveted merchandise of Babylon, and the amazing prehistoric civilization of Asia Minor, sprang from this little recognized source ... Their skilful hands raised Cyclopean walls, dug out mighty lakes and laid imperishable roads that have endured throughout the ages. This was the uniform testimony of ancient records.[79]

Finally, Mr George Wells Parker, in typically majestic style, reminds us that:

> When we ... scan the perfumed literatures of India and Persia [i.e. Elam] and Arabia, let us not forget that the secret, like the secret of all things wonderfully and aesthetically beautiful, lies with Africa, the mother of civilization and of nations.[80]

Notes

[1] Wayne Chandler, *The Jewel in the Lotus,* in *African Presence in Early Asia,* ed Runoko Rashidi, US, Transaction Publishers, 1995, pp.90-1.

[2] Ibid., pp.89-90.

[3] S. G. Blaxland Stubbs, *Wonder Cities of Most Ancient India,* in *Wonders of the Past: Second Volume,* ed Sir J. A. Hammerton, UK, The Amalgamated Press, no date given but probably 1937, p.659.

[4] Wayne Chandler, *The Jewel in the Lotus,* in *African Presence in Early Asia,* p.91 and Walter A. Fairservis, *The Script of the Indus Valley Civilization,* in *African Presence in Early Asia,* ed Runoko Rashidi, US, Transaction Publishers, 1995, pp.65-6 and Runoko Rashidi, *Africans in Early Asian Civilizations: An Overview,* in *African Presence in Early Asia,* ed Runoko Rashidi, US, Transaction Publishers, 1995, p.40.

[5] Wayne Chandler, *The Jewel in the Lotus,* in *African Presence in Early Asia,* p.83.

[6] Sir Mortimer Wheeler, *Civilizations of the Indus Valley and Beyond,* UK, Thames and Hudson, 1965, pp.69-70.

[7] James Baikie, *The Life of the Ancient East,* UK, A. & C. Black, 1923, pp.186-8.

[8] S. G. Blaxland Stubbs, *Wonder Cities of Most Ancient India,* in *Wonders of the Past: Second Volume,* p.666.

[9] Wayne Chandler, *The Jewel in the Lotus,* in *African Presence in Early Asia,* p.91.

[10] Ibid., pp.91-3.

[11] Sir Mortimer Wheeler, *Civilizations of the Indus Valley and Beyond,* pp.18-9.

[12] Ibid., p.18.

[13] Wayne Chandler, *The Jewel in the Lotus,* in *African Presence in Early Asia,* pp.92-3 and S. G. Blaxland Stubbs, *Wonder Cities of Most Ancient India,* in *Wonders of the Past: Second Volume,* pp.663-4.

[14] S. G. Blaxland Stubbs, *Wonder Cities of Most Ancient India,* in *Wonders of the Past: Second Volume,* p.661.

[15] Wayne Chandler, *The Jewel in the Lotus,* in *African Presence in Early Asia,* pp.91-2.

[16] Ibid., p.92.

[17] S. G. Blaxland Stubbs, *Wonder Cities of Most Ancient India,* in *Wonders of the Past: Second Volume,* p.662.

[18] Sir Mortimer Wheeler, *Civilizations of the Indus Valley and Beyond,* p.24.

[19] Walter A. Fairservis, *The Script of the Indus Valley Civilization,* in *African Presence in Early Asia,* p.66.

[20] S. G. Blaxland Stubbs, *Wonder Cities of Most Ancient India,* in *Wonders of the Past: Second Volume,* p.662.

[21] Wayne Chandler, *The Jewel in the Lotus,* in *African Presence in Early Asia,* pp.93-4, Walter A. Fairservis, *The Script of the Indus Valley Civilization,* in *African Presence in Early Asia,* p.66 and Sir Mortimer Wheeler, *Civilizations of the Indus Valley and Beyond,* p.64.

[22] Quoted in Wayne Chandler, *The Jewel in the Lotus*, in *African Presence in Early Asia*, p.83.

[23] Walter A. Fairservis, *The Script of the Indus Valley Civilization*, in *African Presence in Early Asia*, p.65. See also p.72.

[24] Sir Mortimer Wheeler, *Civilizations of the Indus Valley and Beyond*, p.40.

[25] Quoted in S. G. Blaxland Stubbs, *Wonder Cities of Most Ancient India*, in *Wonders of the Past: Second Volume*, p.665.

[26] S. G. Blaxland Stubbs, *Wonder Cities of Most Ancient India*, in *Wonders of the Past: Second Volume*, pp.665-6.

[27] Walter A. Fairservis, *The Script of the Indus Valley Civilization*, in *African Presence in Early Asia*, p.66.

[28] Wayne Chandler, *The Jewel in the Lotus*, in *African Presence in Early Asia*, pp.101-3.

[29] W. E. B. DuBois, *The World and Africa*, US, International Publishers, 1965, p.177.

[30] Wayne Chandler, *The Jewel in the Lotus*, in *African Presence in Early Asia*, p.102

[31] Ibid., pp.83 and 104 and Runoko Rashidi, *Africans in Early Asian Civilizations: An Overview*, in *African Presence in Early Asia*, p.42.

[32] Runoko Rashidi, *Africans in Early Asian Civilizations: An Overview*, in *African Presence in Early Asia*, p.42.

[33] V. T. Rajshekar, *The Black Untouchables of India: Reclaiming our cultural heritage*, in *African Presence in Early Asia*, ed Runoko Rashidi, US, Transaction Publishers, 1995, p.235.

[34] See George Rawlinson, *The Origin of Nations*, UK, John Murray, 1878, p.212.

[35] Runoko Rashidi, *Africans in Early Asian Civilizations: An Overview*, in *African Presence in Early Asia*, pp.28-9.

[36] Sir Richmond Palmer, *The Bornu Sahara and Sudan*, UK, John Murray, 1936, p.1

[37] Runoko Rashidi, *Africans in Early Asian Civilizations: An Overview*, in *African Presence in Early Asia*, p.29.

[38] John Baldwin, *Pre-Historic Nations*, quoted in John G. Jackson, *Introduction to African Civilizations*, US, Citadel Press, 1970, p.70.

[39] Runoko Rashidi, *Africans in Early Asian Civilizations: An Overview*, in *African Presence in Early Asia*, p.29 and Drusilla Dunjee Houston, *Wonderful Ethiopians of the Ancient Cushite Empire*, US, Black Classic Press, 1985 (original 1926), pp.111-3.

[40] Runoko Rashidi, *Africans in Early Asian Civilizations: An Overview*, in *African Presence in Early Asia*, p.29 and Cheikh Anta Diop, *African Origin of Civilization: Myth or Reality?* US, Lawrence Hill Books, 1974, p.124.

[41] Joseph E. Harris ed, *Pillars in Ethiopian History: The William Leo Hansberry African History Notebook, Volume 1*, US, Howard University Press, 1974, pp.51-2.

[42] Ibid., p.53.

[43] Ibid., pp.33-59.

[44] Larry Williams and Charles S. Finch, *The Great Queens of Ethiopia*, in *Black Women in Antiquity*, ed Ivan Van Sertima, US, Transaction Publishers, 1988, pp.16-20 and pp.34-5.

[45] Ibid., pp.16-20 and pp.34-5.

[46] Runoko Rashidi, *Africans in Early Asian Civilizations: An Overview*, in *African Presence in Early Asia*, p.30 and Wayne Chandler, *Ebony and Bronze*, in *African Presence in Early Asia*, ed Runoko Rashidi, US, Transaction Publishers, 1995, p.272 and Anthony Geffen (producer), *Queen of Sheba: Behind the Myth*, television programme, UK, BBC Television, 2003.

[47] *Encyclopaedia Britannica*, quoted in Drusilla Dunjee Houston, *Wonderful Ethiopians of the Ancient Cushite Empire*, pp.120-1.

[48] Runoko Rashidi, *Africans in Early Asian Civilizations: An Overview*, in *African Presence in Early Asia*, p.30 and Drusilla Dunjee Houston, *Wonderful Ethiopians of the Ancient Cushite Empire*, p.119.

[49] Runoko Rashidi, *Research Notes: Ancient Cities Beneath the Arabian Sands*, in *African Presence in Early Asia*, ed Runoko Rashidi, US, Transaction Publishers, 1995, p.313.

[50] Herbert Wendt, *It began in Babel*, UK, Weidenfeld and Nicholson, 1963, p.109.

[51] Quoted in Runoko Rashidi, *Africans in Early Asian Civilizations: An Overview*, in *African Presence in Early Asia*, pp.30-1.

[52] *Holy Bible*, Ezekiel, Chapter 27: 22-24.

[53] Sir Richmond Palmer, *The Bornu Sahara and Sudan*, p.1.

[54] Runoko Rashidi, *Africans in Early Asian Civilizations: An Overview*, in *African Presence in Early Asia*, pp.31-2.

[55] Peter Garlake, *Great Zimbabwe*, UK, Thames and Hudson, 1973, pp.31-2.

[56] Anthony Geffen (producer), *Queen of Sheba: Behind the Myth*.

[57] Ibidem and Runoko Rashidi, *Africans in Early Asian Civilizations: An Overview*, in *African Presence in Early Asia*, p.32.

[58] Anthony Geffen (producer), *Queen of Sheba: Behind the Myth*.

[59] Nicholas Clapp quoted in Anthony Geffen (producer), *Queen of Sheba: Behind the Myth*, television programme.

[60] Runoko Rashidi, *Africans in Early Asian Civilizations: An Overview*, in *African Presence in Early Asia*, p.32.

[61] Drusilla Dunjee Houston, *Wonderful Ethiopians of the Ancient Cushite Empire*, pp.132-3.

[62] Anthony Geffen (producer), *Queen of Sheba: Behind the Myth*.

[63] Runoko Rashidi, *Research Notes: Ancient Cities Beneath the Arabian Sands*, in *African Presence in Early Asia*, p.312.

[64] Quoted in Drusilla Dunjee Houston, *Wonderful Ethiopians of the Ancient Cushite Empire*, p.131.

[65] Quoted in ibid., p.128.

[66] Quoted in ibid., p.129.

[67] Quoted in Basil Davidson, *Old Africa Rediscovered*, UK, Victor Gollancz, 1959, pp.148-9.

[68] Herbert Wendt, *It began in Babel*, p.110 and Wayne Chandler, *Ebony and Bronze*, in *African Presence in Early Asia*, p.273.

[69] Cf. Runoko Rashidi, *Africans in Early Asian Civilizations: An Overview*, in *African Presence in Early Asia*, p.34.

[70] Ibidem and Anthony Geffen (producer), *Queen of Sheba: Behind the Myth*.

[71] John G. Jackson, *Introduction to African Civilizations*, US, Citadel Press, 1970, p.272.

[72] R. A. Caulk, *North-East Africa before the rise of Islam*, in *The Cambridge Encyclopaedia of Africa*, ed Roland Oliver and Michael Crowder, UK, Cambridge University Press, 1981, p.110.

[73] E. A. Wallis Budge, *A History of Ethiopia, Nubia & Abyssinia, Volume I-B*, US, ECA Associates, 1991 (original 1928), p.266.

[74] R. A. Caulk, *North-East Africa before the rise of Islam*, in *The Cambridge Encyclopaedia of Africa*, p.110 and Runoko Rashidi, *Africans in Early Asian Civilizations: An Overview*, in *African Presence in Early Asia*, p.35.

[75] Runoko Rashidi, *Africans in Early Asian Civilizations: An Overview*, in *African Presence in Early Asia*, p.35.

[76] Norris & Ross McWhirter, *Guinness Book of Records, 21st Edition,* UK, Guinness Superlatives Limited, October 1974, p.117.

[77] Drusilla Dunjee Houston, *Wonderful Ethiopians of the Ancient Cushite Empire,* p.131.

[78] James W. Thompson, *Economic and Social History of the Middle Ages,* quoted in John G. Jackson, *Ages of Gold and Silver,* US, A. A. Press, 1990, pp.117-8.

[79] Drusilla Dunjee Houston, *Wonderful Ethiopians of the Ancient Cushite Empire,* p.15.

[80] George Wells Parker, *The Children of the Sun,* US, Black Classic Press, 1981, p.22.

AFTERWORD: WHERE FROM HERE?

BY FARI SUPIYA

Norman Worlds and Saxon Futures

1. The Writing of History
The writing of history involves the discovery of evidence, the interpretation of evidence, and the chronicling of both the evidence and the deductions thereof. Every stage of the production line of evidence takes place within a social context. We shall outline the social context in order to examine how it impacts on the final product that is history.

2. The Mechanics of Power
In 1066 an invasion from Normandy, in northern France, conquered Anglo-Saxon England. A colonial system of administration was set up. It was based on a castle in every Saxon region of England, and the recording and taxing of every Saxon asset by the Normans. The newcomers suppressed the population from these castles and logged every Saxon asset in what became known as the *Domesday Book*.

With every passing decade, the Norman view of the 'lower' Saxon hardened. The Saxons would have assimilated this Norman attitude and with every passing decade they would have become more accepting of Norman supremacy. All national communication, and thus media, was controlled by Normans. Power structures seek to perpetuate their existence by maintaining and expanding themselves. This means resisting changes to the psychological status quo that makes their existence possible.

Imagine a situation where Norman domination continued into the twenty-first century and had covered the globe. The whole world would be composed of 'Saxon' peoples under their domination. A simple task such as the writing of Saxon history would become needlessly complicated at every stage of production because both overlord and Saxon would, by reflex, avoid any revelation, interpretation, or conclusion that supported Saxon independence and thus challenge the psycho-status quo.

3. The Production Line
Historical evidence is discovered by such activities as archaeological excavations, linguistic research and the collecting of oral traditions. We shall

use archaeological evidence as an example. The production line of evidence begins with the discovery of artefacts, then comes cataloguing, packing, transportation, storage, display and finally, textbook exposure. Where the production line of evidence stops, the production line of history continues - with the interpretation of the evidence and the deductions thereof. 'Normans' would form the bulk of any profession and the production of evidence would take place in a socio-economic environment that they control. At any point in the production line, evidence can be conveniently damaged, lost, or sold on the illegal market (no doubt called a 'Saxon' market in a 'Norman' world). Sold items might not even make it into the excavation catalogue. The same would apply to the collecting of oral traditions and also linguistic research. Of all traditions heard, which are recorded? Which are given prominence and what interpretation is given to them? Which languages are compared to each other and which are never compared? What deductions are made thereof?

4. Pre-Production
Evidence also has a pre-production stage, referring to what happens before evidence is discovered. 'Normans' decide whether a particular region gets excavated at all. If so, which of that region's sites get excavated and to what extent? 'Saxons' choosing their own excavation sites or deciding to excavate the remaining 90% of ancient Meroë, for example, had better make plans to secure their own funding because 'Normans' control excavation funding. Who controls access to excavation sites? Directly or indirectly 'Normans' do. In countries where 'Normans' predominate they control access directly. In 'Saxon' countries, however, Saxon governments will give the permissions but their universities are likely to be heavily staffed and funded by 'Normans'. 'Saxon' governments are also very likely to be heavily subsidised by 'Norman' NGOs (so-called non-governmental organisations) which would almost certainly frown on anything that looks like it may disturb the psycho-status quo. So 'Saxon' governments may not want to jeopardise their subsidies by granting excavation permissions to 'Saxon' 'radicals'. But are such 'radicals' likely to be in a position to apply in the first place? Only qualified people will be in a position to apply for excavation permissions. Furthermore, to become qualified one has to win a university place, get through the course, preferably become university staff, win promotion and then be in a position to apply. Assuming of course one can find funding. Any 'Saxon' with subversive views is less likely to survive the pre-production line. The result is that even when 'Saxons' appear to be in charge of archaeology, the difference between their version of history and that of the 'Norman' historians in general may be negligible. All of this does not deal with what happens prior to pre-production, such as who has the better access to previous educational opportunities that

give the best preparation for higher education. Nor does this deal with post-production; 'Normans' own and staff museums, and control access to artefacts; control promotion of history books through media; and control whether major retail outlets stock a particular book. If you think this sounds very bad for the 'Saxons' read on.

5. Behavioural Complications Arising From Domination

Domination of one population by another has two tangible consequences. The first is a lower life expectancy of the dominated group owing to poorer access to resources. Inevitably, the dominated group also have a poorer material quality of life. The attitude of the 'Norman' and the 'Saxon' towards intense pleasure would thus predictably be different. Such pleasure almost always comes with serious risks but if you already think you are not getting past 50 years old, the risks are less of an issue. One can thus predict that the more brutal the domination the greater the likelihood of 'Saxons' choosing an 8% alcoholic beverage over a 4% one. Moreover, there would be a much greater risk of drug addiction in a 'Saxon' population. The combination of lower life expectancy and poor material quality of life also create a negative attitude towards long-term commitment. Unfortunately the most fruitful human endeavours all require long-term commitment. Even the rather simple achievements of getting an education and becoming married become complicated in such a situation. Both, of course, require long-term commitment. 'Normans' would have low expectations of 'Saxons' and they, in turn, would have low expectations of themselves. An independent history could play a crucial role in helping 'Saxons' out of their situation by showing evidence of when circumstances and behaviour were different. For most 'Saxons', however, writing an independent history would be a long-term commitment which could not compete against short-term pleasure.

How History Should Be Written

There will always be a few 'Saxons' who will come forward to explore their historical heritage. How should they proceed? History should be written based on ALL retrieved evidence with ALL interpretations of such evidence being the most probable interpretations thereof. It is not impossible for the 'Saxons' to achieve this.

1. Knowledge vs Impression

History should be a systematic discipline based on precise knowledge of what the sources present and not a mere impression of what is presented. 'Knowledge' of history is when information is possessed at one of three levels of actionability. For example, a statement such as:

A 'Saxon' invented the traffic lights.

is unactionable because there is not enough accurate information contained in the statement to enable fruitful research. The only unit of information that would have been researchable "invented the traffic lights" is an error because it was actually the 'automatic signal system'. The person who utters the above statement has obviously heard some information but has totally failed to convey it.

An example of the first level of actionability might be:

A 'Saxon' named Garret A. Morgan invented the traffic lights.

That is a level 1 statement of knowledge. It has units of accurate information (a) there was a man named Garret A. Morgan, and (b) he was a 'Saxon'. Both data units are researchable. People hearing researchable units of data are more likely to believe them. 'Knowledge' is conveyable, it is believable, and it is researchable so it can grow. He did not invent the traffic lights but the research made possible by the two data units make this fact discoverable:

A 'Saxon' named Garret A. Morgan invented the automatic signal system in 1923 and appears as patent no 1,475,024 in US Patent Office Records.

This statement represents level 2 knowledge. There is much more detail and the information is accurate. It is also easier to research as there are several reference points. It is also more believable than the level 1 knowledge. Disputing it requires counter-evidence that is also at level 2 or else this kind of evidence is impossible to dispute successfully. When the conveyor possesses enough information to replicate the achievement then we have reached level 3 actionability. Level 3 may have the detail of level 2 but it is the technical knowledge of the actual invention which is definitive. Some of the detail of level 2, such as the patent number, would become an irrelevance at level 3 because of the knowledge of how to replicate the achievement. Details which add believability are more of an issue when one cannot recreate an achievement. If 'Saxons' were able to build pyramids today, it would not matter to them whether or not 'Normans' credit them with creating Ancient Egypt and its glories.

2. The Path to Level 3

The question naturally arises of how one gets from level 2 to level 3. It involves two broad steps; one is to remedy the problems outlined facing 'Saxons', and the second is to acknowledge that there are other problems faced by the group which they are not fully aware of. They need to be identified in great detail and categorised before being addressed. The second step requires a great deal of humility, dropping any pretension to knowing it all, and the associated self-righteousness - given that the two go hand in hand.

The first step can be outlined broadly. In order to tackle our history adequately, we need to train ourselves beyond our often meagre qualifications. The first target should be in acquiring the skills to interpret evidence retrieved from excavations and data on languages. For instance, reports on skeletal remains from various parts of the world can be accessed, as can textbooks instructing students on how to interpret such data. The next stage would be to actually examine skeletal remains in museums, take measurements and make deductions based on the evidence collected. One can then compare this with the conclusions of previous researchers and see whether 'Saxon' primary research in this area is necessary. Once you are able to do this, you have reached level 3. We no longer have to speak of 'the anthropologist Shomarka Keita examined Ancient Egyptian remains and showed them to possess certain affinities'. We can now replicate the achievement ourselves. This is level 3. Of course there is a difference between one 'Saxon' reaching level 3 and a community of 'Saxons' gaining level 3 skills in a variety of disciplines whether in medical research, physical anthropology, media operations or architecture. All this requires a high degree of precision planning. A self-taught researcher must figure out ways of keeping abreast of the latest theories in their discipline and remain aware of any rebuttals or challenges to those latest theories. In the case of skeletal evidence, they must plan how to access materials in museums. Ultimately, the aim of such self-taught research must be for the next generation to enter 'Norman' institutions, such as universities, and become a presence to be reckoned with. At this stage it must be clear to 'Saxons' that failure to enter such institutions does not mean the end of progress, as they can always revert to self-taught skills and still apply these. The presence of self-taught individuals with a detailed knowledge of anthropology and linguistics would change the writing of history. Not only 'Saxons', but the whole of humanity would be perceived differently.

The Mismeasure of Man

The human capacity is underestimated. It is often implicitly assumed that certain groups of people were, or are, less capable than others. Regular recipients of such attitudes include Africans, in particular the Khoi, the first Australians, the Negritoes of southeast Asia, the indigenous people of eastern South America and prehistoric humanity. Almost everyone takes part in this mismeasure in one way or another, including those who are already mismeasured. Africans, for example, link Ancient Egypt with the origins of astronomy, anatomy, medicine, and so forth, without giving much thought to the implications of their declarations.

1. An Inductive Challenge to the Mismeasure of Prehistoric Humanity
The populations of Europe and Asia had their origins in bands that left Africa between 100,000 and 30,000 years ago. Did these first people possess astronomy, anatomy, medicine, geology, climatology and mineral usage? A cursory glance at their subsistence strategies will indicate answers to these questions.

Early humans were nomadic hunter-gatherers. This means that they were high mobility groups. Modern Khoi hunters have been known to run over 100 km in a day while tracking an animal. It is therefore a conservative estimate to posit that they may have travelled as much as 1,000 km in a year in pursuit of ideal hunter-gathering locations. At the same time, we know they had rituals. Some ceremonies will undoubtedly require different clans meeting at a ritual centre. How did they find their way from as far as a thousand kilometres away? How would a hunter walking back for 100 km find his way home? High mobility requires the use of landmark navigation, which necessarily involves learning what today's high school students would call geology. It is not enough to say 'we passed a hill and a rock outcrop' because over 100 km there may be a number of such structures. One has to be familiar with different kinds of hills and rock outcrops. We are continually told that they were in the Stone Age and we never give any thought to where they obtained the stone for their tools. Lithology refers to the physical characteristics of a rock. It is impossible to be Stone Age people without having lithologists. Some tools are for cutting, others are for chopping, others still for scraping. Different kinds of stone suit the different functions. Soft stone types, such as soapstone and limestone, are not ideal for the above functions. For that purpose we would expect igneous rocks such as granite and schist to be used. If one is using a stone tip for a spear, should one use the heaviest or the lightest hard rock available? Other properties such as the permeability, or rate at which water is absorbed by rock, would also need to be known, particularly if a group lives in a heavy rainfall environment or frequently has to cross water bodies. Such groups would also need to be aware of the relationship between stone types that predominate in a certain area and the soil type found there. It is during such activities that people would have noticed that some rocks contained minerals which could be extracted and used as a dye like hematite. When humans started using metals it was these earlier prospecting skills that were used to find metal-containing ores. The other technological elements needed to work metal, such as the use of fire and the ability to build a small clay structure to use as a furnace, predated the metal-using era by tens of thousands of years. The intellectual difference between a metal-using and a stone-using community is negligible. All the elements needed to make metallurgy possible were already present in every Stone Age community.

A high mobility lifestyle also requires the observation of celestial bodies. Geological landmarks and their lithological properties are easier to detect in daylight. At night, one is better off supplementing landmark navigation with stellar navigation. Groupings of stars would therefore have been identified, which we now call constellations.

People would have also noticed atmospheric phenomena. They would have seen that the shape and form of clouds indicated whether they were observing them before, during, or after the rainy season. This would have been the beginning of prehistoric weather forecasting.

Gathering would gradually have taught early humans that certain plants thrived in certain soils of a particular colour or texture. This would have happened because the human mind is designed to notice co-occurrence. Co-occurrence is when two phenomena occur together. If red soils have a concentration of certain plant types in one location it will be noticed not at some distant point but very quickly. This design is innate in humans and can be detected in young children. An experiment that all are free to replicate is to get a child with a particular name and middle name combination, say Jarrod and Terry. How many other children named Jarrod would he have to meet before asking one of them whether their other name was Terry? Co-occurrence is not just noticed by children. It is assumed. Since children would have participated in subsistence activities, and more likely gathering than hunting, we can deduce that soil type – vegetation type co-occurrences would have been known for as long as modern human intelligence has existed. By the time agriculture was developed, it would have long been known what the optimum conditions of soil type and (one can infer) rain quantity were needed for certain crops. Chemical properties of certain gathered plants would also have been discovered such as slow and fast acting poisons and herbal remedies. Some of these poisons would have been added to spear tips and used against animals. This was the precursor of chemical warfare.

Hunting would also have aided the development of medicine. Game killed on the hunt would have been skinned and dissected. It would have been realised very early on that all animals have organs in similar positions. All organs would have been known simply from observation. Any extraneous growth such as an abscess or tumour would have been identifiable by prehistoric humans. Anatomy is clearly something that has always existed. Men wounded during hunting would have quickly figured out that a cut artery bleeds in time with the heartbeat. Circulation is but a small leap from such very ancient knowledge.

It is very important to point out that this knowledge would not just have been possessed by early Africans. Since Africans spread out all over the globe, today's Europeans and Asians would have had ancestors who were as much heirs to this knowledge as the humans that remained in Africa. This is why it is not surprising to discover that Africans from Liberia were practising smallpox inoculation in the sixteenth century and similar techniques were also used in Turkey and parts of Asia. Just how far back does knowledge of inoculation go? How did we get from such a situation to one where it was possible to credit Harvey and Jenner with 'discovering' circulation and vaccination respectively in relatively recent times? In other words, how did the majority of Europeans lose this information?

During the start of a settled and urban lifestyle, specialisation of occupations meant that the majority of people no longer engaged in activities that would teach them anatomy, medicine, chemical warfare, etc. Occupations formed guilds where they guarded their accumulated knowledge and its various applications. Guilders might even spread misinformation amongst non-guild members. The last thing they wanted was a situation where people could cure themselves of illnesses or perform surgical operations on family members. In Europe most people knew of cities because of the Roman Empire, even if they did not live in them. Roman sources describe priestly and other trade guilds in Gaul, Britain, Iberia and Germania. Even so people still knew more then than they did in seventeenth century Europe. The death knell rang when State Christianity was introduced into Europe. The Church wanted absolute centralisation of power which meant absolute centralisation of knowledge. Guilds where individuals would have known about anatomy, astronomy, chemical warfare, etc. would have either been absorbed by the Church, or ruthlessly destroyed in what has been called the Inquisition. Whichever be the case, any African historians today who see knowledge as intrinsic to Africa, and ignorance as intrinsic to Europe, are simply mismeasuring Europeans.

2. A Material Evidence-Based Challenge to Mismeasure

We have just shown that without any archaeological evidence we can still make inductions and deductions that show early humans to have been the intellectual and, as far as the basics go, the technological equals of modern twenty-first century humans. It is possible to use archaeological evidence to back at least some of these assertions.

The usual sequence of material development for *Homo Sapiens Sapiens* given in textbooks is (note that BP means 'Before the Present'):

Middle Stone Age (MSA) I	200,000-127,000 BP
MSA II	127,000-80,000 BP

MSA III	80,000-21,000 BP
New Stone Age (NSA)	21,000 BP –

What is called the New Stone Age (i.e. NSA) in Sub-Saharan Africa is referred to as the Epipalaeolithic or Microlithic period in North Africa and Western Asia. This name comes from the common use of microlithic or bladelet technology. These microblades were often with hafts or handles, as evidenced by their backed shape and notches for attachment. The tool-kit of this period also included micro-knife blades, grooved micro-blades, crescent-shaped points, arrowheads, ground and polished awls, stone-weighted digging sticks, ostrich eggshells and the beads made thereof. Microlithic tool-kits imply bow and arrow technology which allow the specialised hunting of large game with a high meat yield. Such animals had been more difficult to hunt with spears. The intense exploitation of large game, like wild cattle, is thought to have led to cattle domestication. Stone-weighted digging sticks allowed for more efficient exploitation of roots and tubers, which led to the first experimentation with agriculture. This was soon followed by intense seed exploitation which is also thought to have led to agriculture. It is not difficult to see why a Microlithic period precedes the beginning of agronomy and animal husbandry everywhere.

Microblades, spatula and needles meant large animals could be processed with increasing ease and that surgical operations on humans were possible. They could be cut open with fine instruments and sewn back with delicate needles. Pictures of such tools recovered resemble surgical instruments in their appearance. Ostrich eggshells were certainly the precursor of cups, pottery, plates and baskets. From their beads came an early form of jewellery. The first evidence of this New or Late Stone Age period is from East and Southern Africa from about 22,000 BP. However, sporadic use of microliths emerged many thousands of years earlier. An account of this situation is given by Peter Mitchell in *The Archaeology of Southern Africa*:

> In North-Western Botswana's Tsodilo Hills a microlithic technology involving some element of bladelet production was already in place before the Last Glacial Maximum [i.e. 18,000 BP]. Further south at Gi this may extend back to 33,000 BP ... in Zambia transitional MSA/LSA assemblages at Kalemba and Leopard's Hill dating *c.*22,000 BP ... but in East Africa the exceptionally well-dated sequence from the Enkapune ya Moto registers this switch >46,000 BP consistent with recently obtained dates for other sites in the region. Such a widespread replacement of MSA technology seems to demand a major technological innovation, perhaps the introduction of the bow and arrow. (pp.117-9).

Clearly the transition from MSA to microlithic technology is first recorded in East Africa 46,000 BP. The earliest evidence of microlithic technology outside Africa is in Jordan and southern Palestine around 20,000 BP. This is the part of Asia closest to Africa. In southeastern Europe, it is 11,000 BP. Finally, in northern Europe, the Microlithic or Epipalaeolithic occurs 10,000 to 8,000 BP. With this in mind, the following is even more astounding:

> Barbed and unbarbed points are also known from apparently MSA contexts at Semliki in Eastern Congo bracketed between 174,000 ± 8000 and 82,000 ± 8,000 BP ... they and the Blombos finds suggest that bone tools similar to those made by LSA people also formed part of MSA toolkits. (p.91).

The archaeological record thus shows that the ingenuity that made civilisation possible has been present since between 182,000 and 74,000 BP. Debates, ironically found in the same book, about whether the modern human mind developed before 40,000 BP, are thus clearly misled and devoid of common sense.

The Testimony of Historical Linguistics

Linguistic science allows us to identify closely related languages and reconstruct their ancestor. An example would be Bantu languages like KiSwahili, IsiZulu, ChiShona and KiKongo which all descend from a common ancestor called Proto-Bantu. Germanic languages like Dutch, English, Swedish and German, likewise, all descend from Proto-Germanic. The relationships are established by demonstrating that these languages share specific words which have regularly corresponding sounds or phonemes. These shared words are called cognates and the corresponding sounds are called reflexes, meaning that they are reflections of an original sound which can be reconstructed in the ancestral language called a proto-language. An easy example is the Kiswahili item for 'three', *tatu,* which is identical to the ChiShona item *tatu,* 'three', and can be found with minor variation across almost 600 Bantu languages. In some languages, it occurs as -*tato.* From these facts, linguists have deduced that the ancestor, or proto-item, was *-tatU* 'three' with a 2nd degree *'U'* which had a tendency to develop into both 'u' in some Bantu languages, and 'o' in others. The asterix (*) that precedes the proto-item indicates that this word is a scholarly reconstruction.

A more complex example of how an original Proto-Bantu (or PB) sound can evolve into modern Bantu reflexes are given as follows:

ChiShona
-*pona* get cured, recover

Gekoyo
-*hona* recover, get cured

-pona be saved, escape	*-hona* be saved, escape
-pora recover from illness	*-hora* recover from disease
-pora become cold	*-hora* become cold

From these, the following reconstructions have been suggested for the ancestral language of both ChiShona and Gekoyo - Proto-Bantu:

Proto-Bantu (PB)
*-*pon-* get cured of illness
*-*pon-* be saved, escape
*-*pod-* recover (illness)
*-*pod-* become cold

The correspondence of the ChiShona /p/ with the Gekoyo /h/, as seen in the above examples, are too orderly to be accidental. In phonology, the study of the sounds that make up languages, /p/ is known to change to /h/, in a process called lenition or weakening, but the reverse is far less likely. We thus reconstruct the ancestor with a */-p/ and not an */-h/. This /p/ was maintained in ChiShona but lenited to /h/ in Gekoyo. The PB */-d/ developed into /-r/ in both languages.

From the items that can be reconstructed for any proto-language, the researcher can learn something about the speakers and their lifestyles. The more widespread the occurrences of the reflexes, the more likely we are to be dealing with a Proto-Bantu (PB) item or word. This is particularly so when we find a reconstruction with reflexes in the north western corner of Bantu-speaking Africa and also in the rest of the Bantu-speaking region. Scholars arbitrarily call the north western corner - zones A, B and C. Furthermore, they call the other Bantu-speaking regions - zones D to S. Reconstructions whose reflexes *only* occur in zones A-C *or* zones D-S may also date back to the initial period but they could also be later innovations. Unless they are backed by cognates in languages related to PB, likely to be located in West Africa, it is impossible to be certain.

1. Material Culture of PB-Speakers
The material culture of PB-speakers is revealed by certain reconstructions such as the following and the zones in which they occur:

-kum- be honoured; be rich	ABCDEFLMNS
-kum-u rich person	ABCGHJKLMNPRS
-kum-u chief; medicine man	ABCGHJKLMNPRS
-ganda house; village; chief's enclosure	BCEGHJKLMNR

*-*dambU* tribute	CDKLMPR
*-*cod-* pay tax	CJ
*-*dIdo* boundary	ABCHJR

The reconstructions, and the distribution of their reflexes, imply a sequence of events. PB-speakers obviously recognised political authority, whose leaders were associated with medicine and magic. Leading politicians would appear to have been medicine-men who used their knowledge of psychology to accumulate great wealth. They used their wealth to gain political control and then used this to further increase their wealth by tax and tribute. The presence of all these terms in PB suggests that these developments occured before the formation of PB or else in PB-prehistory. This means before 3000 BC, the date now agreed as the dispersal date of the Bantu speakers. In other words, all of these elements - wealthy individuals, honoured people, houses, tribute, taxation and agreed territorial boundaries - were standard features of PB societies by at least 3000 BC or possibly earlier! This raises a question: What would happen to those who refused to pay the tribute and taxation?

| *-*kond-o* war | EGKLMNPS |
| *-*kod-I* captive | BNP |

Since we know the consequences - war and captivity - clearly the wise option would have been to pay the tribute and taxation.

How did these prehistoric politicians become rich in the first place?

*-*dand-* buy	AKLR
*-*cUmb-* buy	ABCHL
*-*tu-* fix the price, cost, be worth	ACDEFGJMS
*-*cimbI* iron, cowry	FGJKLMS

The buying and selling of goods allowed prehistoric doctors to accumulate great wealth. The last reconstruction, iron and cowries, only has reflexes in Central and East Africa. For this reason, it cannot ordinarily be assigned to the PB period with any certainty. However, cowries are a currency in West Africa and since the PB-speakers arose in West Africa and spread to Central and East Africa there is a rather logical possibility that cowries (or a shell currency precursor) were used by PB-speakers while they were in West Africa. They later migrated to Central and East Africa but the descendent Bantu languages in the west and northwest have since lost this particular item while the others have preserved it. In support of this is the equation of cowry and iron which, outside of the context of both being historically used as currencies, does not make sense. If evidence were found for the existence of iron in PB times this would make this hypothesis even stronger. We are therefore pleased to reveal the following:

*-*tud-* hammer, forge	16z (all zones - A to S)
*-*tud-i* smith	CFJLMS
*-*tade* iron ore, iron, wire	ABCHJKLMNPRS
*-*duk-Ut-* work the bellows	CEGJKMNP
*-*guba* smithy	ABC
*-*guba* bellows	EFGJMPS
*-*dĺbo* small bell	ABCHLR

The equation of hammer and forge occurs in every Bantu zone. One could argue that the original term meant 'stone hammer' which was later transferred to 'forge' when iron was discovered. This is almost certainly what happened. The question is whether the transfer happened during PB times or some time after this period. Other terms such as 'work the bellows' and 'iron ore' having a distribution showing PB occurrence, means that the most logical interpretation of the evidence is that iron-producing terminology existed in eastern Nigeria and southern Cameroon around 3000 BC and possibly before that date. It would appear that iron and cowries being used as currency is a strong hypothesis. In addition, another reconstruction *-*bamba* means both 'fish scale' and 'cowry' and has a distribution in zones A, L and S. This is from the northwest tip in Cameroon and Gabon, to the southeast tip of Zimbabwe, Mozambique and South Africa. So we now have evidence that cowries (or a shell currency precursor) were known in PB times as was iron. We also have an equation of the two in a reconstruction of limited distribution. It is the simplest, and therefore the most scientifically acceptable view, to see the equation as a sporadic preservation of the memory of a dual currency that existed in PB times.

Now we have an idea of what they were buying with: What were they actually buying? Money is, after all, a means of accessing wealth and is not the actual wealth itself. Anyone who lives through an economic depression can confirm this.

*-*gombe* cattle	16z (all Bantu zones)
*-*budi* goat	16z
*-*kanga* guinea-fowl	16z

Whoever owned the most domestic animals, simply put, had the keys to the Oval Office. A surplus of cattle meant the ability to feed large numbers of people during food shortages. It also meant beasts could be loaned (i) to fertilize fields with dung, (ii) bulls could be loaned to breed cows and (iii) to provide milk for those without milk. A lender would ask for not just the loaned animal but any offspring that it may produce, because (a) the offspring would, by right, partially belong to the lender, and (b) the offspring would compensate him for the period when he was without the animal. Once the concept of interest creeps in, there is the very real temptation not to return the goods at all. Of course if the lender is your doctor and protector against bad magic, you may very well not want to do this. Over time the lender accumulated a lot more wealth than any other individual. In a number of Bantu kingdoms the theory was that all cattle belonged to the king, as did all land. A more socially benign perception would be that the king held all land and cattle in 'trust' of the people. In both views, however, distribution is in the hands of the king. A parallel may be seen in the position of banks in Western Society which, in many cases, are the actual owners of houses until the mortgage is fully paid.

All the 'buying' and 'price-fixing' implies commerce on a scale. This necessitates record-keeping of one kind or another;

*-kanda skin, cloth	BFGHJLMNPS
*-kanda strap, belt	AEGJKLP
*-kanda letter	BCHKLR
*-con- draw a line, write	BCGHJLMS

The items 'letter', 'skin', 'cloth' and 'strap', 'belt' all have a distribution suggesting a PB occurrence. The items also suggest a sequence of development in PB-prehistory. *-Kanda first meant 'skin' which then transferred to 'cloth', 'strap' or 'belt' and finally to 'letter' either during or before the PB period (i.e. 3000 BC). When writing was invented (*-con-) during, or even before the PB period, skins were used in the absence of paper - hence the connection between 'letter' and 'skin'. The continued use of skin as an indigenous writing material was reported among the Nupe of Central Nigeria.

2. The Mismeasure of Zimbabwe

An oral tradition was once related to this author, by his father, concerning the manufacture of guns in precolonial Zimbabwe. According to the tradition, gunpowder was made from the urine of a rock-rabbit. While few Zimbabweans have been able to confirm this, the author S. Gozo, in his rather informative *The Material Culture of Zimbabwe* observed:

> The guns that were imported to Zimbabwe and exchanged for trade goods became highly prized possessions ... During the 19th century, the Shona made copies of these imported weapons, and these became known as *zvigidi* [plural]

or *chigidi* [singular] (from the sound of firing). These weapons were used effectively in the Chindunduma of 1896 [i.e. war of liberation] ... Who exactly discovered the secret of locally manufactured gunpowder will perhaps never be known but *unga* (powder) was certainly produced. (pp.57-8).

The colonial settlers were aware of these guns. After all, they were being used on them. The British South Africa Company tried to disarm Africans after their defeat in 1897, but it took decades. In Malawi the Nyanja people were only totally disarmed in 1930. The Ndebele of Zimbabwe could actually manufacture bullets for specific kinds of European rifles such as the Lee Metford and the Martini-Henry. This way, both African-made guns and those confiscated from Europeans could still be used. In order to replicate European rifles or their bullets, a feat known as reverse engineering, a culture needs a sophisticated understanding of metallurgy. As impressive as reverse engineering is, does it account for all the evidence? There are two post-PB reconstructions which suggest the guns predate the nineteenth century:

-putI gun	GMNPS
-bIda rock-rabbit	LMNPS

Interestingly, nearly all the zones of occurrence, except one, coincide! Furthermore, both reconstructions have reflexes in ChiShona, the predominant language in Zimbabwe (*-pfuti* 'gun', *m-bira* 'rock-rabbit'). Bantu-speaking Africans are famous for their migrations and long-distance travel so the item *-putI* could be interpreted as an old loan from the sixteenth century when Bantu-speaking Africans first came into contact with Europeans. When reverse engineering occurred in areas where rock-rabbits were found, they utilised their urine for gunpowder. It just so happens that urine is rich in ammonia which is flammable and can be used as an explosive. There is also the distinct possibility that gunpowder alone had been discovered during some point of the Eastern Bantu expansion and almost certainly before the sixteenth century. There is another historical example of this. An invention of gunpowder without the invention of guns occurred in China.

3. Genetic Relations of PB
Proto-Bantu must itself have had a shared ancestry with certain other languages. Its closest relations were in Cameroon and eastern Nigeria. Today these languages are called Bantoid. Also closely related are the Cross River languages such as Efik, spoken by 80% of the people of Cross River State, Nigeria. Together with some other languages, these form the Benue-Congo family. Proto-Benue-Congo (PBC) is thought to have existed around 5000 and 4000 BC. The Kwa languages, which include Akanic languages like Twi, and

also Potou languages, like Tano, are spoken in Ghana and the Ivory Coast. They share a common ancestor with Benue-Congo languages, which linguists call Proto-Benue-Kwa, which predates PBC by at least 1,000 years (i.e. 6000-5000 BC). Eventually we reach the North Atlantic languages of Senegambia, whose shared ancestor with PB dates to at least 8000 to 6000 BC. The North Atlantic languages include Wolof and Fulfulde (also called Fula).

We must note that it *is* possible to show similar words between any two languages whether they are related or not. Sporadic similarities, however, do not recur and they are therefore not regular. An example of sporadic similarities can be seen between Hawaiian and Greek.

Hawaiian	Greek
aeto eagle	*aetos* eagle
kia pillar	*kion* pillar
lahui people	*laos* people
meli honey	*meli* honey
noonoo thought	*nous* thought

In the textbook by R. Larry Trask, *Historical Linguistics* - from where these examples were taken, there were a few other compared items but the compared meanings were not exact matches. It is best to first compare the exact meanings and see whether any patterns or recurrences are established. In our two languages, we have only one exact semantic sense with initial /m/ items. To have a recurrence there would have to be *another* such example of initial /m/ items so long as the other segments are also showing recurring correspondences. Hawaiian and Greek provide no other examples, however. It is easier to find items with *related* rather than *exact* meanings with initial /m/ hence:

manao think	*manthano* learn

Because the probability of finding related words is higher than finding words of exactly the same meaning, it is better to stick to exact-meaning items when trying to prove a linguistic relationship. An example of this can be shown in a hitherto unattempted comparison between PB and Wolof.

PB	Wolof
-bIcI fresh	*bees* fresh
-bUm- kill	*boom* to kill
-cing- clench teeth	*siiny* open lips with clenched teeth

*-co- sunset	*so* to set (sun)
*-daka language	*laka* language
*-damI tongue	*laameny* tongue
*-dI- eat	*leeka* eat
*-jedI-Id float	*weer* to hang
*-jed-i moon; month	*weer* moon, month
*-kad- tear, cut	*xar* to tear, cut
*-kada charcoal, ember	*xal* embers, hot coals
*-kodo heart	*xol* heart
*-gend- go	*geena* to go out
*-men- sprout	*meeny* to sprout
*-pind- be black	*findi* to blacken
*-pudo foam	*fuur* foam
*-tamba walk, travel	*taama* to walk, travel
*-teek- put, put on fire, cook	*tek* to put, start cooking

Looking at the above examples of PB and Wolof, one finds five examples of recurring initial-segment correspondences which are followed by corresponding vowels and corresponding second consonants. This is *not* sporadic and indicates that the words *do* have a relationship, that is, they share a common ancestor. This implies that the languages as a whole share a common ancestor. Hence vowel */I/ corresponds to /e/, */i/ to /i/, */o/ to /o/, */a/ to /a/ and so on. Such recurrences form patterns which could not have arisen by chance. We therefore conclude these are not chance resemblances but genetic ones. In the case of initial */k-/, the strongest pattern has emerged. In these items, the PB */k/ has become the Wolof /x/. In the case of the items 'eat' and 'tongue' there are extra segments in Wolof that have been lost in Bantu. We know this by comparing them with other related languages from West Africa and occasionally seeing these segments appearing in the same items.

Additional evidence of the relationship between Wolof and PB will come from comparing PB with Wolof's closest relation, a language known as Fulfulde (also called Fula). They too should be related.

PB	Fula
*-bada open space, field	*baar-ol* field
*-bImbI waves	*bempe-YYe* waves
*-can- to comb	*san-c-aa-de* to comb
*-cenge sand	*seen-al* sand
*-cUb- urinate	*soof-de* to urinate
*-cUmb- buy	*som-aa-de* to buy
*-dIm- cultivate	*rem-de* to cultivate

*-dInd- wait	*reen-aa-de* to wait
*-jed-i moon, month	*lew-ru* moon, month
*-jed-i moonlight	*lewlew-al* moonlight
*-jed-U clear ground	*lew-re* cleared land
*-kad- be bitter	*haaD-de* to be bitter
*-kam- squeeze	*ham-Yu-de* squeeze
*-kam- wring	*ham-de* to wring out clothing
*-kec- cut	*hes-u-de* to cut
*-kond-o war	*hon-de* to war, raid
*-kun-Ik- cover	*huun-a* to cover
*-kad- be difficult, hard	*saD-de* be difficult, hard
*-kek- cut	*seek-de* to cut up

Looking at the above, we see that the pattern of the vowels in the PB-Wolof comparison is replicated here. In 2 examples, the PB word-initial */b-/ corresponds with the Fula /b/. In addition, there are 4 examples where */c-/ corresponds with /s/, 2 examples where */d-/ corresponds with /r/, 3 examples where */j-/ corresponds with /w/, 6 examples where */k-/ corresponds with /h/, and finally 2 examples where /k/ corresponds with /s/.

The reason why */d-/ and */k-/ in PB have two correspondences in Fula, and very likely in other languages from West Africa, is because a number of consonants in the immediate ancestor of PB merged, making it impossible to distinguish (without external assistance) between one kind of /k-/ or /d-/ and the other. The ancestral sounds of Fula /h/ and /s/, which correspond to PB */k/, both merged in pre-PB so that both sounds appeared in PB as */k/. Another interesting observation we make, is that the Fula items for 'moon' and 'moonlight' look different from the Wolof item but in fact the consonants have just been switched around. This is known as metathesis. The correspondence therefore is not */j-/ becomes /l-/ but instead */j-/ corresponds to /w/ and */d/ corresponds to /l/. Even where mergers have occurred in pre-PB consonants, the PB consonant in question simply shows more than one co-occurrence or recurrence and not several individual or sporadic correspondences.

4. Sumerian: A Linguistic Isolate?
It is often assumed that sub-Saharan Africans never migrated outside of Africa within recent prehistoric times. Despite this common perception, the linguist Joseph Greenberg demonstrated a genetic relationship between the Semitic languages, and Chadic (which includes Hausa), Cushitic (includes Oromo, Somali), Omotic (includes Hamar), Ancient Egyptian and Berber (includes Tamasheq spoken by the Tuaregs). Since all these language families are spoken in Africa and only Semitic is spoken in both Africa and Asia, the logical

conclusion has been that at some point within the last ten thousand years, the ancestors of the Semitic peoples left Africa and entered Asia. The question thus arises as to whether there were any other languages that left Africa for Asia within the last ten thousand years. Is Sumerian one such example?

Sumerian was spoken in ancient southern Mesopotamia between 3000 and 2000 BC in what is today southern Iraq. The language was discovered when the cuneiform tablets from the earliest cities of Mesopotamia were deciphered in the nineteenth century AD. The Sumerian language has been compared to a great many language families, usually by amateurs, looking for sporadic similarities. To this day, no wholly convincing relationship has been demonstrated between Sumerian and any known language family, although we must note that the Father of Assyriology, Sir Henry Rawlinson, theorised that Sumerian was of Cushitic origins and therefore originated in East Africa. Languages which are not related to any other known languages are called isolates. Is Sumerian really an isolate?

This author will proceed to compare Sumerian to PB to see whether any recurring correspondences can be detected in the same way that Wolof and Fula can be fruitfully compared to PB. Firstly, PB is ideal for making comparisons because it is a reconstruction based on hundreds of Bantu languages and therefore has a richer source of comparison material than individual Bantu languages such as KiSwahili or IsiZulu. We must, however, note that Reverend Willibald Wanger attempted just such a comparison between IsiZulu and Sumerian in 1935. Secondly, PB is also ideal in that it was spoken at around about the same time as Sumerian (i.e. 3000 BC).

PB	Sumerian
*-*bad-Ud-* to split; burst open	*bar* to cut open, slit, split
*-*badI* liver	*bar* liver
*-*cad-* to hurry	*sar* to run, hasten
*-*cUb-* to rub	*sub* to rub
*-*cI* ground; earth; country	*ki* ground, earth, country
*-*ciici* ant	*kiši* ant
*-*dIa* that, those	*re* that
*-*dI-* eat	*rig* eat
*-*dUm-e* male	*urum* male
*-*dem-* to create, make	*dim₂* to create
*-*dem-* to be heavy	*idim* (to be) heavy
*-*dong-* to speak	*dug₄* to speak
*-*dongo* pot [derived from 'clay']	*dug* (clay) pot
*-*dUng-I* good	*dug* (to be) good
*-*ged-* to pass along	*gid₂* to tow, drag, to pass along

*-ged-o to measure   gid to survey, measure a field
*-jadi oil   li₂ oil
*-jigI door   ig door
*-kad-im- to shine   had (to be) bright; to shine
*-kum- to be honoured   hum to honour
*-ku- to die   uš to die
*-kut- to cover   šuš to cover
*-paca twin   maš twin
*-pad- spread, scatter   mar to winnow; scatter

We see exact meaning matches between 2 examples of word-initial */b/; 2 of
*/c/ corresponding with an /s/ and 2 of */c/ to /k/; 3 of */d/ to /r/ and 5 of */d/
to /d/; 2 of */g/ to /g/; 2 of */j/ to /Ø/; 2 of */k/ to /h/; 2 of */k/ to /š/ and 2 of
*/p/ to /m/.

There are also a few examples of correspondences that only occur once with
an exact meaning but where remaining segments were regular.

*-gend- to go   g~en to walk
*-kUt-o skin   kuš skin
*-mUd-Ik- to shine; radiate mul to shine, radiate
*-to soup   tu₇ soup
*-tU alone   ušu alone

Not all cognates have regularly corresponding vowels. Sometimes vowels
shift in pronunciation sporadically and other times under certain phonological
conditions. The e/i attenuation with /u/ is quite common in Niger-Congo
languages.

*-bed- to cut   bur to cut
*-beede breast   ubur breast
*-jed- to shine   ul to shine
*-kec- to cut; harvest   šuš to cut, fell
*-jijIb- to know   zu to know
*-jija fire   izi fire
*-cUkI hair   siki hair
*-dug- to boil; cook   rig to boil down
*-kod- be strong   kalag (to be) strong
*-oko one   aš one
*-kingo neck, voice   šeg voice, cry
*-nyo- drink   nag~ drink (see also page 668)
*-tika cold weather   šeg cold weather; frost; ice

   Despite the vowel shifts, putative cognates can still be identified because the consonants will conform to already established correspondences. Sometimes the meaning of a cognate may change from that of a generic noun, like 'dog' to that of a specific breed or type, like 'hound'. Other meaning shifts involve verb to noun associations like 'fly' to 'bird'. There are also some close meaning correspondences between PB and Sumerian.

*-badu side of body; side	bar outside; (other) side
*-bodo penis	bur₈ crotch
*-co- sunset	su to sink, go down
*-con- be bashful	sun (to be) humble
*-dai far	ri (to be) distant
*-dago house	dag dwelling, seat
*-dem- be honoured	idim important
*-dem-ad- be lame; be injured	dim₃ (to be) helpless
*-dem-a physically disabled person	idim weak, helpless (person)
*-dong- to teach	dug₄ to order
*-dub- fish	lub a salt-water fish
*-kodi- light a fire	kur to burn, to light up
*-kodi bird of prey; hawk	hurin eagle
*-kUd- to scrape	hur to scratch
*-kom- to kill	šum to slaughter
*-kUt-e overcast weather	šuš to cloud over
*-tad- to cut open	tar to cut down
*-tUndU basket	tun container; bag
*-tup- to give a gift	šum to give

   Putative cognates sharing a similar semantic sense can be identified because they conform to recurrent correspondences established with exact semantic sense items. There are also items in Sumerian and PB with a similar semantic sense and sharing established phonemic recurrences where the PB items reflect a previous stage in cultural development compared to the Sumerian term, which shows a later stage of cultural development. In some cases, both items reflect the same developmental stage.

*-cad- to cut, incise; tattoo	sar to write
*-doba mud; clay	dub (clay) tablet
*-jene chief	en lord
*-tUng- to sew; thread on a string	tug cloth, textile

In the first comparative pair the direction of semantic shift logically would be from 'incise' to 'write'. Interestingly, early Sumerian writing did indeed involve making incisions in clay, hence the transfer of meaning in the second comparative pair. The English word 'write' itself has such an ancestry because it descends from the Proto-Germanic *writan* meaning 'to tear, cut, incise'. In this instance, the ancestor of both reflexes, Sumerian and PB, would date back to Proto-Niger-Congo (i.e. 10,000-8000 BC) or possibly Proto-Benue-Congo (i.e. 6000 to 5000 BC). The items for 'chief' and 'lord' appear to be reflexes of an item in Proto-Benue-Kwa which indicated the political head of a settlement. In Akan this became –*hInI* from where we derive *Asantehene*, 'chief or lord of Asante'. In PB it indicated the political head of a settlement or group of settlements and eventually becomes the ChiShona *Mw-ene* as in *Mwenemutapa*. In Sumerian it became the *en* 'lord' of any one of its many cities. The first king of Kish, for whom we have archaeological evidence, is *En-Mebaragesi* or Lord-Mebaragesi. The gods of Sumer were called *En-lil*, lord-wind, *En-ki*, lord-earth and so on. The last example has a PB item which is inherited in Bantu languages like KiKongo with the double-meaning 'weave' and 'build'. One can derive a PB reconstruction for 'house', the product of building by suffixing the root with –*o*, *-tUng-o*. Sumerian lacks this suffixing principle to derive nouns from verbs. We therefore postulate that *tug* 'cloth', 'textile' is derived from 'sew', 'to weave' in the same way as PB *-tUng-o* is derived from 'to build'. These hypotheses are plausible explanations for the semantic shift in PB and Sumerian reflexes and reflect processes which can be seen in PB and Niger-Congo.

The recurrent correspondences between PB and Sumerian cannot be deemed sporadic any more than those between PB and Wolof, or PB and Fula. There are also a number of the shared reflexes for which reflexes have been identified in a third language, known to be related to PB, and where the reflex has expected correspondences:

-beede	breast	PB
i-bal	breast	Konyagi (North Atlantic)
ubur	breast	Sumerian
-bodo	penis	PB
-bollo	penis	Kisi (South Atlantic)
-foro	penis	Bambara (Mande)
-foto	penis	Mandinka (Mande)
bur	crotch	Sumerian

*-ciici	ant	PB
sisingdo	ant	Kisi (South Atlantic)
kiši	ant	Sumerian
*-cUb-	to rub	PB
suuwo	to rub	Kisi (South Atlantic)
sub	to rub	Sumerian
*-dI-	eat	PB
dio	eat	Kisi (South Atlantic)
di	eat	Ewe (Kwa)
lekk	eat	Wolof (North Atlantic)
rig	eat	Sumerian
*-dongo	pot	PB
longio	cooking pot	Kisi (South Atlantic)
dug	pot	Sumerian
*-dug-	to boil; be cooked	PB
louwo	be cooked	Kisi (South Atlantic)
digi	be cooked, to boil	Buli (Gur)
rig	to boil down	Sumerian
*-jijIb-	to know	PB
sebi	to know	Buli (Gur)
jibe	to know	Mandinka (Mande)
jube	to know	Mandinka
zu	to know	Sumerian
*-cUki	hair	PB
cokk	pubic hair	Wolof
kok	hair	Buli
siki	hair	Sumerian
*-co-	sunset	PB
so	sunset	Wolof
su	to go down, sink	Sumerian
*-gend-	to go	PB
genn	to go, come	Wolof
g~en	to go	Sumerian

*-nyo-	to drink	PB
naan	to drink	Wolof
nwong	to drink	Efik (Lower Cross)
nag~	to drink	Sumerian

*-kodi	bird of prey; hawk	PB
cooli, ceeli	kite	Wolof
koli	hawk	Akan (Kwa)
kudei~	kite	Proto-Ijoid
hurin	eagle	Sumerian

*-cad-	to hurry	PB
chali	to run; rush	Buli
sar	to run, hasten	Sumerian

*-mUd-Ik-	to shine; give light	PB
moolim	to shine excessively	Buli (Gur)
mole	to be bright	Yoruba
mul	to shine, radiate	Sumerian

*-med-o	throat	PB
mI~l~I~	throat	Proto-Potou-Akanic-Bantu
meli	neck	Sumerian

Joseph Greenberg, the originator of the Niger-Congo (NC) hypothesis, included the Konyagi item in his examples of probable cognates with the PB item. This was done on the basis of two corresponding consonants. The PB stem *-bodo 'penis' has a limited distribution but its presence in Mande and South Atlantic demonstrates that it is a Proto-Niger-Congo reflex. Sumerian rig 'to eat' in comparison to PB *-dI- 'to eat', appears to have an extra segment. However a comparison with Wolof allows the sound positing of a velar in word-final position for the PNC item, which was subsequently lost in most NC languages, but kept in Wolof and Sumerian. PB *-dug- 'to boil' and Sumerian rig 'to boil down', is best explained as the back-front vowel alternation that occurs in NC and is evidenced by a back version being found in Kisi and a front version in Buli. A similar kind of additional evidence comes from Mandinka which has an /i/ and /u/ alteration for the item 'to know'. The word-final /b/ is posited by the author as lost in Sumerian by a sporadic lenition from /b/ to /w/ to /Ø/. In the PB *-nyo- and Sumerian nag~ (pronounced 'nang' - the 'ng' is pronounced the same as in 'sing') for 'to drink', we appear to have another extra segment in Sumerian but Wolof and Efik furnish a word-final nasal to show that the PNC item almost certainly had a word-final nasal which was lost in PB. The PB *-kodi* hawk, kite, bird of prey, compared to Sumerian *hurin* 'eagle', provides yet another extra segment. Here Proto-Ijoid, one of the oldest branches of NC provides *kudei~* and a sound solution. The final vowel in the Proto-Ijoid item is nasalised, hence the wave next to the /i/. Nasalisation of a vowel often happens when the word-final nasal consonant has been lost. Famous cases known to every linguist include French nasal vowels in items such as *vi~* 'wine' spelt *vin* because the nasal consonant is preserved in the traditional and conservative spelling system just as the /s/ in 'Paris'. A phonologically sound hypothesis would thus be the PNC item having a word-final nasal consonant. It was lost very early on with the adjacent vowels nasalised. Gradually the nasalised vowels were denasalised, with only Proto-Ijoid retaining a phonological memory of the word-final nasal consonant and Sumerian retaining the consonant. Thus by including languages from other branches of NC, *all* extra segments in Sumerian relative to PB have been explained with phonologically sound hypotheses.

5. Conclusion

This gives us 65 recurrent correspondences between Proto-Bantu and Sumerian of which 24 have recurrent correspondences of all segments and share exact semantic sense; 5 have sporadic correspondence of first consonant amongst items with exact semantic sense but have all other segments recurring correspondingly; 13 have recurrent correspondences of consonants but the vowels are irregular but accountable; 19 have recurrent correspondences of all segments but semantic sense is inexact; and lastly 4 cultural items showing previously established correspondences in all segments but displaying semantic shifts expected with urban development. This situation of 52 comparative pairs with regular vowels, and 13 with irregular vowels, can be compared with other African languages when *they* are compared with PB. Buli, for example, has 40 regular vowel comparative pairs and 20 with irregular vowels. Kisi has a ratio of 42:19, Wolof has 59:17, Efik has 49:12 and Bambara has 21:8.

Of course, it should be clear this is a study in progress, and thus these figures are likely to slightly increase but they show Sumerian to have an affinity to PB comparable to the South Atlantic or the Gur languages. The estimation for the period when the ancestors of the Sumerians were separated from the ancestors of the Proto-Bantu speakers would be around 8000 and 7000 BC. Whatever else can be said we can say that Sumerian is as much a Niger-Congo language lexically as any Niger-Congo language. Sumerian is thus shown to be a language of African origin and cannot be seen any longer as an isolate.

Conclusion

The writing of a proper history for any group of people must take account of the contemporary power relationships that the particular group has with the other major groups on the planet. This is important because history is always written within a given psycho-social context. Such a history must also take into account the real potential and capacity of prehistoric humans, without which we cannot properly measure the downtrodden and seemingly hopeless of today. It falls to 'Saxon' historians to execute this task to the level 3 standards outlined here if the 'Saxons' want an accurate historical memory as a precursor to building a brighter future.

Bibliography

Yvonne Bastin et al (ed), *Bantu Lexical Reconstructions,* internet site, March 2003 see http://linguistics.africamuseum.be/BLR3.html

Lyle Campbell, *Historical Linguistics,* UK, Edinburgh University Press, 1998

S. Gozo, *The Material Culture of Zimbabwe,* Zimbabwe, Longman Zimbabwe, 1984

Peter Mitchell, *The Archaeology of Southern Africa,* UK, Cambridge University Press, 2002

R. L. Trask, *Historical Linguistics,* UK, Arnold, 1996

University Museum of Pennsylvania, *The Pennsylvania Sumerian Dictionary Project,* internet site, see http://psd.museum.upenn.edu/epsd/

Rev. Willibald Wanger, *A Comparative Lexical Study of Sumerian and NTU ("Bantu"): Sumerian the "Sanscrit" of the African Ntu Languages,* Germany, W. Kohlhammer, 1935

CHRONOLOGICAL TABLE

Nile Valley and North Africa Dates BC	West and Central Africa Dates BC	South and East Africa Dates BC
	c.88000 BC Fishing-based culture flourishes at Katanda in Congo. This is the first known culture on earth.	c.41200 BC Hematite mining is conducted in the Ngwenya mountain range of Swaziland.
		c.27000 Rock art is painted in Namibia.
		c.26000 Manganese mining is conducted at Chowa in Zambia.
	c.23000 Ishango bone carved in Congo showing early evidence of arithmetic and the use of the calendar.	c.13000 Cattle is domesticated in the Lukenya Hill District of Kenya.
c.10000 BC Crops of barley, capers, chick-peas, etc, are cultivated at Wadi Kubbaniya in Egypt.		

*c.*7438 First known mummification takes place at Uan Muhuggiag in Libya.

*c.*5900 Birth of kingship in Ta-Seti - the first kings on earth.

*c.*5900 East African incense is exported to Ta-Seti.

5660 Mena becomes the first king of a unified Egypt. He begins the Old Kingdom Period that lasts until 4188 BC.

*c.*5581 Queen Neith-Hotep of Egypt rules as Queen-Regent.

5094-5046 Pharaoh Khasekemui is the first great monument builder of Egypt.

5018 Djoser becomes king of Egypt. He later builds the Funerary Complex in the city of Saqqara.

4872 Sneferu becomes king of Egypt. He begins a golden age of wealth and prosperity.

c.4200 Kush becomes a great power centred on the city of Kerma.

c.4290 Settlements are established at Nok.

4188-3448 The First Intermediate Period of Egypt.

3448 Mentuhotep II reunifies Egypt and begins the Middle Kingdom Period that lasts until 3182 BC.

3182-1709 The Second Intermediate Period of Egypt.

c.3008 Pharaoh Khatire becomes the first known non-African to rule in Egypt.

2545 The Hyksos rule Egypt until 1709 BC.

c.2000 Iron smelting conducted at Nok.

1709 Pharaoh Ahmose and Queen Ahmose-Nefertari reunify Egypt and begin the New Kingdom Period that lasts until 1095 BC.

1615 Queen Hatshepsut declares herself Pharaoh of Egypt.

1230 Rameses III becomes king of Egypt. He later launches voyages across the Atlantic to Ancient America.

1101 The Phoenicians establish Utica on the North African coast.

c.1100 Earliest stone masonry villages emerge in the Dhar Tichitt-Walata region.

1005 Makeda becomes ruler of Ethiopia (and Yemen).

c.1000 Walled villages emerge in the Dhar Tichitt-Walata region.

c.1000 Great art is produced at Nok.

814 The Phoenicians establish Carthage on the North African coast.

663 The Assyrians conquer Egypt.

654 Carthage establishes a colony in Ibiza.

c.550 Temple of Almaqah is built in the city of Yeha.

525 The Persians conquer Egypt.

509 Carthage and Rome sign a treaty.

480 The Greeks defeat Carthage in battle.

c.450 Kingdoms emerge in Numidia.

383 Carthage agrees a peace treaty with the Greeks.

c.350 Earliest known So settlements in the Central Sahara region.

332 The Greeks conquer Egypt.

c.300 The lunar calendar is in use at Namoratunga II in Kenya.

c.250 Cities emerge in the Djenné region.

264-241 The First Punic War between Carthage and Rome. Carthage loses.

218-202 The Second Punic War between Carthage and Rome. The Carthaginians are again defeated.

c.200 Great art is produced at Sokoto and Katsina.

c.186 Lusu Culture flourishes in Zambia.

149-146 The Third Punic War between Carthage and Rome. The Carthaginians are defeated. The Romans destroy their city.

148 Micipsa becomes King of Numidia.

150 The *Adulis Inscription* indicates that Axum held sway over a vast territory.

183 Gadara, King of Axum, exerts strong influence in South Arabia.

330 Ezana, King of Axum, converts to Christianity.

370 Axumites withdraw from Yemen.

609 The Ka'aba of Mecca is rebuilt.

c.300 AD Ghana becomes a kingdom.

c.550 Glass is manufactured in the Yoruba city of Ile-Ife.

c.350 Emperor Ezana of Axum invades Kush.

c.450 Silko, King of Nobadia, writes a famous and controversial inscription.

531 Emperor Justinian of Byzantium decides to spread Christianity to Nubia.

573 Makuria sends a delegation to Byzantium.

639 Arabians invade and occupy Egypt.

c.641 Arabian invasion of Makuria fails.

652 Second Arabian invasion of Makuria fails. A peace treaty is agreed between them.

690 The Dia Dynasty rule as the first kings of Songhai.

705 Queen Dahia al-Kahina of Mauritania is defeated by the Arabs.

*c.*700 The Kingdom of Ancient Ghana becomes an empire.

707 Faras Cathedral is constructed in Makuria.

710 Tarif, the Moor, leads an invasion of Spain.

748 Emperor Cyriacus of Makuria invades Egypt.

*c.*750 Mosques appear for the first time on the East African coast.

756 Abd-al-Rahman I becomes ruler of Spain.

*c.*800 The Keita Dynasty rule as the first kings of Mali.

*c.*800 The Dugawa Dynasty rule as the first kings of Kanem.

*c.*800 Leopard's Kopje I Culture flourishes in southern Africa.

833 Emperor Zakaria of Makuria sends a delegation to the Caliph of Baghdad.

*c.*800 City of Eredo is built in southwestern Nigeria.

*c.*850 The Igbo-Ukwu Culture flourishes in eastern Nigeria.

872 Al-Yaqubi reports that Kanem possessed no towns. He also said that Songhai was the greatest empire of the Blacks.

*c.*900 Igodo establishes the First Dynasty of Benin.

951 Ibn Haukal describes the Ghanaian emperor as the richest king on earth.

985 Al-Muhallabi reports that Kanem possessed two towns, Manan and Tarazaki.

999 Bagauda became the first king of Kano.

886 Ibn Hordadbeh mentions the East African coast.

916 Al-Masudi visits the East African coast and reports on its trade in ivory with India, Oman and China.

940 Judith seizes the throne of Axum. She destroys the city and massacres Christians.

956 Makuria attempts an invasion of Egypt.

*c.*1000 Queen Oluwo paves the city of Ile-Ife with decorations made from American corncobs.

1009 Dia Kossoi becomes the first Islamic ruler of Songhai.

1048 Yahya ibn Ibrahim, the Berber leader, makes a pilgrimage to Mecca.

1050 Baranmindanah becomes the first Islamic ruler of Mali.

1067 Queen Hawwa becomes the first Islamic ruler of Kanem.

*c.*1070 Ali ibn Al Hasan establishes the Shirazi Dynasty of Kilwa.

1075 Humé Jilmi establishes the Sefuwa Dynasty in Kanem.

1076 Almoravides invade Ghana.

1086 The Almoravides defeat the Spaniards at the Battle of Zalakah.

*c.*1085 First walls of the Acropolis are built at Great Zimbabwe.

1116 Castle with glass windows is built (or rebuilt) in Kumbi-Saleh.

1147 The Almohades seize Marrakech from the Almoravides.

*c.*1170 Prince Oranmiyan establishes the Second Dynasty of Benin that lasts until 1897.

1153 Al Idrissi records that East Africans export superior iron (i.e. steel).

1180 Sosso becomes a dominant city in the Ancient Ghana region.

1204 Koy Konboro of Djenné founds the Great Mosque of Djenné.

1210 Dunama ibn Salma becomes ruler of Kanem. He ushers in the first golden age of the empire.

1240 The Malians destroy the Ghanaian capital of Kumbi-Saleh.

1246 Dunama II of Kanem exchanges embassies with the king of Tunis.

c.1300 The Yoruba cities emerge with walls.

1324 Mansa Musa of Mali (and 60,000 others) go on pilgrimage to Mecca - the greatest pilgrimage in history.

1316 Kanz ed-Dawla places Makuria under direct political control.

1180 Emperor Lalibela begins the construction of the underground churches in the city of Roha.

c.1200 Mutota brings most of southern Africa under his sway.

1209 Lalibela sends an embassy to the Sultan of Egypt.

1300 The Abu al-Mawahib Dynasty established at Kilwa.

1335 Abu l-Hasan Ali becomes ruler of Morocco.

1365 The Juhanya Arabs occupy Makuria.

1338 Ali Kolon establishes the Sonni Dynasty of Songhai.

1352-3 Ibn Battuta visits Mali.

1355 The Songhai city of Gao finally becomes independent of Mali.

c.1433 The Tuaregs gain control of Timbuktu.

c.1440 Eware the Great becomes ruler of Benin. He rules until c.1473.

1441 The Portuguese begin the raids on Africa to mass enslave people. This ultimately culminates in the transatlantic slave trade.

c.1444 Muhammad Korau becomes ruler of Katsina. He later builds the Gobirau Minaret.

1463 Muhammad Rumfa becomes ruler of Kano. He becomes one of the greatest Hausa rulers.

1331 Ibn Battuta visits the East African coast and remarks that Kilwa was "one of the most beautiful and well constructed cities in the world."

1414 The city of Malindi sends a giraffe to the Imperial Court of China.

1464 Sonni Ali becomes king of Songhai and begins its second golden age.

1465 Ali ibn Dunama becomes ruler of Kanem.

1482 The Portuguese build Elmina Castle - the first slave dungeon.

1493 Mohammed Toure seizes the throne of Songhai.

1505 Portuguese forces burn the Swahili cities of Kilwa and Mombasa.

1512 The Portuguese write the *Regimento*.

1514 Songhai annexes the Hausa Cities of Kano and Katsina.

1526 King Affonso I of Kongo writes to Portugal requesting an end to enslavement.

1536 Bakwa Turunku founds Zaria City.

c.1490 The Arabs conquer Alwa.

1492 Sultan Abu Abdallah of Granada surrenders the city to the Spaniards.

African Diaspora	West and Central Africa	South and East Africa
		1561 Death of a Portuguese missionary at the Court of Munhumutapa creates a diplomatic incident.
	1562 Englishman Sir John Hawkins becomes an important slave trader.	
	1564 Idris Alooma becomes ruler of Kanem Borno. He becomes the greatest ruler of the empire.	
	1576 Amina becomes ruler of Zaria. She conquers vast territories in the Nigeria region.	1571 Portuguese forces invade Munhumutapa.
	1591 The Moroccans invade Songhai.	
	1623 Ann Nzinga becomes Ngola of Ndongo. She is a great opponent of mass enslavement.	1629 Emperor Mavhura becomes puppet ruler of Munhumutapa on behalf of the Portuguese.
1595 Africans in Brazil establish the Palmares state.	1658 Ngazargamu has a population of 250,000 people.	1652 The Dutch occupy territory in South Africa.
1655 Maroon Community established in Jamaica.		
1712 Africans and Native Americans revolt in New York City.		

1742 Barbari becomes an important Hausa ruler.

1791 Africans in Haiti begin the revolution that ultimately ends the mass enslavement of Africans.

1806 The British occupy territory in South Africa.

1812 Uthman Dan Fodio triumphs over the Hausa rulers.

1884-1885 The European powers at the Berlin Conference agree a plan to seize control of all Africa.

1884-1885 The European powers at the Berlin Conference agree a plan to seize control of all Africa.

1901-1902 Most of Africa's colonial borders are established by European conquest. Only Ethiopia escapes.

1901-1902 Most of Africa's colonial borders are established by European conquest.

1900 Henry Sylvester Williams leads the First Pan-African Conference in London.

1914 The Honourable Marcus Garvey establishes the UNIA and ACL.

1919 Dr DuBois leads the first of five Pan African Congress meetings. At the fifth conference, in 1945, they call for African independence.

1955 Dr King leads the civil rights struggle in the United States to get rights for Africans in America.

1957 Dr Nkrumah becomes first president of an independent Ghana. Most of Africa follows suit within the next few years.

1963 Organisation of African Unity is established. Its headquarters are in Ethiopia.

1994 Nelson Mandela is elected president of South Africa, ending years of Dutch domination. Direct European rule over any part of Africa is now over.

BIBLIOGRAPHY

Books

W. Marsham Adams, *The Book of the Master,* US, ECA Associates, 1990

Abu 'Uthman 'Amr Ibn Bahr Al-Jahiz, *The Book of the Glory of the Blacks Over the Whites,* (Translated by Vincent J. Cornell), US, ECA Associates, 1990

Robert Ardrey, *African Genesis,* UK, William Collins, 1961

Garba Ashiwaju ed, *Cities of the Savannah,* Nigeria, The Nigeria Magazine, no date given for publication

J. A. Atanda, *An Introduction to Yoruba History,* Nigeria, Ibadan University Press, 1980

Guy Atkins ed, *Manding Art and Civilisation,* UK, Studio International, 1972

Rev. James Baikie, *The Life of the Ancient East,* UK, A. & C. Black, 1923

Georges Balandier, *Daily Life in the Kingdom of the Kongo,* UK, George Allen & Unwin, 1968

Rev. C. J. Ball ed, *Light from the East,* UK, Eyre and Spottiswoode, 1899

Ishakamusa Barashango, *Afrikan Genesis, Volume I,* US, IVth Dynasty Publishing Co., 1991

Bawuro M. Barkindo ed, *Kano and Some of Her Neighbours,* Nigeria, Ahmadu Bello University Press, 1989

Leonard Barrett, *The Rastafarians,* US, Beacon, 1988

Henry Barth, *Travels and Discoveries in North and Central Africa, Volumes I, II & III,* UK, Longman, Brown, Green, Longmans & Roberts, 1857 and 1858

Mariane Barucand and Achim Bednorz, *Moorish Architecture in Andalusia,* Germany, Tashen, 1992

Robert Bauval and Graham Hancock, *Keeper of Genesis,* UK, Mandarin, 1996

Ayele Bekerie, *Ethiopic: An African Writing System,* US, Red Sea Press, 1997

Benaebi Benatari, *The Document of African Civilisation*, UK, Unpublished Paper, 1999

Yosef A. A. ben-Jochannan, *Africa! Mother of Western Civilization*, US, Black Classic Press, 1971

Yosef A. A. ben-Jochannan, *Abu Simbel to Gizeh*, US, Black Classic Press, 1989

Yosef A. A. ben-Jochannan, *We the Black Jews*, US, Black Classic Press, 1993

J. Theodore Bent, *The Ruined Cities of Mashonaland, 3rd Edition*, UK, Longmans, Green, and Co., 1902

Martin Bernal, *Black Athena: Volumes I and II*, UK, Free Association, 1987 and 1991

Saburi O. Biobaku ed, *The Living Culture of Nigeria*, Nigeria, Thomas Nelson & Sons, 1976

Tony Blair et al, *Our Common Interest: Report of the Commission for Africa*, UK, March 2005

Suzanne Preston Blier, *Royal Arts of Africa*, UK, Lawrence King, 1998

James Henry Breasted, *A History of Egypt*, US, Bantam Books, 1967

James Henry Breasted, *Ancient Records of Egypt: Volume I*, US, University of Chicago Press, 1906

Don Brothwell and Eric Higgs ed, *Science and Archaeology*, UK, Thames and Hudson, 1963

Anthony T. Browder, *Nile Valley Contributions to Civilization*, US, Institute of Karmic Guidance, 1992

E. A. Wallis Budge, *A History of Ethiopia, Nubia & Abyssinia, Volume I (A & B)*, US, ECA Associates 1991

E. A. Wallis Budge, *Egypt in the Neolithic and Archaic Periods*, UK, Kegan Paul, Trench, Trübner & Co., 1902

E. A. Wallis Budge, *The Book of the Dead*, US, University Books, 1960

John Lewis Burckhardt, *Travels in Nubia*, UK, John Murray, 1819

David Buxton, *The Abyssinians*, UK, Thames and Hudson, 1970

Camerapix, *Ethiopia: A Tourist Paradise*, Ethiopia, Ethiopian Tourist Commission, 1996

Jacob Carruthers, *Essays in Ancient Egyptian Studies*, US, Timbuktu Press, 1984

Jacob Carruthers, *The Irritated Genie,* US, The Kemetic Institute, 1985

Frederic G. Cassidy, *Jamaica Talk,* UK, Macmillan, 1961

G. Caton-Thompson ed, *The Zimbabwe Culture,* UK, The Clarendon Press, 1931

Chinweizu, personal communication

H. N. Chittick, *A Guide to the Ruins of Kilwa,* Tanzania, Ministry of Community Development and Culture, 1965

Daniel Chu and Elliott Skinner, *A Glorious Age in Africa,* US, Africa World Press, 1990

Albert Churchward, *The Origin and Evolution of Freemasonry connected with the Origin and Evolution of the Human Race,* US, ECA Associates, 1990 reprint

Albert Churchward, *The Signs and Symbols of Primordial Man, 2nd Edition,* UK, George Allen & Co., 1913

Bodo Cichy ed, *Architecture of the Ancient Civilizations in Colour,* UK, Thames and Hudson, 1966

Somers Clarke, *Christian Antiquities in the Nile Valley,* UK, Clarendon Press, 1912

Ronald Cohen, *The Kanuri of Bornu,* US, Holt, Rinehart and Winston, 1967

Anthony Coleman ed, *Millennium: A Thousand Years of History,* UK, Bantam Press, 1999

Cynthia Crossen, *The Rich and How They Got That Way,* UK, Nicholas Brealey, 2000

Nancy Cunard ed, *Negro: An Anthology,* US, Frederick Ungar Publishing Co., 1970

Charles Darwin, *The Descent of Man, Volume I,* UK, John Murray, 1871

Basil Davidson, *Africa in History,* UK, Macmillan, 1991

Basil Davidson ed, *African Civilization Revisited,* US, Africa World Press, 1991

Basil Davidson, *African Kingdoms,* Netherlands, Time-Life Books, 1967

Basil Davidson, *A Guide to African History,* US, Zenith Books, 1965

Basil Davidson, *A History of West Africa 1000-1800,* UK, Longmans, 1977

Basil Davidson, *Old Africa Rediscovered,* UK, Victor Gollancz, 1959

Basil Davidson, *The African Slave Trade,* US, Little, Brown and Co., 1980

Basil Davidson, *The Lost Cities of Africa,* UK, Little, Brown, & Co., 1987

Vivian Davies and Renée Friedman, *Egypt,* UK, British Museum Press, 1998

J. C. DeGraft-Johnson, *African Glory,* UK, Watts & Co., 1954

Bernard de Grunne, *The Birth of Art in Black Africa,* France and Luxembourg, Adam Biro & Banque Generale du Luxembourg, 1998

R. A. Schwaller De Lubicz, *Sacred Science,* US, Inner Traditions, 1982

Major Dixon Denham et al, *Narrative of Travels and Discoveries in Northern and Central Africa,* UK, James Murray, 1826

Susan Denyer, *African Traditional Architecture,* UK, Heinemann, 1978

Leo Depuydt, *Civil Calendar and Lunar Calendar in Ancient Egypt,* Belgium, Peeters Publishers & Department of Oriental Studies, 1997

Christiane Desroches-Noblecourt, *Tutankhamen,* UK, Penguin, 1971

Cheikh Anta Diop, *African Origin of Civilization: Myth or Reality?* US, Lawrence Hill Books, 1974

Cheikh Anta Diop, *Civilization or Barbarism,* US, Lawrence Hill Books, 1991

Cheikh Anta Diop, *Precolonial Black Africa,* US, Lawrence Hill Books, 1987

Cheikh Anta Diop, *The Cultural Unity of Black Africa,* UK, Karnak House, 1989

Roland B. Dixon, *The Racial History of Man,* US, Charles Scribners' Sons, 1923

Z. R. Dmochowski, *Northern Nigeria: An Introduction to Nigerian Traditional Architecture,* Volume 1, Nigeria, National Commission for Museums and Monuments, 1990

Sergio Domian, *Architecture Soudanaise: Vitalite d'une tradition urbaine et monumentale,* France, Éditions L'Harmattan, 1989

Abdias Do Nascimento, *Brazil: Mixture or Massacre?* US, The Majority Press, 1989

Major Felix Dubois, *Timbuctoo the Mysterious,* UK, William Heinemann, 1897

W. E. B. DuBois, *The World and Africa,* US, International Publishers, 1965

Charles Dupuis, *The Origin of All Religious Worship,* US, New Orleans, 1872

Jacob Egharevba, *A Short History of Benin,* Nigeria, Ibadan University Press, 1968

Christopher Ehret, *The Civilizations of Africa,* UK, James Currey, 2002

Nnamdi Elleh, *African Architecture: Evolution and Transformation,* US, McGraw-Hill, 1997

H. Ellert, *The Material Culture of Zimbabwe,* Zimbabwe, Longman Zimbabwe, 1984

Walter B. Emery, *Egypt in Nubia,* UK, Hutchinson, 1965

Carl Engel, *The Music of the Most Ancient Nations,* UK, John Murray, 1864

Adolf Erman, *Life in Ancient Egypt,* US, Dover, 1971

Adolf Erman, *The Literature of the Ancient Egyptians,* UK, Methuen & Co, 1927

Mrs Stuart Erskine, *Vanished Cities in Northern Africa,* UK, Hutchinson & Co., no date given for publication

Ekpo Eyo, *Two Thousand Years of Nigerian Art,* UK & Nigeria, Ethnographica and The National Commission for Museums and Monuments, 1977

Ekpo Eyo and Frank Willett, *Treasures of Ancient Nigeria,* UK, William Collins & Sons, 1980

J. D. Fage ed, *The Cambridge History of Africa, Volume 2,* UK, Cambridge University Press, 1978

J. D. Fage and R. A. Oliver ed, *Papers in African Prehistory,* UK, Cambridge University Press, 1970

Bernard Fagg, *Nok Terracottas,* UK & Nigeria, Ethnographica and The National Commission for Museums and Monuments, 1990

William Fagg ed, *The Living Arts of Nigeria,* UK, Studio Vista, 1971

W. A. Fairservis, *The Ancient Kingdoms of the Nile,* US, New American Library, 1962

Charles Finch, *Africa and the Birth of Science and Technology,* US, Khenti, 1992

Charles S. Finch, *Echoes of the Old Darkland,* US, Khenti, 1991

Charles S. Finch, *The Star of Deep Beginnings,* US, Khenti, 1998

G. S. P. Freeman-Grenville ed, *East African Coast, Select Documents,* UK, The Clarendon Press, 1962

Leo Frobenius, *The Voice of Africa: Volumes I and II,* UK, Hutchinson & Co., 1913

Richard N. Frye ed, *The History of Iran,* Germany, Verlagsbachhandlung München, 1984

Moustafa Gadalla, *Exiled Egyptians: The Heart of Africa,* US, Tehuti Research Foundation, 1999

Galen, *Selected Works,* translated by P. N. Singer, UK, Oxford University Press, 1997

René Gardi, *Indigenous African Architecture,* US, Van Nostrand Reinhold Company, 1973

Alan H. Gardiner, *The Royal Canon of Turin,* UK, Griffith Institute, 1959

Peter Garlake, *Early Art and Architecture of Africa,* UK, Oxford University Press, 2002

Peter Garlake, *Great Zimbabwe,* UK, Thames and Hudson, 1973

Peter Garlake, *Great Zimbabwe Described and Explained, Zimbabwe,* Zimbabwe Publishing House, 1985

Peter Garlake, *Life at Great Zimbabwe,* Zimbabwe, Mambo Press, 1982

Peter Garlake, *The Kingdoms of Africa,* UK, Elsevier-Phaidon, 1978

P. Raffaele Garrucci, *Le Monete Dell'Italia Antica,* Italy, 1885

Werner Gillon, *A Short History of African Art,* UK, Penguin, 1984

Anna Melissa Graves, *Africa, the Wonder and the Glory,* US, Black Classic Press, (originally 1942)

Roderick Grierson ed, *African Zion,* US, InterCultura, 1993

Francis Griffith & Herbert Thompson ed, *The Leyden Papyrus: An Egyptian Magical Book,* US, Dover Press, 1974

Count Adam Gurowski, *America and Europe,* US, D. Appleton & Co, 1857

Joseph Gwilt (translator), *The Architecture of Marcus Vitruvius Pollio,* UK, Priestly and Weale, 1826

R. N. Hall and W. G. Neal, *Ancient Ruins of Rhodesia: Second Edition,* UK, Methuen & Co., 1904

Saïd Hamdun & Noël King, *Ibn Battuta in Black Africa,* US, Markus Wiener Publishers, 1993

Sir J. A. Hammerton ed, *Wonders of the Past, Volume 2,* UK, Amalgamated Press, 1937

Graham Hancock, *The Beauty of Historic Ethiopia,* Kenya, Camerapix, 1996

Joseph E. Harris ed, *Pillars in Ethiopian History: The William Leo Hansberry African History Notebook, Volume 1,* US, Howard University Press, 1974

Joseph E. Harris ed, *Africa and Africans as Seen by Classical Writers: The William Leo Hansberry African History Notebook, Volume II,* US, Howard University Press, 1981

Markus Hattstein and Peter Delius ed, *Islam: Art and Architecture,* Germany, Konemann, 2000

D. E. L. Haynes, *Antiquities of Tripolitania,* Libya, The Antiquities Department of Tripolitania, 1959

A. H. L. Heeren, *Historical Researches into the Politics, Intercourse, and Trade of the Carthaginians, Ethiopians, and Egyptians, Volume I,* UK, D. A. Talboys, 1832

Heliodorus, *An Æthiopian History, 2nd Edition,* UK, Chapman & Dodd, no date given for publication

Godfrey Higgins, *Anacalypsis, Volumes I and II,* US, A & B Books, 1992

Cecilia Hill, *Moorish Towns in Spain,* UK, Methuen & Co., 1931

Walther Hinz, *The Lost World of Elam,* UK, Sidgwick & Jackson, 1972

Erik Hornung, *History of Ancient Egypt,* UK, Edinburgh University Press, 1999

Drusilla Dunjee Houston, *Wonderful Ethiopians of the Ancient Cushite Empire,* US, Black Classic Press, 1985

W. W. How and J. Wells, *A Commentary on Herodotus, Volume 1,* UK, Clarendon Press, 1912

John O. Hunwick, *Timbuktu and the Songhay Empire: Al-Sadi's Tarikh al-Sudan down to 1613 and other Contemporary Documents,* Netherlands, Brill, 1999

Ibn Battuta, *Travels in Asia and Africa,* (Translated by H. A. R. Gibb), UK, George Routeledge & Sons, 1929

Indus Khamit-Kush, *What They Never Told You in History Class,* US, Luxorr Publications, 1983

John G. Jackson, *Ages of Gold and Silver,* US, American Atheist Press, 1990

John G. Jackson, *Christianity before Christ,* US, American Atheist Press, 1985

John G. Jackson, *Ethiopia and the Origin of Civilization,* US, Black Classic Press, (original 1939)

John G. Jackson, *Introduction to African Civilizations,* US, Citadel Press, 1970

John G. Jackson, *Man, God and Civilization,* US, Citadel Press, 1972

Rafique Jairazbhoy, *Rameses III: Father of Ancient America,* UK, Karnak House, 1992

Richard Jobson, *The Golden Trade or A Discovery of the River Gambra, and the Golden Trade of the Aethiopians,* UK, The Penguin Press, 1932.

Rev. Samuel Johnson, *The History of the Yorubas,* Nigeria, CSS Bookshops, 1921

Sir Harry Johnston, *The Uganda Protectorate, Volume II,* UK, Hutchinson & Co., 1902

Maulana Karenga, *Introduction to Black Studies,* US, University of Sankore Press, 1982

Maulana Karenga, *Selections from The Husia,* US, University of Sankore Press, 1984

Maulana Karenga and Jacob Carruthers ed, *Kemet and the African Worldview,* US, University of Sankore Press, 1986

F. George Kay, *The Shameful Trade,* UK, Frederick Muller, 1967

Philip Koslow, *Hausaland: The Fortress Kingdoms,* US, Chelsea House, 1995

Philip Koslow, *Kanem-Borno: 1,000 Years of Splendor,* US, Chelsea House, 1995

D. Krencker et al, *Deutsche Aksum-Expedition, Book II,* Germany, Georg Reimer, 1913

Serge Lancel, *Carthage: A History,* UK, Basil Blackwell, 1995

Stanley Lane-Poole, *The Story of the Moors in Spain,* US, Black Classic Press, 1990

Richard Leakey & Roger Lewin, *Origins Reconsidered,* UK, Little, Brown & Co., 1992

Colin Legum, *Pan-Africanism: A Short Political Guide,* UK, Pal Mall Press, 1962

Julius Lester, *To Be a Slave,* UK, Longman Group, 1968

Nehemia Levtzion, *Ancient Ghana and Mali,* UK, Methuen & Co., 1973

Henri Lhote, *The Search for the Tassili Frescoes,* UK, Hutchinson of London, 1959

Adam Lively, *Masks: Blackness, Race and the Imagination,* UK, Vintage, 1998

J. Norman Lockyer, *The Dawn of Astronomy,* UK, Cassell & Co., 1894

Lady Lugard, *A Tropical Dependency,* UK, James Nisbet & Co., 1906

Pierre Maas et al, *Djenné: Chef D'Oeuvre Architectural,* Netherlands, Universite de Technologie, Eindhoven, 1992

Duncan MacNaughton, *A Scheme of Babylonian Chronology*, UK, Luzac & Co., 1929

Duncan MacNaughton, *A Scheme of Egyptian Chronology*, UK, Luzac & Co., 1932

David Mac Ritchie, *Ancient and Modern Britons: A Retrospect, Volume I*, US, William Preston, 1985

R. R. Madden, *Travels in Turkey, Egypt, Nubia and Palestine in 1824, 1825, 1826, and 1827: Volume II*, UK, Henry Colburn, 1829

Gerald Massey, *Ancient Egypt: The Light of the World, Volume I*, UK, T. Fisher Unwin, 1907

Gerald Massey, *Gerald Massey's Lectures*, US, Samuel Weiser, 1974

P. C. Mazikana and I. J. Johnstone, *Zimbabwean Epic*, Zimbabwe, National Archives of Zimbabwe, 1984

Anu M'Bantu, *The Blackheads: A History of Mesopotamia*, UK, Anu-Enlil-Enki Publishing, 2001

Joseph McCabe, *The Golden Ages of History*, UK, Watts & Co., 1940

Colin McEvedy, *Penguin Atlas of African History*, UK, Penguin, 1980

Norris & Ross McWhirter, *Guinness Book of Records, 21st Edition*, UK, Guinness Superlatives Limited, October 1974

G. R. S. Mead, *Thrice Greatest Hermes, Volumes I and III*, UK, John M. Watkins, 1949

Kurt Mendelssohn, *The Riddle of the Pyramids*, UK, Thames and Hudson, 1974

Laure Meyer, *Art and Craft in Africa*, France, Éditions Pierre Terrail, 1995

Laure Meyer, *Black Africa: Masks, Sculpture, Jewelry*, France, Éditions Pierre Terrail, 1992

George Michell ed, *Architecture of the Islamic World*, UK, Thames and Hudson, 1978

Geoffrey S. Mileham, *Churches in Lower Nubia*, US, University of Philadelphia, 1910

Siaf Millar, *Afrikan Enslavement: The Numbers Game*, UK, Unpublished Paper, 1995

James Morris and Suzanne Preston Blier, *Butabu: Adobe Architecture of West Africa*, US, Princetown Architectural Press, 2004

R. W. Morris, *Our Commonwealth in the Old World*, UK, George Allen and Unwin, no date given

J. C. Moughtin, *Hausa Architecture,* UK, Ethnographica, 1985

S. I. G. Mudenge, *Political History of Munhumutapa c 1400-1902,* Zimbabwe, Zimbabwe Publishing House, 1988

Mwalimu I. Mwadilifu ed, *European Scholars on the African Origins of the Africans of Antiquity,* US, ECA Associates, 1991

M. Nesturkh, *The Races of Mankind,* U.S.S.R., Foreign Languages Publishing, 1966

C. H. Oldfather (translator), *Diodorus Siculus. Library of History, Volumes II and III,* US, Loeb Classical Library, 1967

Paul Oliver ed, *Shelter in Africa,* UK, Barrie & Jenkins, 1971

Roland Oliver ed, *The Dawn of African History,* UK, Oxford University Press, 1961

Roland Oliver and Anthony Atmore, *Medieval Africa: 1250 - 1800,* UK, Cambridge University Press, 2001

Roland Oliver and Michael Crowder ed, *The Cambridge Encyclopedia of Africa,* UK, Cambridge University Press, 1981

Roland Oliver and Brian Fagan, *Africa in the Iron Age,* UK, Cambridge University Press, 1975

Isaac D. Osabutey-Aguedze, *Principles Underlying African Religion and Philosophy,* Kenya, Maillu Publishing House, 1990

W. G. Palgrave, *Dutch Guiana,* UK, Macmillan & Co., 1876

Sir Richmond Palmer, *The Bornu Sahara and Sudan,* UK, John Murray, 1936

George Wells Parker, *The Children of the Sun,* US, Black Classic Press, 1981

William Peck, *A Popular Handbook and Atlas of Astronomy,* UK, Gall & Inglis, 1890

W. J. Perry, *The Growth of Civilisation, 2nd Edition,* UK, Penguin Books, 1937

W. M. Flinders Petrie, *Researches in Sinai,* UK, John Murray, 1906

D. W. Phillipson, *Ancient Ethiopia,* UK, The British Museum Press, 1998

Gilbert Picard, *Carthage,* UK, Elek Books, 1964

Pliny the Elder, *Natural History, Book II,* UK, William Heinemann, 1938

André Pochan, *L'Enigme de la Grande Pyramide,* France, Éditions Robert Laffont, 1971

Richard Poe, *Black Spark: White Fire,* US, Prima Publishing, 1997

Marco Polo, *The Travels,* UK, Penguin, 1958

Zénaïde Ragozin, *Chaldea: The Story of the Nations,* US, G. P. Putnam's Sons, 1886

David Randall-Maciver, *Mediæval Rhodesia,* US, Negro Universities Press, 1969

Runoko Rashidi ed, *African Presence in Early Asia,* US, Transaction Publishers, 1995

George Rawlinson, *Ancient Egypt: The Story of the Nations,* UK, T. Fisher Unwin, 1888

George Rawlinson, *Five Great Monarchies of the Ancient Eastern World, Fourth Edition, Volumes I, II and III,* UK, John Murray, 1879

George Rawlinson (translator), *History of Herodotus: Volumes I, II and IV,* Third Edition, UK, John Murray, 1875

George Rawlinson, *Phœnicia: The Story of the Nations,* UK, T. Fisher Unwin, 1889

George Rawlinson, *The Origin of Nations,* UK, John Murray, 1878

Winwood Reade, *The Martyrdom of Man,* UK, Watts & Co., 1934 edition

Donald B. Redford, *Egypt, Canaan and Israel in Ancient Times,* US, Princetown University Press, 1992

Michael Rice, *Egypt's Making,* UK, Routledge, 1991

Charles Henry Robinson, *Nigeria: Our Latest Protectorate,* UK, Horace Marshall & Son, 1900

Walter Rodney, *The Groundings with my Brothers,* UK, Bogle L'Ouverture publications, 1975

James Rodway, *The West Indies and the Spanish Main,* UK, T. Fisher Unwin, 1896

J. A. Rogers, *100 Amazing Facts about the Negro,* US, Helga M. Rogers, 1957

J. A. Rogers, *From "Superman" to Man,* US, Helga M. Rogers, 1990

J. A. Rogers, *Nature Knows No Color-Line,* US, Helga M. Rogers, 1952

J. A. Rogers, *Sex and Race: Volume I,* US, Helga M. Rogers, 1968

J. A. Rogers, *World's Great Men of Color, Volume I,* US, Macmillan, 1972

David M. Rohl, *A Test of Time (Volume One): The Bible - From Myth to History,* UK, Century, 1995

David M. Rohl, *A Test of Time (Volume Two): Legend - The Genesis of Civilisation,* UK, Century, 1998

H. Ling Roth, *Great Benin: Its Customs, Art and Horrors,* UK, F. King and Sons, 1903

George Roux, *Ancient Iraq, Third Edition,* UK, Penguin Books, 1992

John Ruffle, *Heritage of the Pharaohs,* UK, Phaidon Press, 1977

The Rev. Michael Russell, *History and Present Condition of the Barbary States,* UK, Oliver & Boyd, 1835

A. H. Sayce, *The Ancient Empires of the East: Herodotos I-III,* UK, Macmillan and Co., 1883

A. H. Sayce, *The Archæology of the Cuneiform Inscriptions,* UK, S. P. C. K., 1907

Alan Scholefield, *The Dark Kingdoms,* UK, Heinemann, 1975

Charles Seignobos, *History of Ancient Civilization,* UK, T. Fisher Unwin, 1907

Alastair Service, *Lost Worlds,* UK, Collins, 1981

Diodorus Siculus, *Library of History, Volume II,* US, Loeb Classical Library, 1967

Philip Smith, *The Ancient History of the East,* UK, John Murray, 1871

R. Bosworth Smith, *Carthage and the Carthaginians,* New Edition, UK, Longmans, Green and Co., 1894

H. G. Spearing, *The Childhood of Art,* UK, Kegan Paul, Trench, Trübner & Co., 1912

Wilhelm Spiegelberg, *The Credibility of Herodotus' Account of Egypt in the Light of the Egyptian Monuments,* US, ECA Associates, 1990

Captain C. H. Stigand, *The Land of Zinj,* UK, Constable & Company, 1913

G. T. Stride & Caroline Ifeka, *Peoples and Empires of West Africa,* UK, Thomas Nelson and Sons, 1971

John E. G. Sutton, *A Thousand Years of East Africa,* Kenya, British Institute of Eastern Africa, 1990

The Museum of Fine Arts, *The Olmec Tradition* (catalogue), US, The Museum of Fine Arts, Houston Texas, 1963

Bertram Thomas, *Arabia Felix,* UK, Jonathan Cape, 1932

Bertram Thomas, *The Arabs,* UK, Thornton Butterworth, 1937

Gloria Thomas-Emeagwali ed, *African Systems of Science, Technology & Art,* UK, Karnak House, 1993

Peter Tompkins, *Secrets of the Great Pyramid,* US, Harper Colophon, 1978

J. Spencer Trimingham, *A History of Islam in West Africa,* UK, Cambridge University Press, 1962

UNESCO, *General History of Africa, Volume I,* ed J. Ki-Zerbo, UK, Heinemann, 1981

UNESCO, *General History of Africa, Volume II,* ed G. Mokhtar, UK, James Currey, 1990

UNESCO, *General History of Africa: Volume III,* ed M. Al Fasi, UK, Heinemann, 1988

UNESCO, *General History of Africa: Volume IV,* ed D. T. Niane, UK, Heinemann, 1984

UNESCO, *General History of Africa: Volume V,* ed B. A. Ogot, US, Heinemann, 1992

Bala Usman & Nur Alkali ed, *Studies in the History of Pre-Colonial Borno,* Nigeria, Northern Nigeria Publishing Company, 1983

Ivan Van Sertima ed, *African Presence in Early America,* US, Transaction Publishers, 1992

Ivan Van Sertima ed, *African Presence in Early Europe,* US, Transaction Publishers, 1985

Ivan Van Sertima ed, *Black Women in Antiquity,* US, Transaction Publishers, 1988

Ivan Van Sertima ed, *Blacks in Science: Ancient and Modern,* US, Transaction Publishers, 1983

Ivan Van Sertima, *Early America Revisited,* US, Transaction Publishers, 1998

Ivan Van Sertima ed, *Egypt: Child of Africa,* US, Transaction Publishers, 1994

Ivan Van Sertima ed, *Egypt Revisited,* US, Transaction Publishers, 1989

Ivan Van Sertima ed, *Golden Age of the Moor,* US, Transaction Publishers, 1992

Ivan Van Sertima ed, *Great Black Leaders,* US, Transaction Publishers, 1988

Ivan Van Sertima, *They Came Before Columbus,* US, Random House, 1976

Jan Vansina, *Kingdoms of the Savanna,* US, University of Wisconsin Press, 1966

Monica Blackmun Visonà et al, *A History of Art in Africa,* UK, Thames and Hudson, 2000

C. F. Volney, *The Ruins of Empires,* US, Peter Eckler, 1890

Alexander Von Wuthenau, *Art of the World: Pre-Columbian Terracottas,* UK, Methuen & Co., 1969

W. G. Waddell (translator), *Manetho,* UK, William Heinemann, 1940

Barbara G. Walker, *Women's Encyclopedia of Myths and Secrets,* US, Harper & Row, 1983

Gordon Waterford, *Egypt,* UK, Thames & Hudson, 1967

Barbara Watterson, *The Egyptians,* UK, Blackwell Publishers, 1997

Derek A. Welsby, *The Kingdom of Kush,* US, Marcus Wiener, 1996

Derek A. Welsby, *The Medieval Kingdoms of Nubia,* UK, The British Museum Press, 2002

Herbert Wendt, *It Began in Babel,* UK, Weidenfield and Nicholson, 1963

Sir Mortimer Wheeler, *Civilizations of the Indus Valley and Beyond,* UK, Thames and Hudson, 1965

F. D. P. Wicker, *Egypt and the Mountains of the Moon,* UK, Merlin Books, 1990

Donald L. Wiedner, *A History of Africa South of the Sahara,* US, Random House, 1962

Leo Wiener, *Africa and the Discovery of America, Volume III,* US, Innes & Sons, 1922

Dietrich Wildung, *Egypt from Prehistory to the Romans,* Germany, Taschen, 1997

Dietrich Wildung ed, *Sudan: Ancient Kingdoms of the Nile,* France, The Institut du monde arabe, 1997

Bruce Beyer Williams, *The A-Group Royal Cemetery at Qustul: Cemetery L,* US, The Oriental Institute of the University of Chicago, 1986

Chancellor Williams, *The Destruction of Black Civilization,* US, Third World Press, 1987

Eric Williams, *Capitalism and Slavery,* UK, Andre Deutsch, 1944

Hon A. Wilmot, *Monomotapa: Its Monuments and its History,* UK, T. Fisher Unwin, 1896

Freda Wolfson ed, *Pageant of Ghana,* UK, Oxford University Press, 1958

Leonard Woolley, *Ur of the Chaldees,* UK, Pelican Books, 1938

Claudia Zaslavsky, *Africa Counts,* US, Lawrence Hill Books, 1973

Journals, Newspapers, Television, Video, etc

Africa had societies, in Metro, UK, 22 February 2001, p.15

Alarm Promotions, *The Great Debate* (video), UK, Nekhebet Productions, 1998

Jean-Louis Bourgeois, *The Great Mosque of Djenné,* Mali, US, Internet Article, 1996

Bruce Boyer, *African finds revise cultural roots,* in *Science News Online: Editors' Picks,* 29 April 1995, http://www.sciencenews.org/sn_edpik/aa_2.htm

C. Loring Brace et al, *Clines and Clusters Versus Race,* in *Yearbook of Physical Anthropology, Volume 36,* 1993

Kathy Brewis, *Writings in the Sand,* in *The Sunday Times Magazine,* UK, 28 January 2001, pp.32-5

Michael Butcher, *Mauritania's Slavery Shame,* in *The Voice,* UK, Voice Communications, 10 January 1995, p.13

Rebecca Cann et al, *Mitochondrial DNA and human evolution,* in *Nature,* UK, 1 January 1987

J. Michael Crichton, *A Multiple Discriminant Analysis of Egyptian and African Negro Crania,* US, The Peabody Museum, 1966

Basil Davidson, *Africa,* television series part 1: *Different but Equal,* UK, Michael Beazley, Rm Arts, Channel Four Television & Nigerian Television, 1984

Basil Davidson, *Africa,* television series part 3: *Caravans of Gold,* UK, Michael Beazley, Rm Arts, Channel Four Television & Nigerian Television, 1984

Basil Davidson, *Africa,* television series part 4: *The King and the City,* UK, Michael Beazley, Rm Arts, Channel Four Television & Nigerian Television, 1984

Jessica Davies, *Is this the Mother of us all?* in *Daily Mail,* UK, 11 May 1995

Laurance R. Doyle, *Astronomy of Africa in Encyclopaedia of the History of Science, Technology and Medicine in Non-Western Cultures,* internet article, http://www.safaris.cc/8art.encyclo.htm.

David Dugan, *Time Life's Lost Civilizations,* video series, *Africa, A History Denied,* Holland, Time Life Video, 1995

Marc R. Feldesman and Robert L. Fountain, *"Race" Specificity and the Femur/Stature Ratio,* in *American Journal of Physical Anthropology, Volume 100,* June 1996

Henry Field, *Papers of the Peabody Museum, Volume 48,* US, Harvard University Press, 1953

Arthur M. Foyle, *Nigerian Architecture,* in *The Geographical Magazine, Volume XXII: Number 5,* ed Michael Huxley, UK, January 1951

Khshatrapa Gandasa, *Four-Nation Theory: Sakastan, Dalitstan, Mughalstan and Hindu Rashtra,* see http://www.dalitstan.org/books/gandasa/gandasa8.html

Henry Louis Gates, *Into Africa,* television series part 2: *The Road to Timbuktu,* UK, BBC Television, 1999

Anthony Geffen (producer), *Queen of Sheba: Behind the Myth,* television programme, UK, BBC Television, 2003

Georg Gerster, *Threatened Treasures of the Nile,* in *National Geographic, Volume 124: Number 4,* ed Melville Bell Grosvenor, US, National Geographic Society, October 1963, pp.586-621

Bernard Hamilton, *Spreading the Gospel in the Middle Ages,* in *History Today, Volume 53 (1),* ed Peter Furtado, UK, History Today Limited, January 2003, p.45

Fekri Hassan, *Ancient Apocalypse* (television programme), UK, BBC Television, 2001

Roger Highfield (Science Editor), *Britons explore 'Queen of Sheba's monument',* in *The Daily Telegraph,* 26 May 1999, p.13

Jeremy Isaacs (producer), *Millennium: The 14th Century,* Television Series, UK, BBC Television, 1999

Jeremy Isaacs (producer), *Millennium: The 15th Century,* Television Series, UK, BBC Television, 1999

Professor M. D. W. Jeffreys, *The Negro Enigma,* in *The West Africa Review,* September 1951, p.1049

S. O. Y. Keita, *Further Analysis of Crania from Ancient Northern Africa,* in *American Journal of Physical Anthropology, Volume 87,* 1992

Timothy Kendall, *Kingdom of Kush,* in *National Geographic, Volume 178, Number 5,* ed William Graves, US, National Geographic Society, November 1990, pp.112-4

David Keys, *Fossils could reveal origins of humanity,* in *The Independent,* UK, 22 September 1994

Christina Lamb, *The Eden Project,* in *The Sunday Times Magazine,* UK, 27 July 2003, p.26

Joao Lavinha et al, *Importation Route of the Sickle Cell trait into Portugal: Contribution of Molecular Epidemiology,* in *Human Biology: Volume 64, Number 6,* ed Michael H. Crawford, US, Wayne State University Press, December 1992

Mark Macaskill, *Jungle reveals traces of Sheba's fabled kingdom*, in *The Sunday Times*, 23 May 1999, p.10

Laura Marshall (producer), *Timewatch: White Slaves, Pirate Gold*, UK, BBC Television, 2003

Anu M'Bantu & Fari Supiya, *Ethiopia's First Christian Emperor: Ezana of Axum*, in *West Africa, Issue 4303*, UK, Afrimedia International, 26 November - 2 December 2001, p.43

Anu M'Bantu and Fari Supiya, *The Elliptical Building: Master builders of Zimbabwe*, in *West Africa, Issue 4300*, UK, Afrimedia International, 5-11 November 2001, p.43

Mark McCarron, *Khufu or NOT Khufu ... that is the Question?* Internet article, http://www.gizapyramid.com/McCarron-C14.htm.

S. K. McIntosh and R. J. McIntosh, *The Early City in West Africa: towards an understanding*, in *The African Archaeological Review: Volume 2*, UK, Cambridge University Press, 1984

Siaf Millar, *In The Name of Civilisation*, in *The Alarm: Issue 18*, ed Pascoe Sawyers, UK, Alarm Promotions, May-June 1996

Alan Mitchell, *Imhotep: He Who Comes in Peace*, in *The Alarm Journal*, ed Robin Walker, UK, Alarm Promotions, Spring/Summer 1997

Gillian Mosely (producer), *The Black Mummy Mystery*, (television programme), UK, Fulcrum TV, 2003

Patrick J. Munson, *Archaeology and the Prehistoric Origins of the Ghana Empire*, in *Journal of African History, Volume 21: No.4*, UK, Cambridge University Press, 1980

Uthaya Naidu, *The Bible of Aryan Invasions, Volume II*, see http://www.light1998.com/The-Bible-of-Aryan-Invasions/ bibai2.html

news.telegraph.co.uk, internet article, http://www.telegraph.co.uk/news/main.jhtml?xml=/news/2003/01/27/db2701.xml

David Northrup, *The Growth of Trade among the Igbo Before 1800*, in *Journal of African History, Volume 13: No.2*, UK, Cambridge University Press, 1972

Nwanna Nzewunwa, *Prehistoric Pavements in West Africa*, in *West African Journal of Archaeology: Volume 19*, ed Bassey W. Andah and Ikechukwu Okpoko, Nigeria, Association Quest Africaine d'Archaeologie, 1989

S. D. Ousely and R. L. Jantz, *FORDISC 2.0, Personal Computer Forensic Discriminant Functions*, US, University of Tennessee, 1996

Michael Palin, *Sahara*, television series part 3: *Absolute Desert*, UK, BBC Worldwide Linited, 2002

Barnaby Phillips (BBC), *Nigeria's hidden wonder,* BBC Online (Internet), 9 June 1999

Reginald Stuart Poole, *The Egyptian Classification of the Races of Man,* in *The Journal of the Anthropological Institute, Volume XVI,* UK, Trübner & Co., 1887

Tracy L. Prowse and Nancy C. Lovell, *Concordance of Cranial and Dental Morphological Traits and Evidence for Endogamy in Ancient Egypt,* in *American Journal of Physical Anthropology, Volume 101,* October 1996

Radiocarbon Web-Info, http://www.c14dating.com/k12.html

Boyce Rensberger, *Nubian Monarchy Called Oldest,* in *New York Times,* 1 March 1979, pp.1 and 16

Rosemary Righter, *Great wonders from the wild heart of Africa,* in *The Times,* UK, 26 January 2002, p.21

Gay Robins and C. C. D. Shute, *The Physical Proportions and Living Stature of New Kingdom Pharaohs,* in *Journal of Human Biology, Volume 12,* 1983

Statement of Aims and Objectives [Mughalstan Nation], see http://www.geocities.com/mughalstan/mn/aimobjec.html

F. M. C. Stokes, *Zimbabwe,* in *The Geographical Magazine, Volume II: No.2,* ed Michael Huxley, UK, The Geographical Magazine, December 1935

Sudan Human Rights Voice, UK, Sudan Human Rights Organisation, October 1993

Curt Suplee, *DNA Refutes Neanderthal Link,* in *washingtonpost.com,* 11 July 1997, http://www.washingtonpost.com

The Economist, UK, 24 December 1994 - 6 January 1995, p.123

The Search for Adam and Eve, in *Newsweek,* US, 11 January 1988, p.38

We've all just got 40,000 years older, in *Metro,* UK, 17 February 2005, p.9

John Noble Wilford, *The Latest Riddle of the Sphinx,* in *International Herald Tribune,* US, 25 October 1991

Lieutenant Francis Wilford, *On Egypt and the Nile From the Ancient Books of the Hindus,* in *Asiatick Researches, Volume III,* ed Sir William Jones, India, 1792, p.536

H. E. Winlock, *The Origin of the Ancient Egyptian Calendar,* US, Proceedings of the American Philosophical Society: Volume 83, No.3, September 1940

Women in Ancient Egypt, internet article, http://www.crystalinks.com/egyptianwomen.html

Gary Younge, *Nights on the tiles,* in *The Guardian (Travel),* UK, 2 January 1999, p.15

INDEX

230311-100-2-60W